D0467908

MACROECONOMICS

Second Edition

MACROECONOMICS

Second Edition

Charles I. Jones
Stanford University, Graduate School of Business

W. W. NORTON & COMPANY
NEW YORK LONDON

W. W. Norton & Company has been independent since its founding in 1923, when William Warder Norton and Mary D. Herter Norton first published lectures delivered at the People's Institute, the adult education division of New York City's Cooper Union. The firm soon expanded its program beyond the Institute, publishing books by celebrated academics from America and abroad. By mid-century, the two major pillars of Norton's publishing program—trade books and college texts—were firmly established. In the 1950s, the Norton family transferred control of the company to its employees, and today—with a staff of four hundred and a comparable number of trade, college, and professional titles published each year—W. W. Norton & Company stands as the largest and oldest publishing house owned wholly by its employees.

Printed in the United States of America

Editor: Jack Repcheck
Developmental Editor: Susan Gaustad
Managing Editor, College: Marian Johnson
Project Editor: Melissa Atkin
Production Manager: Christopher Granville
Copyeditors: Richard Mickey, Carol Flechner
Emedia Editor: Dan Jost
Editorial Assistant: Jason Spears
Art Director: Rubina Yeh
Artist: John McAusland
Designer: Lissi Sigillo
Composition: Matrix Publishing Services
Manufacturing: Courier Companies

Library of Congress Cataloging-in-Publication Data
Jones, Charles I. (Charles Irving)
Macroeconomics / Charles I. Jones.—2nd ed.
p. cm.
Includes bibliographical references and index.
ISBN 978-0-393-93423-6 (hardcover)
1. Macroeconomics. I. Title.
HB172.5.J65 2011
339—dc22 2010041083

W. W. Norton & Company, Inc., 500 Fifth Avenue, New York, NY 10110
wwnorton.com
W. W. Norton & Company Ltd., Castle House, 75/76 Wells Street, London W1T 3QT
1 2 3 4 5 6 7 8 9 0

To Terry; for Audrey and Charlie

BRIEF CONTENTS

CONTENTS

PREFACE TO THE SECOND EDITION

The macroeconomic events of the last several years are truly breathtaking—a once-in-a-lifetime (we hope) occurrence. While the basics of how economists understand the macroeconomy remain solid, the global financial crisis and the Great Recession take us into waters that, if not uncharted, at least haven't been visited in recent decades. The remarkable collapse in housing prices, the large rise in the financial risk premium, the massive expansion of the Federal Reserve's balance sheet, and the global nature of the financial crisis are among the novel changes in the macroeconomy.

It was just last year that we published the "Economic Crisis Update" to the first edition, introducing two new chapters to address the financial crisis and the global recession that ensued. But the rest of the text was untouched. This second edition features revisions throughout the text, including updates to the two chapters on the Great Recession, two entirely new chapters on consumption (Chapter 15) and investment (Chapter 16), many new case studies and exercises, extensive updates to tables and figures to reflect the most current data, and improvements on nearly every page in the text.

It is a fascinating time to study macroeconomics, and I look forward to sharing astounding facts about the macroeconomy with you and to discussing the Nobel-caliber ideas that help us understand them.

1. Innovations

(This section will make the most sense to readers with some familiarity with macroeconomics, especially instructors. Students new to the subject might skip to the Guided Tour.)

The most popular textbooks for teaching intermediate macroeconomics were first written fifteen or twenty years ago. Our understanding of the macroeconomy has improved substantially since then. This textbook provides an accessible and yet modern treatment. Its order and structure will feel familiar to instructors, but the execution, examples, and pedagogy have been updated to incorporate the best that macroeconomics instruction has to offer.

What's special about this book? Innovations occur throughout, but the key ones are described below.

Two Chapters on the Great Recession

The global financial crisis and the Great Recession that followed are obviously the most important macroeconomic events in decades. While these events are discussed throughout the section of the book devoted to the short-run, two chapters explicitly focus on recent events. Chapter 10 (The Great Recession: A First Look) follows immediately after the fist introductory chapter on the short-run, exposing students to the facts of the last several years and to critical concepts like leverage, balance sheets, and securitization. Chapter 14 (The Great Recession and the Short-Run Model) is the last chapter of the short-run section of the book. It provides a detailed application of the short-run model to recent events, explaining in the process the unconventional aspects of monetary and fiscal policy that have been featured prominently in the government's response to the crisis.

Rich Treatment of Economic Growth

Economic growth is the first major topic explored in the book. After an overview chapter describes the facts and some tools, Chapter 4 presents a (static) model based on a Cobb-Douglas production function. Students learn what a model is with this simple structure, and they see it applied to understanding the 50-fold differences in the per capita GDP that we see across countries. Chapter 5 presents the Solow model but with no technological change or population growth—which simplifies the presentation. Instead, students learn Robert Solow's insight that capital accumulation cannot serve as the engine for long-run economic growth.

Chapter 6 then offers something absent in most other intermediate macro books: a thorough exposition of the economics of ideas and Paul Romer's insight that the discovery of new ideas can drive long-run growth.

The approach taken here is to explain the macroeconomics of the long run before turning to the short run. It is much easier to understand fluctuations in macroeconomic aggregates when one understands how those aggregates behave in normal times.

Familiar Yet Updated Short-Run Model

The "modern" version of the short-run AS/AD model is the crowning achievement of the short-run section. By modern, I mean several things. First and foremost, the AS/AD graph is drawn with inflation on the vertical axis rather than the price level—perfect for teaching students about the threat of deflation that has reared its head following the Great Recession, the Volcker disinflation, and the Great Inflation of the 1970s. All the short-run analysis—including explicit dynamics—can be performed in this single graph.

Another innovation in getting to the AS/AD framework is a focus on interest rates and the absence of an LM curve. The central bank sets the interest rate in Chapter 12. Chapter 13 introduces a simple version of John Taylor's monetary policy rule to get the AD curve.

A final innovation in the short-run model is that it features an open economy from the start. Business cycles in the rest of the world are one source of shocks to the home economy. To keep things simple, however, the initial short-run model does not include exchange rates.

Interplay Between Models and Data

A tight connection between models and data is a feature of modern macroeconomics, and this connection pervades the book. Many exercises ask students to work with real data. Some of this is available in the book itself; some is obtained by using the online *Economic Report of the President*; and some is available in a new data tool I've put together: Country Snapshots. This is a pdf file available from www.norton.com/college/econ/macroeconomics2/snapshots.aspx that contains a page of graphs for each country in the world. The data underlying the graphs can be obtained as a spreadsheet simply by clicking on a link at the top of each page.

Worked Exercises at the End of Each Chapter

One of the most effective ways to learn is by working through problems, and a carefully chosen collection of exercises is included at the end of each chapter. From among these, one or two are selected and worked out in detail. Students are encouraged to attempt these exercises on their own before turning to the full solution.

More Emphasis on the World Economy

Relative to many intermediate macro books, this text features more emphasis on the world economy. This occurs in three ways. First, the long-run growth chapters are a main emphasis in the book, and these inherently involve international comparisons. Second, the short-run model features an open economy (albeit without exchange rates) from the very beginning. Finally, the book includes two international chapters in Part 4: in addition to the standard international finance chapter that appears as Chapter 19, Chapter 18 is entirely devoted to international trade.

Better Applications and Microfoundations

Part 4 includes five chapters of applications and microfoundations. The basic structure of this part is traditional; there is a chapter for each component of the national income identity: consumption, investment, the government, and the international economy. However, the material inside this part is modern and novel. For example, the consumption chapter (Chapter 15) is centered around the famous Euler equation that lies at the heart of today's macroeconomics. The investment chapter (Chapter 16) highlights the strong parallels between investment in physical capital and financial investments in the stock market, using the "arbitrage equation" approach. The chapter on the government and the macroeconomy (Chapter 17) includes an application to what I call "The Fiscal Problem of the Twenty-First Century"—how to finance the growing expenditures on health care. And, as mentioned above, the international section features two chapters, one on international trade and one on international finance. These chapters are not essential, and some instructors may wish to skip one or both of them depending on time constraints.

A Guided Tour

The book consists of three main parts: The Long Run, The Short Run, and Applications and Microfoundations. Surrounding these are an introductory section (Preliminaries) and a concluding chapter (Parting Thoughts).

This organization reflects an increasing appreciation in the profession of the importance of long-run macroeconomics. In addition, it makes sense from a pedagogical standpoint to put the long run first: this way students understand what it is that the economy fluctuates *around* when we get to the short-run chapters.

A brief overview of each part follows.

Part 1: Preliminaries

We begin with an overview of macroeconomics: what kind of questions macroeconomics addresses and how it goes about its business. A second chapter then discusses the data of macroeconomics in more detail, with a focus on national income accounting.

Part 2: The Long Run

The second part of the book consists of Chapters 3 through 8, and these chapters consider the macroeconomy in the long run. Chapter 3 presents an overview of the facts and tools that economists use to study long-run macroeconomics, with special attention to economic growth. Chapter 4 introduces the Cobb-Douglas production function as a way to understand the enormous differences in standards of living that we see across countries. The interplay between theory and data that is central to macroeconomics makes a starring appearance in this chapter.

Chapter 5 considers the Solow model of economic growth, one of the workhorse models of macroeconomics. We study the extent to which the Solow model can help us understand (a) why some countries are rich while others are poor, and (b) why people in the advanced countries of the world are so much richer today than they were a hundred years ago. Somewhat to our surprise, we will see that the model does not do a good job of explaining long-run economic growth.

For this explanation, we turn in Chapter 6 to the Romer model, which emphasizes the role played by the discovery of new ideas. Thinking about the economics of ideas leads to profound changes in the way we understand many areas of economics.

Chapter 7 studies the most important market in modern economies, the labor market. We learn about the determination of the unemployment rate in the long run and discover that many readers of this book are already, in some sense, millionaires.

Chapter 8 concludes the long-run portion of the book by considering inflation. The quantity theory of money provides a long-run theory of inflation, which, according to Milton Friedman, occurs because of "too much money chasing too few goods."

Part 3: The Short Run

Part 3 is devoted to the branch of macroeconomics that students are probably most familiar with: the study of booms, recessions, and the rise and fall of inflation in the short run. The five chapters of this part form a tight unit that develops our short-run model and applies it to current events.

Chapter 9 provides an overview of the macroeconomy in the short run, summarizing the key facts and providing an introduction to the short-run model that will explain these facts. Chapter 10 provides a "first look" at the financial crisis and the Great Recession, carefully laying out the facts of how the crisis evolved and introducing the important concepts of "leverage" and "balance sheets."

The next three chapters then develop the short-run model. Chapter 11 introduces the IS curve, a key building block of the short-run model. The IS curve reveals that a fundamental determinant of output in the short run is the real interest rate. Chapter 12 shows how the central bank in an economy can move the interest rate in order to keep the economy close to full employment. Chapter 12 also provides the link between the real economy and inflation, called the Phillips curve.

Chapter 13 looks at our short-run model in an aggregate supply/aggregate demand (AS/AD) framework. This framework allows the complete dynamics of the economy in the short run to be studied in a single graph. Using this framework, the chapter emphasizes the key roles played by expectations, credibility, and time consistency in modern macroeconomic policymaking.

Chapter 14 culminates the short-run section of the book. It uses the short-run model to help us understand the financial crisis and the Great Recession and discusses the macroeconomic prospects going forward.

Part 4: Applications and Microfoundations

Part 4 includes five chapters of applications and microfoundations. While it may be unapparent to the student new to macroeconomics, the organization of these chapters follows the "national income identity," a concept discussed early in the book. These chapters include a number of important topics. For example, Chapter 15 studies how individuals make their lifetime consumption plans. Chapter 16 considers the pricing of financial assets, such as stocks and houses, in the context of a broader chapter on investment.

Chapter 17 studies the role played by the government in the macroeconomy, including the role of budget deficits and the government's budget constraint. The chapter also considers a key problem that governments around the world will face in coming decades: how to finance the enormous increases in health spending that have occurred for the last fifty years and that seem likely to continue.

Both the long-run and the short-run parts of the book place the study of macroeconomics in an international context. Indeed, the short-run model includes open economy forces from the very beginning. The final two applications of the book, however, go even farther in this direction.

Chapter 18 focuses on international trade. Why do countries trade? Are trade deficits good or bad? How have globalization and outsourcing affected the macroeconomy? Chapter 19 studies international finance, including the determination of the exchange rate.

Parting Thoughts

Chapter 20 concludes our study of macroeconomics. We summarize the important lessons learned in the book, and we offer a brief guide to the key questions that remain less than well understood.

Learning Aids

- *Overview*: The opening page of each chapter provides an overview of the main points that will be covered.
- *Boxes around key equations*: Key equations are boxed to highlight their importance.
- *Graphs and tables*: The main point of each figure is summarized in an accompanying text box. Tables are used to summarize the key equations of a model.
- *Guide to notation*: The inside back cover contains a guide to notation, listing each symbol, its meaning, and the chapter in which it first appears.
- *Case studies*: Case studies in each chapter highlight items of interest.
- *Chapter summaries in list form*: The main points of each chapter are listed for easy reference and review.
- *Key concepts*: Important economic concepts are presented in bold type when they first appear. At the end of the chapter, they are listed together for review.
- *Review questions*: Review questions allow students to quiz themselves on what they've learned.
- *Exercises*: Carefully chosen exercises reinforce the material from the chapter

and are intended to be used for homework assignments. These exercises include many different kinds of problems. Some require graphical solutions, others use numbers. Some ask you to look for economic data online and interpret it in a particular way. Others ask you to write a position paper for a presidential candidate or to pretend you are advising the chair of the Federal Reserve.

- *Worked exercises*: From the exercises, one or two are selected and worked out in detail at the end of each chapter. These exercises are indicated by the "worked exercise" icon in the margin. You will find these answers most helpful if you consult them only after you have tried to work through each exercise on your own.
- *Glossary*: An extensive glossary at the end of the book defines terms and provides page numbers where more information can be found.

Supplements for Students

Student Studyspace

David Agrawal, *University of Michigan*
www.wwnorton.com/college/econ/macroeconomics2/

The student StudySpace for *Macroeconomics* is a free and open resource for students to review key concepts and test themselves prior to midterms and finals. It contains a link to the SmartWork homework problems.

The StudySpace offers the following features:

- **Chapter Outlines**
- **Quiz+ Assessment**: Quiz+ presents students with a targeted study plan that offers specific page references, links to the ebook, and other online learning tools.
- **Interactive Graphs**: interactive versions of the graphs presented in the text
- **Data Plotter**: a set of tools to compare and contrast real economic data to better understand trends and concepts related to data models
- **Interactive Concept Tutorials**: These interactive tutorials provide students with the extra help they need to learn the most challenging concepts in the course, and they offer opportunities for students to demonstrate critical-thinking skills and comprehension to their instructors.
- **Short-Answer Review Questions**
- **An Economics in the News RSS feed**

COUNTRY SNAPSHOTS

www.wwnorton.com/college/econ/macroeconomics2/snapshots.aspx

To accompany the book, I've put together a resource containing data from more than 200 countries. Each page of the file snapshots.pdf corresponds to a country and provides graphs of that country's key macroeconomics statistics. Moreover, the data underlying the graphs can be obtained as a spreadsheet simply by selecting a link at the top of each page. Whenever you read about a particular country in the newspaper or in this book, detailed macroeconomics statistics are only a click away.

Supplements for Instructors

SmartWork

Online Homework and Tutorial Program with an Integrated Ebook.

Developed by university educators, SmartWork is the most intuitive online tutorial and homework-management system available for the intermediate macroeconomics course. The powerful assessment engine supports a wide range of questions, including multiple-choice, interactive graphing, and macroeconomics equations.

Answer-specific feedback, tutorial questions, and hints coach students through solving problems, while links to the integrated ebook encourage active reading and provide easy reference to the concepts discussed in the text. Assigning, editing, and administering homework is easy with SmartWork's intuitive authoring tools, which allow instructors to modify existing problems or create their own.

Completely revised and updated, the new SmartWork course for *Macroeconomics* Second Edition features new homework questions, more worked solutions, additional answer-specific feedback, and more algorithmically-generated questions. The entire SmartWork system has been updated with an improved user interface that is more intuitive for both instructors and students.

SmartWork highlights:

- An intuitive and easy-to-use interface with extensive hinting and answer-specific feedback, including multistep guided tutorial problems
- A wide range of question types, including interactive graphs, multiple-choice questions, and economics equations
- Intuitive authoring tools that give instructors an easy-to-use environment for modifying existing problems or creating their own
- An easy-to-use math palette for composing graphs and mathematical expressions
- Algorithmically generated variables so each student sees a slightly different version of the same problem
- An at-a-glance gradebook that offers a visual summary of students' work
- A full complement of tools for managing assignments and grades

Lecture PowerPoints

This set of PowerPoint slides includes every graph and table from the text, along with insightful annotations and suggestions for lecture content. It also contains PowerPoint slides covering each key concept presented in the chapter, thus providing a lecture-ready resource for the instructor.

Instructor's Resouce Site

Downloadable resources will include the test bank in rich-text, Blackboard, and ExamView formats, graphs in jpeg format and as PowerPoints, lecture PowerPoints, and chapter quizzes in WebCT and Blackboard format.

Instructor's Manual

Anthony Laramie, *Boston College*, with contributions from Pavel Kapinos, *Carleton College*, and Kenneth Kuttner, *Williams College*

This valuable instructor's resource includes for each chapter an overview, a suggested approach to the chapter lecture, expanded case studies, additional case studies, and complete answers to the end-of-chapter problems. Updated for the second edition, the instructor's manual now includes numerical examples and simulations, as well as Excel-based problems that will make an excellent supplement to any lecture.

Test Bank

Robert Sonora, *Fort Lewis College*, with contributions from Todd Knoop, *Cornell College*, and Dietrich Vollrath, *University of Houston*

Available on CD-ROM or for download in rich-text, Blackboard Learning System, and *ExamView® Assessment Suite* formats, the updated test bank includes over 1,800 carefully constructed true/false and multiple-choice questions. And, new for the second edition, over 100 short answer/numerical questions.

ACKNOWLEDGMENTS

This book could not have been written without the tremendous support, encouragement, and assistance that I have received from many people. I am especially grateful to my colleagues in the economics profession for many insights, comments, and suggestions for improving the manuscript:

David Aadland
University of Wyoming

Yamin S. Ahmad
University of Wisconsin, Whitewater

Ehsan Ahmed
James Madison University

Francisco Alvarez-Cuadrado
McGill University

William Bennett
Loyola University

Jules van Binsbergen
Stanford University

Peter Bondarenko
University of Chicago

Ronald Britto
Binghamton, SUNY

Robin Burgess
London School of Economics

Miki Brunyer
West Virginia University

Colleen M. Callahan
American University

Gabriele Camera
Purdue University

Tiago Cavalcanti
Purdue University

Betty C, Daniel
University of Albany, SUNY

Steven Davis
University of Chicago, Booth School of Business

A. Edward Day
University of Texas, Dallas

Robert J. Derrell
Manhattanville College

Robert A. Driskill
Vanderbilt University

Ryan Edwards
Queens College, CUNY

J. Peter Ferderer
Macalester College

John Fernald
Federal Reserve Bank of San Francisco

Edward N. Gamber
Lafayette College

David H. Gillette
Truman State University

Pierre-Olivier Gourinchas
University of California, Berkeley

Kristin Harnett
Univeristy of Pittsburgh

William R. Hauk, Jr.
Washington University

Williams Hawkins
University of Rochester

Denise Hazlett
Whitman College

Ryan Herzog
Gonzaga University

Christopher L. House
University of Michigan

Chang-Tai Hsieh
University of Chicago, Booth School of Business

Murat F. Iyigun
University of Colorado, Boulder

Garett B. Jones
George Mason University

Louis D. Johnston
College of Saint Benedic/ Saint John's University

Oscar Jorda
University of California, Davis

Pavel Kapinos,
Carleton College

Cem Karayalcin
Florida International University

John W. Keating
Kansas University

Manfred Keil
Claremont McKenna College

Young Se Kim
University of North Texas

Miles Kimball
University of Michigan

Pete Klenow
Stanford University

Ken Kletzer
University of California, Santa Cruz

Todd Knoop
Cornell College

Per Krusell
Princeton University

Corinne M. Krupp
Duke University

James Kwak
Baseline Scenario

George Langelett
South Dakota State University

Man-Lui Lau
University of San Francisco

Junsoo Lee
University of Alabama

Dennis Patrick Leyden
University of North Carolina, Greensboro

Shu Lin
University of Oklahoma

Stephen A. McCafferty
Ohio State University

Ken McCormick
University of Northern Iowa

Ted Miguel
University of California, Berkeley

Fabio Milani
University of California, Irvine

Jenny A. Minier
University of Kentucky

Sergey Mityakov
Clemson University

Bruck M. Mizrach
Rutgers University

John A. Neri
University of Maryland

Phacharaphot Nuntramas
San Diego State University

Ann Owen
Hamilton College

Christakis Papageorgiou
Louisiana State University

Bruce Preston
Gérard Roland
University of California, Berkeley

David Romer
University of California, Berkeley

Paul Romer
Stanford University

Benjamin Russo
University of North Carolina, Charlotte

John E. Sabelhaus
Congressional Budget Office and University of Maryland

Dean Scrimgeour
Colgate University

Mark V. Siegler
California State University, Sacramento

Robert I. Sonora
Fort Lewis College

Eric Swanson
Federal Reserve Bank of San Francisco

Kevin F. Sylwester
Southern Illinois University

Timothy D. Terrell
Wofford College

Victor J. Valcarcel
Texas Tech University

Dietrich Vollrath
University of Houston

Andre Watteyne
Katholieke Universiteit Leuven

John Williams
Federal Reserve Bank of San Francisco

Wei Xiao
University of New Orleans

Steven Yamarik
Tufts University

Several research and teaching assistants helped in many ways, including David Agrawal, Mark Borgschulte, Dean Scrimgeour, Josie Smith, Luke Stein, and William Vijverberg. El Lee and Tina Bernard provided excellent advice and assistance on many facets of the book.

The people at W. W. Norton & Company have been exceptionally supportive, dedicated, and thorough. For the second edition, I am once again most indebted to Jack Repcheck, my editor, for his constant enthusiasm and excellent suggestions. Melissa Atkin expertly coordinated all our efforts as managing editor and kept us solidly on track. The stellar Norton team again did a tremendous job, for which I am extremely grateful: Christopher Granville, Lorraine Klimowich, Jason Spears, and Rubina Yeh.

For the first edition, I am most grateful to Jack Repcheck, who did an outstanding job spearheading the project; I could not ask for a better editor. Marian Johnson was magnificent as managing editor. Thanks also to Susan Gaustad for her developmental editing. I would also like to thank Matt Arnold, Mik Awake, Christopher Granville, Richard Mickey, Dan Jost, John McAusland, Brian Sisco, Jason Spears, and Rubina Yeh for their excellent work. I am also extremely grateful to my colleagues who prepared the superb supplements for students and instructors: David Agrawal, Elias Aravantinos, Ryan Edwards, David Gillette, Anthony Laramie, and Robert Sonora.

Finally, I would like to thank my family, near and far, for everything.

ABOUT THE AUTHOR

CHARLES I. JONES (Ph.D. MIT, 1993) is the STANCO 25 Professor of Economics at the Stanford University Graduate School of Business and a Research Associate of the National Bureau of Economic Research. Professor Jones's main research contributions are to the study of long-run economic growth. In particular, he has examined theoretically and empirically the fundamental sources of growth in per capita income over time and the reasons underlying the enormous differences in standards of living across countries. In recent years, he has used his expertise in macroeconomic methods to study the economic causes of the rise in health spending and longevity. He is the author of *Introduction to Economic Growth*, Second Edition, also published by W. W. Norton & Company.

MACROECONOMICS

Second Edition

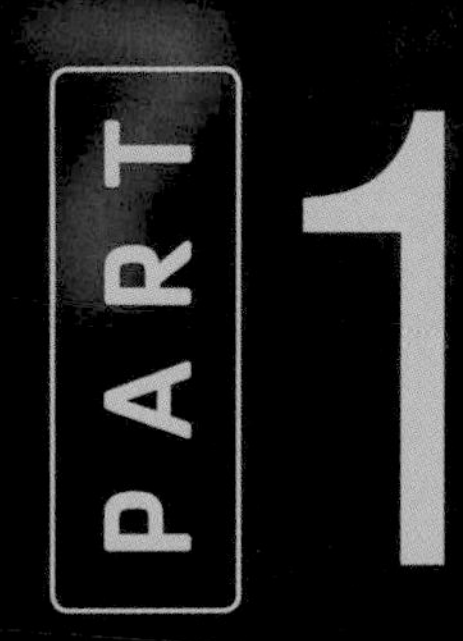

PRELIMINARIES

CHAPTER 1

INTRODUCTION TO MACROECONOMICS

OVERVIEW

In this chapter, we learn

- what macroeconomics is and consider some macroeconomic questions: What determines the wealth of nations? How do we understand the recent global financial crisis and the Great Recession that resulted? What caused the Great Inflation of the 1970s, and why has inflation been so much lower in recent decades?
- how macroeconomics uses models to answer such questions.
- the book's basic three-part structure: the long run, the short run, and issues for the future.

> We shall not cease from exploration
> And the end of all our exploring
> Will be to arrive where we started
> And know the place for the first time.
>
> –T. S. ELIOT, *FOUR QUARTETS*

1.1 What Is Macroeconomics?

Macroeconomics is the study of collections of people and firms and how their interactions through markets determine the overall economic activity in a country or region. The other main area of economics, microeconomics, focuses on the study of individual people, firms, or markets. These two branches, however, are much closer than their standard separation into different courses would lead you to believe. Just as cosmologists who study black holes draw on concepts both large (general relativity) and small (quantum mechanics), macroeconomists look to individual behavior—which economists refer to as "microfoundations"—in creating their theories of aggregate economic activity. In this sense, macroeconomics is just one large black hole!

One good way to get a sense of macroeconomics is to consider the questions it deals with, some of the most important in all of economics:

- Why is the typical American today more than 10 times richer than the typical American a century ago?
- Why is the American of today 50 times richer than the typical Ethiopian? Some of the data that motivate these first two questions are shown in Figure 1.1, a graph of GDP per person since 1870 for seven countries. (GDP stands for gross domestic product, an overall measure of income that we will study in more detail in Chapter 2.)
- How do we understand the global financial crisis and the Great Recession that has followed in recent years? As shown in Figure 1.2, this recession has seen the largest sustained decline in employment in the United States in many decades. More generally, what causes recessions and booms in the overall economy?
- What determines the rate of inflation—that is, what determines how rapidly prices are increasing in an economy? Why was inflation so high in much of the world in the 1970s, and why has it fallen so dramatically in many of the richest countries since the early 1980s? These facts are shown in Figure 1.3. Why do some countries experience hyperinflation, where the price level can explode and rise by a thousand-fold or more, essentially rendering the currency worthless?
- Why has the unemployment rate—the fraction of the labor force that would like to work but does not currently have a job—been nearly twice as high in

As we will see in Chapter 2, per capita GDP is a useful, though imperfect, measure of economic welfare. Notice both the large differences across countries as well as the increases in per capita GDP over time.

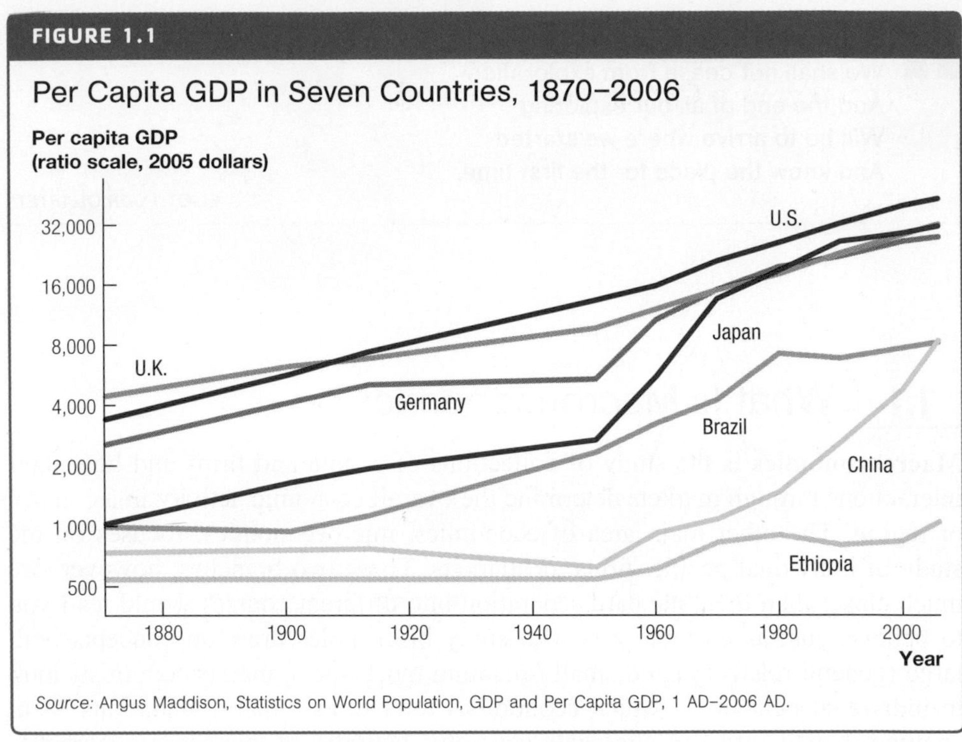

Source: Angus Maddison, Statistics on World Population, GDP and Per Capita GDP, 1 AD–2006 AD.

Employment typically rises each month. But the latest recession has led to the largest sustained decline in employment in many decades.

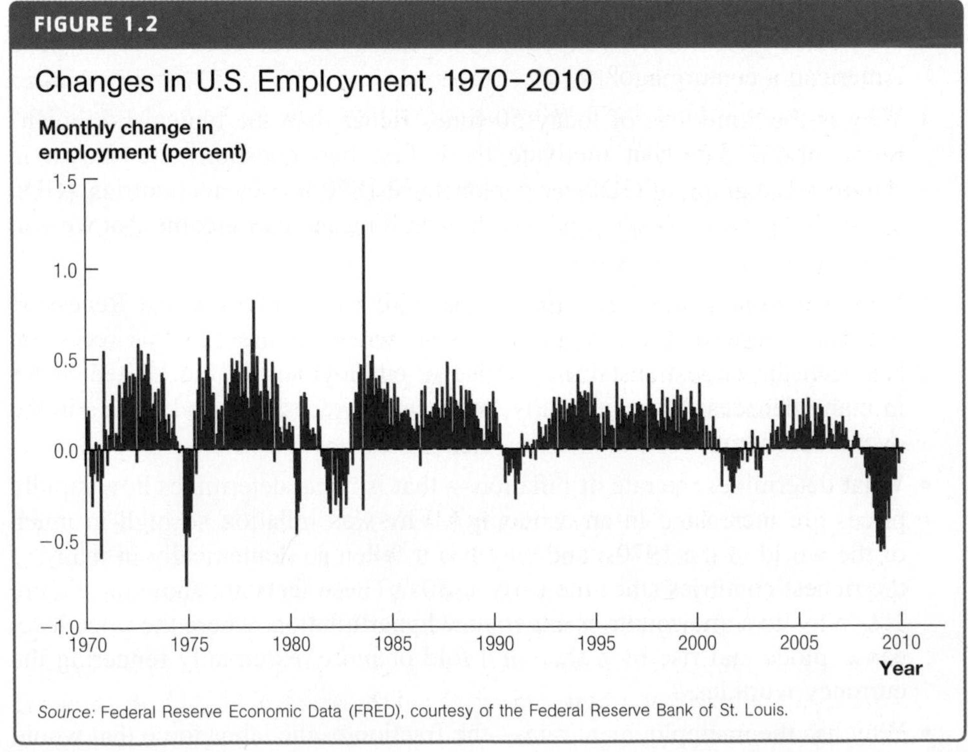

Source: Federal Reserve Economic Data (FRED), courtesy of the Federal Reserve Bank of St. Louis.

FIGURE 1.3

Inflation Rates in Certain Rich Countries, 1970–2009

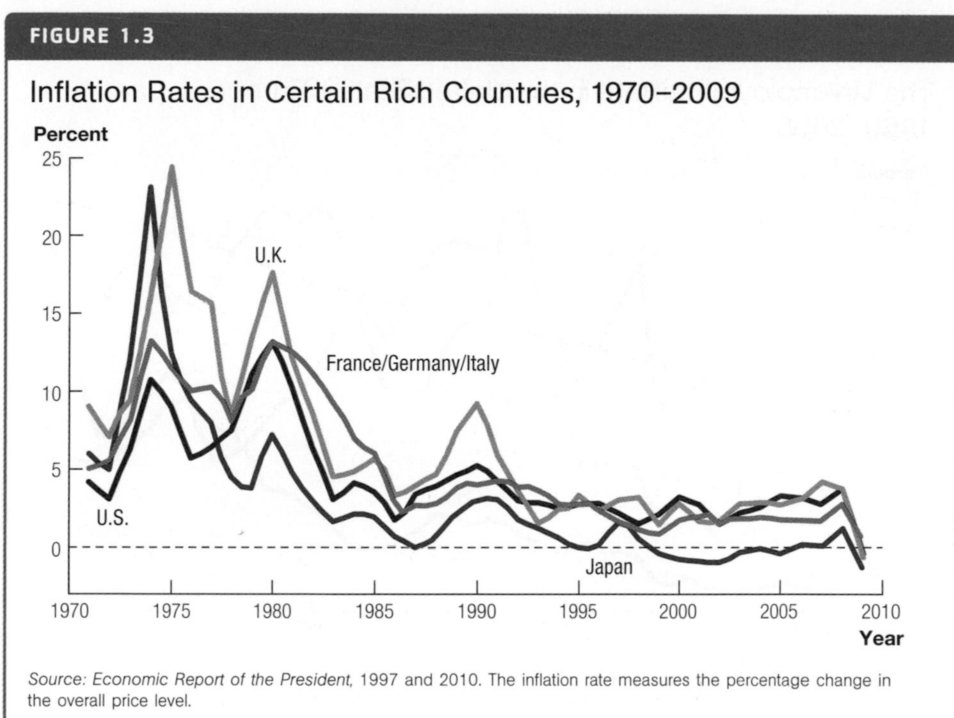

Source: Economic Report of the President, 1997 and 2010. The inflation rate measures the percentage change in the overall price level.

In many rich countries, inflation was high in the 1970s and has been low since the late 1980s.

Europe as in the United States the last two decades? Consider the evidence shown in Figure 1.4. This experience is particularly surprising in light of the fact that unemployment rates in Europe were much lower than in the United States up until about 1980. Why has unemployment in Japan been so low for most of this period?

- What role does the government, both the fiscal authority and the monetary authority, play in recessions and booms and in determining the rate of inflation?
- Budget deficits result when the government borrows money to finance its spending. Trade deficits result when one economy borrows from another. Why would an economy run a high budget deficit or a high trade deficit, or both? What are the consequences of these deficits? Figure 1.5 shows the evolution of both deficits in the United States since 1960. Are large deficits a problem?
- What prompted the currency crises in Mexico in the mid-1990s and in many Asian economies at the end of the 1990s? What are the consequences of the recent decision by China to let its currency, the renminbi, appreciate, after it was fixed for many years relative to the dollar?
- What role do financial markets like the stock market play in an economy? What is a "bubble," and how can we tell if the stock market or the housing market is in one?

What explains the very different histories of the unemployment rate in the United States, Europe, and Japan?

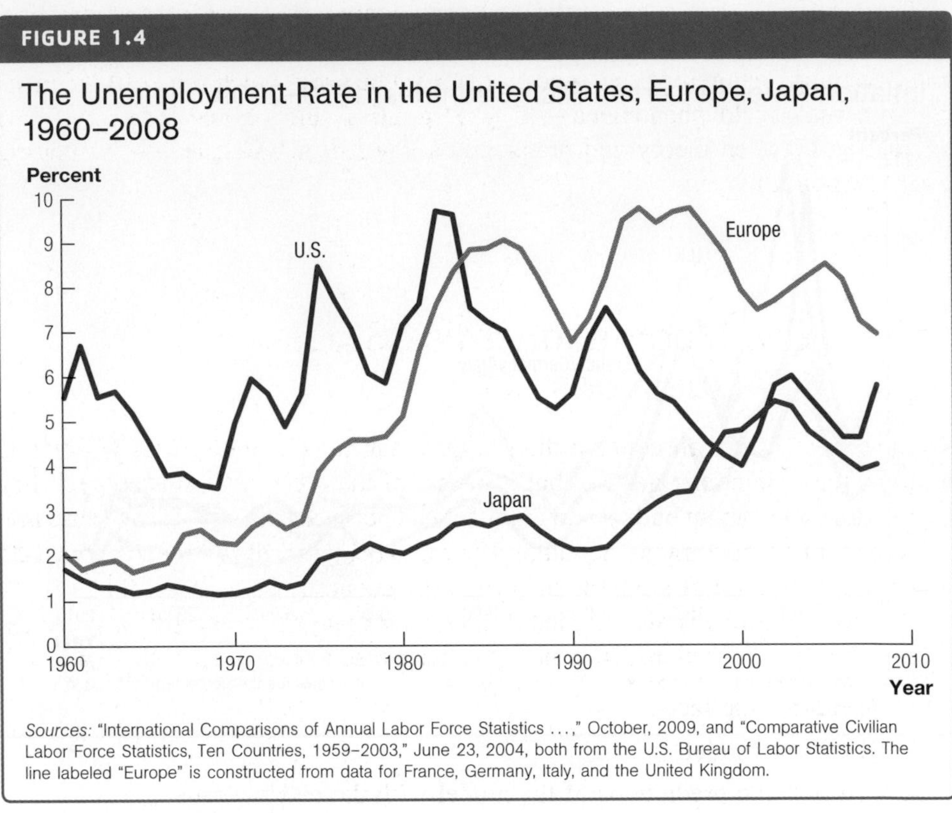

FIGURE 1.4

The Unemployment Rate in the United States, Europe, Japan, 1960–2008

Sources: "International Comparisons of Annual Labor Force Statistics . . . ," October, 2009, and "Comparative Civilian Labor Force Statistics, Ten Countries, 1959–2003," June 23, 2004, both from the U.S. Bureau of Labor Statistics. The line labeled "Europe" is constructed from data for France, Germany, Italy, and the United Kingdom.

The U.S. budget and trade deficits have been relatively high in recent years.

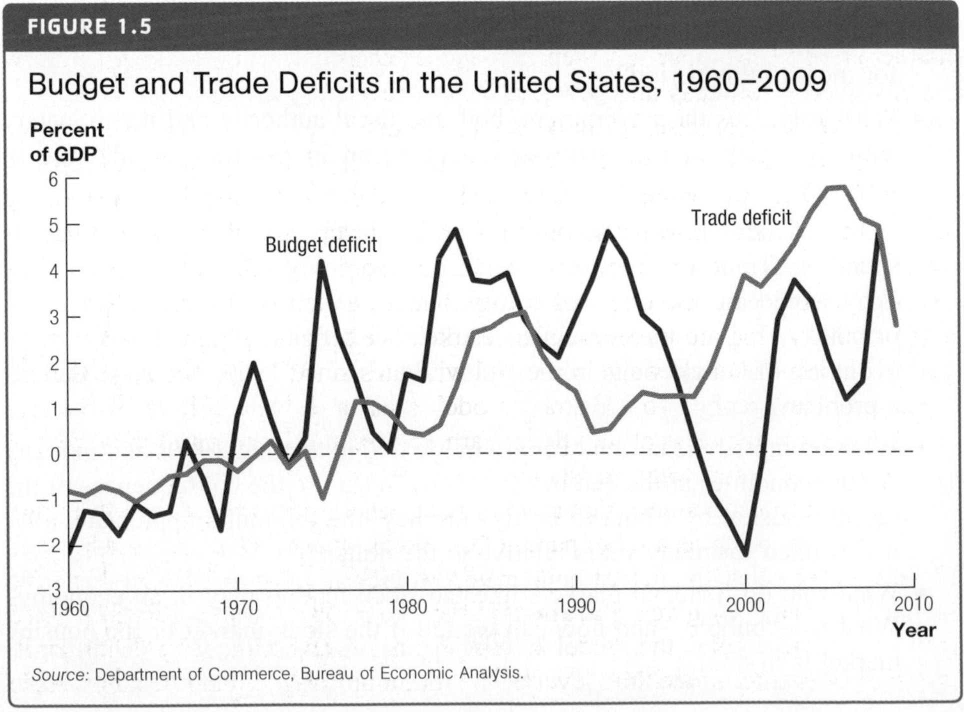

FIGURE 1.5

Budget and Trade Deficits in the United States, 1960–2009

Source: Department of Commerce, Bureau of Economic Analysis.

To study questions such as these, macroeconomists construct mathematical models, similar in spirit to the models used in microeconomics. Yet one of the most exciting features of macroeconomics is the way it combines these models with real-world phenomena—history, politics, and economic policy. This interaction between theory and practice is a key reason students enjoy studying macroeconomics.

1.2 How Macroeconomics Studies Key Questions

The questions above all concern the economy taken as a whole. This is obvious in the case of economic growth, but it is true of the other questions as well. For example, we care about budget and trade deficits because they may affect standards of living for the economy in the future. We care about bubbles in financial markets because the collapse of a bubble may send the economy into a recession.

Macroeconomics is also unified in a different way: by the approach it takes to studying these questions. In general, this approach consists of four steps:

1. Document the facts.
2. Develop a model.
3. Compare the predictions of the model with the original facts.
4. Use the model to make other predictions that may eventually be tested.

1. First, we document the key facts related to the question we want to consider. For example, suppose we ask, "Why are people in Europe so much richer today than a century ago?" Our first step is to gather economic *data* to document how rich Europeans are today and how rich they were a hundred years ago. With such data we can make precise, quantitative statements.

2. Next, we develop a model. You are already familiar with one of the most important models in economics, that of supply and demand. Models are extremely useful because they allow us to abstract from the nearly infinite number of forces at play in the real world in order to focus on those that are most relevant. For example, in studying the effect of a minimum wage law, economists will use a supply-and-demand model of the labor market. We act as if there is a single labor market that pays a single wage in a world with no schooling decisions, on-the-job training, or geography. This abstract model is an unrealistic picture of the real world, but it nevertheless allows us to learn important lessons about the effect of introducing minimum wage legislation.

All models in economics share an important general structure, shown in Figure 1.6. Each takes as inputs a set of parameters and exogenous variables: the features of the economy that the model builder gets to pick in advance, features that are outside the model, or given. **Parameter** refers to an input that is generally fixed over time, except when the model builder decides to experiment by changing it. In our labor market model, the level of the minimum wage would be an example

A model takes some inputs, called parameters and exogenous variables, and determines some outcomes—called endogenous variables. For example, a labor market model may take the level of the minimum wage and the number of people in the economy as parameters and determine the wage and the level of employment (the endogenous variables).

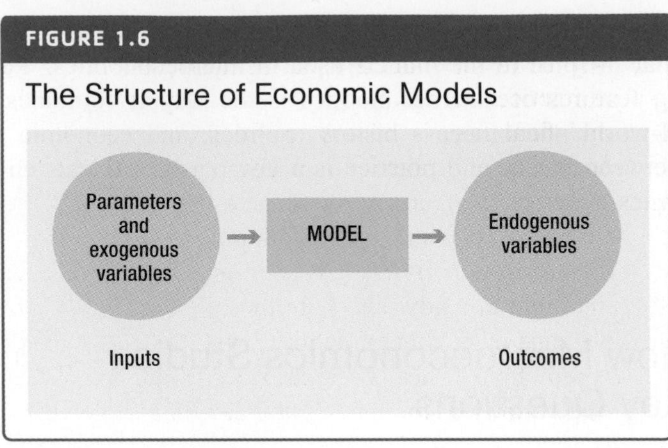

FIGURE 1.6
The Structure of Economic Models

of a parameter. **Exogenous variable** ("exo-" means "outside") refers to an input that is allowed to change over time, but in a way that is completely determined ahead of time by the model builder. For example, we might assume the population in the economy grows over time at a constant, exogenous rate, regardless of what happens in the labor market. Population then would be an example of an exogenous variable.

A model operates on the exogenous variables and parameters in order to generate outcomes, called **endogenous variables** ("endo-" means "within": within, or explained by, the model). For example, in the labor market model, the level of the wage and the level of employment would be endogenous variables (outcomes) determined by supply and demand.

Unlike what you may have seen in an introductory economics class, the models we develop in this book will consist of a set of mathematical equations and a set of unknowns (the endogenous variables). Solving a model is in principle as simple as solving the equations for the values of the unknowns. For example, an equation describing labor supply and an equation describing labor demand constitute the mathematical version of the labor market model. Both equations involve our two endogenous variables, the wage and the level of employment. So we have two equations and two unknowns. Equilibrium in the labor market occurs when labor supply is equal to labor demand at the market wage, and the solution to these equations gives us the equilibrium levels of the wage and employment.

The end of each chapter contains one or two worked exercises to help you learn the material.

At the moment, this is all admittedly very abstract. A worked exercise at the end of this chapter will take you through the labor market example in more detail. Later, in Chapter 4, we will develop our first model in order to understand why some countries are so much richer than others. That example will go a long way toward helping you understand exactly what a model is and why models are useful. You can then build on that knowledge as you work with other models throughout the book.

3. The third step is to consider how well our model helps us understand the facts we began with. A successful model of why some countries are so much richer than others, for example, should predict that countries will have different levels of income. But that is not enough. To be truly successful, the model should also get the *quantitative* predictions right as well: that is, it should not only predict that the United States will be richer than Ethiopia, but also give the 50-fold difference that we observe in practice.

4. The fourth and final step is related to the third: using the model to run "experiments." Once we have a model in hand, the model builder is free to change the underlying parameters in order to analyze how this change affects the endogenous variables. For example, we might change a tax rate and study the response of investment and standards of living. Or we might consider lowering a short-term nominal interest rate to study the evolution of inflation and unemployment over time. The advantage of having an explicit mathematical model is that it can make quantitative predictions. These predictions can then be compared with real evidence to judge the validity of the model, and can be used to analyze particular policy changes.

1.3 An Overview of the Book

Figure 1.7, a graph of per capita GDP for the United States, is one of the most famous and intriguing graphs of macroeconomics, and it serves as an organizing device for this book. There are three important features of the graph that parallel the three main sections of the text.

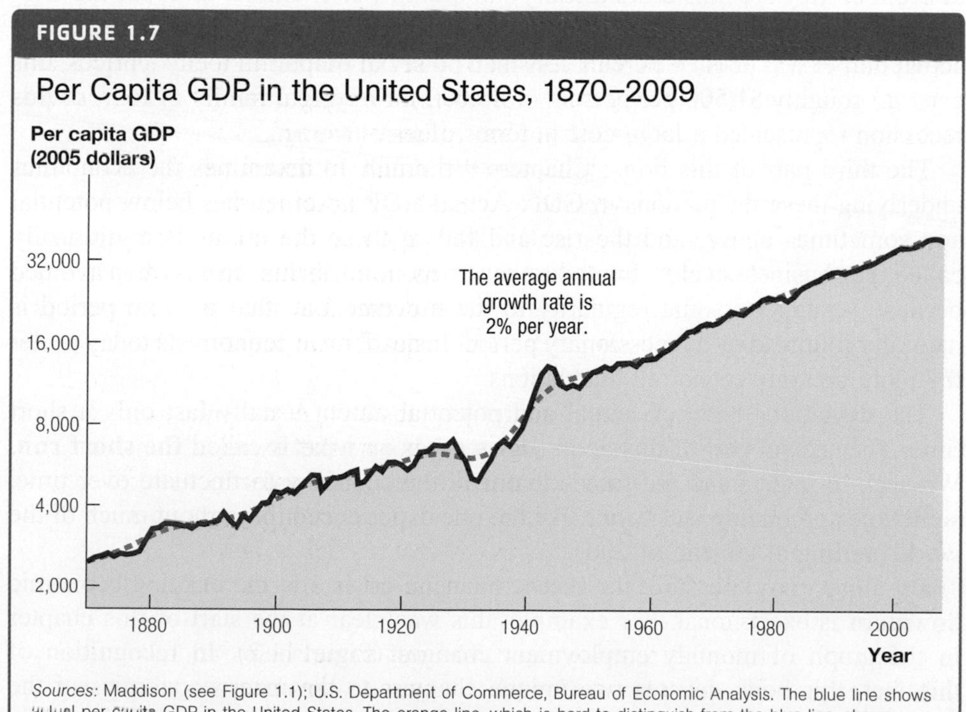

FIGURE 1.7

Per Capita GDP in the United States, 1870–2009

Sources: Maddison (see Figure 1.1); U.S. Department of Commerce, Bureau of Economic Analysis. The blue line shows actual per capita GDP in the United States. The orange line, which is hard to distinguish from the blue line, shows potential output. The difference between actual and potential output is a measure of short-run fluctuations in GDP.

Three features of the graph stand out: (1) the overall upward trend due to economic growth, (2) the short-run fluctuations in economic activity, and (3) the suggested question of what the future holds. These features reflect the structure of the book.

The Long Run

The most impressive feature of the graph is the enormous increase in standards of living over the years. Income per person began at $2,800 in 1870 and rose by more than a factor of 15 to $44,000 in 2008. Why have living standards grown so dramatically in the United States? And why have some regions of the world, like Ethiopia (as we saw earlier), not experienced a similar revolutionary change? These are among the most important questions in macroeconomics. The first part of this book—Chapters 3 through 6—develops the answers that macroeconomics currently offers. More generally, this first section is concerned with economic growth and the determinants of the macroeconomy in **the long run**. Chapter 7 then turns to the labor market in the long run, and Chapter 8 considers the long-run causes of inflation. A solid understanding of the macroeconomics of the long run turns out to be essential to understanding everything else that follows.

The Short Run

Notice that in Figure 1.7 two lines are plotted: the blue line is actual per capita GDP, or output, while the orange line, a "smoothed" version of the solid line, is called **potential output**. Potential output measures the way per capita GDP would evolve if prices were completely flexible and resources were fully employed. The second important feature of the figure is that actual output deviates from potential output. Other than the Great Depression of the 1930s, these deviations are hard to see, but they are still economically important. For example, in 1982, the U.S. economy suffered one of the largest recessions of the post–World War II era, and actual output was about 5 percent less than potential output. In today's prices, this gap was roughly $1,500 per person, or $6,000 for a typical family of four, so this recession represented a large cost in terms of lost income.

The third part of this book, Chapters 9 through 14, examines the economics underlying these fluctuations in GDP. Actual GDP is sometimes below potential and sometimes above, and the rise and fall of these deviations is traditionally called the "business cycle." In modern macroeconomics, this term is often avoided because it suggests some regularity to the movements—that a boom period is naturally followed by a recessionary period. Instead, most economists today prefer the more neutral "economic fluctuations."

The deviations between actual and potential output usually last only a short time. The second part of this book thus focuses on what is called **the short run**. We seek to understand the forces that lead the economy to fluctuate over time, sometimes producing recessions like the one experienced throughout much of the world starting at the end of 2007.

By almost any measure, the recent financial crisis and the ensuing economic downturn is exceptional. For example, this was clear at the start of this chapter in the graph of monthly employment changes (Figure 1.2). In recognition of this fact, this book devotes two unique chapters to the macroeconomics of the financial crisis, Chapters 10 and 14. These chapters explain the facts of the crisis, introduce several important concepts like balance sheets and leverage, and use the basic macroeconomics of the short run to shed light on the events surrounding the crisis.

A central topic of short-run macroeconomics that is not conveyed by our organizing graph is the role of inflation. As we will see, economic fluctuations and inflation are connected in an important way: one reason economic activity fluctuates is that the central bank leads the economy into a recession in order to bring down inflation. Chapters 9 through 14 develop a model of how inflation and GDP are jointly determined in the short run.

The fact that the fluctuations in GDP are somewhat difficult to see in Figure 1.7 is itself worthy of note. Even the worst crisis—the Great Depression of the 1930s—painful as it was, proved to be temporary, and the overwhelming fact of twentieth-century macroeconomics was one of sustained economic growth. Over the long term, economic growth swamps economic fluctuations.

Issues for the Future

Finally, the natural question raised by Figure 1.7 concerns the future. We can't help but look at the sustained rise in income and wonder if it will continue. Will the next century see another 10-fold increase in per capita GDP, so that our great-grandchildren will earn an average of $440,000 per year?

This theme of what the future holds—or of macroeconomics beyond economic growth and fluctuations—is one way of thinking about the last section of the book. Chapter 15 explores the microfoundations that underlie the modern understanding of consumption. What determines how much the economy consumes or saves in any given year? Chapter 16 studies investment. One very important type of investment, central to macroeconomics, is investment in physical capital—machine tools, computers, and buildings, for example. We explore how firms determine how much to invest in physical capital. Another key theme of this chapter, though, is that many kinds of investment can be understood in the same way. So this chapter also studies the determinants of financial investment and prices in the stock market.

Chapter 17 discusses the government budget constraint and the size of the current deficit and debt. A key point of this chapter is that major decisions about government spending and taxation, especially regarding health care, will have to be made in the coming decades. Virtually all economists agree that current policies cannot be sustained.

Chapters 18 and 19 explore another key theme related to the future of the macroeconomy: the rise of globalization. The United States is but one (albeit large and important) member of the world economy. Earlier chapters in the book explicitly recognize this fact and explore its implications: for example, the discovery of new ideas in a distant part of the world affects potential output in *every* country, and changes in the demand for U.S. exports can be a source of short-run fluctuations. Here, however, we make globalization a focus.

Chapter 18 explores the theory of international trade: why do economies trade with each other, and what are the consequences of this trade? Chapter 19 studies exchange rates and international finance. Both chapters help us think about the effects of globalization on the macroeconomy and the consequences of the high trade deficits seen in recent years in the United States. Finally, in Chapter 20 we look back at the ground we have covered and consider the important questions that remain.

Macroeconomics is a fascinating and intriguing subject. Understanding the answers to the questions it poses offers the possibility of enormous improvements in welfare throughout the world. If we understand the sources of economic growth, perhaps all countries can unleash its powerful engine. If we understand why hyperinflations or depressions occur, perhaps we can prevent them from recurring. Education is the first step to a better future.

CHAPTER REVIEW

SUMMARY

1. Macroeconomics is the study of collections of people and firms and how their interactions through markets determine the overall performance of the economy.
2. Many of the most important questions in economics require macroeconomic analysis: What determines the wealth of nations? How do we understand the recent global financial crisis and the Great Recession that resulted? What caused the Great Inflation of the 1970s, and why has inflation been so much lower for the last decade? What are the consequences of trade deficits and budget deficits?
3. Macroeconomics studies these questions in four steps: document the relevant facts, develop a model, compare the predictions of the model with the facts, use the model to make and test other predictions.
4. A model is a collection of mathematical equations that are used to study a particular economic issue. Models determine the value of endogenous variables, like the price and quantity of computers sold or the rate of economic growth.
5. This book is organized around a key graph, Figure 1.7. The first part focuses on macroeconomics in the long run, the second part deals with the short run, and the third part takes up a number of important topics that will concern us in the future.

KEY CONCEPTS

endogenous variables
exogenous variables
the long run
macroeconomics
parameters
potential output
the short run

REVIEW QUESTIONS

1. Which questions in macroeconomics interest you the most? Why?
2. Given your current knowledge, what do you think are the answers to these questions?
3. How does macroeconomics study these questions?
4. What are the key ingredients of an economic model, and why are models useful?

EXERCISES

smartwork.wwnorton.com 

1. **Macroeconomic questions and answers:** Select one of the macroeconomic questions in this chapter. Describe what you think the answer is.
2. **The macroeconomics of your favorite country:** Pick a country that you find interesting, and learn some basic facts about its economy. Summarize these facts in a half-page essay. You may find the following resources to be helpful; feel free to explore others on your own.
   —The *CIA World Factbook:* www.cia.gov/cia/publications/factbook
   —Wikipedia: wikipedia.org
   —The "Country Snapshots" file, snapshots.pdf, which should be available on your course web page, or from the web address in the next question.
3. **Country snapshots:** Download the file snapshots.pdf from wwnorton.com/college/econ/chad and answer the following. (At the moment, the latest year in the data file is 2007. Over time, this year will advance, so please use the latest year available in the Country Snapshots file whenever the year 2007 appears in questions below.)
   - (a) What was the ratio of per capita income in each of the following countries to that in the United States in the year 2007: Ethiopia, Mexico, India, and Japan?
   - (b) Which country had the faster average annual growth rate of per capita GDP between 1960 and 2007, Botswana or China?
   - (c) Rank these countries in order of population: Bangladesh, Brazil, Indonesia, Nigeria, Russia, the United States.
   - (d) Which is larger as a share of GDP in most rich countries, investment or government purchases? What about in most poor countries?
   - (e) Exchange rates are reported as units of domestic currency (like the Japanese yen or the British pound) per U.S. dollar. Look at the exchange rate for several countries. Do you detect any overall pattern? Why might that be?
4. **Making graphs (spreadsheet):** Use the snapshots.pdf file, together with its hyperlinks to the underlying spreadsheet data. Use a spreadsheet program of your choice to complete the following.
   - (a) Make a plot of per capita GDP (in dollars) for the years 1950 to 2007 for a country of your choice. Label the x-axis "year" and the y-axis "per capita GDP."

(b) Make a plot of per capita GDP relative to the United States (U.S. = 100) for the years 1950 to 2007 that includes the United States and three other countries of your choice, all on the same graph. Be sure to label the lines on the graph in some informative way so that each line can be associated with its country.

5. The labor market model (I): Suppose the following equations characterize supply and demand in the labor market model:

$$\text{labor supply: } L^s = 2 \times w + 30$$
$$\text{labor demand: } L^d = 60 - w$$

Equilibrium occurs at an employment level L^* and a wage w^*, so that the labor market clears. That is, supply is equal to demand: $L^s = L^d$.

(a) What are the endogenous variables in the labor market model?
(b) Solve for the equilibrium values of these endogenous variables.

6. The labor market model (II): Now we add some parameters to the labor market model:

$$\text{labor supply: } L^s = \bar{a} \times w + \bar{\ell}$$
$$\text{labor demand: } L^d = \bar{f} - w$$

The parameters in this setup are $\bar{a}$, $\bar{\ell}$, and $\bar{f}$. (Notice that parameters are denoted with an overbar, a convention we will maintain throughout the book.) The parameter $\bar{\ell}$ represents the number of hours workers would supply to the market even if the wage were zero; it therefore reflects the inherent amount of time people like to work. The parameter $\bar{f}$, on the other hand, reflects the amount of labor the firm would like to hire if the wage were zero. It might be thought of as some inherent capacity of the firm (perhaps because the firm owns a given amount of land and capital that cannot be altered).

(a) What is the economic interpretation of $\bar{a}$?
(b) What are the endogenous variables in this model?
(c) Solve for the equilibrium of the labor market. That is, solve for the endogenous variables as a function of the parameters of the model.
(d) If $\bar{\ell}$ increases, what happens to the equilibrium wage and employment levels? Does this make sense? (*Hint:* Think about what happens in the supply-and-demand diagram for the labor market.)
(e) Answer the same questions in (d) for an increase in $\bar{f}$.

7. Models: Apply the supply-and-demand model to the following markets. In each case, state the key endogenous variables in the market as well as some important exogenous variables or parameters. Also, express each model as a system of mathematical equations. As an example, $Q = F(P, \bar{X})$ might be the demand curve in the computer market, where $\bar{X}$ captures some exogenous variables like the availability of the iPod or computer games. How many equations are there within each example? How many unknowns?

(a) The computer market.
(b) The market for your favorite music.
(c) The market for a particular currency, such as the dollar, the yen, or the euro. (*Hint:* This last example suggests an important point about "exogenous

variables": what is exogenous in one model, as in a narrow study of the supply and demand for dollars, may be endogenous in a richer model—like a study of the entire U.S. macroeconomy.)

WORKED EXERCISES

Here and in each following chapter, you will find the worked exercises most helpful if you try to work through them completely on your own before consulting the answers.

5. The labor market model:

(a) The endogenous variables are the price and quantity: the wage w and the quantity of labor L. Another way to think about this problem is that we have three equations and three unknowns, the unknowns being the wage, labor supply, and labor demand. However, since the "third" equation is that labor supply equals labor demand, this naturally reduces our model to two equations in w and L.

(b) The equilibrium of the labor market is shown in Figure 1.8. To solve for this equilibrium, we first find the wage rate that equates supply and demand. This wage solves

$$2w + 30 = 60 - w.$$

(The left side is labor supply and the right side is labor demand.) The solution to this equation is $w^* = 10$. Substituting this wage into either the labor supply equation or the labor demand equation, we find that the equilibrium quantity of labor is $L^* = 50$.

FIGURE 1.8

The Labor Market

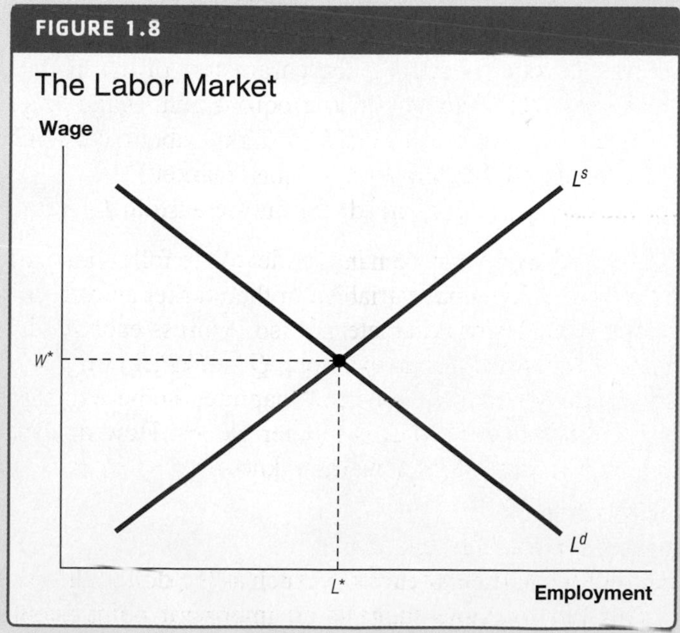

CHAPTER 2

MEASURING THE MACROECONOMY

OVERVIEW

In this chapter, we learn

- the importance of gross domestic product (GDP), and how it is measured.
- the composition of GDP, and how it has changed over time.
- how to use GDP to measure the evolution of living standards over time.
- how to use GDP to measure differences in living standards across countries.

> While the GDP and the rest of the national income accounts may seem to be arcane concepts, they are truly among the great inventions of the twentieth century.
>
> —PAUL A. SAMUELSON AND WILLIAM D. NORDHAUS

2.1 Introduction

Exactly how severe was the Great Depression? Perhaps surprisingly, it was difficult for policymakers in the early 1930s to know. Stock prices, railroad freight reports, and some limited measures of industrial production did signal problems. But no broad-based measure of economic activity was available to quantify the Depression or to indicate the effectiveness of steps designed to spur economic recovery. This ignorance in the face of such an important phenomenon led Simon Kuznets and his colleagues at the U.S. Department of Commerce to create the National Income and Product Accounts that same decade. The development of "national income accounting," together with improvements made subsequently, stands as one of the fundamental contributions of economics during the twentieth century.[1]

National income accounting provides a systematic method for aggregating the production of cars, computers, health care, and music into a single measure of overall economic activity. Moreover, it relates this measure of aggregate production to the total amount of income earned by every person in the economy and to all the spending that occurs. In one of the most beautiful accounting relations in economics, total production equals total income equals total spending; in this chapter, we will see how.

National accounting allows us to take a detailed snapshot of the state of the economy at a given point in time. But it also shows us how these snapshots can be linked together over time to provide a picture of economic growth. Further, pictures for different countries can be lined up to help us understand how economic performance varies throughout the world.

This chapter discusses the central elements of national accounting and how these pictures of economic performance are created. The accounting theory is presented with real-world examples, so that you simultaneously learn the economic concepts as well as important empirical facts about economic activity in the United States and other countries.

2.2 Measuring the State of the Economy

The key measure of the state of the economy is called **gross domestic product**, or GDP for short. Gross domestic product is defined as the market value of the

Epigraph: From "GDP: One of the Great Inventions of the 20th Century," *Survey of Current Business* (January 2000), pp. 6–14.

[1] This history is discussed in detail in the article cited in the epigraph.

final goods and services produced in an economy over a certain period. If you add together the value of all the cars, clothes, peanut butter, airline travel, musical performances, magazine articles, and everything else produced in a year, you will get GDP. In 2008, GDP in the United States was equal to $14.4 trillion, or about $47,000 per person.

Production = Expenditure = Income

Like nearly all other accounting systems, national income accounting involves a large number of detailed definitions and constructs. Its overall principles, however, are elegantly straightforward. We can see how they work by considering a simple example.

Suppose the economy consists of only a single family farm with a small fruit stand in the front yard. Our farmers, Homer and Marge, grow tangerines on the land, hire some workers to help them with the harvest, and then sell the tangerines at the fruit stand. GDP in this simple economy is the total number of tangerines Homer and Marge produce in a year. This is the *production* measure of GDP, and we could compute it by following the farm workers through the orchard and counting the tangerines as they get picked.

An alternative way to measure this GDP is by focusing on sales at the fruit stand. Consumers visit the stand each day to buy tangerines, and the total purchases represent the *expenditure* approach to measuring GDP. As long as all the tangerines that are picked end up being sold, these two measures will be equal.[2]

Finally, the workers in this tangerine economy are paid a wage, and Homer and Marge also earn some income—the "profits" that are not paid out as wages to the workers. The *income* approach to measuring GDP adds up all the income earned in the economy. On the farm, all production gets paid out to someone as income—either to the workers as wages or to Homer and Marge as "profits"—so the production measure of GDP must also be equal to the income measure.

According to national income accounting, GDP in an economy equals production, expenditure, and income. We exploit this result repeatedly throughout the book.

This example illustrates a fundamental principle in national income accounting: *production equals expenditure equals income*. These terms reflect the three different ways to compute GDP in any economy, and all three are defined so that they will give identical values.

Why is "profits" in quotation marks above? The reason has to do with the distinction between the common use of the word—as in the profits Homer and Marge earn—and the "economic profits" referred to by economists. The profits earned by Homer and Marge are really just a normal, competitive return on their own labor, farm, and fruit stand. **Economic profits** are the above-normal returns associated with prices that exceed those that prevail under perfect competition. An important lesson from microeconomics is that unless there is some market power by which firms charge prices above marginal cost, economic profits are zero.

We now look at each approach to GDP in turn.

---

[2] In practice, you can imagine some firms producing goods—like dump trucks or airplanes—that are not sold during the same year in which they are produced. National accounting treats these goods as *inventories* and counts them as investment expenditures so that the production and expenditure measures of GDP are equal.

The Expenditure Approach to GDP

The national income accounts divide the goods and services that are purchased into several categories. This breakdown appears in one of the fundamental accounting equations, called the **national income identity**:

$$Y = C + I + G + NX \tag{2.1}$$

where

$$\begin{aligned} \boldsymbol{Y} &= \text{GDP (in dollars)}, \\ \boldsymbol{C} &= \text{consumption}, \\ \boldsymbol{I} &= \text{investment}, \\ \boldsymbol{G} &= \text{government purchases, and} \\ \boldsymbol{NX} &= \text{net exports} = \text{exports} - \text{imports}. \end{aligned}$$

This equation, representing the *expenditure approach* to GDP, illustrates how expenditures are divided according to their purpose. Goods and services can be consumed, invested by the private sector, bought by the government, or shipped abroad for foreigners to use.

Table 2.1 shows the actual breakdown of U.S. GDP in 2008. Consumption expenditures accounted for 70 percent of GDP. Examples include expenditures on motor vehicles, food, housing services, and medical care, with consumption of the last two categories each exceeding 10 percent of GDP. Investment expenditures made up about 15 percent of GDP. This category includes purchases by

TABLE 2.1

The Expenditure Approach to U.S. GDP in 2008

	Total (billions of dollars)	Share of GDP (percent)	Per person (dollars)
Gross domestic product	14,440	100.0	47,010
Consumption	10,130	70.2	32,970
Motor vehicles and parts	340	2.4	1,110
Food	780	5.4	2,550
Housing	1,840	12.7	6,000
Medical care	1,550	10.7	5,060
Investment	2,140	14.8	6,950
Structures (nonresidential)	610	4.2	1,980
Equipment and software	1,080	7.5	3,530
Residential	480	3.3	1,550
Government purchases	2,880	19.9	9,380
National defense	740	5.1	2,400
Net exports	−710	−4.9	−2,300
Exports	1,830	12.7	5,960
Imports	2,540	17.6	8,260

Source: U.S. Department of Commerce, Bureau of Economic Analysis, www.bea.gov.

GDP is the sum of consumption, investment, government purchases, and net exports. Some examples of these expenditure categories are listed.

businesses of structures like office buildings and equipment such as computers and machine tools. The construction of new homes ("Residential") is also counted as part of investment.

Government purchases, which totaled 20 percent of GDP, include expenditures on public schools, highways, government-funded research, and national defense. There is an important and sometimes confusing distinction between government purchases and government spending. Government spending includes purchases of goods and services, but also "transfer" payments (like Social Security and Medicare) and interest payments on any outstanding government debt. To see this distinction more clearly, suppose the government taxes businesses and pays out the proceeds to the unemployed in the form of unemployment insurance. Both taxes and government spending are then higher, but is a flow of GDP generated? No: there is simply a transfer of resources from one group to another. In 2008, government purchases accounted for about two-thirds of government spending, with the remainder consisting of transfers and interest payments. It is only the purchases that directly involve new production and are properly recorded as GDP.

Finally, 12.7 percent of the goods and services produced by U.S. businesses were shipped abroad and sold to foreigners; these sales are exports. At the same time, U.S. consumers and businesses imported goods and services from abroad equal in magnitude to 17.6 percent of GDP. Imports included cars, cell phones, machine tools, and financial services. On net, then, the United States imported more than it exported, so that "net exports"—exports minus imports—were equal to −4.9 percent of GDP. Another common name for net exports is the **trade balance**, and when the trade balance is negative, as in 2008, we say there is a trade deficit.

How have these percentages changed over time? The answer is shown in Figure 2.1. Broadly speaking, for the last seventy-five years or so, the composition

This expenditure-side decomposition of GDP shows the general stability of the shares over much of the twentieth century.

FIGURE 2.1

Composition of U.S. GDP, 1929–2009

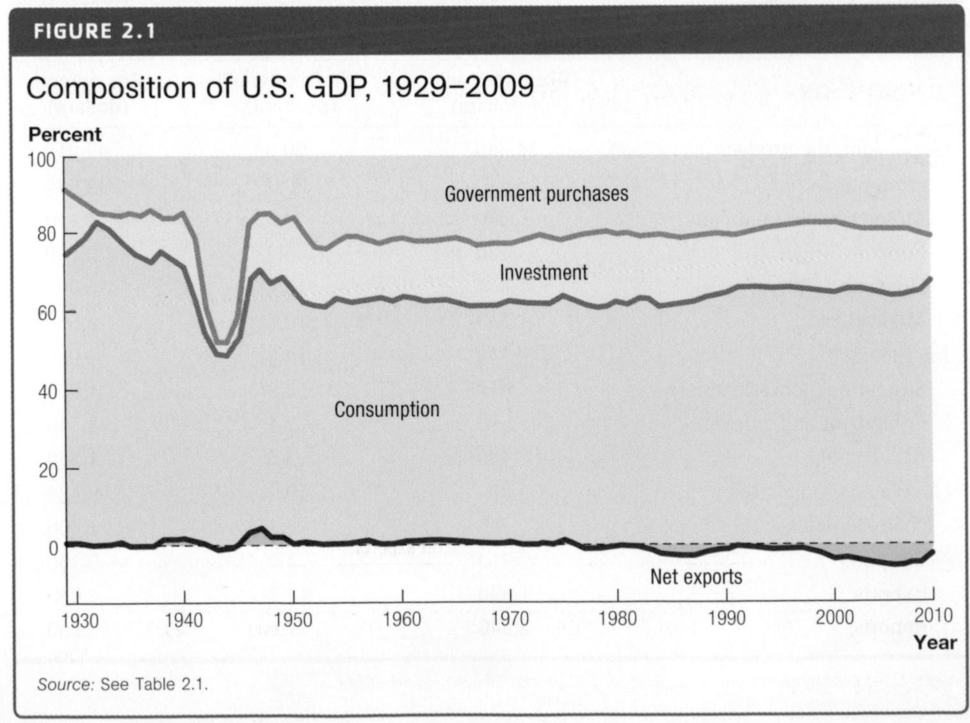

Source: See Table 2.1.

of GDP has been relatively stable. The consumption share of GDP is roughly 65 percent, government purchases just under 20 percent, and investment about 15 percent. We can also see from the figure that a big change occurred during World War II (1939–45), when government purchases for national defense expanded sharply and crowded out private investment and consumption. During the Great Depression of the 1930s, the consumption share was relatively high and the investment share relatively low. Finally, the trade deficits of the last three decades are a recent phenomenon, and the deficit reached nearly 6 percent of GDP in 2006 before declining during the Great Recession. Before 1980, the U.S. economy almost always had a trade balance that was zero or slightly positive. Why did it change? The next figure begins to address this question.

The broad stability of shares of GDP suggested by Figure 2.1 masks some of the more recent movements. Figure 2.2, which plots the shares since 1970, shows that the consumption share of GDP has actually been rising since about 1980: in 1970, it was under 63 percent, but by 2009 it had risen to more than 70 percent. At an accounting level, this rise is mirrored by a decline in the trade balance through 2006, from roughly 0 to −5.7 percent of GDP, and by a decline in government purchases from 22.5 percent to 19 percent. To some extent, then, the trade deficit is caused by the rise in consumption.

The economic explanation for these changes is not clear. On the one hand, if the government decides to reduce its share in the economy, more is left over for private consumption. On the other hand, the rising trade deficit should make us wary. A trade deficit is basically a way to borrow goods and services from another economy: the rest of the world sends more goods to the United States than we send in return. The only way they will agree to do this is if we promise to repay the "loan" in the future. This repayment will show up in the form of future trade

FIGURE 2.2

Expenditure Shares of U.S. GDP, 1970–2009

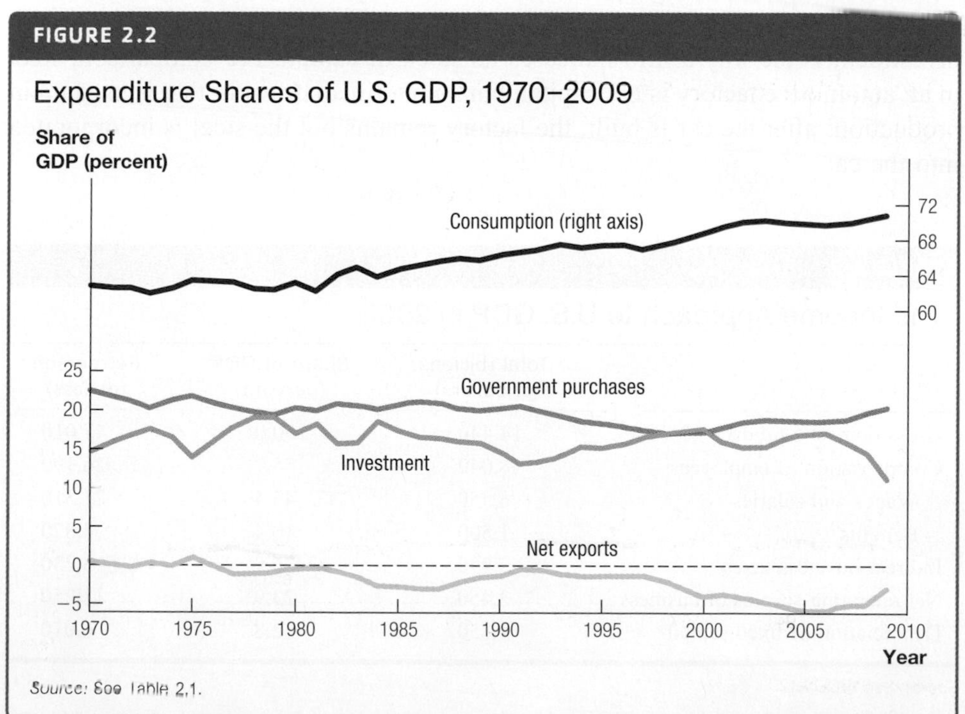

Source: See Table 2.1.

The steady rise in the consumption share is associated with a slight decline in government purchases and the emergence of a large trade deficit (at least prior to the recent recession).

surpluses, at which time there will be less GDP available for consumption, investment, and government purchases.

And the rise in consumption raises another question: what changes to the economy have U.S. consumers seen that lead them to want to increase their consumption share now at the expense of what will likely be a lower consumption share in the future? One possibility is a positive "technology shock" that will make the United States a richer country in the future (the Internet revolution? biotech?). Another possibility, however, is that easy credit card access and easy methods of borrowing are leading people to consume too much and save too little. Exactly how much of the increased consumption share is due to each of these possibilities is unclear. This important issue will be explored in more detail in Chapter 18.

The Income Approach to GDP

An important lesson from national income accounting is that for every dollar of product sold there is a dollar of income earned. That is, as we saw with Homer and Marge, GDP is equal to the value of all goods and services produced in the economy, but it is also equal to the sum of all income earned in the economy.

Table 2.2 shows the income approach to U.S. GDP in 2008. A large part of income, just under 60 percent, came in the form of compensation to employees—wages and salaries as well as the (growing) category of benefits, including health and retirement benefits. The bulk of the remainder was the net operating surplus of businesses, a fancy name for the "profits" earned by Homer and Marge.

A much smaller category, depreciation of capital, constituted just over 10 percent of GDP. **Capital** refers to the inputs into production other than labor that are not completely used up in the production process. Examples include structures like a factory or office building and equipment like computers or copying machines. If this sounds like our description of investment (from Table 2.1), that is intentional: investment is the way a firm increases its stock of capital. For comparison, steel in an automotive factory is not capital, but an intermediate input that is used up in production: after the car is built, the factory remains but the steel is incorporated into the car.

TABLE 2.2

The Income Approach to U.S. GDP in 2008

	Total (billions of dollars)	Share of GDP (percent)	Per person (dollars)
Gross domestic product	14,440	100.0	47,010
Compensation of employees	8,040	55.7	26,190
Wages and salaries	6,550	45.4	21,310
Benefits	1,500	10.4	4,870
Indirect business taxes	990	6.9	3,230
Net operating surplus of business	3,450	23.9	11,250
Depreciation of fixed capital	1,850	12.8	6,010

Source: See Table 2.1.

FIGURE 2.3

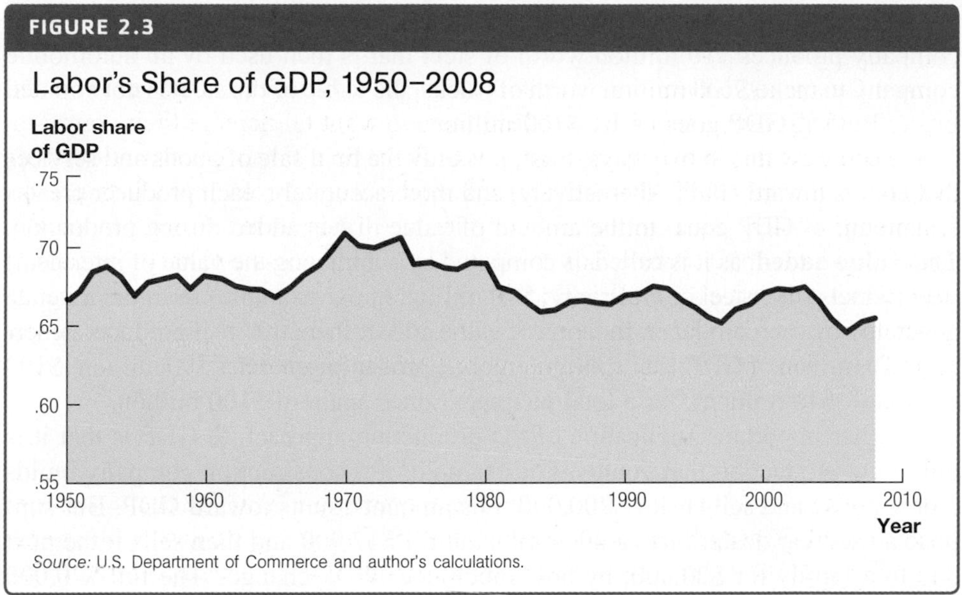

Source: U.S. Department of Commerce and author's calculations.

Labor income as a share of GDP is about two-thirds.

When Homer and Marge run their fruit stand for a year, the shelving, light fixtures, and wooden structure all endure some wear and tear. These items are part of the farm's capital stock, and the wear and tear is called **depreciation**. Some of their income is implicitly a compensation for this wear and tear—that is, for the depreciation of the farm's capital. The presence of this depreciation accounts for the label "gross domestic product"; if we subtract out the depreciation, then the remainder is referred to as "net domestic product." Finally, indirect business taxes, the smallest component of income, include sales and property taxes paid by the business sector.

Another convenient way of presenting these income numbers is to assign all income to either labor or capital. If we do this, we discover two important things.[3] First, the fraction of GDP earned by labor is approximately two-thirds, or 67 percent; this leaves one-third as income to capital. Second, as we can see in Figure 2.3, the labor share fluctuates very little over time, lying between about 65 and 70 percent of GDP. This is an important fact for a number of reasons. For one, it indicates that there is no general trend to capital's share or labor's share of income: it is not the case that corporations or shareholders are getting rich at the expense of labor, or vice versa. The relative stability of labor's share will also play an important role in helping us think about production in the chapters on long-run growth.

The Production Approach to GDP

The stated definition of GDP—the value of the goods and services produced in an economy during a given period—is correct in a general way, but it misses one important qualifier. When GDP is computed as the value of goods and services

[3] The main difficulty in making this assignment is that the net operating surplus of business—such as the profits of Homer and Marge—includes both labor income (e.g., for Homer and Marge) and capital income (e.g., land rent).

produced in an economy, there is no double counting. For example, if a steel company produces $10 million worth of steel that is then used by an automobile company to make $100 million worth of trucks, the value of the steel is not counted twice. Rather, GDP goes up by $100 million.

We can view this in two ways. First, it is only the final sale of goods and services that counts toward GDP. Alternatively, and more accurately, each producer creates an amount of GDP equal to the amount of value that is added during production. This **value added**, as it is called, is computed by subtracting the value of intermediate products (like steel or electricity; $10 million in our example) from the revenue generated by each producer. In terms of value added, then, the steel producer generates $10 million of GDP, while the automobile producer generates $90 million ($100 million − $10 million), for a total increment once again of $100 million.

Another important implication of the production approach to GDP is that it is only new production that counts. For example, if a construction company builds a new house and sells it for $200,000, this amount counts toward GDP. But suppose a used-car dealer buys a 2004 minivan for $17,000 and then sells it the next day to a family for $20,000; by how much does GDP change? The full $20,000 does not count toward this year's GDP: the car already existed and does not represent new production. However, the "profit" of $3,000 earned by the dealer does count toward GDP: the product is the service of finding a match for minivan and family.

What Is Included in GDP and What's Not?

A key way to understand more thoroughly the usefulness of GDP is to examine some of its limitations. The first thing to note is that GDP includes only goods and services that transact in markets. If your family goes out to dinner at a nice restaurant, the entire amount you spend there is counted as GDP. On the other hand, if your parents pick up some ingredients at the local market and spend an hour preparing a gourmet meal, only the purchase of the ingredients contributes to GDP—not the value of the time they spend cooking. Similarly, if Aunt Zoe and Uncle Elmo put their kids in day care while they work, the day-care service gets counted as GDP, but if Uncle Bert stays home to care for his kids, no market transaction occurs and no contribution to GDP is recorded.[4]

Another important omission from GDP is the health of a nation's people. Over the last century, life expectancy has risen in virtually every country in the world. This increase is quantitatively very significant. In fact, William Nordhaus calculates that the rise in U.S. life expectancy in the twentieth century had roughly the same impact on the country's economic welfare as the entire gain in per capita consumption over that century.[5] To judge the validity of this calculation, ask yourself the following: would you rather have the per capita income of the United

---

[4] A prominent exception to the market rule is the benefit associated with owner-occupied housing. If you rent your home, the rental income is captured in GDP. But if you own your home, there is no annual income like the rent. National accountants estimate a rental equivalent in this case and include it in GDP.

[5] William Nordhaus, "The Health of Nations: The Contribution of Improved Health to Living Standards," in Kevin M. Murphy and Robert Topel, eds., *Measuring the Gains from Medical Research: An Economic Approach* (Chicago: University of Chicago Press, 2003).

States from 1900 together with the medical technology of 2000, or the per capita income from 2000 with the medical technology of 1900? Conventional measures of GDP do not incorporate this change in health. To take another example, the specter of the AIDS epidemic in Africa threatens to kill millions of people in the coming decades and has reduced life expectancy significantly in many sub-Saharan countries. The effect of this tragedy on measured GDP, however, will likely be relatively small.[6]

A third potentially significant limitation of GDP is that it doesn't include changes in environmental resources. For example, air and water pollution generated by factories as by-products of their manufacturing do not reduce GDP. Similarly, when nonrenewable natural resources like oil and natural gas are extracted, GDP goes up because of the productive effort spent turning the reserves into products, but there is no deduction from GDP associated with the reduction of oil and natural gas reserves. Interestingly, Martin Weitzman has calculated that the economic value of this depletion may be smaller than one might have expected: the price data used to measure the scarcity of these resources suggest that the overall cost of the finite nature of our nonrenewable resources is less than 1 percent of annual consumption.[7]

2.3 Measuring Changes over Time

Measuring GDP in any given year is primarily a matter of careful counting. Measuring how GDP changes over time or comparing GDP between two countries is substantially harder. Each process involves separating out changes in prices and quantities.

Economists use the word "nominal" to refer to a measure like GDP when prices and quantities have not been separated out, and "real" to refer only to the actual quantity of goods and services. **Nominal** and **real GDP** are related by a simple equation:

$$\text{nominal GDP} = \text{price level} \times \text{real GDP} \tag{2.2}$$

If an economy produces 37 cell phones and nothing else, and if the price of each is $100, then nominal GDP would equal $3,700, while real GDP would equal 37 cell phones.

Nominal GDP can go up either because the price level has gone up or because real GDP has gone up. For example, nominal GDP in 2008 in the United States was $14.4 trillion, and in 1995 only $7.4 trillion. How many more goods and services—that is, how much more real GDP—were produced in 2008 than in 1995?

[6] See, for example, Alwyn Young, "The Gift of the Dying: The Tragedy of AIDS and the Welfare of Future African Generations," *Quarterly Journal of Economics*, vol. 120 (May 2005), pp. 423–66.

[7] Martin L. Weitzman, "Pricing the Limits to Growth from Minerals Depletion," *Quarterly Journal of Economics*, vol. 114 (May 1999), pp. 691–706.

What makes this question difficult is that prices have changed over the 13 years. It is possible, for example, that all the increase in GDP is accounted for by higher prices and real GDP has not changed. Alternatively, it is equally possible that prices haven't changed at all and all the increase is explained by an increase in the quantity of real GDP. The truth lies somewhere in between, and the challenge is to figure out exactly where.

A Simple Example: Where Real GDP Doesn't Change

Imagine a simple economy in which there are two goods, apples and computers. Nominal GDP in this economy is the sum of the values of apples and computers that are produced:

$$\text{nominal GDP} = (\text{price of apples} \times \text{quantity of apples}) + (\text{price of computers} \times \text{quantity of computers}).$$

Suppose that in 2008, an apple costs \$1, a computer costs \$900, and the economy produces 500 apples and 5 computers. Then nominal GDP in this economy is

$$\frac{\$1}{\text{apple}} \times 500 \text{ apples} + \frac{\$900}{\text{computer}} \times 5 \text{ computers} = \$5{,}000.$$

These numbers are shown in Table 2.3.

Now suppose that in 2009, the economy still produces 500 apples and 5 computers, but an apple now costs \$2 while a computer costs \$1,000. Nominal GDP in 2009 is then

$$\frac{\$2}{\text{apple}} \times 500 \text{ apples} + \frac{\$1{,}000}{\text{computer}} \times 5 \text{ computers} = \$6{,}000.$$

Nominal GDP is higher by \$1,000 in 2009, but we know that nothing "real" has changed: the economy is producing the same number of apples and computers. Here, all the change in nominal GDP occurs because of changes in prices.

What about real GDP in this economy? In our 37–cell phone example, real GDP was easy to measure: it was just the number of cell phones produced. Here,

The table shows the calculation of real and nominal GDP for our apple and computer example. The question marks are entries that you will fill in yourself in an exercise at the end of the chapter.

TABLE 2.3

Real and Nominal GDP in a Simple Economy, 2008–2010

	2008	2009	2010	Percentage change 2009–2010
Quantity of apples	500	500	550	10
Quantity of computers	5	5	6	20
Price of apples (dollars)	1	2	3	50
Price of computers (dollars)	900	1,000	1,000	0
Nominal GDP	5,000	6,000	7,650	27.5
Real GDP in 2008 prices	5,000	5,000	?	?
Real GDP in 2009 prices	6,000	6,000	7,100	18.3
Real GDP in 2010 prices	?	6,500	7,650	17.7
Real GDP in chained prices, benchmarked to 2010	?	6,483	7,650	18.0

though, things are more complicated because we have two goods. How can we construct a summary statistic that adds these two goods together but controls for the change in prices that occurred from 2008 to 2009? The answer is that we use the *same* set of prices to compute real GDP in each of the two years—either the 2008 prices or the 2009 prices. If we use the 2009 prices, we will measure real GDP to be \$6,000 in both years. If we use the 2008 prices, we will measure real GDP to be \$5,000 in both years. Both approaches yield the right answer that real GDP is unchanged. (The calculations are exactly the same as the ones we carried out at the beginning of this section.)

Notice that, perhaps confusingly, real GDP is measured in dollars, just like nominal GDP. This is because there is more than one good in the economy, so we can't just count the number of cell phones produced. To distinguish nominal from real variables, we measure nominal variables in "current dollars" and real variables in, say, "2009 prices" or "2009 dollars."

A Second Example: Where Real GDP Changes

Now consider an example where real GDP does change. Suppose that in 2010 the economy looks like this: an apple costs \$3, a computer still costs \$1,000, and the economy produces 550 apples and 6 computers. If you calculate nominal GDP for this economy, you will find that the answer is \$7,650 (\$6,000 + \$1,650).

But what about real GDP? Relative to 2009, the economy is producing 50 more apples and 1 more computer, so real GDP should be higher, but by how much? If we use the 2009 prices, we find that real GDP in 2010 is

$$\frac{\$2}{\text{apple}} \times 550 \text{ apples} + \frac{\$1{,}000}{\text{computer}} \times 6 \text{ computers} = \$7{,}100.$$

Measured in 2009 prices, real GDP in 2009 is equal to nominal GDP, which was \$6,000. So according to this calculation, real GDP in 2010 is higher by \$1,100 (\$7,100 − \$6,000), or by 1,100/6,000 = 18.3 percent (see Table 2.3).

Alternatively, suppose we compute real GDP using the 2010 prices. Real GDP in 2010 is then equal to nominal GDP in 2010, or \$7,650. Real GDP in 2009 is

$$\frac{\$3}{\text{apple}} \times 500 \text{ apples} + \frac{\$1{,}000}{\text{computer}} \times 5 \text{ computers} = \$6{,}500 \text{ (in 2010 prices)}.$$

So using 2010 prices, we find that real GDP is higher in 2010 by \$1,150 (\$7,650 − \$6,500), or by 1,150/6,500 = 17.7 percent.

This second example, then, reveals that the change in real GDP differs, although only slightly, depending on whether we use the initial 2009 prices or the final 2010 prices.

Quantity Indexes: Laspeyres, Paasche, and Chain Weighting

The method of computing the change in real GDP with the initial prices is called the **Laspeyres index**, while the method that uses the final prices is called the **Paasche index**. (To keep these straight, you might remember that the alphabetical order of Laspeyres and Paasche corresponds to the initial versus final order.) In general, these approaches give different answers, and the size of the difference depends on the extent to which relative prices have changed. If we are comparing two consecutive years in an economy, then the differences usually aren't great. But if we are comparing real GDP across a long period such as a decade, or if we are looking at any economy with high inflation, the differences can be substantial.

A third, preferred, approach to computing real GDP is called the *Fisher index*, or **chain weighting**. To compute the chain-weighted index of real GDP, first compute the Laspeyres and Paasche indexes, then calculate the average of the two growth rates. In our Table 2.3 example, this approach gives a growth rate of $1/2 \times (18.3\% + 17.7\%) = 18.0\%$. The chain-weighted index therefore says that real GDP is 18 percent higher in 2010 than in 2009.[8] The level of real chain-weighted GDP in 2009 is then computed by finding the level x such that if it were to grow at 18 percent, it would equal the 2010 level of GDP. That is,

$$x \times (1 + 0.180) = 7{,}650 \Rightarrow x \times 7{,}650/1.180 = 6{,}483.$$

National income accountants would say that real chain-weighted GDP in 2009 is therefore equal to \$6,483. These calculations are reported in the last line of Table 2.3.

Modern national income statisticians generally prefer to use chain weighting when comparing real GDP over time, particularly when the time period is a long one. Why? Suppose we are comparing real GDP in 1960 with real GDP in 2010. The Laspeyres index would make the comparison using 1960 prices. In 1960, computers were extremely expensive relative to apples, so they would get a very high weight in this comparison. A Paasche index would make the comparison using 2010 prices, when computers were relatively cheap. Because computer output has grown so rapidly, the Laspeyres index (1960 weights) would produce very fast growth for real GDP, while the Paasche index (2010 weights) would produce much slower growth. Chain weighting gives us an average of these two extremes and in general provides a more accurate view of how standards of living change over time.[9]

More generally, real chain-weighted GDP is computed by applying the Fisher index on a year-by-year basis. To construct the chain index over the period 1960 to 2010, we compute real GDP in *each* year: real GDP in 2010 is computed using both the 2009 and the 2010 prices, real GDP in 2009 is computed using both the 2008 and 2009 prices, and so on. In other words, the 1960 level of real GDP is based on prices that were applicable in 1960, while 2010 real GDP is computed using prices that were applicable around 2010. Chain weighting therefore produces a more accurate portrayal of how real GDP changes over time.

[8] To be more precise, the Fisher index actually involves taking the geometric average of the "gross" percentage changes, i.e., $\sqrt{1.183 \times 1.177} = 1.180$, to get the 18.0% growth rate. As long as relative prices are not changing too rapidly, the arithmetic average used in the text will give a similar answer.

[9] See Jack E. Triplett, "Economic Theory and BEA's Alternative Quantity and Price Indexes," *Survey of Current Business* (April 1992), pp. 49–52.

Price Indexes and Inflation

For each quantity index—Laspeyres, Paasche, and chain weighting—there is a corresponding price index. Recall the basic formula for nominal GDP:

$$\text{nominal GDP} = \text{price level} \times \text{real GDP}. \tag{2.3}$$

In the national accounts, the price level that satisfies this equation is called the **GDP deflator**. This name captures the fact that real GDP can be computed by "deflating" nominal GDP—that is, by dividing by the price level. Similar deflators exist for the various components of GDP, such as consumption and investment.

We *could* compute the percentage change in the price level by applying the formula in equation (2.3) in two different years. But there's a simple mathematical trick that makes this even easier; in fact, this trick is just one of the basic rules for computing growth rates that we will learn in Chapter 3. The percentage change in a mathematical product is approximately equal to the sum of the percentage changes of the components. Applying this formula to equation (2.3) means that

$$\begin{array}{c}\text{percentage}\\ \text{change in}\\ \text{nominal GDP}\end{array} \approx \begin{array}{c}\text{percentage}\\ \text{change in}\\ \text{price level}\end{array} + \begin{array}{c}\text{percentage}\\ \text{change in}\\ \text{real GDP.}\end{array}$$

We saw above in our simple example that the chain-weighted index of real GDP grew at a rate of 18.0 percent between 2009 and 2010. If we compute the change in nominal GDP, we discover a change of 27.5 percent. This means that the change in the price level between these two periods was 27.5 − 18.0 = 9.5 percent. Another name for the percentage change in the price level is the **inflation rate**.

Using Chain-Weighted Data

The U.S. Department of Commerce introduced chain weighting into the national accounts in the late 1990s. One of the main motivations was the fact that relative prices for goods that involve semiconductors were falling rapidly. For example, the price of computers relative to the price of other nondurable consumer goods has fallen at a rate of more than 15 percent per year when you adjust for the improvements in the quality of computers, like the speed of the processor and the storage capacity. In calculating real GDP growth over a period of 5 or 10 years, these changes in relative prices are large enough to cause large errors in Laspeyres or Paasche indexes. (This is especially true since an increasing fraction of our GDP benefits from "Moore's law," the assertion by the former CEO of Intel, Gordon Moore, that the number of transistors on a computer chip is doubling about every 18 months.) Chain weighting eliminates these errors.

The main downside to chain weighting in national accounts is that we must be careful when adding together the components of real GDP. Recall that the sum of nominal consumption, investment, government purchases, and net exports is equal to nominal GDP. Unfortunately, this is not true for the chain-weighted numbers: the sum of *real* chain-weighted consumption, investment, government purchases, and net exports does not generally equal real chain-weighted

GDP. (The reason is that different prices are used in constructing the different components.) The important lesson to remember is this: *if you are interested in particular shares, like the share of investment in GDP, then you want to look at the ratio of nominal variables, since the nominal shares will add up. If you are interested in real rates of economic growth, then you want to use the chain-weighted real measures.*

2.4 Comparing Economic Performance across Countries

With the help of local statistical agencies, the United Nations assembles national income accounts data for nearly every country in the world. With this data, economists can make comparisons of GDP across countries and over time. Such comparisons are important in helping us answer basic questions like "How large is the gap between incomes in the richest and poorest countries?" and "How has this gap changed over time?" We will explore these questions in detail in the next few chapters.

When we try to compare GDP across countries, we will need to separate quantities and prices as we did with comparisons of GDP over time. Say, for example, we want to determine how large China's economy is in comparison with the U.S. economy. The national accounts for the two countries show that U.S. GDP was \$13.7 trillion in 2007, while China's GDP was 26.4 trillion yuan. The first problem we are confronted with, then, is that the countries use different currencies.

As almost anyone who has traveled internationally knows, there are markets that allow you to exchange dollars for yuan, pesos for euros, or rubles for pounds. The price at which one of these exchanges occurs is called the **exchange rate**. For example, the exchange rate between the Chinese yuan and the U.S. dollar in 2007 was about 7.6 yuan per dollar: at the airport in Shanghai, you could receive 7.6 yuan for every dollar traded (or probably a little bit less, as the company doing the exchange takes a commission, and commissions at airports are notoriously high), and in San Francisco you would have to give up 7.6 yuan for every dollar you wanted to buy.

If we use the 2007 exchange rate to convert China's GDP of 26.4 trillion yuan into dollars, we get

$$26.4 \text{ trillion yuan} \times \frac{\$1}{7.6 \text{ yuan}} = \$3.5 \text{ trillion.}$$

And since U.S. GDP in 2007 was \$13.7 trillion, we conclude that China's economy was about one-quarter the size of the U.S. economy that year (3.5/13.7 = 0.26).

Is that the final answer? Well, not really. We saw in Section 2.3 that the problem comparing GDP over time is that prices might change. If we want a fair comparison, we need to make sure we are applying the same prices in the two periods. Otherwise, the quantities of all the goods produced might be the same, and any difference we see in GDP might just be due to the different prices.

Exactly the same problem exists in comparing GDP across different countries. To see this more clearly, consider an extreme example in which only a single good, rice, is produced in China and the United States. Now suppose that for some reason rice is less expensive in China than in the United States: at current exchange rates, a bag of rice costs \$1 in Shanghai but \$3 in New York. Even if China and the United States produce identical quantities of rice (so that their real GDPs are the same), we will find differences in GDP if we use the local prices to compute it. The right way to correct for this, as we did over time, is to use a common set of prices to calculate real GDP in each country.

Recall the equation relating nominal and real GDP:

$$\text{nominal GDP} = \text{price level} \times \text{real GDP}. \tag{2.4}$$

Say we'd like to compute China's GDP using U.S. prices rather than Chinese prices. (We could alternatively compute U.S. GDP using Chinese prices; these are the spatial equivalents of the Laspeyres and Paasche quantity indexes. In reality, we will use international prices, representing the average of world prices.) Here's how we do this:

$$\text{real GDP}^{\text{U.S. prices}}_{\text{China}} = \text{price level}_{\text{U.S.}} \times \text{real GDP}_{\text{China}}. \tag{2.5}$$

For this example, you may find it helpful to think of real $\text{GDP}_{\text{China}}$ as being measured in kilograms of rice.

Next, since equation (2.4) tells us that real GDP in China is also equal to nominal GDP divided by the price level, we can substitute this result into equation (2.5) to get

$$\begin{aligned} \text{real GDP}^{\text{U.S. prices}}_{\text{China}} &= \text{price level}_{\text{U.S.}} \times \frac{\text{nominal GDP}^{\text{dollars}}_{\text{China}}}{\text{price level}_{\text{China}}} \\ &= \frac{\text{price level}_{\text{U.S.}}}{\text{price level}_{\text{China}}} \times \text{nominal GDP}^{\text{dollars}}_{\text{China}}. \end{aligned} \tag{2.6}$$

That is, to measure China's GDP in U.S. prices, we need to adjust for the relative price level of goods in the United States versus China.

The United Nations International Comparisons Program collects price data from different countries in order to facilitate this comparison. And the Penn World Tables data set incorporates these prices to construct measures of real GDP that are comparable across countries. These data will be used here and in the remainder of the book.[10]

According to these data, the rice example is not far from the truth. Goods in China, on average, cost about 30 percent of goods in the United States. That is, $\text{price level}_{\text{U.S.}}/\text{price level}_{\text{China}}$ is roughly equal to 1/0.30. Therefore, the formula above says that real GDP in China is about \$11.7 trillion (3.5/0.30). In other words, at common prices, the Chinese economy is much larger than it first appeared: about 85 percent of the size of the U.S. economy instead of 25 percent. Indeed, as of 2007, China had the second largest economy in the world, and several more years of rapid growth should be more than enough to move it into first place.

[10] Alan Heston, Robert Summers, and Bettina Aten, Penn World Tables, Version 6.35, Center for International Comparisons at the University of Pennsylvania (CICUP), August 2009. Available at pwt.econ.upenn.edu/

In general, rich countries tend to have higher price levels than poor countries. The main reason is that the low wage rate in poor countries translates into lower prices for goods like haircuts or other services that are difficult to trade, or products that involve a retail or distribution channel that uses labor extensively, like restaurant meals or clothing. In practice, this means that, as we saw in the China–U.S. example, comparisons of GDP based on exchange rates tend to yield larger differences across countries than comparisons based on common prices. We will explore comparisons like these in much more detail in the coming chapters.

CHAPTER REVIEW

SUMMARY

1. National income accounting provides systematic measures of aggregate economic activity. Gross domestic product (GDP) is the key overall measure of economic activity in an economy. It can be viewed as total expenditure, total income, or total production in an economy.
2. The expenditure approach to GDP makes use of a fundamental *national income identity*, $Y = C + I + G + NX$, which says that total spending is the sum of spending on consumption, investment, government purchases, and net exports.
3. A key lesson of the income approach is that labor's share of GDP is relatively stable over time at about two-thirds.
4. In the production approach, it is only the value of final production that counts. Equivalently, GDP is the sum of *value added* at each stage of production.
5. Nominal GDP refers to the value of GDP measured in current prices in a given year. Real GDP involves computing GDP in two different years using the *same* set of prices. Changes in real GDP therefore reflect changes in actual production rather than changes in prices.
6. Chain weighting allows us to compare real GDP in 1950, for example, with real GDP in 2010 by gradually updating the prices: 1950 and 1951 prices are used to compare 1950 and 1951 real GDPs, 1951 and 1952 prices are then used to compare 1951 and 1952 real GDPs, and so on. By linking the chain of comparisons in this way, we construct a more accurate measure of real GDP. (If we used 2010 prices to value production in 1950, we'd get a distorted picture: telephone service that was extremely valuable and expensive in 1950, for example, would be valued according to the cheap modern prices.)
7. International comparisons of GDP involve two conversions. First, we need exchange rates to convert the measures into a common currency. Second, just as we need to use common prices to measure real GDP over time, we also need to use common prices to compare real GDP across countries.

KEY CONCEPTS

capital
chain weighting
depreciation
economic profits
exchange rate
expenditure
GDP deflator
gross domestic product
income
inflation
inflation rate
labor's share of GDP
Laspeyres index
national income identity
nominal versus real GDP
Paasche index
production
trade balance
value added

REVIEW QUESTIONS

1. What is GDP, and why is it a useful measure? What are the most important components of GDP in the U.S. economy today?
2. What are net exports, and how is this concept related to the trade deficit?
3. What are some problems with using GDP as a measure of overall economic welfare?
4. What is the difference between real and nominal GDP? How do you compare GDPs over time within an economy? How do you compare GDPs across different economies?

EXERCISES

smartwork.wwnorton.com 

1. **What counts as GDP (I)?** By how much does GDP rise in each of the following scenarios? Explain.
   (a) You spend $5,000 on college tuition this semester.
   (b) You buy a used car from a friend for $2,500.
   (c) The government spends $100 million to build a dam.
   (d) Foreign graduate students work as teaching assistants at the local university and earn $5,000 each.
2. **What counts as GDP (II)?** By how much does GDP rise in each of the following scenarios? Explain.
   (a) A computer company buys parts from a local distributor for $1 million, assembles the parts, and sells the resulting computers for $2 million.
   (b) A real estate agent sells a house for $200,000 that the previous owners had bought 10 years earlier for $100,000. The agent earns a commission of $6,000.
   (c) During a recession, the government raises unemployment benefits by $100 million.
   (d) A new U.S. airline purchases and imports $50 million worth of airplanes from the European company Airbus.

(e) A new European airline purchases \$50 million worth of airplanes from the American company Boeing.
(f) A store buys \$100,000 of chocolate from Belgium and sells it to consumers in the United States for \$125,000.

3. **National accounting over time (I):** Look back at Table 2.3. Some missing entries are labeled with question marks. Compute the values that belong in these positions.

4. **National accounting over time (II):** Consider an economy that produces oranges and boomerangs. The prices and quantities of these goods in two different years are reported in the table below. Fill in the missing entries.

	2016	2017	Percentage change 2016–2017
Quantity of oranges	100	105	?
Quantity of boomerangs	20	22	?
Price of oranges (dollars)	1	1.10	?
Price of boomerangs (dollars)	3	3.10	?
Nominal GDP	?	?	?
Real GDP in 2016 prices	?	?	?
Real GDP in 2017 prices	?	?	?
Real GDP in chained prices, benchmarked to 2017	?	?	?

5. **Inflation in the orange and boomerang economy:** Consider the economy from exercise 4. Calculate the inflation rate for the 2016–2017 period using the GDP deflator based on the Laspeyres, Paasche, and chain-weighted indexes of GDP.

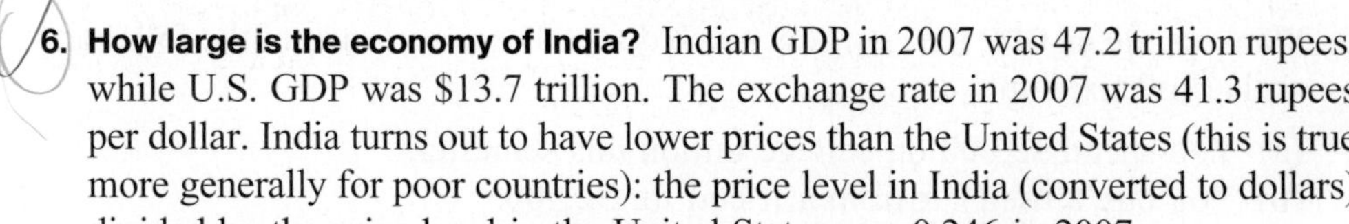

6. **How large is the economy of India?** Indian GDP in 2007 was 47.2 trillion rupees, while U.S. GDP was \$13.7 trillion. The exchange rate in 2007 was 41.3 rupees per dollar. India turns out to have lower prices than the United States (this is true more generally for poor countries): the price level in India (converted to dollars) divided by the price level in the United States was 0.246 in 2007.
   (a) What is the ratio of Indian GDP to U.S. GDP if we don't take into account the differences in relative prices and simply use the exchange rate to make the conversion?
   (b) What is the ratio of real GDP in India to real GDP in the United States in common prices?
   (c) Why are these two numbers different?

7. **How large is the economy of Japan?** Japanese GDP in 2007 was 517 trillion yen (U.S. GDP, again, was \$13.7 trillion). The exchange rate in 2007 was 118 yen per dollar. Contrary to China and India, however, Japan had higher prices than the United States: the price level in Japan (converted to dollars) divided by the price level in the United States was 1.074 in 2007.
   (a) What is the ratio of Japanese GDP to U.S. GDP if we don't take into account the differences in relative prices and simply use the exchange rate to make the conversion?

(b) What is the ratio of GDP in Japan to real GDP in the United States in common prices?
(c) Why are these two numbers different?

8. **Earthquakes and GDP:** Suppose the rural part of a country is hit by a major earthquake that destroys 10 percent of the country's housing stock. The government and private sector respond with a major construction effort to help rebuild houses. Discuss how this episode is likely to affect (a) the economic well-being of the people in the country, and (b) the economy's measured GDP.

WORKED EXERCISES

1. **What counts as GDP (I)?**

   (a) GDP rises by the $5,000 amount of your tuition payment. This is the purchase of a service (education) that is produced this semester.

   (b) The purchase of used goods does not involve new production. This example is just the transfer of an existing good, so GDP is unchanged. If you bought the used car from a used-car dealer, the service of selling the car would represent new production—so something like $200 of the $2,500 might be included in GDP.

   (c) The new dam is new production, and the government spending of $100 million is counted as GDP. Notice that if the spending were spread over several years, then the flow of new production (and GDP) would also be spread over time.

   (d) Foreign graduate students working in the United States contribute to production that occurs within the United States, and this is included in GDP. So GDP goes up by $5,000 for each student.

PART 2
THE LONG RUN

CHAPTER 3

AN OVERVIEW OF LONG-RUN ECONOMIC GROWTH

OVERVIEW

In this chapter, we learn

- some facts related to economic growth that later chapters will seek to explain.
- how economic growth has dramatically improved welfare around the world.
- that this growth is actually a relatively recent phenomenon.
- some tools used to study economic growth, including how to calculate growth rates and why a "ratio scale" makes plots of per capita GDP easier to understand.

> The first step in making things better is to understand why things are the way they are.
>
> —ANONYMOUS

3.1 Introduction

Let's play a game. I'll describe some economic characteristics of a country, and you tell me which country I am describing. In this country, life expectancy at birth is under 50 years, and 1 out of every 10 infants dies before reaching a first birthday. More than 90 percent of households have no electricity, refrigerator, telephone, or car. Fewer than 10 percent of young adults have graduated from high school. Is it Kenya, or Bangladesh, or perhaps North Korea? All good guesses, but in fact the country is the United States, not today but at the end of the nineteenth century.

Such is the power of economic growth: in just over a century, the United States has been completely transformed. Almost all households have electricity, refrigerators, telephones, and cars. The overwhelming majority of young adults have graduated from high school, with many going on to college. But this only hints at the scale of the transformation. Think of the new goods that were nearly unimaginable a hundred years ago: air-conditioning, dishwashers, skyscrapers, jet airplanes, satellites, television, movie theaters, DVDs, computers and the Internet, portable music players, and the multitude of other goods available in supermarkets, restaurants, and superstores.

The tremendous gains in health are equally impressive. Life expectancy at birth in the United States is 50 percent higher than a century ago, at more than 78 years. The great European financier Nathan Rothschild, the richest man in the world in the early 1800s, died from an infection that $10 of antibiotics could cure today.

Not all countries in the world have experienced this rapid growth. The fact that the United States of a century ago could be mistaken for Kenya or Bangladesh today is testimony to an enormous lost opportunity.

This chapter provides an overview of the basic facts of economic growth. We use statistics on GDP per person to quantify the large differences in economic performance between the present and the past, and between the rich and poor countries of the world today. In the process, we develop a number of mathematical tools that are extremely useful in studying macroeconomics. Subsequent chapters in the long-run portion of this book will draw on these tools to provide economic theories that help us understand the facts of economic growth.

3.2 Growth over the Very Long Run

One of the most important facts of economic growth is that sustained increases in standards of living are a remarkably recent phenomenon. Figure 3.1 makes this point by showing estimates of per capita GDP over the last 2,000 years

On a long time scale, economic growth is so recent that a plot of per capita GDP looks like a hockey stick, and the lines for different countries are hard to distinguish.

FIGURE 3.1

Economic Growth over the Very Long Run in Six Countries

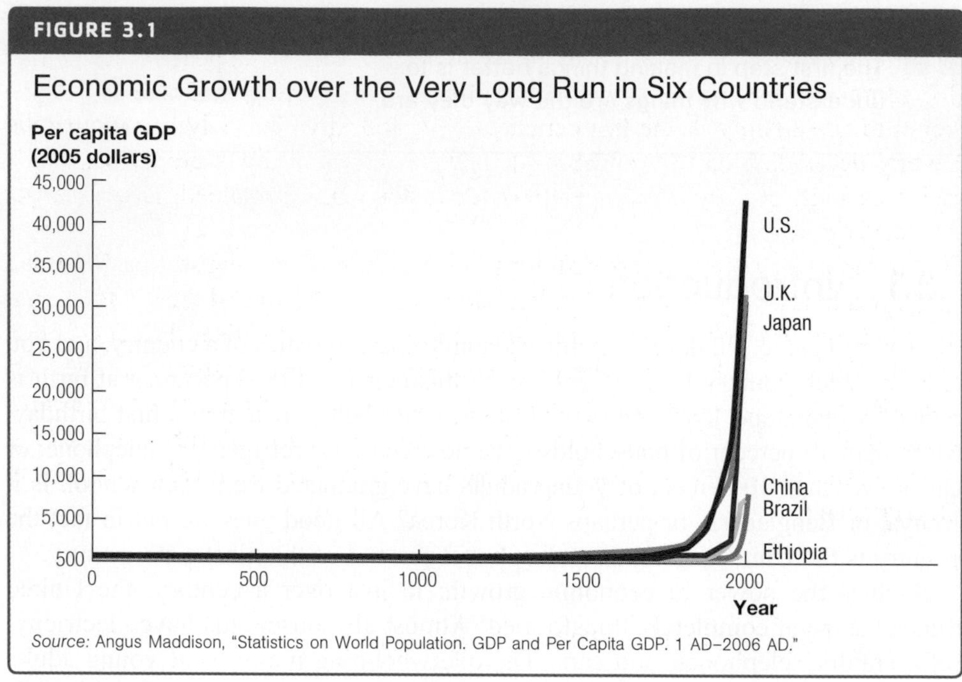

Source: Angus Maddison, "Statistics on World Population. GDP and Per Capita GDP. 1 AD–2006 AD."

for six countries. For most of history, standards of living were extremely low, not much different from that in Ethiopia today. The figure shows this going back for 2,000 years, but it is surely true going back even farther. Up until about 12,000 years ago, humans were hunters and gatherers, living a nomadic existence. Then around 10,000 B.C. came an agricultural revolution, which led to the emergence of settlements and eventually cities. Yet even the sporadic peaks of economic achievement that followed were characterized by low average standards of living. Evidence suggests, for example, that wages in ancient Greece and Rome were approximately equal to wages in Britain in the fifteenth century or France in the seventeenth, periods distinctly prior to the emergence of modern economic growth.[1]

It is only in the most recent two or three centuries that modern economic growth emerges, but when it appears, the results are stunning. In the words of seventeenth-century English philosopher Thomas Hobbes, life was "nasty, brutish, and short" for hundreds of thousands of years. Since 1700, however, living standards in the richest countries have risen from roughly $500 per person to something approaching $45,000 per person today. Incomes have exploded by a factor of 90 during a period that is but a flash in the pan of human history. If the 130,000-year period since modern humans made their first appearance were compressed into a single day, the era of modern growth would have begun only in the last 3 minutes.

[1] For more on this evidence, see Robert E. Lucas Jr., *Lectures on Economic Growth* (Cambridge, Mass.: Harvard University Press, 2004); and Charles I. Jones, "Was an Industrial Revolution Inevitable? Economic Growth over the Very Long Run," *Advances in Macroeconomics*, 2001.

Another point to be gleaned from Figure 3.1 is that sustained growth emerges in different places at different times. Growth first starts to appear in the United Kingdom and then in the United States. Standards of living in Brazil and Japan begin to rise mainly in the last century or so, and in China only during the last several decades. Finally, standards of living in Ethiopia today are perhaps only twice as high as they were over most of history, and sustained growth is not especially evident.

An important result of these differences in timing is that living standards around the world today vary dramatically. Per capita GDP in Japan and the United Kingdom is about 3/4 that in the United States; for Brazil and China, the ratio is 1/5, and for Ethiopia only 1/40. These differences are especially stunning when we consider that living standards around the world probably differed by no more than a factor of 2 or 3 before the year 1700. In the last three centuries, standards of living have diverged dramatically, a phenomenon that has been called **the Great Divergence**.[2]

3.3 Modern Economic Growth

On a scale of thousands of years like that shown in Figure 3.1, the era of modern economic growth is so compressed that incomes almost appear to rise as a vertical line. But if we stretch out the time scale and focus on the last 140 years or so, we get a fuller picture of what has been occurring. Figure 3.2 does this for the United States.

Measured in year 2005 prices, per capita GDP in the United States was about \$2,800 in 1870 and rose to more than \$42,000 by 2009, almost a 15-fold increase. A more mundane way to appreciate this rate of change is to compare GDP in the year you were born with GDP in the year your parents were born. In 1990, for example, per capita income was just over \$32,000. Thirty years earlier it was under \$16,000. Assuming this economic growth continues, the typical American college student today will earn a lifetime income about twice that of his or her parents.

The Definition of Economic Growth

Up to this point, the phrase "economic growth" has been used generically to refer to increases in living standards. However, "growth" also has a more precise meaning, related to the exact rate of change of per capita GDP.

Notice that the slope of the income series shown in Figure 3.2 has been rising over time: our incomes are rising by an ever-increasing amount each year. In fact, these income changes are roughly proportional to the level of per capita income at any particular time.

---

[2] See Lant Pritchett, "Divergence, Big Time," *Journal of Economic Perspectives*, vol. 11 (Summer 1997), pp. 3–17, as well as Robert E. Lucas Jr., "Some Macroeconomics for the 21st Century," *Journal of Economic Perspectives*, vol. 14 (Winter 2000), pp. 159–68. The term "Great Divergence" is borrowed from Kenneth Pomeranz, *The Great Divergence: China, Europe, and the Making of the Modern World Economy* (Princeton, N.J.: Princeton University Press, 2000).

Per capita GDP in the United States has risen by nearly a factor of 15 since 1870.

FIGURE 3.2

Per Capita GDP in the United States, 1870–2009

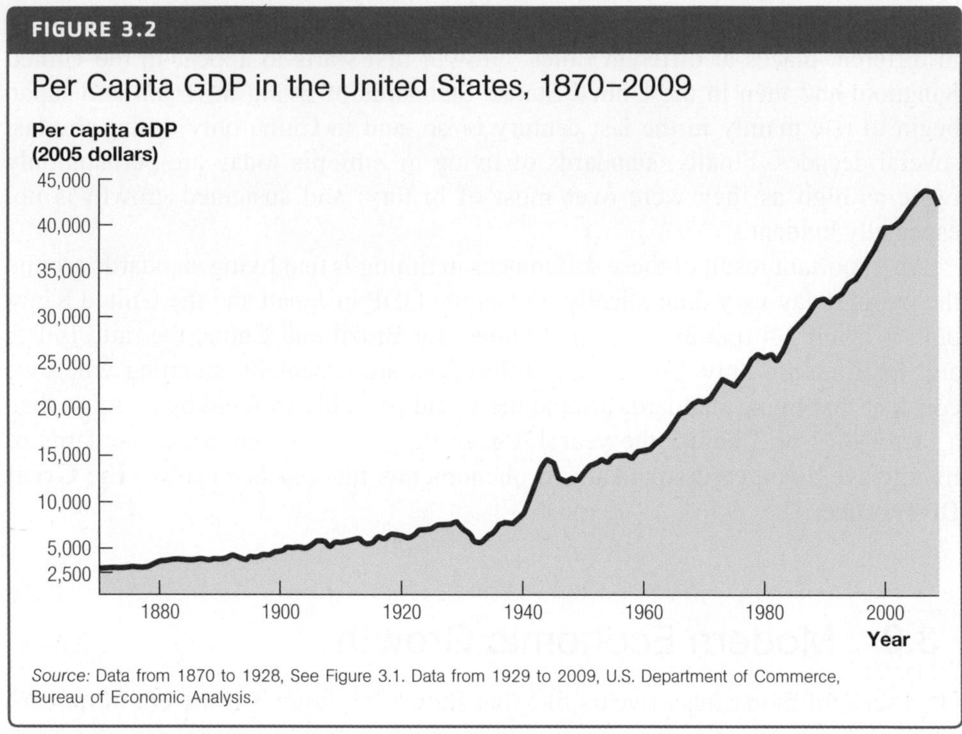

Source: Data from 1870 to 1928, See Figure 3.1. Data from 1929 to 2009, U.S. Department of Commerce, Bureau of Economic Analysis.

Some algebra may help us see what this statement means. Let y stand for per capita income. Then, at least as an approximation,

$$y_{2007} - y_{2006} = \bar{g} \times y_{2006},$$

where, as we will see, the numerical value for $\bar{g}$ turns out to be about 0.02. That is, the change in per capita income between 2006 and 2007 is roughly proportional to the level of per capita income in 2006, where the factor of proportionality is 2 percent.

Dividing both sides of this equation by income in 2006, we discover another way of expressing this relationship:

$$\frac{y_{2007} - y_{2006}}{y_{2006}} = \bar{g}.$$

The left-hand side of this equation is the *percentage change* in per capita income. This expression says that the percentage change in per capita income is the constant $\bar{g}$, and it is this percentage change that we call a growth rate.

We can look at the growth rate between any two consecutive years. Suppose y_t is income in some period. Then we could study the growth rate between 2009 and 2010, or 1950 and 1951, or more generally between year t and year $t + 1$. This leads us to the following general definition: a **growth rate** in some variable y is the percentage change in that variable. The growth rate between period t and $t + 1$ is

$$\frac{y_{t+1} - y_t}{y_t}.$$

From this definition of a growth rate as a percentage change, we can derive a number of useful insights. For example, if the growth rate of per capita income happens to equal some number $\bar{g}$, then we can express the level of per capita income as

$$y_{t+1} = y_t(1 + \bar{g}). \tag{3.1}$$

This equation is useful because it allows us to determine the value of per capita income tomorrow if we know the value today and the growth rate.

A Population Growth Example

To see equation (3.1) in action, consider the following example. Suppose the population of the world is given by L_0; we might suppose L_0 is equal to 6 billion, to reflect the number of people in the world in the year 2000. Now consider the possibility that population growth will be constant over the next century at a rate given by $\bar{n}$. For example, $\bar{n}$ might equal 0.02, implying that the world's population will grow at 2 percent per year. Under these assumptions, what will the level of the population be 100 years from now?

Inserting our population notation into equation (3.1), we have

$$L_{t+1} = L_t(1 + \bar{n}). \tag{3.2}$$

The population next year is equal to the population this year multiplied by (1 plus the growth rate). Why? Well, the 1 simply reflects the fact that we carry over the people who were already alive. In addition, for every person at the start, $\bar{n}$ new people are added, so we must add $\bar{n}L_t$ people to the original population L_t.

Let's apply this equation to our example. We begin at year 0 with L_0 people. Then at year 1 we have

$$L_1 = L_0(1 + \bar{n}). \tag{3.3}$$

Similarly, we can calculate the population in year 2 as

$$L_2 = L_1(1 + \bar{n}).$$

But we already know the value of L_1 from equation (3.3). Substituting from this equation, we have

$$L_2 = L_0(1 + \bar{n})(1 + \bar{n}) = L_0(1 + \bar{n})^2. \tag{3.4}$$

What about the population in year 3? Again, we take our basic growth equation, $L_3 = L_2(1 + \bar{n})$, and substitute the expression for L_2 from equation (3.4), which gives

$$L_3 = (L_0(1 + \bar{n})^2)(1 + \bar{n}) = L_0(1 + \bar{n})^3. \tag{3.5}$$

At this point, you should start to see a pattern. In particular, this process suggests that the population in any arbitrary year t is

$$L_t = L_0(1 + \bar{n})^t. \tag{3.6}$$

This is the key expression that we need to answer our original question: given values for L_0 and $\bar{n}$, what will the world population be 100 years from now? Evaluating equation (3.6) at $t = 100$, we get

$$L_{100} = L_0(1 + \bar{n})^{100}.$$

With $L_0 = 6$ billion and $\bar{n} = 0.02$, we thus find that the population 100 years from now would equal 43.5 billion.

More generally, this example illustrates the following important result, known as the **constant growth rule**: if a variable starts at some initial value y_0 at time 0 and grows at a constant rate $\bar{g}$, then the value of the variable at some future time t is given by

$$y_t = y_0(1 + \bar{g})^t \tag{3.7}$$

There is one more lesson to be learned from our simple population example. Equation (3.6) provides us with the size of the population at any time t, not just $t = 100$. In principle, we can use it to produce a plot of the population at each point in time. What do you think such a plot would look like? Try making one on your own, with a calculator and a judicious choice of a few years, or even with a computer spreadsheet program. You should end up with a plot that looks like Figure 3.3. Where have you seen a graph that looked something like this before? While the numbers are different, the signature growth curve here looks a lot like the pattern of per capita GDP in the United States, shown in Figure 3.2. It is this similarity that we explore next.

The Rule of 70 and the Ratio Scale

A major shortcoming of a figure like 3.2 or 3.3 is that it's difficult to "see" the rate of growth in the figure. For example, is it possible to tell from Figure 3.3 that the rate of growth of the world population is constant over the 100 years? Not really. In Figure 3.2, is the average growth rate increasing, decreasing, or constant? Again, it's nearly impossible to tell.

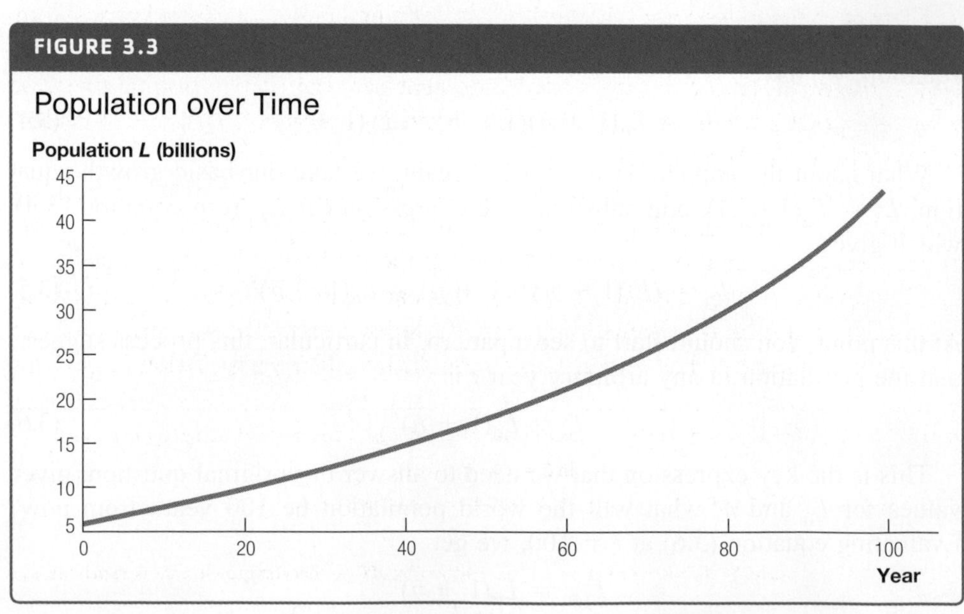

FIGURE 3.3

Population over Time

This graph shows the level of the population computed according to $L_t = L_0(1 + \bar{n})^t$ for $L_0 = 6$ and $\bar{n} = 0.02$.

Fortunately, there is an alternative way of plotting these figures, called a "ratio scale," that makes it much easier to see what is happening to the growth rate. Suppose a country called Utopia has a per capita income that exhibits a constant growth rate $\bar{g}$. How many years does it take before income doubles? If income starts at y_0, we are asking how many years it takes until $y_t = 2 \times y_0$. We know from the constant growth rule in equation (3.7) that $y_t = y_0(1 + \bar{g})^t$. So per capita income will double when

$$\begin{aligned} y_t = 2y_0 &= y_0(1 + \bar{g})^t \\ \Rightarrow 2 &= (1 + \bar{g})^t. \end{aligned} \tag{3.8}$$

That is, if income is growing at rate $\bar{g}$, then the number of years it takes until income doubles is the value of t such that $2 = (1 + \bar{g})^t$. Solving this equation for t requires you to take the logarithm of both sides of the equation. Here, it is sufficient for us simply to note the bottom line, which is important enough to have its own name, the **Rule of 70**: if y_t grows at a rate of g percent per year, then the number of years it takes y_t to double is approximately equal to $70/g$. For example, if y_t grows at 2 percent per year, then it doubles about every $70/2 = 35$ years.[3]

There are two points to note about the Rule of 70. First, it is very informative in its own right. If a country's income grows at 1 percent per year, then it takes about 70 years for income to double. On the other hand, if growth is slightly faster at 5 percent per year, then income doubles every 14 (70/5) years. Seemingly small differences in growth rates lead to quite different outcomes when compounded over time. This is a point we will return to often throughout the next several chapters.

The second implication of the Rule of 70 is that the time it takes for income to double depends only on the growth rate, not on the current level of income. If a country's income grows at 2 percent per year, then it doubles every 35 years, regardless of whether the initial income is \$500 or \$25,000.

How does this observation help us? First, let's go back to our population example, reproduced in a slightly different way in Figure 3.4. In part (a), because population is growing at a constant rate of 2 percent per year, it will double every 35 years; the points when the population hits 6 billion (today), 12 billion, 24 billion, and 48 billion are highlighted.

Now consider what happens if we "squish" the vertical axis of the population plot so that the key doubling points—the 6, 12, 24, and 48 billion points—are equally far apart. That is, rather than labeling the vertical axis in the usual "1, 2, 3, 4" fashion, we label it as "1, 2, 4, 8" so that each interval represents a doubling; this is shown in part (b). Something remarkable happens: what was previously an ever-steepening curve has turned into a straight line. If the population is growing

---

[3]Logarithms help you see how this rule is derived. Taking natural logs of both sides of equation (3.8) gives

$$\ln 2 = t \times \ln(1 + \bar{g}).$$

Next, note that $\ln 2 \approx 0.7$ and $\ln(1 + \bar{g}) \approx \bar{g}$, so this equation can be written as

$$t = 0.7/\bar{g}.$$

To get our rule, we multiply the top and bottom of this fraction by 100 so that the growth rate is expressed as a percent.

These graphs show the level of the population computed according to $L_t = L_0 (1 + \bar{n})^t$ for $L_0 = 6$ and $\bar{n} = 0.02$. The vertical scale in part (b) is a *ratio scale*, so that equally spaced intervals are associated with a doubling of population.

FIGURE 3.4

Population over Time, Revisited

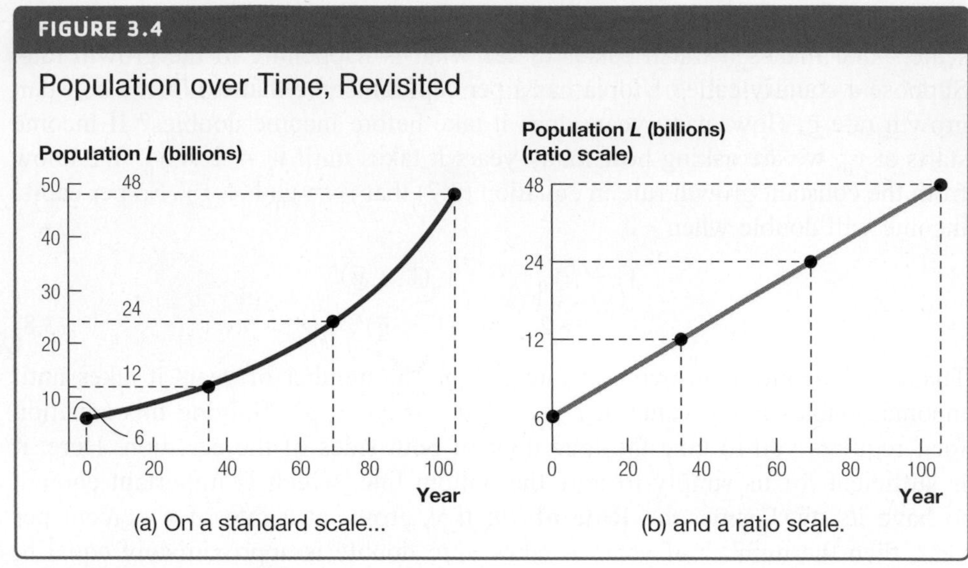

at a constant rate, we should hit our equally spaced markers every 35 years, and this is exactly what happens.

Squishing the vertical axis this way creates a **ratio scale**:[4] a plot where equally spaced tick marks on the vertical axis are labeled consecutively with numbers that exhibit a constant ratio, like "1, 2, 4, 8, . . ." (a constant ratio of 2) or "10, 100, 1,000, 10,000, . . ." (a constant ratio of 10). Plotted on a ratio scale, a variable growing at a constant rate appears as a straight line.

U.S. GDP on a Ratio Scale

The ratio scale is a tool that allows us to quickly read growth rates from a graph. For example, consider what we can learn by plotting U.S. per capita GDP on a ratio scale. If income grows at a constant rate, then the data points should lie on a straight line. Alternatively, if growth rates are rising, we would expect the slope between consecutive data points to be increasing.

Figure 3.5 shows the same data as Figure 3.2, per capita GDP in the United States, but now on a ratio scale. Notice that the vertical axis here is labeled "2, 4, 8, 16"—doubling over equally spaced intervals. Quite remarkably, the data series lies close to a line that exhibits a constant slope of 2.0 percent per year. This means that to a first approximation, per capita GDP in the United States has been growing at a relatively constant annual rate of 2.0 percent over the last 140 years.

A closer look at the figure reveals that the growth rate in the first half of the sample was slightly lower than this. For example, the slope between 1870 and 1929 is slightly lower than that of the 2.0 percent line, while the slope between 1950 and 2009 is slightly higher. These are points that we can easily see on a ratio scale, as opposed to the standard linear scale in Figure 3.2.

[4] In computer spreadsheet programs, a ratio scale is sometimes called a "logarithmic" scale.

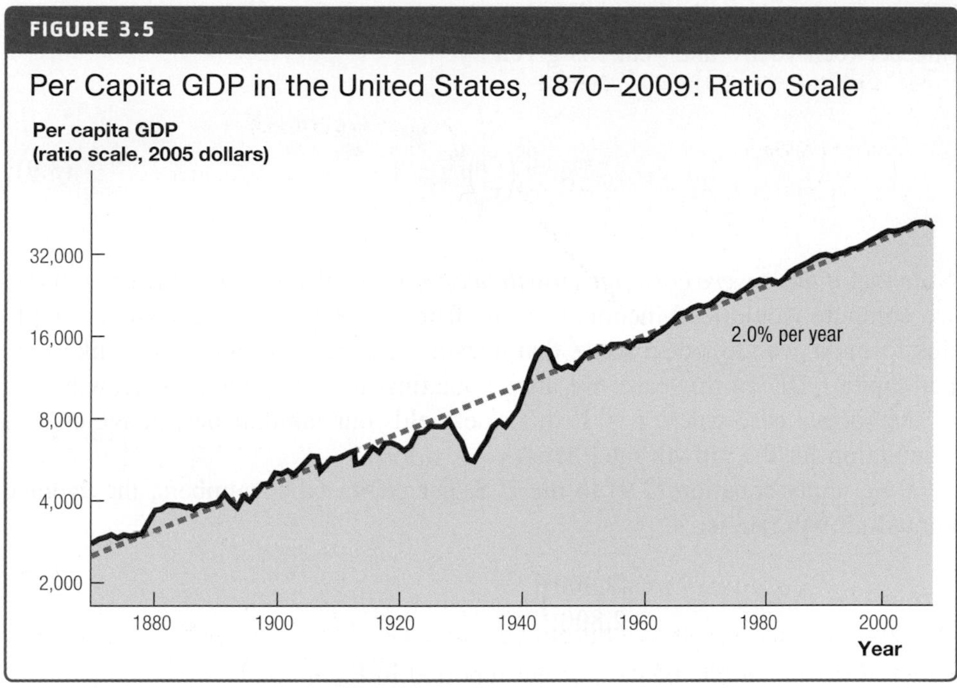

This is the same data shown in Figure 3.2, but plotted using a *ratio scale*. Notice that the ratios of the equally spaced labels on the vertical axis are all the same, in this case equal to 2. The dashed line exhibits constant growth at a rate of 2.0 percent per year.

Calculating Growth Rates

Figure 3.5 raises a couple of interesting questions. How can we tell that the growth rate associated with the straight line is 2 percent instead of 5 percent or 1 percent? More generally, given some data on income or population, how do we compute a growth rate?

First, the fact that the graph is a straight line on a ratio scale tells us that the growth rate is constant. To get the actual rate of 2 percent, there are two approaches. For a quick estimate, we can use the Rule of 70. If you look closely at Figure 3.5, you will see that the straight line is doubling about every 35 years. For example, between 1900 and 1935, the line rises from about \$4,000 to about \$8,000; between 1935 and 1970, it doubles again to about \$16,000. From our Rule of 70, we know that a process that doubles every 35 years is growing at 2 percent per year (70/35 = 2).

To get a more precise measure of the growth rate, we need the raw data. If the data for every year are available, we could compute the percentage change across each annual period, and this would be a fine way to measure growth. But what if instead we are given data only for the start and end of this series? For example, suppose we know that U.S. per capita GDP was \$2,800 in 1870 and \$42,000 in 2009. What is the average annual growth rate over these 139 years?

The answer can be found by applying the constant growth rule in equation (3.7): that is, for a quantity growing at a constant rate, the level in year t is given by $y_t = y_0(1 + \bar{g})^t$. When we encountered this rule earlier, we assumed we knew y_0 and $\bar{g}$ and wanted to solve for the value of y at some future date t. Now, though, we are given values of y_t and y_0 and asked to solve for $\bar{g}$. The way to do this is to rearrange the equation and then take the tth root of the ratio of the two incomes, as explained in the **rule for computing growth rates**: the average annual growth rate between year 0 and year t is given by

$$\bar{g} = \left(\frac{y_t}{y_0}\right)^{1/t} - 1 \qquad (3.9)$$

Note that *if there were constant growth between year 0 and year t*, the growth rate we compute would lead income to grow from y_0 to y_t. We can, however, apply this formula even to a data series that does not exhibit constant growth, like U.S. per capita GDP. In this case, we are calculating an average annual growth rate. In the special case where $t = 1$, this rule yields our familiar percentage change calculation for the growth rate, here $(y_1 - y_0)/y_0$.

If we apply equation (3.9) to the U.S. per capita GDP numbers, the average annual growth rate is

$$\left(\frac{42{,}000}{2{,}800}\right)^{1/139} - 1 = 0.0197,$$

which justifies the rate of 2.0 percent reported in Figure 3.5.

3.4 Modern Growth around the World

Figure 3.6 uses the ratio scale to examine the behavior of per capita GDP in seven countries over the last century. In the late nineteenth century, the United Kingdom was the richest country in the world, but it slipped from this position several decades later because it grew substantially slower than the United States. Notice how flat the per capita income line is for the U.K. relative to the United States. Since 1950, the United States and the U.K. have grown at more or less the same rate (indicated by the parallel lines), with income in the U.K. staying at about 3/4 the U.S. level.

Germany and Japan are examples of countries whose incomes lagged substantially behind those of the United Kingdom and the United States over most of the last 135 years. Following World War II, however, growth in both countries accelerated sharply, with growth in Japan averaging nearly 6 percent per year between 1950 and 1990. The rapid growth gradually slowed in both, and incomes have stabilized at something like 3/4 the U.S. level for the last two decades, similar to the income level in the United Kingdom. This catch-up behavior is related to an important concept in the study of economic growth known as **convergence**. You might say that income levels in Germany and Japan have converged to the level in the United Kingdom during the postwar period.

Economic growth in Brazil shows a different pattern, one that, to make a vast and somewhat unfair generalization, is more typical of growth in Latin America. Between 1900 and 1980, the country exhibited substantial economic growth, with

FIGURE 3.6

Per Capita GDP in Seven Countries, 1870–2006

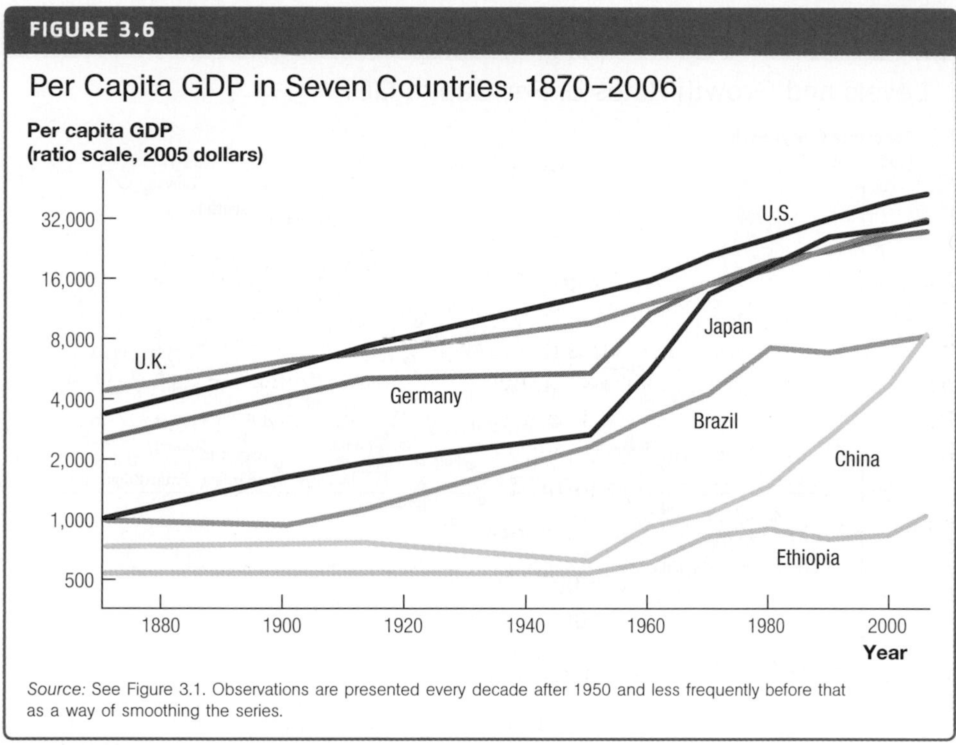

Source: See Figure 3.1. Observations are presented every decade after 1950 and less frequently before that as a way of smoothing the series.

The ratio scale applied to incomes in several countries . . .

income reaching nearly 1/3 the U.S. level. Since 1980, however, growth has slowed considerably, so that by 2006 income relative to the United States was just over 1/5.

China shows something of the opposite pattern, with growth really picking up after 1978 and reaching rates of more than 7 percent per year for the last two decades. A country often grouped with China in such discussions is India, in part because the two countries together account for more than 40 percent of the world's population. India's per capita GDP (not shown in the graph) looks somewhat similar to China's, especially before 1980. But since then, its growth has been slower, averaging 3.7 percent per year between 1986 and 2006. By 2006, China's per capita income was about 1/5 the U.S. level, while India's was just under 1/12.

These last numbers may come as a surprise if you take only a casual glance at Figure 3.6; at first it appears that by 2006 China's income was more than half the U.S. level. But remember that the graph is plotted on a ratio scale: look at the corresponding numbers on the vertical axis.

A Broad Sample of Countries

Figure 3.7 shows income levels and growth rates for a much larger sample of countries. The horizontal axis represents per capita GDP in the year 2007 relative to the United States. (Hong Kong, Norway, Singapore, and the United States had the highest per capita GDP in the world that year. Other rich countries include

Growth rates between 1960 and 2007 range from −3% to +6% per year. Per capita GDP in 2007 varies by about a factor of 64 across countries.

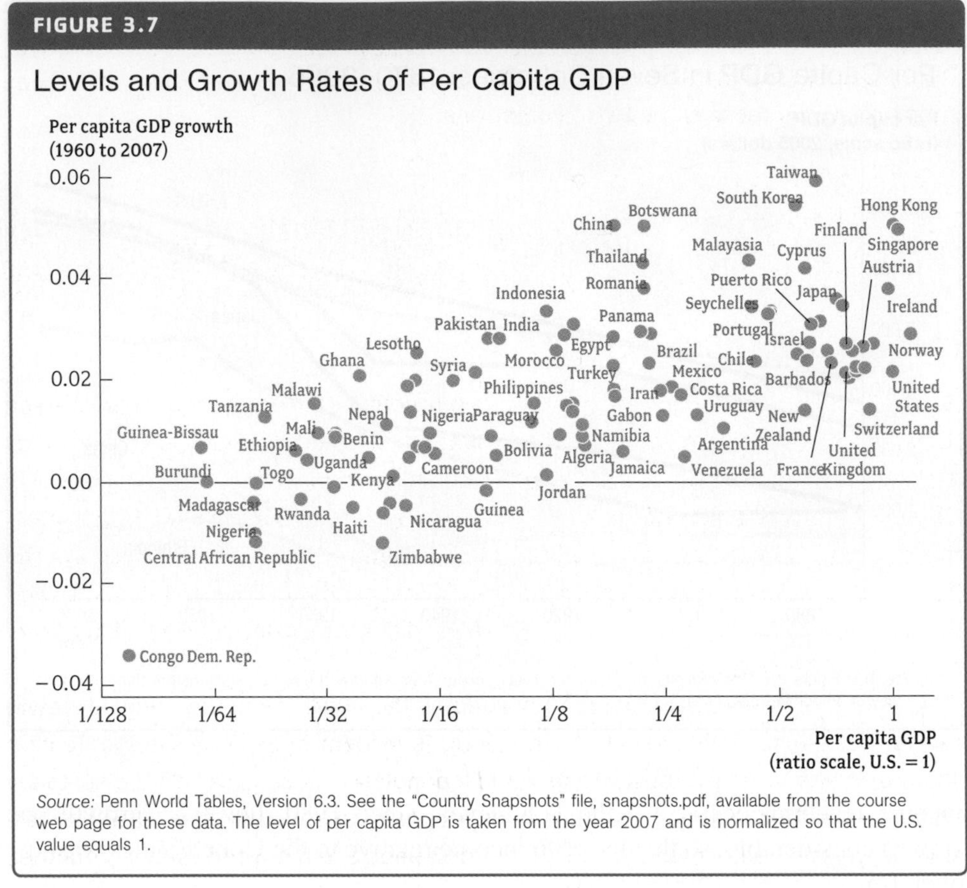

FIGURE 3.7

Levels and Growth Rates of Per Capita GDP

Source: Penn World Tables, Version 6.3. See the "Country Snapshots" file, snapshots.pdf, available from the course web page for these data. The level of per capita GDP is taken from the year 2007 and is normalized so that the U.S. value equals 1.

Ireland, Israel, Japan, South Korea, and Spain, with incomes greater than 1/2 the U.S. level. Middle-income countries like Honduras, Mexico, and Argentina had incomes about 1/3 the U.S. level. China, India, and Indonesia are examples of countries with relative incomes between 1/16 and 1/5. Finally, Burundi, Niger, and Tanzania, among the poorest countries of the world in 2007, had incomes as low as 1/64 the U.S. level.

The vertical axis illustrates the wide range of growth rates that countries have experienced since 1960. The fastest-growing countries over this period include South Korea, Hong Kong, Thailand, China, Botswana, and Japan, all with average growth rates between 4 and 6 percent per year. At the other end of the spectrum are the Central African Republic, the Democratic Republic of the Congo, Niger, and Zimbabwe, each of which exhibited *negative* average growth over this half century. The bulk of the countries lie between these two extremes. For example, growth rates in Sweden, Colombia, Turkey, Mexico, and the United Kingdom all hover around 2 percent. A number of poor countries saw growth rates above this average, including Brazil, Egypt, India, Indonesia, and Mauritius.

The importance of these differences in growth rates is hard to overestimate. In Taiwan, for example, which is growing at 6 percent per year, incomes will double every 12 years (remember the Rule of 70). Over the course of a half century—about two generations—incomes will increase by a factor of $2^4 = 16$. In a country like Taiwan, young adults are 16 times richer than their grandparents. But in countries like Nicaragua and Madagascar standards of living have been stagnant across these same two generations.

CASE STUDY

People versus Countries

Figure 3.8 takes a different perspective on economic growth and treats the *person* rather than the *country* as the unit of observation. Rather than letting China count as 1 observation out of 150 countries, for example, we count the 1.3 billion people in China as about one-fifth of the world's population. The figure, in other words, plots the distribution of the world's population according to per capita GDP. It shows the fraction of people living in countries that have a per capita GDP below the number on the horizontal axis. Importantly, this per capita GDP is measured as a fraction of U.S. per capita GDP in the year 2007.

A couple of interesting facts are revealed by the figure. First, the general growth rate of per capita GDP throughout the world is evident in the way the distribution shifts out over time. The bulk of the world's population is substantially richer today than it was in 1960. Second, the fraction of people living in poverty has fallen dramatically in the last half century. In 1960, 2 out of 3 people in the world lived in countries

FIGURE 3.8

The Distribution of World Population by Per Capita GDP, 1960 and 2007

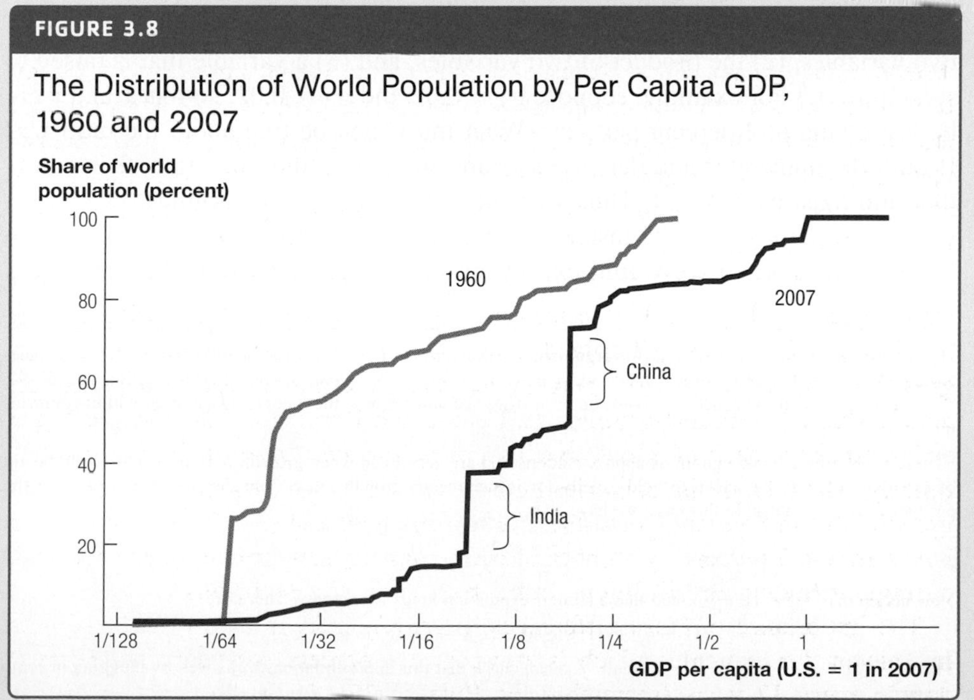

The graph shows, for 1960 and 2007, the percentage of the world's population living in countries with a per capita GDP less than or equal to the number on the horizontal axis. This per capita GDP is relative to the United States *in the year 2007* for both lines.

with a per capita GDP less than 5 percent of the 2007 U.S. level. In other words, in today's prices, these people made about $5 per day. By 2007, the fraction living in this kind of poverty had fallen to less than 1 out of 12. If the distribution had remained unchanged from its 1960 level, more than 4 billion people would fall below this poverty threshold today. Instead, because of economic growth, only about 600 million do. One of the major reasons for this has been the rapid economic growth in India and China, which together account for more than a third of the world's population.[5]

3.5 Some Useful Properties of Growth Rates

As we develop models of economic growth, three simple properties of growth rates will prove extremely valuable. These properties are summarized below.

Growth rates of ratios, products, and powers: Suppose two variables x and y have average annual growth rates of g_x and g_y, respectively. Then the following rules apply:

1. If $z = x/y$, then $g_z = g_x - g_y$.
2. If $z = x \times y$, then $g_z = g_x + g_y$.
3. If $z = x^a$, then $g_z = a \times g_x$.

In these expressions, g_z is the average annual growth rate of z.

These simple rules explain how to compute the growth rate of (1) the ratio of two variables, (2) the product of two variables, and (3) a variable that is raised to some power.[6] For example, suppose $g_x = 0.02$ and $g_y = 0.02$, so that x and y are both growing at 2 percent per year. What must then be true about the ratio x/y? If both the numerator and denominator are growing at the same rate, then surely the ratio must be constant. This is exactly what the first rule implies.

Now suppose $g_x = 0.05$ instead. In this case, the numerator grows faster than the denominator, so we would expect the ratio to grow as well. In fact, rule 1

---

[5] For a more sophisticated version of this argument, see Xavier Sala-i-Martin, "The World Distribution of Income: Falling Poverty and . . . Convergence, Period," *Quarterly Journal of Economics*, vol. 121 (May 2006), pp. 351–97. The paper shows that the conclusion holds up even if we account for how the income distribution within countries may have changed.

[6] These rules should be thought of as approximations that are very good when growth rates are small. With the aid of calculus, they can be shown to hold exactly for instantaneous growth rates. Consider the second rule, for the product of two variables. In this case, we have

$$\frac{z_{t+1}}{z_t} = \frac{x_{t+1}}{x_t} \times \frac{y_{t+1}}{y_t}.$$

Now notice that $\frac{z_{t+1}}{z_t} = (1 + g_z)$, and that a similar expression holds for x and y. Therefore,

$$(1 + g_z) = (1 + g_x)(1 + g_y) = 1 + g_x + g_y + g_x g_y.$$

Then $g_z \approx g_x + g_y$ as long as $g_x g_y$ is small. You can check that this approximation works well by plugging in some numbers.

TABLE 3.1

Examples of Growth Rate Calculations

Suppose x grows at rate $g_x = 0.10$ and y grows at rate $g_y = 0.03$.
What is the growth rate of z in the following cases?

$z = x \times y$	$\Rightarrow$	$g_z = g_x + g_y = .13$
$z = x/y$	$\Rightarrow$	$g_z = g_x - g_y = .07$
$z = y/x$	$\Rightarrow$	$g_z = g_y - g_x = -.07$
$z = x^2$	$\Rightarrow$	$g_z = 2 \times g_x = .20$
$z = y^{1/2}$	$\Rightarrow$	$g_z = .5 \times g_y = .015$
$z = x^{1/2}y^{-1/4}$	$\Rightarrow$	$g_z = .5 \times g_x - .25 \times g_y = .0425$

says the growth rate of the ratio should equal $g_x - g_y = 0.05 - 0.02 = 0.03$, so the ratio of x to y will now grow at 3 percent per year.

Next, consider the second rule. If $g_x = 0.04$ and $g_y = 0.02$, what will the growth rate of $z = x \times y$ be? Surely z must grow faster than x, since we've multiplied x by something that is growing. Rule 2 says that the growth rate of the product of two variables is the *sum* of the two growth rates.

These first two rules illustrate an elegant property of growth rates: growth rates obey mathematical operations that are one level "simpler" than the operation on the original variables. Division of the variables becomes subtraction of the growth rates; multiplication of the variables becomes addition of the growth rates.

As rule 3 shows, this same kind of simplification occurs when we look at exponentiation. To begin with a simple example, suppose y grows at rate g_y. What is the growth rate of $z = y^2$? Since $y^2 = y \times y$, we can apply our multiplication rule to see that $g_z = g_y + g_y = 2 \times g_y$. Similarly, the growth rate of y^3 will be $3 \times g_y$, and the growth rate of y^{10} will be $10 \times g_y$. This result generalizes to any exponent, including negative ones.

Table 3.1 shows some ways to apply these rules, and Figure 3.9 gives a practical example. Total GDP in an economy is equal to the product of per capita GDP and the population. Therefore the growth rate of GDP is the *sum* of the growth rates of per capita GDP and population. This can be seen graphically in the figure in the three different slopes. We will use these growth rules extensively in the chapters that follow, so you should memorize them and be prepared to apply them.

CASE STUDY

Growth Rules in a Famous Example, $Y_t = A_t K_t^{1/3} L_t^{2/3}$

This well-known example incorporates one of the key equations of macroeconomics, which we will return to often in coming chapters. For now, we'll see how it illustrates our growth rules.

Suppose we have an equation that says a variable Y_t is a function of some other variables A_t, K_t, and L_t. In particular, this function is

$$Y_t = A_t K_t^{1/3} L_t^{2/3}.$$

What is the growth rate of Y_t in terms of the growth rates of A_t, K_t, and L_t?

Here's where we apply our growth rules. Our second rule says that the growth rate of the product of certain variables is the sum of the variables' growth rates.[7] So

$$g(Y_t) = g(A_t) + g(K_t^{1/3}) + g(L_t^{2/3}).$$

(We write Y_t, A_t, and so on in parentheses here rather than as a subscript to avoid the awkward notation that would result.) Next, we can use the third rule to compute the growth rates of the last two terms in this expression: the growth rate of a variable raised to some power is equal to that power times the growth rate of the variable. Therefore, we have

$$g(Y_t) = g(A_t) + \tfrac{1}{3} \times g(K_t) + \tfrac{2}{3} \times g(L_t).$$

And that's the answer we are looking for. As we will see in later chapters, this equation says that the growth rate of output Y can be decomposed into the growth rate of a productivity term A and the contributions to growth from capital K and labor L.

The growth rate of total GDP is the sum of the growth rate of per capita GDP and the growth rate of the population.

FIGURE 3.9

U.S. Population, GDP, and Per Capita GDP, 1870–2009

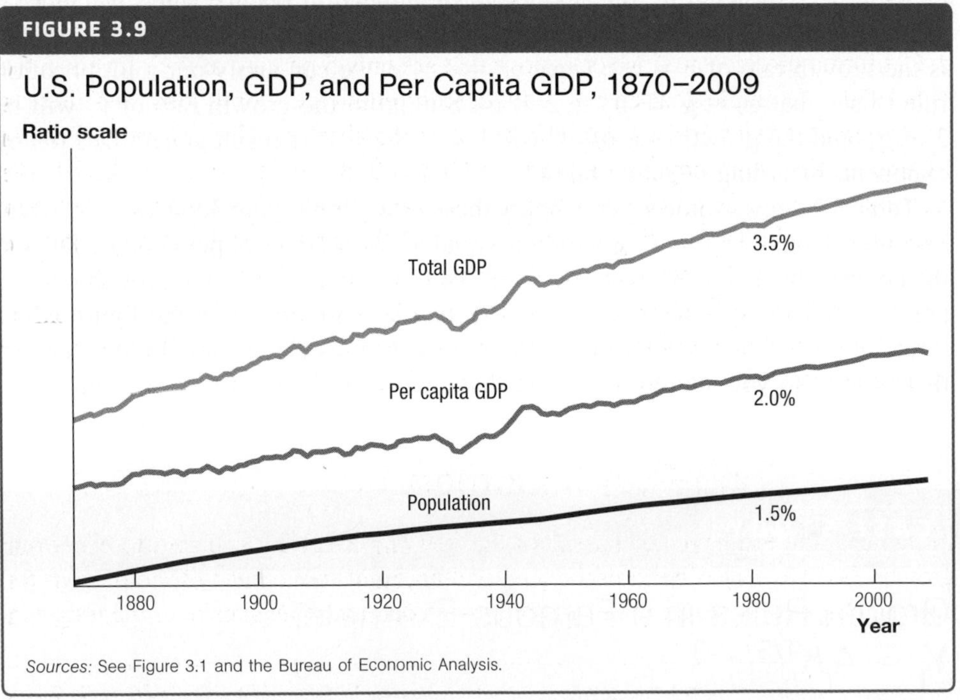

Sources: See Figure 3.1 and the Bureau of Economic Analysis.

[7] Although the original rule applied to the product of two variables, it applies equally well to three or more variables. For example, if $z = wxy$, then $g(z) = g(w) + g(xy) = g(w) + g(x) + g(y)$.

3.6 The Costs of Economic Growth

When we consider economic growth, what usually comes to mind are the enormous benefits it brings: increases in life expectancy, reductions in infant mortality, higher incomes, an expansion in the range of goods and services available, and so on. But what about the costs of economic growth? High on the list of costs are environmental problems such as pollution, the depletion of natural resources, and even global warming. Another by-product of economic growth during the last century is increased income inequality—certainly across countries and perhaps even within countries. Technological advances may also lead to the loss of certain jobs and industries. For example, automobiles decimated the horse-and-buggy industry; telephone operators and secretaries have seen their jobs redefined as information technology improves. More than 40 percent of U.S. workers were employed in agriculture in 1900; today the fraction is less than 2 percent.

The general consensus among economists who have studied these costs is that they are substantially outweighed by the overall benefits. In the poorest regions of the world, this is clear. When 20 percent of children die before the age of 5—as they do in much of Africa—the essential problem is not pollution or too much technological progress, but rather the absence of economic growth.

But the benefits also outweigh the costs in richer countries. For example, while pollution is often associated with the early stages of economic growth—as in London in the mid-1800s or Mexico City today—environmental economists have documented an inverse-U shape for this relationship. Pollution grows worse initially as an economy develops, but it often gets better eventually. Smog levels in Los Angeles are substantially less today than they were 30 years ago; one reason may be that cars in California produce noxious emissions that are only 5 percent of their levels in the mid-1970s. Technological change undoubtedly eliminates some jobs, and there is no denying the hardship that this can cause in the short run. But as we will see in Chapter 7, the unemployment rate in the United States today—at least before the recent recession—is on par with the levels in the 1960s. Jobs disappear, but new ones are created. The decline in agriculture and the demise of the family farm are the flip side of the tremendous rise in agricultural productivity.

It is indisputable that economic growth entails costs, especially in certain times and certain places and for certain people. In general, however, these costs are more than offset by the benefits of economic growth.[8]

3.7 A Long-Run Roadmap

In this chapter, we have seen some of the key empirical facts related to economic growth. We have also been introduced to important tools that will help us in the coming chapters as we build models of how an economy behaves over the long run.

[8] For more on the costs and benefits of growth, see the following: E. J. Mishan, *The Costs of Economic Growth* (New York: Praeger, 1993); Charles I. Jones, *Introduction to Economic Growth* (New York: Norton, 2002), Chapter 9; William Nordhaus, "Lethal Model 2: The Limits to Growth Revisited," *Brookings Papers on Economic Activity*, vol. 2 (1992), pp. 1–59. The facts about smog in California are from the California Air Resources Board, "Fact Sheet: Reducing Emissions from California Vehicles," February 23, 2004.

The next three chapters are primarily concerned with developing theories that help us understand the facts of economic growth. Chapter 4 focuses on explaining differences in levels of income across countries using production functions. Chapter 5 develops one of the canonical models of macroeconomics, the Solow growth model. And Chapter 6 studies the economics of knowledge itself to provide a richer understanding of the sources of growth and income differences. The last two chapters of the "long run" section of this book then turn away from economic growth to consider the labor market and the determination of wages and the unemployment rate in the long run (Chapter 7) and the long-run determinants of inflation (Chapter 8).

It should be clear at this point that the study of economic growth is of far more than academic interest. The United States of a century or two ago doesn't look that different from the poorest countries in the world today. But Americans today are more than 50 times richer on average than people in these poor regions. The rapid growth exhibited by Japan after World War II or by China in recent decades has the power to eliminate poverty there in a single generation: growing at 6 percent per year, incomes will double in 12 years, quadruple in 24 years, and increase by a factor of 8 in 36 years. At these rates, even a 50-fold gap could be closed in three generations.

In 1985, Robert E. Lucas Jr.—who would go on to win the Nobel Prize in Economics in 1995—delivered his now-famous Marshall Lectures at Cambridge University. These lectures, which laid out the facts of economic growth, much as in this chapter, were instrumental in stimulating an explosion of research on the subject in the decades that followed.[9] There is perhaps no better way to conclude this chapter than to let Lucas himself have the last word:

> I do not see how one can look at figures like these without seeing them as representing *possibilities*. Is there some action a government of India could take that would lead the Indian economy to grow like Indonesia's or Egypt's? If so, *what* exactly? If not, what is it about the "nature of India" that makes it so? The consequences for human welfare involved in questions like these are simply staggering: Once one starts to think about them, it is hard to think about anything else.[10]

3.8 Additional Resources

You may find these additional resources of interest. For articles published in academic journals, try Google Scholar (scholar.google.com): just type in the author's name and a word from the title of the paper. Many universities have online subscriptions to academic journals.

---

[9] The other important stimulus was a set of papers by Paul Romer on the economics of ideas. This work will be discussed extensively in Chapter 6.

[10] From "On the Mechanics of Economic Growth," *Journal of Monetary Economics*, vol. 22 (1988), p. 5.

W. Michael Cox and Richard Alm, *Time Well Spent: The Declining Real Cost of Living in America*, 1997 Annual Report, Federal Reserve Bank of Dallas, www.dallasfed.org/fed/annual/1999p/ar97.pdf

Robert E. Lucas Jr., "Some Macroeconomics for the 21st Century," *Journal of Economic Perspectives*, vol. 14 (Winter 2000), pp. 159–68.

Much of the data in this chapter, especially from before 1950, is taken from an online data collection of Angus Maddison, "Statistics on World Population, GDP and Per Capita GDP, 1 AD–2006 AD." These data are available from the "Historical Statistics" section of Maddison's web page at www.ggdc.net/maddison/.

Data on per capita income and growth rates since 1950 for most of the countries in the world can be found in the "Country Snapshots" file, *snapshots.pdf*, available from wwnorton.com/college/econ/chad.

CIA World Factbook, www.cia.gov/library/publications/the-world-factbook/.

CHAPTER REVIEW

SUMMARY

1. Viewed over the long course of history, sustained growth in standards of living is a very recent phenomenon. If the 130,000 years of human history were warped and collapsed into a single year, modern economic growth would have begun only at sunrise on the last day of the year.
2. Modern economic growth has taken hold in different places at different times. Since several hundred years ago, when standards of living across countries varied by no more than a factor of 2 or 3, there has been a "Great Divergence." Standards of living across countries today vary by more than a factor of 60.
3. Incomes in the poorest countries of the world are probably no more than twice as high as average incomes around the world a thousand years ago.
4. Since 1870, growth in per capita GDP has averaged about 2 percent per year in the United States. Per capita GDP has risen from about $2,800 in 1870 to more than $42,000 today.
5. Growth rates throughout the world since 1960 show substantial variation, ranging from negative growth in many poor countries to rates as high as 6 percent per year in several newly industrializing countries, most of which are in Asia.
6. Growth rates typically change over time. In Germany and Japan, growth picked up considerably after World War II as incomes in these countries converged to levels in the United Kingdom. Growth rates have slowed down as this convergence occurred. Brazil exhibited rapid growth in the 1950s and 1960s and slow growth in the 1980s and 1990s. China showed the opposite pattern.

7. Economic growth, especially in India and China, has dramatically reduced poverty in the world. In 1960, 2 out of 3 people in the world lived on less than \$5 per day (in today's prices). By 2007, this number had fallen to only 1 in 12.

GROWTH RULES

The important tools we will use extensively in the coming chapters are listed below for your convenience.

- Calculating a growth rate as a percentage change: $(y_{t+1} - y_t)/y_t$.
- The constant growth rule: $y_t = y_0(1 + \bar{g})^t$ if y grows at the constant rate $\bar{g}$.
- The Rule of 70: if income grows at g percent per year, it doubles roughly every $70/g$ years.
- The ratio scale for graphs, where a variable growing at a constant rate produces a straight line.
- The formula for computing average growth rates: $g = (y_t/y_0)^{1/t} - 1$.
- The rules for computing growth rates of ratios, products, and exponentials.

    1. If $z = x/y$, then $g_z = g_x - g_y$.
    2. If $z = xy$, then $g_z = g_x + g_y$.
    3. If $z = x^a$, then $g_z = ag_x$.

KEY CONCEPTS

constant growth rule
convergence
economic growth
the Great Divergence
growth rate
ratio scale
rule for computing growth rates
Rule of 70

REVIEW QUESTIONS

1. When and where did sustained economic growth first begin? How much inequality in per capita income was there throughout the countries of the world a thousand years ago? How much is there today?
2. How much richer is the typical 40-year-old today than the typical 40-year-old 35 years ago in the United States? What about in South Korea or China?
3. This question is not addressed in the chapter—and in fact is still debated among economists—but it is interesting to think about: Why do you suppose growth in living standards was virtually nonexistent for thousands of years? Why did this situation change in recent centuries?
4. Why are the Rule of 70 and the ratio scale useful tools? How do they work together?

5. Why, and in what sense, do the three growth rates shown in Figure 3.9 add up?
6. What are some costs and benefits of economic growth?

EXERCISES

smartwork.wwnorton.com 

1. **Growth and development:** In 2007, Ethiopia had a per capita income of \$1,100, about \$3 per day. Compute per capita income in Ethiopia for the year 2050 assuming average annual growth is
   (a) 1% per year.
   (b) 2% per year.
   (c) 4% per year.
   (d) 6% per year.

   (For comparison, per capita income in Mexico in the year 2007 was nearly \$11,000, about 1/4 the U.S. level.)

2. **Population growth:** Suppose the world population today is 7 billion, and suppose this population grows at a constant rate of 3% per year from now on. (This rate is almost certainly much faster than the future population growth rate; the high rate used here is useful for pedagogy. If you like, you can use a spreadsheet program to help you with this question.)
   (a) What would the population equal 100 years from now?
   (b) Compute the level of the population for $t = 0$, $t = 1$, $t = 2$, $t = 10$, $t = 25$, and $t = 50$.
   (c) Make a graph of population versus time (on a standard scale).
   (d) Now make the same graph on a ratio scale.

3. **Interest on your bank balance:** Suppose your bank account has a balance today of \$100. Consider the following time periods: $t = 0$, $t = 1$, $t = 2$, $t = 12$, $t = 24$, $t = 48$, and $t = 60$. Assume there are no deposits or withdrawals in this account other than the interest that accumulates. (If you like, use a spreadsheet program to help you with this question.)
   (a) Compute your bank balance for these time periods assuming the interest rate is 1%.
   (b) Do the same thing for an interest rate of 6%.
   (c) Plot your bank balances for these two scenarios on a standard scale.
   (d) Do the same thing with a ratio scale.

4. **Stock returns and your retirement account:** Suppose your retirement account has a balance today of \$10,000 and you are 20 years old. If you are invested in a diversified portfolio of stocks, you might hope that the historical return of about 6% continues into the future. Consider how the balance in your retirement account evolves as you age under the different assumptions below. (If you like, use a spreadsheet program to help you with this question.)
   (a) Compute the balance in your retirement account when you will be 25, 30, 40, 50, and 65 years old assuming the average annual rate of return is 6%. Assume there are no deposits or withdrawals in this account, so the original balance just accumulates.

(b) Do the same thing for rate of return of 5% and 7%. How sensitive is the calculation to the rate of return?
(c) Plot your retirement account balance for these three scenarios (6%, 5%, 7%) on a standard scale.
(d) Do the same thing with a ratio scale.

5. **The ratio scale:** Plot the following scenarios for per capita GDP on a ratio scale. Assume that per capita GDP in the year 2000 is equal to $10,000. You should not need a calculator or computer program. Use the Rule of 70 to label the value of per capita GDP on the graph in the years listed below.
   (a) Per capita GDP grows at a constant rate of 5% per year between 2000 and 2070.
   (b) Per capita GDP grows at 2% per year between 2000 and 2070, speeds up to 7% per year for the next 20 years, and then slows down to 5% per year for the next 28 years.
   (c) Per capita GDP grows at 7% per year for 50 years and then slows down to 1% per year for the next 140 years.

6. **U.S. growth:** On page 48, we noted that the growth rate of per capita GDP in the United States between 1870 and 1929 was slightly lower than 2.0%, while the growth rate between 1950 and 2009 was slightly higher. Using the following table, calculate the actual average annual growth rates during these two periods.

Year	U.S. income
1870	$2,840
1929	$8,020
1950	$13,225
2009	$42,240

7. **Growth rates of per capita GDP:** Compute the average annual growth rate of per capita GDP in each of the cases below. The levels are provided for 1980 and 2007, measured in constant 2005 dollars.

	1980	2007
United States	24,537	42,887
Canada	21,781	36,168
France	19,698	29,633
Germany	20,000	31,306
Japan	18,820	30,585
Italy	18,383	28,815
United Kingdom	16,681	31,181
Ireland	13,699	41,624
Mexico	9,288	11,204
Brazil	8,458	9,646
Indonesia	2,205	5,186
Kenya	1,932	2,025
India	1,429	3,826
China	1,133	7,868
Ethiopia	964	1,110

8. **The costs of economic growth?** In addition to the benefits of economic growth, there are also potentially costs. What are some of these costs? Write a paragraph arguing that the benefits exceed the costs. Write a paragraph arguing the opposite, that the costs exceed the benefits. Which argument do you find more convincing, and why?

9. **Computing growth rates (I):** Suppose $x_t = (1.05)^t$ and $y_t = (1.02)^t$. Calculate the growth rate of z_t in each of the following cases:
   (a) $z = xy$
   (b) $z = x/y$
   (c) $z = y/x$
   (d) $z = x^{1/2}y^{1/2}$
   (e) $z = (x/y)^2$
   (f) $z = x^{-1/3}y^{2/3}$

10. **Computing growth rates (II):** Suppose k, l, and m grow at constant rates given by $\bar{g}_k$, $\bar{g}_l$, and $\bar{g}_m$. What is the growth rate of y in each of the following cases?
   (a) $y = k^{1/3}$
   (b) $y = k^{1/3}l^{2/3}$
   (c) $y = mk^{1/3}l^{2/3}$
   (d) $y = mk^{1/4}l^{3/4}$
   (e) $y = mk^{3/4}l^{1/4}$
   (f) $y = (klm)^{1/2}$
   (g) $y = (kl)^{1/4}(1/m)^{3/4}$

11. **Computing levels:** Suppose x_t grows at 2% per year and y_t grows at 4% per year, with $x_0 = 2$ and $y_0 = 1$. Calculate the numerical values of z_t for $t = 0$, $t = 1$, $t = 2$, $t = 10$, $t = 17$, and $t = 35$ for the following cases:
   (a) $z = x$
   (b) $z = y$
   (c) $z = x^{3/4}y^{1/4}$

12. **(Harder) An alternative way of computing growth rates?** In exercise 6, the correct way to compute the average growth rate is to apply equation (3.9). An alternative way is to take the percentage change divided by the number of years: for example,

$$\frac{1}{T} \times \frac{y_T - y_0}{y_0}.$$

   Compute the growth rates with this formula; they should be substantially different from what you got before. What is the explanation for this difference?

13. **How can we measure growth over the very long run?** The poorest countries in the world have a per capita income of about $600 today. We can reasonably assume that it is nearly impossible to live on an income below half this level (below $300). Per capita income in the United States in 2009 was about $42,000. With this information in mind, consider the following questions.
   (a) For how long is it possible that per capita income in the United States has been growing at an average annual rate of 2% per year?

(b) Some economists have argued that growth rates are mismeasured. For example, it may be difficult to compare per capita income today with per capita income a century ago when so many of the goods we can buy today were not available *at any price* then. Suppose the true growth rate in the last century was 3% per year rather than 2%. What would the level of per capita income in 1800 have been in this case? Is this answer plausible?

WORKED EXERCISES

3. Interest on your bank balance:

(a) To calculate your bank balance in any period, we use the formula from the constant growth rule in equation (3.7) on page 46:

$$y_t = y_0(1 + \bar{g})^t.$$

Let B_t denote the bank balance and $\bar{r}$ denote the interest rate. Then your bank balance satisfies

$$B_t = B_0(1 + \bar{r})^t.$$

With $B_0 = \$100$ and $\bar{r} = 0.01$, the bank balances are shown in the second column of Table 3.2 below. For example, after 60 years, the bank balance has reached \$182, not quite double the original value (recall that according to the Rule of 70, it will take 70 years for the bank balance to double if the interest rate is 1%).

(b) We use the same formula with $\bar{r} = 0.06$ to calculate the bank balances with a 6% interest rate. These are shown in the last column of Table 3.2. Notice that the Rule of 70 applies here as well, so the bank balance doubles about every 12 years. (This is why those somewhat odd-looking times were chosen, rather than $t = 5$, $t = 10$, etc.) Notice how the seemingly small difference in interest rates—1% versus 6%—turns into enormous differences

TABLE 3.2

Bank Balances

Time	Interest rate $\bar{r} = 0.01$	Interest rate $\bar{r} = 0.06$
0	100	100
1	101	106
2	102	112
12	113	201
24	127	405
48	161	1,639
60	182	3,299

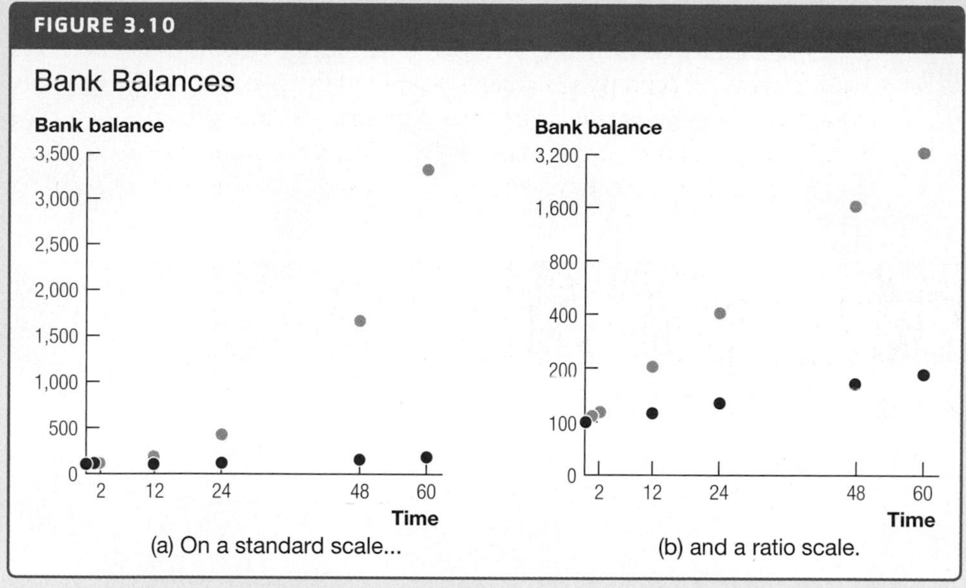

(a) On a standard scale... (b) and a ratio scale.

in your bank balance. After 60 years, the balance is nearly \$3,300 when the interest rate is 6%.

(c) and (d) Figure 3.10 shows the bank balances on a standard scale and a ratio scale (also called a "logarithmic scale" in some spreadsheet programs). On the standard scale, we see the data points curve upward, following the standard pattern of economic growth. Because the interest rate is constant, the upward curve turns into a straight line on the ratio scale. This is what you need to keep in mind when you are making the plot on the ratio scale: if you are not using a spreadsheet program, you just draw the straight line and label the points as in the table.

6. U.S. growth:

To compute the average annual growth rate, we use the formula from equation (3.9) on page 50:

$$\bar{g} = \left(\frac{y_t}{y_0}\right)^{1/t} - 1.$$

Notice that this formula is derived from the familiar expression $y_t = y_0(1 + \bar{g})^t$.

For the period 1870 to 1929, the formula yields a growth rate of

$$\bar{g} = \left(\frac{8{,}020}{2{,}840}\right)^{1/(1929-1870)} - 1 = 0.0178.$$

So the growth rate in this initial period averaged 1.78% per year.

For the period 1950 to 2009, the formula yields a growth rate of

$$\bar{g} = \left(\frac{42{,}220}{13{,}225}\right)^{1/(2009-1950)} - 1 = 0.0199.$$

So the growth rate in the more recent period averaged 1.99% per year.

CHAPTER 4

A MODEL OF PRODUCTION

OVERVIEW

In this chapter, we learn

- how to set up and solve a macroeconomic model.
- how a production function can help us understand differences in per capita GDP across countries.
- the relative importance of capital per person versus total factor productivity in accounting for these differences.
- the relevance of "returns to scale" and "diminishing marginal products."
- how to look at economic data through the lens of a macroeconomic model.

If we understand the process of economic growth—or of anything else—we ought to be capable of demonstrating this knowledge by creating it in these pen and paper (and computer-equipped) laboratories of ours. If we know what an economic miracle is, we ought to be able to make one.

—ROBERT E. LUCAS JR.

What I cannot create, I do not understand.

—ATTRIBUTED TO RICHARD P. FEYNMAN

4.1 Introduction

As noted in Chapter 3, people in the United States today are roughly 3 times richer than people in Argentina, 5 times richer than people in China, and more than 50 times richer than people in the poorest countries of the world. How do we explain these enormous differences in standards of living across countries?

This chapter provides a first answer. It comes in the form of a *model*, like many of the answers in modern economics. For example, the model that is likely most familiar to you is the standard supply-and-demand framework of economics. This framework can help us understand why water is relatively cheap, why diamonds are relatively expensive, why the price of computer chips is falling over time, and why college tuition continues to rise faster than inflation.[1]

A **model** is a mathematical representation of a hypothetical world that we use to study economic phenomena. To take a simple analogy, imagine building a toy world with Lego Mindstorm robots. As the model builder, you determine what actions the robots can take, and you provide the raw materials that fill the robot world. After constructing the world, you switch on a power source and watch what happens. Economists do the same thing with our "pen and paper (and computer-equipped) laboratories," in Lucas's words. We build a toy economy and see how it behaves. If we really understand why some countries are so much richer than others, we ought to be able to make this happen in one of our toy worlds.

Mathematically, a model is no more than a set of equations, like those you've studied since your first class in algebra. For example, a supply-and-demand model consists of two equations and two unknowns. What makes this much more exciting than algebra, however, is that we are not particularly concerned with the mathematics of solving equations; that is what you learned long ago. Rather, our equations and variables have real-world interpretations—like the supply-and-demand equations and the quantity and price of diamonds. What is fascinating about the best economic models is that they use simple equations to shed light on some of the most fundamental questions in economics.

Epigraph: Lucas, "Making a Miracle," *Econometrica* 1993, p. 271.

[1] The water, diamond, and computer chip examples are all things you should be able to figure out for yourself. We will return to the college tuition example in Chapter 7.

The general approach just outlined captures the essence of modern macroeconomics. We document a set of facts, build a model to understand those facts, and then examine our model to see how effective it is at "explaining" the facts we began with. If we happen to find a model that is consistent with the facts, that doesn't mean it is the right model. There may be others that are also consistent, and we may need new facts to distinguish among them. But that is a layer of complexity for another time. For the moment, we are interested in crafting at least *one* model that can help us to understand why Americans are 40 times richer than Ethiopians. By the end of the chapter, we will have done so.

4.2 A Model of Production

First we start with ice cream. Consider a single, closed economy where ice cream is the only consumption good. In the economy as a whole, there are a fixed number of people and a given number of ice cream machines. Firms decide how many workers to hire and how many machines to rent. They engage in production, pay their workers, and sell the ice cream to consumers. We will formalize this simple model with mathematics and then solve the model to see how much ice cream each person gets to eat.

No one would mistake this toy model for the United States and the tens of thousands of goods it produces, or even for the poorest country of the world. Still, even though it's a vast oversimplification of the real world, this model will provide important insights.

Setting Up the Model

In this toy world, we assume there are a certain number of people available to make ice cream. This number will be denoted by the symbol $\bar{L}$ (for "labor"). We also assume there are a certain number of ice cream machines, given by $\bar{K}$ (for "capital"). For example, $\bar{L}$ might equal 10 million people and $\bar{K}$ might equal 1 million machines. Throughout this book, letters with a bar over them, like $\bar{L}$ and $\bar{K}$, denote parameters that are fixed and exogenously given in the model. They simply stand in for some fixed constant.

A **production function** tells us how much ice cream Y can be produced if L workers are combined with K machines. We assume this production function is given by

$$Y = F(K,L) = \bar{A}K^{1/3}L^{2/3} \quad (4.1)$$

where $\bar{A}$ is some positive constant. We refer to $\bar{A}$ as a *productivity* parameter since, as we will see later, a higher value of $\bar{A}$ means the firm produces more ice cream, other things being equal. Notice that the K and L here do not have bars over them. That is intentional. The production function describes how *any* amounts of capital and labor can be combined to generate output, not just the particular amount that our toy economy possesses.

The first part of equation (4.1) says that the production function is some mathematical function $F(K,L)$; with K machines and L workers, the economy can produce $F(K,L)$ tons of ice cream. The second part specializes our production function to a particular form, one of the most common in all of economics, called **the Cobb-Douglas production function**. You may have seen it written before as $Y = K^a L^{1-a}$. Here, we are focusing on the case where a takes the particular value 1/3 (why the value is 1/3 will be explained later). Because we will return to this production function over and over again, it is worth spending some time to get to know it better.

First, let's make sure we understand what the production function says. Suppose we measure output in tons of ice cream per year, and let's assume $\bar{A} = 1$ to keep our example simple. How much ice cream can a firm produce with 27 workers and 8 ice cream machines? The answer is

$$Y = 8^{1/3} \cdot 27^{2/3} = 2 \cdot 9 = 18.$$

That is, each year, the firm produces 18 tons of ice cream.

Second, notice that this production function exhibits **constant returns to scale**. That is, if we double the amount of each input, we will double the amount of ice cream produced. You can check this by noting that

$$\begin{aligned} F(2K,2L) &= \bar{A}(2K)^{1/3}(2L)^{2/3} \\ &= 2^{1/3}2^{2/3}\bar{A}K^{1/3}L^{2/3} \\ &= 2^{1/3+2/3}F(K,L) \\ &= 2 \cdot F(K,L). \end{aligned}$$

It is the fact that the exponents sum to 1 (1/3 + 2/3 = 1) that delivers constant returns to scale. If the exponents summed to more than 1, then doubling the inputs would *more* than double the amount of ice cream produced; in this case, there would be **increasing returns to scale**. Conversely, if the exponents summed to less than 1, doubling the inputs would *less* than double output, and we would say production exhibits **decreasing returns to scale**.

How can we justify our assumption that the ice cream production function exhibits constant returns? Suppose you are the owner of an ice cream company and, because the weather is warm and times are good in the ice cream business, you decide you would like to double your production. How could you do this? A moment's reflection suggests one way: you find a similar piece of land, build an identical factory, hire identical workers, and exactly double your stocks of cream, sugar, rock salt, and strawberries. That is, one way to double your production would be to replicate exactly your current setup. Intuitively, this makes sense—and you have just illustrated the constant returns principle: if you double all the inputs of production, you double output. This justification for constant returns is known as **the standard replication argument**.

Allocating Resources

Up until this point, we've outlined the production possibilities of our ice cream economy. A production function combines labor and machines to make ice cream, and we can employ any amount of labor up to $\bar{L}$ and any amount of capital up to $\bar{K}$. Now we need to figure out how many workers and machines to use.

Let's assume our economy is perfectly competitive. A large number of identical ice cream–making firms take prices as given and then decide how much labor and capital to use. They choose these inputs to maximize profits.

A typical firm in this economy will solve the following problem:

$$\max_{K,L} \Pi = F(K,L) - rK - wL, \tag{4.2}$$

taking the wage w and the rental price of capital r as given. That is, the firm chooses the amount of capital K to rent and labor L to hire in order to maximize profits Π. Notice that we've normalized the price of ice cream to 1. That is, all prices—w, r, and the price of ice cream itself—are expressed in tons of ice cream. We have to choose some good—pieces of paper, total GDP, or ice cream—in which to express prices, and economists call this good the **numéraire**. Profits are equal to the amount of ice cream produced less the total payments to capital and labor.

The solution to this maximization problem tells the firm how much capital and labor to hire to maximize profits. How do we obtain this solution? If you have already taken a course in intermediate microeconomics, you are probably familiar with the answer. If not, the following discussion will walk you through it.

The solution to the firm's problem is to hire capital until the marginal product of capital is equal to the rental price r, and to hire labor until the marginal product of labor equals the wage w. That's quite a mouthful, so let's take it one step at a time. We'll start with capital: *The* ***marginal product of capital (MPK)*** *is the extra amount of output that is produced when one unit of capital is added, holding all the other inputs constant.* The production function and the marginal product of capital are shown graphically in Figure 4.1.

In the figure, L is held constant. Notice that each additional unit of capital employed (the horizontal axis) increases output by less and less. For example, increasing capital from 7 to 8 units raises output by much less than increasing

This figure shows the Cobb-Douglas production function, $Y = \bar{A}K^{1/3}L^{2/3}$, where L is held constant. Notice that each additional unit of K increases output by less and less. This is the diminishing marginal product of capital.

FIGURE 4.1

The Diminishing Marginal Product of Capital in Production

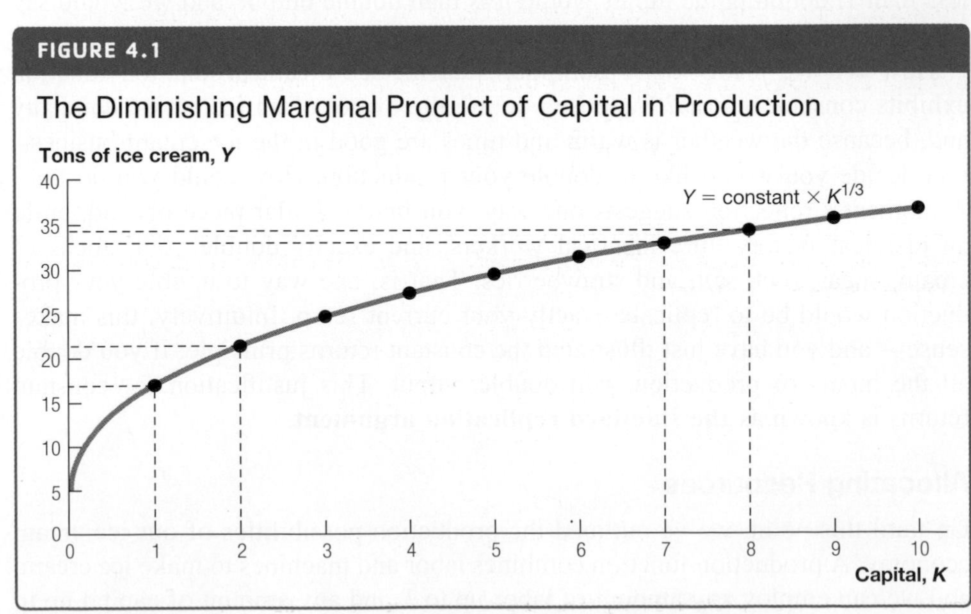

capital from 1 to 2 units. Because our production function exhibits constant returns to scale in K and L *together*, it must exhibit decreasing returns in K alone: doubling both K and L will double output, so doubling K by itself will *less* than double output.

As an illustration, suppose we have five workers. The first five ice cream machines are thus very valuable, as each worker can be matched with a single machine. The next five machines are less valuable—it's hard for a worker to oversee two machines simultaneously. Eventually, once each individual worker is paired with nine or ten machines, additional machines are essentially useless and do not significantly increase production.

For our Cobb-Douglas production function, the marginal product of capital is given by[2]

$$MPK = \frac{1}{3} \cdot \bar{A} \cdot \left(\frac{L}{K}\right)^{2/3} = \frac{1}{3} \cdot \frac{Y}{K}. \tag{4.3}$$

This equation has a nice form: the marginal product of capital is proportional to the average amount that each unit of capital produces, Y/K, where the factor of proportionality is 1/3, the Cobb-Douglas exponent. In fact, in Cobb-Douglas production functions generally, the marginal product of a factor is the product of the factor's exponent and the average amount that each unit of the factor produces.

The first equality in equation (4.3) confirms the diminishing marginal product. The marginal product of capital depends on the ratio L/K. Therefore, MPK declines as K rises.

Everything you've just read about capital turns out to be true for labor as well. *The* ***marginal product of labor (MPL)*** *is the extra amount of output that is produced when one unit of labor is added, holding all the other inputs constant.* If we hold K constant, the marginal product of labor declines as we increase the number of workers at the firm. Why? Suppose we have five ice cream machines. The first five people we hire are very productive. But as we add more and more workers, there is less for them to do with only five machines among them.

Referring back to equation (4.3), you should be able to figure out the marginal product of labor in this case. In particular, you should find that

$$MPL = \frac{2}{3} \cdot \bar{A} \cdot \left(\frac{K}{L}\right)^{1/3} = \frac{2}{3} \cdot \frac{Y}{L}. \tag{4.4}$$

---

[2]Showing this requires basic calculus. The marginal product of capital is the derivative of $F(K,L)$ with respect to K, treating L as a constant. That is,

$$\begin{aligned}\frac{\partial Y}{\partial K} &= \frac{\partial(\bar{A}K^{1/3}L^{2/3})}{\partial K}\\ &= \frac{1}{3} \cdot \bar{A}K^{1/3-1}L^{2/3}\\ &= \frac{1}{3} \cdot \bar{A}K^{-2/3}L^{2/3}\\ &= \frac{1}{3} \cdot \bar{A} \cdot \left(\frac{L}{K}\right)^{2/3}\\ &= \frac{1}{3} \cdot \frac{Y}{K}.\end{aligned}$$

Notice that this last equality follows directly from the production function, $Y = \bar{A}K^{1/3}L^{2/3}$.

The marginal product of labor is proportional to the average amount each worker produces, Y/L, where the factor of proportionality is the Cobb-Douglas exponent, 2/3.

Now let's return to our profit-maximization problem. As mentioned above, the solution is to hire capital and labor until their marginal products fall to equal r and w, respectively. This can be summarized as

$$MPK \equiv \frac{1}{3} \cdot \frac{Y}{K} > r \Rightarrow \text{hire more capital, until } MPK = r.$$

$$MPL \equiv \frac{2}{3} \cdot \frac{Y}{L} > w \Rightarrow \text{hire more labor, until } MPL = w.$$

Why does this solution make sense? If the marginal product of labor is higher than the wage, the ice cream produced by an additional worker exceeds the wage she must be paid (recall that the price of output is normalized to 1), so profits will increase. This remains true until the cost of hiring a worker is exactly equal to the amount of extra ice cream the worker produces. The same reasoning holds for capital.

Solving the Model: General Equilibrium

Our model is summarized in Table 4.1. There are five exogenous variables, or "unknowns": three quantities (output Y and the amount of capital K and labor L hired by firms) and two prices (the wage w and the rental price of capital r). These are the variables our model must determine.

To pin down the values of our endogenous variables, we have five equations: the production function, the two rules for hiring capital and labor, and finally the "supply equals demand" equations for the capital and labor markets. A simplification we have made is that the number of perfectly competitive firms in this economy is exactly equal to 1 (a common simplification in macroeconomic models), so that in the solution of our model, the demand by our representative firm is equal to the aggregate quantity of capital in the economy. A similar result holds for

TABLE 4.1

The Production Model: 5 Equations and 5 Unknowns

Unknowns/endogenous variables: Y, K, L, r, w

Production function	$Y = \bar{A}K^{1/3}L^{2/3}$
Rule for hiring capital	$\frac{1}{3} \cdot \frac{Y}{K} = r$
Rule for hiring labor	$\frac{2}{3} \cdot \frac{Y}{L} = w$
Demand = supply for capital	$K = \bar{K}$
Demand = supply for labor	$L = \bar{L}$

Parameters/exogenous variables: $\bar{A}, \bar{K}, \bar{L}$

labor. We could have more firms if we wished and nothing would change, since our model features constant returns to scale. These five equations also depend on the model's parameters: the productivity parameter $\bar{A}$ and the exogenous supplies of capital and labor, $\bar{K}$ and $\bar{L}$.

The solution of this model is called the **equilibrium**. In fact, we might call it the **general equilibrium**, because we have more than a single market that is clearing. In microeconomics, when supply and demand in a single market determine the price and quantity sold in the market, it's called a partial equilibrium. Here, we have a capital market, a labor market, and a model of the entire economy, hence a general equilibrium.

Mathematically, the equilibrium of the model is obtained by solving these five equations for the values of our five unknowns. A solution of the model is a new set of equations, with the unknowns on the left side and the parameters and exogenous variables on the right side.

The solution is perhaps easiest seen in a graph of supply and demand for the capital and labor markets, as shown in Figure 4.2. Since the supplies of capital and labor are exogenously given, the supply curves are vertical lines at the values $\bar{K}$ and $\bar{L}$. The demand curves for capital and labor are based on the hiring rules that we derived from the firm's profit-maximization problem. These demand curves trace out exactly the marginal product schedules for capital and labor: at any given wage, the amount of labor the firm wishes to hire is such that the marginal product of labor equals that wage.

The equilibrium prices and quantities, marked with an asterisk (*), are found at the intersections of these supply and demand curves. At these intersections, supply is equal to demand and the markets for capital and labor clear. In equilibrium, all the labor and all the capital in the economy are fully employed, and the equilibrium wage and rental price are given by the marginal products of labor and capital at the points where $K^* = \bar{K}$ and $L^* = \bar{L}$. The amount of output produced (Y^*) is then given by the production function. You can see this solution in equation form in Table 4.2.

FIGURE 4.2

Supply and Demand in the Capital and Labor Markets

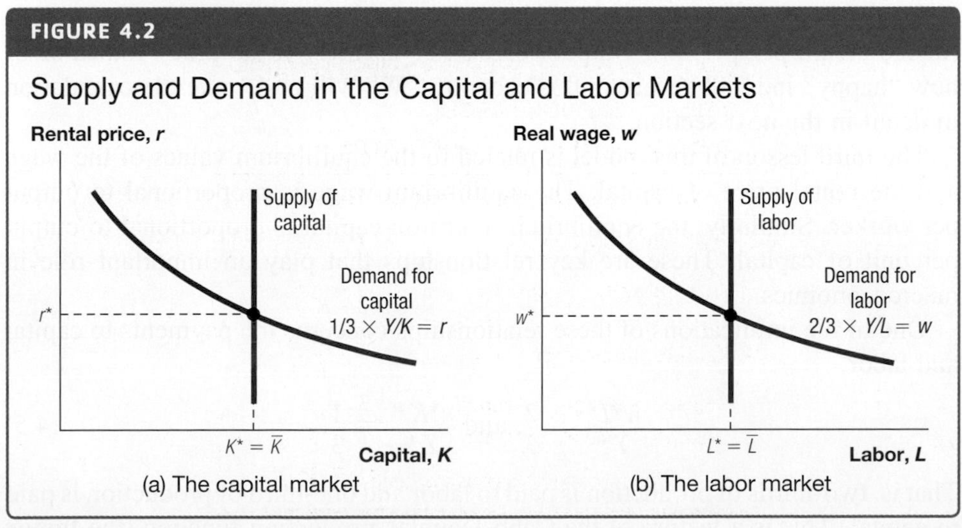

(a) The capital market (b) The labor market

The capital and labor markets clear when supply equals demand, determining the wage and the rental price of capital.

The solution of the production model: the equilibrium values for the endogenous variables are given as a function of the parameters and exogenous variables.

TABLE 4.2

The Solution of the Production Model

Capital	$K^* = \bar{K}$
Labor	$L^* = \bar{L}$
Rental rate	$r^* = \frac{1}{3} \cdot \frac{Y^*}{K^*} = \frac{1}{3} \cdot \bar{A} \cdot \left(\frac{\bar{L}}{\bar{K}}\right)^{2/3}$
Wage	$w^* = \frac{2}{3} \cdot \frac{Y^*}{L^*} = \frac{2}{3} \cdot \bar{A} \cdot \left(\frac{\bar{K}}{\bar{L}}\right)^{1/3}$
Output	$Y^* = \bar{A}\bar{K}^{1/3}\bar{L}^{2/3}$

While there is quite a bit of algebra going on in this table, the solution is actually extremely simple. The firms employ all the capital and labor in the economy, so that total production in the economy is given by the production function evaluated at $\bar{K}$ and $\bar{L}$. Then the wage and the rental price of capital are just the marginal product of labor and the marginal product of capital.

Interpreting the Solution

What do we learn from the production model? Three things. First, we learn how to set up a model and what it means to solve one. In future chapters, we will be adding elements to this basic framework to create more sophisticated models.

Second, we actually learn a great deal about what makes a country rich or poor. At some level, the answer is already apparent in the production function:

$$Y^* = F(\bar{K},\bar{L}) = \bar{A}\bar{K}^{1/3}\bar{L}^{2/3}.$$

The total amount of output—in this case, ice cream—is determined by the total amount of capital and the total amount of labor available in the economy. If the economy is endowed with more machines and/or more people, it will achieve a higher level of production.

On a related point, our solution also allows us to calculate output per worker (or ice cream per person). Output per worker is likely to be a key indicator of how "happy" individuals are in this economy. We will undertake the calculation in detail in the next section.

The third lesson of this model is related to the equilibrium values of the wage and the rental price of capital. The equilibrium wage is proportional to output per worker. Similarly, the equilibrium return on capital is proportional to output per unit of capital. These are key relationships that play an important role in macroeconomics.

One of the implications of these relationships concerns the payments to capital and labor:

$$\frac{w^*L^*}{Y^*} = \frac{2}{3}, \text{ and } \frac{r^*K^*}{Y^*} = \frac{1}{3}. \quad (4.5)$$

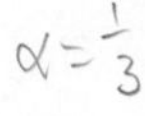

That is, two-thirds of production is paid to labor and one-third of production is paid to capital. This is a feature of the Cobb-Douglas production function (the **factor**

shares of income, as the payments to capital and labor are called, are equal to the Cobb-Douglas exponents), and is true regardless of how much capital or labor there is in the economy. It turns out that this two-thirds/one-third split holds true empirically, at least as a fair approximation. In the United States, about one-third of GDP is paid to capital and about two-thirds is paid to labor, and these shares are reasonably stable over time. This fact was documented more thoroughly back in Chapter 2 (see Figure 2.3), and it explains why we chose the exponent of one-third for capital in our production function.[3]

These factor share equations imply in turn that

$$w^*L^* + r^*K^* = Y^*. \tag{4.6}$$

That is, the sum of payments to capital and labor is exactly equal to total production in the economy. If we look back at the profit-maximization problem in equation (4.2), we see that this means that profits in the economy are equal to zero. At some level, this should come as no surprise. We knew from the beginning that we were looking at the allocation of resources in a perfectly competitive economy, and one of the implications of perfect competition is zero profits. We have thus just verified this implication in our production model.

More important, equation (4.6) says that total income in the economy is equal to total production—one of the fundamental relationships of national income accounting. It's nice to see this verified in our model. Moreover, the other fundamental relationship—that production and income are equal to spending—also holds. The toy model includes no investment, government purchases, imports, or exports (ice cream is for consumption only). So the model verifies national income accounting: production equals spending equals income.

CASE STUDY

What Is the Stock Market?

Although it may come as a surprise to you, this is the perfect place to pause and reflect on what the stock market is. Figure 4.3 shows the value of the S&P (Standard and Poor's) 500 stock price index for the last half century. But what do these numbers mean? What does the stock market value?

The answer turns out to be related to the capital income we have just been investigating. To see this more clearly, we need to distinguish between economic profit and accounting profit. **Economic profit** refers to the amount left over when total payments for inputs are subtracted from total revenues. In models with perfect competition, economic profits are zero. As we just saw in equation (4.6), all of production

[3]An interesting paper by Douglas Gollin examines the division of factor payments in a wide range of countries at different stages of development. Gollin finds that the factor shares in these countries are close to the one-third/two-thirds split. See Douglas Gollin, "Getting Income Shares Right," *Journal of Political Economy*, vol. 110 (April 2002), pp. 458–74.

The S&P 500 index is a measure of the stock market value of 500 large corporations traded on U.S. stock exchanges. The real index is equal to the nominal index divided by the Consumer Price Index.

FIGURE 4.3

The S&P 500 Stock Price Index, 1950–2010

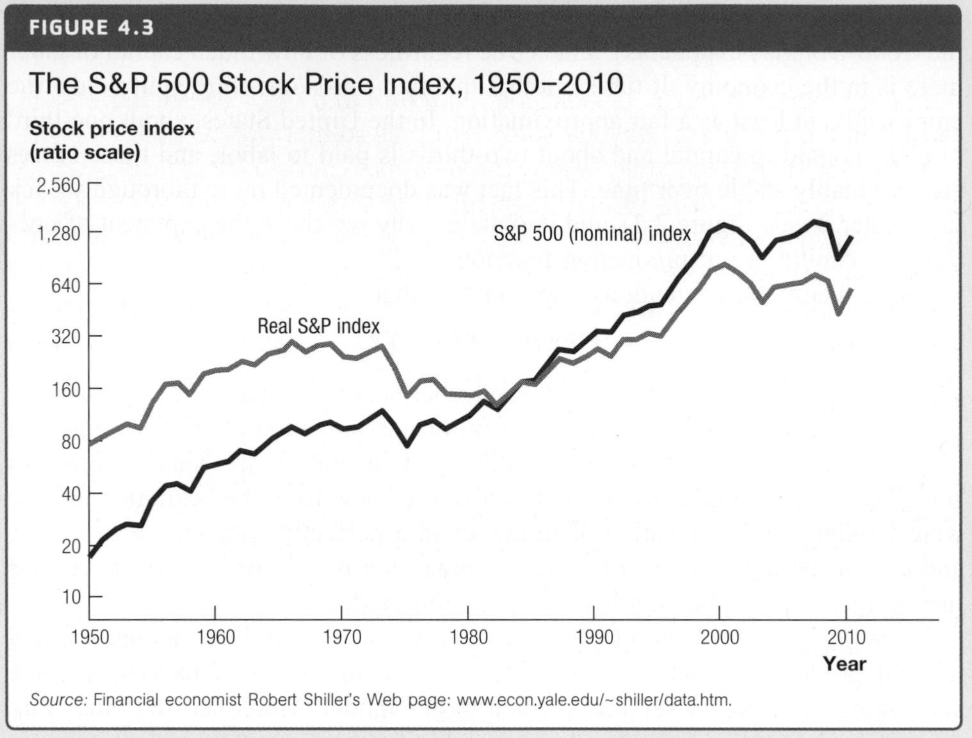

Source: Financial economist Robert Shiller's Web page: www.econ.yale.edu/~shiller/data.htm.

is paid out to capital and labor in our simple production model, so economic profits are zero.

In contrast, **accounting profit** is a term used in accounting and finance to describe payments to capital. It is equal to total revenues less payments to labor (and any other inputs other than capital). In our production model, accounting profit is equal to r^*K^*, total payments to capital – equal to one-third of output.

A firm's stock market value is the total value of its current and future accounting profits.[4] The stock market as a whole, then, can be viewed as the value of the economy's capital stock (or at least the part that is owned by publicly traded corporations). At a basic level, that is how you should understand a stock price index, like the S&P 500 or the Dow Jones Industrial Average commonly reported in the news. When people trade shares of a company's stock, they are just trading claims to the firm's future capital income.

For fun, look again at the graph in Figure 4.3. Notice the important difference between the real price index and the nominal price index. By how much did the index change over your lifetime? How about between 1965 and 1995? The value of the S&P 500 index was about 1,150 in January 2010. What is its value today?

[4] More precisely, the stock market value is the *present discounted value* of current and future profits—the total value of profits viewed from the standpoint of today. This concept will be discussed in more detail in Chapter 7.

4.3 Analyzing the Production Model

With our production model in hand, we can return to the key question that motivated it in the first place: why are some countries so much richer than others?

Notice that our question is a statement about per capita GDP. So far, we have solved the model in terms of *total* (aggregate) output, but a country's welfare is determined by output *per person*. This fact suggests that we have a little more work to do: we need to solve the model for output per person.

(A word about terms: "per capita" means per person, while "per worker" means per member of the labor force. In our production model, the number of workers is equal to the number of people, so these concepts are the same. In reality, of course, not all people work. Economists often refer to output per worker when discussing how successful the production process is. They speak of output per capita, or per person, to indicate some notion of economic welfare, since this measure is more closely related to consumption per person in the economy.)

To solve for output per person, let's define two new variables, $y \equiv Y/L$ and $k \equiv K/L$. The first, y, is output per person, and this is the main variable we want to characterize. The second, k, is capital per person. Looking back at Table 4.2, we can calculate output per person in equilibrium as

$$\begin{aligned} y^* \equiv \frac{Y^*}{L^*} &= \frac{\overline{A}\overline{K}^{1/3}\overline{L}^{2/3}}{\overline{L}} \\ &= \frac{\overline{A}\overline{K}^{1/3}}{\overline{L}^{1/3}} \\ &= \overline{A}\overline{k}^{1/3}. \end{aligned} \tag{4.7}$$

Output per person is thus the product of two terms. The first is the productivity parameter $\overline{A}$. Recall that a higher value of $\overline{A}$ means the economy is more productive. Here, this productivity translates into higher output per person. The second term, $\overline{k}^{1/3}$, is capital per person raised to the power 1/3. Renting more ice cream machines for the workers raises output per person. However, increasing capital per person leads to diminishing returns: the first ice cream machine is more valuable than the second, and so on. If we were to double the amount of capital per person in the economy, the equilibrium quantity of output per person would less than double.

Equation (4.7), then, teaches us an important lesson about what makes a country rich or poor: *Output per person tends to be higher when (1) the productivity parameter is higher and (2) the amount of capital per person is higher.* We now turn to some data on capital per person and output per person to check how well these predictions hold up empirically.

Comparing Models with Data

In our toy model, ice cream is produced in a simple robot world. But countries produce far more goods than ice cream, and they certainly have at their disposal a broader collection of inputs than just a single type of labor and a single type of capital. How can we justify using our ice cream model to study per capita GDP across countries of widely differing income levels?

This is a good question to ask of any model. There is always a healthy tension between economic models and the real world. All models make vast simplifying assumptions that divorce them from reality; that's why we call them models. For example, scientists forecast global climate change over the next century ignoring local features of geography like rivers and mountain ranges. Astronomers compute the orbits of asteroids ignoring the gravitational impact of distant planets. The best models are those that, despite this chasm, turn out to be especially insightful about how the world works.

For any given model, this goal may or may not be met, and a healthy dose of skepticism is warranted. Interestingly, what often turns out to be true is that if the gap between the model and the world is too large, you will see this failure when you confront the model with the data. Typically, the failure will suggest ways in which the model can be improved. This interplay between modeling and data is an important feature of modern macroeconomics.

The Empirical Fit of the Production Model

We are now about to make an enormous leap: we will apply the production function in our model to the aggregate economies in the United States and the other countries of the world. In this exercise, called **development accounting**, we use the model to account for differences in incomes across countries. We will match up ice cream per person y with per capita GDP. Capital in the model will be measured as the economy's stock of housing, factories, tractors, computers, machine tools, and other capital goods. We divide this measure by population to obtain $\bar{k}$ for each country. (Exactly how we measure capital is discussed more in Chapter 5.)

Repeating the final line of equation (4.7), per capita GDP should thus be proportional to capital per person raised to the 1/3 power:

$$y^* = \bar{A}\bar{k}^{1/3} \tag{4.8}$$

Before we can apply this equation, we have to decide how to treat $\bar{A}$. Up until now, it has mainly been an extra parameter we've had to carry around. It will remain this way for another page or two; then we will put it to use. For now, simply assume that $\bar{A} = 1$ for every country, so that per capita GDP should be determined solely by the amount of capital per person in the economy. That is,

$$y^* = \bar{k}^{1/3}. \tag{4.9}$$

Table 4.3 shows capital per person and per capita GDP in the year 2007 for a sample of economies. To make comparisons easy, we set the U.S. values of both of these variables equal to 1.00. For example, in 2007, Japan's per capita GDP was 71.3 percent of the level in the United States (column 3). Interestingly, capital per person in Japan (column 1) was 17.3 percent *higher* than in the United States, so that $\bar{k} = 1.173$.

TABLE 4.3

The Model's Prediction for Per Capita GDP (U.S. = 1)

Country	Observed capital per person, $\bar{k}$	Predicted per capita GDP $y = \bar{k}^{1/3}$	Observed per capita GDP
United States	1.000	1.000	1.000
Switzerland	1.287	1.088	0.870
Japan	1.173	1.055	0.713
Italy	0.927	0.975	0.672
Spain	0.908	0.968	0.733
United Kingdom	0.661	0.871	0.750
Brazil	0.134	0.512	0.225
China	0.127	0.502	0.183
South Africa	0.098	0.461	0.244
India	0.044	0.352	0.089
Burundi	0.003	0.149	0.015

Predicted per capita GDP is computed as $\bar{k}^{1/3}$, that is, assuming no differences in productivity across countries. Data correspond to the year 2007 and are divided by the values for the United States.
Source: Penn World Tables, Version 6.3.

With no difference in productivity, the model predicts smaller differences in income across countries than we observe.

What does our model predict about per capita GDP in Japan? Because capital per person was higher in Japan than in the United States, the model predicts that Japan should also have a higher per capita GDP. But how much higher—1.17 times the U.S. level, or more or less than this amount? Because of diminishing returns to capital, the answer is less. In the model, the answer is given by $1.173^{1/3} = 1.055$, so Japan is predicted to have an income about 5.5 percent greater than the United States'.

What about the other countries? One way of illustrating the results of the model is to plot the production function that underlies equation (4.9). This is shown in Figure 4.4. As we saw in the table, capital per person varies tremendously across countries, ranging from a low in Burundi of less than 1 percent of the U.S. value to a high in Switzerland of almost 30 percent higher. These differences translate into much smaller differences in predicted GDP, however, because of **diminishing returns to capital**. The production function is sharply curved, indicating that countries with little capital, like Burundi, have a high marginal product of capital and get a lot from the little capital they have. However, because of diminishing returns, having a lot more capital per person doesn't raise per capita GDP by that much. For example, Japan has roughly twice as much capital per person as the U.K., but because of diminishing returns, this advantage translates into a relatively small difference in predicted income.

How well do the model's predictions hold up empirically? Table 4.3 shows that for many countries there is a fairly large gap between actual per capita GDP and the model's predictions. In fact, the model systematically predicts that countries should be richer than they are. Burundi, for example, is predicted to have an income about 15 percent of the U.S. level, whereas the actual value is 1.5 percent.

The figure shows the model's predictions for per capita GDP, assuming $\bar{A} = 1$ (that is, based on the equation $y^* = \bar{k}^{1/3}$). Both capital per person and predicted per capita GDP are expressed relative to the U.S. values (U.S. = 1).

FIGURE 4.4

Predicted Per Capita GDP in the Production Model

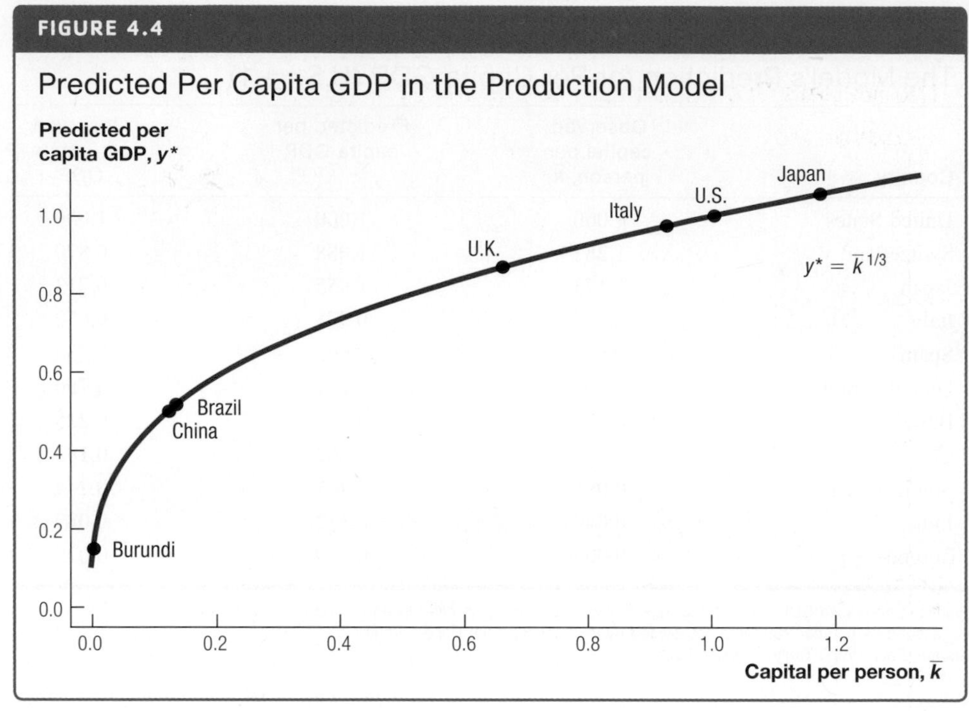

Japan, as we have seen, has an income of only 71 percent of the U.S. level, substantially less than the model's prediction that Japan should be richer.

Figure 4.5 illustrates the gap between the model and the data for an even larger sample of countries. Actual per capita GDP relative to the United States is shown on the horizontal axis, with the model's predictions given on the vertical axis. If the model is successful, the countries should line up close to the solid 45-degree line, suggesting that the model and the data give the same answers. But in fact, the data points lie significantly above the 45-degree line; countries are systematically poorer than our model predicts.

What's going on? In general, the model correctly suggests that countries will be rich or poor according to how much capital per person they have. But it goes wrong in two main ways. First, it gets the magnitudes wrong. As we saw in Table 4.3, India has just over 4 percent of the U.S. capital per person, but because of diminishing returns to capital, the model predicts India to have 35 percent of the U.S. income. In reality, Indian per capita GDP is only 9 percent of the U.S. level. Second, the model mistakenly predicts that a number of countries, such as Switzerland, Japan, and Norway, should be as rich as or even richer than the United States.

A close look at the first and third columns of Table 4.3 suggests how we might improve the fit of the model. Roughly speaking, capital per person varies by just as much as or even more than per capita GDP across countries. Look back at equation (4.9). If the exponent on capital were equal to 1 instead of 1/3, the model would predict that $y = k$, so that incomes would vary by as much as capital does. But with this approach, while the model might fit better for the poorest countries, it would miss by even more for the richer countries: it would predict,

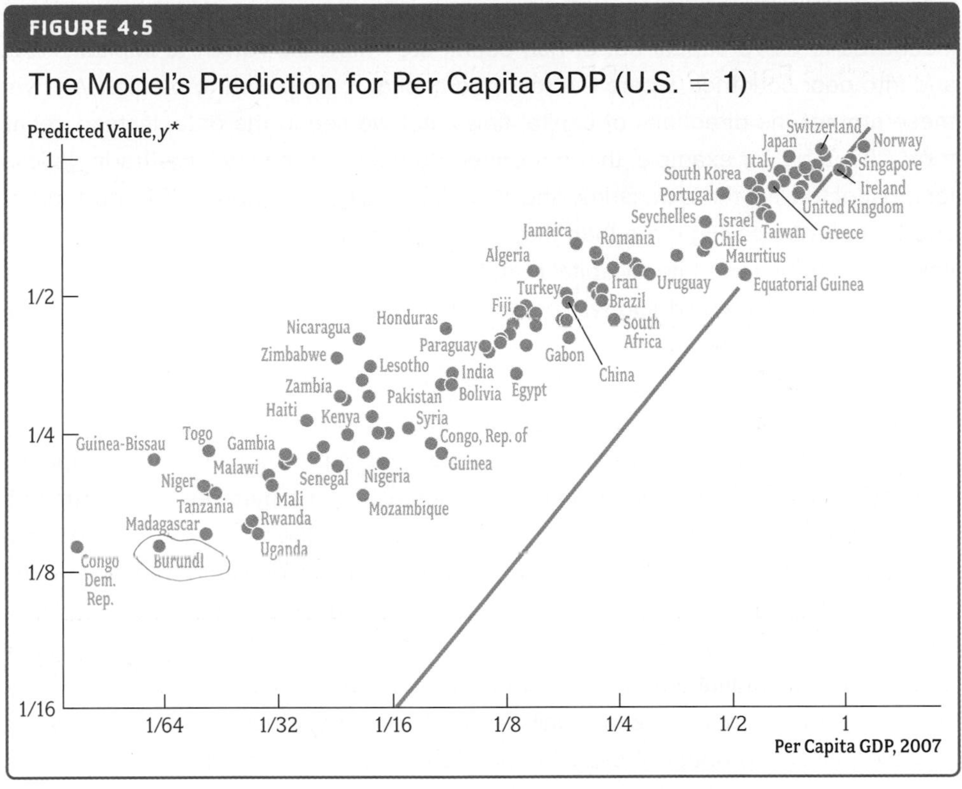

FIGURE 4.5

The Model's Prediction for Per Capita GDP (U.S. = 1)

The vertical axis shows our model's predictions for per capita GDP relative to that in the United States, assuming $\bar{A} = 1$ in all countries. Countries should lie close to the solid 45-degree line if the model is doing a good job of explaining incomes. Instead, the model predicts that most countries should be substantially richer than they are.

for example, that Japan should be 17 percent richer than the United States rather than 5 percent.

Perhaps more important, however, we did not arrive at the exponent of 1/3 for capital arbitrarily. This value was motivated by the fact that capital's share of income over time in the United States and in countries across the world lies fairly close to 1/3; it is certainly far from a value of 1. Sharply raising the exponent on capital is therefore not an appealing option for improving the model.

CASE STUDY

Why Doesn't Capital Flow from Rich to Poor Countries?

In 1990, Robert Lucas of the University of Chicago published one of his many famous papers, bearing the title of this case study. Lucas was motivated by a graph like that shown in Figure 4.4, and he drew attention to a puzzling fact: poor countries—those with low levels of capital per person—should have *high* marginal products of capital. This is easily seen in Figure 4.4. Compare Burundi and Japan, and notice the *slope* of the production function around those countries. At the very low level of capital possessed by Burundi, the slope is steep: the marginal product of capital is very high. In contrast, at high levels of capital like those seen in Japan or even the United States, the slope—the marginal product of capital—is much lower.

If this were true, how would firms and entrepreneurs respond? They would have incentives to move capital out of rich countries, where the return to capital is low, and into poor countries, where the return to capital is supposed to be high. And yet these are not the directions of capital flows that we see in the data. Instead, recall from Chapter 2, for example, that the United States has run very large trade deficits for most of the last three decades. And, in fact, China has an enormous trade surplus. The Chinese are saving more than they are investing, and much of that difference is flowing to the United States. Capital is flowing "backward" relative to what the simple story in Figure 4.4 would suggest. Hence, the Lucas question: why doesn't capital flow from rich to poor countries?

The short answer is that the simple production model with no differences in productivity across countries is misguided. We will pursue this explanation in detail below.

A very useful insight into the explanation, however, is provided in a recent paper by Francesco Caselli of the London School of Economics and James Feyrer of Dartmouth College. Caselli and Feyrer use data on GDP, capital, and the shape of the production function to measure the marginal product of capital directly for many countries around the world. What they find is striking: the marginal product of capital is quite similar across a range of countries. In fact, the marginal product in rich countries is slightly *more* than the marginal product in poor countries, at 8.4 and 6.9 percent, respectively. The puzzle, then, is not why capital fails to flow to poor countries. The puzzle is, rather, why the marginal product of capital in poor countries is not much higher, given that they have so little capital. A key part of the explanation turns out to be that poor countries have low levels of the productivity parameter, as we discuss next.[5]

Productivity Differences: Improving the Fit of the Model

Recent research in macroeconomics has employed the production model in a different way to explain differences in incomes across countries. This approach is based on the up-to-now mysterious parameter $\bar{A}$.[6] Recall our original production function:

$$Y = F(K,L) = \bar{A}K^{1/3}L^{2/3}.$$

If a country has a high value of $\bar{A}$, it will have a higher level of output for any given values of K and L. What is $\bar{A}$? We can interpret it as an efficiency or productivity parameter: it measures how productive countries are at using their factor inputs (in this case K and L) to produce output. For this reason, $\bar{A}$ is often referred to as **total factor productivity**, or **TFP**.[7]

---

[5] For more details related to this case study, see Robert E. Lucas, Jr., "Why Doesn't Capital Flow from Rich to Poor Countries?" *American Economic Review Papers and Proceedings*, vol. 80 (May 1990), pp. 92–96; and Francesco Caselli and James Feyrer, "The Marginal Product of Capital," *Quarterly Journal of Economics*, vol. 122 (May 2007), pp. 535–568.

[6] It is also sometimes called multifactor productivity.

[7] See, for example, Peter Klenow and Andrés Rodríguez, "The Neoclassical Revival in Growth Economics: Has It Gone Too Far?" *NBER Macroeconomics Annual*, Ben Bernanke and Julio Rotemberg, eds. (Cambridge, Mass.: MIT Press, 1997), pp. 73–102; and Robert E. Hall and Charles I. Jones, "Why Do Some Countries Produce So Much More Output per Worker Than Others?" *Quarterly Journal of Economics*, February 1999, pp. 83–116.

Now recall how this parameter shows up in the equilibrium of our production model:

$$y^* = \bar{A}\bar{k}^{1/3}. \tag{4.10}$$

What we have seen so far is that if $\bar{A} = 1$ for all countries, the model predicts that most countries should be substantially richer than they are. One way of explaining why they are not so rich, then, is by assigning them values of $\bar{A}$ that are less than 1. Countries can be rich either because they have a high level of capital per person or because they use their capital and labor very efficiently and therefore exhibit a high level of TFP ($\bar{A}$).

An important limitation on our ability to implement the production model with TFP is that we have no independent measure of this efficiency parameter. For capital, we could count the number of machines, factories, computers, and so on in the economy, but for TFP there is nothing comparable we can do.

Instead, we exploit the fact that we *do* possess data on per capita GDP and capital per person. That is, we have data on every term in equation (4.10) *other than TFP*. As a way of moving forward, then, we can assume our model is correct and calculate the level of TFP for each country that would be needed to make equation (4.10) hold exactly.

This is best understood in the context of an example. Recall from Table 4.3 that Japan's capital per person is equal to 1.17 times the U.S. level but its GDP is only about 0.71 times the U.S. level. Now we take this information and apply it to equation (4.10). That is, we compute

$$\bar{A} = \frac{y^*}{\bar{k}^{1/3}}. \tag{4.11}$$

$\bar{A}$ for Japan is thus equal to 0.68 times the U.S. level, since $0.713/(1.173)^{1/3} = 0.68$. It must be the case that Japan is significantly less efficient in using its machines than the United States is, at least if the model is correct.

Because we don't have independent measures of $\bar{A}$ but rather compute it assuming the model holds, we can also think of $\bar{A}$ as a measure of how big the gap is between our model and the data. In addition to being called TFP, therefore, $\bar{A}$ is sometimes also referred to as "the residual" or "a measure of our ignorance."

Table 4.4 shows the TFP measures for the same countries as in Table 4.3. Per capita GDP in the first column is equal to the product of capital per person (raised to the 1/3 power) in the second column and "implied TFP" in the third. As we saw earlier, if countries differed only in terms of capital per person, we would expect the poorest countries to be much richer. The fact that they are not suggests that they must have TFP levels that are substantially below that in the United States.

For example, given its capital per person, we would expect China to have a per capita income of about 50 percent of the U.S. level if its TFP were the same as the United States'. Instead, its income is only 18 percent of the U.S. level. Our model suggests that the way to understand China's lower income is that its TFP is only about 1/3 (0.365) the U.S. level. So if we gave China the same amount of capital per person as the United States, we would still expect its per capita GDP to be only 1/3 that in the United States.

In order for our model to match the data, poor countries must be very inefficient in production—that is, they must have low TFP.

TABLE 4.4

Measuring TFP So the Model Fits Exactly

Country	Per capita GDP (y)	$\bar{k}^{1/3}$	Implied TFP ($\bar{A}$)
United States	1.000	1.000	1.000
Switzerland	0.870	1.088	0.800
United Kingdom	0.750	0.871	0.861
Spain	0.733	0.968	0.757
Japan	0.713	1.055	0.676
Italy	0.672	0.975	0.689
South Africa	0.244	0.461	0.530
Brazil	0.225	0.512	0.439
China	0.183	0.502	0.365
India	0.089	0.352	0.253
Burundi	0.015	0.149	0.101

Calculations are based on the equation $y = \bar{A}\bar{k}^{1/3}$. Implied productivity $\bar{A}$ is calculated from data on y and $\bar{k}$ for the year 2007, so that this equation holds exactly as $\bar{A} = y/\bar{k}^{1/3}$.

The comparison between China and the United States is shown graphically in Figure 4.6. With a TFP level equal to about 1/3 the U.S. level, China's production function is shifted down substantially relative to the U.S. production function: at any given level of capital per person, Chinese workers produce only 1/3 the output of their U.S. counterparts.

Figure 4.7 shows the TFP levels that are implied by our model for a large sample of countries. From the figure, we can see that there is a high correlation between per capita GDP and TFP. Rich countries tend to have high levels of

The figure shows the production functions for China ($\bar{A}_{China} = 0.365$) and the United States ($\bar{A}_{US} = 1$). With its capital per person, if China were as efficient as the United States at producing output, Chinese GDP per person would be 50% the U.S. level. Instead, with its lower TFP, Chinese per capita GDP is only 18% of the U.S. level.

FIGURE 4.6

The U.S. and Chinese Production Functions

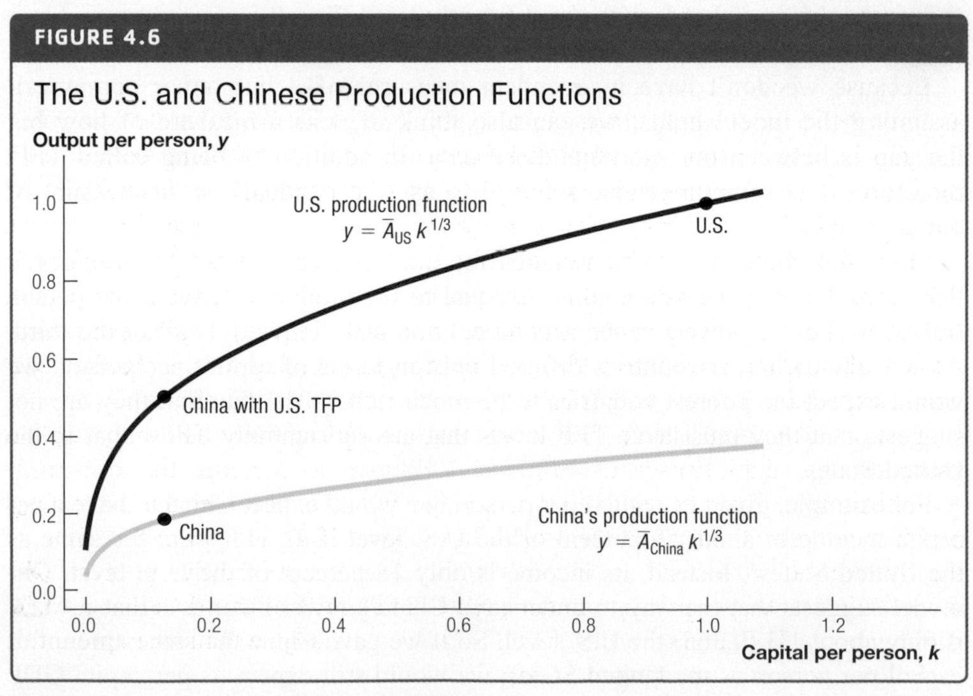

FIGURE 4.7

Measuring TFP So the Model Fits Exactly

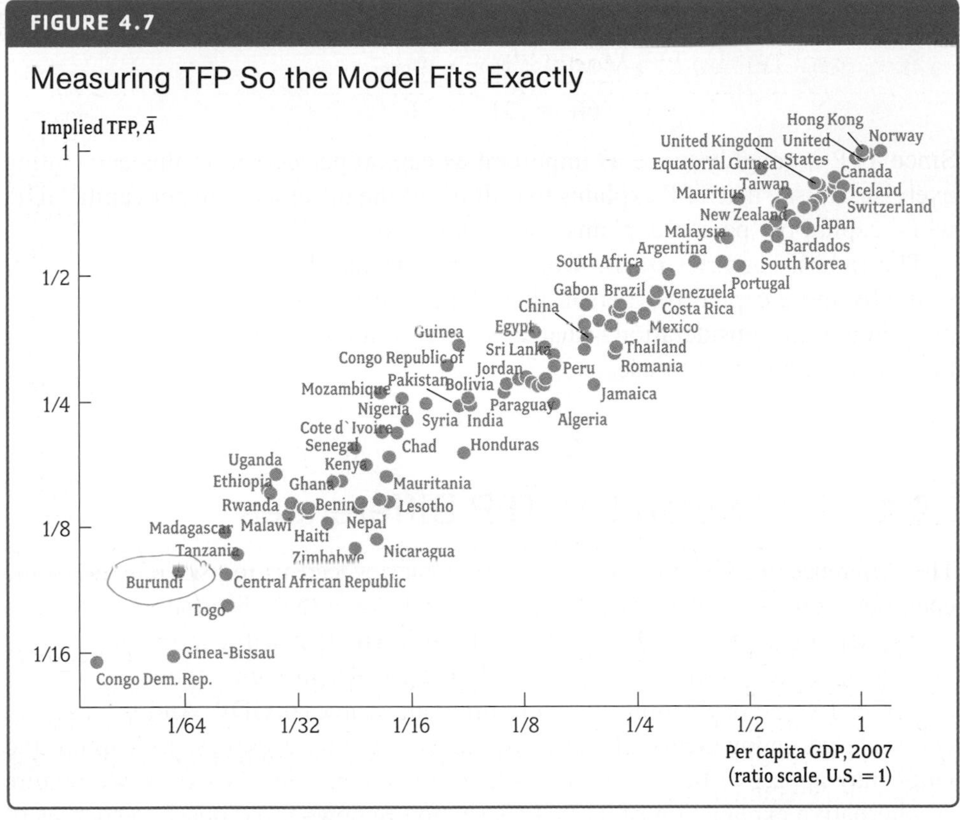

Measured TFP is closely related to per capita GDP and varies substantially across countries.

TFP, and poor countries tend to have low levels. Also, the differences in TFP across countries are great. If our production model is correct in explaining the differences in incomes, it must be the case that TFP in the poorest countries is less than 1/10 the U.S. level.

In development accounting, which is the more important force in explaining differences in incomes: differences in capital per person or differences in TFP? The answer can be seen by comparing Figures 4.5 and 4.7. If there were no TFP differences, just differences in capital per person, the ratio of per capita GDP in Burundi to that in the United States would be about 1/5 or 1/6 (see Figure 4.5). On the other hand, if the differences were only in TFP and not capital (Figure 4.7), then the income ratio of GDP between Burundi and the United States would be about 1/10. As a rough approximation, then, differences in capital per person explain about one-third of the difference in income between the richest and poorest countries, while differences in TFP explain the remaining two-thirds.

This calculation can be applied to any two countries; while TFP may explain more or less than two-thirds of their difference in income, the one-third/two-thirds breakdown is relatively typical. For instance, consider the five richest and five poorest countries of the world. In the year 2007, the per capita GDP of the five richest countries was 66 times higher than that of the five poorest. Differences in capital per person explain a factor of about 6 of this difference, while differences in TFP explain a factor of 11. Mathematically, we might express this as follows, drawing on equation (4.10):

$$\underbrace{\frac{y^*_{\text{rich}}}{y^*_{\text{poor}}}}_{66} = \underbrace{\frac{\bar{A}_{\text{rich}}}{\bar{A}_{\text{poor}}}}_{11} \cdot \underbrace{\left(\frac{\bar{k}_{\text{rich}}}{\bar{k}_{\text{poor}}}\right)^{1/3}}_{6} \quad (4.12)$$

$$66 = 11 \times 6$$

Since TFP is roughly twice as important as capital per person in this accounting exercise, we say that TFP explains two-thirds of the differences in per capita GDP, while capital per person explains about one-third.

The richest countries of the world are rich in part because they possess substantially more capital per person than the poorest countries. However, an even more important consideration is that they are substantially more efficient in putting their labor and capital to use.

4.4 Understanding TFP Differences

The differences in TFP that we see across countries lead us to ask: *Why* are some countries more efficient at using the capital and labor at their disposal than others?

As mentioned earlier, TFP is a kind of "residual" that will capture any factors omitted from the production function. For example, in some countries, natural resources like oil or diamonds are an important source of GDP. And if a country enjoys large endowments of these expensive natural resources, its capital and labor may appear to be very productive. In most countries, however, we require an alternative explanation of TFP. This section reviews three possible sources of differences in efficiency: human capital, technology, and institutions. As we will see, all three likely play a role in explaining TFP differences.

Human Capital

A significant omission from our model is "human capital." Recall that physical capital is the stock of machines and buildings that an economy accumulates to help in production. **Human capital**, in contrast, is the stock of skills that individuals accumulate to make them more productive. An obvious example of human capital is a college education: right now you are acquiring knowledge and skills that will, among other things, make you a more productive member of society. Human capital is also accumulated when first-graders learn to read, when construction workers learn to operate a tower crane, and when doctors master a new surgical technique. Part of the difference in TFP across countries may be explained by the fact that workers in different countries possess different quantities of human capital.[8]

One type of human capital that is relatively straightforward to incorporate into the model is education. To what extent can educational differences across countries explain differences in TFP and income? The average number of years American adults have spent in school is just under 13, while the average in the

[8] For more on human capital, a useful reference is a classic book by Gary Becker of the University of Chicago, who won the Nobel Prize in economics in 1992: *Human Capital: A Theoretical and Empirical Analysis, with Special Reference to Education*, 3rd ed. (Chicago: University of Chicago Press, 1994). Becker's colleague and fellow Nobel Prize winner Robert E. Lucas Jr. proposes that human capital can explain income differences across countries in his classic paper "On the Mechanics of Economic Development," *Journal of Monetary Economics*, vol. 22 (1988), pp. 3–42.

poorest countries is about 4. This is a fairly large gap of nearly 9 years. But what does it imply about differences in income?

One way economists have answered this question is by looking at the **returns to education** within a country. In the United States, for example, each year of education seems to increase a person's future wages by something like 7 percent. A 4-year college education, then, might be expected to raise your wages by about 28 percent over your entire lifetime (this will be discussed further in Chapter 7). In developing countries, these returns can be even higher—up to 10 percent or even 13 percent per year. One reason is that the typical student is learning the basic skills associated with literacy and arithmetic, and the returns to these skills may be even higher than the returns to a college education.

To make a rough calculation, suppose the additional 9 years of school in the United States is associated with an average return to education of 10 percent per year. As a result, we might expect wages to be higher in the United States by 90 percent. Now recall from Table 4.2 that the equilibrium wage is proportional to output per person. We might thus expect per capita GDP in the United States to be about 1.9 times as high as income in the poorest countries if the only difference were education. Differences in level of education do help us understand the large TFP differences across countries, perhaps reducing the "residual" from a factor of 11 to a factor of 6 (11/1.9 = 5.8). Nevertheless, the remaining differences in TFP are still large.

Technology

Another possible reason for differences in TFP is that rich and poor countries are producing with different *technologies*. Goods such as state-of-the-art computer chips, software, new pharmaceuticals, supersonic military jets, and skyscrapers, as well as production techniques such as just-in-time inventory methods, information technology, and tightly integrated transport networks, are much more prevalent in rich countries than in poor. The possibility that differences in TFP partly reflect technological differences in production is an important one and will be discussed in more detail in Chapter 6.

Institutions

Rich countries may be rich because of their physical capital, human capital, and state-of-the-art technologies, but we still need to ask, Why do they have these advantages? What keeps poor countries from enjoying similar high levels of capital and technology?

Differences in **institutions** may be an important part of the answer. Mancur Olson, in a lecture published in the *Journal of Economic Perspectives* in 1996,[9] provided one of the most compelling demonstrations of the importance of institutions. Olson observed that accidents of history, especially wars, provide us with interesting "natural experiments" relating to institutions and government policies. For example, consider North and South Korea, East and West Germany, and Hong Kong and mainland China. Historically, each pair was once a single

[9] Mancur Olson, "Distinguished Lecture on Economics in Government. Big Bills Left on the Sidewalk: Why Some Nations Are Rich, and Others Poor," *Journal of Economic Perspectives*, vol. 10, no. 2 (Spring 1996), pp. 3–24.

country (and, in the case of Germany, is today). The people in each region share similar cultures, and there are no obvious advantages in geography on one side or the other. Moreover, these neighbors had relatively similar incomes. At the end of various wars, though, the regions were separated into distinct countries with different governments and institutions.

Over the course of just a few generations, enormous differences in income emerged between these siblings. North Korea is one of the poorest regions of the world today, while South Korea is one of the growth miracles. At the time of the collapse of the Berlin Wall in 1989, standards of living in East and West Germany were substantially different. And even after rapid growth in China during the last two decades, per capita GDP in Hong Kong is estimated to be 5 times higher than in China.

What explains these sharp differences in economic performance? The obvious answer—obvious largely because this is the only clear difference between the neighboring countries—is the differences in government policies and in the rules and regulations that economists call "institutions."

To see the importance of institutions, imagine that you set up two computer companies, one in a rich country and the other in a poor country. In a typical rich country, there is a well-defined set of laws you have to follow to establish your business, and the rules are the same for everyone. You may have to pay license fees and taxes, but these are longstanding and explicit. To a great extent, your company succeeds or fails on its own merit, and you profit directly from your own success.

In contrast, you may run into numerous obstacles in the poor country. Corruption and bribes may make it difficult to set up the business in the first place. Importing the computer components may be a challenge—once the parts have arrived into port, they may be held hostage for additional "fees." Profits that you earn may not be secure: they may be taxed away or even stolen because of insufficient property rights. If your company succeeds, it may even be taken over by the government—as Bolivia did to foreign firms when it nationalized the oil and gas industries in 2006. Finally, even if your profits are secure for several years, a coup or war could change the environment overnight. Not only your profits but even your life may be at risk.

Property rights, the rule of law, contract enforcement, and the separation of powers are essential for economic success. In their absence, the costs of investing in physical capital, human capital, and technology may exceed the benefit, and as a result the investments may not be made. These institutional differences appear to be an important part of the explanation for differences in TFP and capital across countries.

The study of the relationship between institutions and economic performance is at the frontier of current research in economics. At the moment, elegant and quantifiable models like our production model do not exist in the study of institutions. It's to be hoped that this research will reach a point in the near future where its insights can be gleaned as easily as those of the production model (or the growth models in the next two chapters). But unfortunately, we are not there yet.[10]

[10] Important work on this topic has been carried out by Douglass North, Mancur Olson, Nathan Rosenberg, Stephen Parente, Edward Prescott, Andrei Shleifer, Robert Vishny, Robert Hall, William Easterly, Daron Acemoglu, Edward Glaeser, Simon Johnson, James Robinson, and others. A section at the end of Chapter 6 includes additional readings for students wishing to pursue this topic further.

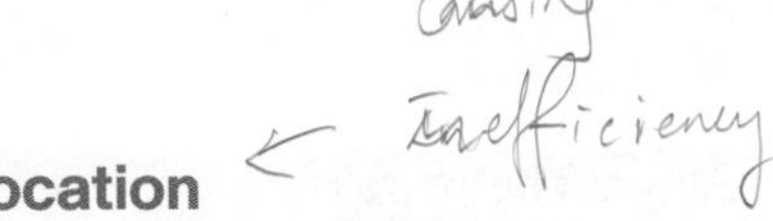

Misallocation

In recent years, another explanation for TFP differences across countries has been put forward: misallocation. To see the effects of misallocation, consider a country that has only two firms that import and resell automotive parts—for example, sparkplugs, engine fluids, and brake pads. One firm is a new start-up that is seeking to use modern inventory management techniques. The other is an older, established company run by the prime minister's cousin. Allowed to compete freely, the new start-up would probably thrive, taking substantial business away from the established firm and increasing the economy's productivity. However, perhaps political connections prevent this from happening: the new firm cannot get the necessary licenses to import parts from abroad and is not allowed to expand. The result is that the new firm gets too little capital and labor, while the old firm gets too much. This misallocation means the industry's capital and labor is less productive than it otherwise should be. That is, it has lower TFP.

A recent paper by Chang-Tai Hsieh of the University of Chicago and Pete Klenow of Stanford University suggests that the effects of misallocation can be substantial. The authors compare the marginal products of labor and capital across manufacturing firms in China and India. If capital and labor are allocated efficiently, their marginal products should be equated across firms. However, Hsieh and Klenow document substantial variation in marginal products. They estimate that reallocating capital and labor to equate marginal products across the Arms within each country could raise TFP in China and India by about 40 percent. Interestingly, they also show that improvements in the allocation of capital and labor in China—for example, shifts away from state-owned enterprises and toward private firms—can explain some of China's rapid growth.[11]

CASE STUDY

A "Big Bang" or Gradualism? Economic Reforms in Russia and China

The fall of the Berlin Wall in November 1989 was a historic event that will be remembered a hundred years from now as symbolic of the decline of communism in countries of Eastern Europe and the former Soviet Union. Some of the world's top economists served as advisers for these economies during the 1990s as they made the transition to capitalism. Many economists thought that a "big bang" approach to reform–in which old institutions would be swept away and replaced quickly by democracy and markets–would usher in an era of economic success. Combining the economic incentives of capitalism with the highly educated populations of Eastern Europe and the former Soviet Union seemed like a perfect recipe for raising incomes in these countries to the levels set by Western Europe and the United States.

[11] Chang-Tai Hsieh and Peter Klenow, "Misallocation and Manufacturing TFP in China and India," *Quarterly Journal of Economics*, vol. 124 (November 2009), pp. 1403–48.

FIGURE 4.8

Per Capita GDP in China and Russia, 1990–2007

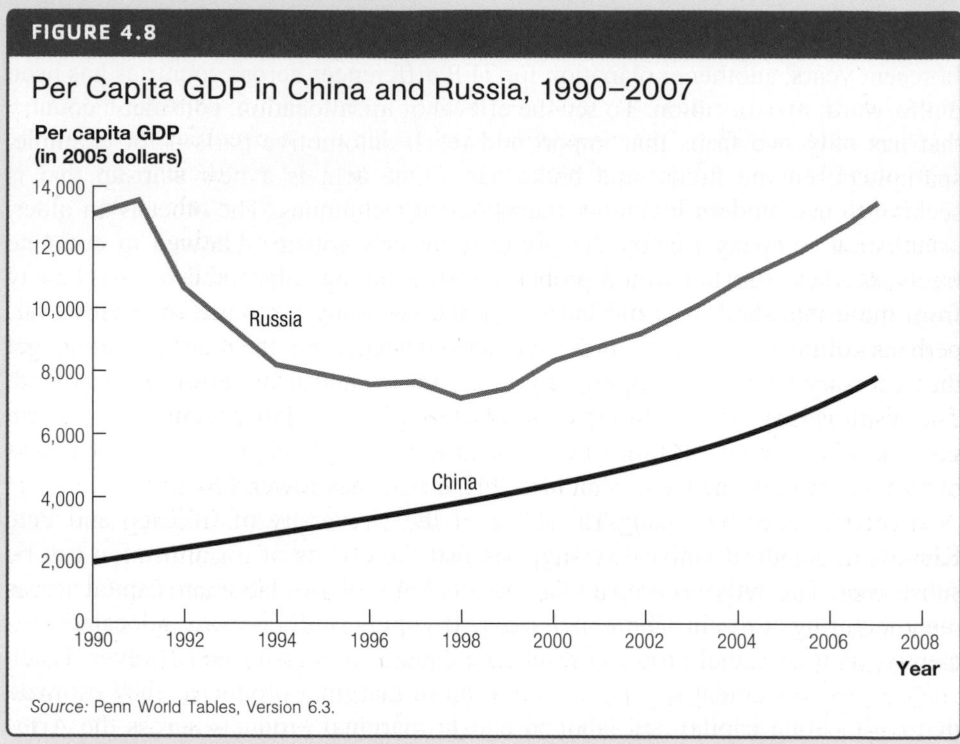

Source: Penn World Tables, Version 6.3.

With the benefit of hindsight, it is clear that nearly all economists were too optimistic and somewhat naive about the prospects for these transition economies. Figure 4.8 shows the surprising performance of per capita GDP in Russia since 1990. Starting from a baseline of more than $13,000 per person, GDP actually declined over the next 7 years, falling by more than 40 percent in total. Economic growth has resumed in recent years so that by 2007 the original level of per capita GDP had almost been recovered.

China's economy serves as a useful foil to the Russian example. Many observers in the 1980s thought that China's gradual, piecemeal approach to economic reform—largely occurring in the absence of political reform—would have trouble generating significant increases in economic performance. As shown in the figure, however, the Chinese economy has grown rapidly in recent decades. Between 1990 and 2007, for example, per capita GDP in China rose from just over $1,900 to more than $7,800, a growth rate of more than 8 percent per year.

The examples of Russia and China illustrate that the process of economic reform is much more complicated than any simple model can convey. Developing a common framework that explains these two fascinating cases is an important goal of current economic research.[12]

[12] These examples are discussed in more detail in two recent papers: Gérard Roland, "The Political Economy of Transition," *Journal of Economic Perspectives*, vol. 16 (Winter 2002), pp. 29–50; and Andrei Shleifer and Daniel Treisman, "A Normal Country: Russia after Communism," *Journal of Economic Perspectives*, vol. 19 (Winter 2005), pp. 151–74.

4.5 Evaluating the Production Model

What does our production model—summarized by the expression $y^* = \bar{A}k^{1/3}$—teach us? First, per capita GDP will be higher in countries that (1) have high quantities of capital per person and (2) use that capital efficiently.

Second, our production function features constant returns to scale in capital and labor. That is, we could double a firm's production by replicating it: we set up an identical firm with identical amounts of capital and labor. This is the standard replication argument, one of the main justifications for constant returns to scale in production. An implication of constant returns is that output per person can be written as a function of capital per person. Importantly, *this* relationship features diminishing returns: if we double the amount of capital per person in a firm, the amount of output per person will less than double.

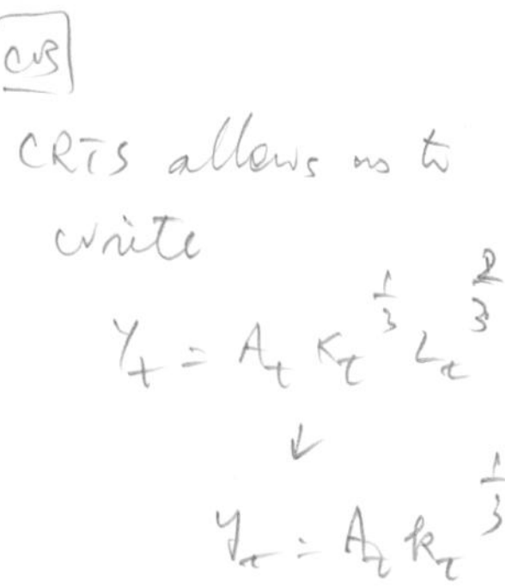

In fact, the exponent on capital in the production function is about 1/3—far below the constant-returns value of 1. This means that the diminishing returns to capital are quite strong. And we see the implications of these diminishing returns in the empirical fit of our production model. The large differences in capital per person that we see across countries (larger than the differences in output per person) explain only about one-third of the differences in per capita GDP.

Our production model, then, is only partially an empirical success. It helps us understand which countries are rich and poor, but in the absence of TFP differences, it vastly underpredicts the differences in income. Moreover, the model provides little guidance about why countries exhibit different TFP levels and different amounts of capital per person. The next two chapters address this issue in the context of one of the great questions of economics: Why do economies grow over time?

CHAPTER REVIEW

SUMMARY

1. Per capita GDP varies by more than a factor of 50 between the richest and poorest countries of the world. If we really understand why this is the case, we ought to be able to build a toy world in which this enormous difference can be observed.

2. The key equation in our production model is the Cobb-Douglas production function: $Y = \bar{A}K^{1/3}L^{2/3}$. Output Y depends on the productivity parameter $\bar{A}$, the capital stock K, and labor L.

3. The exponents in this production function indicate that about one-third of GDP is paid out to capital and two-thirds is paid to labor. The fact that these exponents sum to 1 implies that the production function exhibits constant returns to scale in capital and labor.

4. The complete production model consists of five equations and five unknowns: the quantities Y, K, and L, and the prices w (wage) and r (the rental price of capital).

5. The solution to this model is called an equilibrium. The prices are determined by the clearing of the labor and capital markets, the quantities of capital and labor are pinned down by the exogenous factor supplies, and output is determined by the production function.

6. The production model implies that output per person in equilibrium is the product of two key forces, total factor productivity (TFP) and capital per person raised to the power 1/3: $y^* = \bar{A}k^{1/3}$.

7. Assuming the productivity parameter $\bar{A}$, or TFP, is the same across countries, the model predicts that income differences should be substantially smaller than we observe. Capital per person actually varies enormously across countries, but the sharp diminishing returns to capital per person in the production model overwhelm these differences.

8. Making the production model fit the data requires large differences in TFP across countries. Empirically, these differences "explain" about two-thirds of the differences in income, while differences in capital per person explain about one-third. This "explanation" really just assigns values to $\bar{A}$ that make the model hold; for this reason, economists also refer to TFP as the residual, or a measure of our ignorance.

9. Understanding why TFP differs so much across countries is an important question at the frontier of current economic research. Differences in human capital (such as education) are one reason, as are differences in technologies. These differences in turn can be partly explained by a lack of institutions and property rights in poorer countries.

KEY CONCEPTS

accounting profit
the Cobb-Douglas production function
constant returns to scale
development accounting
diminishing returns to capital
economic profit
equilibrium
factor shares
general equilibrium
human capital
increasing and decreasing returns to scale
marginal products of capital and labor
model
numéraire
production function
returns to education
the standard replication argument
total factor productivity

REVIEW QUESTIONS

1. What is the purpose of macroeconomic models? How can a model of ice cream production be used to explain 50-fold income differences across countries?

2. Explain the rule that profit-maximizing firms follow when they decide how much capital and labor to hire.

3. What is an equilibrium in the ice cream model?
4. How does the national income identity show up in the ice cream model?
5. Look back at Table 4.3. Why do such large differences in capital lead to relatively small differences in predicted GDP across countries?
6. What might explain why TFP differs so much across countries?

EXERCISES

smartwork.wwnorton.com 

1. **Returns to scale in production:** Do the following production functions exhibit increasing, constant, or decreasing returns to scale in K and L? (Assume $\bar{A}$ is some fixed positive number.)
   (a) $Y = K^{1/2}L^{1/2}$
   (b) $Y = K^{2/3}L^{2/3}$
   (c) $Y = K^{1/3}L^{1/2}$
   (d) $Y = K + L$
   (e) $Y = K + K^{1/3}L^{1/3}$
   (f) $Y = K^{1/3}L^{2/3} + \bar{A}$
   (g) $Y = K^{1/3}L^{2/3} - \bar{A}$

2. **The "per person" versions of production functions:** Write each production function given below in terms of output per person $y \equiv Y/L$ and capital per person $k \equiv K/L$. Show what these "per person" versions look like in a graph with k on the horizontal axis and y on the vertical axis. (Assume $\bar{A}$ is some fixed positive number.)
   (a) $Y = K^{1/3}L^{2/3}$ and $Y = K^{3/4}L^{1/4}$ (on the same graph)
   (b) $Y = K$
   (c) $Y = K + \bar{A}L$
   (d) $Y = K - \bar{A}L$

3. **The Black Death:** In the middle of the fourteenth century, an epidemic known as the Black Death killed about a third of Europe's population, about 34 million people. While this was an enormous tragedy, the macroeconomic consequences might surprise you: Over the next century, wages are estimated to have been *higher* than before the Black Death.
   (a) Use the production model to explain why wages might have been higher.
   (b) Can you attach a number to your explanation? In the model, by how much would wages rise if a third of the population died from disease?

4. **Solving the production model:** Suppose the production function at the core of our model is given by $Y = \bar{A}K^{3/4}L^{1/4}$ (that is, assume the exponents on capital and labor are 3/4 and 1/4 rather than 1/3 and 2/3).
   (a) Create a new version of Table 4.1 for the new version of the model. What are the five equations and five unknowns? (*Hint:* The hiring rules for capital and labor will change in the obvious way.)
   (b) Now solve these equations to get the solution to the model. Put your solution in the same form as Table 4.2.
   (c) What is the solution for the equilibrium level of output per person?

5. **The empirical fit of the production model:** The table below reports per capita GDP and capital per person in the year 2007 for 10 countries. Your task is to fill in the missing columns of the table.
   (a) Given the values in columns 1 and 2, fill in columns 3 and 4. That is, compute per capita GDP and capital per person relative to the U.S. values.
   (b) In column 5, use the production model (with a capital exponent of 1/3) to compute predicted per capita GDP for each country relative to the United States, assuming there are no TFP differences.
   (c) In column 6, compute the level of TFP for each country that is needed to match up the model and the data.
   (d) Comment on the general results you find.

	In 2005 dollars		Relative to the U.S. values (U.S. = 1)			
Country	(1) Capital per person	(2) Per capita GDP	(3) Capital per person	(4) Per capita GDP	(5) Predicted y^*	(6) Implied TFP to match data
United States	135,877	42,887	1.000	1.000	1.000	1.000
Canada	116,188	36,168				
France	109,023	29,633				
Hong Kong	123,268	43,121				
South Korea	104,864	23,850				
Indonesia	9,957	5,186				
Argentina	35,182	15,275				
Mexico	33,168	11,204				
Kenya	2,379	2,025				
Ethiopia	584	1,110				

6. **Fitting the model with a higher capital share:** Repeat exercise 5, but this time assume the production function is given by $Y = \bar{A}K^{3/4}L^{1/4}$. That is, assume the exponent on capital is 3/4 rather than 1/3 so that the diminishing returns to capital are less. In part (d), be sure to compare the results here with those in exercise 5, where the capital exponent was 1/3. Why do you think the results are different? Is it reasonable to assume a capital share of 3/4 in the model?

7. **The importance of capital versus TFP:** Create a new table that contains only the last three columns of the table in exercise 5. This time, instead of reporting the numbers relative to the U.S. value, report the inverse of these numbers. For example, you should have found that per capita GDP in Kenya relative to that in the United States was 0.047. Now express this number as the ratio of U.S. per capita GDP to Kenya's per capita GDP: $1/0.047 \approx 21$. Fill in all three columns for the remaining countries.
   (a) Explain in general how to interpret these numbers and in particular how the three columns are related.
   (b) In the chapter, we found that about one-third of the differences in per capita GDP across countries were due to differences in capital per person and about two-thirds were due to differences in TFP. Carry out this calculation for Kenya. The United States is 21 times richer than Kenya; what fraction

of this factor of 21 is due to differences in capital per person and what fraction is due to differences in TFP?

(c) Repeat part (b) for Ethiopia.

8. **Institutions and economic performance:** Read the article on institutions by Mancur Olson, cited in footnote 8. (You may be able to find it on the Web by typing the author's name and a few words from the title into Google Scholar.) The last sentence of that paper says that "individual rationality is very far indeed from being sufficient for social rationality." What does Olson mean by this statement?

WORKED EXERCISES

1. **Returns to scale in production:**

Recall that a production function $F(K,L)$ exhibits constant returns to scale if doubling the inputs leads to a doubling of output. If it leads to more than doubling of output, there are increasing returns to scale; if it leads to less than doubling of output, there are decreasing returns to scale. The answers to parts (a) and (f) are worked out below.

(a) $Y = K^{1/2}L^{1/2}$. If we double K and L, output is

$$(2K)^{1/2}(2L)^{1/2} = 2^{1/2}2^{1/2}K^{1/2}L^{1/2} = 2^{1/2+1/2}K^{1/2}L^{1/2} = 2K^{1/2}L^{1/2}.$$

So output exactly doubles, and there are constant returns to scale.

(f) $Y = K^{1/3}L^{2/3} + \bar{A}$. This production function says you get $\bar{A}$ units of output "for free," that is, even if there is no capital and no labor. Then you produce on top of that with a Cobb-Douglas production function.

If we double K and L, output is

$$(2K)^{1/3}(2L)^{2/3} + \bar{A} = 2^{1/3+2/3}K^{1/3}L^{2/3} + \bar{A} = 2K^{1/3}L^{2/3} + \bar{A}.$$

Notice that the first term is doubled, but the output we got for free (the $\bar{A}$) is left unchanged. Therefore, output is less than doubled, and this production function exhibits decreasing returns to scale.

3. **The Black Death:**

(a) Wages were higher after the Black Death because of *diminishing returns*. Our production model exhibits diminishing returns to labor: each additional unit of labor increases output by less and less. So if the amount of labor is reduced, the marginal product of labor—and hence the wage—increases. The reason is that capital stays the same: each remaining worker is able to work with more machines, so his productivity rises. In fourteenth-century Europe, the marginal workers could move to better land and discard old broken-down tools.

Graphically, this can be seen by considering the supply-and-demand diagram for labor in Figure 4.2(b). If the supply of labor shifts back (because a large number of workers die), the equilibrium wage rate increases. Draw this graph—including the shift in the labor supply curve—to see the result for yourself.

Mathematically, the result can be seen in the solution for the wage rate in our production model, shown in Table 4.2 and reproduced here:

$$w^* = \frac{2}{3} \cdot \frac{Y^*}{L^*} = \frac{2}{3} \cdot \bar{A} \cdot \left(\frac{\bar{K}}{\bar{L}}\right)^{1/3}$$

Holding capital constant, a decrease in labor $\bar{L}$ will increase the wage.

It is important to notice that Y^* is an endogenous variable in the equation above. So we can't use the first part of the equation to answer this question: Y^* itself changes when there is a decrease in labor.

(b) The European population fell by one-third, so two-thirds of the population remained: $\bar{L}$ fell to $2\bar{L}/3$. Plugging the quantity into the wage equation above shows that the wage would be expected to increase by a factor of $(3/2)^{1/3} \approx 1.14$, or by about 14%.

CHAPTER 5

THE SOLOW GROWTH MODEL

OVERVIEW

In this chapter, we learn

- how capital accumulates over time, helping us understand economic growth.
- the role of the diminishing marginal product of capital in explaining differences in growth rates across countries.
- the principle of transition dynamics: the farther below its steady state a country is, the faster the country will grow.
- the limitations of capital accumulation, and how it leaves a significant part of economic growth unexplained.

> All theory depends on assumptions which are not quite true. That is what makes it theory. The art of successful theorizing is to make the inevitable simplifying assumptions in such a way that the final results are not very sensitive.
>
> —ROBERT SOLOW

5.1 Introduction

In 1960, South Korea and the Philippines were similar in many respects. Both were relatively poor countries: per capita GDP was about \$1,800 in Korea and \$2,200 in the Philippines, less than 15 percent of the U.S. level. Both had populations on the order of 25 million, about half of whom were of working age. Similar fractions of the population in both countries worked in industry and agriculture. About 5 percent of Koreans in their early twenties attended college, versus 13 percent of Filipinos.

Between 1960 and 2007, however, the paths of these two countries diverged dramatically. In the Philippines, per capita GDP grew at a relatively modest rate of about 1.7 percent per year. In contrast, South Korea became one of the world's fastest-growing economies, with growth just under 6 percent per year. By 2007, per capita GDP in Korea had risen to nearly \$24,000, more than half the U.S. level. In contrast, per capita GDP in the Philippines was only \$5,000.[1]

How do we understand this astounding difference in economic performance between two countries that on the surface looked relatively similar? Why was growth in South Korea so much faster?

The starting point in economics for thinking about these questions is what's known as **the Solow growth model**. This model was developed in the mid-1950s by Robert Solow of MIT and was the basis for the Nobel Prize he received in 1987. Since the 1950s, the model has been extended in a number of important directions and is now probably the most widely used in all of macroeconomics.

The Solow framework builds on the production model we developed in Chapter 4, but introduces a new element: a theory of capital accumulation. Rather than the capital stock being given at some exogenous level, agents in the economy can accumulate tools, machines, computers, and buildings over time. This accumulation of capital is *endogenized* in the Solow model—it is converted from an exogenous variable into an endogenous variable. Other than this one change, the Solow model *is* the production model, so the insights we developed in Chapter 4 will serve us well here.

Epigraph: From "A Contribution to the Theory of Economic Growth," *Quarterly Journal of Economics*, vol. 70, 1956, p. 65.

[1] This line of argument is taken from the introduction to Robert E. Lucas Jr., "Making a Miracle," *Econometrica*, vol. 61, 1993, pp. 251–72.

The Solow model allows us to consider the accumulation of capital as a possible engine of long-run economic growth. Perhaps standards of living have increased by a factor of 10 in the last century because we have increased the amount of capital available for each worker. Perhaps some countries are richer than others because they invest more in accumulating capital. This chapter develops and evaluates these insights.

5.2 Setting Up the Model

Before diving into equations, let's consider a simple representation of the Solow model. Think of the economy as a large family farm that grows a single crop, corn. To begin, the farm has a silo containing several bags of seed corn. The family farmers plant some kernels in the spring, tend their crop over the summer, and then harvest it as autumn draws near. They reserve three-fourths of the corn for eating over the course of the year and store the remaining fourth in their silo, to plant the next year. Key to this process is that one kernel of seed corn produces ten ears of corn, each containing hundreds of kernels that can be eaten or planted the following year. So as the years pass, the size of the harvest grows larger and larger, as does the quantity of corn kernels stored in the silo. That in a nutshell—or a corn kernel—is the Solow model we will develop.

We start with our familiar production model and add an equation describing the accumulation of capital over time. This capital accumulation will proceed much like the collection of seed corn on the family farm.

Production

As in the production model, the farm produces a final output good Y, using the capital stock K and labor L:

$$Y_t = F(K_t, L_t) = \bar{A}K_t^{1/3}L_t^{2/3}. \tag{5.1}$$

We assume this production function is Cobb-Douglas and exhibits constant returns to scale in K and L. Moreover, the exponent on capital is again 1/3—recall that this exponent reflects the fact that one-third of GDP is paid to capital. Notice that here we add the time subscript t to our production function. Output, capital, and labor can all potentially change over time.

In our toy economy, the output can be used for one of two purposes, consumption or investment:

$$C_t + I_t = Y_t. \tag{5.2}$$

C_t is the amount of output the family chooses to eat, while I_t is the amount invested for the future. Such an equation is called a **resource constraint**: it describes a fundamental constraint on how the economy can use its resources. We are assuming the farm is a closed economy: there are no imports or exports in this equation.

Capital Accumulation

The seed corn invested for the future (I_t) determines the accumulation of capital, as can be seen in the following equation:

$$K_{t+1} = K_t + I_t - \bar{d}K_t.$$

This **capital accumulation equation** says that the capital stock next year, K_{t+1}, is equal to the sum of three terms. The first term (K_t) is the amount of capital we started with this year. The second term (I_t) is the amount of investment undertaken using this year's production. Finally, the last term ($\bar{d}K_t$) subtracts off **depreciation**. A constant fraction $\bar{d}$ of the capital stock is assumed to wear out each period; typically, economists think of this depreciation rate as taking on a value of 0.07 or 0.10, so that 7 percent or 10 percent of the capital stock is used up in the production process each period. On the family farm, you might think of $\bar{d}$ as the fraction of the seed corn in the silo that gets eaten by rats before it can be planted. The capital accumulation equation, then, says that the amount of corn in the silo next spring will be equal to the amount in the silo this year, plus the new additions of seed corn from this year's harvest, less the amount the rats eat.

One way in which the farm analogy is not perfect is that in our model, capital survives from one period to the next. It's more like a tractor that remains available in the next period than like seed corn that gets planted and used up every year. However, if you think of the seed corn as being recovered at the end of each harvest (since one kernel of seed corn leads to a bucket of kernels at harvest), the analogy works.

We can also express the capital accumulation equation in a different form. Let $\Delta K_{t+1} \equiv K_{t+1} - K_t$ represent the change in the capital stock between today, period t, and next year, period $t + 1$ (Δ is the "change over time" operator). Then

$$\Delta K_{t+1} = I_t - \bar{d}K_t. \tag{5.3}$$

The change in the capital stock is equal to new investment I less the amount of capital that depreciates in production.

Notice that today's capital stock is the result of investments undertaken in the past. This works fine for all periods in the model other than the first. To get the model started, we simply assume that the economy is endowed with some initial capital $\bar{K}_0$ and the model begins at date $t = 0$.

CASE STUDY

An Example of Capital Accumulation

To understand the capital accumulation equation (5.3), suppose the economy begins with a capital stock of $\bar{K}_0 = 1{,}000$ bushels of corn, has a depreciation rate of $\bar{d} = 0.10$, and invests a constant amount of 200 bushels each year. How does the capital stock evolve over time? The answer is shown in Table 5.1.

TABLE 5.1

A Capital Accumulation Example

Time, t	Capital, K_t	Investment, I_t	Depreciation, $\bar{d}K_t$	Change in capital, ΔK_{t+1}
0	1,000	200	100	100
1	1,100	200	110	90
2	1,190	200	119	81
3	1,271	200	127	73
4	1,344	200	134	66
5	1,410	200	141	59

The last column is found by applying the capital accumulation equation: $\Delta K_{t+1} = I_t - \bar{d}K_t$. That is, it is computed by taking the difference between the two prior columns. The next period's capital stock is then the sum of K_t and ΔK_{t+1}.

To read this table, start with the first row and go across, from left to right. The farm economy begins with 1,000 bushels of corn and invests 200 more. The depreciation rate is 10 percent, so during the course of production in year 0, 100 (= 0.10 · 1,000) bushels get eaten by rats. Investment net of (minus) depreciation is therefore 200 − 100 = 100 bushels. The capital stock rises by this amount, so the amount of corn in the silo at the start of period 1 is 1,100 bushels. In year 1, 10 percent of this higher stock is lost again to rats, so investment net of depreciation in this year is 200 − 110 = 90, and so on.

A key insight from this table is that the capital stock is simply the sum of past investments: the capital stock in an economy today consists of machines and buildings that were purchased in previous decades. Economists often compute the capital stock in an economy with this basic approach: we make an educated guess about an initial stock of capital at some date long ago and then add up the amount of investment that occurs each year, net of depreciation. Because the stock from long ago will mostly have depreciated by today, this approach is not particularly sensitive to (does not vary much with) the initial educated guess.

While Table 5.1 is just an example, it reveals something fundamental about the Solow model: the amount by which the capital stock increases each period, ΔK_{t+1} is smaller and smaller each year. Why do you think this happens? (We will learn why later in the chapter.)

Labor

We *could* include labor supply and labor demand explicitly in the model, but in the spirit of keeping it simple, we won't. Instead, we assume the amount of labor working on the family farm is given exogenously at the constant level $\bar{L}$.

TABLE 5.2

The Solow Model: 5 Equations and 5 Unknowns

Unknowns/endogenous variables: Y_t, K_t, L_t, C_t, I_t

Production function	$Y_t = \bar{A}K_t^{1/3}L_t^{2/3}$
Capital accumulation	$\Delta K_{t+1} = I_t - \bar{d}K_t$
Labor force	$L_t = \bar{L}$
Resource constraint	$C_t + I_t = Y_t$
Allocation of resources	$I_t = \bar{s}Y_t$

Parameters: $\bar{A}, \bar{s}, \bar{d}, \bar{L}, \bar{K}_0$

Investment

Our description of the economy is nearly complete, but we're still one equation short. In particular, we have not yet specified a rule for allocating resources. The family farm uses the output Y for consumption or investment, but how does the family choose how much to consume and how much to invest?

We'll assume the family farmers eat a constant fraction of the output each period and invest the remainder. Let $\bar{s}$ denote the fraction invested, so that

$$I_t = \bar{s}Y_t. \tag{5.4}$$

The fact that total output is used for either consumption or investment implies that $C_t = (1 - \bar{s})Y_t$. Although in our corn example $\bar{s}$ is equal to 1/4, for the model we allow this to be any number between 0 and 1.

The Model Summarized

That completes our setup of the Solow growth model, summarized in Table 5.2: there are essentially five equations and five unknowns. Here, though, we have a *dynamic* model, so these five equations hold at each point in time, starting at $t = 0$ and lasting for $t = 1, t = 2, \ldots$ —as long as we'd like the model to run.

CASE STUDY

Some Questions about the Solow Model

What about wages and the rental price of capital?

If you compare the Solow model with the model of production presented in Chapter 4, you'll notice several differences. The main one is that we have added dynamics to the model in the form of capital accumulation. But we have also left out the markets for capital and labor and the corresponding prices—the rental price of capital and the wage rate. This is a simplification that makes the model easier to work with; its reasoning will be discussed in more detail in Section 5.3.

Why isn't $C_t = (1 - \bar{s})Y_t$ part of Table 5.2?

Why do we include the investment allocation equation $I_t = \bar{s}Y_t$ but not the consumption equation $C_t = (1 - \bar{s})Y_t$? Take a minute to think about this question before reading on.

First, this consumption equation is part of the model, but we do not need to add it to the list in Table 5.2 because it would be redundant. The equations for the resource constraint $C_t + I_t = Y_t$ and the allocation of investment $I_t = \bar{s}Y_t$ together *imply* that the consumption relation holds, so it's not necessary to specify that equation in the table. Second, by leaving the equation out, we preserve our counting: we have five equations and five unknowns. If we were to include the redundant equation, we would have six equations, one of which is unnecessary, and five unknowns.

What are stocks and flows?

You'll have noticed that we refer to K_t as the capital stock. Economists often find it helpful to distinguish between *stocks* and *flows*. A **stock** is a quantity that survives from period to period—a tractor, house, or semiconductor factory, for example. We also speak of the stock of government debt, a debt that persists over time unless it is paid off. In contrast, a **flow** is a quantity that lasts for a single period—the breakfast you ate this morning, or a withdrawal you make from your bank's ATM. Stocks and flows are intimately related. Stocks satisfy an accumulation equation, like the capital accumulation equation in this model. The change in a stock is a flow: the change in the capital stock, for example, is the flow of investment, and the change in your bank balance (a stock) is the flow of deposits and withdrawals you make.

5.3 Prices and the Real Interest Rate

We've left prices—the rental price of capital and the wage rate for labor—out of our Solow model to keep the model as simple as possible. If we added those elements back in, we would end up with two more endogenous variables and two more equations. These would pin down the wage as the marginal product of labor and the rental price of capital as the marginal product of capital, just as in the production model of Chapter 4. Otherwise, though, nothing would change. You might think about these additional elements as lying in the background of our Solow model. They are available in case we ever need them, but it is simpler for most of this chapter to leave them there.

For now, however, there is one other important price to consider, called the real interest rate. The real interest rate in an economy is equal to the rental price of capital, which in turn is given by the marginal product of capital.

Let's take this statement in pieces. First, *the* ***real interest rate*** *is the amount a person can earn by saving one unit of output for a year, or equivalently the amount a person must pay to borrow one unit of output for a year*. We say that it is real because it is measured in units of output (or constant dollars) rather than in nominal dollars.

Why is this rate equal to the rental price of capital? Consider the source of the supply of capital in an economy. In Chapter 4, we simply assumed the existence of a fixed amount of capital. In this chapter, we understand that capital comes from the decision by households to forgo consumption and save instead. This saving is equal to investment, which becomes the capital supplied in the economy.

On the family farm, our farmers forgo consuming some corn (they *save* the corn) and place it in the silo to be used as next year's seed (investment). Now consider the national income identity for our Solow model, which we've already seen in equation (5.2): $Y_t = C_t + I_t$. Subtracting consumption from both sides gives

$$\underbrace{Y_t - C_t}_{\text{saving}} = \underbrace{I_t}_{\text{investment}}.$$

The left side of this expression is **saving**: the difference between income and consumption. The right side is investment. So the equation tells us that saving equals investment in this economy.

We've already defined the real interest rate as the amount a person can earn by saving one unit of output. We now see that the unit of saving gets used as a unit of investment, and a unit of investment becomes a unit of capital. Therefore, the return on saving is equal to the price at which the unit of capital can be rented.

Finally, we saw in Chapter 4 that the rental price of capital is given by the marginal product of capital in equilibrium. Therefore, we have the following result: *the real interest rate equals the rental price of capital that clears the capital market, which in turn is equal to the marginal product of capital.*

5.4 Solving the Solow Model

To solve the Solow model completely, we need to write the endogenous variables—Y_t, K_t, L_t, C_t, I_t—as functions of the parameters of the model. Furthermore, we need to do this not just for a single time period, but for every point in time.

It turns out that the model cannot be solved algebraically in this fashion. However, we *can* make some progress in two complementary ways. First, we can show graphically what the solution looks like. Second, we can solve the model "in the long run," a phrase that will take on more meaning once we've studied the model more carefully. Keep a pencil and some paper handy as you read through the solution of the Solow model below; working through the equations yourself as we go along is one of the most effective ways of learning the model.

The first step is to combine equations in a way that will take us as far as we can go algebraically. Thus, we combine the investment allocation equation (5.4) with the capital accumulation equation (5.3) to get

$$\underbrace{\Delta K_{t+1}}_{\text{change in capital}} = \underbrace{\bar{s}Y_t - \bar{d}K_t}_{\text{net investment}}. \qquad (5.5)$$

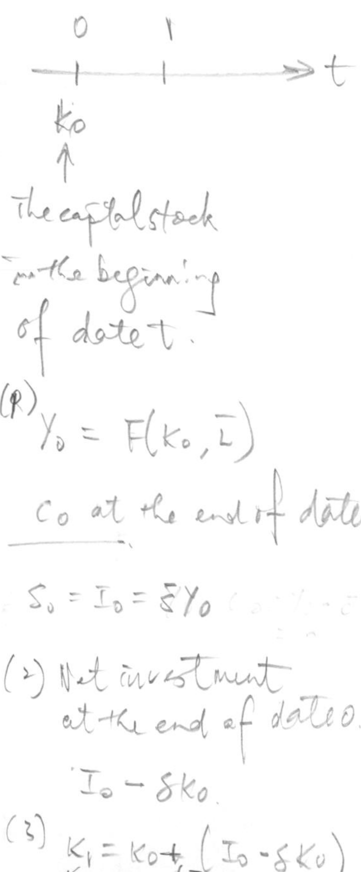

This equation has a nice economic interpretation: the change in the capital stock is equal to investment $I_t = \bar{s}K_t$ less depreciation $\bar{d}K_t$. For this reason, the quantity $I_t - \bar{d}K_t$ is often called **net investment**: it is investment net of (minus) depreciation.

Another key equation of the model is the production function. Recall that the amount of labor in the economy is fixed ($L_t = \bar{L}$), so we have

$$Y_t = \bar{A}K_t^{1/3}\bar{L}^{2/3}. \qquad (5.6)$$

At this point, we have reduced our system of five equations and five unknowns to two equations and two unknowns (K_t and Y_t). Moreover, it should be clear that we could simply plug in the production function for output into equation (5.5) if we wished. Then we would have a single dynamic equation describing the evolution of the capital stock. While this equation cannot be solved algebraically, we can learn a lot about it by analyzing it graphically. The key graph to draw is called **the Solow diagram**, shown in Figure 5.1.

The Solow diagram plots the two terms ($\bar{s}Y$ and $\bar{d}K$) that govern the change in the capital stock, according to the capital accumulation equation (5.5). New investment (the curved line) depends on production and can be written as $\bar{s}Y = \bar{s}\bar{A}K^{1/3}\bar{L}^{2/3}$. Notice that this function is basically proportional to $K^{1/3}$, so the graph of $\bar{s}Y$ looks much like the production functions we graphed in Chapter 4, scaled down by the investment rate $\bar{s}$.

FIGURE 5.1

The Solow Diagram

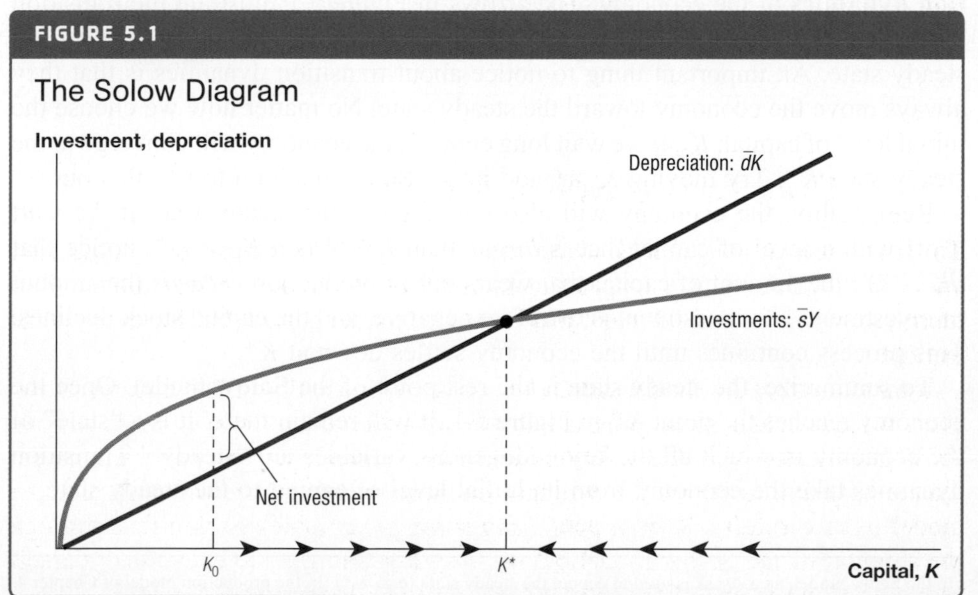

The Solow diagram plots two curves, which are both functions of capital K. The first curve is new investment $\bar{s}Y$. Because the production function is increasing in K but with diminishing returns, investment shows this same curvature. The second curve is depreciation $\bar{d}K$, which is just a linear function of K. The change in the capital stock – net investment – is the vertical difference between these two curves. Arrows on the horizontal axis indicate how the capital stock changes.

The second line shows the amount of capital that depreciates, $\bar{d}K$. This is just a linear function of capital, so its graph is a straight line.

Using the Solow Diagram

Now we are ready to put the Solow diagram to work. Suppose the economy begins with some starting level of capital, $\bar{K}_0$, as shown on the graph. What happens over time? At the level $\bar{K}_0$, the amount of investment, $\bar{s}Y$, exceeds the amount of depreciation, $\bar{d}K_0$. In other words, the amount of seed corn we add to the silo exceeds the amount that gets eaten by rats, so the total amount of seed corn in the silo rises. Mathematically, $\Delta K_{t+1} = \bar{s}Y - \bar{d}K$ is greater than zero, so the capital stock increases. (Recall that $\Delta K_{t+1} = K_{t+1} - K_t$, so that if ΔK_{t+1} is greater than zero, $K_{t+1} > K_t$.)

This means that K_1 will be a little bit higher than $\bar{K}_0$, just to the right of $\bar{K}_0$ in the graph. What then happens in period 1? It remains true that the $\bar{s}Y$ curve lies above the $\bar{d}K$ curve, so investment again exceeds depreciation. Net investment is positive, and the capital stock increases once again.

This process continues—and the economy moves in the direction of the arrows—until the economy reaches a capital level K^*. At this point, the two curves in the Solow diagram intersect so that $\bar{s}Y = \bar{d}K$. This means that the amount of investment being undertaken is exactly equal to the amount of capital that wears out through depreciation. And since investment equals depreciation, the change in the capital stock is equal to zero ($K_{t+1} = K_t$), and the capital stock remains constant. In the absence of any shocks, the capital stock will remain at K^* forever, as each period's investment is just enough to offset the depreciation that occurs during production. This rest point is called the **steady state** of the Solow model.[2]

We call the behavior of the economy *away* from its steady state the **transition dynamics** of the economy. The arrows in Figure 5.1 illustrate the transition dynamics in the basic Solow model—that is, as the economy "transits" to its steady state. An important thing to notice about transition dynamics is that they always move the economy toward the steady state. No matter how we choose the initial level of capital, $\bar{K}_0$, if we wait long enough, the economy will converge to the steady state K^*. Try moving $\bar{K}_0$ around in the Solow diagram to test this out.

Remarkably, the economy will also converge to the steady state if we start it off with a level of capital that is *larger* than K^*. When $K_t > K^*$, notice that $\bar{d}K > \bar{s}Y$: the amount of capital that wears out in production *exceeds* the amount of investment. Net investment is therefore negative, and the capital stock declines. This process continues until the economy settles down at K^*.

To summarize, the steady state is the rest point of the Solow model. Once the economy reaches the point K^* in Figure 5.1, it will remain there: it is a "state" of the economy in which all the key endogenous variables are "steady." Transition dynamics take the economy from its initial level of capital to the steady state.

---

[2] In the Solow model, an asterisk is used to denote the steady state (e.g., K^*). In the production model of Chapter 4, we used an asterisk to denote an equilibrium value. These uses are different. An equilibrium is a solution to a model, even when it is not constant. A steady state occurs when the equilibrium settles down to constant values.

Output and Consumption in the Solow Diagram

What about the behavior of output, Y? Recall that according to equation (5.6), output is a Cobb-Douglas function of capital: $Y_t = \bar{A}K_t^{1/3}\bar{L}^{2/3}$. We can plot this production function on the Solow diagram as well, and it allows us to see how output evolves over time (see Figure 5.2). As transition dynamics take the economy from K_0 to K^*, output rises over time from Y_0 to its steady-state level, Y^*.

Finally, the level of consumption can also be seen in the Solow diagram. From the resource constraint, $C_t + I_t = Y_t$, so consumption is the difference between output and investment: $C_t = Y_t - I_t$.

Solving Mathematically for the Steady State

As mentioned earlier, we can't solve the Solow model mathematically for the level of capital at each point in time. The Solow diagram helps us understand what is going on in the absence of an exact mathematical expression. But we *can* solve mathematically for the steady-state level of capital, and this is what we do now.

According to the Solow diagram, the steady-state level of capital is such that $\bar{s}Y^* = \bar{d}K^*$. Substituting from the production function, equation (5.6), we see that

$$\bar{s}\bar{A}K^{*1/3}\bar{L}^{2/3} = \bar{d}K^*.$$

And solving this equation for K^* by collecting the K^* terms on the right-hand side and raising both sides of the equation to the 3/2 power yields

$$K^* = \left(\frac{\bar{s}\bar{A}}{\bar{d}}\right)^{3/2}\bar{L}. \tag{5.7}$$

FIGURE 5.2

The Solow Diagram with Output

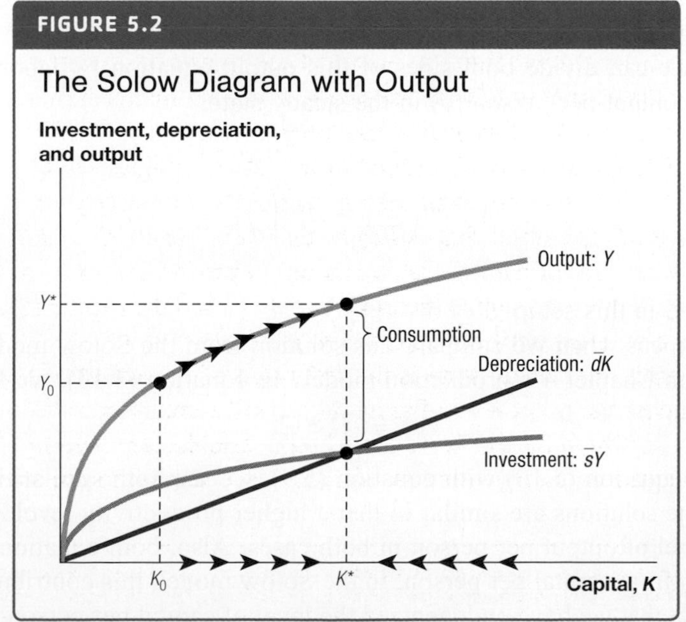

Here, the production function is added to the Solow diagram: $Y_t = \bar{A}K_t^{1/3}\bar{L}^{2/3}$, plotting Y as a function of K. Output rises as the economy transits from K_0 to the steady state K^*. Consumption is the difference between output and investment.

This equation pins down the steady-state level of capital K^* as a function of the underlying parameters of the model, and it's worth pausing to make sure you understand the result. A higher investment rate $\bar{s}$ leads to a higher steady-state capital stock: if we invest 20 percent of our harvest as seed corn rather than 10 percent, more seed will accumulate in the silo.

The steady-state level of capital also increases if the underlying level of productivity $\bar{A}$ is higher. This might seem surprising at first—why does the level of capital depend on how productive the economy is? The answer is that if the farm is more productive, the harvest will be larger, and the larger harvest will translate into more seed corn in the silo.

Finally, the steady-state capital stock also depends on the depreciation rate and the size of the workforce. A higher rate of depreciation reduces the capital stock, as the rats gobble more of the seed corn. A larger workforce produces more output, which leads to more investment and hence more capital in the steady state.

Associated with the steady-state level of capital K^* is a steady-state level of production Y^*, given by the production function:

$$Y^* = \bar{A}K^{*\,1/3}\bar{L}^{2/3}.$$

Substituting our solution for K^* into this equation yields the expression for steady-state production:

$$Y^* = \left(\frac{\bar{s}}{\bar{d}}\right)^{1/2}\bar{A}^{3/2}\bar{L}. \tag{5.8}$$

As with the steady-state capital stock, a higher rate of investment ($\bar{s}$) and higher productivity ($\bar{A}$) lead to a higher steady-state level of production, but faster depreciation ($\bar{d}$) lowers it. The constant returns to scale of the underlying production function show up in that doubling labor leads in the long run to a doubling of steady-state production. As with the capital stock equation, (5.7), make sure you understand how each of the parameters in equation (5.8) affects steady-state output.

Finally, we can divide both sides of this output equation by labor to get our solution for output per person (y) in the steady state:

$$y^* \equiv \left(\frac{Y^*}{L^*}\right) = \bar{A}^{3/2}\left(\frac{\bar{s}}{\bar{d}}\right)^{1/2} \tag{5.9}$$

since $L^* = \bar{L}$ in this setup.

What happens when we compare this solution from the Solow model with the solution from Chapter 4's production model? In equation (4.10), we found that

$$y^* = \bar{A}k^{*\,1/3}. \tag{5.10}$$

Comparing equation (5.10) with equation (5.9), we see both similarities and differences. The solutions are similar in that a higher productivity level $\bar{A}$ raises the long-run level of output per person in both cases. Also, both equations include a contribution from capital per person. In the Solow model, this contribution shows up in the fact that we have endogenized the level of capital per person; as implied by equation (5.7), capital per person in the steady state depends on the investment rate ($\bar{s}$), productivity ($\bar{A}$), and depreciation ($\bar{d}$). These are the terms that appear in equation (5.9) in place of $\bar{k}$.

An interesting difference between these two equations is the role of the productivity parameter $\bar{A}$. In the production model, it enters with an exponent of 1, while in the Solow model it enters with an exponent of 3/2. Why the difference? The answer is that the level of the capital stock itself depends on productivity. In the Solow model, a higher productivity parameter raises output directly just as in the production model. But there is an additional effect in the Solow model. The higher productivity level leads the economy to accumulate more capital as well. This explains the larger exponent in the Solow framework.

5.5 Looking at Data through the Lens of the Solow Model

The Capital-Output Ratio

The key difference between the Solow model and the production model in Chapter 4 is that the Solow model endogenizes the process of capital accumulation: it explains where the capital stock comes from. We can examine this key element of the model empirically by focusing on the capital accumulation equation. As we have learned, the model predicts that in steady state, $\bar{s}Y^* = \bar{d}K^*$. This implies that the capital-output ratio in steady state is given by

$$\frac{K^*}{Y^*} = \frac{\bar{s}}{\bar{d}}. \tag{5.11}$$

In reality, different countries have different investment rates—different values of $\bar{s}$. Over the last 30 years, the investment rate in Japan has averaged more than 35 percent of GDP, while the rate in the United States has been about 24 percent. In the poorest countries of the world, investment rates are only 5 percent or so. It is conventional to assume that the depreciation rate is relatively similar across countries; a typical value would be about 7 percent.

According to equation (5.11), countries with high investment rates should have high capital-output ratios. Figure 5.3 examines this prediction empirically, by plotting the capital-output ratio in 2007 against the average investment rate for a sample of countries. It turns out that the Solow prediction holds up remarkably well. Countries like Japan and Norway experience high average investment rates and high capital-output ratios. The United States lies somewhere in the center, with an investment rate of 24 percent and a capital-output ratio of 3. Uganda and Egypt have low investment rates and low capital-output ratios.

Differences in *Y/L*

Recall that in Chapter 4's production model, we found that most of the differences in per capita GDP across countries were explained by differences in total factor productivity (TFP), with a modest contribution from differences in capital per

Just as the Solow model predicts, a key determinant of a country's capital-output ratio is its investment rate.

FIGURE 5.3

Explaining Capital in the Solow Model

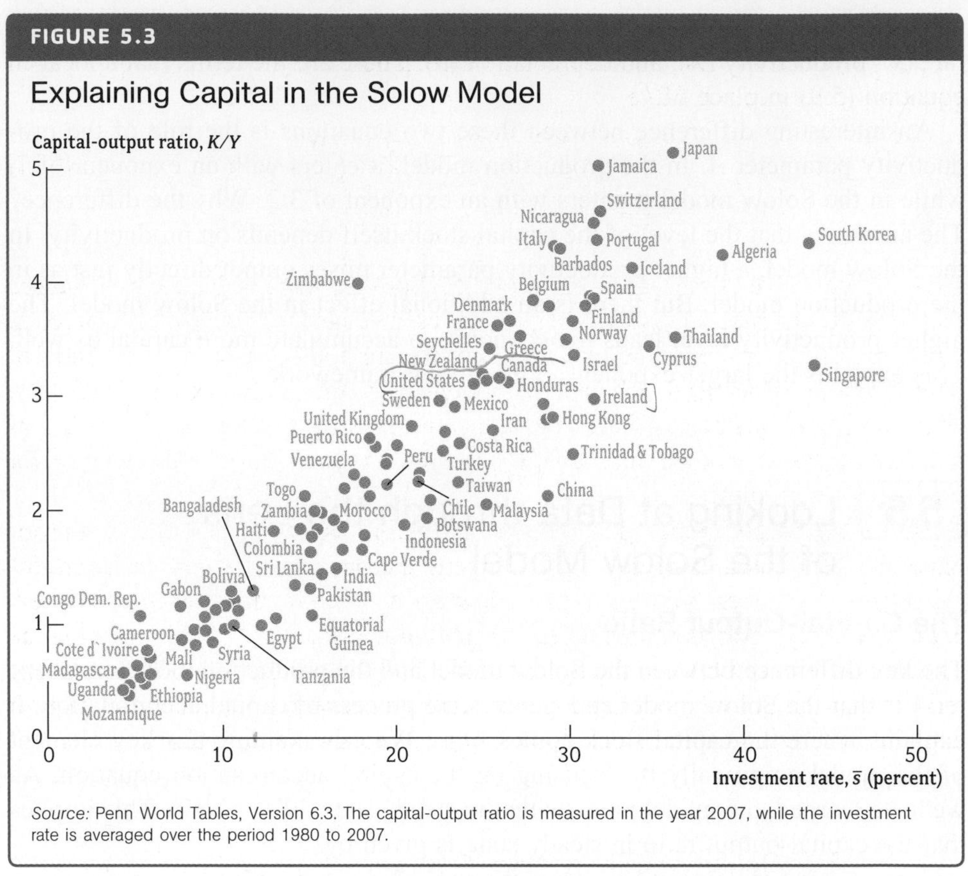

Source: Penn World Tables, Version 6.3. The capital-output ratio is measured in the year 2007, while the investment rate is averaged over the period 1980 to 2007.

person. What the Solow model does is to endogenize these differences in capital per person. Since it adds nothing new regarding TFP differences, we would expect that they remain as a key explanatory factor.

In fact, the Solow model leads to an even more important role for TFP differences. Why? Look back at equation (5.7). Notice that differences in capital are explained in part by differences in investment rate $\bar{s}$ and in part by differences in the productivity parameter $\bar{A}$. That is, some of the differences we observe in capital per person across countries are *themselves* due to differences in productivity. This means that the Solow model gives an even larger role to TFP than our production model did.

One way to see this is to look back at the equation for output per person in steady state, equation (5.9). As was pointed out earlier, the exponent on the productivity parameter $\bar{A}$ is now larger than 1, suggesting a more important role for productivity.

A second way to see the larger role of TFP in the Solow model, though, is to calculate how important differences in investment rates are for explaining differences in y^*. In Chapter 4, we found that the ratio of per capita GDP in the five richest countries to GDP in the five poorest countries was a factor of 66. With the production model, a factor of 11 of this difference was attributed to productivity and a factor of 6 to capital.

We can do this same accounting exercise with the steady-state equation for output per person (5.9). Assuming the depreciation rate is the same in the rich and poor countries, we have

$$\underbrace{\frac{y^*_{\text{rich}}}{y^*_{\text{poor}}}}_{66} = \underbrace{\left(\frac{\bar{A}_{\text{rich}}}{\bar{A}_{\text{poor}}}\right)^{3/2}}_{\approx\ 26} \times \underbrace{\left(\frac{\bar{s}_{\text{rich}}}{\bar{s}_{\text{poor}}}\right)^{1/2}}_{\times\ 2.5}. \tag{5.12}$$

How do we arrive at the figures 26 and 2.5? Looking back at Figure 5.3, we see that investment rates in the richest countries average about 25 or 30 percent, while investment rates in the poorest countries are about 5 percent. The ratio of investment rates between rich and poor countries is thus no more than $30/5 = 6$, suggesting that differences in investment rates explain a factor of $\sqrt{6} \approx 2.5$ of the differences in income, and leaving an even larger factor of $66/2.5 = 26$ for productivity differences.

While the Solow model is successful in helping us understand why countries have different amounts of capital, it deepens the puzzle of why some countries are so much richer than others. Since it assigns an even larger role to TFP differences than our production model did, we are led to ask again, Why is it that some countries use their inputs so much more efficiently than others? This is one of the most important questions at the current frontier of research on economic growth and development, and we'll get closer to an answer in the next chapter.

5.6 Understanding the Steady State

The steady-state result—that the Solow model eventually approaches a constant level of capital K^* and a constant level of production Y^* no matter where it begins—is quite remarkable. It is therefore worth spending some time thinking about where this result comes from and what it means.

First, why does the economy settle down to a steady state? As we've seen, at the steady state, $\bar{s}Y^* = \bar{d}K^*$. Back on the farm, in other words, the amount of new seed corn we add to the silo is just enough to offset the amount that's eaten by rats, keeping the amount of seed corn in the silo at the same level just before each spring planting. The reason the economy settles down is that the $\bar{s}Y$ curve exhibits **diminishing returns** (see Figure 5.1). As we increase the capital stock, production rises and therefore investment rises. But the *amount* by which production and investment rise gets smaller as the capital stock grows, a fact embedded in our production function: $Y = \bar{A}K^{1/3}\bar{L}^{2/3}$. In contrast, a constant fraction of the capital stock depreciates every period, so the amount of depreciation rises one-for-one with capital.

The fact that production exhibits diminishing returns to capital accumulation means that each addition to the capital stock increases production—and therefore investment—by less and less. But it increases depreciation by the same amount, $\bar{d}$. Eventually, the amount of investment the economy generates is equal to the amount of capital that depreciates. Net investment is zero, and the economy stabilizes at the steady state.

The fact that the model settles down to a steady state is thus intimately linked to the presence of diminishing returns to capital.

5.7 Economic Growth in the Solow Model

One of the most important implications of the steady-state result is that *there is no long-run growth in the Solow model*. In the long run, the economy settles down to a constant level of production Y^* and a constant amount of capital K^*. Output per person $y^* \equiv Y^*/\bar{L}$ is constant as well, as is consumption per person $c^* = (1 - \bar{s})y^*$. As we see in the Solow diagram, this basic version of the Solow model can lead to economic growth for a while—for example, as the economy grows from $\bar{K}_0$ to K^*—but eventually growth stops as the capital stock and production converge to constant levels.

Let's contrast this theoretical prediction with the facts of economic growth that we observed in Chapter 3. There we saw that economic growth was a widespread phenomenon, both across countries and over time. Per capita GDP in the United States, for example, has grown at an average annual rate of 2 percent per year for more than a century. Moreover, this rate of growth is higher than the growth rate in previous centuries. Economic growth shows no signs of disappearing, but in the Solow model, this is exactly what happens.

One of the central lessons of the Solow model therefore comes as something of a surprise: capital accumulation cannot serve as the engine of long-run economic growth. The fact that we save and invest in additional factories, machine tools, computers, and bulldozers does lead output to grow in the medium run. But in the long run, the diminishing returns to capital accumulation cause the return to these investments to fall. Eventually depreciation and new investment offset each other, and the economy settles down to a constant level of output per person.

Although we can't help but feel disappointed by this result, it is a testimony to the importance of *other* results we will derive in the Solow model that it still remains one of the most important models in macroeconomics. The capital accumulation hypothesis is an important one to explore, but in the end, the Solow model teaches us that it is not the answer to the question of what causes long-run growth.

Meanwhile, Back on the Family Farm

In our farm example, the family of corn farmers eat a constant fraction of their harvest and plant the remainder as seed for next year's crop. Our model suggests that starting from a small stock of seed corn, the harvest grows larger and larger each year, at least for a while. Eventually, though, the harvest settles down to some constant level: the farm produces 1,500 bushels of corn every year. Why does this occur? Why doesn't the process of planting seed corn year after year, each kernel of which can produce ten ears of corn, lead to an ever-growing harvest?

The amount of corn that can be successfully harvested is limited by the amount of labor the farmers can provide. As we add more and more corn plants to the farm, the amount that a family of six can harvest may rise, but it runs into **diminishing returns**: six farmers can effectively harvest 6 acres or 600 acres, but what about 600,000 acres? Eventually a fixed number of farmers simply cannot harvest all the corn that's planted, and growth stops. This is inherent in our production function: harvest $=$ (seed corn)$^{1/3}$(farmers)$^{2/3}$. Diminishing returns to the amount of corn a given number of farmers can cultivate lead to a situation where the new investment—which is proportional to each year's harvest—is exactly offset by depreciation, just as in the Solow diagram.

CASE STUDY

Population Growth in the Solow Model

What would happen if the number of farmers we could employ on the family farm were to grow? Can growth in the labor force lead to overall economic growth? The short answer is that it can in the *aggregate*, but not in output per person. That is, total capital and total production can grow as the labor force grows. But the presence of diminishing returns leads capital per person and output per person to settle down in a steady state; fundamentally, the amount of corn each farmer can produce runs into diminishing returns as well: $y = \bar{A}k^{1/3}$. At first, one farmer can tend to 100 acres, 1,000 acres, and maybe even 10,000 acres of corn. But as the number of acres per farmer grows, eventually she has no time to cultivate the additional crop. Investment per farmer falls to equal depreciation per farmer, and growth in output per farmer stops. An increase in labor by itself doesn't really change the lessons of the Solow model: even with more workers, the economy eventually settles down to a steady state with no growth in output per person.

An intuitive way to understand this result is to recall that the Solow economy exhibits constant returns to scale. Adding more family farms won't affect the analysis of a single farm (recall the standard replication argument). Therefore each farm ends up in a steady state with constant output per farm, just as in the Solow model.[3]

5.8 Some Economic Experiments

While the Solow model leads us to look elsewhere for a source of long-run economic growth, it nevertheless helps us understand some of the other facts of growth documented in Chapter 3. For example, it *does* help us understand differences in

[3] The mathematics of the Solow model with population growth is slightly harder than without. For example, see Chapter 2 of Charles I. Jones, *Introduction to Economic Growth* (New York: Norton, 2002).

growth rates between countries like South Korea and the Philippines. Developing these results will occupy the remainder of the chapter; we return to the question of the source of long-run growth in the next chapter.

One of the best ways to understand how an economic model works is to experiment by changing some of the parameter values. After building a toy world populated by little robots, the economist-god is free to watch the world for a while and then change it suddenly to see how it responds. Such experiments can reveal useful insights, as we will now see in a couple of examples.

An Increase in the Investment Rate

Suppose an economy begins in steady state. Then, for exogenous reasons (outside the model), the investment rate increases permanently. For example, we might be contemplating a change in tax regulations that would encourage investment. How would the economy respond to such a change?

Figure 5.4 shows the answer in terms of the Solow diagram. The economy begins at K^*, the steady state associated with the investment rate $\bar{s}$. Then the investment rate rises to $\bar{s}'$. This causes the $\bar{s}Y$ curve to rotate upward. Why? Recall that this curve is a plot of $\bar{s}\bar{A}\bar{L}^{2/3}K^{1/3}$. When $\bar{s}$ increases, the amount of investment rises for any given level of the capital stock, so the new $\bar{s}'Y$ curve lies above the old $\bar{s}Y$ curve. The $\bar{d}K$ curve does not shift, since that expression does not involve $\bar{s}$.

At the old investment rate, the economy was in steady state: the amount of investment just equaled the amount of depreciation. At the new, higher investment rate, though, the amount of investment rises and exceeds the amount of depreciation. This causes the capital stock to increase over time, until it reaches the new steady-state level K^{**}.

What happens to output in response to this increase in the investment rate? The answer is shown in Figure 5.5(a). The rise in investment leads capital to

Starting from K^*, new investment exceeds depreciation when the investment rate rises to $\bar{s}'$. This causes the capital stock to increase, until the economy reaches the new steady state at K^{**}.

FIGURE 5.4

An Increase in the Investment Rate

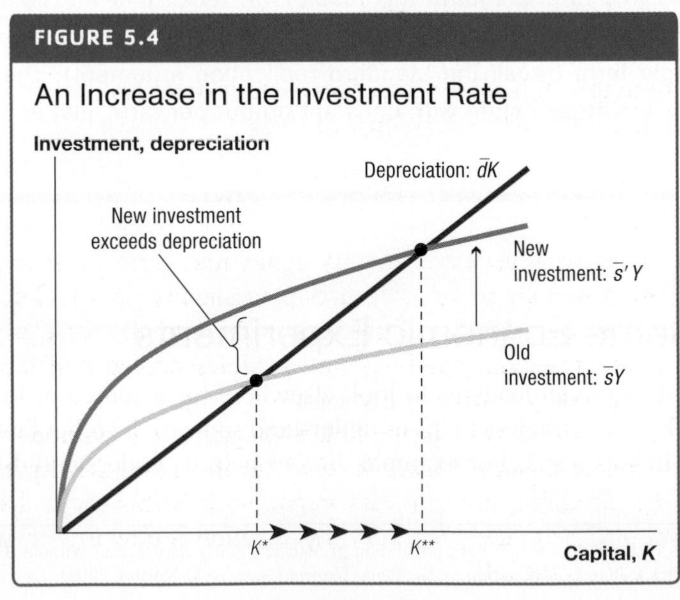

FIGURE 5.5

The Behavior of Output Following an Increase in $\bar{s}$

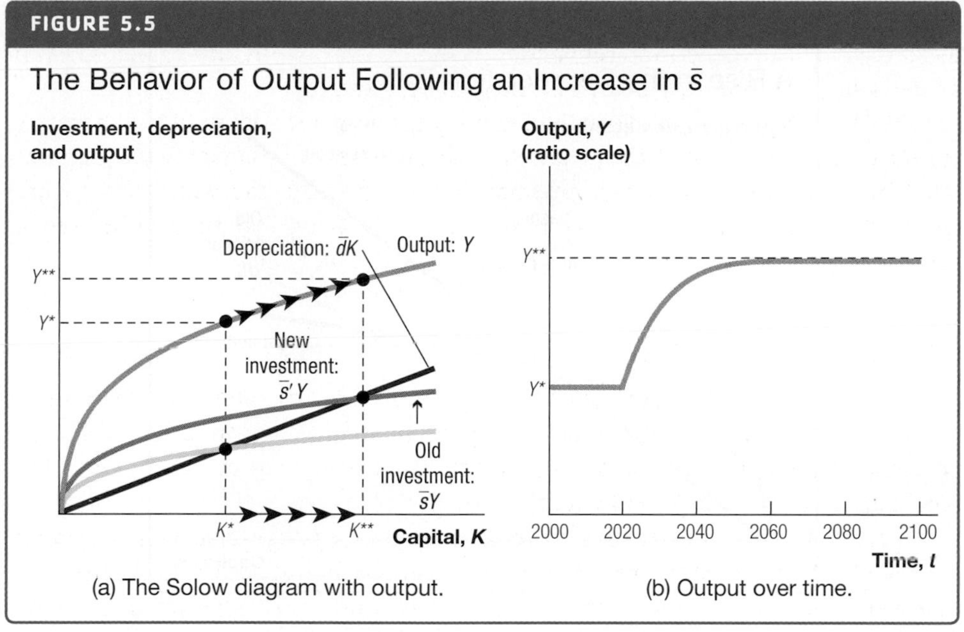

(a) The Solow diagram with output.

(b) Output over time.

A permanent increase in the investment rate causes output to grow over time until it reaches its new steady-state level Y^{**}.

accumulate over time. This higher capital causes output to rise as well. Output increases from its initial steady-state level Y^* to the new steady state Y^{**}. Part (b) shows the hypothetical behavior of output over time, assuming that the increase in the investment rate occurs in the year 2020. Notice that output grows fastest immediately following the change in the investment rate. Then over time, the growth rate of output falls, and the economy converges smoothly to its new steady state. We will explore these transition dynamics in more detail later in the chapter.

A key point to appreciate from this example is that the increase in the investment rate causes the economy to grow over time, at least until the new steady state is reached. In the long run, both steady-state capital and steady-state production are higher. Because labor is constant, this also means the level of output per person is permanently higher as well. In fact, these steady-state results can be seen just by looking back at equations (5.7) through (5.9).

A Rise in the Depreciation Rate

As a second experiment, let the economy again start from its steady state, but now suppose the depreciation rate increases permanently. In a real economy, we might imagine this could happen if changes in the climate, for example, led to more severe weather so that buildings and vehicles depreciated more quickly. How would the economy evolve in this case?

Figure 5.6 shows the answer in the Solow diagram. We assume the depreciation rate rises from $\bar{d}$ to some higher level $\bar{d}'$. In this case, the depreciation rate shows up in the $\bar{d}K$ curve, not in the $\bar{s}Y$ curve, so it is this curve that shifts. At any given level of capital, the amount of depreciation is now higher, so the curve rotates upward and to the left.

Starting from K^*, depreciation exceeds new investment when the depreciation rate rises to $\bar{d}'$. This causes the capital stock to decline, until the economy reaches the new steady state at K^{**}.

FIGURE 5.6

A Rise in the Depreciation Rate

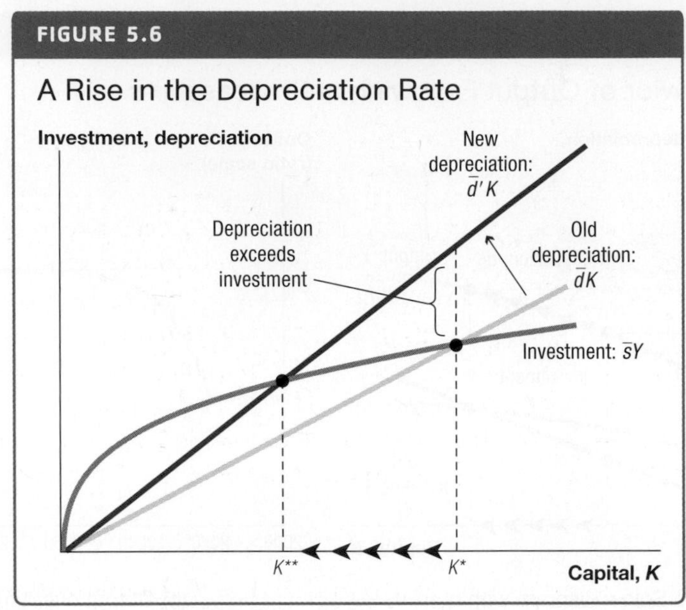

At the original rate of depreciation, the amount of investment was just enough to offset the wear and tear of the capital stock. Now, since depreciation has increased, $\bar{d}'K$ exceeds $\bar{s}Y$. This means that the change in the capital stock is negative, since $\Delta K_{t+1} = \bar{s}Y_t - \bar{d}'K_t$, so the capital stock declines and the economy moves slightly to the left (following the arrows). At this new quantity of capital, though, it's still true that depreciation exceeds new investment, so the capital stock continues to decline until the economy reaches the new, lower steady state K^{**}, where $\bar{s}Y = \bar{d}'K$.

What happens to output in response to this increase in the depreciation rate? The answer is shown in Figure 5.7. The decline in capital reduces output as well.

A permanent increase in the depreciation rate causes output to decline over time until it reaches its new steady-state level Y^{**}.

FIGURE 5.7

The Behavior of Output Following an Increase in $\bar{d}$

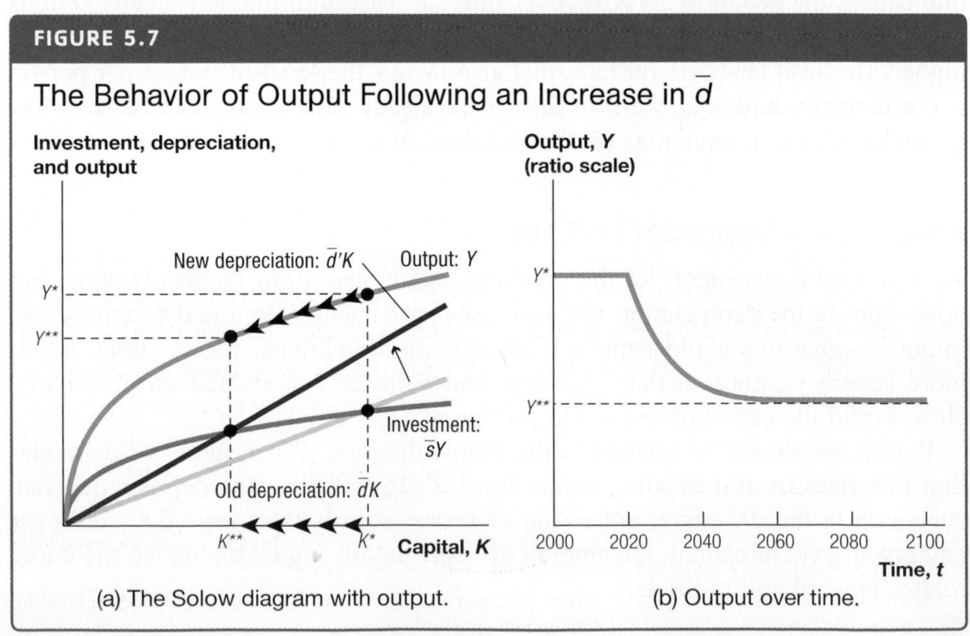

(a) The Solow diagram with output.

(b) Output over time.

Output declines rapidly at first, and then gradually settles down at its new, lower steady-state level Y^{**}. Once again, the algebra underlying this result can be seen in equations (5.7) through (5.9).

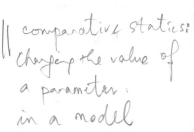

Experiments on Your Own

To conduct other experiments with the Solow model, change one (or more) of the parameters and see what happens. You'll do this in exercises at the end of the chapter, drawing on the parameters $\bar{s}$, $\bar{d}$, $\bar{A}$, $\bar{L}$, and $\bar{K}_0$ as listed in Table 5.2. As you work through your own experiments, refer to the template provided by the examples we've just studied. First, figure out which curve (depreciation or investment), if either, shifts in response to the parameter change.[4] Then follow the dynamics of the Solow diagram to determine what happens. Finally, consult the algebraic solutions for the steady-state values of K^*, Y^*, and y^*.

CASE STUDY

Wars and Economic Recovery

Wars are horrible tragedies. Life is the most valuable "asset" that people possess, and the lives lost in wars represent an extraordinary personal, social, and economic loss.

Above and beyond the loss of life, however, what can we say about the economic consequences of war? Does war have a long-lasting detrimental effect on economic performance that persists for decades after the war ends? Most of us would guess that the answer is yes. But in fact, some recent research calls that instinct into question, offering some intriguing evidence.

Donald Davis and David Weinstein of Columbia University have considered the effect of the nuclear bombs that were dropped on the Japanese cities of Hiroshima and Nagasaki near the end of World War II.[5] The bombing of Hiroshima leveled over two-thirds of the city and in short order killed perhaps more than 20 percent of the population, with more casualties following over time from radiation poisoning. The explosion over Nagasaki was twice as powerful, but hilly geography and a missed target lessened the destruction. Perhaps 40 percent of the city was destroyed and about 8.5 percent of the population killed. Despite this devastating loss of life and economic capability, however, Hiroshima and Nagasaki recovered relatively quickly. In just a few decades, these cities had returned to close to their original economic position relative to other Japanese cities—by 1960 for Nagasaki and by 1975 for Hiroshima.

---

[4] Figuring out whether or not a curve shifts is best done by thinking about the underlying mathematics. In a plot of y versus x, if the curve is $y = ax + b$, then changes in a and b shift the curve—at any given level of x, the amount of y changes. Changes in x, on the other hand, lead to movements *along* the curve.

[5] Donald R. Davis and David E. Weinstein, "Bones, Bombs, and Break Points: The Geography of Economic Activity," *American Economic Review*, vol. 92 (December 2002), pp. 1269–89.

Edward Miguel and Gérard Roland of the University of California at Berkeley have studied the effect on subsequent economic development of the most intense bombing campaign in military history—the U.S. bombing of Vietnam from 1964 to 1973.[6] The heaviest bombing occurred in the central region of the country in Quang Tri province, and the infrastructure of this region was virtually destroyed: of 3,500 villages in the region, only 11 were left untouched by bombing. Despite the enormous humanitarian and economic losses, however, Miguel and Roland find that by 2002—about 30 years after the war—poverty rates, consumption levels, literacy, and population density in this region look much like those in other areas of Vietnam that were not bombed.

These studies should in no way be read as an argument that minimizes the costs of war. And as long as war and the threat of war persist, the negative economic consequences appear to be large. However, the research suggests that economies (and people) are surprisingly robust. Once wars are completely ended, economies can at least sometimes recover from massive destruction over the course of a single generation.

Can you relate these studies to what you've learned in the Solow model? As a hint, imagine that a war destroys half of an economy's capital stock. What happens in the long run?

5.9 The Principle of Transition Dynamics

The experiments we have just conducted with the Solow model suggest yet another possible explanation for differences in growth rates across countries. Notice that if an economy is "below" its steady state—in the sense that $K_t < K^*$—it grows rapidly. On the other hand, if it is "above" its steady state, its growth rate is negative. Perhaps, then, differences in growth rates reflect how near or far countries are from their steady states. That's where we are headed in this section.

Take a look back at Figures 5.5(b) and 5.7(b), showing how output evolves over time. In these graphs, output is drawn on a ratio scale. This means that the growth rate of output can be inferred from the slope of the output path (see Chapter 3 for an explanation of the ratio scale). In Figure 5.5, immediately following the change in the investment rate, output grows rapidly, and then gradually declines as the economy approaches its new steady state. Similarly, when the depreciation rate increases in Figure 5.7, the growth rate is initially a large negative number. Once again, though, as the economy approaches its steady state, the growth rate moves smoothly back to zero.

[6] Edward Miguel and Gérard Roland, "The Long Run Impact of Bombing Vietnam," NBER Working Paper No. 11954, January 2006.

These patterns apply more generally. The overall result is important enough that we give it a name, **the principle of transition dynamics**: the farther below its steady state an economy is (in percentage terms), the faster the economy will grow; similarly, the farther above its steady state, the slower it will grow.[7]

Consider two economies, one just a little below its steady state, say 5 percent below, and another far below its steady state, say 50 percent. The principle of transition dynamics says that not only will both economies grow, but the economy that is 50 percent below will grow faster.

One of the most important traits of the principle of transition dynamics is that it gives us a coherent way of understanding why countries may grow at different rates—why China is growing rapidly, for example, while Argentina is growing slowly. We now look at this phenomenon in more detail.

Understanding Differences in Growth Rates

With the principle of transition dynamics in mind, let's take a look at the evidence on growth rates across countries. Figure 5.8 plots the growth rate of per capita GDP between 1960 and 2007 for 24 countries belonging to the Organization for Economic Cooperation and Development (OECD). This group is made up of relatively rich countries, mostly from Western Europe, but also includes Australia, Japan, New Zealand, and the United States. The x-axis shows the level of per capita GDP in these countries in 1960.

We can see quite a remarkable regularity in the figure. Countries that were relatively poor in 1960, including Japan, Ireland, Portugal, and Spain, grew quickly. In contrast, countries that were relatively rich in 1960—including New Zealand, Switzerland, and the United States—were among the slowest-growing countries in the OECD.

How do we understand these facts? The principle of transition dynamics suggests a possible explanation. Suppose all the countries of the OECD will have

---

7 If you are interested in the mathematics behind this principle, consider dividing the capital accumulation equation (5.5) by K_t:

$$\frac{\Delta K_{t+1}}{K_t} = \bar{s}\frac{Y_t}{K_t} - \bar{d}.$$

Next, note that from equation (5.11) the depreciation rate can be written as a function of the steady-state capital-output ratio as $\bar{d} = \bar{s}Y^*/K^*$, yielding

$$\frac{\Delta K_{t+1}}{K_t} = \bar{s} \times \left(\frac{Y_t}{K_t} - \frac{Y^*}{K^*}\right).$$

We can multiply and divide the right side by Y^*/K^* to get

$$\frac{\Delta K_{t+1}}{K_t} = \bar{s}\frac{Y^*}{K^*} \times \left(\frac{Y_t/K_t}{Y^*/K^*} - 1\right).$$

Finally, substitute in from the production function in equation (5.6) to see that

$$\frac{\Delta K_{t+1}}{K_t} = \bar{s}\frac{Y^*}{K^*} \times \left(\frac{K^{*2/3}}{K_t^{2/3}} - 1\right).$$

This equation gives us one version of the principle of transition dynamics: if $K_t < K^*$, the capital stock grows, and the growth rate is higher the greater the distance below the steady state.

Among OECD countries, those that were poor in 1960 grew the fastest, and those that were rich in 1960 grew the slowest.

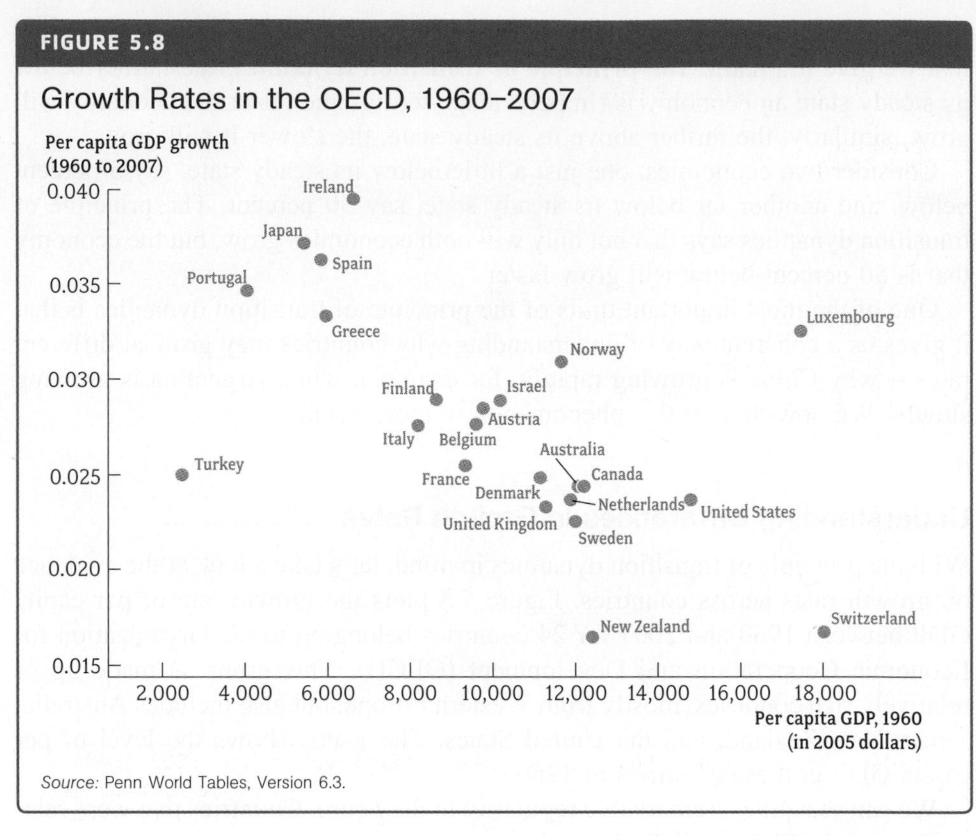

FIGURE 5.8

Growth Rates in the OECD, 1960–2007

Source: Penn World Tables, Version 6.3.

similar incomes in the long run. In this case, countries that are poor in 1960 would be far below their steady state, while countries that are rich would be closer to (or even above) their steady state. The principle of transition dynamics predicts that the poorest countries should grow quickly while the richest should grow slowly. This is exactly what the negative slope of the countries in Figure 5.8 shows.

Figure 5.9 moves beyond the OECD to consider growth rates for the world as a whole. Here, the picture is very different: there is essentially no correlation between how rich a country is and how fast it grows. The fact that, on average, rich and poor countries grow at the same rate suggests that *most countries—both rich and poor—have already reached their steady states.* Most poor countries are not poor because they received a bad shock and have fallen below their steady state; if this were the case, we would expect them to grow faster than rich countries—as relatively poor OECD countries did, for example, in Figure 5.8. Instead, the poor countries of the world are typically poor because, according to the Solow model, the determinants of their steady states—investment rates and total factor productivity levels—are substantially lower than in rich countries. Without some change in these determinants, we can't expect most poor countries to grow rapidly.

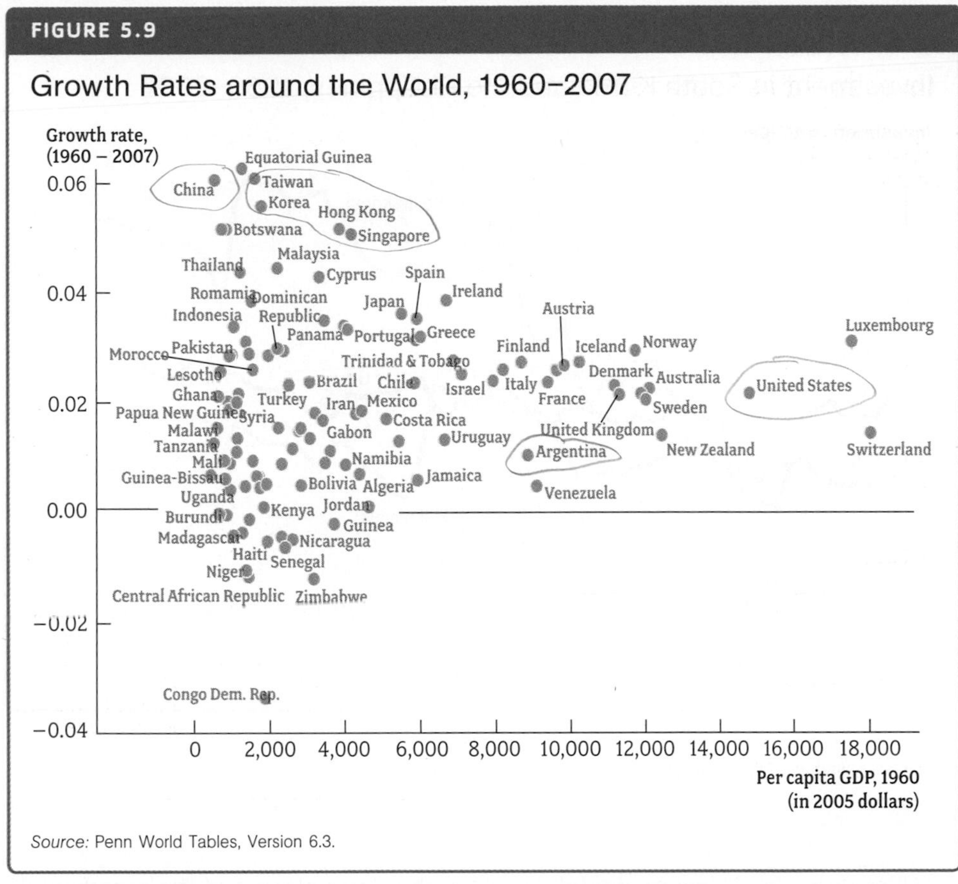

FIGURE 5.9

Growth Rates around the World, 1960–2007

Source: Penn World Tables, Version 6.3.

For the world as a whole, growth rates are largely unrelated to initial per capita GDP. This suggests that most poor countries are poor because of a low steady state income, not because some shock has pushed them below their steady state.

CASE STUDY

South Korea and the Philippines

We began this chapter by asking: Why has South Korea grown so much faster (6 percent per year) than the Philippines (1.7 percent per year) in the last half century? We can now apply the principle of transition dynamics to suggest an answer. Perhaps starting in the 1960s, changes in the investment rate and productivity took place in Korea that moved the country's steady-state income to a much higher level. Starting from around 15 percent of U.S. income in 1960, maybe Korea's steady-state level moved up to 50 or 75 percent while the Philippines' level remained at 15 percent. This scenario means that Korea in 1960 would have been far below its steady state, so we would expect its economy to grow quickly. And the Philippines, in contrast, would have been roughly at its steady state, and we would expect that economy to grow at about the same rate as the United States, preserving its ratio of 15 percent.

The investment rate in South Korea rose sharply between 1960 and 1990, while it remained relatively stable in the United States and the Philippines.

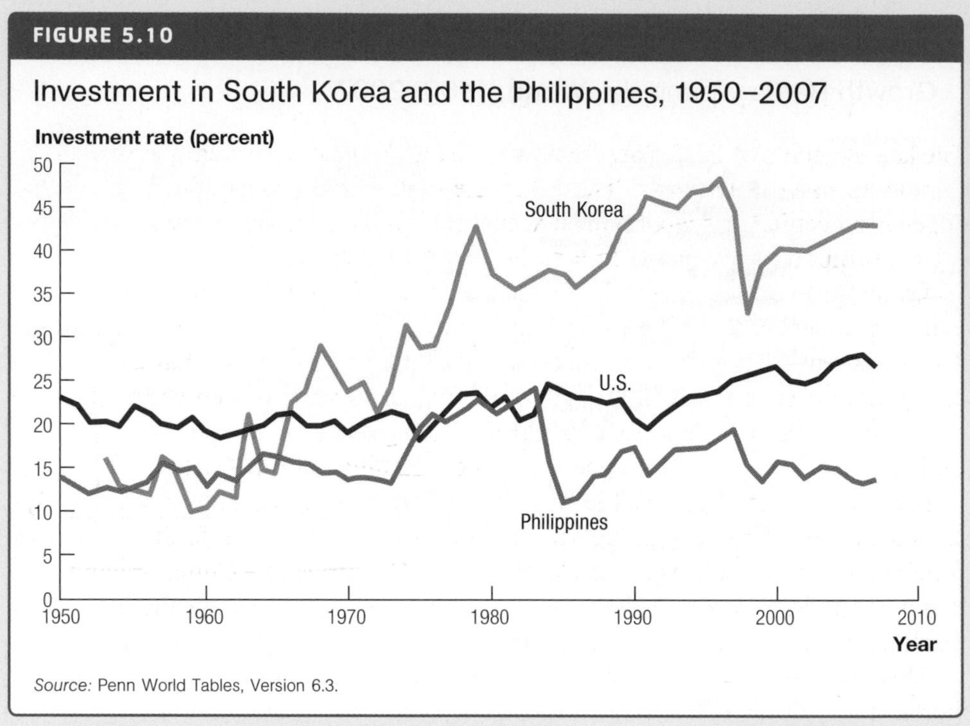

Source: Penn World Tables, Version 6.3.

What does the Solow model tell us about the determinants of the steady-state ratio of income in South Korea to income in the United States? Assuming these economies have the same rate of depreciation, the ratio of their steady-state incomes is given by

$$\frac{y^*_{\text{Korea}}}{y^*_{\text{US}}} = \left(\frac{\bar{A}_{\text{Korea}}}{\bar{A}_{\text{US}}}\right)^{3/2} \times \left(\frac{\bar{s}_{\text{Korea}}}{\bar{s}_{\text{US}}}\right)^{1/2} \tag{5.13}$$

That is, the long-run ratio of per capita incomes depends on the ratio of productivities (TFP levels) and the ratio of investment rates.

Figure 5.10 shows the investment rates in the United States, South Korea, and the Philippines over the last 50 years. While the U.S. rate is relatively stable, the rate in Korea rises dramatically, from about 12 percent in the 1950s to more than 40 percent in the early 1990s. According to the Solow model, this rise should significantly increase Korea's steady-state income. The principle of transition dynamics then tells us that the Korean economy will grow rapidly as it makes the transition to its new, higher level. In contrast, the relatively stable investment rate in the Philippines suggests that the steady state in this economy is not changing, and the principle of transition dynamics then implies that the Philippines will not grow rapidly over this period.

5.10 Strengths and Weaknesses of the Solow Model

The key elements of the Solow framework lie at the heart of virtually every model in modern macroeconomics. These key elements are a production function that depends on capital and labor and an accumulation equation that shows how forgoing consumption today leads to a higher capital stock tomorrow.

There are two main strengths of the Solow model. First, it provides a theory that determines how rich a country is in the long run—that is, in the steady state. As we saw in equation (5.9), countries will be rich to the extent that they have a high rate of investment, a high TFP level, and a low rate of depreciation. If we extended the Solow model, we might add a high rate of investment in human capital—including education and on-the-job training—to this list.

Second, through the principle of transition dynamics, the Solow model helps us understand differences in growth rates across countries. The farther a country is below its steady state, the faster it will grow. Countries like China, Ireland, and South Korea have grown rapidly between 1960 and 2007 because the key determinants of their steady-state income (investment rates, TFP levels) have risen.

Along with these strengths, though, come three basic shortcomings of the Solow model. First, the main mechanism studied in the model is investment in physical capital, but our quantitative analysis showed that differences in investment rates explain only a small fraction of the differences in income across countries. Instead, TFP differences—which remain something of a mystery—are even more important here in explaining income differences than they were in the production model.

Second, why is it that countries have different productivity levels and different investment rates? If one of the key reasons for increased growth is a rise in the investment rate, the Solow model doesn't explain why, for example, the investment rate rose in South Korea but not in the Philippines. On this question, the economics literature provides some insight. Economists extending the Solow model have endogenized the investment rate—that is, they have made $\bar{s}$ an endogenous variable. In these models, the long-run investment rate depends on how patient people are and on the taxes and subsidies that a government levies on investment, among other things; we will study the determinants of investment in more detail in Chapter 16. It is possible, then, that the Korean government removed substantial barriers to investment, while the Philippines maintained these barriers. Such a story may go part of the way toward understanding the Korean growth miracle.[8]

The final and perhaps most important shortcoming of the Solow model is that it does not provide a theory of long-run growth. We might have thought that the mechanism by which saving leads to investment in computers, factories, and machine tools could serve as an engine of long-run growth. However, what we have seen in this chapter is that the diminishing returns to capital accumulation

[8] As you might anticipate given the significant role of TFP in explaining differences in income across countries, increases in TFP also play a key role in understanding the Korean growth miracle. But explaining why TFP would rise is something the Solow model is not equipped to do.

in the production function mean that capital accumulation by itself cannot sustain growth. As an economy accumulates capital, the marginal product of capital declines. Each additional unit of capital produces a smaller and smaller gain in output, so that eventually the additional output produced by investment is only just enough to offset the wear and tear associated with depreciation. At this point, growth stops in the Solow model.

Since the Solow growth model leaves long-run growth unexplained, what does account for the sustained rise in living standards in much of the world over the last two centuries? The next chapter will address this question head-on.

CHAPTER REVIEW

SUMMARY

1. The starting point for the Solow model is the production model of Chapter 4. To that framework, the Solow model adds a theory of capital accumulation. That is, it makes the capital stock an endogenous variable.
2. The capital stock is the sum of past investments. The capital stock today consists of machines and buildings that were bought over the last several decades.
3. The goal of the Solow model is to deepen our understanding of economic growth, but in this it's only partially successful. The fact that capital runs into diminishing returns means that the model does not lead to sustained economic growth. As the economy accumulates more capital, depreciation rises one-for-one, but output and therefore investment rise less than one-for-one because of the diminishing marginal product of capital. Eventually, the new investment is only just sufficient to offset depreciation, and the capital stock ceases to grow. Output stops growing as well, and the economy settles down to a steady state.
4. There are two major accomplishments of the Solow model. First, it provides a successful theory of the determination of capital, by predicting that the capital-output ratio is equal to the investment-depreciation ratio. Countries with high investment rates should thus have high capital-output ratios, and this prediction holds up well in the data.
5. The second major accomplishment of the Solow model is the principle of transition dynamics, which states that the farther below its steady state an economy is, the faster it will grow. While the model cannot explain long-run growth, the principle of transition dynamics provides a nice theory of differences in growth rates across countries. Increases in the investment rate or total factor productivity can increase a country's steady-state position and therefore increase growth, at least for a number of years. These changes can be analyzed with the help of the Solow diagram.

6. In general, most poor countries have low TFP levels and low investment rates, the two key determinants of steady-state incomes. If a country maintained good fundamentals but was poor because it had received a bad shock, we would see it grow rapidly, according to the principle of transition dynamics.

KEY CONCEPTS

- the capital accumulation equation
- depreciation
- diminishing returns
- net investment
- real interest rate
- resource constraint
- saving
- the principle of transition dynamics
- the Solow diagram
- the Solow growth model
- steady state
- stocks versus flows
- transition dynamics

REVIEW QUESTIONS

1. What is the mechanism in the Solow model that generates growth? Why is this an appealing mechanism? Why does it fail to deliver economic growth in the long run?
2. Add another line, period 6, to Table 5.1. What are the values of K_6, I_6, $\bar{d}K_6$, and ΔK_6?
3. What is the economic meaning of the vertical gap between the investment curve and the depreciation curve in the Solow diagram?
4. What is the solution of the Solow model for consumption per person in the steady state, $c^* \equiv C^*/L^*$? How does each parameter in the solution affect c^*, and why?
5. The Solow model implies that differences in total factor productivity are even more important in explaining differences in income across countries than the production model of Chapter 4 suggested. Why?
6. What determines whether a curve shifts in the Solow diagram? Make a list of the parameters of the Solow model, and state whether a change in each parameter shifts a curve (which one?) or is simply a movement along both curves.
7. What is the principle of transition dynamics? Why does the Solow model lead to this principle, and why is it useful?

EXERCISES

smartwork.wwnorton.com 

1. **A decrease in the investment rate:** Suppose a country enacts a tax policy that discourages investment: suppose the policy reduces the investment rate immediately and permanently from $\bar{s}$ to $\bar{s}'$. Assuming the economy starts in its initial steady state, use the Solow model to explain what happens to the economy over time and in the long run. Draw a graph showing how output evolves over time (put Y_t on the vertical axis with a ratio scale, and time on the horizontal axis), and explain what happens to economic growth over time.

2. **An increase in total factor productivity:** Suppose the level of TFP in an economy rises permanently from $\bar{A}$ to $\bar{A}'$.
   - **(a)** Assuming the economy starts in its initial steady state, use the Solow model to explain what happens to the economy over time and in the long run.
   - **(b)** Draw a graph showing how output evolves over time, and explain what happens to the level and growth rate of per capita income.
   - **(c)** Suppose that $\bar{A}$ grew at a constant rate, instead of being constant. Explain in words what you think would happen to GDP over time.
   - **(d)** How is the response of the economy to an increase in TFP different from the economy's response to an increase in the investment rate? (*Hint*: Think about what happens to consumption.)

3. **An earthquake:** Consider a Solow economy that begins in steady state. Then a strong earthquake destroys half the capital stock. Use a Solow diagram to explain how the economy behaves over time. Draw a graph showing how output evolves over time, and explain what happens to the level and growth rate of per capita GDP. (*Hint*: Pay close attention to footnote 4 on page 117—does any curve shift?)

4. **An increase in the labor force:** Consider a one-time change in government policy that immediately and permanently increases the level of the labor force in an economy (such as a more generous immigration policy). In particular, suppose it rises permanently from $\bar{L}$ to $\bar{L}'$. Assuming the economy starts in its initial steady state, use the Solow model to explain what happens to the economy over time and in the long run. In particular, comment on what happens to the level and growth rate of per capita GDP.

5. **Foreign aid:** Consider a Solow economy that begins with a capital stock equal to \$300 billion, and suppose its steady-state level of capital is \$500 billion. To its pleasant surprise, the economy receives a generous gift of foreign aid in the form of \$100 billion worth of capital (electric power plants, machine tools, etc.).
   - **(a)** Use the Solow diagram, other graphs, and the mathematics of the Solow model to explain what happens to the economy, both immediately and over time. By what proportion does consumption per person initially increase? What happens to consumption in the long run?
   - **(b)** Suppose instead of starting below its steady state, the economy begins in steady state, with a capital stock equal to \$500 billion. Answer part (a) for this case.
   - **(c)** Summarize what this exercise teaches you about the possible consequences of foreign aid. In this example, does foreign aid exert a long-run effect on the welfare of poor countries? What is the benefit of foreign aid?

6. Predicting steady states and growth rates: Consider the data in this table.

Country	Per capita GDP, 2000	Investment Rate $\bar{s}$ (%)	TFP $\bar{A}$
United States	1.000	24.5	1.000
Ireland	0.971	31.5	0.995
France	0.691	25.9	0.744
Japan	0.713	36.1	0.676
South Korea	0.556	43.9	0.606
Spain	0.733	31.4	0.757
Argentina	0.356	18.0	0.559
Mexico	0.261	23.5	0.418
China	0.183	28.8	0.365
India	0.089	16.5	0.253
Zimbabwe	0.044	17.6	0.115
Uganda	0.027	4.2	0.173

(You may find it easier to answer these questions using a spreadsheet program.)

(a) Assuming no differences in TFP (ignore the last column) or the rate of depreciation across countries, use the data in the table to predict the ratio of per capita GDP in each country relative to that in the United States in steady state.

(b) Now do the same exercise assuming TFP is given by the levels in the last column. Discuss briefly the differences you find in these two approaches.

(c) Based on the numbers you find with the TFP differences, compute the percentage gap between the steady-state income ratio and the ratio in 2007 (as shown in the table). Use the actual 2007 ratio in the denominator.

(d) Apply the principle of transition dynamics to rank the countries in order of expected growth rate over the coming decades, from fastest to slowest.

7. Per capita GDP in the long run: Suppose an economy begins in steady state. By what proportion does per capita GDP change in the long run in response to each of the following changes?

(a) The investment rate doubles.

(b) The depreciation rate falls by 10%.

(c) The productivity level rises by 10%.

(d) An earthquake destroys 75% of the capital stock.

(e) A more generous immigration policy leads the population to double.

8. Growth rates in the Solow model (I):

(a) Use the production function in equation (5.6) and the rules for computing growth rates from page 49 of Chapter 3 to write the growth rate of per capita GDP as a function of the growth rate of the capital stock. (*Hint*: Because the labor force is constant, the growth rates of GDP and per capita GDP are the same.)

(b) Combine this result with the last equation in footnote 7 (section 5.9) to get a solution for the growth rate of per capita GDP as a function of the current level of capital K_t. Be sure to write your answer in terms of K_t and parameters of the model only. For example, use the fact that $\bar{s}Y^*/K^* = \bar{d}$.

9. Growth rates in the Solow model (II): Suppose an economy begins in steady state and is characterized by the following parameter values: $\bar{s} = .2$, $\bar{d} = .1$, $\bar{A} = 1$, $\bar{L} = 100$. Apply your answer to question 8 to calculate the growth of per capita GDP in the period immediately following each of the changes listed below. (*Hint*: Since the economy begins in steady state, its growth rate is initially zero and $K_t = K^*$.)

(a) The investment rate doubles.
(b) The productivity level rises by 10%.
(c) An earthquake destroys 75% of the capital stock.
(d) A more generous immigration policy leads the population to double.

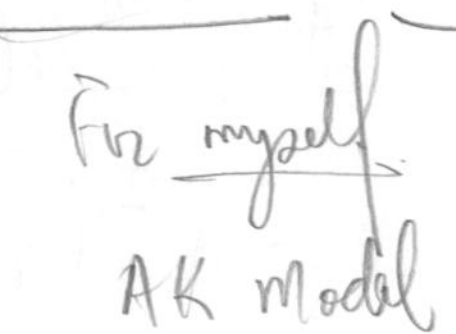

10. What happens with no diminishing returns? Consider a Solow model where the production function no longer exhibits diminishing returns to capital accumulation. This is not particularly realistic, for reasons discussed in Chapter 4. But it is interesting to consider this case nonetheless because of what it tells us about the workings of the Solow model. Assume the production function is now $Y_t = \bar{A}K_t$. The rest of the model is unchanged.

(a) Draw the Solow diagram in this case.
(b) Suppose the economy begins with capital $\bar{K}_0$, and show how the economy evolves over time in the Solow model.
(c) What happens to the growth rate of per capita GDP over time?

WORKED EXERCISES

3. An earthquake:

The key to this exercise is recognizing that an earthquake that reduces the capital stock creates a *movement along the curves* in the Solow diagram, rather than shifting the curves. Recall that the Solow diagram shows investment and depreciation at each level of capital that could exist in the economy. Since we are just changing the capital stock, we move down the *x*-axis of the graph and read off the investment and depreciation that prevail in the economy.

As shown in Figure 5.11, the economy begins in steady state, with capital equal to K^*. After the earthquake, the economy's capital drops to half, and the economy jumps down to $K^*/2$ (illustrated by the long left arrow). At this level of capital, investment exceeds depreciation. The economy is now below its steady state, and the principle of transition dynamics takes over. Capital accumulates, and the economy grows until it returns once again to the original steady-state level.

FIGURE 5.11

The Solow Diagram

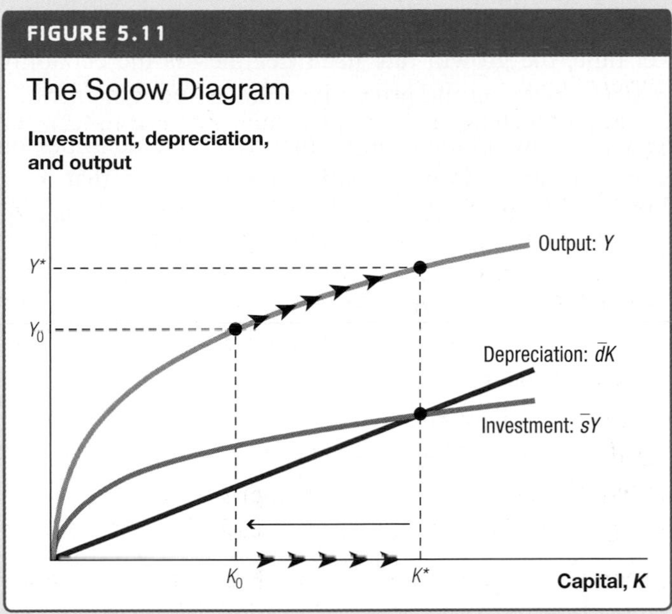

It is important to notice that since there has been no change in the investment rate, the productivity parameter, or the depreciation rate, there is no change in the steady-state level of capital. Therefore the economy just returns to where it began.

The dynamics of output can be read from the production function in the Solow diagram. Figure 5.12 shows this level of output over time, assuming the shock occurs in the year 2020. Output jumps down immediately because

FIGURE 5.12

Output over Time, 2000–2100

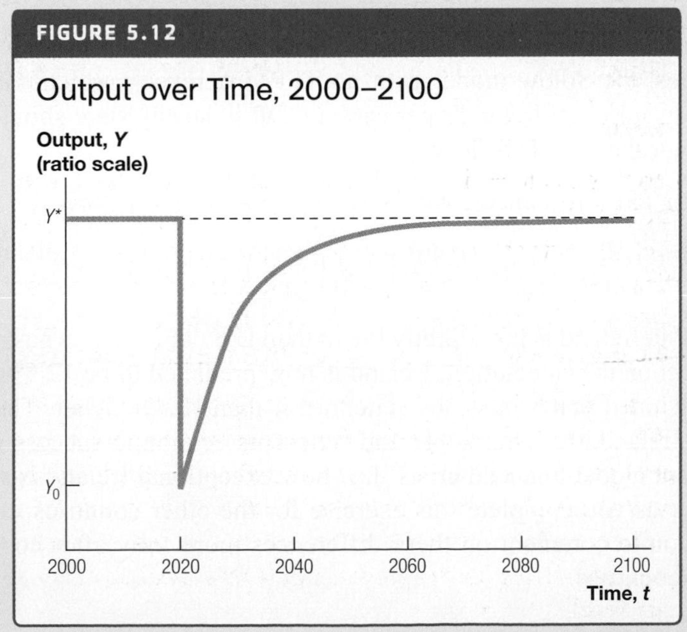

of the decline in capital. The economy then begins to grow to return to steady state. Over time, the growth rate itself declines as the economy approaches its steady state—obeying the principle of transition dynamics.

An interesting follow-up question is this: by how much does output decline when the capital stock drops in half? The answer is that $Y_0 = (1/2)^{1/3} \times Y^* \approx 0.79 \times Y^*$, so that output falls by just over 20%. What is the intuition for why a 50% decline in capital leads to only a 20% decline in output?

6. **Predicting steady states and growth rates:** The answer is given here for Ireland only.

(a) This first question asks us to calculate the steady-state ratio of per capita GDP between Ireland and the United States assuming no differences in TFP or depreciation. The key equation for this entire exercise is equation (5.9), reproduced here:

$$y^* \equiv \frac{Y^*}{L^*} = \bar{A}^{3/2}\left(\frac{\bar{s}}{\bar{d}}\right)^{1/2}.$$

The ratio of steady-state per capita GDP between the United States and Ireland is given by:

$$\frac{y_{\text{I}}^*}{y_{\text{US}}^*} = \left(\frac{\bar{A}_{\text{I}}}{\bar{A}_{\text{US}}}\right)^{3/2} \times \left(\frac{\bar{s}_{\text{I}}}{\bar{s}_{\text{US}}}\right)^{1/2}.$$

Notice that we keep the TFP term ($\bar{A}$) in this equation since it will be useful in part (b); the depreciation rates are the same, so they cancel out.

With no differences in TFP, the ratio of per capita GDP is given by the square root of the ratio of investment rates:

$$\frac{y_{\text{I}}^*}{y_{\text{US}}^*} = \left(\frac{31.5}{24.5}\right)^{1/2} = 1.134.$$

Because Ireland actually has a higher investment rate than the United States, the Solow model with no TFP difference predicts that it should be even richer: Ireland's per capita GDP in steady state should be 13.4% higher than the U.S. level.

(b) With TFP differences, we apply the same formula. Now the answer is

$$\frac{y_{\text{I}}^*}{y_{\text{US}}^*} = \left(\frac{0.995}{1.0}\right)^{3/2} \times \left(\frac{31.5}{24.5}\right)^{1/2} = 1.125.$$

TFP in Ireland is just slightly lower than U.S. TFP, so this has only a small effect on the calculation. Ireland is now predicted to be 12.5% richer than the United States in steady state, rather than 13.4% richer. These findings for Ireland are remarkable and reflect its economic success prior to the recent global financial crisis. Just how exceptional Ireland is will become clear as you complete this exercise for the other countries. It will be up to you to comment on these differences more fully after considering all the countries.

(c) Ireland's current income ratio (as of 2007) is 97.1%. Allowing for TFP differences, part (b) told us that in steady state, Ireland would be at 112.5%. So the gap between its current position and its steady-state position is

$$\frac{112.5 - 97.1}{97.1} = 15.9\%.$$

According to these calculations, Ireland is substantially below its steady-state position.

(d) Because Ireland's gap is so large—because it is well below its steady state—the principle of transition dynamics predicts that it should grow rapidly in coming decades. How does this growth compare with the other countries?

CHAPTER 6

GROWTH AND IDEAS

OVERVIEW

In this chapter, we learn

- why new ideas—new ways of using existing resources—are the key to sustained long-run growth.
- why "nonrivalry" makes ideas different from other economic goods in a crucial way.
- how the economics of ideas involves increasing returns and leads to problems with Adam Smith's invisible hand.
- a new model of economic growth: the Romer model.
- how to combine the Romer and Solow models to get a full theory of long-run economic performance.

Every generation has perceived the limits to growth that finite resources and undesirable side effects would pose if no new recipes or ideas were discovered. And every generation has underestimated the potential for finding new recipes and ideas. We consistently fail to grasp how many ideas remain to be discovered.

—PAUL ROMER

6.1 Introduction

As we have seen, all models abstract from features of the world in order to highlight a few crucial economic concepts. The Solow model, for example, draws a sharp distinction between capital and labor and focuses on capital accumulation as a possible engine of economic growth. What we saw in Chapter 5 is that this model leads to valuable insights but ultimately fails to provide a theory of sustained growth.

In a famous paper published in 1990, Paul Romer suggested an even more fundamental distinction by dividing the world of economic goods into objects and ideas.[1] **Objects** include most goods we are familiar with: land, cell phones, oil, jet planes, computers, pencils, and paper, as well as capital and labor from the Solow model. **Ideas**, on the other hand, are instructions, or recipes. Ideas include designs for *making* objects. For example, sand (silicon dioxide) has always been of value to beachgoers, kids with shovels, and glassblowers. But with the discovery around 1960 of the recipe for converting sand into computer chips, a new and especially productive use for sand was created. Other ideas include the design of a cell phone or jet engine, the manufacturing technique for turning petroleum into plastic, and the set of instructions for changing trees into paper.

Ideas need not be confined to feats of engineering, however. The management techniques that make Wal-Mart the largest private employer in the United States are ideas. So are the just-in-time inventory methods of Japanese automakers and the quadratic formula of algebra.

The division of economic goods into objects and ideas leads to the modern theory of economic growth. This theory turns out to have wide-ranging implications for many areas of economics, including intellectual property, antitrust policies, international trade, and economic development. Romer's "idea about ideas" is one of the most important contributions of economics during the last two decades of the twentieth century.

In the first part of this chapter, we get an overview of the economics of ideas, and develop a number of key insights in the process. Next, we construct a simple

Epigraph: From "Economic Growth," *The Concise Encyclopedia of Economics*, David R. Henderson, ed. (Indianapolis: Liberty Fund, 2008).

[1] Romer's original paper is a classic, although the mathematics after the first several pages is challenging: Paul M. Romer, "Endogenous Technological Change," *Journal of Political Economy*, vol. 98 (October 1990), pp. S71–S102.

model of idea-based economic growth that exploits these insights. Finally, we learn how this model can be combined with the Solow model to generate a rich theory of long-run economic performance.

6.2 The Economics of Ideas

The economics of objects, which has been studied for centuries, forms the basis of Adam Smith's invisible-hand theorem: that perfectly competitive markets lead to the best of all possible worlds. The economics of ideas turns out to be different, as we will see, and the differences are what make sustained economic growth possible.[2]

As a guide to our discussion, consider the following **idea diagram**:

ideas → nonrivalry → increasing returns → problems with pure competition

We will consider each element in this diagram in turn.

Ideas

One way of viewing the distinction between objects and ideas is to consider objects as the raw materials of the universe—atoms of carbon, oxygen, silicon, iron, and so on—and ideas as instructions for using these atoms in different ways. Depending on the instructions, these raw materials can yield a diamond, a computer chip, a powerful new antibiotic, or the manuscript for Einstein's theory of relativity. New ideas are new ways of arranging raw materials in ways that are economically useful.

How many potential ideas are there? Suppose we limit ourselves to instructions that can be written in a single paragraph of 100 words or less, about the length of the abstract to most scientific papers. The English language contains more than 20,000 words. How many different idea paragraphs can we create? The answer is $(20{,}000)^{100}$, which is larger than 10^{430}, or a 1 followed by 430 zeros. Although most of these word combinations will be complete gibberish, some will describe the fundamental theorem of calculus, Charles Darwin's theory of evolution, Louis Pasteur's germ theory of disease, the chemical formula for penicillin, the double helix structure of DNA, and perhaps even a warp drive to power spaceships in the future. To put this huge number into context, suppose only 1 in 10^{100} of these paragraphs contains a coherent idea. That would still leave 10^{330} possible paragraphs, which is gazillions of times larger than the number of particles in the known universe.[3]

---

[2] While Paul Romer took the most important step in developing idea-based growth theory, many other researchers also share credit. In the 1960s, Kenneth Arrow, Zvi Griliches, Dale Jorgenson, William Nordhaus, Edmund Phelps, Karl Shell, Hirofumi Uzawa, and others made substantial progress. Important advances following Romer's work have been made by Philippe Aghion, Robert Barro, Gene Grossman, Elhanan Helpman, Peter Howitt, Robert Lucas, and Martin Weitzman, among others.

[3] Scientists estimate that there are on the order of 4×10^{77} particles in the universe.

The amount of raw material in the universe—the sand, oil, atoms of carbon, oxygen, and so on—is finite. But the number of ways of arranging these raw materials is so large as to be virtually infinite. Economic growth occurs as we discover better and better ways to use the finite resources available to us. In other words, sustained economic growth occurs because we discover new ideas.

Nonrivalry

Objects like cell phones, chalkboards, and professors are **rivalrous**: that is, one person's use of a particular object reduces its inherent usefulness to someone else. If you are talking on your cell phone, I can't use it. If the economics professor is writing on a particular chalkboard at a particular time, the mathematicians can't write on it simultaneously. Most goods in economics are rivalrous objects, and it is this characteristic that gives rise to scarcity, the central subject of economics.

The notion that objects are rivalrous is so natural that it barely needs explaining. However, it comes into sharp relief when compared with the fact that ideas are **nonrivalrous**. My use of an idea doesn't inherently reduce the "amount" of the idea available for you. The quadratic formula is not itself scarce, and the fact that I am relying on the formula to solve an equation doesn't make it any less available for you to do the same. Opera companies around the world can perform Mozart's *Magic Flute* simultaneously: once the opera has been composed, one company's performance doesn't make the composition itself more scarce in any sense.

Because nonrivalry may be a new concept, let's go through an example carefully. Consider the difference between the design of a computer and the computer itself. The computer is certainly rivalrous: if you are using particular CPU (central processing unit) cycles to browse your favorite Web site, those cycles can't be used by me to listen to my favorite song or by your friend Joe to estimate an econometric model of stock prices. Your use of the computer reduces the potential benefit to Joe and me from using that same computer.

The design for the computer is different, however. Suppose there's a factory in Taiwan that follows a particular design for producing a computer. The factory includes 27 assembly lines running full time, with each assembly line working from the same design. We don't need to invent a new design for each assembly line, and if we want to add another assembly line, that line just follows the same set of instructions. The design for the computer does not have to be reinvented for each production line. As an idea, the design is nonrivalrous: it can be used by any number of people without reducing its inherent usefulness.[4]

We should be careful with the concept of scarcity. New ideas surely are scarce: it would always be nice to have faster computers or better batteries or improved medical treatments. But *existing* ideas are not inherently scarce themselves. Once an idea has been introduced, it can be employed by an arbitrary number of people without anyone's use being degraded.

We should also distinguish between nonrivalry and "excludability." **Excludability** refers to the extent to which someone has property rights over a good—possibly

[4] If each assembly line requires its own physical set of blueprints, that's fine. The blueprints from another line can be photocopied. The paper they are printed on is a rivalrous object, but the design itself is the idea and nonrivalrous.

an idea—and is legally allowed to restrict the use of that good. Nonrivalry simply says that it is feasible for ideas to be used by numerous people simultaneously. As we will see shortly, societies often grant intellectual property rights that restrict the use of ideas. But this doesn't change the fact that the ideas themselves are nonrivalrous.

Increasing Returns

The fact that particular designs and instructions are not scarce in the same way that objects are scarce is the first clue that the economics of ideas is different from the economics of objects. This becomes clear in the idea diagram's next link, **increasing returns**.

Consider the production of a new antibiotic. Coming up with the precise chemical formula and manufacturing technique is the hard part. Indeed, current estimates suggest that the average cost of developing a new drug is on the order of $800 million.[5] Once the antibiotic has been developed, though, it is reasonable to think of a standard constant-returns-to-scale production function. After all, doses of the antibiotic are just some *object*, and we have already considered the production of objects in the previous two chapters.

Suppose a factory with a given workforce and given raw materials for inputs can produce 100 doses of the antibiotic per day. If we wish to double the daily production of the antibiotic, we can simply build an identical factory, employ an identical collection of workers, and buy the same quantity of raw materials. Doubling all these inputs will exactly double production. This is the *standard replication argument*, as we learned in Chapter 4. If each of the first 100 doses costs $10 to produce, then each of the second 100 doses will also cost $10.

But now consider the entire chain of production, starting from the invention of the antibiotic. The first $800 million goes to conduct the necessary research to create the instructions for making the antibiotic, producing no actual doses of the drug. To get one dose, we spend $800 million for the design plus $10 in manufacturing costs. After that, if we spend another $800 million, we produce 80 million doses. Doubling inputs leads to much more than a doubling of outputs. Therefore, the production function is characterized by *increasing* returns to scale, once we include the fixed cost of creating the drug in the first place.

Figure 6.1 illustrates this example graphically. Panel (a) shows the constant-returns-to-scale production function for producing the antibiotic once the formula has been created. For each $10 spent, one dose of the drug is produced. Letting X denote the amount of money spent producing the antibiotic, average production per dollar spent, Y/X, is constant; it doesn't vary with the scale of production. Doubling the inputs exactly doubles the output.[6]

[5] For an interesting discussion of this number, see the recent review by John P. Moore of Merrill Goozner's book *The $800 Million Pill: The Truth behind the Cost of New Drugs*, in the *Journal of Clinical Investigation*, vol. 114 (2004), p. 1182.

[6] To be strictly correct, we should specify the production function in terms of the actual labor and raw materials that are needed to produce the antibiotic, rather than in terms of dollars.

FIGURE 6.1

How a Fixed Cost Leads to Increasing Returns: The Antibiotic Example

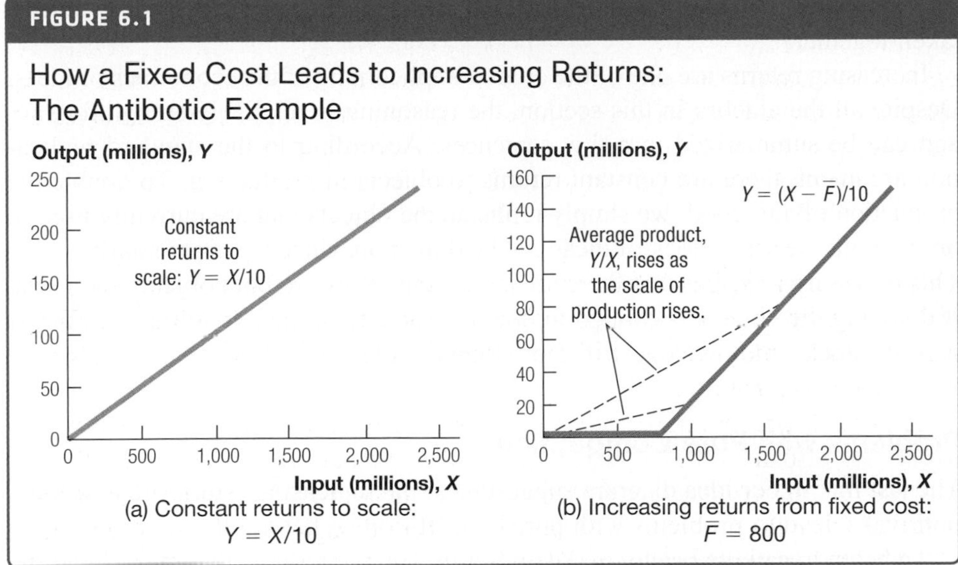

(a) Constant returns to scale: $Y = X/10$

(b) Increasing returns from fixed cost: $\bar{F} = 800$

Panel (a) shows a constant-returns-to-scale production function, $Y = X/10$; the average product Y/X is constant. Panel (b) shows the same production function, but this time with an additional fixed cost $\bar{F}$ of \$800 million that must be paid before production can occur. This leads to increasing returns to scale. The average product of the input, Y/X, now increases as the scale of production rises.

Panel (b) shows this same production formula, but now including the fixed cost of $\bar{F}$ = \$800 million that must be paid before any of the antibiotic can be produced. The production function including this fixed cost is $Y = (X - \bar{F})/10$, once X is larger than $\bar{F}$. In this case, the average production per dollar spent, Y/X, is increasing as the scale of production rises. We can also note this in an equation: $Y/X = (1 - \bar{F}/X)/10$, which increases as X gets larger.

If we want to be more precise, we can return to our standard production function. Suppose output Y is produced using capital K and labor L. But suppose there is also another input called "knowledge," or the stock of ideas. Denote this stock of ideas by A. As in previous chapters, let our production function be

$$Y_t = F(K_t, L_t, A_t) = A_t K_t^{1/3} L_t^{2/3}. \tag{6.1}$$

The only difference between this production function and the one from Chapters 4 and 5 is that we have replaced the TFP parameter $\bar{A}$ with the stock of ideas A_t. We have given it a new name and a time subscript.

This new production function exhibits constant returns to scale in K and L. If we want to double the amount of antibiotic produced, we can just build another factory and double the amount of capital and labor. By the standard replication argument, we only need to double the "objects" involved in production. Because knowledge—the chemical formula for the antibiotic in this case—is nonrivalrous, it can be used by *both* factories we set up; we certainly don't need to reinvent the chemical formula for the new factory.

Notice what this implies about the returns to scale to all the inputs, both objects and ideas. If we double capital, labor, *and* knowledge, we will more than double the amount of output:

$$\begin{aligned} F(2K, 2L, 2A) &= 2A(2K)^{1/3}(2L)^{2/3} = 2 \cdot 2^{1/3} \cdot 2^{2/3} \cdot AK^{1/3}L^{2/3} \\ &= 4 \cdot AK^{1/3}L^{2/3} = 4 \cdot F(K, L, A). \end{aligned}$$

This production function thus exhibits increasing returns to ideas and objects taken together.

Increasing returns are one of the crucial implications of the economics of ideas. Despite all the algebra in this section, the reasoning is relatively straightforward and can be summarized in a few sentences. According to the standard replication argument, there are constant returns to objects in production. To double the production of any good, we simply replicate the objects that are currently used in production; the same stock of ideas can be drawn on, since ideas are nonrivalrous. This necessarily implies that there are increasing returns to both objects and ideas: if doubling the objects is enough to double production, then doubling the objects *and* the stock of knowledge will more than double production.

Problems with Pure Competition

The last link in our idea diagram suggests that the increasing returns generated by nonrivalry lead to problems with pure competition. What are these problems?

To begin, recall the beauty of Adam Smith's invisible-hand theorem. Under the assumption of perfect competition, markets lead to an allocation that is **Pareto optimal**: there is no way to change the allocation to make someone better off without making someone else worse off. In this sense, markets produce the best of all possible worlds.[7] Perfectly competitive markets achieve this optimal allocation by equating marginal costs and marginal benefits through a price system. Prices allocate scarce resources to their appropriate uses. And this is where the problem occurs when there are increasing returns to scale.

In our antibiotic example, what would happen if the pharmaceutical company were forced to charge a price equal to marginal cost? At first, it appears nothing goes wrong. The marginal cost of producing a dose is \$10, and if the firm sells the antibiotic at \$10, it just breaks even, leading to one of the hallmarks of perfect competition, zero profits.

But to go back one stage earlier, suppose the pharmaceutical company has not yet invented the new drug. Will it undertake the \$800 million research effort to discover the chemical formula for the new antibiotic? If it does, it sinks \$800 million, discovers the formula, and then sells the drug at marginal cost. Including the original research expenditures, the firm loses \$800 million. So *if prices are equal to marginal cost, no firm will undertake the costly research that is necessary to invent new ideas*. Pharmaceuticals must sell at a price greater than marginal cost in order to allow the producer to eventually recoup the original research expenditures.

This point is much more general than the antibiotics example. Any time new ideas are invented, there is a fixed cost to produce the new set of instructions. After that, production proceeds with constant returns to scale and therefore constant marginal cost. But in order for the innovator to be compensated for the original research that led to the new idea, there must be some wedge between price and marginal cost at some point down the line. This is true for drugs, computer

[7] A limitation of this theorem, also known as the first fundamental theorem of welfare economics, is that it says nothing about equity. For example, your owning *everything* in the economy is still Pareto optimal: we can't make me better off without making you worse off.

software, music, cars, soft drinks, and even economics textbooks. One of the main reasons new goods are invented is because of the incentives embedded in the wedge between price and marginal cost.

This wedge means that markets cannot be characterized by pure competition if we are to have innovation. This is one justification for the patent and copyright systems. Patents reward innovators with monopoly power for 20 years in exchange for the inventor making the knowledge underlying the discovery public. This monopoly power provides a temporary wedge between price and marginal cost that leads to profits. The profits, in turn, provide the incentive for the innovator to seek out the new idea in the first place.

How can we best encourage innovation? Patents and copyrights are one approach. Where patents are uncommon, such as in industries like financial services and retailing, one way to generate a wedge between price and marginal cost is through trade secrets—withholding the details of a particular idea from competitors.

CASE STUDY

Open Source Software and Altruism

Profits are not the only incentive for people to create new ideas. One of the more interesting alternatives is the open source movement in computer software. Linux (a computer operating system) and Apache (a program for running Web sites) are examples of sophisticated software programs that are available for free. This price equals the marginal cost of making additional copies of the software, which is essentially zero.

How are the large research costs of creating this software financed, if not from the subsequent profits associated with a price greater than marginal cost? The answer is that many people willingly spend their free time writing and improving such computer programs, although some financing does come from existing companies. Feelings of altruism may account for part of the motivation, as well as a desire to show off programming skills to other people, including potential employers or venture capitalists.[8]

Incentives for innovation that require prices to be greater than marginal cost carry an important negative consequence. Consider a pharmaceutical company that invests $1 billion in developing a new cancer drug. Suppose the marginal cost of producing the drug is only $1,000 for a year's worth of treatments. In

[8] See Josh Lerner and Jean Tirole, "Some Simple Economics of Open Source," *Journal of Industrial Economics*, vol. 50 (2002), pp. 197–234.

order to cover the cost of the research, the drug company may charge a price much greater than marginal cost—say $10,000 per year—for treatment. However, there will always be people who could afford the drug at $1,000, but not at the monopoly price of $10,000. These people are priced out of the market, resulting in a (potentially large) loss in welfare, or economic well-being. A single price cannot simultaneously provide the appropriate incentives for innovation *and* allocate scarce resources efficiently.

Other approaches may avoid the distortion associated with prices that are above marginal costs. For example, governments provide incentives for certain research by spending tax revenue to fund the research. Successful examples of this approach include the National Science Foundation, the National Institutes of Health, and the Department of Defense's ArpaNet, a precursor to today's World Wide Web.

Prizes provide yet another alternative. In the 1920s, hotel magnate Raymond Orteig offered $25,000 to the first person to fly nonstop between New York and Paris. Charles Lindbergh, flying *The Spirit of St. Louis*, won in 1927, and the prize is credited with spurring substantial progress in aviation. More recently, the $10 million Ansari X Prize for private space travel has had a similar effect. Michael Kremer of Harvard University has even proposed that organizations fund large prizes as a way to spur innovation in creating vaccines for AIDS and malaria in developing countries.[9]

Which of these mechanisms—patents, trade secrets, government funding, or prizes—provide the best incentives for innovation and maximize welfare? Note that the mechanisms themselves are ideas that were created at some point. Patents, for example, first appeared in England in the seventeenth century, although with limited application and enforcement. It seems likely that we have not yet discovered the best approaches for providing incentives for innovation. Such "meta-ideas" (ideas to spur other ideas) may be among the most valuable discoveries we can make.[10]

CASE STUDY

Intellectual Property Rights in Developing Countries

Should firms in China be allowed to pirate the latest Hollywood blockbuster DVD or hot-selling video game? This question may be easy to answer, but consider a more difficult one: Should firms in India ignore patents filed on U.S. pharmaceuticals and produce cheap HIV treatments to sell in poor countries?[11] One of the important

[9] See J. R. Minkel, "Dangling a Carrot for Vaccines," *Scientific American*, July 2006.

[10] For some interesting thoughts on this question, see Michael Kremer, "Patent Buyouts: A Mechanism for Encouraging Innovation," *Quarterly Journal of Economics* (November 1998), pp. 1137–67; also Suzanne Scotchmer, *Innovation and Incentives* (Cambridge: MIT Press, 2004).

[11] Jean O. Lanjouw, "The Introduction of Pharmaceutical Product Patents in India: Heartless Exploitation of the Poor and Suffering?" NBER Working Paper No. 6366, January 1998.

policy issues in recent years related to intellectual property rights—patents, copyrights, and trademarks—is the extent to which poor countries should respect the intellectual property rights of rich countries.

The United States and other industrialized countries have recently been pushing for stronger international protection. As a result of global trade negotiations in 1994, members of the World Trade Organization must now adhere to an agreement called Trade-Related Aspects of Intellectual Property Rights (or the TRIPs accord). But are such arrangements in the interest of developing countries?

Historically, intellectual property rights were relatively weak. When the United States was an up-and-coming nation on the world economic scene, it was a notorious pirate of intellectual property. A classic example is the willful flaunting of foreign copyrights. In the eighteenth century, Benjamin Franklin republished writings by British authors without permission and without paying royalties. In the following century, Charles Dickens railed against the thousands of cheap reprints of his work that were pirated in America nearly as soon as they were published in Britain.[12]

The gains from ignoring intellectual property rights are clear: poor countries may obtain pharmaceuticals, literature, and other technologies more cheaply if they do not have to pay the premiums associated with intellectual property rights. However, there are also good arguments in favor of respecting these property rights: doing so may encourage multinational firms to locate in developing countries and may facilitate the transfer of new technologies.[13]

It is fair to say that economists disagree on the extent to which the intellectual property rights of industrialized countries should be respected by developing countries. This is a question at the frontier of economic research, and more work will be needed to sort out the answer.

6.3 The Romer Model

To truly understand the causes of sustained growth, we need a model that emphasizes the distinction between ideas and objects; and because of the nonrivalry of ideas, this model must incorporate increasing returns. We need, in other words, **the Romer model**.

To get a feel for this model, let's return to our corn farmers from Chapter 5. As in the Solow economy, the farmers of the Romer model use their labor (and land, tractors, and seed) to produce corn. However, they also have a new use for their time: they can devote effort to inventing more efficient technologies

[12] See Philip V. Allingham, "Dickens's 1842 Reading Tour: Launching the Copyright Question in Tempestuous Seas," www.victorianweb.org/authors/dickens/pva/pva75.html.

[13] Lee Branstetter, Raymond Fisman, and C. Fritz Foley, "Do Stronger Intellectual Property Rights Increase International Technology Transfer? Empirical Evidence from U.S. Firm-Level Panel Data," *Quarterly Journal of Economics*, vol. 121 (February 2006), pp. 321–49.

for growing corn. They may begin with hoes and ox-drawn plows, but they can discover combine tractors, fertilizer, and pest-resistant seed to make them much more productive. Because of nonrivalry, the discovery of these new ideas is able to sustain growth in a way that capital accumulation in the Solow model could not.

In our model, we follow Romer's logic and emphasize the distinction between ideas and objects. We will downplay Solow's distinction between capital and labor in order to bring out the key role played by ideas. In fact, in the main model that follows, we omit capital completely to keep things simple. Section 6.9 will reintroduce capital, so don't let this omission bother you.

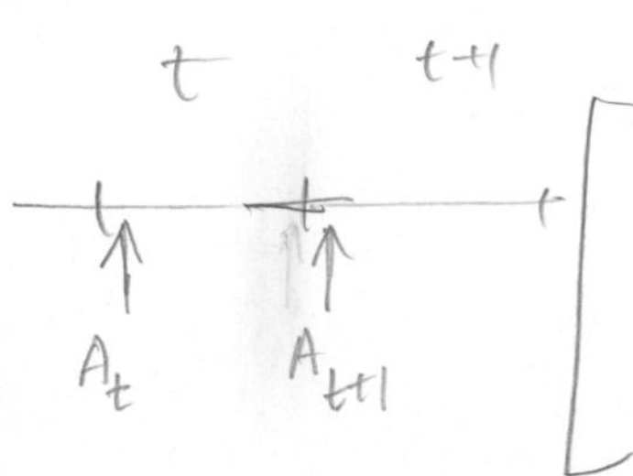

To translate Romer's story into a mathematical model, we first consider the production functions for the consumption good—corn, in our example—and for new ideas:

$$Y_t = A_t L_{yt} \tag{6.2}$$

$$\Delta A_{t+1} = \bar{z} A_t L_{at}. \tag{6.3}$$

Briefly, these two equations say that people and the existing stock of ideas can be used to produce corn or to produce new ideas. The first equation is the production function for output Y_t. Output is produced using the stock of existing knowledge A_t and labor L_{yt}. Notice that this production function features all the key properties discussed in the previous section. In particular, there are constant returns to *objects* (workers): if we want to double output, we simply double the number of workers. Because ideas are nonrivalrous, the new workers can use the existing stock of ideas. There are therefore increasing returns to ideas *and* objects in this production function.

The second equation, (6.3), is the production function for *new* ideas. A_t is the stock of ideas at time t. Recall that Δ is the "change over time" operator, so that $\Delta A_{t+1} \equiv A_{t+1} - A_t$ is the change in the stock of ideas. In other words, ΔA_{t+1} is the number of new ideas produced during period t. Our second equation, then, says that new ideas are produced using existing ideas A_t and workers L_{at}. The only difference between the two production functions is that the second one includes a productivity parameter $\bar{z}$. This allows us to conduct experiments in which the economy gets better at producing ideas. We also assume the economy starts out at date $t = 0$ with an existing stock of ideas $\bar{A}_0$.

Notice that the same stock of ideas features in both the production of output and the production of new ideas. Again, this is because ideas are nonrivalrous: they can be used by many people for many different purposes simultaneously. In contrast, workers are an object. If a worker spends her time producing automobiles, that time can't simultaneously be spent conducting research on new antibiotics. In our model, this rivalry shows up as a resource constraint:

$$L_{yt} + L_{at} = \bar{L}. \tag{6.4}$$

That is, the number of workers producing output and the number of workers producing ideas (engaged in research) add up to the total population $\bar{L}$, which we take to be a constant parameter.

Let's pause now to count equations and endogenous variables. Our model includes three equations at this point: the two production functions and the resource

TABLE 6.1

The Romer Model: 4 Equations and 4 Unknowns

Unknowns/endogenous variables: Y_t, A_t, L_{yt}, L_{at}	
Output production function	$Y_t = A_t L_{yt}$
Idea production function	$\Delta A_{t+1} = \bar{z} A_t L_{at}$
Resource constraint	$L_{yt} + L_{at} = \bar{L}$
Allocation of labor	$L_{at} = \bar{l}\bar{L}$
Parameters: $\bar{z}$, $\bar{L}$, $\bar{l}$, $\bar{A}_0$	

constraint. As for endogenous variables, we have Y_t, A_t, L_{yt}, and L_{at}. (Recall that ΔA_{t+1} is just a function of A_t, so we don't need to count it separately.) We need one more equation to close the model.

Think about the economics of the model, and ask yourself what's missing (don't read any farther if you want to figure it out for yourself). The answer is that we need an equation that describes how labor is allocated to its two uses. How much labor produces output, and how much is engaged in research?

Here is where we make another useful simplification. In Romer's original model, he set up markets for labor and output, introduced patents and monopoly power to deal with increasing returns, and let the markets determine the allocation of labor. What Romer discovered is fascinating, and you may have already figured it out. He found that unregulated markets in this model do *not* lead to the best of all possible worlds. There is a tendency for markets to provide too little innovation relative to what is optimal. In the presence of increasing returns, Adam Smith's invisible hand may fail to get things right.[14]

Going through the full analysis with markets, patents, and monopoly power is informative, but unfortunately beyond the scope of this text.[15] Instead, we make a simplifying assumption and allocate labor through a rule of thumb, the same way Solow allocated output to consumption and investment. We assume that the constant fraction $\bar{\ell}$ of the population works in research, leaving $1 - \bar{\ell}$ to work in producing output. For example, we might set $\bar{\ell} = 0.05$, so that 5 percent of the population works to produce new ideas while 95 percent works to produce the consumption good. Our fourth equation is therefore

$$L_{at} = \bar{\ell}\bar{L}. \tag{6.5}$$

This completes our description of the Romer model, summarized in Table 6.1.

[14] The result that the market allocation provides too little incentive for research depends on the exact model and the exact institutions for allocating resources that are introduced into the model. Nevertheless, most empirical work that has looked at this question has concluded that advanced economies like the United States probably underinvest in research. For a survey of recent research, see Vania Sena, "The Return of the Prince of Denmark: A Survey on Recent Developments in the Economics of Innovation," *The Economic Journal*, vol. 114 (June 2004), pp. F312–32.

[15] The interested reader might find it helpful to look at Chapter 5 of my textbook on growth, *Introduction to Economic Growth* (New York: Norton, 2002), which works through this analysis.

Solving the Romer Model

To solve this model, we need to express our four endogenous variables as functions of the parameters of the model and of time. Fortunately, our model is simple enough that this can be done easily. First, notice that $L_{at} = \bar{\ell}\bar{L}$ and $L_{yt} = (1 - \bar{\ell})\bar{L}$. Those are the solutions for two of our endogenous variables.

Next, applying the production function in equation (6.2), output per person can be written as

$$y_t \equiv \frac{Y_t}{\bar{L}} = A_t(1 - \bar{\ell}). \tag{6.6}$$

This equation says that output per person is proportional to A_t. That is, output *per person* depends on the *total* stock of knowledge. So a new idea that increases A_t will raise the output of each person in the economy. This feature of the model reflects the nonrivalry of ideas: when a new combine tractor or drought-resistant seed is invented, all farmers benefit from the new technology. In the Solow model, in contrast, output *per person* depended on capital per person rather than on the total capital stock.

Finally, to complete our solution, we need to solve for the stock of knowledge A_t at each point in time. Dividing the production function for ideas in equation (6.3) by A_t yields

$$\frac{\Delta A_{t+1}}{A_t} = \bar{z}L_{at} = \bar{z}\bar{\ell}\bar{L}. \tag{6.7}$$

This equation says that the growth rate of knowledge is constant over time. It is proportional to the number of researchers in the economy L_{at}, which in turn is proportional to the population of the economy $\bar{L}$. It is helpful to define this particular combination of parameters as $\bar{g} \equiv \bar{z}\bar{\ell}\bar{L}$, so that we don't have to keep writing out each term.

Since the growth rate of knowledge is constant over time, even starting from time 0, the stock of knowledge is therefore given by

$$A_t = \bar{A}_0(1 + \bar{g})^t. \tag{6.8}$$

where the growth rate $\bar{g}$ is defined above. If you have trouble understanding where this equation comes from, notice that it's just an application of the *constant growth rule* from Chapter 3 (page 45). That is, since we know A_t grows at a constant rate, the level of A_t is equal to its initial value multiplied by $(1 + \bar{g})^t$, where $\bar{g}$ is the growth rate.

This last equation, together with equation (6.6) for output per person, completes the solution to the Romer model. In particular, combining these two equations, we have

$$y_t = \bar{A}_0(1 - \bar{\ell})(1 + \bar{g})^t \tag{6.9}$$

where, again, $\bar{g} \equiv \bar{z}\bar{\ell}\bar{L}$. The level of output per person is now written entirely as a function of the parameters of the model. Figure 6.2 uses this solution to plot output per person over time for the Romer model. It shows up as a straight line on a ratio scale, since it grows at a constant rate at all times.

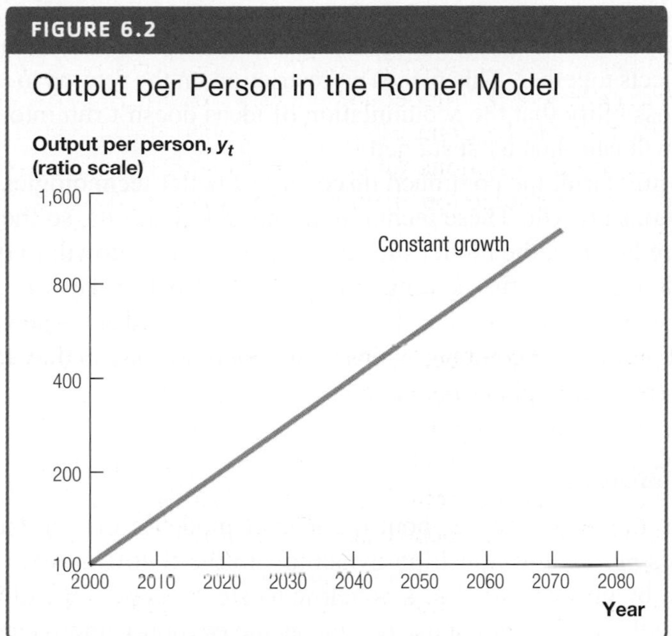

Output per person grows at a constant rate in the Romer model, so it appears as a straight line on this graph with a ratio scale. (The value of 100 in the year 2000 is simply a normalization.)

Why Is There Growth in the Romer Model?

Now that we have solved the Romer model, let's think about what the solution means. First and foremost, we have the holy grail we have been searching for over the last several chapters: a theory of sustained growth in per capita GDP.

This is the main result of this chapter, and you should pause to appreciate its elegance and importance. The nonrivalry of ideas means that per capita GDP depends on the *total* stock of ideas. Researchers produce new ideas, and the sustained production of these new ideas leads to the sustained growth of income over time. Romer's division of goods into objects and ideas thus opens up a theory of long-run growth in a way that Solow's division of goods into capital and labor did not.

Why is this the case? Recall that in the Solow model, the accumulation of capital runs into diminishing returns: each new addition to the capital stock increases output—and therefore investment—by less and less. Eventually, these additions are just enough to offset the depreciation of capital. Since new investment and depreciation offset, capital stops growing, and so does income.

In the Romer model, consider the production function for new ideas, equation (6.3):

$$\Delta A_{t+1} = \bar{z} A_t L_{at}.$$

There are no diminishing returns to the existing stock of ideas here—the exponent on A is equal to 1. As we accumulate more knowledge, the return to knowledge does not fall. Old ideas continue to help us produce new ideas in a virtuous circle that sustains economic growth.

Why does capital run into diminishing returns in the Solow model but not ideas in the Romer model? The answer is nonrivalry. Capital and labor are objects, and the standard replication argument tells us there are constant returns to all objects taken together. Therefore, there are diminishing returns to capital by itself.

In contrast, the nonrivalry of ideas means that there are increasing returns to ideas and objects together. This places no restriction on the returns to ideas, allowing for the possibility that the accumulation of ideas doesn't run into diminishing returns. Growth can thus be sustained.

On the family farm, the continued discovery of better technologies for producing corn sustains growth. These technologies are nonrivalrous, so they benefit all farmers. More broadly, the model suggests that economic growth in the economy as a whole is driven by the continued discovery of better ways to convert our labor and resources into consumption and utility. New ideas—new antibiotics, fuel cells, jet planes, and computer chips—are nonrivalrous, so they raise average per capita income throughout the economy.

Balanced Growth

An important thing to observe about the Romer model is that unlike the Solow model, it does *not* exhibit transition dynamics. In the Solow model, an economy may start out by growing (if it begins below its steady state, for example). However, the growth rate will gradually decline as the economy approaches its steady state. In the Romer model, in contrast, the growth rate is constant and equal to $\bar{g} = \bar{z}\bar{\ell}\bar{L}$ at all points in time—look back at equation (6.9). Since the growth rate never rises or falls, in some sense the economy could be said to be in its steady state from the start.

Because the model features sustained growth, it seems a little odd to call this a steady state. For this reason, economists refer to such an economy as being on a **balanced growth path**, where the growth rates of all endogenous variables are constant. The Romer economy is on its balanced growth path at all times. Actually, this statement requires one qualification: as long as the parameter values are not changing, the Romer economy features constant growth. In the experiments that we look at next, however, changes in some parameters of the model can change the growth rate.

CASE STUDY

A Model of World Knowledge

How should we think about applying the Romer model to the world? This is an important question that should be considered carefully. For example, suppose we applied the model to each country individually. What would we learn about the difference between, say, Luxembourg and the United States?

Luxembourg's population is fewer than half a million, while the United States' is more than 600 times larger. According to statistics from the National Science Foundation, there are actually more researchers in the United States than Luxembourg has people. Since the growth rate of per capita GDP in the model is tied to the number of researchers, the model would seem to predict that the United States should grow at a rate several hundred times larger than the growth rate of Luxembourg. This is obviously not true. Between 1960 and 2007, the growth rate of per capita GDP in the United States averaged 2.3 percent per year, while growth in Luxembourg was nearly a full percentage point faster, at 3.2 percent.

A moment's thought, though, reveals why. It is not the case that the economy of Luxembourg grows only because of ideas invented in Luxembourg, or even that the United States grows only because of ideas discovered by U.S. researchers. Instead, virtually all countries in the world benefit from ideas created throughout the world. International trade, multinational corporations, licensing agreements, international patent filings, the migration of students and workers, and the open flow of information ensure that an idea created in one place can impact economies worldwide.

We would do better to think of the Romer model as a model of the world's stock of ideas. Through the spread of these ideas, growth in the world's store of knowledge drives long-run growth in every country in the world. Why, then, do countries grow at different rates? We will learn more about this in the next section.

Experiments in the Romer Model

What happens if we set up a Romer economy, watch it evolve for a while, and then change one of the underlying parameter values? There are four parameters in the model: $\bar{L}$, $\bar{\ell}$, $\bar{z}$, and $\bar{A}_0$. We will consider the first two here and leave the others for exercises at the end of the chapter.

Experiment #1: Changing the Population, $\bar{L}$

For our first experiment, we consider an exogenous increase in the population $\bar{L}$, holding all other parameter values constant. In the solution to the Romer model in equation (6.9), $\bar{L}$ shows up in one place, the growth rate of knowledge ($\bar{g} = \bar{z}\bar{\ell}\bar{L}$). Because the research share $\bar{\ell}$ is held constant, a larger population means there are more researchers. More researchers produce more ideas, and this leads to faster growth: a Romer economy with more researchers actually grows faster over time. Figure 6.3 shows the effect of this experiment on the time path for output per person.

In the case study "A Model of World Knowledge," we determined that rather than applying the Romer model on a country-by-country basis, it's better to view it as a model of the world as a whole. With this perspective, the model may also help us understand economic growth over the long course of history. Recall from Figure 3.1 in Chapter 3 that over the last several thousand years, growth rates have been rising. Michael Kremer of Harvard University has suggested that this could be the result of a virtuous circle between ideas and population. People create new ideas, and new ideas make it possible for finite resources to support a larger population. The larger population in turn creates even more ideas, and so on.[16]

[16] Michael Kremer, "Population Growth and Technological Change: One Million B.C. to 1990," *Quarterly Journal of Economics*, vol. 108 (August 1993), pp. 681–716.

A one-time, permanent increase in $\bar{L}$ in the year 2030 immediately and permanently raises the growth rate in the Romer model.

FIGURE 6.3

Output per Person after an Increase in $\bar{L}$

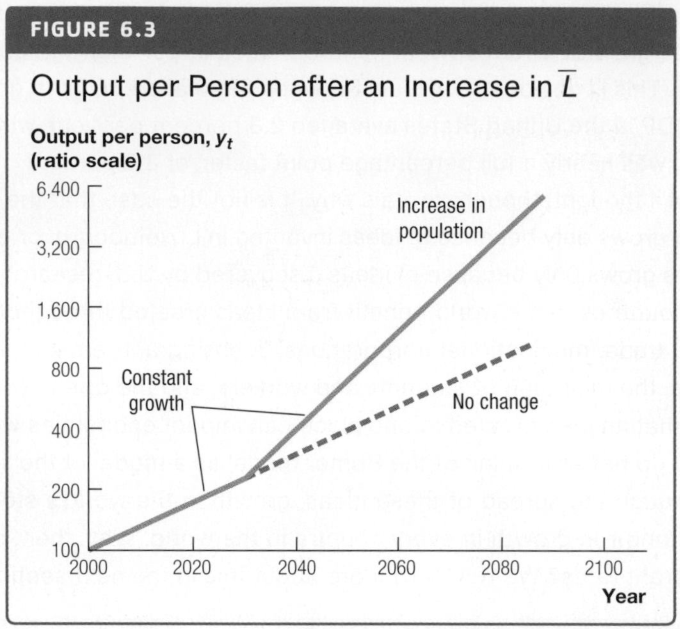

That said, the careful reader may challenge the validity of this prediction for the last century or so. Both the world population and the overall number of researchers in the world increased dramatically during the twentieth century. According to the Romer model, the growth rate of per capita GDP should therefore have risen sharply as well, but this is clearly not the case. For example, we found that U.S. growth rates have been relatively stable over the last hundred years. Fortunately, extensions of the Romer model can render it consistent with this evidence, as we'll see below.

Experiment #2: Changing the Research Share, $\bar{\ell}$

Now suppose the fraction of labor working in the ideas sector, $\bar{\ell}$, increases. Look back at the solution in equation (6.9) to see what happens. There are two effects. First, since there are now more researchers, more new ideas are produced each year. This leads the growth rate of knowledge, $\bar{g} = \bar{z}\bar{\ell}\bar{L}$, to rise. Equation (6.9) tells us that this also causes the growth of per capita GDP to rise, just as in our previous experiment.

The second effect is less obvious, but it can also be seen in equation (6.9). If more people are working to produce ideas, fewer are available to produce the consumption good (corn, in our example). This means that the *level* of output per person declines. Increasing the research share thus involves a tradeoff: current consumption declines, but the growth rate of consumption is higher, so future consumption is higher as well.[17] The results of this experiment are shown graphically in Figure 6.4.

[17] With some additional mathematics, we could think about the optimal value for the research share, but for now we will simply note that the optimal value is at some midpoint: an economy needs researchers to produce ideas in order to raise future income, but it also needs workers to produce output today in order to satisfy current consumption.

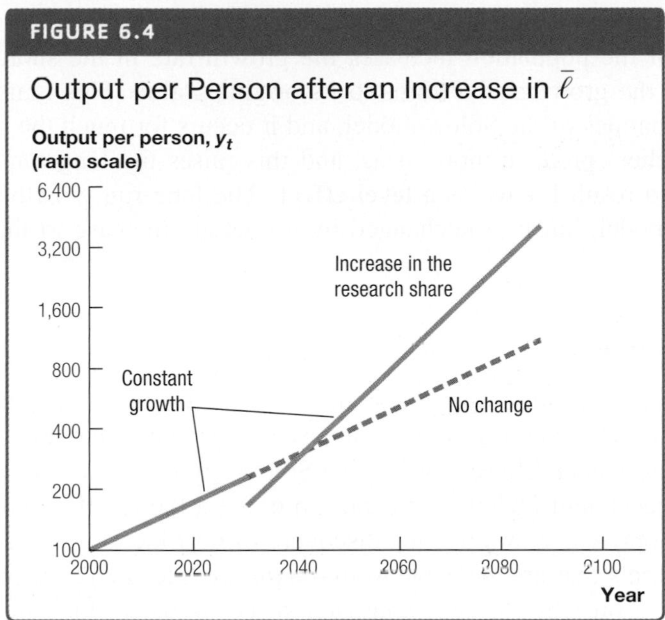

FIGURE 6.4

Output per Person after an Increase in $\bar{\ell}$

The figure considers a one-time, permanent increase in $\bar{\ell}$ that occurs in the year 2030. Two things happen. First, the growth rate is higher: more researchers produce more ideas, leading to faster growth. Second, the initial level of output per person declines: there are fewer workers in the consumption goods sector, so production per person must fall initially.

Growth Effects versus Level Effects

Our discussion of the importance of increasing returns in generating sustained growth finessed one important issue. You may have noticed that in the two production functions of the Romer model, not only are there increasing returns to ideas and objects, but the degree of increasing returns is especially strong. (Look back at Table 6.1 to review these production functions.) The standard replication argument tells us that there should be constant returns to objects (labor) in these production functions, and therefore increasing returns to labor and ideas together. This means that the exponent on labor should be 1, but the argument says nothing about what the exponent on ideas should be, other than positive.

So what would happen if the exponent on ideas were equal to some number less than 1? For example, what if $\Delta A_{t+1} = \bar{z} A_t^{1/2} L_{at}$? Notice that there would still be increasing returns overall (the exponents add to more than 1), but there would also be diminishing returns to ideas alone.

This is an important question, and the answer comes in two parts. First, the ability of the Romer model to generate sustained growth in per capita GDP is not sensitive to the degree of increasing returns. The general point of this chapter—that the nonrivalry of ideas leads to increasing returns, and thus to a theory of sustained growth—does not depend on the "strength" of increasing returns. The Romer framework provides a robust theory of long-run growth.

The second part, though, is that other predictions of the Romer model *are* sensitive to the degree of increasing returns. In the two experiments we just considered, changes in parameters led to permanent increases in the rate of growth of per capita GDP, results known as **growth effects**. These growth effects can be eliminated in models when the degree of increasing returns is not strong. If the exponent on ideas is less than 1, increases in ideas run into diminishing returns.

In this alternative version of the Romer model, an increase in the research share or the size of the population increases the growth rate in the short run, but in the long run the growth rate returns to its original value. This is much like the transition dynamics of the Solow model, and it occurs for much the same reason. More researchers produce more ideas, and this raises the long-run *level* of per capita GDP, a result known as a **level effect**. The long-run growth rate is positive in this model, but it is unchanged by a onetime increase in the number of researchers.[18]

Recapping Romer

The Romer model divides economic goods into two categories, objects and ideas. Objects are the raw materials available in an economy, and ideas are ways of using these raw materials in different ways. The Solow approach studies a model based solely on objects, and finds that it cannot provide a theory of sustained growth. The Romer approach shows that the discovery of new ideas—better ways to use the raw materials that are available to us—*can* provide such a theory.

The key reason why the idea approach succeeds where the object approach fails is that ideas are nonrivalrous: the same idea can be used by one, two, or a hundred people or production lines. By the standard replication argument, there are constant returns to scale to objects, but this means that there are increasing returns to objects and ideas taken together.

Because of nonrivalry and increasing returns, each new idea has the potential to increase the income of every person in an economy. It's not "ideas per person" that matter for an individual's income and well-being, but rather the total stock of ideas in the economy. Sustained growth in the *stock* of knowledge, then, is the key to sustained growth in per capita GDP.

CASE STUDY

Globalization and Ideas

By almost any measure, the world is a much more integrated place today than it was previously. International trade, foreign direct investment, urbanization, and global communications through technologies such as the Internet are all substantially higher now than they were fifty years ago.

An important consequence of this integration is that ideas can be shared more easily. Ideas invented in one place can, at least potentially, be used to increase incomes throughout the world. And it is clear that some of the gains from globalization are being realized. To take one simple example, consider oral rehydration therapy. Combining water, salt, and sugar in just the right proportions can rehydrate

[18] Many of the general results in this chapter hold in this alternative version of the Romer model. As this section hints, however, there are some important differences as well. The interested reader may consult Chapter 5 of Charles I. Jones, *Introduction to Economic Growth* (New York: Norton, 2002), and "R&D-Based Models of Economic Growth," *Journal of Political Economy*, vol. 103 (August 1995), pp. 759–84.

a child who would otherwise die from diarrhea. This simple idea, shared around the world by public health organizations, now saves countless lives each year. Another powerful example comes from telephony. Sub-Saharan Africa has fewer than 3 landline telephones for every 100 people. But in the last decade, use of a new idea—mobile telephones—has exploded, and there are now more than 10 mobile phones for every landline in this region.[19]

The benefits from the worldwide flow of ideas are by no means limited to developing countries, however. About half of all patents granted by the U.S. Patent and Trademark Office go to foreigners as opposed to domestic residents, just one indication of the substantial benefits that the United States receives from ideas created elsewhere. And the benefits from the worldwide flow of ideas seem likely to increase in the future. China and India each have a population that is roughly the same as that of the United States, Japan, and Western Europe combined. As these economies continue to develop, they will increasingly help to advance the technological frontier, creating ideas that benefit people everywhere.

6.4 Combining Solow and Romer: Overview

In the Romer model, we made the simplifying assumption that there was no capital in the economy, which helped us see how growth can be sustained in the long run. However, because the Solow model also helps us answer many questions about economic growth, it's important to understand how to combine the two frameworks.

An appendix at the end of the chapter (Section 6.9) details how the insights of Solow and Romer can be combined in a single model of economic growth. All the results we have learned from both models continue to hold in the combined model. However, as the appendix incorporates algebra more intensively than elsewhere in the book, it's optional. The (nonmathematical) summary provided here is for readers who will not be working through the appendix.

In the combined Solow-Romer model, the nonrivalry of ideas is once again the key to long-run growth. The most important element contributed by the Solow side is the principle of transition dynamics. In the combined model, if an economy starts out below its balanced growth path, it will grow rapidly in order to catch up to this path; if an economy begins above its balanced growth path, it will grow slowly for a period of time.

The Romer model helps us see the overall trend in incomes around the world and why growth is possible. The transition dynamics of the Solow model help us understand why Japan and South Korea have grown faster than the United States for the last half century. In the long run, all countries grow at the same rate. But because of transition dynamics, actual growth rates can differ across countries for long periods of time.

---

[19] See Jenny C. Aker and Isaac M. Mbiti, "Mobile Phones and Economic Development in Africa," *Journal of Economic Perspectives*, vol. 24 (Summer 2010).

6.5 Growth Accounting

One of the many ways in which growth models like the combined Solow-Romer model have been applied is to determine the sources of growth in a particular economy and how they may have changed over time. This particular application is called **growth accounting**. Robert Solow was one of the early economists to apply it to the United States.[20]

To see how growth accounting works, consider a production function that includes both capital and ideas:

$$Y_t = A_t K_t^{1/3} L_{yt}^{2/3}. \tag{6.10}$$

A_t can be thought of as the stock of ideas, as in the Romer model, or more generally as the level of total factor productivity (TFP).

We now apply the rules for computing growth rates that we developed in Chapter 3; in fact, one of the examples we worked out in Section 3.5 is exactly the problem we have before us now. Recall rules 2 and 3 from Section 3.5: the growth rate of the product of several variables is the sum of the variables' growth rates, and the growth rate of a variable raised to some power is that power times the growth rate of the variable. Applied to the production function in equation (6.10), we have

$$g_{Yt} = g_{At} + \frac{1}{3} g_{Kt} + \frac{2}{3} g_{Lyt}, \tag{6.11}$$

where $g_{Yt} \equiv \Delta Y_{t+1}/Y_t$ and the other growth rates are defined in a similar way ($g_{At} \equiv \Delta A_{t+1}/A_t$, and so on).

Equation (6.11) is really just the growth rate version of the production function. It says that the growth rate of output is the sum of three terms: the growth rate of TFP, the growth contribution from capital, and the growth contribution from workers. Notice that the growth contributions of capital and workers are weighted by their exponents, reflecting the diminishing returns to each of these inputs.

Suppose, as is true in practice, that the number of hours worked by the labor force can change over time: when the economy is booming, people may work more hours per week than when the economy is in a recession. Let L_t denote the aggregate number of hours worked by everyone in the economy, and let g_{Lt} denote the growth rate of hours worked. Now, subtract g_{Lt} from both sides of equation (6.11) above to get

$$\underbrace{g_{Yt} - g_{Lt}}_{\text{growth of } Y/L} = \underbrace{\frac{1}{3}(g_{Kt} - g_{Lt})}_{\text{contribution from } K/L} + \underbrace{\frac{2}{3}(g_{Lyt} - g_{Lt})}_{\text{labor composition}} + \underbrace{g_{At}}_{\text{TFP growth}}. \tag{6.12}$$

In this equation, the right side uses the fact that $g_L = 1/3 \times g_L + 2/3 \times g_L$. Also, we've moved the TFP term to the end.

[20] See Robert M. Solow, "Technological Change and the Aggregate Production Function," *Review of Economics and Statistics*, vol. 39 (1957), pp. 312–20. Other important early contributors to growth accounting include Edward Denison and Dale Jorgenson. The Bureau of Labor Statistics now conducts these growth-accounting exercises at regular intervals for the United States.

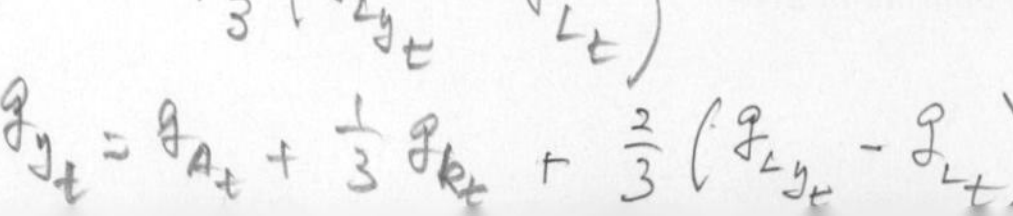

TABLE 6.2

Growth Accounting for the United States

	1948–2008	1948–73	1973–95	1995–2008
Output per hour, Y/L	2.5	3.3	1.5	2.6
Contribution of K/L	0.9	0.9	0.7	1.0
Contribution of labor composition	0.2	0.2	0.3	0.2
Contribution of TFP, A	1.4	2.2	0.5	1.4

The table shows the average annual growth rate (in percent) for different variables.
Source: Bureau of Labor Statistics, *Multifactor Productivity Trends.*

As in equation (6.12), the growth rate of output per hour can be decomposed into contributions from capital, labor, and TFP.

The equation tells us that the growth rate of output per hour, Y/L, over a time period can be viewed as the sum of three terms. The first term is the contribution from the growth of capital per hour worked by the labor force. As capital per hour rises, output per hour rises as well, but this effect is reduced according to the degree of diminishing returns to capital, 1/3. We've written the second term as the growth rate of workers less the growth rate of total hours, but in actual applications of growth accounting, this term can also include increases in education or changes in the age distribution of the workforce. We therefore call it "labor composition." Finally, the last term is the growth rate of TFP. Faster productivity growth also raises the growth rate of output per hour.

By measuring the growth rates of output per hour, capital per hour, and the labor force composition term, we can let this equation account for the sources of growth in any given country. In practice, since we can observe everything *other* than TFP, we use our equation as a way to *measure* the unobserved TFP growth. For this reason, TFP growth is also sometimes called "the residual." (You may recall a similar point being discussed when we used the production function to account for differences in levels of per capita GDP in Chapter 4.)

Table 6.2 shows the four terms of equation (6.12) for the United States, first for the entire period 1948 to 2008, and then for particular subperiods. Output per hour grew at an average annual rate of 2.5 percent between 1948 and 2008. Of this 2.5 percent, 0.9 percentage points were due to an increase in the capital-labor ratio, K/L, and an additional 0.2 percentage points came from changes in the composition of the labor force, including increased years of education. This means that the residual, TFP growth, accounted for the majority of growth, at 1.4 percentage points.

These numbers have changed over time in interesting ways. The period 1948 to 1973 featured the fastest growth in output per hour, at 3.3 percent per year, while the years 1973 to 1995 saw output per hour grow less than half as fast, at 1.5 percent. What accounted for the slowdown? It's nearly entirely explained by a decline in TFP growth, from a rapid rate of 2.2 percent before 1973 to an anemic 0.5 percent after. Economists refer to this particular episode as **the productivity slowdown**. It has been studied in great detail in an effort to understand exactly what caused productivity growth to decline so dramatically. The list of potential explanations is long and includes the oil price shocks of the 1970s, a decline in the fraction of GDP spent on research and development, and a change in the sectoral composition of the economy away from manufacturing and toward services. But though each of these factors seems to have contributed to the slowdown, the exact cause(s) remain elusive.[21]

Just as remarkable as the slowdown, however, is the dramatic resurgence of growth that has occurred since 1995. Between 1995 and 2008, output per hour grew at an annual rate of 2.6 percent, nearly as rapidly as before the productivity slowdown. This era, of course, was marked by the rise of the World Wide Web and the dot-com boom in the stock market, followed by the sharp decline in stock prices in 2001. Some commentators have labeled this era **the new economy**.

What explains the resumption of relatively rapid growth? In the accounting exercise, the increase in growth is accounted for in roughly equal parts by capital accumulation and TFP. The contribution of capital rose from 0.7 to 1.0 percent, while TFP growth increased from 0.5 to 1.4 percent. Economists studying this productivity boom generally conclude that at least half of it can be explained by purchases of computers and by rapid growth in the sectors that produce information technology. That is, there is a link between the new economy and information technology.[22]

6.6 Concluding Our Study of Long-Run Growth

The key to sustained growth in per capita GDP is the discovery of new ideas, which increase a country's total stock of knowledge. Because ideas are nonrivalrous, it is not ideas per person that matter, but rather this total stock of ideas. Increases in the stock of knowledge lead to sustained economic growth for countries that have access to that knowledge. This is the lesson of the Romer model.

Combining the insights of the Solow and Romer models leads to our full theory of long-run economic performance. Think of each country as a Solow economy that sits on top of the overall trend in world knowledge that's generated by a Romer model. Growth in the stock of knowledge accounts for the overall trend in per capita GDP over time. Transition dynamics associated with the Solow model then allow us to understand differences in growth rates across countries that persist for several decades.

The United States and South Korea have both experienced sustained growth in per capita GDP, driven in large part by the increase in the world's stock of knowledge. South Korea has grown faster than the United States during the last four decades because structural changes in the economy have shifted its balanced growth path sharply upward. Whereas in 1950 the steady-state ratio of per capita GDP in Korea to per capita GDP in the United States may have been 10 or 15 percent, the ratio today is probably something like 80 percent (the exact number depends on Korea's

[21] See the Fall 1998 issue of the *Journal of Economic Perspectives* for a more detailed discussion of the productivity slowdown.

[22] For a discussion of the causes and consequences of the recent boom in productivity growth, see William Nordhaus, "The Sources of the Productivity Rebound and the Manufacturing Employment Puzzle," NBER Working Paper No. 11354, May 2005; and Robert J. Gordon, "Five Puzzles in the Behavior of Productivity, Investment, and Innovation," NBER Working Paper No. 10660, August 2004.

investment rate and productivity level, among other things). The Korean economy has thus grown rapidly during the last several decades as it makes the transition from its initial low steady-state income ratio to its eventual high ratio.

Nigeria, on the other hand, is almost the opposite story. In the 1950s and early 1960s, the country's per capita GDP was just under 10 percent of the U.S. level. Since then, however, Nigeria's economy has steadily deteriorated so that by 2000, per capita GDP was only slightly more than 2 percent of the U.S. level and about the same level it was in 1950. A half century of lost growth is a tremendous lost opportunity; this is the same period when U.S. living standards more than tripled while those in South Korea rose by a factor of 12. The Solow model suggests that this tragedy has its roots in a decline in the investment rate in physical capital and a decline in productivity, at least relative to the rest of the world. And part of this decline in productivity may come from a change in the degree to which Nigerians can access the world's stock of ideas, a point suggested by the Romer model.

Exactly what caused these changes in South Korea and Nigeria is a critical subject that our growth model does not speak to. As we saw in Chapter 4, *institutions*—the extent to which property rights are protected and contractual agreements are enforced by the law—appear to play an important role. In the absence of these institutions, firms may be unwilling to invest in an economy, and the transfer of knowledge that often seems to come with trade and foreign investment may be hindered. At the same time, improvements in these institutions may help explain the increase in investment and TFP levels that our Solow-Romer model suggests is associated with rapid growth.

This is where our study of economic growth leaves off. The Solow and Romer frameworks provide a sound foundation for understanding why some countries are so much richer than others and why economies grow over time. They don't provide the final answers: questions of *why* countries exhibit different investment rates and TFP levels remain unanswered and remain at the frontier of economic research. But there is more macroeconomics to cover, and our time is short.

CASE STUDY

Institutions, Ideas, and Charter Cities

The institutions that govern how people interact—property rights, the justice system, and the rules and regulations of a country, for example—are themselves ideas. They are nonrival: if one country has a freedom-of-speech clause in its constitution, that does not mean there is "less" of the free-speech clause available for other countries.

One approach to raising incomes in the world's poorest countries seeks to encourage those countries to adopt good institutions. But that approach has proven difficult. For reasons that are not well understood, it does not seem to be in the interest of the heads of the poorest countries to adopt the rules and institutions that would substantially boost economic performance.

An intriguing alternative has recently been suggested by Paul Romer of Stanford University. If it is hard to move good institutions to poor people, perhaps poor people can move to places with good institutions. Successful economies, however, often restrict immigration. Drawing inspiration from the historical experience of Hong Kong, Professor Romer suggests that new cities be established. In these **charter cities,** advanced economies would agree to set the rules by which the new city is administered. People from throughout the world would then be free to live and work in the new city. Such cities could even be established in developing countries with a charter that grants administrative rights to one or more advanced economies. There are, of course, many important issues to be worked out before this idea could be implemented. But the success of Hong Kong and the enormous number of people living in impoverished countries suggest that charter cities may be an idea worth trying.[23]

6.7 A Postscript on Solow and Romer

The Solow and Romer models have been simplified here in ways that don't do justice to the richness of either of the original papers. For one thing, the basic production model presented in Chapter 4 is itself a contribution of the original Solow paper. For another, we saw that Solow endogenized capital accumulation and found that capital could not provide the engine of economic growth, but he went further in postulating that exogenous improvements in technology—"exogenous technological progress"—*could* explain growth. That is, he included an equation like $\Delta A_{t+1}/A_t = 0.02$, allowing productivity to grow at a constant, exogenous rate of 2 percent per year. The limitation of this approach, however, is that the growth was simply assumed rather than explained within the model. Solow intuited that growth must be related to technological improvements, but he took these to be exogenous, like rain falling from the sky.

In his original paper, Romer included capital accumulation in his model. More important, he solved a significant puzzle related to increasing returns. That is, if increasing returns are the key to growth, why wouldn't the economy come to be dominated by a single, very large firm? After all, such a firm would enjoy the best advantage of increasing returns. Romer's answer was to incorporate the modern theory of monopolistic competition into his idea model. In this theory, the economy contains many monopolists, each producing a slightly different good. They compete with each other to sell us different varieties of music, books, computers, and airplanes. Their size, as Adam Smith said, is limited by the extent of the market as well as by competition with each other.

[23] More discussion can be found at chartercities.org as well as in Paul Romer, "For Richer, for Poorer," *Prospect*, January 27, 2010.

6.8 Additional Resources

Ideas:

Paul Romer's Web page contains links to a number of short articles on economic growth and ideas: www.stanford.edu/~promer. The quote that begins this chapter is taken from an encyclopedia article he wrote on economic growth. It can be found at www.stanford.edu/~promer/EconomicGrowth.pdf.

Joel Mokyr. *The Gifts of Athena: Historical Origins of the Knowledge Economy*. Princeton, N.J.: Princeton University Press, 2002.

Julian L. Simon. *The Ultimate Resource* 2. Princeton, N.J.: Princeton University Press, 1998.

David Warsh. *Knowledge and the Wealth of Nations: A Story of Economic Discovery*. New York: Norton, 2006.

Institutions and economic growth:

Daron Acemoglu and James A. Robinson. *Economic Origins of Dictatorship and Democracy*. Cambridge: Cambridge University Press, 2005.

Charles I. Jones. *Introduction to Economic Growth*. New York: Norton, 2001. Chapter 7.

Douglass C. North and Robert P. Thomas. *Institutions, Institutional Change, and Economic Performance*. Cambridge: Cambridge University Press, 1990.

Mancur Olson. "Distinguished Lecture on Economics in Government. Big Bills Left on the Sidewalk: Why Some Nations Are Rich, and Others Poor." *Journal of Economic Perspectives*, vol. 10, no. 2 (Spring 1996), pp. 3–24.

Stephen L. Parente and Edward C. Prescott. *Barriers to Riches*. Cambridge, Mass.: MIT Press, 2000.

Other references:

Jared Diamond. *Guns, Germs, and Steel*. New York: Norton, 1997.

William Easterly. *The Elusive Quest for Growth: Economists' Adventures and Misadventures in the Tropics*. Cambridge, Mass.: MIT Press, 2001.

Elhanan Helpman. *The Mystery of Economic Growth*. Cambridge, Mass.: Belknap Press, 2004.

CHAPTER REVIEW

SUMMARY

1. Whereas Solow divides the world into capital and labor, Romer divides the world into ideas and objects. This distinction proves to be essential for understanding the engine of growth.

2. *Ideas* are instructions for using objects in different ways. They are *nonrivalrous*; they are not scarce in the same way that objects are, but can be used by any number of people simultaneously without anyone's use being degraded.
3. This nonrivalry implies that the economy is characterized by increasing returns to ideas and objects taken together. There are fixed costs associated with research (finding new ideas), and these are a reflection of the increasing returns.
4. Increasing returns imply that Adam Smith's invisible hand may not lead to the best of all possible worlds. Prices must be above marginal cost in some places in order for firms to recoup the cost of research. If a pharmaceutical company were to charge marginal cost for its drugs, it would never be able to cover the large cost of inventing drugs in the first place.
5. Growth eventually ceases in the Solow model because capital runs into diminishing returns. Because of nonrivalry, ideas need not run into diminishing returns, and this allows growth to be sustained.
6. Combining the insights from Solow and Romer leads to a rich theory of economic growth. The growth of world knowledge explains the underlying upward trend in incomes. Countries may grow faster or slower than this world trend because of the principle of transition dynamics.

KEY CONCEPTS

balanced growth path
charter cities
excludability
fixed costs
growth accounting
growth effects
idea diagram
increasing returns
level effects
the new economy
objects versus ideas
Pareto optimal
the principle of transition dynamics
problems with perfect competition
the productivity slowdown
rivalrous versus nonrivalrous
the Romer model

REVIEW QUESTIONS

1. How are ideas different from objects? What are some examples of each?
2. What is nonrivalry, and how does it lead to increasing returns? In your answer, what role does the standard replication argument play? Is national defense rivalrous or nonrivalrous?
3. Suppose a friend of yours decides to write a novel. Explain how ideas and objects are involved in this process. Where do nonrivalry and increasing returns play a role? What happens if the novel is sold at marginal cost?
4. Explain how nonrivalry leads to increasing returns in the two key production functions of the Romer model.
5. The growth rate of output in the Romer model is $\bar{z}\bar{\ell}\bar{L}$. Why does each of these parameters belong in the solution?
6. Why is growth accounting useful?

EXERCISES

smartwork.wwnorton.com 

1. **Nonrivalry:** Explain whether the following goods are rivalrous or nonrivalrous: (a) Beethoven's Fifth Symphony, (b) a portable music player, (c) Monet's painting *Water Lilies*, (d) the method of public key cryptography, (e) fish in the ocean.

2. **Increasing returns and imperfect competition:** Suppose a new piece of computer software—say a word processor with perfect speech recognition—can be created for a onetime cost of \$100 million. Suppose that once it's created, copies of the software can be distributed at a cost of \$1 each.

   (a) If Y denotes the number of copies of the computer program produced and X denotes the amount spent on production, what is the production function—that is, the relation between Y and X?
   (b) Make a graph of this production function. Does it exhibit increasing returns? Why or why not?
   (c) Suppose the firm charges a price equal to marginal cost (\$1) and sells a million copies of the software. What are its profits?
   (d) Suppose the firm charges a price of \$20. How many copies does it have to sell in order to break even? What if the price is \$100 per copy?
   (e) Why does the scale of the market—the number of copies the firm could sell—matter?

3. **Calculating growth rates:** What is the growth rate of output per person in Figure 6.2? What are the growth rates of output per person before and after the changes in the parameter values in Figures 6.3 and 6.4?

4. **An increase in research productivity:** Suppose the economy is on a balanced growth path in the Romer model, and then, in the year 2030, research productivity $\bar{z}$ rises immediately and permanently to the new level $\bar{z}'$.

   (a) Solve for the new growth rate of knowledge and y_t.
   (b) Make a graph of y_t over time using a ratio scale.
   (c) Why might research productivity increase in an economy?

5. **An increase in the initial stock of knowledge:** Suppose we have two economies—let's call them Earth and Mars—that are identical, except that one begins with a stock of ideas that is twice as large as the other: $\bar{A}_0^{\text{Earth}} = 2 \times \bar{A}_0^{\text{Mars}}$. The two economies are so far apart that they don't share ideas, and each evolves as a separate Romer economy. On a single graph (with a ratio scale), plot the behavior of per capita GDP on Earth and Mars over time. What is the effect of starting out with more knowledge?

6. **Numbers in the Romer model (I):** Suppose the parameters of the Romer model take the following values: $\bar{A}_0 = 100$, $\bar{\ell} = 0.10$, $\bar{z} = 1/500$, and $\bar{L} = 100$.

   (a) What is the growth rate of output per person in this economy?
   (b) What is the initial level of output per person? What is the level of output per person after 100 years?
   (c) Suppose the research share were to double. How would you answer parts (a) and (b)?

7. **Numbers in the Romer model (II):** Now suppose the parameters of the model take the following values: $\bar{A}_0 = 100$, $\bar{\ell} = 0.06$, $\bar{z} = 1/3{,}000$, and $\bar{L} = 1{,}000$.
   - **(a)** What is the growth rate of output per person in this economy?
   - **(b)** What is the initial level of output per person? What is the level of output per person after 100 years?
   - **(c)** Now consider the following changes, one at a time: a doubling of the initial stock of knowledge $\bar{A}_0$, a doubling of the research share $\bar{\ell}$, a doubling of research productivity $\bar{z}$, and a doubling of the population $\bar{L}$. How would your answer to parts (a) and (b) change in each case?
   - **(d)** If you could advocate one of the changes considered in part (c), which would you choose? Write a paragraph arguing for your choice.

8. **A variation on the Romer model:** Consider the following variation:

$$Y_t = A_t^{1/2} L_{yt},$$
$$\Delta A_{t+1} = \bar{z} A_t L_{at},$$
$$L_{yt} + L_{at} = \bar{L},$$
$$L_{at} = \bar{\ell} \bar{L}.$$

   There is only a single difference: we've changed the exponent on A_t in the production of the output good so that there is now a diminishing marginal product to ideas in that sector.
   - **(a)** Provide an economic interpretation for each equation.
   - **(b)** What is the growth rate of knowledge in this economy?
   - **(c)** What is the growth rate of output per person in this economy?
   - **(d)** Solve for the level of output per person at each point in time.

Important:

9. **Growth accounting:** Consider the following (made-up) statistics for some economies. Assume the exponent on capital is 1/3 and that the labor composition is unchanged. For each economy, compute the growth rate of TFP.
   - **(a)** A European economy: $g_{Y/L} = 0.03$, $g_{K/L} = 0.03$.
   - **(b)** A Latin American economy: $g_{Y/L} = 0.02$, $g_{K/L} = 0.01$.
   - **(c)** An Asian economy: $g_{Y/L} = 0.06$, $g_{K/L} = 0.15$.

WORKED EXERCISES

2. **Increasing returns and imperfect competition:**
   - **(a)** The production function for the word processor is

$$Y = X - 100 \text{ million}$$

   if X is larger than 100 million, and zero otherwise. By spending \$100 million, you create the first copy, and then \$1 must be spent distributing it (say for the DVD it comes on). For each dollar spent over this amount, you can create another copy of the software.

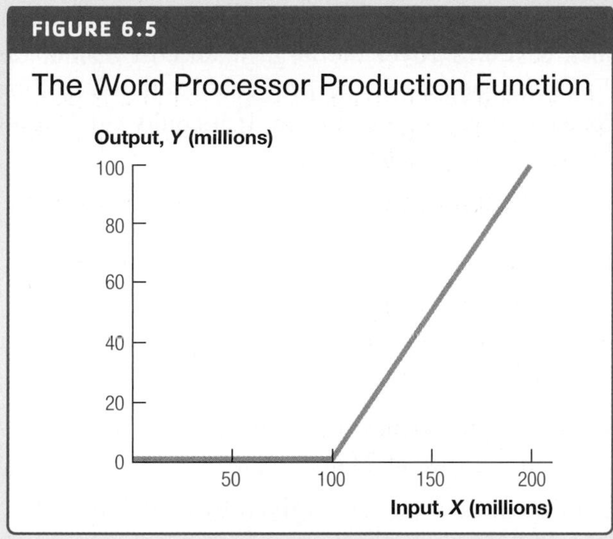

FIGURE 6.5
The Word Processor Production Function

(b) The production function is plotted in Figure 6.5. Output is zero whenever X is less than 100 million. Does this production function exhibit increasing returns? Yes. We spend \$100 million (plus \$1) to get the first copy, but doubling our spending will lead to 100 million copies (plus 2). So there is a huge degree of increasing returns here. Graphically, this can be seen by noting that the production function "curves up" starting from an input of zero, a common characteristic of production functions exhibiting increasing returns. (Constant returns would be a straight line starting from zero; decreasing returns would curve down more sharply than a straight line.)

(c) If the firm charges a price equal to marginal cost (i.e. equal to \$1) and sells a million copies, then revenues are \$1 million, while costs are \$101 million. Profits are therefore negative \$100 million. That is, if the firm charges marginal cost, it loses an amount equal to the fixed cost of developing the software.

(d) Selling at price p, revenue is pX, and cost is \$100 million + X dollars. To break even so that revenue is equal to cost, the firm must sell X copies, where

$$pX = 100 \text{ million} + X.$$

Solving this equation yields

$$X = \frac{100 \text{ million}}{p - 1}.$$

At $p = 20$, this gives $X = 5.26$ million copies. At $p = 100$, this gives $X = 1.01$ million copies. Notice that the answer is approximately 100 million divided by the price, since the marginal cost is small.

(e) The fact that this production function exhibits increasing returns to scale is a strong hint that "scale matters." Increasing returns to scale means that larger firms are more productive. In this case, everything is about covering the fixed cost of creating the software. If the software can be sold all over the world, it will be much easier to cover the large fixed cost than if the software can only be sold to a few people. If the firm could sell 100 million copies of the software at $2 each, it would break even. If it could sell 200 million copies at that price, it would make lots of money.

6. Numbers in the Romer model (I):

(a) The growth rate of output per person in the Romer economy is equal to the growth rate of ideas, given by the formula in equation (6.7):

$$\frac{\Delta A_{t+1}}{A_t} = \bar{z}L_{at} = \bar{z}\bar{\ell}\bar{L}.$$

With the given parameter values, this growth rate is $0.10 \times 1/500 \times 100 = 0.02$, so the economy grows at 2% per year.

(b) The level of output per person is given by equation (6.9):

$$y_t = \bar{A}_0(1 - \bar{\ell})(1 + \bar{g})^t,$$

where $\bar{g} \equiv \bar{z}\bar{\ell}\bar{L} = 0.02$. Substituting in the relevant parameter values, we find

$$y_0 = 100 \times (1 - 0.10) = 90,$$

and

$$y_{100} = 100 \times (1 - 0.10) \times (1.02)^{100} = 652.$$

(c) If the research share doubles to 20%, the economy behaves as follows. The growth rate doubles to 4% per year, and the income levels are given by

$$y_0 = 100 \times (1 - 0.20) = 80,$$

and

$$y_{100} = 100 \times (1 - 0.20) \times (1.04)^{100} = 4{,}040.$$

The output of the consumption good is lower in the short run because more people are engaged in research. The economy grows faster as a result; however, incomes in the future are much higher. This exercise is the numerical version of the change considered in the second experiment in Section 6.3 (Figure 6.4).

6.9 Appendix: Combining Solow and Romer (Algebraically)

This appendix shows how the insights of Solow and Romer can be combined in a single model of economic growth. Mathematically, the combination is relatively straightforward. Intuitively, all the results we have learned from both models continue to hold in the combined model.

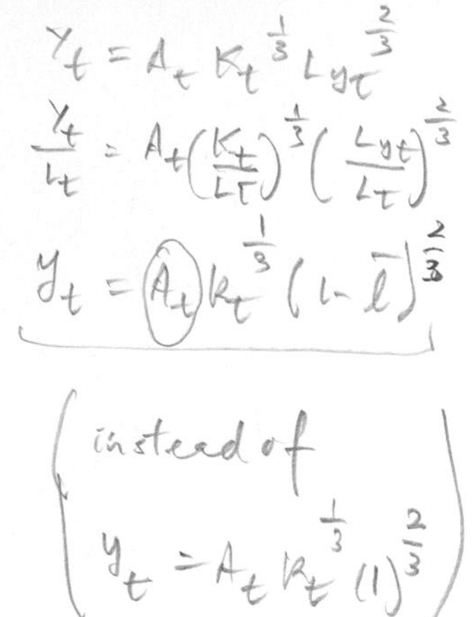

Setting Up the Combined Model

We start with the Romer model and then add capital back in. The combined model features five equations and five unknowns. The equations are

$$Y_t = A_t K_t^{1/3} L_{yt}^{2/3}, \tag{6.13}$$

$$\Delta K_{t+1} = \bar{s} Y_t - \bar{d} K_t, \tag{6.14}$$

$$\Delta A_{t+1} = \bar{z} A_t L_{at}, \tag{6.15}$$

$$L_{yt} + L_{at} = \bar{L}, \tag{6.16}$$

$$L_{at} = \bar{\ell} \bar{L}. \tag{6.17}$$

Our five unknowns are output Y_t, capital K_t, knowledge A_t, workers L_{yt}, and researchers L_{at}.

Equation (6.13) is the production function for output. Notice that it exhibits constant returns to objects—capital and workers. Because of the nonrivalry of ideas, however, it exhibits increasing returns to objects and ideas together.

Equation (6.14) describes the accumulation of capital over time. The change in the capital stock is equal to new investment $\bar{s}Y_t$ less depreciation $\bar{d}K_t$. As in the Solow model, the investment rate $\bar{s}$ is an exogenously given parameter.

The last three equations are all directly imported from the Romer model. New ideas, equation (6.15), are produced using the existing stock of ideas and researchers. Here we leave capital out, but only because it makes the model easier to solve; nothing of substance would change if we instead let capital and researchers combine with knowledge to produce new ideas. Equation (6.16) says that the numbers of workers and researchers sum to equal the total population. And equation (6.17) captures our assumption that a constant fraction of the population, $\bar{\ell}$, works as researchers. This implies that the fraction $1 - \bar{\ell}$ works to produce the output good.

Solving the Combined Model

One thing to notice about the combined model is that it is much like our original Solow model. In the original Solow model, however, the productivity level $\bar{A}$ was a constant parameter. A onetime increase in this productivity level produced transition dynamics that led the economy to grow for a while before settling down at its new steady state. Now, A_t increases continuously over time. In a Solow diagram, this would show up as the $\bar{s}Y$ curve shifting upward each period, leading the capital stock to increase each period as new investment exceeded depreciation.

This result means two things. First, it helps us understand how capital and output will continue to grow in our combined model. Rather than achieving a steady state with a constant level of capital, we will get a balanced growth path, where capital grows at a constant rate. Second, linking the combined model to the Solow diagram suggests that transition dynamics are likely to be important; this turns out to be correct. In what follows, we begin by showing how to solve for the balanced growth path, then take up the issue of transition dynamics.

Long-Run Growth

Inspired by the Romer model, let's look for a balanced growth path—that is, for a situation in the combined model where output, capital, and the stock of ideas all grow at constant rates. The first step is to apply the rules for computing growth rates that we developed in Chapter 3 (Section 3.5) to the production function for output. As in Section 6.5, we use rules 2 and 3: the growth rate of the product of several variables is the sum of the variables' growth rates, and the growth rate of a variable raised to some power is that power times the growth rate of the variable. Applied to the production function for output in equation (6.13), we have

$$g_{Yt} = g_{At} + \frac{1}{3}g_{Kt} + \frac{2}{3}g_{Lyt} \tag{6.18}$$

where $g_{Yt} \equiv \Delta Y_{t+1}/Y_t$ and the other growth rates are defined in a similar way. Notice that g_Y, g_A, and g_K are all endogenous variables; they are just the growth rates of our regular endogenous variables.

Equation (6.18) is the growth rate version of the production function. It says that the growth rate of output is the sum of three terms: the growth rate of knowledge, the growth contribution from capital, and the growth contribution from workers.

To solve for the growth rate of output, we need to know the growth rate of the three terms on the right-hand side of this equation. The growth rate of knowledge, g_A, turns out to be easy to obtain. Just as in the Romer model, it comes directly from dividing the production function for new ideas by the level of knowledge:

$$g_{At} = \frac{\Delta A_{t+1}}{A_t} = \bar{z}L_{at} = \bar{z}\bar{\ell}\bar{L}. \tag{6.19}$$

Knowledge grows because researchers invent new ideas. It turns out to be convenient to define $\bar{g} \equiv \bar{z}\bar{\ell}\bar{L}$ here, just as we did in the Romer model.

We can learn about the growth rate of capital, the second term in equation (6.18), by looking back at the capital accumulation equation, (6.14). Dividing that equation by K_t yields

$$g_{Kt} = \frac{\Delta K_{t+1}}{K_t} = \bar{s}\frac{Y_t}{K_t} - \bar{d}. \tag{6.20}$$

This equation still has two endogenous variables on the right side, so it's not yet a solution. But we can still learn something important from it. What must be true about Y_t and K_t in order for g_K to be constant over time? Since the other terms in equation (6.20), $\bar{s}$ and $\bar{d}$, are constant along a balanced growth path, Y_t/K_t must be constant as well. But the only way it can be constant is if Y_t and K_t grow at the same rate. For example, if Y_t grew faster than K_t, then the ratio would grow over time, causing g_K to increase. This means we must have $g_K^* = g_Y^*$, where the asterisk (*) denotes the fact that these variables are evaluated along a balanced growth path. At this point, we don't know the value of either g_Y^* or g_K^*, but if we can figure out one of them, we will know the other.

The last term in equation (6.18) is the growth rate of the number of workers. We've assumed the number of workers is a constant fraction of the population, and we've assumed the population itself is constant. This means that the growth rate of the number of workers must be equal to zero: $g_{Lyt} = 0$.

Now we are ready to plug our three results back into the growth rate version of the production function. In particular, we have $g_{A_t} = \bar{z}\bar{\ell}\bar{L} = \bar{g}$, $g_K^* = g_Y^*$, and $g_{Lyt} = 0$. Substituting these three results into equation (6.18) and evaluating that expression along a balanced growth path yields

$$g_Y^* = \bar{g} + \frac{1}{3} g_Y^* + \frac{2}{3} \cdot 0.$$

And since this equation involves just a single endogenous variable, g_Y^*, we can solve this equation for g_Y^* to find[24]

$$g_Y^* = \frac{3}{2}\bar{g} = \frac{3}{2}\bar{z}\bar{\ell}\bar{L} \tag{6.21}$$

This equation pins down the growth rate of output—and the growth rate of output per person, since there is no population growth—in the long run of the combined model. Compare this solution with what we found in the Romer model. In equation (6.9), we found that the growth rate of output per person in the Romer model was exactly equal to $\bar{g}$. In the combined model, growth in the long run is even faster, at $3/2 \cdot \bar{g}$. Why the difference?

The answer must be related to capital accumulation, since that's the only real difference between the Romer model and the combined model. Indeed, recall from the Solow diagram what happens when productivity increases in the Solow model: the level of capital increases. So output rises for *two* reasons: (1) there is an increase in productivity itself (a direct effect); (2) the productivity increase leads to a higher capital stock, which in turn leads to an even higher level of output (an indirect effect). This is exactly what happens in our combined model. There is a direct effect of growth in knowledge on output growth; this was clear back in equation (6.18). But then the growth in output leads to capital accumulation, which in turn leads to more output growth.

So while capital can't itself serve as an engine of economic growth, it helps to amplify the underlying growth in knowledge. Long-run growth in output per person is therefore higher in the combined model than in the Romer model.

Output per Person

Now that we know the growth rate of output in the combined model, we can also solve for the *level* of output per person along a balanced growth path. The process of arriving at this solution is exactly the same as in the original Solow model in Chapter 5.

First, we need an equation for the capital stock. Look back at equation (6.20), and recall that $g_K^* = g_Y^*$ along a balanced growth path. That equation can be solved for the capital-output ratio along a balanced growth path:

$$\frac{K_t^*}{Y_t^*} = \frac{\bar{s}}{g_y^* + \bar{d}}. \tag{6.22}$$

[24] Subtract $1/3 \cdot g_Y^*$ from both sides to find $2/3 \cdot g_Y^* = \bar{g}$, and then multiply both sides by 3/2 to get the solution.

This equation says that the capital-output ratio is proportional to the investment rate $\bar{s}$ along a balanced growth path.

If we view this solution for the capital-output ratio as an equation giving K_t^* as a function of Y_t^*, we can substitute it back into the production function, equation (6.13), and solve to find[25]

$$y_t^* \equiv \frac{Y_t^*}{\bar{L}} = \left(\frac{\bar{s}}{g_y^* + \bar{d}}\right)^{1/2} A_t^{*3/2}\,(1 - \bar{\ell}) \qquad (6.23)$$

Compare this equation with our solutions for the Romer model in equation (6.9) and the Solow model in equation (5.9) (on page 106 in Chapter 5). As in the Romer model, output per person depends on the stock of knowledge. Because of nonrivalry, a new idea raises the income of every person in the economy. (By the way, we can solve this equation further by noting that the stock of ideas A_t^* is given by the same equation as in the Romer model, equation [6.8].) Growth in A_t leads to sustained growth in output per person along the balanced growth path.

As in the Solow model, output depends on the square root of the investment rate. A higher investment rate raises the *level* of output per person along a balanced growth path; this result is discussed further below in the context of transition dynamics.

Transition Dynamics

What in the original Solow model led to the presence of transition dynamics? This is an important question, and you should make sure you remember the answer: diminishing returns to capital. As capital accumulates, each additional increment to the capital stock raises the level of output—and investment—by less and less, causing the growth rate to decline as the economy approaches its steady state from below.

In the combined Romer and Solow model, the production function still exhibits diminishing returns to capital, so the principle of transition dynamics applies in this richer model as well. The following paragraphs discuss the transition dynamics of the combined model without the mathematics; at this point, it is sufficient for you to follow the intuition behind the basic result.

In the Solow model, the principle of transition dynamics said that the farther below its steady state an economy was, the faster it would grow. In the combined Solow-Romer model, there is no longer a steady state; instead, the economy grows at a constant rate in the long run. Nevertheless, a similar statement still applies. For

---

[25] Here is the algebra for the solution. First, the substitution for K_t^* from equation (6.22) gives

$$Y_t^* = A_t \left(\frac{\bar{s}}{g_y^* + \bar{d}} \cdot Y_t^*\right)^{1/3} L_{yt}^{2/3}.$$

Collecting the Y_t terms on the left side yields

$$Y_t^{*2/3} = A_t \left(\frac{\bar{s}}{g_y^* + \bar{d}}\right)^{1/3} L_{yt}^{2/3}.$$

Finally, raise both sides to the power 3/2 and divide by $\bar{L}$ to get equation (6.23).

the combined model, the **principle of transition dynamics** can be expressed as follows: The farther below its balanced growth path an economy is (in percentage terms), the faster the economy will grow. Similarly, the farther above its balanced growth path an economy is, the slower it will grow.

To understand our new version of this principle, consider an example. Suppose the economy starts out on its balanced growth path, but then the investment rate $\bar{s}$ is increased to a permanently higher value. How does the economy evolve over time? According to equation (6.23), the increase in the investment rate means that the balanced-growth-path level of income is now higher. Since current income is unchanged, the economy is now below its balanced growth path, and we should expect it to grow rapidly to "catch up" to this path.

This example is shown graphically in Figure 6.6. A key thing to notice here is that output per person is plotted on a ratio scale. Recall that this means that the slope of the output path is related to the growth rate of y_t. Before the increase in the investment rate, y_t is growing at a constant rate: the path is a straight line. After the increase in the year 2030, the growth rate rises immediately—the slope of the path increases sharply. Over time, the growth rate declines until eventually it exhibits the same slope as the original path. That is, the growth rate returns to $\bar{g}$, which does not depend on $\bar{s}$. Notice also that the level of output per person is permanently higher as a result of the increase in the investment rate, but the growth rate is unchanged. This is sometimes called a long-run "level effect." Overall, this graph shows the principle of transition dynamics at work in the combined model.

What changes in the combined model lead to transition dynamics? The answer is that changing any parameter of the model—$\bar{s}$, $\bar{d}$, $\bar{z}$, $\bar{L}$, $\bar{\ell}$, $\bar{K}_0$, or $\bar{A}_0$—will create transition dynamics. Why? If you look back at equations (6.21) and (6.23), you'll see that all these parameters affect either the level of output along the balanced

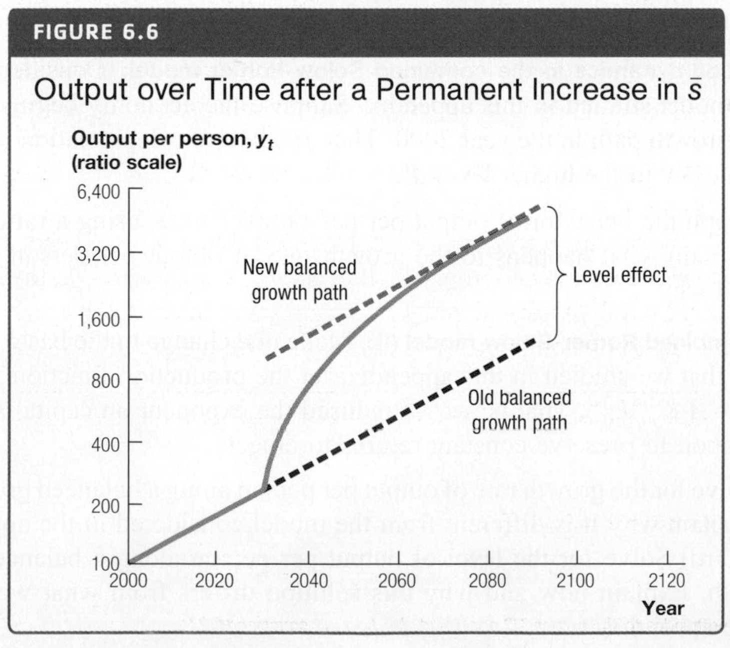

FIGURE 6.6

Output over Time after a Permanent Increase in $\bar{s}$

The economy begins on a balanced growth path. Then, in the year 2030, there is a permanent increase in the investment rate $\bar{s}$, which raises the balanced growth path. Since the economy is now below its new balanced growth path, the principle of transition dynamics says that the economy will grow rapidly. Notice that y_t is plotted on a ratio scale, so the slope of the path is the growth rate.

growth path or the level of current output. A change in any of these parameter values will create a gap between current output and the balanced growth path, just like the one we see in Figure 6.6. Once this gap is created, the principle of transition dynamics takes over and the economy grows to close the gap.

The principle of transition dynamics was the key to understanding differences in growth rates across countries in the Solow model. Now we see that this explanation continues to apply in the combined model. We have a theory of long-run growth driven by the discovery of new ideas throughout the world *and* a theory of differences in growth rates across countries based on transition dynamics. Our model predicts that in the long run, all countries should grow at the same rate, given by $\bar{g}$, the growth rate of world knowledge. However, over any given period of time, we may observe differences in growth rates across countries based on the fact that not all countries have reached their balanced growth paths. Changes in policies that change the parameters of the model—like the investment rate—can thus lead to differences in growth rates over long periods of time.

MORE EXERCISES

1. **Transition dynamics:** What is the principle of transition dynamics in the combined Solow-Romer model?

2. **Long-run growth:** Growth in the combined Solow-Romer model is faster than growth in the Romer model. In what sense is this true? Why is it true?

3. **Balanced growth:** Suppose we observe the following growth rates in various economies. Discuss whether or not each economy is on its balanced growth path.
   (a) A European economy: $g_{Y/L} = 0.03$, $g_{K/L} = 0.03$.
   (b) A Latin American economy: $g_{Y/L} = 0.02$, $g_{K/L} = 0.01$.
   (c) An Asian economy: $g_{Y/L} = 0.06$, $g_{K/L} = 0.15$.

4. **Transition dynamics in the combined Solow-Romer model:** Consider the combined model studied in this appendix. Suppose the economy begins on a balanced growth path in the year 2000. Then in 2030, the depreciation rate $\bar{d}$ rises permanently to the higher level $\bar{d}'$.

   (a) Graph the behavior of output per person over time, using a ratio scale.
   (b) Explain what happens to the growth rate of output per person over time and why.

5. **The combined Romer-Solow model (I):** Make one change to the basic combined model that we studied in this appendix: let the production function for output be $Y_t = A_t K_t^{1/4} L_{yt}^{3/4}$. That is, we've reduced the exponent on capital and raised it on labor, to preserve constant returns to objects.

   (a) Solve for the growth rate of output per person along a balanced growth path. Explain why it is different from the model considered in the appendix.
   (b) (Hard) Solve for the level of output per person along a balanced growth path. Explain how and why this solution differs from what we found in the appendix.

6. **The combined Solow-Romer model (II, hard):** Now let the production function for output be $Y_t = A_t K_t^{\alpha} L_{yt}^{1-\alpha}$. That is, we've made the exponent on capital a parameter (α) rather than keeping it as a specific number. Notice that this affects the exponent on labor as well, in order to preserve constant returns to objects.
   - **(a)** Solve for the growth rate of output per person along a balanced growth path. Explain how it relates to the solution of the model considered in the appendix.
   - **(b)** Solve for the level of output per person along a balanced growth path. Explain how it relates to the solution of the model considered in the appendix.
   - **(c)** The formula for a geometric series is $1 + \alpha + \alpha^2 + \alpha^3 + \cdots = 1/(1 - \alpha)$ if α is some number between 0 and 1. How and why is this formula related to your answers to parts (a) and (b)? (*Hint*: Think about how an increase in output today affects capital in the future.)

CHAPTER 7

THE LABOR MARKET, WAGES, AND UNEMPLOYMENT

OVERVIEW

In this chapter, we learn

- how a basic supply-and-demand model helps us understand the labor market.
- how labor market distortions like taxes and firing costs affect employment in the long run.
- how to compute present discounted values, and how to value your human capital.
- a key fact about the labor market: the return to a college education has risen enormously over the last half-century.

> It's a recession when your neighbor loses his job; it's a depression when you lose yours.
>
> —HARRY S TRUMAN

7.1 Introduction

The most significant interaction most of us have with markets occurs in the labor market. Over the course of a lifetime, the typical worker will spend approximately 90,000 hours at a job. The wages earned by a person who starts her career this year in the United States and works for the next 45 years will altogether be worth more than $1 million in today's dollars. In a sense that will become clear in this chapter, many of you reading this sentence are already millionaires!

This chapter and the next—the last two chapters of the "long run" section of the book—examine two important topics in macroeconomics: the labor market and inflation. You might say that these chapters provide the long-run theory of unemployment and inflation. In this view, they are a natural transition to the "short run" chapters that follow, which are concerned with economic fluctuations in unemployment, output, and inflation.

Our focus on the labor market allows us to explore a number of key issues in economics. We begin, in Section 7.2, by documenting some basic facts about the U.S. labor market. Section 7.3 then presents a standard supply-and-demand model of the labor market showing how wages and employment are determined in an economy. This framework will be used in the remainder of the chapter as we seek to understand two other important facts about labor markets: the large differences in unemployment rates and hours worked among the advanced countries of the world (Section 7.4) and the tremendous increase in the return to education that has occurred in the United States over the last half-century (Section 7.6). Workers with a college education today earn nearly twice the wage paid to a worker with only a high school education, a premium that has nearly doubled since the early 1960s. Understanding why this is the case leads to significant implications for public policy and for our understanding of economic growth.

This chapter includes a discussion of an important tool in economics, the concept of *present discounted value*. By the end, you will understand the sense in which you are already a millionaire. You will also gain a new appreciation for how much your college education is worth.

7.2 The U.S. Labor Market

The labor market determines both the price of labor—the wage—and the quantity of labor, employment. But before we start analyzing this market in detail, let's take a general look at how wages and employment have changed over time.

Recall from Chapter 2 (Section 2.2) that wages account for about two-thirds of per capita GDP, a share that's stable over time. We also know that average wages have grown at a rate of almost 2 percent per year for the last century. So this is our first key fact: workers are getting richer and richer over time, at least on average. (Among individuals, there are significant differences in wages, but we can set this inequality aside for the moment, to be examined more carefully later in the context of differences in education.)

What about the quantity of labor, employment? There are two measurements that prove useful here: the ratio of employment to the population, and the unemployment rate. Figure 7.1 shows the **employment-population ratio** for the United States, from 1960 to 2010. The first thing that strikes us is the general increase in the employment-population ratio during the last 50 years. About 56 percent of people over the age of 16 worked in 1960, but more than 63 percent worked in 2007, before the start of the latest recession. As you might expect, this rise in employment was driven entirely by the increase in female workers: the employment-population ratio was about 35 percent for women in 1960 and rose to 56 percent by 2005. In contrast, the fraction of the male population that works has actually declined, from about 79 percent in 1960 to about 70 percent in 2005.

Another fact that stands out in Figure 7.1 is the sharp decline in employment that occurs surrounding a recession (the shaded areas). In March 2007, the employment-population ratio peaked at 63.4 percent. By January 2010, it had fallen all the way to 58.4 percent, a decline of 5 percentage points. We should be careful not to forget that actual jobs are attached to these percentages. Because

Both the trend and the fluctuations in the employment-population ratio are significant. The trend reflects the growing participation of women in the labor market. Fluctuations reveal recessions, which are shaded.

FIGURE 7.1

The Ratio of Employment to Population in the United States, 1960–2010

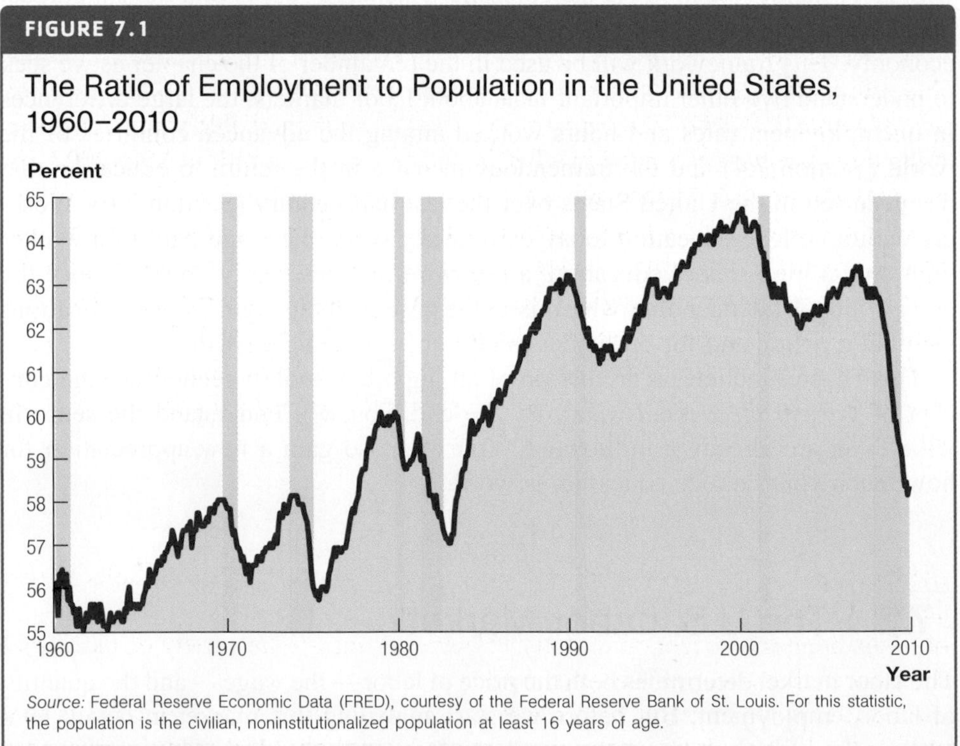

Source: Federal Reserve Economic Data (FRED), courtesy of the Federal Reserve Bank of St. Louis. For this statistic, the population is the civilian, noninstitutionalized population at least 16 years of age.

TABLE 7.1

The Composition of the U.S. Labor Force, January 2010

Civilian population, aged 16 and over	237 million
Labor force	153 million
Employed	138 million
Unemployed	14.8 million
Not in the labor force	84 million

Source: Bureau of Labor Statistics, Economic News Release, February 5, 2010.

the civilian population aged 16 and over in 2010 was approximately 240 million, each percentage point corresponds to 2.4 million missing jobs.

A common statistic for analyzing the slackness of the labor market is the **unemployment rate**, the fraction of the labor force that is unemployed. A person is said to be unemployed if she doesn't have a job that pays a wage or salary, she actively looked for such a job during the 4 weeks before the rate was measured, and she is currently available to work. The labor force is defined as the sum of the employed and the unemployed. Table 7.1 shows the breakdown of the U.S. population in January 2010 along these lines.

The unemployment rate in January 2010 was 9.7 percent, which from Table 7.1 is equal to 14.8/153. To put this rate into perspective, Figure 7.2 shows the unemployment rate since 1950. The unemployment rate peaked at 10.1 percent in October 2009, during the recession associated with the recent financial crisis. This rate is extraordinarily high, having been exceeded only in 1982–83, when unemployment reached 10.8 percent. The rise is also remarkable when compared to the low rates that prevailed just before the recession started: in May 2007, for example, the unemployment rate was just 4.4 percent.

Another interesting fact that stands out in Figure 7.2 is the general upward and then downward swing in the average rate of unemployment, at least prior to the recent recession. After averaging between 4 and 5 percent during the 1950s and 1960s, the unemployment rate crept steadily higher during the 1970s, peaking at 10.8 percent during the 1982 recession. The 1980s and 1990s then witnessed two very long expansions when the unemployment rate dropped substantially, marred only by the recessions in 1990–91 and 2001.

The Dynamics of the Labor Market

The fact that the unemployment rate in January 2010 was 9.7 percent tells us that almost 10 percent of people who would have liked to be working didn't have a job. This blunt macroeconomic statistic, however, masks the variety of individual experiences that occur in the labor market.

A fundamental property of economies that is important to appreciate is that even in the best of times, many workers are losing jobs, and many workers are

The dashed line plots a measure of the "natural" rate of unemployment, constructed by averaging the rate over the previous and next 5 years.

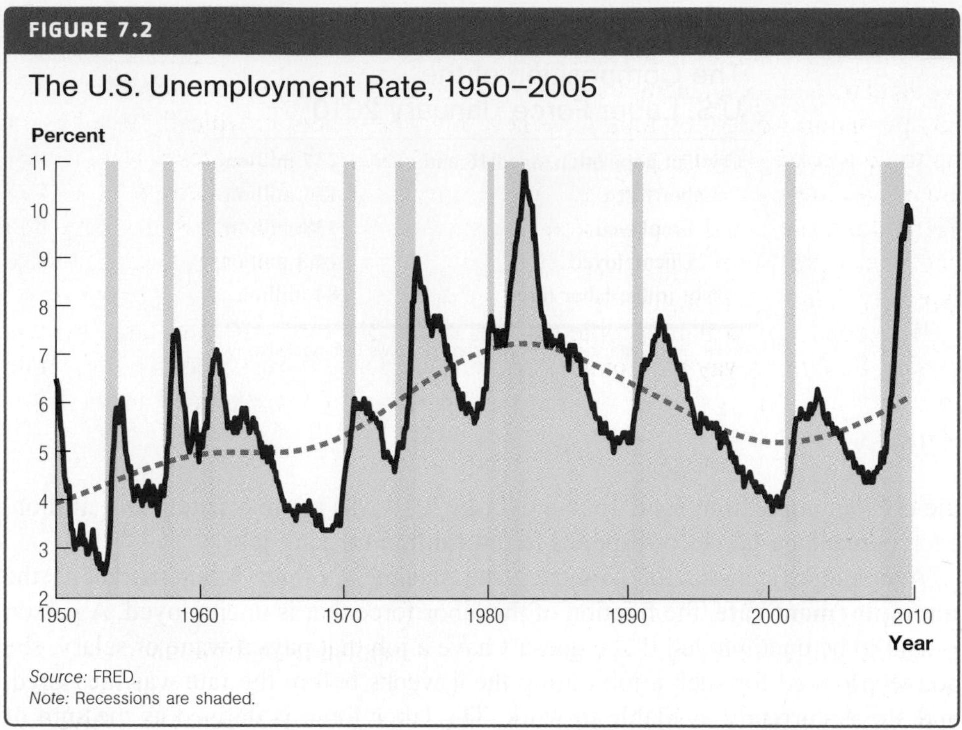

FIGURE 7.2

The U.S. Unemployment Rate, 1950–2005

Source: FRED.
Note: Recessions are shaded.

finding new ones. For example, consider a time when the labor market was booming: between September and December of 2005, 8 million new jobs were created and 7.4 million old jobs were lost. The net change during this quarter was thus a small increase of 0.6 million jobs. In a famous paper written in the early 1990s, Steven Davis and John Haltiwanger highlighted the importance of what they called **job creation** and **job destruction**, or "gross flows," in understanding the labor market.[1] Large quantities of jobs are being created and destroyed every month as part of the normal, dynamic nature of the U.S. economy.

Associated with this churning labor market are two key facts about individual spells of unemployment. First, most spells of unemployment are relatively short. Each month, about 25 percent of people who are unemployed will find a job, and this high job-finding rate means that most spells of unemployment are not too long—less than 3 months for most people. This in no way implies that being unemployed is anything but an extremely unpleasant experience. However, for most people, the unpleasant experience will be over within several months, at least in normal times.

The second key fact is that most of the total weeks of lost work are accounted for by people who are unemployed for a long period of time. While most people can find a job within several months, a significant fraction remain unemployed for an extended period of time. In January 2010, just under half of the unemployed had been out of work for less than 14 weeks, but more than 40 percent had been unemployed for more than 6 months.

[1] Steven J. Davis and John Haltiwanger, "Gross Job Creation, Gross Job Destruction, and Employment Reallocation," *Quarterly Journal of Economics*, vol. 107 (August 1992), pp. 819–63.

Most societies have developed social safety nets to assist people when they lose their job. In the United States, for example, unemployment insurance allows workers who become unemployed through no fault of their own to receive weekly compensation while they look for a new job. The benefit is typically payable for up to 26 weeks, although this period is often extended by Congress during recessions. The insurance payment is based on an individual's past earnings, and in 2009, the average payment was on the order of $300 per week. Some European countries offer benefits that are substantially more generous, but these countries typically exhibit higher unemployment rates as well.

Not surprisingly, many people manage to find a job shortly after their benefits expire. Finding a way to provide adequate insurance while encouraging people to return to work is one of the most important challenges related to the labor market.

7.3 Supply and Demand

What determines the ratio of employment to population and the unemployment rate in the long run? Why do these statistics change over time? To answer these questions, we begin with the most important tool in economics: the analysis of supply and demand. Figure 7.3 shows a basic supply-and-demand diagram for the labor market. Employment (the quantity of labor, denoted L) is on the horizontal axis, and the wage (the price of labor) on the vertical axis.

Recall from Chapter 4 that the labor demand curve is derived from the firm's profit-maximization problem. This curve says that firms continue to hire new

FIGURE 7.3

The Labor Market

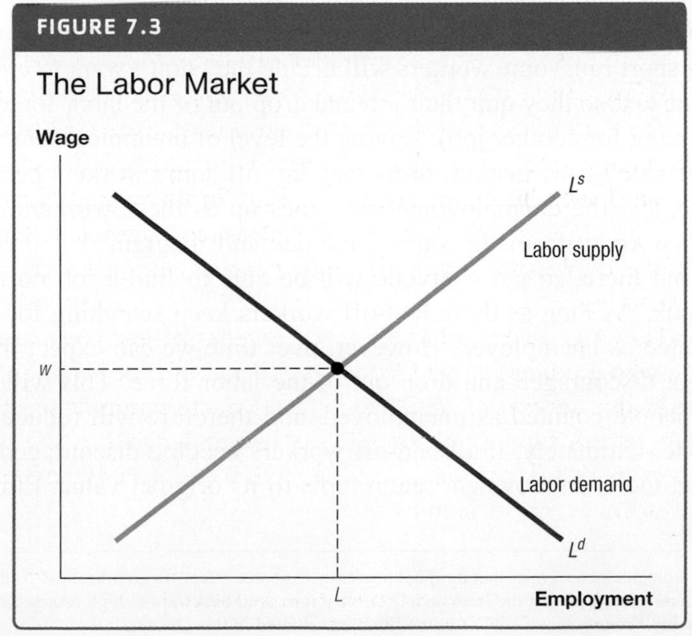

The labor market clears at the wage w and level of employment L such that the amount of labor supplied by workers equals the amount demanded by firms.

workers until the additional output produced by the last worker (the marginal product of labor) equals the cost of hiring that worker—the wage. The labor demand curve slopes downward because of the diminishing marginal product of labor: as we add more workers (holding the other inputs fixed), each additional worker produces less and less.

The labor supply curve slopes upward. At higher wage rates, individuals are willing to work more. Why? At higher wages, the price of leisure (of not working) is higher, so people consume less leisure and work more.[2]

The intersection of labor supply and labor demand determines the level of employment and the wage. If we assume there is a fixed population of people, say N, then this intersection also determines the employment-population ratio L/N.

Why might the level of employment in the economy change? The natural answer is because of changes in the supply and the demand for labor. We now consider each of these in turn.

A Change in Labor Supply

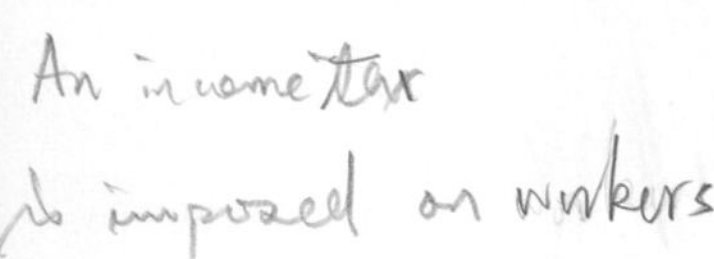

Consider first a shift in the labor supply curve. Suppose, for example, that the government levies an income tax on workers, so that for each dollar earned, the worker has to pay τ cents in taxes. Another way of saying this is that while the firm pays a wage w, the worker gets to keep only $(1 - \tau)w$, with the difference going to the government.

Figure 7.4 shows how this tax appears in the supply-and-demand framework. Here, the labor supply curve shifts back. For any given wage w that the firm pays, the worker receives less, and therefore supplies less labor. In practice, some workers may quit their job while others continue to work full-time. This reduction in labor supply raises the wage the firm has to pay to w' and reduces the level of employment to L'. A labor income tax, then, can be expected to reduce the employment-population ratio.

How would such a tax affect the unemployment rate? The answer is not entirely clear. In the short run, some workers will decide they don't want to work because of the income tax, so they quit their job and drop out of the labor force altogether (without looking for another job), leaving the level of unemployment unchanged. On the other side of the market, firms may lay off some workers because of the higher wage, and the unemployment rate goes up as these workers do look for new jobs. We know from the supply-and-demand diagram that there are now fewer jobs out there, so not everyone will be able to find a job no matter how hard they look. As long as these laid-off workers keep searching for a job, they will be counted as unemployed. However, over time we can expect that some of them will get discouraged and drop out of the labor force. This will reduce the number of people counted as unemployed, and therefore will reduce the unemployment rate. Ultimately, if all laid-off workers become discouraged, the effect could be that the unemployment rate returns to its original value. Empirically, it

[2] You may recall from microeconomics that it is possible for the "income effect" to dominate the "substitution effect" in determining labor supply, so that the labor supply curve might bend backward at high wages. This phenomenon is important in some circumstances, but not in the situations studied in this chapter.

FIGURE 7.4

An Income Tax at Rate τ

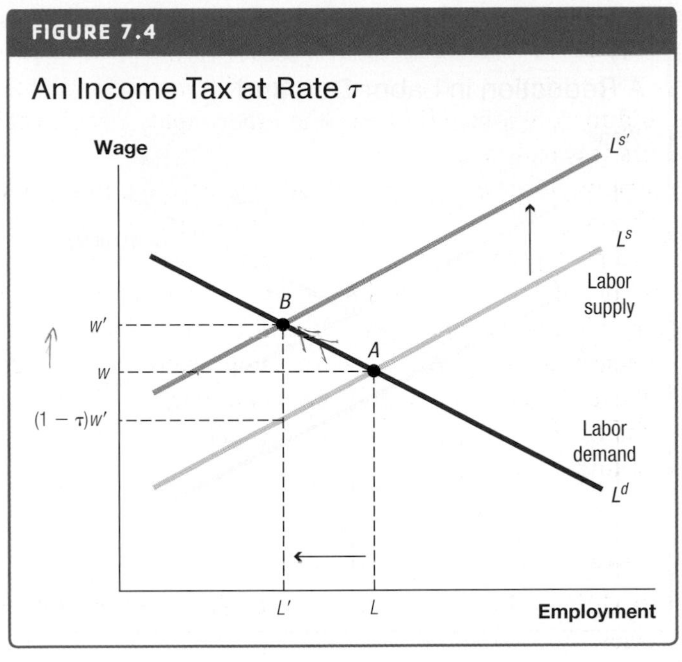

A tax on labor supply creates a wedge between the wage paid by firms and the wage received by workers. This can be understood as a shift back in the labor supply curve: at a given wage paid by firms, workers receive less and supply less labor.

doesn't appear that actual labor markets are so extreme, but the point is that the unemployment rate is not a perfect measure of the state of the labor market. This is one reason why it is helpful to look at alternative statistics as well, like the employment-population ratio.[3]

A Change in Labor Demand

A number of different changes in the economy can cause a reduction in labor demand. For example, there could be an increase in the price of an input like oil. For our purposes, though, let's suppose the government introduces regulations that make it difficult to fire workers. In the short run, such a change may reduce firings. For example, if the economy undergoes a recession just after the regulations are introduced, the firm will not be able to reduce employment as easily. But this situation may make firms less willing to hire labor in the first place, reducing the demand for labor in the long run.

Figure 7.5 shows the effect of a decline in labor demand. When the labor demand curve shifts back, the wage falls to w' and employment falls to L'. The employment-population ratio therefore also declines; the economy moves from its starting point A to the new equilibrium point B. As we saw in the context of the labor supply shock, we would expect the unemployment rate to rise initially in this case, and then perhaps to recover somewhat as discouraged workers drop out of the labor force.

[3] The Bureau of Labor Statistics also collects data on these so-called "discouraged workers" and on workers who take temporary or part-time jobs. So it is possible to look at additional measures of underemployment as well.

A reduction in labor demand causes both the equilibrium wage and the level of employment to decline.

FIGURE 7.5

A Reduction in Labor Demand

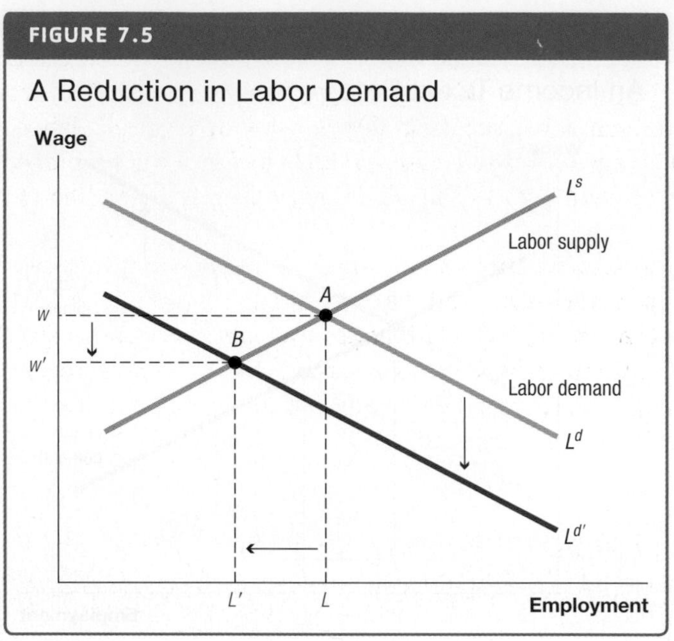

3. ## Wage Rigidity

This example of a shift in the labor demand curve provides a nice laboratory for exploring an important theme in macroeconomics: what happens if wages are rigid for some reason and fail to adjust to clear the labor market? Rather than falling in response to the decline in labor demand, suppose the wage remains unchanged at its original level.

The results are shown in Figure 7.6. While in Figure 7.5 the wage declined and the economy moved from point *A* to point *B*, here the wage does *not* decline

If wages are rigid for some reason and don't fall to clear the labor market, the result is an even larger reduction in employment (compare points *B* and *C*). Notice also that at the original wage $\overline{w}$, labor supply exceeds labor demand: more people would like to work than are able to find jobs.

FIGURE 7.6

A Reduction in Labor Demand with Wage Rigidity

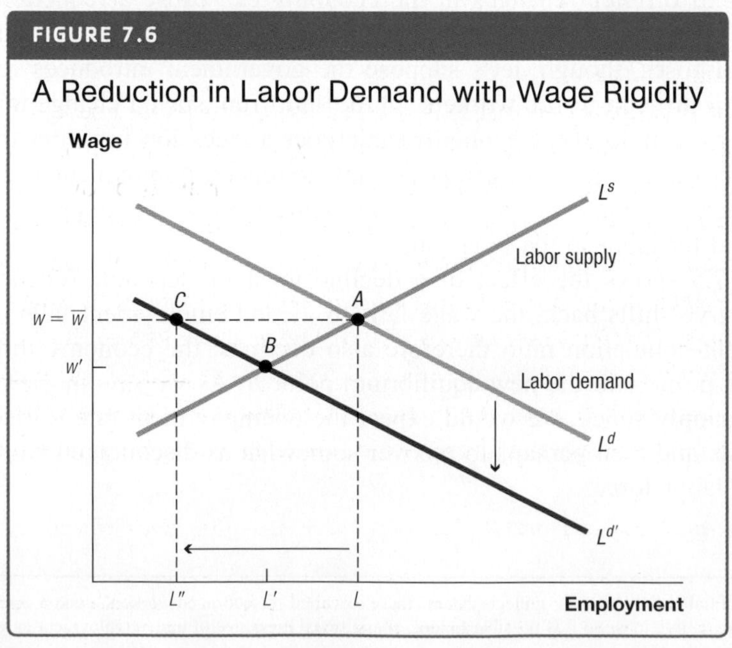

in response to the reduction in labor demand, and the economy moves to point C instead. At the original high wage, firms would like to hire much less labor than before. Notice that at this high wage, many more workers would like jobs than can find them: labor supply at the high wage $\overline{w}$ exceeds labor demand. The failure of the wage to fall to clear the labor market leads to a *larger* adjustment in employment: employment falls to L'', significantly below the market-clearing level L'.

The point of this experiment is to show that **wage rigidities** can lead to large movements in employment. Indeed, they are the reason John Maynard Keynes gave, in *The General Theory of Employment, Interest, and Money* (1936), for the high unemployment of the Great Depression. In modern macroeconomics, wage rigidities often play an important role in our understanding of economic fluctuations, as we will see in Chapter 11.

CASE STUDY

Supply and Demand Shocks in the U.S. Labor Market

The supply-and-demand framework can shed light on the changes in the employment-population ratio and in the unemployment rate that we observed in Section 7.2. There, we learned that the rise in the employment-population ratio is largely explained by the increase in female workers. This increase in turn can be interpreted as resulting from a combination of supply and demand shocks. On the supply side, changing social norms and technological progress in managing fertility are shocks that have likely increased the supply of labor for women. On the demand side, reduced discrimination in the workplace might be thought of as a positive shock to labor demand.

As for the unemployment rate, the gradual rise in the 1960s and 1970s and then the subsequent decline since 1980 appears, at least partly, to be due to a different force on the supply side. Robert Shimer of the University of Chicago suggests that the demographic bulge associated with the baby boom can explain about half the movement in the unemployment rate.[4] Shimer argues that because teenage and young-adult unemployment rates are much higher than those for middle-aged workers, the entry of baby boomers into the labor force in the 1960s and 1970s raised the unemployment rate by about 2 percentage points. As these workers matured, however, their individual unemployment rates declined, and this maturing explains about 1.5 percentage points of the decline in unemployment in the 1980s and 1990s.

---

[4]Robert Shimer, "Why Is the U.S. Unemployment Rate So Much Lower?" in B. Bernanke and J. Rotemberg, eds., *NBER Macroeconomics Annual*, vol. 13 (Cambridge, Mass.: MIT Press, 1998), pp. 11–61.

Different Kinds of Unemployment

Because changes in demographics or unemployment insurance can generate medium-run changes in the unemployment rate, economists divide unemployment into two kinds. The **natural rate of unemployment** is the rate that would prevail if the economy was in neither a boom nor a recession. **Cyclical unemployment** is the difference between the actual rate and the natural rate and is associated with short-run fluctuations, such as occur in booms and recessions. In Figure 7.2, the dashed line representing the natural rate is calculated by taking the average of the unemployment rates in the surrounding periods; it averages out the cyclical component.

In some ways, the so-called natural rate is poorly named, as there is nothing particularly natural about its level. Economists decompose this natural rate into two smaller parts: frictional and structural unemployment. **Frictional unemployment** inevitably results when workers are changing jobs in a dynamic economy. As mentioned at the beginning of the chapter, large numbers of jobs are created and destroyed every month in the course of normal economic activity. Many workers, then, need to change jobs each month, and the process of searching for a new job may certainly involve a spell of unemployment. This is frictional unemployment, and is likely to occur even in a smoothly operating labor market as workers change jobs.[5]

While there is something "natural" about frictional unemployment, the same can't be said about the other component of the natural rate. **Structural unemployment** results from the labor market institutions that match up workers and firms in the labor market. Examples include hiring and firing costs, the level of unemployment benefits, and the level of the minimum wage.

With these terms defined, you can see that the following relationship holds:

$$\text{actual unemployment} = \underbrace{\text{frictional} + \text{structural}}_{\text{natural}} + \text{cyclical}. \tag{7.1}$$

How large are the components on the right side in practice? The conventional wisdom is that most of the natural rate of unemployment in the U.S. economy is frictional in nature. That is, the labor market is viewed as functioning smoothly, so that there is little structural unemployment. Europe, however, is another story, as we will see in the next section.

7.4 The Bathtub Model of Unemployment

Oftentimes in economics, a simple and elegant model can shed useful insight into some aspect of the economy. Such is the **bathtub model** of unemployment. In a way that will become clear, the unemployment rate is in some ways similar to the height of water in a bathtub.[6]

---

[5] One of the most promising current approaches to the macroeconomics of unemployment is based on search theory, which carefully studies the process by which workers and firms match up to produce output. Important contributors to this literature include Olivier Blanchard, Peter Diamond, Robert Hall, Lars Ljungqvist, Dale Mortensen, Christopher Pissarides, Richard Rogerson, Thomas Sargent, and Robert Shimer.

[6] See Robert E. Hall, "A Theory of the Natural Unemployment Rate and the Duration of Employment," *Journal of Monetary Economics*, vol. 5 (April 1979), pp. 153–169.

The bathtub model is based on two simple equations:

$$E_t + U_t = \bar{L} \tag{7.2}$$

$$\Delta U_{t+1} = \underbrace{\bar{s}E_t}_{\substack{\text{employed people}\\ \text{who lose their jobs}}} - \underbrace{\bar{f}U_t}_{\substack{\text{unemployed people}\\ \text{who find new jobs}}} \tag{7.3}$$

The first equation just says that the number of people in the labor force, $\bar{L}$, is the sum of employment, E_t, plus the number of people unemployed, U_t. For this model, we assume that the size of the labor force is some given constant, like 135 million people (hence the "bar" over L).

The second equation is the heart of the bathtub model. It describes how unemployment changes over time. The first term on the right side of equation (7.3) raises unemployment. This term captures the number of employed people who lose their jobs: it is the product of the **job separation rate**, $\bar{s}$, and the number of people who start out with jobs, E_t. Empirically, the job loss rate is a relatively small number: most people who have jobs in one month do not become unemployed the next. A typical value for this rate is something like 1.3 percent: just over 1.0 percent of the people who are employed lose their jobs each month in the United States.

The second term on the right side is the number of unemployed people who find a new job. This term equals the product of $\bar{f}$, the **job finding rate**, and the number of unemployed people, U_t. The job finding rate is the fraction of unemployed who find a job every month; as we discussed earlier, this is a surprisingly high number—about 25 percent. When unemployed people find new jobs, the number of unemployed declines.

In the bathtub model, there are two endogenous variables, E_t and U_t, and two equations. The model tells us how employment and unemployment evolve over time.

Given our earlier work with growth models, it probably won't surprise you that this bathtub model features a steady state where the number of people employed and unemployed is constant. This steady state occurs when $\Delta U_{t+1} = 0$—that is, the change in unemployment is zero. And according to equation (7.3), something quite intuitive happens in the steady state: the number of people losing jobs exactly equals the number of people finding new jobs.

This is where the bathtub analogy shines. Imagine a bathtub with the drain open and the faucet turned on: the height of water in your bathtub will be constant when the amount of water coming in from the faucet equals the amount of water flowing down the drain. Moreover, when the water drains quickly and the faucet is running slowly, the steady state level of water in the bathtub will be low—that is, unemployment will be small. This is precisely the prediction that emerges from the model, as we shall see.

To solve mathematically, just set ΔU_{t+1} equal to zero, and then use equation (7.2) to eliminate E_t from the equation:

$$\begin{aligned} 0 &= \bar{s}E_t - \bar{f}U_t \\ &= \bar{s}(\bar{L} - U_t) - \bar{f}U_t \\ &= \bar{s}\bar{L} - (\bar{f} + \bar{s})U_t \end{aligned}$$

Solving this last equation for U_t gives the number of people unemployed in steady state:

$$U^* = \frac{\bar{s}\bar{L}}{\bar{f} + \bar{s}}.$$

Finally, recall that the unemployment rate is defined as the fraction of the labor force that is unemployed. Therefore,

$$u^* \equiv \frac{U^*}{\bar{L}} = \frac{\bar{s}}{\bar{f} + \bar{s}} \tag{7.4}$$

Because this equation holds in the steady state—the long run—think of the bathtub model as determining the natural rate of unemployment: the rate that prevails when the economy is neither in a boom nor a recession.

To see this equation at work, let's plug in the values for the job loss rate and the job separation rate mentioned above. We said that in a typical month, 25 percent of the unemployed find new jobs, suggesting $\bar{f} = 0.25$. Also, 1.3 percent of the employed lose their jobs, suggesting $\bar{s} = 0.013$. For these values, the natural rate of unemployment equals

$$u^* = \frac{0.013}{0.25 + 0.013} = 0.049.$$

That is, these values imply a natural rate of unemployment of just under 5 percent. Notice that these parameter values suggest a bathtub with a slow-running faucet (only a small fraction of employed people lose their jobs each month) and a quick drain (a large fraction of the unemployed find work each month). The unemployment rate—the amount of water in the bathtub in steady state—is correspondingly low.

An important insight of the bathtub model is that the only way to alter the natural rate of unemployment is to change the job finding rate or the job separation rate. Unfortunately, well-intentioned policies along these lines can have unintended consequences. For example, one may try to reduce the job separation rate by imposing firing costs on firms: any firm that fires a worker must pay one year's salary as a severance payment. If the only thing that happened was a reduction in the separation rate, then this would indeed reduce the natural rate of unemployment. But firms could then become reluctant to hire new workers, reducing the job finding rate. The net of these effects could be to increase the natural rate of unemployment rather than to decrease it.

7.5 Labor Markets around the World

To what extent is the U.S. labor market typical of labor markets in other countries? The answer turns out to be quite interesting. Figure 7.7 shows the unemployment rate for the United States, a set of four European countries, and Japan during the last 50 years. The rates in the United States and Japan in 2005 were relatively

FIGURE 7.7

Unemployment in the United States, Europe, and Japan, 1960–2008

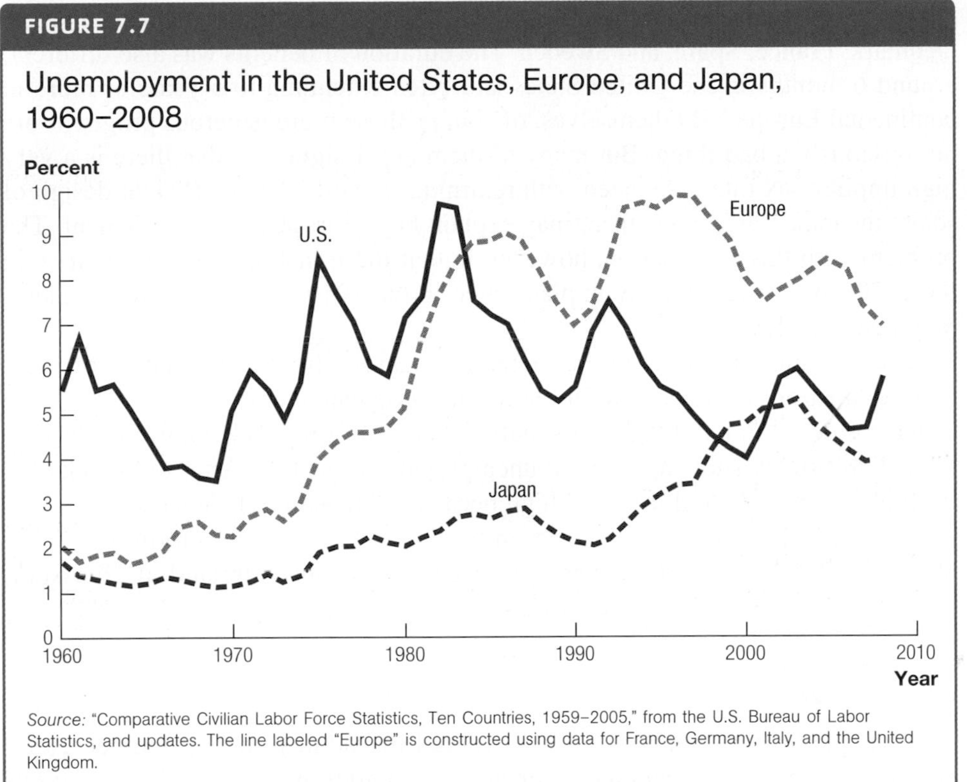

Source: "Comparative Civilian Labor Force Statistics, Ten Countries, 1959–2005," from the U.S. Bureau of Labor Statistics, and updates. The line labeled "Europe" is constructed using data for France, Germany, Italy, and the United Kingdom.

European unemployment has been substantially higher than that in the United States in recent decades. Unemployment in Japan, after being low for many decades, began approaching U.S. levels in the 2000s.

similar, at 5.1 percent and 4.5 percent, respectively. In contrast, the unemployment rate in Europe was substantially higher, at 8.2 percent. This high level has persisted in Europe for the last two decades, while Japan's unemployment rate has been substantially below that in the United States and Europe until recent years.

Unemployment rates were not always so high in Europe. In fact, up until 1975, its rate was well below that in the United States, averaging about 2.5 percent. Then between 1975 and 1985, the rate skyrocketed, and it has remained relatively high ever since.

What explains this enormous rise in European unemployment?[7] Two potential explanations might be labeled "adverse shocks" and "inefficient labor market institutions." The adverse shocks explanation recognizes that in the 1970s, European economies were hit by a worldwide productivity slowdown and by high oil prices. The problem with this explanation, of course, is that other economies such as the United States and Japan were also hit by these shocks but did not experience such a large and protracted rise in unemployment.

The inefficient labor market institutions explanation points to social insurance programs like unemployment and welfare benefits, which are significantly more generous in some European countries than in the United States or Japan. For example, in recent decades, unemployment insurance replaced between 20 and 30 percent of labor income in the United States, Japan, and the United Kingdom

[7] A useful survey of the explanations is Stephen Nickell, "Unemployment and Labor Market Rigidities: Europe versus North America," *Journal of Economic Perspectives*, vol. 11, no. 3 (Summer 1997), pp. 55–74.

during the first few months of unemployment, but about 60 percent or more in Denmark, France, Spain, and Sweden. The duration of benefits was also different: around 6 months in the United States and often extending to 5 years or more in continental Europe.[8] By themselves, of course, these more generous programs are not obviously a bad thing. But many of them are designed so that there is a very high implicit tax rate associated with returning to work. The inefficient design of social insurance programs, then, may explain high European unemployment. The problem with this explanation, however, is that these institutions did not arise in the 1970s, but were typically in place even in the 1950s and 1960s, when unemployment was low.

An emerging consensus in the literature suggests that a combination of these two explanations may account for the rise in European unemployment. Before the adverse shocks hit in the 1970s, the inefficiencies of Europe's labor market institutions didn't really show up because unemployment was low. After the shocks hit, unemployment rose and it stayed high because of these inefficiencies.[9]

In recent years, different countries in Europe have sought to reform their labor market institutions. As a result, unemployment rates in Spain, Ireland, and the Netherlands, for example, have decreased substantially from levels in the 1980s.

Hours of Work

The average annual number of hours worked per adult provides another useful perspective on the international labor market. In addition to capturing variations in labor force participation and unemployment, hours worked also incorporates differences in the intensity of work—for example, either through differences in hours worked per week or through differences in weeks of vacation taken during the year.

Table 7.2 shows this measure for seven different countries at the start of the 1970s and during the mid-1990s. To simplify comparisons, the value for the United States is normalized to 100 in both periods. In the 1970s, hours worked per person in Europe were slightly higher than in the United States (Italy being the exception). Hours worked in Japan were even higher, 27 percent above those in the United States. By the 1990s, however, hours worked had fallen substantially relative to the United States in every country in the table. Hours in Japan were roughly the same as in the United States, while hours in Europe were about three-fourths of the U.S. level.

Indeed, a substantial part of the explanation for why per capita GDP is lower in Europe than in the United States is simply that Europeans work fewer hours. GDP per hour turns out to be not that different between these countries. Is working fewer hours good or bad? The answer isn't clear. If this is a voluntary choice by Europeans to enjoy more leisure, then it has likely improved their welfare. On the other hand, if it is caused by an increase in distortions such as adverse

[8] For these and other facts, see Stephen Nickell, "A Picture of European Unemployment: Success and Failure," working paper, London School of Economics, June 2004.

[9] See, for example, Olivier Blanchard and Lawrence Summers, "Hysteresis in Unemployment," *European Economic Review*, vol. 31 (1987), pp. 288–95; and Lars Ljungqvist and Thomas J. Sargent, "The European Unemployment Dilemma," *Journal of Political Economy*, vol. 106 (1998), pp. 514–50.

TABLE 7.2

Hours Worked per Person Aged 16–64 (U.S. = 100)

	1970–74	1993–96
Italy	82	64
France	105	68
Germany	105	75
Canada	94	88
United Kingdom	110	88
United States	100	100
Japan	127	104

Source: Edward Prescott, "Why Do Americans Work So Much More Than Europeans?" Federal Reserve Bank of Minneapolis, *Quarterly Review*, vol. 28 (July 2004), pp. 2–13.

shocks and inefficient labor market institutions, then it may not be such a good thing. Edward Prescott, winner of the 2004 Nobel Prize in economics, has recently proposed that changes in the tax systems in Europe can help explain why workers in these countries work fewer hours (see source note to Table 7.2).

CASE STUDY

Efficiency Wages and Henry Ford's Five-Dollar-a-Day Plan

In 1914, automaker Henry Ford instituted a five-dollar-a-day minimum wage for his workers, a change that *doubled* the wage of most of them. Why would an astute businessperson pay such high wages when they clearly were not necessary, since these workers were already employed? Ford himself answered, in 1922, "There was . . . no charity in any way involved. . . . We wanted to pay these wages so the business would be on a lasting foundation. We were building for the future. A low wage business is always insecure. . . . The payment of five dollars a day for an eight hour day was one of the finest cost cutting moves we ever made."[10]

Echoing Ford's reasoning, the theory of *efficiency wages* recognizes that it may increase a firm's profits to pay a wage greater than the wage needed to retain workers. There are (at least) three possible reasons for this. First, especially in poor countries, workers may be so poor that paying a higher wage will allow them to eat more, and thus become healthier, more energetic, and more productive. Second,

[10] Daniel M. G. Raff and Lawrence H. Summers, "Did Henry Ford Pay Efficiency Wages?" *Journal of Labor Economics*, vol. 5 (October 1987), pp. S57–86.

when it is difficult for the firm to monitor a worker's effort on the job, paying a higher wage can ensure high effort. The higher wage makes the job more valuable to the worker, so he is less likely to "shirk" and risk being fired. Finally, the higher wage may attract more able workers to that company, making the firm more productive.[11]

7.6 How Much Is Your Human Capital Worth?

So do you feel like a millionaire yet? If your college experience is anything like mine was, your days are generally happy—economists would say you have a "high flow of utility"—but it would be extremely hard to tell you are a millionaire from the appearance of your dorm room. How can we justify this seemingly crazy claim?

The answer is that the "present discounted value" of your lifetime income is (likely) greater than $1 million. To understand this statement, we turn now to this very important tool in economics, finance, accounting, and business: the notion of present discounted value.

Present Discounted Value

Say you win a prize of $1,000 but you won't receive it for another 5 years. If the interest rate is 10 percent, how much is that $1,000 worth today? In other words, how much money would you have to put into the bank today so that your bank balance in 5 years' time is equal to $1,000? The answer is called the **present discounted value** of the prize, computed in the following way. If *pdv* denotes the answer and R is a constant interest rate, then

$$pdv \times (1 + R)^5 = \$1{,}000. \tag{7.5}$$

Rearranging, we see that the present value is given by

$$pdv = \frac{\$1{,}000}{(1 + R)^5}. \tag{7.6}$$

If the interest rate is 10 percent, we discover that the present discounted value of $1,000 in 5 years' time is equal to about $621. That's the amount of money you would have to deposit today in order to have $1,000 five years from now.

As this example illustrates, the present discounted value tells us how much a future payment or stream of payments is worth today (the present). It is discounted in the sense that income in the future is worth less than income today, because of the extra interest that income today can earn. The general formula for computing the present discounted value of a payment that occurs T periods in the future is

$$\text{present discounted value} = \frac{\text{future value}}{(1 + \text{interest rate})^T}. \tag{7.7}$$

[11] For more on efficiency wages, see Lawrence F. Katz, "Efficiency Wage Theories: A Partial Evaluation," *NBER Macroeconomics Annual*, vol. 1 (1986), pp. 235–76.

Now imagine a different prize. Rather than a single payment of \$1,000, this one pays out \$100 every year, starting today, for 20 years. Which prize is more valuable? We've seen that the first one was worth \$621; how much is the second worth?

To answer this question, we compute the present discounted value of each of the 20 payments and add them together. Today's payment is obviously worth \$100; call this amount *pdv*0. Based on the formula in equation (7.6), the payment next year is worth

$$pdv1 = \frac{\$100}{(1+R)^1}. \tag{7.8}$$

Similarly, the payment two years from now is worth

$$pdv2 = \frac{\$100}{(1+R)^2}, \tag{7.9}$$

and so on. Therefore, the entire stream of twenty payments is worth

$$pdv = pdv0 + pdv1 + pdv2 + \ldots + pdv19 \tag{7.10}$$

$$= \$100 + \frac{\$100}{(1+R)} + \frac{\$100}{(1+R)^2} + \ldots + \frac{\$100}{(1+R)^{19}}, \tag{7.11}$$

Most computer spreadsheet programs feature a function called PDV that can compute the solution. Alternatively, there are some clever algebraic tricks that can be employed. For example, recall the formula for a geometric series. If a is some number between 0 and 1, then

$$1 + a + a^2 + \ldots + a^n = \frac{1 - a^{n+1}}{1 - a}. \tag{7.12}$$

We can rewrite equation (7.11) to exploit this formula:

$$pdv = \$100 \times \left[1 + \frac{1}{(1+R)} + \frac{1}{(1+R)^2} + \ldots + \frac{1}{(1+R)^{19}}\right] \tag{7.13}$$

Now let $a = 1/(1+R)$, and apply this to the formula for the geometric series:

$$pdv = \$100 \times \frac{1 - \left(\frac{1}{(1+R)}\right)^{20}}{1 - \frac{1}{(1+R)}}. \tag{7.14}$$

Plugging in $R = 0.10$, the calculation reveals that the *pdv* for this second prize is equal to \$936, so the second prize is significantly more valuable!

Your Human Capital

How does the concept of present discounted value help us see that you are a millionaire? Over the course of your lifetime, you will earn a stream of income from your work. The value of this stream is the value of your current and future human capital: it incorporates the value of your education as well as the value of any skills you may learn on the job in the future. How much is this stream worth today?

To keep things simple, suppose you're an average worker in the economy. The average annual wage is currently about $63,000.[12] Let's suppose you start working now, say at age 22, and retire at age 67, so you work 45 years. We'll ignore growth in wages and discount the future at an interest rate of 3 percent. (Chapter 8 will discuss this 3 percent figure in more detail.)

Applying $R = 0.03$ to equation (7.14), you should find that the value of your human capital is given by

$$pdv = \$63{,}000 \times \frac{1 - \left(\frac{1}{1+R}\right)^{45}}{1 - \frac{1}{1+R}}. \qquad (7.15)$$

$$= \$1.59 \text{ million.} \qquad (7.16)$$

That is, even ignoring future wage growth, the present discounted value of your labor income is almost $1.6 million!

Several exercises at the end of the chapter will help you become comfortable with present discounted value. This is a tool that you will likely find valuable in the future, both in economics classes and in your professional career. It is used in the theory of consumption (consumption depends on the present discounted value of income, as we'll see in Chapter 10), in financial economics (the value of a stock is the presented discounted value of the dividends that it will pay in the future), and in accounting and business. You might say that the tool itself has a high present discounted value to you!

7.7 The Rising Return to Education

How valuable is a college education? Tuition is expensive and has been rising rapidly in recent decades. Is the education worth it?

One of the most important facts we can observe about the labor market is that the return to a college education is large and has been rising over time. Figure 7.8 illustrates this by plotting the average wage for a worker with a college-level education relative to the average wage for a high school graduate. In 1963, the typical college graduate earned about 50 percent more than the typical high school graduate—the ratio shown in Figure 7.8 is 1.5. This by itself is a large premium. But the figure also shows that this premium has generally been trending upward over time, especially since 1980. By 2002, the college wage premium was about 90 percent. Indeed, the rise in the return to a college education is one of the main factors underlying the rapid increase in the cost of college tuition.

Suppose the average college-educated worker earns $70,000 per year, while the typical worker with a high school education earns $40,000 per year (this premium

[12] U.S. per capita GDP in 2007—before the financial crisis—was about $47,000. Approximately half of the population works, so GDP per worker is about twice per capita income. Recall also that about two-thirds of GDP is paid as labor income. So the average payment to the typical worker in the United States in 2007 was $47,000 × 2 × 2/3 = $63,000.

FIGURE 7.8

College Versus High School Wages and Employment, 1960–2005

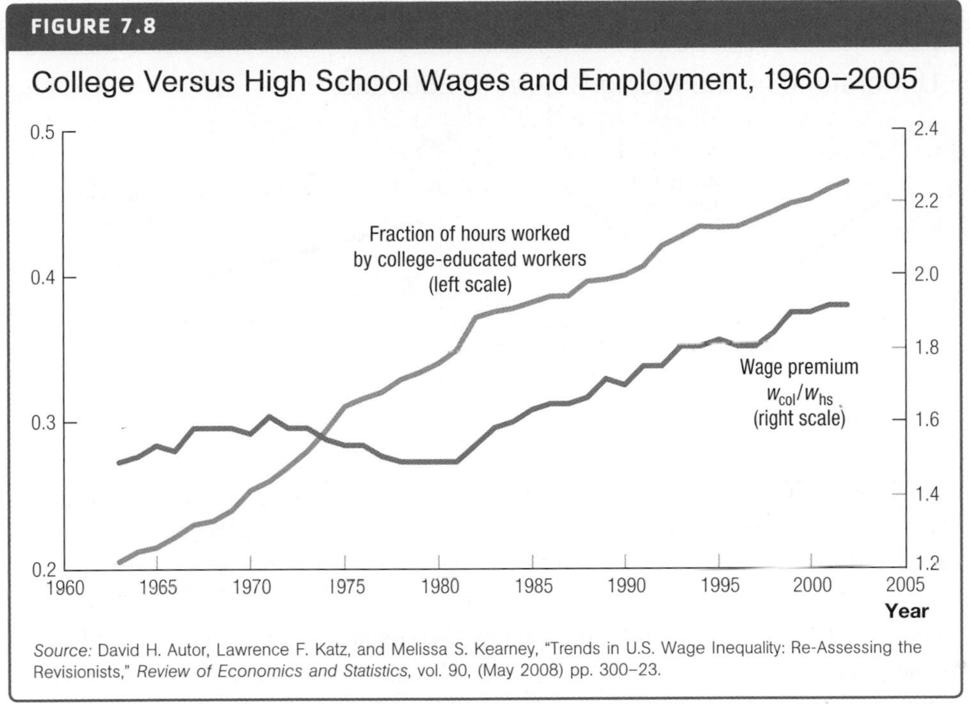

Source: David H. Autor, Lawrence F. Katz, and Melissa S. Kearney, "Trends in U.S. Wage Inequality: Re-Assessing the Revisionists," *Review of Economics and Statistics*, vol. 90, (May 2008) pp. 300–23.

is only 75 percent, so it underestimates the true premium of 90 percent but it keeps the numbers simple). This means the college education is worth \$30,000 per year more in wages, and this amount grows over time. Of course, by going to college in the first place, a worker would give up 4 years of earnings, valued at roughly \$160,000 if we don't adjust for growth and discounting. But over the course of a career of 45 years, the additional wages earned from college clearly dominate the cost of tuition and the forgone earnings. An exercise at the end of the chapter asks you to make this comparison more carefully, but for now notice that a \$30,000 advantage for 45 years starting today has a present discounted value of more than \$750,000 (if the interest rate is 3 percent). This is far more than tuition and forgone earnings—at least for everyone other than people like LeBron James and Taylor Swift![13]

Figure 7.8 also plots another variable: the ratio of hours worked by college-educated workers to total hours worked by all workers. This variable measures the relative supply of college-educated workers, and what we see is that this supply has been growing even faster than the relative wage. In 1963, the total amount of labor supplied by college graduates was only about 20 percent of all hours worked. But by 2002, the number had risen to nearly 50 percent.

This situation raises a puzzle for our supply-and-demand framework: if the supply of college-educated workers is growing so rapidly, how is it that the relative

[13] You might have noticed an important limitation of this argument: it assumes that the people who attend college are just like those who don't, except for the fact that they have four extra years of education. In reality, there is significant "self-selection" in who goes to college: they are likely students with better study habits, more discipline, and more aptitude. These traits are also valued by the labor market and thus surely contribute to the college wage premium. For this reason, the analysis in the text overstates the return to a college education. More generally, labor economists typically estimate that each year of education raises wages by about 7 percent.

FIGURE 7.9

Understanding the Rising Return to Education

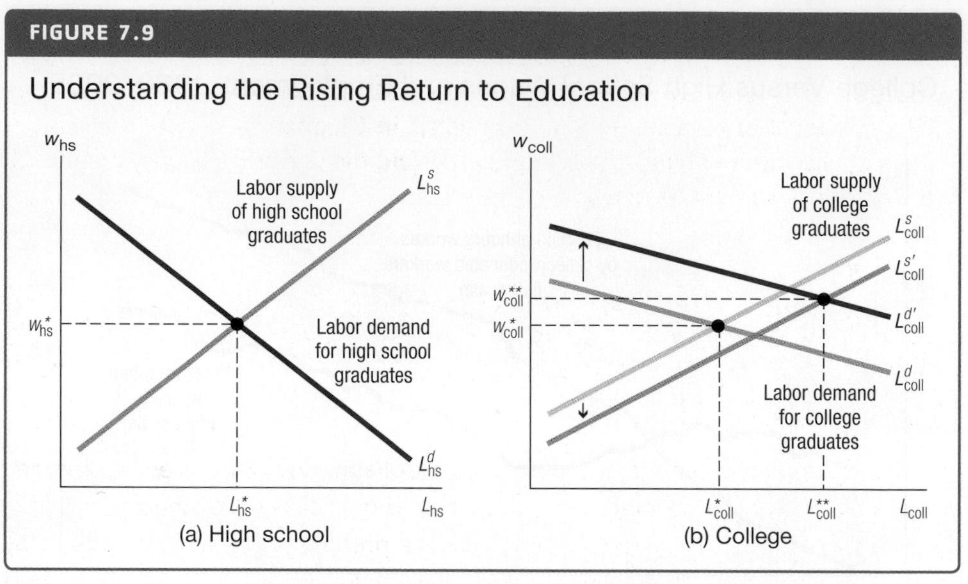

(a) High school (b) College

wage of college graduates is also growing? We usually expect that outward shifts in the supply of a good reduce its price. The answer is shown in Figure 7.9.[14] Panel (a) shows the market for workers with a high school education. For the moment, we assume there are no shocks to supply or demand in this market. Panel (b) shows the market for workers with a college education. Because of the rise in the supply of college workers shown in Figure 7.8, we assume the labor supply curve for college graduates has shifted out. Other things being equal, this would reduce the wage. However, to explain a rise in the wage, it must be the case that the *demand* for college workers has also shifted out, by an amount large enough to more than offset the rise in the supply. With both of these changes, we can understand an increase in the supply of college workers *and* an increase in their relative wage.

It's plausible that the demand curve for high school workers is shifting out as well, and the supply curve may be shifting back as an increasing fraction of the population is getting a college education. The main thing we need to understand, though, is that the shift in the demand for college-educated workers must be large relative to *whatever* shifts are occurring in the market for high school graduates.

So the big question is this: what kind of changes in the economy might have led to a large, sustained shift out in the demand for highly educated workers? The economics literature has focused on two explanations. The first is called **skill-biased technical change**. The idea is that new technologies such as computers, the Internet, and new kinds of software are more effective at improving productivity when used by highly skilled, educated workers, and so the demand for such workers has risen.

The second explanation is related to **globalization**. Before globalization, the large supply of educated workers in the United States kept their wage relatively

[14] See also Lawrence Katz and Kevin Murphy, "Changes in Relative Wages, 1963–1987: Supply and Demand Factors," *Quarterly Journal of Economics*, vol. 107 (1993), pp. 35–78.

low. But trade opens up the U.S. economy to a world where highly educated workers are much more scarce, and this relative scarcity has caused their wages to rise. We will consider this explanation—and the consequences for workers with a low level of education—in more detail in Chapter 14.[15]

Presumably both explanations are at work, and the relative importance of each is a continuing subject of research.

CASE STUDY

Income Inequality

The rise in the wage premium associated with a college education in recent decades is one dimension of rising inequality. A remarkable new data set on income inequality based on tax return data from 1913 to the present has been assembled by Thomas Piketty of the Paris School of Economics, Emmanuel Saez of the University of California at Berkeley, and several others. These data excel at showing how incomes at the very top of the income distribution have changed over time.

An example, shown in Figure 7.10, plots the share of income going to the top 0.1 percent of families—that is, the top 1 in 1,000. In the so-called "Gilded Age"

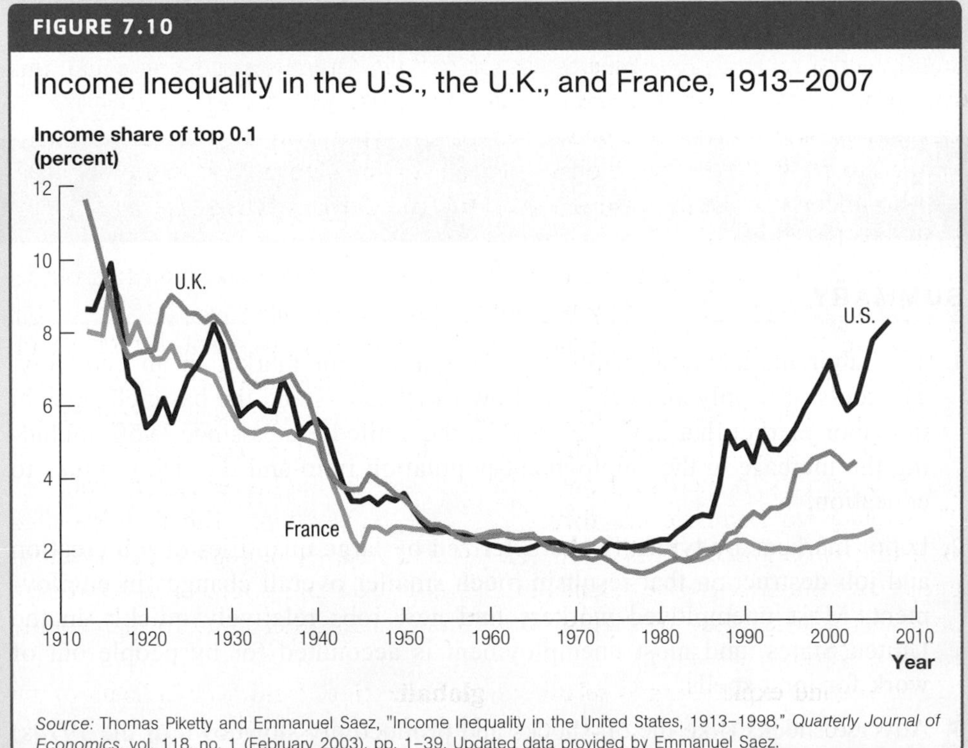

FIGURE 7.10

Income Inequality in the U.S., the U.K., and France, 1913–2007

Source: Thomas Piketty and Emmanuel Saez, "Income Inequality in the United States, 1913–1998," *Quarterly Journal of Economics*, vol. 118, no. 1 (February 2003), pp. 1–39. Updated data provided by Emmanuel Saez.

Income inequality decreased dramatically between 1913 and 1950, with the share earned by the top 1 in 1,000 families falling from about 9 percent to about 2 percent. It remained at this low level until the 1980s, at which point it rose sharply in the United States, reaching more than 8 percent by 2007.

[15] See also the Symposium on Income Inequality and Trade in the *Journal of Economic Perspectives*, Summer 1995.

of the 1910s and 1920s, income inequality according to this measure was high. For example, in the United States, the top 0.1 percent of families earned about 8 percent of all income. This was also true in France and the United Kingdom. During the Great Depression and World War II, inequality declined sharply, with the top income share falling to around 2 percent by the 1950s. It remained at this low level for the next several decades. Then, starting in the early 1980s, the experience in these three countries diverged. While income inequality remained low in France, it rose sharply in the United States, with the top income share returning to more than 8 percent by 2007.

What accounts for these large, persistent movements in income inequality? Piketty and Saez show that in the early part of the twentieth century, much of the inequality was associated with capital income. In contrast, the rise in inequality in the last several decades is largely due to an increase in inequality associated with salaries and business income. For example, a dramatic rise in compensation for CEOs is a significant part of the story.

Whether or not this rise in inequality is good or bad is a much more difficult question to answer. To the extent that it reflects high returns to innovation in a more integrated world economy, for example, it could be beneficial. On the other hand, this kind of polarization in incomes can be problematic, and there is no consensus in the economics profession on how these and other considerations net out.

CHAPTER REVIEW

SUMMARY

1. The labor market is arguably the most important market in an economy. The tools of supply and demand allow us to understand the basic changes in the labor market that have occurred in the United States since 1950, including the increase in the employment-population ratio and the rising return to education.
2. Labor markets are typically characterized by large quantities of job creation and job destruction that result in much smaller overall changes in employment. Most unemployed workers find new jobs relatively quickly in the United States, and most unemployment is accounted for by people out of work for long spells.
3. Adverse shocks (like the oil shocks and productivity slowdown of the 1970s) as well as inefficient labor market institutions appear to play important roles in explaining the relatively high unemployment rates and low hours worked in Europe.

4. Because the labor market is so important, problems like unemployment merit serious responses by society. Designing the right safety net requires balancing the needs for social insurance against the disincentives associated with that insurance.
5. Present discounted values help us compare financial payments received at different times.
6. The rising return to a college education is one of the key facts about the labor market. This college wage premium has risen from about 50 percent in 1963 to about 90 percent by 2002. Another way of viewing this fact is that wage inequality between collegc graduates and high school graduates has increased, mirroring a broader increase in income inequality. Possible explanations include skill-biased technical change and globalization.

KEY CONCEPTS

bathtub model
cyclical unemployment
employment-population ratio
frictional unemployment
globalization
job creation
job destruction
job finding rate
job separation rate
natural rate of unemployment
present discounted value
skill-biased technical change
structural unemployment
unemployment rate
wage rigidity

REVIEW QUESTIONS

1. What explains the general rise in the employment-population ratio in the United States? By how much did the ratio decline around the last recession? How many jobs does this represent?
2. What is the definition of the unemployment rate?
3. What are some examples of changes in the economy that would cause the labor supply curve to shift? What might shift the labor demand curve? How do these changes affect the wage rate and the employment-population ratio?
4. What is the difference between the natural rate of unemployment and cyclical unemployment? How are these related to structural and frictional unemployment?
5. Is the unemployment rate in Europe today higher or lower than in the United States? What about hours worked per person? What are some possible explanations for the differences?
6. Give some examples of economic questions where the concept of present discounted value would be useful.
7. In the last 50 years, both the fraction of hours worked by college graduates and the relative wage of college graduates have gone up. Why?

EXERCISES

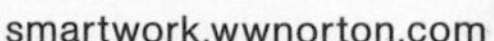

1. **How many missing jobs?** Suppose the U.S. unemployment rate at the start of 2010 had been 6% instead of 9.7%. How many more people would have been working (assuming the labor force remained the same)?

2. **Reducing tax rates:** Suppose the government decides to reform the tax system to reduce the marginal income tax rate across the board. Explain the effect on wages, the employment-population ratio, and unemployment.

3. **A positive oil shock:** Suppose scientists discover a new way to extract oil from deposits that were previously thought to be unrecoverable. The extra supply of oil leads oil prices to decline by $5 per barrel. Explain the effect on wages, the employment-population ratio, and unemployment—all for the overall economy.

4. **Present discounted values (I):** Compute the present discounted value of the following income streams. Assume the interest rate is 3%.
   (a) $50,000, received 1 year from now.
   (b) $50,000, received 10 years from now.
   (c) $100 every year, forever, starting immediately.
   (d) $100 every year, forever, starting 1 year from now.
   (e) $100 every year for the next 50 years, starting immediately.

5. **Present discounted values (II):** Repeat exercise 4 for an interest rate of 1%, then for an interest rate of 5%. Arrange your answers in a table so you can more easily see the difference a change in the interest rate makes.

6. **The value of your human capital:** Review the discussion of the value of a typical worker's human capital in Section 7.5 on pages 182–83.
   (a) Recompute the present discounted value in the following cases: $R = 0.01$, $R = 0.02$, $R = 0.04$, $R = 0.05$.
   (b) What is the economic intuition for why the present discounted value changes when the interest rate changes?

7. **Valuing human capital with wage growth:** To make the calculation of the present discounted value of a worker's human capital more realistic, suppose labor income starts at $50,000 initially, but then grows at a constant rate of 2% per year after that. Let w_t be labor income in year t, so that

$$w_t = \bar{w}_0(1 + \bar{g})^t,$$

where $\bar{w}_0 = \$50{,}000$ and $\bar{g} = 0.02$. The steps below will walk you through the problem.
   (a) If the interest rate is R, what is the formula for the present discounted value today (in year 0) of labor income from a particular future year t?
   (b) Now add up these terms from $t = 0$ to $t = 45$ to get a formula for the present discounted value of labor income. Your answer should look something like that in equation (7.12).
   (c) Write your answer to part (b) so that it takes the form of the geometric series:

$$pdv = \bar{w}_0(1 + a + a^2 + a^3 + \ldots + a^{45}).$$

What is the value of a that you find?

(d) Apply the geometric series formula to compute the present discounted value for the case of $R = 0.04$, $R = 0.03$, and $R = 0.02$. What weird thing happens (and why) when $R = 0.02$?

(e) Comment on your results.

8. **How much is a college education worth?** In the text, we supposed a college education raised a person's wage by $30,000 per year, from $40,000 to $70,000. Assume the interest rate is 3% and there is no growth in wages, and answer the following.

   (a) Suppose you are a high school senior and deciding whether or not to go to college. What is the present discounted value of your labor income if you forgo college and start work immediately?

   (b) As an alternative, you could pay $20,000 per year in college tuition, attend for 4 years, and then earn $70,000 per year after you graduate. What is the present discounted value of your labor earnings under this plan? (Compute this value from the point of view of a high school senior.)

   (c) Discuss the economic value of a college education.

9. **Explaining the college premium in the 1970s:** As shown in Figure 7.8, the college wage premium declined in the 1970s. Using a supply-and-demand graph, explain why this decline might have occurred.

10. **Optimal unemployment insurance:** Consider the following two proposals to reform unemployment insurance. Explain the arguments for and against each reform.

    (a) The insurance payment would be increased so that it replaced 100% of a worker's regular labor income for 26 weeks.

    (b) Each worker would be paid a lump sum equal to 10 weeks of his or her labor income at the start of the spell of unemployment. There would then be no other payments.

11. **GDP per hour:** Assume annual hours worked per person aged 16–64 in the United States is equal to 1,000. Using the data from Table 7.2 and the data from the "Country Snapshots" file (snapshots.pdf), compute GDP per hour for the other countries in Table 7.2 for the year 2000. (You can assume that hours worked was the same in 2000 as in 1993–96.) Comment on what you find.

WORKED EXERCISES

4. **Present discounted values (I):**

   (a) To calculate the present discounted value of $50,000 received one year from now, think about how much money you would have to put in the bank today in order to have $50,000 in one year. The answer—let's call it x—satisfies

$$x(1 + R) = \$50,000.$$

Therefore, the present discounted value is

$$x = \frac{\$50{,}000}{1 + R} = \frac{\$50{,}000}{1.03} = \$48{,}544.$$

(b) Similarly, if the \$50,000 is to be received in 10 years,

$$x(1 + R)^{10} = \$50{,}000.$$

So the present discounted value is

$$x = \frac{\$50{,}000}{(1 + R)^{10}} = \frac{\$50{,}000}{(1.03)^{10}} = \$37{,}205.$$

(c) The present discounted value of \$100 every year forever is

$$\begin{aligned} x &= 100 + \frac{100}{1 + R} + \frac{100}{(1 + R)^2} + \frac{100}{(1 + R)^3} + \ldots \\ &= 100 \times \left[1 + \frac{1}{1 + R} + \frac{1}{(1 + R)^2} + \frac{1}{(1 + R)^3} + \ldots\right] \\ &= 100 \times \frac{1}{1 - \frac{1}{1 + R}} \\ &= 100 \times \frac{1 + R}{R} \\ &= 100 \times \frac{1.03}{0.03} = \$3{,}433. \end{aligned}$$

(d) To find the present value of \$100 every year forever, starting one year from now, we can use a simple trick: the answer to this question is the same as the answer to (c) except that payment is delayed by one year. That is, the answer is

$$\frac{\text{answer to part (c)}}{1 + R}.$$

Now take a look at the answer to part (c) given above, especially in the second-to-last line. Using that result, we see that the present value of \$100 forever, starting one year from now is

$$\frac{1}{1 + R} \times 100 \times \frac{1 + R}{R} = \frac{100}{R}.$$

That is, we get a very elegant answer: we just divide the \$100 by the interest rate. For an interest rate of 3 percent, then, the answer is \$100/.03 = \$3,333.

(e) To calculate this value if the payments stop after 50 years, we use the formula derived in equation (7.14). In this case, it is

$$x = \$100 \times \frac{1 - \left(\frac{1}{1 + R}\right)^{50}}{1 - \frac{1}{1 + R}}.$$

With $R = 0.03$, the present discounted value of the first 50 payments is \$2,650.

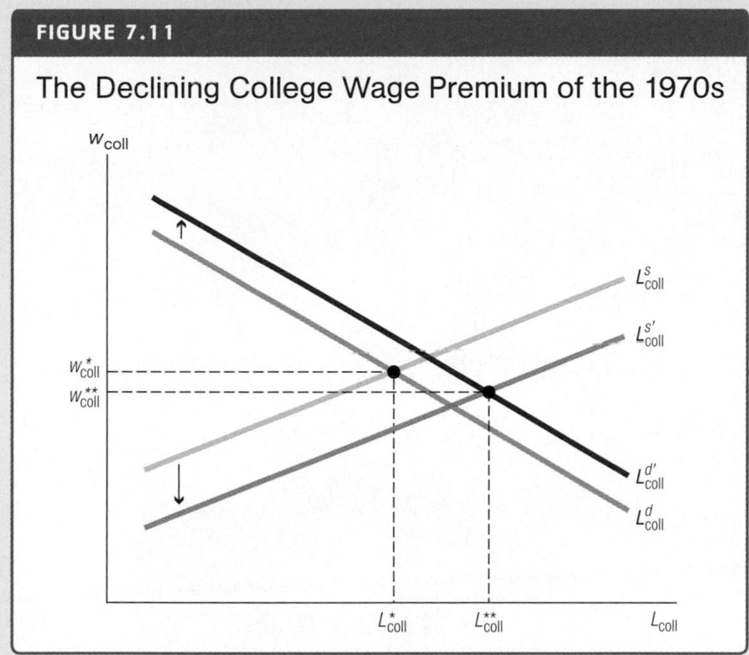

FIGURE 7.11

The Declining College Wage Premium of the 1970s

9. **Explaining the college premium in the 1970s:**

To answer this question, conduct a supply-and-demand analysis of the labor market, as we did in Figure 7.9. Let's assume the labor market for workers with only a high school education does not change, in order to keep things simple. Instead, focus on the labor market for college-educated workers.

Recall that our basic analysis assumes the labor demand curve for college-educated workers is shifting out rapidly because of technological change. Normally, this would lead the wage premium to rise. How can it decline?

A natural way to explain a decline in the wage premium is to have the labor supply curve shift out by *more* than the labor demand curve, as shown in Figure 7.11. If this supply shift is large enough, the wage premium can decline. What might have caused such a large change in supply? Demographic changes and the Vietnam War are two plausible candidates. The 1970s were a period when the baby boomers entered the labor force after college, creating a larger-than-usual increase in the supply of college graduates. In addition, the Vietnam War may have encouraged people to attend college to avoid military service and also created a pool of veterans who returned to college and entered the labor market in the 1970s. The paper by Katz and Murphy cited in footnote 14 (p. 190) discusses these forces in more detail.

CHAPTER 8

INFLATION

OVERVIEW

In this chapter, we learn

- what inflation is, and how costly it can be.
- how the quantity theory of money and the classical dichotomy allow us to understand where inflation comes from.
- how the nominal interest rate, the real interest rate, and inflation are related through the Fisher equation.
- the important link between fiscal policy and high inflation.

Inflation is always and everywhere a monetary phenomenon.

—MILTON FRIEDMAN

Inflation is always and everywhere a fiscal phenomenon.

—THOMAS SARGENT

8.1 Introduction

In late 1919, a loaf of bread in Germany cost about 26 pfennig, or just over a fourth of a mark. By November 1923, the same loaf of bread cost 80 billion marks. More generally, the overall price level in Germany had risen by a factor of *one trillion* in four years. This massive inflation proved enormously costly to German society, and perhaps to the world as a whole. By late 1923, prices were rising 300-fold during the course of a month. The daily price increase was so large at the peak that every day was payday; wages were paid at 11 a.m., and workers immediately dashed with suitcases full of paper money to buy whatever goods they could find. Many people lost their lifetime savings, and many businesses failed. The economic turmoil and strife caused by the German inflation was one of the factors that led to the rise of the Nazi movement.[1]

Inflation is the percentage change in an economy's overall price level, and episodes of extremely high inflation—say greater than 500 percent per year—are known as **hyperinflations**. Hyperinflations have occurred throughout history. The 1980s and 1990s witnessed numerous episodes among the economies of Latin America. The inflation rate in Russia in the early 1990s reached more than 800 percent per year as Russia made the transition to a noncommunist country. And lest we think the United States is immune to such episodes, high inflation has often characterized the U.S. economy during major wars. For example, paper money designed by Benjamin Franklin to help finance the American Revolution in 1776 was printed in such great supply that George Washington remarked, "A wagonload of currency will hardly purchase a wagonload of provisions." Similarly, the rapid printing of Confederate currency during the Civil War led to high rates of inflation in Southern states. By the end of the war, the currency was worthless, and transactions in the South were being conducted largely by barter or with the black-market currency of the North.

While inflation has been relatively tame by comparison in recent decades in the United States and in many other countries, it has still exerted a profound effect on economic policy and well-being. Figure 8.1 shows a graph of the inflation

Epigraphs: Friedman, *Dollars and Deficits: Living with America's Economic Problems* (Englewood Cliffs, N.J.: Prentice Hall, 1968), p. 18. Sargent, quoted in Norman Gall, "King Kong in Brazil," Braudel Paper No. 15 (São Paulo, Brazil: Instituto Fernand Braudel de Economia Mundial, 2003).

[1] See Thomas J. Sargent, "The Ends of Four Big Inflations," in R. E. Hall, ed., *Inflation: Causes and Effects* (Chicago: University of Chicago Press, 1983); and William L. Shirer, *The Rise and Fall of the Third Reich* (New York: Simon and Schuster, 1990 [1960]).

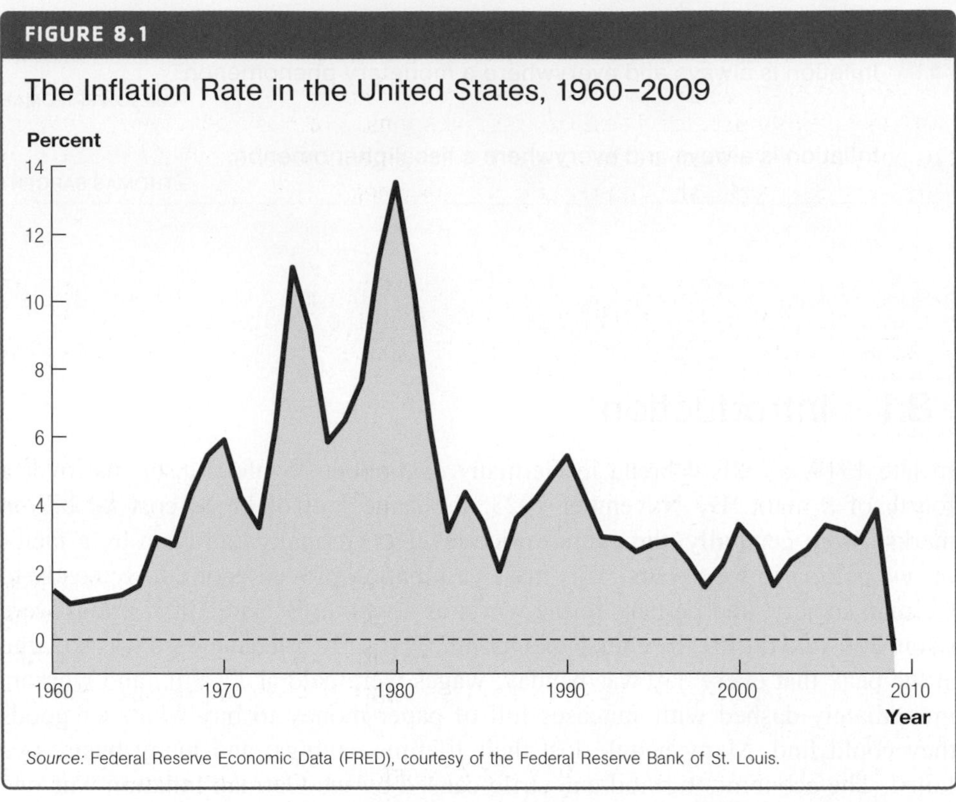

FIGURE 8.1

The Inflation Rate in the United States, 1960–2009

Source: Federal Reserve Economic Data (FRED), courtesy of the Federal Reserve Bank of St. Louis.

Calculated as the annual percentage change in the consumer price index, inflation was low in the early 1960s before rising sharply in the "Great Inflation" of the 1970s. The last 25 years have seen a return to low inflation.

rate for the United States for the last 45 years. If P_t is the price level in year t, then the inflation rate is computed as the annual percentage change in the price level $(P_{t+1} - P_t)/P_t$. For this graph, we use the consumer price index (CPI)—a price index for a bundle of consumer goods—as our measure of the price level. The case study on the next page discusses this and other price indexes that can be used to calculate inflation.

Inflation was relatively low in the first half of the 1960s, continuing a period of calm from the 1950s. The price level increased by a modest amount in these years, on the order of 2 percent per year. Starting in the second half of the 1960s, however, the inflation rate began to rise, leading to what is sometimes referred to as the "Great Inflation" of the 1970s. Inflation peaked in 1980 at 13.5 percent. As we'll see later, this high inflation created arbitrary transfers of wealth between different groups of people and distorted incentives for investment. Businesses that borrowed often found it difficult to repay their loans when interest rates shot to record highs, leading to a spike in bankruptcies. The Great Inflation marked a watershed for both politics and economic policy. In late 1979, President Carter appointed Paul Volcker to head the Federal Reserve Board of Governors, the country's central bank. Volcker made fundamental changes in monetary policy that echo through the present time. Politically, double-digit inflation was a critical factor in the electoral triumph of Ronald Reagan over Jimmy Carter in the United States and the rise of Margaret Thatcher in the United Kingdom.

Inflation rates declined sharply in the early 1980s, and since then they have declined even further. For the last decade or so, inflation has hovered around 2.5 percent.

Where does inflation come from, and what are its costs? If inflation is caused by a country's central bank printing too much money—as 1976 Nobel laureate Milton Friedman suggests at the start of this chapter—why would the central bank make this mistake? These are big questions. We begin to analyze them in this chapter, as we focus on the long-run determinants of inflation. We then return to these issues in the short-run section of this book.

CASE STUDY

How Much Is That?

In 1950, a gallon of gasoline cost 27 cents, while in 2007 it cost around $3 in the United States and even more in Europe. How do we compare these numbers? Was 27 cents in 1950 worth more or less than $3 in 2007?

This problem is an exercise in comparing values at different points in time, similar to the problems we studied in Chapter 2. In this case, we'll use the consumer price index (CPI) to calculate the answer. Data on the CPI are shown in Table 8.1 below:

To obtain the equivalent 2007 value of 27 cents in 1950, we do the following "units" calculation:

$$0.27 \text{ in 1950 dollars} \times \frac{100 \text{ in 2007 dollars}}{11.61 \text{ in 1950 dollars}} = 2.32 \text{ in 2007 dollars.}$$

That is, we start with the unit of "1950 dollars" and then incorporate the fact that $100 in 2007 is equivalent to $11.61 in 1950. The "1950 dollars" units cancel to leave us with the value of $2.32 in 2007 dollars. This calculation reveals that 27 cents in 1950 is worth $2.32 in 2007, so gasoline was noticeably cheaper in 1950, but not by nearly as much as the 27 cents would lead you to believe. The reason gas wasn't *that* much cheaper is that inflation has eroded the value of the dollar.

A nice resource hosted by Samuel H. Williamson through the Economic History Association called "How Much Is That?" allows you to explore these calculations in different ways: see http://eh.net/hmit/. One thing you'll notice if you use this resource or if you pay close attention to the inflation numbers reported in the press

TABLE 8.1

The Consumer Price Index, 1900–2007 (2007 = 100)

Year	CPI	Year	CPI
1900	3.93	1980	39.73
1930	8.05	1990	63.04
1950	11.61	2000	83.05
1960	14.29	2007	100.00
1970	18.73		

Source: John J. McCusker, "Comparing the Purchasing Power of Money in the United States (or Colonies) from 1665 to 2007." Economic History Services, www.eh.net/hmit/ppowerusd/.

This CPI comparison answers the question, How many dollars in a given year have the same purchasing power as $100 in the year 2007?

is that inflation can be measured with different price indexes. One of the most popular measures is the percentage change in the consumer price index. A related measure starts with the CPI but excludes food and energy prices, because these tend to be more volatile. Another popular measure uses the GDP deflator, the price index that relates real and nominal GDP (see Chapter 2).

These different inflation measures are based on different baskets of goods, and therefore have different uses. Workers bargaining with employers over wage increases may focus on the consumer price index. Policymakers concerned about inflation may wish to exclude the volatile food and energy components. By and large, however, these price indexes all give the same picture of inflation over moderately long periods.

8.2 The Quantity Theory of Money

It's hard to think about inflation without also thinking about money, and it turns out there is a tight connection between the two, as we will see in this section. But first, what is money? Over the years, seashells, rocks, and precious metals as well as paper currency have all claimed this status. Even cigarettes have been used as money in prisons and during wartime.[2] To begin, think of money simply as the paper currency with which we are all familiar. In 2009, the amount of U.S. currency in circulation was $862 billion, or more than $2,800 per person.

Why does this paper currency have value? Historically, currency was typically backed by gold or silver: either coins were made of precious metals, or the government made an explicit promise that the paper money could be exchanged for gold or silver. Nowadays, however, this is no longer the case, and paper money in the United States, Europe, Japan, and most other countries is not backed by anything. This currency is called "fiat money," because the government simply declares that certain pieces of paper can be used as money. At the most basic level, these colored pieces of paper with portraits and funny writing on them are valued simply because we expect that other people will value them. A software engineer is willing to accept payment for her long hours of work in the form of colored pieces of paper because she expects that the grocery store and the automobile dealer will accept them in turn in exchange for goods that she'd like to buy. Money is thus valued largely by social convention.

Measures of the Money Supply

How do we measure the amount of money in an economy? The answer depends on how narrowly we want to count. Currency in circulation is a narrow mea-

[2] Neal Stephenson's recent set of historical novels known as the Baroque Cycle (*Quicksilver, The Confusion, The System of the World*) explore, in part, the evolution of money in the years surrounding 1700. If you have not read these books yet, please don't start until after the semester is over—long, excellent fiction can be hazardous to your academic studies!

TABLE 8.2

Different Measures of the Money Supply in 2009 (billions of dollars)

C	Currency	862
MB	Monetary base = currency plus reserves	2,018
M1	Currency plus demand deposits (e.g., checking accounts)	1,693
M2	M1 plus savings deposits and individual money market accounts	8,524

Source: Economic Report of the President, 2010.

sure, which equaled $862 billion in the United States in 2009, as shown in Table 8.2. A broader measure, the **monetary base**, includes not only currency but also accounts that private banks hold with an economy's central bank, which pay no interest. These accounts are called **reserves**, and private banks can exchange these reserves for currency at will. The central bank typically requires private banks to hold some fraction of their deposits as reserves while they lend out the rest in the form of loans to businesses and consumers. These reserves ensure that banks have sufficient resources on hand in case depositors show up all at once asking for their money, as they do to James Stewart's dismay in the 1946 Frank Capra movie *It's a Wonderful Life*.

A different measure known as M1 adds "demand deposits" like checking account balances to the amount of currency, while M2 adds savings account and money market account balances to M1. In general, the broader measures include accounts that are less *liquid*, meaning they are harder to turn into currency in a short period of time.[3]

CASE STUDY

Digital Cash

What do debit cards, travelers' checks, frequent flyer miles, PayPal, and Hong Kong's Octopus card have in common? All are innovations to the financial system that change the way the layperson thinks about money. Frequent flyer miles are a new form of currency that can be used to purchase airline tickets, rental cars, and hotel rooms. PayPal is an electronic currency that allows us to make purchases on the Web. And the 13 million Octopus cards in use in Hong Kong (twice the population) allow people to buy a ticket on the Star Ferry, a chai latte at Starbucks, or lunch at McDonald's simply by waving their wallets by a magnetic reader.

At a fundamental level, however, these innovations don't change the way economists think about money. When I add $25 to my PayPal account, the money is transferred from my bank account into PayPal's bank account, but the aggregate

[3] The Federal Reserve used to construct an aggregate called M3, but it stopped doing so in March 2006, since this broader measure hadn't been used by policymakers for many years.

amount of money in circulation hasn't changed. The same is basically true for these other financial innovations.

Another thing to appreciate is that most money in advanced economies today is *already* digital cash. The balance in your savings account is just a number on a computer. When you use the electronic "bill pay" feature of your bank to pay off a credit card bill, electrons zoom across networks to record the transaction.

The Quantity Equation

The **quantity theory of money** allows us to make the connection between money and inflation. Suppose M_t is the number of green pieces of paper in the economy with the words "One Dollar" written on them. Also, let P_t denote the price level and Y_t denote real GDP. The quantity theory then says that

$$M_t V_t = P_t Y_t \tag{8.1}$$

where V_t is called the **velocity of money**. The velocity of money should be thought of as the average number of times per year that each piece of paper currency is used in a transaction. Equation (8.1) is our **quantity equation**.

The expression on the right-hand side, $P_t Y_t$, is nominal GDP—the amount of goods and services purchased in an economy, valued at current prices. According to the quantity theory, these goods and services are bought with money, and the left-hand side is the amount of money in circulation M_t multiplied by the number of times each piece of paper changes hands V_t. The theory, then, says that nominal GDP is equal to the effective amount of money used in purchases, $M_t V_t$.

As an example, suppose nominal GDP is $1,000 and the amount of currency in circulation is $200. Then it must be the case that each piece of currency is used, on average, in five transactions. The quantity equation in this case is just $200 × 5 = $1,000.

At this point, we have a single, quantity equation and four unknowns: M_t, V_t, P_t, and Y_t. To complete the quantity theory, we need to specify three additional equations, and the four together will provide us with a theory of inflation.

The Classical Dichotomy, Constant Velocity, and the Central Bank

The second equation of the quantity theory turns out to be an assumption we have already been making implicitly throughout this book. This assumption, called **the classical dichotomy**, says that in the long run, the real and nominal sides of the economy are completely separate. In particular, real GDP in the long run is determined solely by real considerations. Indeed, the theory of long-run growth we developed in Chapters 4–6 doesn't depend on money or the aggregate price level. Instead, it depends on real variables like the investment rate, new ideas, and total factor productivity. With this dichotomy in mind, we assume $Y_t = \bar{Y}_t$. That is, real GDP is taken to be an exogenous variable in the quantity theory of money, determined by the forces (investment rate, TFP, and so on) discussed in previous chapters. As usual, the overbar denotes an exogenous variable that's given from outside the model.

The third equation of the quantity theory specifies the velocity of money. Largely because it is extremely convenient, we will assume the velocity of money is an exogenous constant: that is, $V_t = \bar{V}$. There is no time subscript here, since velocity is assumed to be constant over time. In reality, the velocity of the M2 definition of money is approximately constant, so this is not a bad assumption in the long run, at least as a starting point.

The final equation of the quantity theory determines the money supply itself. This supply is a policy variable chosen by the central bank of an economy, one of whose main roles is to determine monetary policy. To keep things simple, we will not specify a model of how Ben Bernanke, the current chair of the Federal Reserve, conducts monetary policy. Instead, we take monetary policy itself as exogenous, so that $M_t = \bar{M}_t$. (We will consider a much richer model of monetary policy in Chapter 11.)

The Quantity Theory for the Price Level

The quantity theory of money is summarized in Table 8.3. Essentially, the model consists of the quantity equation itself. We assume real GDP, velocity, and money are determined exogenously, so the quantity equation is left to pin down the price level.

Solving the model is quite straightforward. Our last three equations give the solutions for Y_t, V_t, and M_t. Plugging these exogenous values into the quantity equation and rearranging, we get the solution for the price level itself:

$$P_t^* = \frac{\bar{M}_t\bar{V}}{\bar{Y}_t} \tag{8.2}$$

This equation says that the price level is determined by the ratio of the effective quantity of money $\bar{M}_t\bar{V}$ divided by the volume of goods $\bar{Y}_t$. An increase in the money supply causes the price level to rise, as does a decrease in real GDP. Or, as a famous phrase summarizes the quantity theory, inflation is caused by too much money chasing too few goods.

TABLE 8.3

The Quantity Theory of Money: 4 Equations and 4 Unknowns

Endogenous variables: M_t, V_t, P_t, Y_t	
The quantity equation	$M_tV_t = P_tY_t$
Real GDP from growth model (classical dichotomy)	$Y_t = \bar{Y}_t$
Exogenous and constant velocity	$V_t = \bar{V}$
Exogenous money supply	$M_t = \bar{M}_t$
Exogenous variables/parameters: $\bar{M}_t$, $\bar{V}$, $\bar{Y}_t$	

Since the velocity of money and the level of real GDP are taken as given in the model, any changes in the supply of money will show up in the long run as changes in prices. If the central bank decides to increase M, the only way the quantity equation can hold is if the aggregate price level P rises as well. This is the essence of the quantity theory of money: *in the long run, a key determinant of the price level is the level of the money supply.*

The Quantity Theory for Inflation

Recall that the inflation rate is defined as the percentage change in the overall (aggregate) price level. So to translate the quantity theory into a statement about inflation, we apply our basic trick for figuring growth rates: the growth rate of the product of two variables is the sum of the growth rates of those variables (see Section 3.5). Applied to the quantity equation, we have

$$\begin{array}{c}\text{percentage}\\\text{change in}\\\text{money supply}\end{array} + \begin{array}{c}\text{percentage}\\\text{change in}\\\text{velocity}\end{array} = \begin{array}{c}\text{percentage}\\\text{change in}\\\text{price level}\end{array} + \begin{array}{c}\text{percentage}\\\text{change in}\\\text{real GDP.}\end{array}$$

Or, using symbols (where, as usual, g denotes a growth rate),

$$\bar{g}_M + \bar{g}_V = g_P + \bar{g}_Y. \tag{8.3}$$

Now, since velocity is constant, $\bar{g}_V = 0$. Also, let's follow the conventional notation in economics and let the Greek letter pi denote the rate of inflation: $\pi \equiv g_P$. Rearranging equation (8.3), we have our second key result from the quantity theory of money:

$$\pi^* = \bar{g}_M - \bar{g}_Y \tag{8.4}$$

The inflation rate is thus equal to the growth rate of money less the growth rate of real GDP. The growth rate of real GDP is some constant in the long run, which we can think of as being determined by the long-run growth theory we developed in Chapters 4–6. The growth rate of money, on the other hand, as mentioned earlier, is a policy variable controlled by the central bank. *The quantity theory implies that in the long run, changes in the growth rate of money lead one-for-one to changes in the inflation rate.*

Let's take an example. If the money supply is growing at a rate of 7 percent per year and if real GDP grows at 4 percent per year, then the inflation rate will be 3 percent per year.

Now suppose the central bank decides to increase the growth rate of money to 10 percent per year. The quantity theory implies that in the long run, this extra money growth will leave the *real* economy unaffected (because of the classical dichotomy), so the only change will be that inflation will be higher, at 6 percent. This general result serves as the main basis for the assertion by Milton Friedman that "inflation is always and everywhere a monetary phenomenon"; it's determined, in other words, by the rate of growth of the money supply.

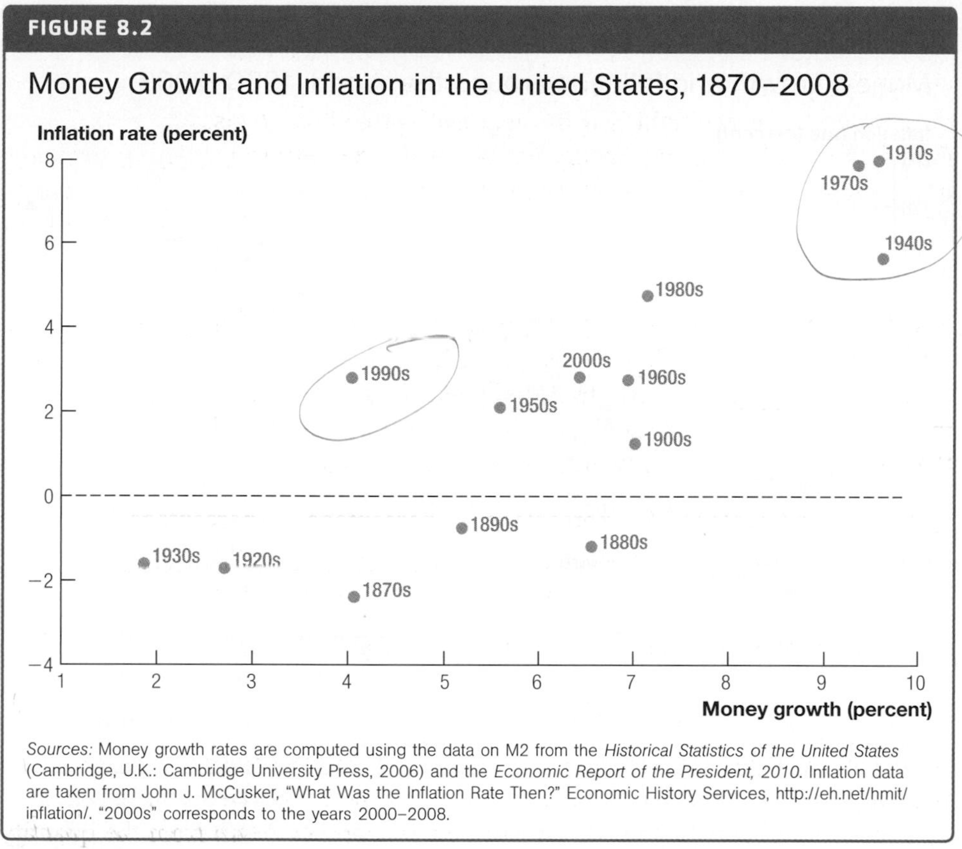

FIGURE 8.2

Money Growth and Inflation in the United States, 1870–2008

Sources: Money growth rates are computed using the data on M2 from the *Historical Statistics of the United States* (Cambridge, U.K.: Cambridge University Press, 2006) and the *Economic Report of the President, 2010*. Inflation data are taken from John J. McCusker, "What Was the Inflation Rate Then?" Economic History Services, http://eh.net/hmit/inflation/. "2000s" corresponds to the years 2000–2008.

The main prediction of the quantity theory holds up in U.S. data: decades of high money growth are decades of high inflation.

Let's see if the quantity theory's prediction holds up empirically. Does a high rate of money growth in fact lead to a high rate of inflation? We analyze this prediction by looking at the United States over time and looking across countries of the world. Figure 8.2, which plots money growth rates and inflation rates by decade for the U.S. economy since the 1870s, confirms the strong relationship between money growth and inflation. Decades of rapid money growth, like the 1970s and the 1910s, also show the highest rates of inflation. Decades when money growth was slow—like the 1920s and the 1930s—have the lowest rates of inflation. In fact, inflation rates were negative during these decades—a phenomenon economists call **deflation**. The overall price level actually declined during the 1920s and 1930s.

Figure 8.3 plots the average annual growth rate of money and the average annual rate of inflation after 1990 across a sample of countries. We see once again that the one-for-one prediction of the quantity theory holds up quite well. Many countries are in a cluster in the lower left corner, with low money growth and low inflation; examples include the United States, with a money growth rate of 4.7 percent and inflation of 2.7 percent; and Denmark, with a money growth rate of 5.1 percent and inflation of 2.2 percent. Countries like Indonesia (18.7 and 12.5 percent) and Mexico (22.8 and 15.2 percent) are in the low to middle range over this period. Sierra Leone and Venezuela show high inflation and money growth, both averaging 25 percent per year or more, while Turkey and Brazil are examples of countries with very high inflation and money growth.

The quantity theory also holds across countries: countries with rapid money growth experience high inflation.

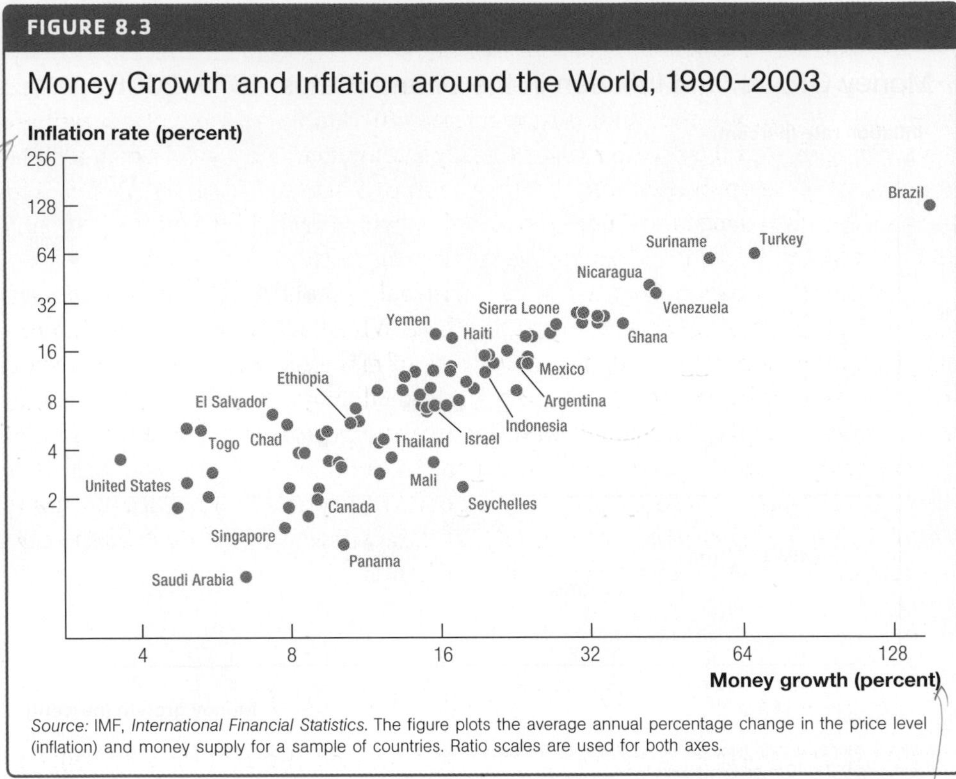

FIGURE 8.3

Money Growth and Inflation around the World, 1990–2003

Source: IMF, *International Financial Statistics*. The figure plots the average annual percentage change in the price level (inflation) and money supply for a sample of countries. Ratio scales are used for both axes.

Revisiting the Classical Dichotomy

With the quantity theory fleshed out, we are now prepared to understand why the classical dichotomy (that the real and nominal sides of the economy are separate in the long run) holds.

Imagine an economy that uses green pieces of paper called dollars for money. The central bank decides to introduce a new currency and replaces each green dollar with a blue one. Does this have any effect on the economy? Suppose all prices and wages (and anything previously expressed in units of green dollars) are immediately converted one-for-one into blue dollars. Whereas a hamburger used to cost one green dollar, now it costs one blue dollar. The *New York Times* best seller that used to cost 20 green dollars now costs 20 blue dollars. And the wage you make working in the undergraduate library, 10 green dollars per hour, becomes 10 blue dollars per hour.

Notice that the change to blue currency leaves the *relative* prices of goods unchanged. Twenty hamburgers could initially be traded for 1 best-selling book, and that's still the case. An hour's work originally bought 10 burgers, and that rate of exchange still holds. Since the relative prices of goods are unchanged, there's no reason for producers and consumers to change their behavior.

What if the central bank replaces each green dollar with 2 blue dollars instead of 1? The same principle applies: all prices can now be doubled and expressed in units of blue dollars, and nothing real will have changed.

Now suppose the central bank is smart and realizes that the color of money is irrelevant. So it keeps the color green and simply doubles the money supply, introducing a second green dollar for every green dollar in the economy. What happens? The story is the same. All prices can still double, relative prices will not have changed, and there's no reason for anyone to change any real behavior: the quantity of goods produced and the allocation of those goods is unaffected. The proposition that changes in the money supply have no real effects on the economy and only affect prices is called **the neutrality of money**.

This kind of reasoning underlies the classical dichotomy, and as a statement about the long run, it seems entirely compelling. What about the short run? Empirically, the evidence suggests that the neutrality of money does not hold in the short run. That is, nominal prices do *not* respond immediately and precisely to changes in the money supply, so changes in the money supply *can* affect the real side of the economy over short horizons. The general consensus among economists is that the classical dichotomy provides a good description of how the economy behaves in the long run but not in the short. Exactly why this should be the case is something we will return to in detail in Chapter 11.

8.3 Real and Nominal Interest Rates

Recall from Chapter 5 that in the long run, the **real interest rate** is equal to the marginal product of capital. That is, the real interest rate is determined by the real return to purchasing a unit of capital, investing it, reaping the return to the investment, and then selling the capital: it is the total amount (in consumption goods) you earn by this process.

However, this real interest rate is not the interest rate earned in a savings account or discussed in the newspaper. The interest rate on a savings account, for example, is the number of dollars you earn by taking $100 and putting it in a savings account for a year. This is a **nominal interest rate**. The real interest rate is paid in goods, while the nominal interest rate is paid in units of currency, like dollars.

We know that the price level P allows us to convert between real GDP and nominal GDP. Since interest rates are the return over the course of a year, it is perhaps not surprising that the difference between the nominal interest rate and the real interest rate is the *change* in the price level—the rate of inflation.

Thus, if we let R denote the real interest rate and i denote the nominal interest rate, these two rates are related by

$$i = R + \pi. \tag{8.5}$$

This formula is called **the Fisher equation** after Irving Fisher, an economist at Yale University in the first half of the twentieth century who first drew a clear distinction between real and nominal interest rates. It says that the nominal interest rate is equal to the sum of the real interest rate and the rate of inflation.

To understand this equation, suppose the real interest rate in the economy is equal to 5 percent and the rate of inflation, determined by the quantity theory, is equal to 3 percent. What is the nominal interest rate? The Fisher equation gives the answer: 8 percent.

To see the economic reasoning behind this equation, consider the following example. Suppose for simplicity that a machine in this same economy costs \$100 today. Since the inflation rate is 3 percent, we know the machine will sell for \$103 a year from now. Now suppose an investor buys a machine, uses it to produce output for a year, and then sells the output and the machine. How much will this investment earn? Since the real interest rate is 5 percent, the output produced by the machine must be worth \$5. And since the machine sells for \$103 at the end of the year, the investor earns an additional \$3 on the value of the machine, for a total nominal return of \$8. As a percentage of the original investment of \$100, this is 8 percent, the nominal interest rate, exactly what the Fisher equation predicts.

As mentioned earlier, the real interest rate is not a statistic we can look up in the newspaper or the *Economic Report of the President*. Instead, economists typically calculate it by applying the Fisher equation. Rewriting that equation, we see that

$$R = i - \pi. \tag{8.6}$$

That is, the real interest rate in the economy is computed by subtracting the inflation rate from the nominal interest rate.

Figure 8.4 shows the nominal and real interest rates for the United States since 1960. As the Fisher equation suggests, the nominal rate is generally high when inflation is high—compare Figures 8.1 and 8.4. For example, the nominal rate reaches its peak in the graph in 1981 at just over 14 percent, close to the 1980 peak of inflation. It's not a coincidence that the nominal interest rate peaks a year later. Think about why that is the case; we will return to this topic in Chapter 11.

The real interest rate is computed by subtracting inflation from the nominal interest rate, according to the Fisher equation.

FIGURE 8.4

Real and Nominal Interest Rates in the United States, 1960–2009

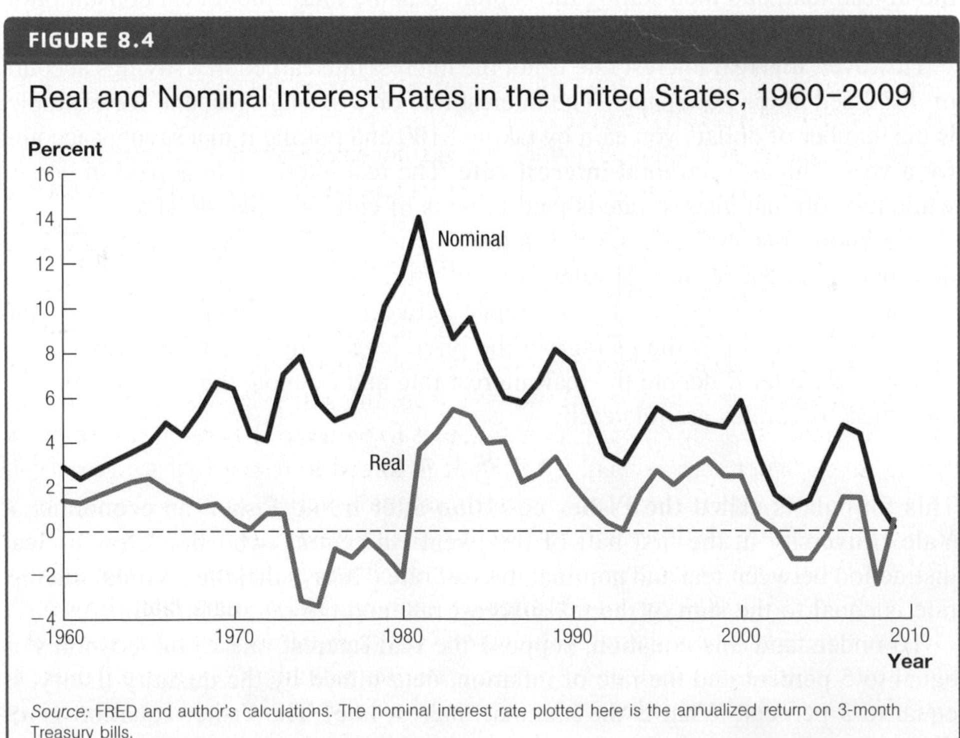

Source: FRED and author's calculations. The nominal interest rate plotted here is the annualized return on 3-month Treasury bills.

In 2009, an interesting event occurred: the real interest rate actually became larger than the nominal interest rate. How could this happen? Consider equation (8.6), and then look at the graph of inflation (Figure 8.1). What happened to inflation in 2009?

The real interest rate generally fluctuates between 0 and 4 percent and takes on an average value of about 1.5 percent during this period. Notice that occasionally it becomes negative. This occurred in the 1970s when inflation was very high and again in 2003 when the nominal interest rate was very low. If the real interest rate were always equal to the marginal product of capital, then these negative rates would be puzzling; the marginal product of capital is the extra amount of output that could be produced by installing an extra unit of capital, and *this* amount is surely not negative. The graph, then, suggests that in the short run, the real interest rate can depart from the marginal product of capital. Once again, this is a subject we will revisit in the short-run section of the book.

8.4 Costs of Inflation

The story of the German hyperinflation in the early 1920s suggests that inflation can be extremely costly to an economy. In this section, we study the costs of inflation in more detail. Consider the following examples, starring three hypothetical characters: Mr. Aiken, Ms. Barrino, and Ms. Clarkson.

Mr. Aiken enters the labor force in the early 1940s to help with the war effort. He continues to work throughout adulthood, and in 1970 he retires with a pension from his lifelong employer that will pay him $10,000 per year. What seems like a nice retirement package in 1970, however, is eroded by inflation, so that by 1983 his fixed income is worth only 40 percent of what it was worth in 1970, the equivalent of $4,000 per year.

Ms. Barrino owns a bank. Her bank accepts deposits from the local community and lends the proceeds back to small businesses and farmers. The savings accounts pay a small rate of interest that moves with the market. Most of the loans are for 5, 10, or 30 years at fixed rates. Now suppose the inflation rate, which had been low and stable for many years, starts rising quickly. Ms. Barrino is forced to match the increases on returns she offers in her savings accounts, as customers have the right to pull their money out at any time. Therefore, her costs rise just as quickly. However, the income she receives from the loans she has made does not rise with inflation—these loans were made at fixed interest rates. Because costs rise so much faster than revenues, her bank is forced to declare bankruptcy.

The rich and successful Ms. Clarkson obtains a variable-rate mortgage in a year when inflation is 3 percent and short-term interest rates are 5 percent. The $100,000 per month mortgage on her beautiful house is expensive, but affordable with her $200,000 per month after-tax income. Three years later, however, and much to everyone's surprise, the rate of inflation jumps up to 8 percent, the short-term interest rate rises to 10 percent, and the monthly mortgage payment is $200,000. Ms. Clarkson is forced to sell her house and become a renter at exactly the time when high interest rates are punishing the housing market.

With the benefit of hindsight, it's easy to see what each character did wrong. Mr. Aiken should have asked for a pension that incorporated cost-of-living increases tied to inflation (not that any firms were offering such pensions before the 1970s). Ms. Barrino should have matched up the terms on her assets and liabilities, or at least hedged these risks in a secondary market (not that this was easy to do before the 1980s). And Ms. Clarkson should have taken a fixed-rate mortgage instead (this experiment is currently being run, so we'll have to see if all the people taking bets with variable-rate mortgages in the first half of this decade end up in or out of the money).

When inflation is low and stable, people and institutions become adapted to the situation. But if the situation changes dramatically, the surprise inflation can lead to a large redistribution of wealth. People with debts that they can pay back with the new, cheaper dollars are winners, while creditors end up as losers. In general, then, we can think of inflation as being particularly costly when it occurs in an unexpected fashion and in an environment that is not prepared for the change.

The United States in the 1970s experienced another cost of inflation as well, related to the interactions between inflation and the tax system. In the United States and most countries, taxes are based on nominal income. In contrast, correct economic decisions are made on the basis of real returns. When inflation is high, your savings account may be earning a high nominal return that gets taxed, even though the real return is low. After you pay the tax, the overall return is even lower, and this distortion is more severe when inflation is high. Similarly, investments in new equipment or research and development (R&D) may look good to businesses when inflation is low and look bad when inflation is high if nominal returns are taxed, so inflation will distort investment decisions. Economists such as Martin Feldstein of Harvard University have argued that the interaction of inflation and the tax code had a large negative effect on investment during the 1970s.

Another important cost of inflation is that inflation distorts relative prices: some prices adjust quickly to inflation, while others adjust slowly. And since relative prices signal to the economy how to allocate resources, these distortions lead to resources being allocated in inefficient ways.

Finally, there are two other kinds of costs traditionally associated with inflation. One is associated with the fact that people want to hold less money when inflation is high, which means they must go to the bank more often. These costs are called "shoe-leather costs" because of the implied cost of wearing out the soles of your shoes walking to the bank. "Menu costs" are the costs to firms (not just restaurants) of changing prices; when inflation is high, prices must be changed more frequently.

The problem with inflation is not that society can't deal with it. If we knew that inflation would be 10 percent per year forever, we would build this into every contract, transaction, and tax law—we would index economic transactions to inflation—and inflation would be little more than a minor annoyance. The problem is that when inflation comes, it often comes in surprising ways that society isn't prepared for. For as long as most of us can remember, there have been 12 inches in a foot and 100 centimeters in a meter. Suppose measuring tapes and rulers around the world were magically shortened or lengthened in an arbitrary fashion once a year on a random day. Inflation does exactly the same thing to the value of a currency.

CASE STUDY

The Wage-Price Spiral and President Nixon's Price Controls

Facing reelection in 1972, Richard Nixon was confronted with an economy that featured rising inflation and relatively high unemployment. After averaging less than 2 percent per year in the 1960s, inflation had reached 5 percent. Similarly, unemployment—which had remained about 3.5 percent during much of the 1960s—had risen to 5 percent. To maximize his chances for reelection, Nixon looked for a policy that would quickly address both problems.

A view at the time was that rising inflation resulted from a *wage-price spiral*: strong unions pressed for higher wages, strong corporations translated these rising costs into higher prices, and strong unions demanded even higher wages, leading to spiraling prices. With this view in mind, President Nixon and his advisers announced a New Economic Policy in August 1971 that would freeze wages and prices at their current levels for a period of 90 days. The goal was to break the wage-price spiral that was producing rising inflation.

After 90 days, the price controls were gradually relaxed, and inflation slowed briefly. Unemployment, however, remained high, leading the Nixon administration to pursue an expansionary policy (exactly what this means will be discussed further in Chapter 12). Combined with increases in the world price of oil, the expansionary policy brought the return of inflation. Price controls were reinstated in June 1973, but the effort to keep prices low only led to rationing. Empty supermarket shelves and long lines for gasoline made the failure of the price controls apparent, and they were abandoned in April 1974.[4]

Superficially, price controls appear to be an obvious remedy for high inflation. However, if the underlying monetary policy generates pressure for prices to rise, such a solution cannot succeed. Pent-up inflation will be released when the price controls are lifted. And until that happens, price controls distort economic decisions. Shortages and long lines are likely to be the main consequence of centralized efforts to control prices. For example, if importers of oil must pay high world prices but are constrained to sell at lower domestic prices, the supply of domestic oil will disappear.

[4]A nice summary of these facts is presented by Daniel Yergin and Joseph Stanislaw in *The Commanding Heights: The Battle Between Government and the Marketplace That Is Remaking the Modern World* (New York: Simon and Schuster, 1998), pp. 60–64; an online excerpt can be found at www.pbs.org/wgbh/commandingheights/shared/minitextlo/ess_nixongold.html.

8.5 The Fiscal Causes of High Inflation

The quantity theory of money tells us the main cause of high inflation is that the central bank prints too much money. But why, given the costs of inflation, would a central bank do this? The answer is that printing money is one way for the government to pay its bills.

To see this, consider the following equation, called **the government budget constraint**:

$$\underbrace{G}_{\text{uses}} = \underbrace{T + \Delta B + \Delta M.}_{\text{sources of funds}} \tag{8.7}$$

That is, the government's uses of funds must equal its sources of funds. According to this equation, the government finances its spending, denoted by G, with three main sources of funds. The first is tax revenue T. The second is borrowing. Let B denote the government's outstanding stock of debt; then ΔB is the change in the stock of debt, which is the amount of new borrowing. Finally, the third source of funds is printing money. Since M is the stock of money, the change in the stock of money ΔM is the amount of new money issued by the government.

The Inflation Tax

To take a concrete example, suppose the government decides to spend an extra \$100 million to provide additional health benefits to Medicare recipients. This spending must be paid for in some way, and the government has limited choices. It can cut some of its other spending or raise taxes. Or it can borrow the \$100 million from U.S. and foreign citizens and promise to pay it back as part of future spending. Or, and this is the intriguing possibility that concerns us here, the Federal Reserve could issue an extra \$100 million of currency which the government could use to pay for the higher spending. The revenue the government obtains by issuing new money (ΔM) is called **seignorage**, or the **inflation tax**.

Who pays the so-called inflation tax? By printing money, the government is taking resources from the rest of the economy, but from whom exactly? Suppose each person in the economy holds \$200 in currency. Now suppose the government decides to double the money supply. It prints an extra \$200 for each person but then spends that currency itself. From the quantity theory of money, we know that the long-run effect of this monetary expansion is to double the price level. Therefore, the \$200 of currency held by the private sector is now worth only half as much in real terms. People must now pay prices that are twice as high. The inflation tax, which shows up as a rise in the price level, is thus paid by people holding currency.

Since everyone in the economy pays higher prices, you might expect that everyone pays the inflation tax, not just holders of currency. However, consider two people. Ralph keeps all his money in his bank account, while Alice holds her wealth in the form of land, by owning a family farm. When the government prints the new currency, causing the price level to double, Ralph now in essence holds pieces of paper that are worth half as much. But Alice sees the price of her farm double as well—recall that inflation causes all prices to double, including the price of land. So in real terms, the farm is just as valuable as it was before the inflation tax hit. Again, the inflation tax is paid by people who are holding money.

In a well-functioning economy, the government finances its spending almost entirely through conventional taxes and borrowing. In certain times and places, however, this may be difficult. Imagine a government that has run a large and growing budget deficit over the last decade: that is, G is larger than T, so the government is spending more than it receives in tax revenue. Suppose also that the government has financed these budget deficits by borrowing in units of the local currency, say dollars. As the debt rises, lenders to the government may start to worry that it will have trouble paying back its debts, and they may charge higher and higher interest rates. Eventually, they may stop lending to the government altogether. If the budget deficit is 5 percent of GDP, the government may also find it difficult for political reasons to raise taxes by this large amount.

In such a situation, the government may well resort to printing currency to pay for its spending and to pay back its loans. That is, when regular taxes and borrowing dry up as sources of revenue, the government may be forced to fall back on the inflation tax. And this validates the concern that debtholders had about the government's ability to pay them back: they are repaid in units of currency that are worth much less than the dollars they lent.

This basic story is at the heart of most episodes of hyperinflation. It has led Thomas Sargent, professor of economics at New York University, to a variation on Milton Friedman's statement: "Persistent high inflation is always and everywhere a fiscal phenomenon" ("fiscal" means pertaining to government expenditures, revenues, or debt). Though Friedman is correct when he says that the root cause of inflation is the central bank's printing too much money, Sargent tells us why a government may allow this: there's no other way to satisfy its budget constraint.

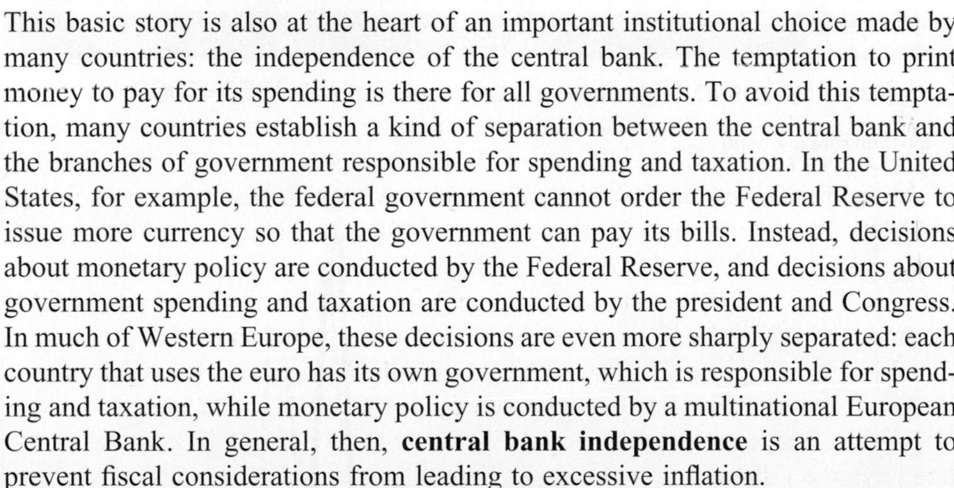

Central Bank Independence

This basic story is also at the heart of an important institutional choice made by many countries: the independence of the central bank. The temptation to print money to pay for its spending is there for all governments. To avoid this temptation, many countries establish a kind of separation between the central bank and the branches of government responsible for spending and taxation. In the United States, for example, the federal government cannot order the Federal Reserve to issue more currency so that the government can pay its bills. Instead, decisions about monetary policy are conducted by the Federal Reserve, and decisions about government spending and taxation are conducted by the president and Congress. In much of Western Europe, these decisions are even more sharply separated: each country that uses the euro has its own government, which is responsible for spending and taxation, while monetary policy is conducted by a multinational European Central Bank. In general, then, **central bank independence** is an attempt to prevent fiscal considerations from leading to excessive inflation.

At some level, though, the central bank is part of the government, and the head of the central bank is typically a political appointee. For example, in the United States, the president appoints the chair of the Federal Reserve. In principle, the president could request the resignation of a Federal Reserve chair and install someone more sympathetic to issuing currency to pay the government's bills. The independence of the central bank, then, is an ideal that invariably comes under threat when there are problems with the government's budget constraint.

CASE STUDY

Episodes of High Inflation

Figure 8.5 shows rates of inflation for Argentina, Brazil, and Russia in recent decades. In Argentina and Brazil, we see two interesting patterns. First, episodes of high inflation tend to recur. Second, hyperinflations can stop just as quickly as they start. Even though inflation rates in the early 1990s were more than 2,000 percent per year in Argentina and Brazil, they dropped to below 5 percent just a few years after the peaks in both countries. And since 2003, all three economies' inflation rates have remained below 15 percent per year. A similar pattern can be seen in Figure 8.6 for Mexico and Nigeria, two countries that experienced high inflation—but probably not what we would call hyperinflation—in the 1980s and 1990s.

How much revenue did these countries raise through the inflation tax? Typically, about 5 percent of GDP or less—making this tax an important source of revenue when you consider that total government spending as a ratio of GDP is often about 20 or 30 percent. Argentina in the late 1970s and early 1980s raised more than 10 percent of GDP through the inflation tax, financing about half its government expenditures this way.

How do episodes of high inflation or hyperinflation end? The answer from the quantity theory is that they end when the rate of money growth falls sharply. The more fundamental analysis of the government's budget constraint, however, reveals that this can only occur when the government makes difficult choices to get its finances in order: typically through a combination of lower spending, higher taxes, and new loans.

Argentina, Brazil, and Russia all experienced hyperinflation over this period. Notice the recurring hyperinflation in Argentina in the late 1970s through the end of the 1980s.

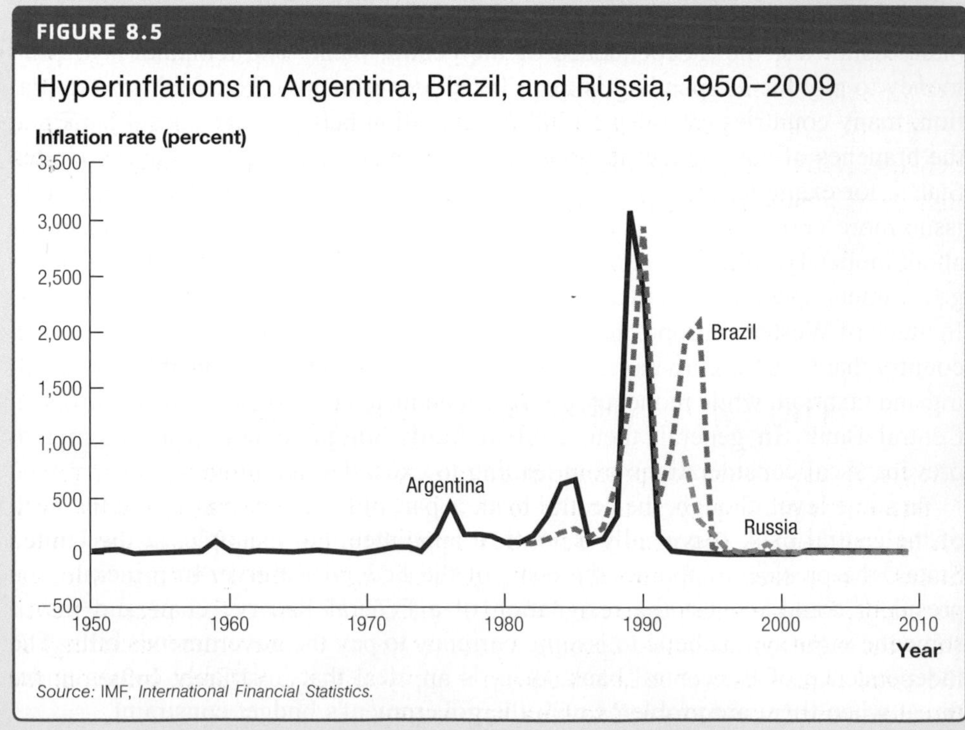

FIGURE 8.5

Hyperinflations in Argentina, Brazil, and Russia, 1950–2009

Source: IMF, *International Financial Statistics*.

FIGURE 8.6

High Inflation in Mexico and Nigeria, 1950–2009

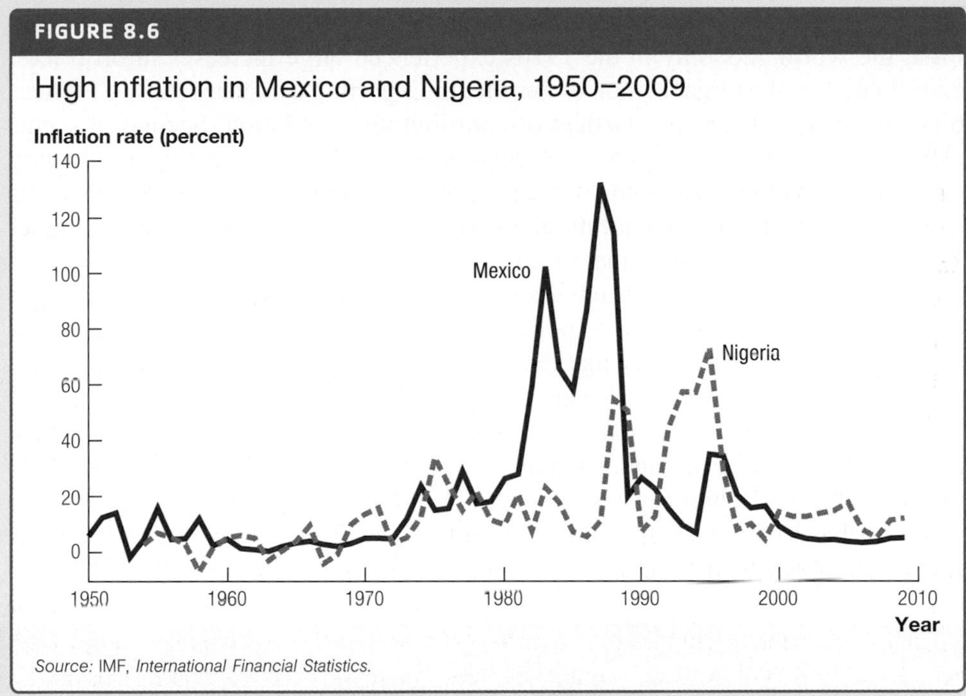

Source: IMF, *International Financial Statistics*.

Mexico and Nigeria experienced high inflation, but not what we would call hyperinflation.

Another difficulty in ending high inflation is what's known as a *coordination problem*. Imagine you are a business owner and you have to choose how to set your prices in the coming week. If the rate of inflation has been high and perhaps rising for the last year, you will build a high and rising rate of inflation into your prices. Other firms will do this as well, as will workers as they bargain over wages. This coordination injects a certain inertia into the inflation process. At some level, all the price setters in the economy have to be convinced that the high inflation of recent years is going to end, and this coordination problem can be hard to solve.

For both these reasons—because fiscal reform involves difficult choices and because of the coordination problem—halting hyperinflations is not easy. They also help us understand why hyperinflations can recur.

8.6 The Great Inflation of the 1970s

The fiscal justification for printing more money—that the government is forced to turn to the printing press in order to satisfy its budget constraint—works well for hyperinflations. But what about the Great Inflation of the 1970s in the United States? Look back at Figure 8.1. Inflation was high in the 1970s by historical standards, but the rate peaked at below 15 percent. Even at this peak, revenue from the inflation tax made up only a tiny fraction of government spending, so the fiscal explanation of inflation does not apply to the U.S. Great Inflation: the revenue earned was too small to be a key factor.

Why, then, did the Federal Reserve let inflation get out of hand in the 1970s? First, the world economy in the 1970s experienced large increases in oil prices, coordinated by the Organization of Petroleum Exporting Countries (OPEC). These oil price shocks had a direct effect of contributing to inflation. Second, it seems clear in hindsight that the Federal Reserve made mistakes in running a monetary policy that was too loose—the money supply grew too rapidly. Exactly why this is the case remains an open question, one we will find easier to analyze in Chapter 12. But we can foreshadow that discussion here.

We know now that a substantial and prolonged productivity slowdown began in the early 1970s. As of 1975, policymakers naturally thought this was a temporary shock to the economy that they might try to offset with a loose monetary policy. At the same time, however, policymakers weren't equipped with a good understanding of how the economy worked. The economic theory that would have given them the necessary understanding was being proposed by Milton Friedman, Edmund Phelps, Robert Lucas, and others in the late 1960s and early 1970s, too recent to have the necessary impact on policy. Their insights serve as the basis for the short-run model we develop in the next section of the book.

CHAPTER REVIEW

SUMMARY

1. Inflation is the annual percentage change in the overall price level in an economy. The fact that identical goods cost significantly more today than 100 years ago is a general reflection of inflation. A dollar today is worth much less than it was a decade or two ago.
2. The quantity theory of money is our basic model for understanding the long-run determinants of the price level and therefore of inflation. There are two ways to express the solution. For the price level, the solution is $P_t^* = \overline{M}_t\overline{V}/\overline{Y}_t$. For the rate of inflation, the solution is $\pi_t^* = \bar{g}_M - \bar{g}_Y$, assuming a constant velocity.
3. The quantity theory says that the main determinant of inflation is the growth rate of money in an economy, or "too much money chasing too few goods."
4. The classical dichotomy, an important part of the quantity theory, states that the real and nominal sides of the economy are largely separate. Real economic variables, like real GDP, are determined only by real forces—like the investment rate and TFP. They are not influenced by nominal changes, such as a change in the money supply. The general consensus among economists is that the classical dichotomy holds in the long run, but not necessarily in the short run.
5. The nominal interest rate in an economy is paid in units of currency, while the real interest rate is paid in goods. These rates are related by the Fisher equation: $i = R + \pi$.
6. Inflation—particularly when it is high and unexpected—can be very costly to an economy. Inflation generally transfers resources from lenders and savers to

borrowers, because borrowers can repay their loans with dollars that are worth less. Other costs include high effective tax rates, distortions to relative prices, shoe-leather costs, and menu costs.

7. The government budget constraint says that the government has three basic ways to finance its spending: through taxes, borrowing, and printing money. When governments find it hard to reduce spending, raise taxes, or borrow, they will be forced to print money to satisfy the budget constraint. Hyperinflations are generally a reflection of such fiscal problems.

KEY CONCEPTS

central bank independence
the classical dichotomy
deflation
the Fisher equation
the government budget constraint
hyperinflation
inflation
the inflation tax (seignorage)
monetary base
the neutrality of money
nominal interest rate
quantity equation
the quantity theory of money
real interest rate
reserves
the velocity of money

REVIEW QUESTIONS

1. What is inflation? Suppose an individual's retirement plan consists of putting $100 into a safe. What effect does inflation have on this plan?
2. A concise summary of the quantity theory of money is that inflation occurs because of too much money chasing too few goods. Explain.
3. Explain how a rise in $\overline{M}_t$, $\overline{V}$, and $\overline{Y}_t$ affects the price level according to the quantity theory.
4. Why do economists think the classical dichotomy holds in the long run?
5. What is the difference between a real interest rate and a nominal interest rate? What is the intuition behind the Fisher equation?
6. What are the costs of inflation, and how can these costs be avoided?
7. What is the government budget constraint? How does it help us understand the causes of high inflation?
8. How can we understand the Great Inflation of the 1970s? Does the government budget constraint help?
9. Who pays the inflation tax?

EXERCISES

smartwork.wwnorton.com 

1. **How much is that?** Using the data on the consumer price index reported in Table 8.1, calculate the value in 2007 of the following items (refer to the nearest year in the table to do each calculation):

   (a) The salary of a worker in 1900: $1,000 per year.
   (b) Babe Ruth's salary in 1932: $80,000.
   (c) A bottle of Coke or Pepsi in the late 1940s: one nickel.

(d) A quarter pounder from McDonald's in 1972: 55 cents.
(e) A movie ticket to see *Star Wars* in 1977: about $2.25.
(f) A pack of M&M candies in 1991: 45 cents.

2. **Calculating inflation:** Compute inflation rates in the following cases.
   (a) Suppose the consumer price index in the future takes the following values: $P_{2015} = 110$, $P_{2016} = 113$, $P_{2017} = 118$, $P_{2018} = 120$, $P_{2019} = 125$. Viewing these price levels as prevailing at the *end* of each year, calculate the inflation rate for the years 2016, 2017, 2018, and 2019.
   (b) Consider the data on the CPI from Table 8.1. Compute the average annual rate of inflation that prevailed between 1980 and 2007. (*Hint*: This calculation is similar to the computation of an average annual growth rate, say for real GDP.)
   (c) Referring to the same CPI data in part (b), compute the average annual inflation rate between 1970 and 1980. What was the rate between 1900 and 2007?

3. **The quantity theory of money:** What is the key endogenous variable in the quantity theory? Explain the effect on this key variable of the following changes:
   (a) The money supply is doubled.
   (b) The velocity of money increases by 10%.
   (c) Real GDP rises by 2%.
   (d) The money supply increases by 3% while real GDP rises by 3% at the same time.

4. **Inflation and the quantity theory:** Suppose velocity is constant, the growth rate of real GDP is 3% per year, and the growth rate of money is 5% per year. Calculate the long-run rate of inflation according to the quantity theory in each of the following cases:
   (a) What is the rate of inflation in this baseline case?
   (b) Suppose the growth rate of money rises to 10% per year.
   (c) Suppose the growth rate of money rises to 100% per year.
   (d) Back to the baseline case, suppose real GDP growth rises to 5% per year.
   (e) What if real GDP growth falls to 2% per year?
   (f) Return to the baseline case and suppose the velocity of money rises at 1% per year. What happens to inflation in this case? Why might velocity change in this fashion?

5. **Price stability:** Suppose you are the head of the central bank and your mandate is to maintain the price level at a constant value. Explain what you would do to the money supply in response to each of the following events:
   (a) Real GDP increases by 4% during a boom.
   (b) Real GDP declines by 1% during a recession.
   (c) Real GDP is growing at 3% per year.
   (d) The velocity of money increases by 2%.
   (e) The velocity of money declines by 1%.

6. **Interest rates:** The Fisher equation relates real (R) and nominal (i) interest rates to the rate of inflation (π). Given two of these values below, calculate the third.

(a) $R = 1\%$, $\pi = 3\%$. What is i?
(b) $\pi = 5\%$, $i = 10\%$. What is R?
(c) $R = 2\%$, $i = 6\%$. What is π?
(d) $R = 1\%$, $\pi = 12\%$. What is i?
(e) $\pi = 6\%$, $i = 2\%$. What is R?
(f) $R = 1\%$, $i = 10\%$. What is π?

7. **Real and nominal interest rates:** Suppose the real return on investing in a machine is 5% and the inflation rate is 4%.
   (a) According to the Fisher equation, what should the nominal interest rate be?
   (b) Suppose bank A charges a nominal interest rate on loans equal to 8%. What happens?
   (c) Suppose bank B advertises its nominal rate on savings accounts as 12%. What happens?

8. **Earning the nominal return:** Suppose the inflation rate is 5%. Suppose the marginal product of capital in a firm is 8% but that in the course of production, 6% of capital is worn out by depreciation. What is the nominal return associated with an investment in capital, and why? What is the Fisher equation in this example?

9. **Can interest rates be negative?** Consider the following two questions.
   (a) Can the real interest rate be negative? In what circumstances?
   (b) Can the nominal interest rate be negative? Discuss.

10. **The costs of inflation:** Consider two possible inflation scenarios. In one, the inflation rate is 100% per year, but it has been at this level for three decades and the central bank says it will keep it there forever. In the other, the inflation rate was 3% for two decades but just this past year rose to 10%. Over the next 5 years, which economy do you think suffers a higher cost of inflation, and why?

11. **Hyperinflations:** Explain some of the costs of hyperinflations. If they are so costly to an economy, why do they occur?

12. **Inflation as fiscal phenomenon:** The complete version of the Thomas Sargent quote that began this chapter is "Persistent high inflation is always and everywhere a fiscal phenomenon." Why did Sargent include the modifiers "persistent high"?

13. **Revenue from the inflation tax:** The amount of money the government raises from the inflation tax is ΔM. Consult the statistical tables at the back of the *Economic Report of the President* (available online) to answer the following questions:
    (a) How much currency was in circulation in 1981? What was the size of the monetary base in 1981?
    (b) If the monetary base is the measure of M, how much revenue was raised from the inflation tax between 1980 and 1981, in dollars? What fraction was this of 1981 GDP?
    (c) Why does this exercise ask you to do these calculations for the year 1981 instead of some other year?

14. **A formula for the inflation tax (hard):** As in exercise 13, the amount of money the government raises from the inflation tax is ΔM.
   (a) Write this amount as a ratio to nominal GDP. Multiply and divide by M to get an expression for the ratio of revenue from the inflation tax to GDP. Your answer should take the form of the product of a growth rate and a different ratio. Interpret this equation.
   (b) Use the quantity theory to replace the growth rate of money in this product with a term that involves the inflation rate.
   (c) How much revenue, as a share of GDP, would the inflation tax raise in the following episodes? Assume the growth rate of real GDP is 2% in these calculations:
      i. The United States in 1981: Use the tables from the *Economic Report of the President* to compute the answer. How does this compare with your answer to exercise 13?
      ii. The United States in 2005.
   (d) Suppose there is a hyperinflation where the inflation rate rises to 2,000%. For a given value of M/Y, the formula you derived in (b) suggests that the inflation tax could raise more than 100% of GDP in revenue. Clearly this could not actually happen. Why not? (*Hint*: Think about what happened in the German hyperinflation example that began this chapter.)

15. **Reflections on a classic:** *A Monetary History of the United States, 1867 to 1960*, by Milton Friedman and Anna Schwartz, is a classic study of monetary policy, published in 1963. Read the interview with Anna Schwartz available at www.minneapolisfed.org/pubs/region/93-09/int939.cfm, and explain what you think the main contribution of this book was. (Other interesting interviews with famous macroeconomists are gathered at http://minneapolisfed.org/pubs/region.)

WORKED EXERCISES

2. **Calculating inflation:**
   (a) The inflation rate is the percentage change in the price level. By convention, we calculate this percentage change relative to the price that prevails in the initial period. Think of the prices reported in the exercise as being "end of year" prices. The inflation rate in the year 2016 is then $\frac{113 - 110}{110} = 0.027$, or 2.7%. In the year 2017, it's $\frac{118 - 113}{113} = 0.044$, or 4.4%.

      Inflation in the other years can be calculated in the same way.
   (b) To calculate the average annual rate of inflation between 1980 and 2007, think of the inflation rate as the average annual growth rate of the price level. That is, we are asked to undertake a growth rate calculation.

From our growth rate rules back in Chapter 3, recall that the average annual growth rate between two periods satisfies

$$p_T = p_0(1 + \pi)^T,$$

where π is the growth rate, p_T is the price level in the final period at date T, and p_0 is the price level in the initial period, date 0. The inflation rate is the growth rate of the price level.

We can solve this equation for the inflation rate to find that

$$\pi = \left(\frac{P_T}{P_0}\right)^{1/T} - 1.$$

Notice the similarity between this equation and the rule for calculating growth rates—for example, look back at equation (3.9) on page 50. Applying this equation to calculate the inflation rate between 1980 and 2007, we find

$$\pi = \left(\frac{100}{39.73}\right)^{1/27} - 1 = 0.035.$$

So the inflation rate averaged 3.5% during this period.

(c) You should now be able to compute these inflation rates using the formulas from part (b).

5. **Price stability:** Consider the quantity theory of money in its growth rate form, shown in equation (8.3):

$$\bar{g}_M + \bar{g}_V = g_P + \bar{g}_Y.$$

Rearranging to solve for the percentage change in the price level, we have

$$g_P = \bar{g}_M + \bar{g}_V - \bar{g}_Y.$$

Our goal is to keep the price level constant, so we want to maintain $g_P = 0$.

(a) If real GDP increases by 4% and the central bank does nothing, then the equation we have just derived says that inflation will be −4%. To restore inflation back to zero, the central bank must increase the money supply by 4% to keep the price level constant. Recall the summary of the quantity theory of inflation as "too much money chasing too few goods." In this case, the number of goods is going up, so we have to raise the amount of money in the economy to keep the price level constant.

(b) The same reasoning applies here. If real GDP falls by 1%, the central bank needs to reduce the money supply by 1% to keep the price level constant.

(c) If real GDP is growing at a constant rate of 3% per year, then the central bank needs to keep the money supply growing at 3% per year to maintain a constant price level (assuming velocity is constant).

(d) The quantity theory in its standard form, $MV = PY$, is especially helpful in seeing what needs to be done when the velocity of money changes. The quantity theory says that nominal GDP equals the "effective" quantity of money, MV. So if velocity changes and we want to keep the price level unchanged, we must move the money supply in the *opposite* direction to keep MV constant. In this problem, velocity increases by 2%, so we need to reduce the money supply by 2% to offset this change.

(e) Finally, if the velocity of money falls by 1%, we need to increase the supply of money by 1% to keep the price level constant.

DIS
MEC
SME

PART 3 THE SHORT RUN

CHAPTER 9

AN INTRODUCTION TO THE SHORT RUN

OVERVIEW

In this chapter, we learn

- how the gap between actual GDP and potential GDP—a gap we call short-run output—is a key measure of the economy's performance in the short run.
- how costly fluctuations in economic activity can be.
- that the rate of inflation tends to decline when the economy is in a recession.
- a simple version of the short-run model that will help us understand these patterns.

> But this "long run" is a misleading guide to current affairs. "In the long run" we are all dead. Economists set themselves too easy, too useless a task if in tempestuous seasons they can only tell us that when the storm is long past the ocean is flat again.
>
> —JOHN MAYNARD KEYNES

9.1 Introduction

The passage quoted above is one of the most well known in economics, penned by one of the great economists of the twentieth century, John Maynard Keynes. The long-run model we developed in the first section of the book is a guide to how the economy will behave on average. But as Keynes points out, at any given time the situation in which an economy finds itself is unlikely to be equal to this long-run average. That was certainly the case in late 2008 and 2009. The financial crisis shocked the economy into its most "tempestuous season" in many decades. Economic growth turned sharply negative throughout much of Europe, Japan, and the United States, and more than 8 million U.S. workers lost their jobs.

Over the next six chapters, we turn to the second main model in this book, the short-run model. This model will help us understand how the normally robust engine of economic growth can sputter, with growth turning negative and unemployment rising sharply. We will devote substantial attention—more than two complete chapters—to the recent financial crisis that has shaken the world economy.

The short-run model developed in fits and starts throughout the last century, with contributions coming from a wide range of economists, many of whom we'll meet in the coming pages. We will begin in this chapter with a brief overview of the short-run model, paring it down to its simplest ingredients. We will learn intuitively how the economy behaves as it deviates from its long-run trend. Chapter 10 will then apply this intuition immediately to the global financial crisis and the major recession that began in 2007. We'll see the basic macroeconomic facts of the financial crisis, including the dramatic run-up and collapse of housing prices, the demise of many of Wall Street's storied financial institutions, and the sharpest contraction in the U.S. and world economies in decades. We will also introduce several key financial concepts, especially balance sheets and leverage, that are crucial for understanding recent events.

Chapters 11 through 13 will consider the building blocks of the short-run model in detail, producing a basic theory of economic fluctuations that can explain the sharp rise in inflation during the 1970s, the booming economy of the late 1990s, and the recessions of the early 1980s, 1990s, and 2000s. Finally, in Chapter 14, we will return to the financial crisis, highlighting the particular features of the crisis that have made it so devastating. We will use the short-run model as a lens through which to view both the crisis itself and the range of monetary and fiscal policies that have been implemented in response to it. In the end, we will see both how far the short-run model can take us in understanding modern economic fluctuations and how our understanding of these fluctuations remains incomplete.

Epigraph: From *A Tract on Monetary Reform*, 1923.

9.2 The Long Run, the Short Run, and Shocks

The following lines encapsulate the general organization of our approach to macroeconomics:

long-run model ⇒ potential output, long-run inflation
short-run model ⇒ current output, current inflation

We think of the long-run model as determining the level of potential output and the long-run rate of inflation. The short-run model, on the other hand, determines the current levels of output and inflation that we observe on a year-to-year or even quarter-to-quarter basis.

Potential output is the amount the economy would produce if all inputs were utilized at their long-run, sustainable levels. Actual output may deviate from potential because the economy is hit by shocks such as sudden changes in oil prices, the seizing of financial markets, changes in taxes and government spending, the development of successful new technologies, the disappointment of new technologies that fail to pan out, natural disasters, or booms or recessions in the rest of the world. The **short run** is defined to be the length of time over which these deviations occur. It may not correspond precisely to a given amount of calendar time, but such deviations typically last for two years or so, as we will see below.

One of the important assumptions underlying the short-run model that we develop over the next several chapters is that the long run is given. We think of potential output and the long-run rate of inflation as being determined by the long-run model, outside the short-run model. In other words, the short-run model takes these two variables as exogenous. What this means for our notation is that these variables will have overbars. For example, potential output is denoted by $\bar{Y}_t$; think of it as being determined by a combined Solow-Romer model. Similarly, the long-run inflation rate is denoted $\bar{\pi}$. It lacks a time subscript because, as we will discuss in more detail in Chapter 13, we think of the long-run inflation rate as a stable parameter that is chosen by policymakers.

The two key endogenous variables in our short-run model are the current level of output, denoted Y_t, and the current inflation rate, denoted π_t. These are the variables that our short-run model will determine. Just like in the recent recession associated with the global financial crisis, current output and current inflation can deviate from their long-run values. Explaining these deviations is the basic goal of the short-run model. To see this, let's focus more precisely on the difference between trends and fluctuations.

Trends and Fluctuations

Actual output in an economy can be viewed as the sum of the **long-run trend** and **short-run fluctuations**:

$$\underbrace{\text{actual output}}_{Y_t} = \underbrace{\text{long-run trend}}_{\bar{Y}_t} + \underbrace{\text{short-run fluctuations}}_{\tilde{Y}_t}. \tag{9.1}$$

The long-run component is potential output $\bar{Y}_t$, accounting for the general trend in overall GDP. Potential output can be thought of as a relatively smooth trend, much like the bar that sits on top of $\overline{Y}_t$. The short-run component captures the fluctuations in GDP, which the short-run model seeks to explain. We will denote the short-run component as $\tilde{Y}_t$, where the tilde (˜) illustrates the "wiggles" of economic fluctuations.

In practice, we specify short-run fluctuations in percentage terms rather than in dollars. For example, suppose actual output falls short of potential output by \$100 million in a given year. Is that a lot or a little? The answer depends on the overall size of the economy—in 1950, \$100 million was a much larger fraction of GDP than it is today. It is typically more informative to say actual output is, for example, 1 percent below potential.

To be more explicit, the fluctuations component of output is measured as

$$\tilde{Y}_t \equiv \frac{Y_t - \overline{Y}_t}{\overline{Y}_t}. \tag{9.2}$$

That is, it is the difference between actual and potential output, expressed as a percentage of potential output. For example, if actual output is \$980 and potential output is \$1,000, then $\tilde{Y}$ is $-20/1{,}000 = -0.02 = -2\%$ (rather than $-\$20$).

Figure 9.1 shows a stylized graph of actual and potential output (panel a), as well as a measure of the implied short-run fluctuations (panel b). A key thing to notice in this figure is that $\tilde{Y}$ looks much like actual output. When we remove the long-run trend associated with economic growth (potential output), what remains are the ups and downs of economic fluctuations (panel b). For this reason, economists often refer to $\tilde{Y}$ as "detrended output," or **short-run output**. When an economy is booming, actual output is above potential, and $\tilde{Y}$ is positive. When an economy is in recession, actual output is less than potential output, and $\tilde{Y}$ is negative.

Short-Run Output in the United States

Figure 9.2 shows actual and potential GDP in the U.S. economy since 1929. Graphed this way, the fluctuations in GDP are relatively hard to see, especially since 1950 or so. There was a large negative gap during **the Great Depression** of the 1930s

FIGURE 9.1

Economic Fluctuations and Short-Run Output

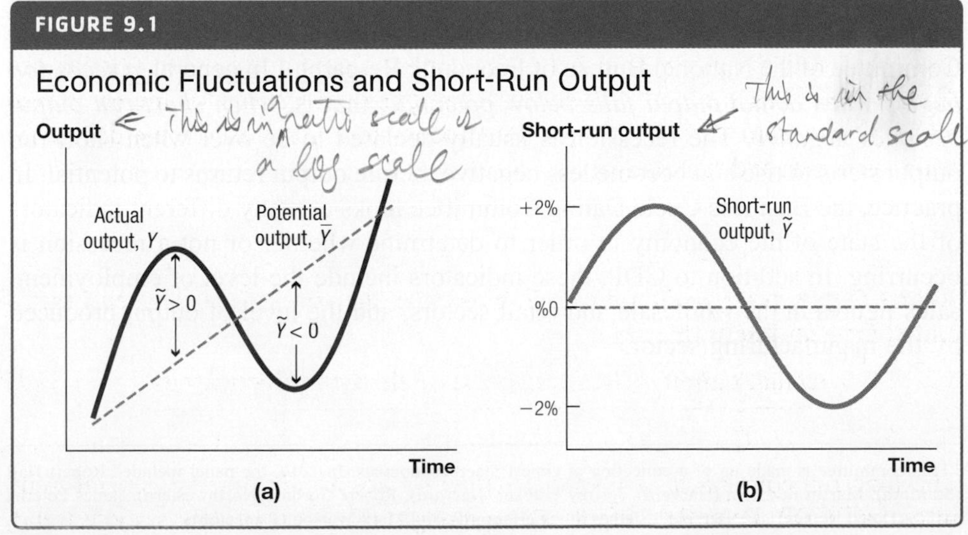

The short-run model studies the deviations of actual output from potential output. When an economy is booming, actual output is above potential, and $\tilde{Y}$ is positive. When an economy is in a recession, actual output is less than potential output, and $\tilde{Y}$ is negative.

Because of the magnitude of economic growth, actual and potential output look quite similar on this time scale.

FIGURE 9.2

U.S. Real GDP, Actual and Potential, 1929–2009

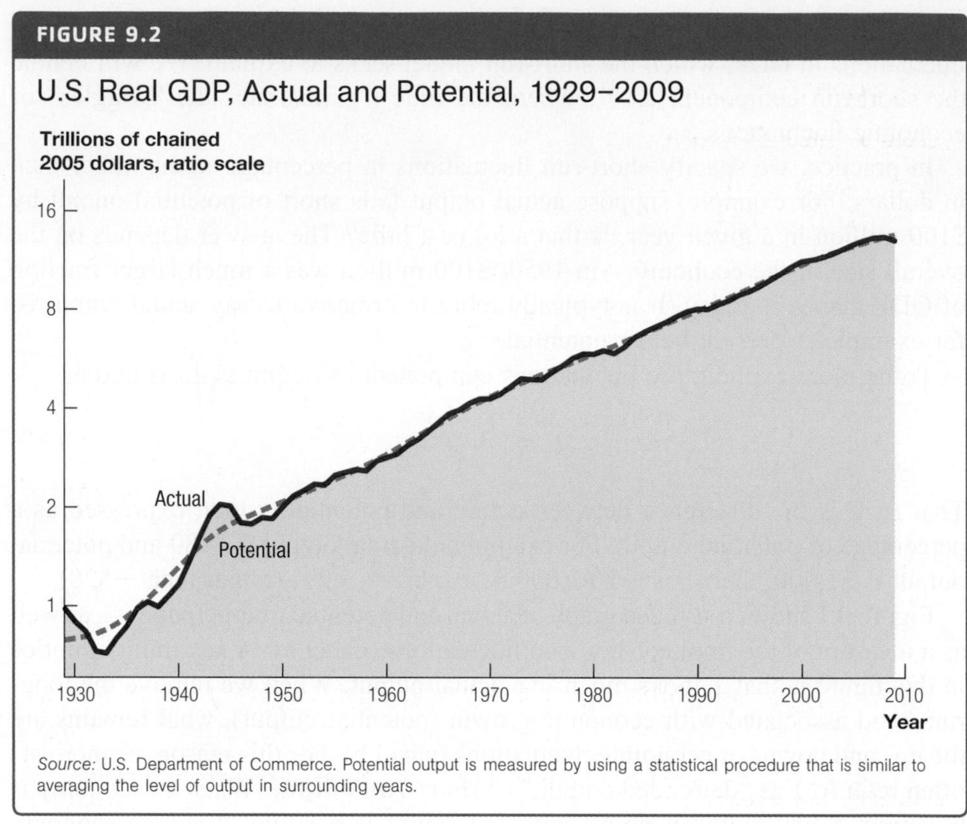

Source: U.S. Department of Commerce. Potential output is measured by using a statistical procedure that is similar to averaging the level of output in surrounding years.

when actual output was dramatically below potential. This situation turned around during the course of World War II, when actual output was above potential. But since then, the two lines appear to have tracked each other closely.

In part, however, this is an illusion of scale, as shown in Figure 9.3. If we compute the difference between actual and potential output from Figure 9.2 and plot it since 1960, the economic fluctuations become visible.

In addition to plotting short-run output, Figure 9.3 also shades periods during which the economy was in a **recession**, determined by the Business Cycle Dating Committee of the National Bureau of Economic Research.[1] In general, *a recession begins when actual output falls below potential*; that is, *when short-run output becomes negative*. The recession is usually declared to be over when short-run output starts to rise and become less negative, before output returns to potential. In practice, the Business Cycle Dating Committee looks at many different indicators of the state of the economy in order to determine whether or not a recession is occurring. In addition to GDP, these indicators include the level of employment, sales figures in the wholesale and retail sectors, and the level of output produced by the manufacturing sector.[2]

[1] This committee is made up of a collection of expert macroeconomists. In 2010, the panel included Robert Hall (Stanford), Martin Feldstein (Harvard), Jeffrey Frankel (Harvard), Robert Gordon (Northwestern), James Poterba (MIT), David Romer (U.C. Berkeley), James Stock (Harvard), and Mark Watson (Princeton).

[2] A more detailed discussion can be found at www.nber.org/cycles/recessions.html.

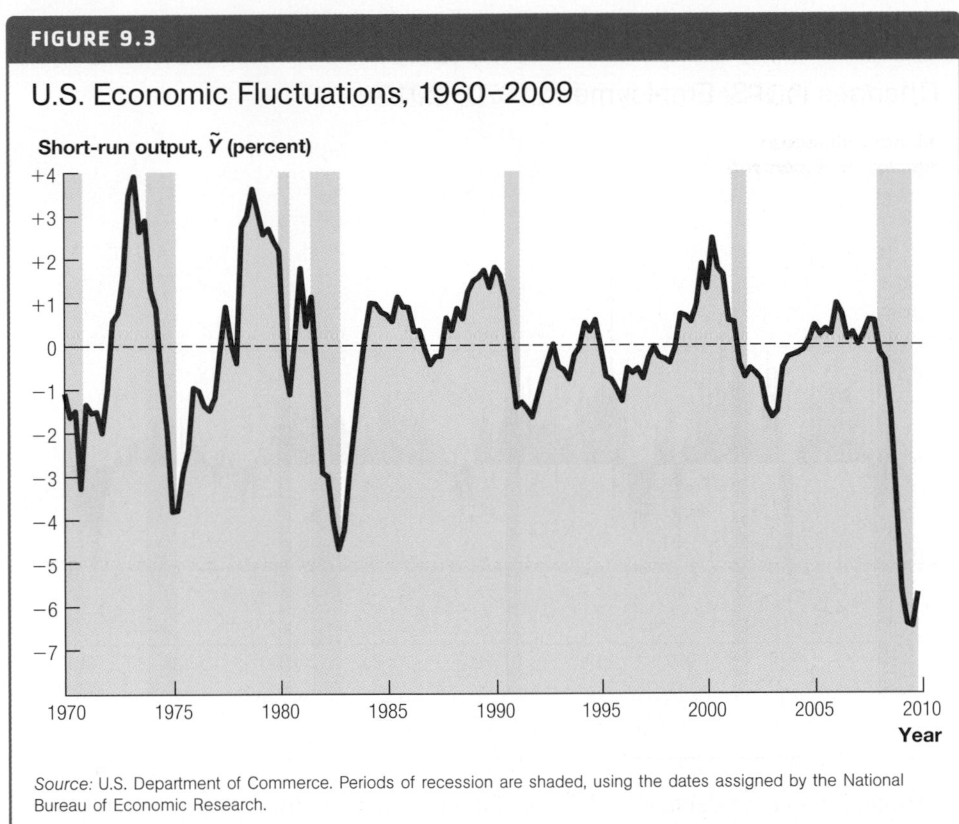

FIGURE 9.3

U.S. Economic Fluctuations, 1960–2009

Source: U.S. Department of Commerce. Periods of recession are shaded, using the dates assigned by the National Bureau of Economic Research.

Short-run output $\tilde{Y}$ is computed as the percentage difference between actual and potential output, as described in the text.

Since 1950, the fluctuations in real GDP have usually ranged from about −4 percent to +4 percent. The deepest recession before the recent financial crisis occurred in 1980–82, when output fell to 5 percent below potential. The recessions in 1990–91 and 2001 were substantially milder.

In contrast, the most recent recession, which began in December 2007, shows a level of output by the end of 2009 that was more than 6 percent below potential. We will discuss this recession—and the financial crisis that precipitated it—in much greater detail in the coming chapter.

In a typical recession, output falls below potential for about 2 years, first during the recession itself and then as the economy recovers back to potential. If we add up the lost output over the entire length of a typical recession, about 6 percent of GDP is forgone. To put this number into perspective, recall that U.S. GDP in 2009 was about \$14 trillion, and 6 percent of this is about \$840 billion. Since the U.S. population is about 300 million, the loss works out to about \$2,800 per person, or about \$11,000 per family of four. On average, then, a recession is quite costly. In addition, the decline in income is typically not spread evenly across the population. To the extent that it's concentrated in particular regions, industries, and families, the costs to those affected can be even larger.

These calculations, however, overstate the costs of economic fluctuations, because they don't incorporate the gains from periods when the economy is booming. If policymakers could eliminate fluctuations in short-run output altogether, the overall gains would be noticeably smaller, because the booms and recessions offset each other to some extent.

Employment typically rises each month. But the latest recession has led to the largest sustained decline in employment in many decades.

FIGURE 9.4

Changes in U.S. Employment, 1970–2010

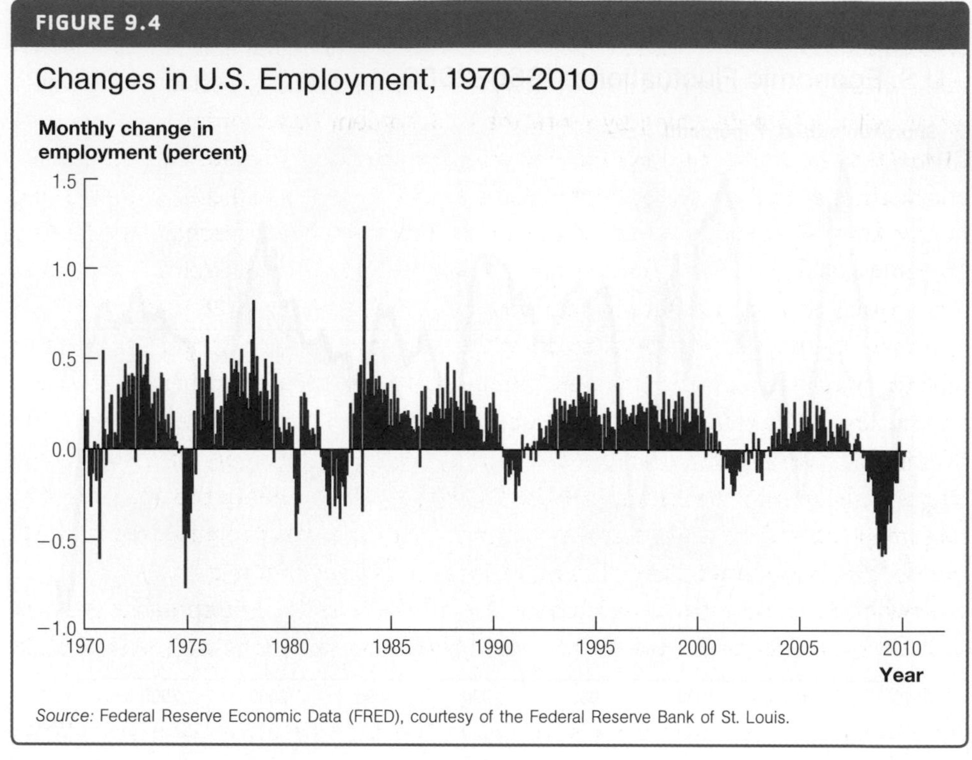

Source: Federal Reserve Economic Data (FRED), courtesy of the Federal Reserve Bank of St. Louis.

Another way to understand the costs of a recession is to think about the number of jobs that are lost. In a typical recession, the unemployment rate rises by one or two percentage points. Since the U.S. labor force consists of about 150 million people (see Chapter 7), between 1.5 and 3 million jobs are "lost" as a result of a recession. It's as if the entire labor force in the San Francisco Bay area becomes unemployed.

Figure 9.4 follows this approach and plots the monthly change in employment since 1970. By this measure, the recent recession looks particularly severe: total employment fell by more than 8.4 million jobs between December 2007 and February 2010, the largest decline in employment in many decades.

As Figure 9.4 suggests, the recent recession is special in many ways. It was precipitated by a large decline in housing prices and by the most severe financial crisis to hit the economy since the 1930s. It will be discussed in more detail in the next chapter.

CASE STUDY

The Great Depression

The Great Depression is to economics what the Big Bang is to physics. As an event, the Depression is largely synonymous with the birth of modern macroeconomics, and it continues to haunt successive generations of economists.

—Robert A. Margo

Epigraph: "Employment and Unemployment in the 1930s," *Journal of Economic Perspectives,* vol. 7 (Spring 1993), p. 41.

The Great Depression of the 1930s was a worldwide calamity. When the U.S. economy bottomed out in 1933, 25 percent of Americans were unemployed, and industrial production had declined by more than 60 percent. The Depression hit the whole world, with output declining by more than 20 percent in countries as diverse as Chile, Canada, Germany, Italy, and Poland.[3] For a contrast to these "dry" statistics, check out the vivid scenes of Depression-era New York City in the 2005 movie *Cinderella Man* (directed by Ron Howard) and the stunning photographs in the Library of Congress collection "America from the Great Depression to World War II" (see memory.loc.gov/ammem/fsahtml and www.loc.gov/rr/print/list/128_migm.html).

As the quotation above indicates, the Great Depression marked the beginning of modern macroeconomics. Chapter 2 noted the impetus the Depression provided for the creation of national income accounting. The Depression also stimulated the development of John Maynard Keynes's *The General Theory of Employment, Interest, and Money*, published in 1936. Keynes's general theory provided the first systematic attempt to understand macroeconomic fluctuations, and elements of his theory form important building blocks of modern macroeconomic analysis.

How does modern macroeconomics understand the Great Depression? Could such an event happen in the world today? These are questions we will explore in Chapters 10–14.

Measuring Potential Output

Current GDP numbers can be obtained quite easily from statistical agencies in virtually any economy: they are simply careful measures of what is actually produced. But how do we measure potential output, an economic construct that is not directly observable? One way is to assume there's a perfectly smooth trend passing through the quarter-to-quarter movements in real GDP. An alternative is to take averages of the surrounding actual GDP numbers.

The fact that there is no directly observed measure of potential output in the economy poses a significant problem for policymakers. Suppose we observe that GDP grew over the last quarter at an annualized rate of 5 percent. (An **annualized rate** is the rate of change that would apply if the growth persisted for an entire year. For example, if GDP increases by 1 percent over a single quarter, we would say it grew at an annualized rate of 4 percent.) How much of this increase in GDP reflects an increase in potential output and how much reflects a short-run fluctuation? Is the economy now above potential, or has potential output grown rapidly?

Macroeconomic policymakers face questions like these on a daily basis, and the answers are usually far from obvious. In practice, economists consult a variety of indicators: data on how quickly the unemployed are finding jobs, surveys revealing economic activity in particular industries, demand by firms for new factories and equipment, and so on. Still, these indicators are far from perfect, and one of the

[3] See Christina D. Romer, "The Nation in Depression," *Journal of Economic Perspectives*, vol. 7 (Spring 1993), pp. 19–39.

The inflation rate typically falls during a recession.

FIGURE 9.5

Inflation in the United States, 1960–2009

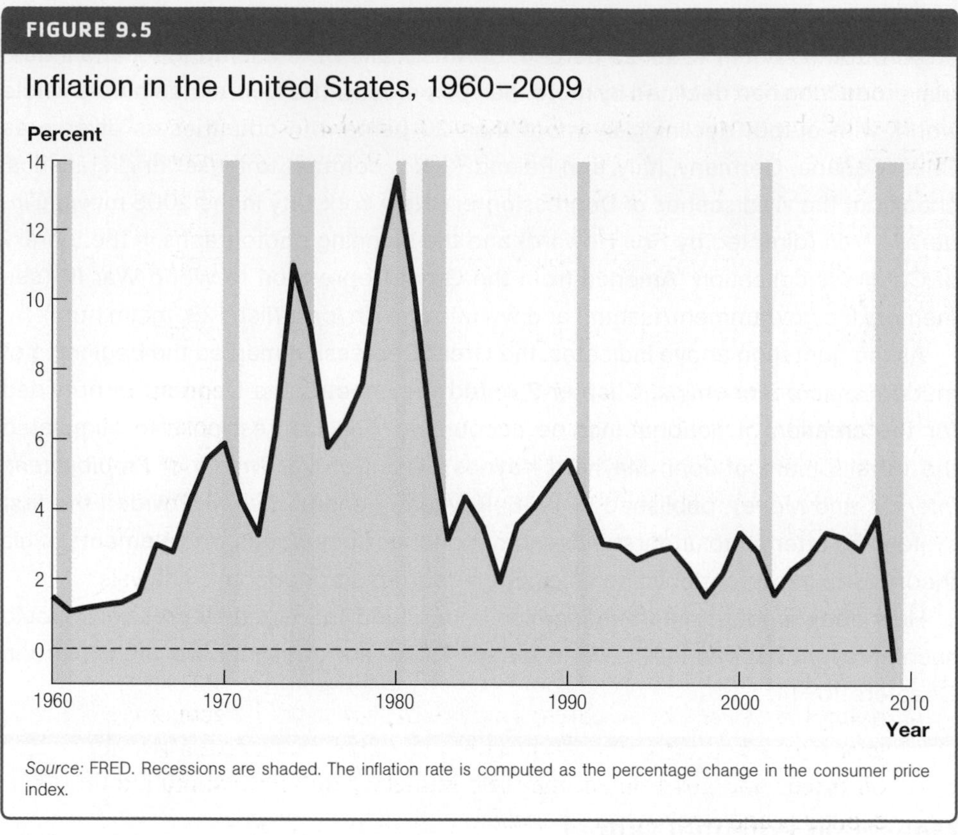

Source: FRED. Recessions are shaded. The inflation rate is computed as the percentage change in the consumer price index.

most difficult tasks faced by policymakers is to decide whether a change in GDP reflects a change in underlying potential output or a short-run fluctuation. Indeed, as we will see later, you could make the case that the high inflation of the 1970s was partly caused by confusion over this issue.

The Inflation Rate

Figure 9.5 shows the annual rate of inflation since 1960 for the U.S. economy. As before, periods in which the economy is in a recession are shaded, and this shading reveals an important fact: *the rate of inflation typically falls during a recession*. For every recession since 1960, we see that the inflation rate peaked at a date very close to the start of the recession and then declined—often sharply—over the course of the recession. This fact turns out to play a central role in the short-run model.

9.3 The Short-Run Model

Why does actual GDP differ from potential output? Why do recessions follow peaks in the rate of inflation? These are among the questions addressed by the model we develop in the next three chapters. Our short-run model describes an economy that exhibits many features we see in the real world. It includes consumers and workers, firms that undertake investments in capital, a government that uses some of the economy's production, and trade with the rest of the world. While a discussion of exchange rates will be delayed until Chapter 19, the short-run model features an open economy where booms and recessions in the rest of the world impact economic activity at home. The economy will exhibit both long-run growth and fluctuations in economic activity. A central bank will manage monetary policy in an effort to smooth out those fluctuations.

More specifically, the short-run model is based on three premises:

1. *The economy is constantly being hit by shocks.* These **economic shocks** include changes in oil prices, disruptions in financial markets, the development of new technologies, changes in military spending, and natural disasters. Such shocks can push actual output away from potential output and/or move the inflation rate away from its long-run value.
2. *Monetary and fiscal policy affect output.* The government has monetary and fiscal tools at its disposal that can affect the amount of economic activity in the short run. In principle, this means policymakers might be able to neutralize shocks to the economy. For example, if the economy is hit with a negative shock like a rise in oil prices, the government may use monetary policy to stimulate the economy and keep output from falling below potential.
3. *There is a dynamic trade-off between output and inflation.* If the government can affect output, wouldn't it try to keep actual GDP as high as possible? This is an important question and goes to the heart of our short-run model. The answer is no, and the reason lies in this trade-off. A booming economy today—in which the economy is producing more than its potential output—leads to an increase in the inflation rate. Conversely, if the inflation rate is high and policymakers want to lower it, a recession is typically required. This trade-off is known as **the Phillips curve**, named after the New Zealand–born economist A. W. Phillips, who first identified this kind of trade-off in 1958 (see the case study in Chapter 12).

A complete development of the short-run model will take us several more chapters, as we explore each of these elements in detail. First, however, we can get an intuitive feel for how the model works.

A Graph of the Short-Run Model

According to the Phillips curve, shown graphically in Figure 9.6, a booming economy leads to an increase in the inflation rate, and a recession leads to a decrease. This shows up in the figure as a positive relationship between the change in the inflation rate and short-run output $\tilde{Y}$. If output is above potential, $\tilde{Y}$ is positive, and the Phillips curve says that the change in inflation $\Delta\pi$ will also be

The Phillips curve relates the change in the inflation rate to the amount of economic activity. In a booming economy ($\tilde{Y} > 0$), inflation rises. In a slumping economy ($\tilde{Y} < 0$), inflation falls.

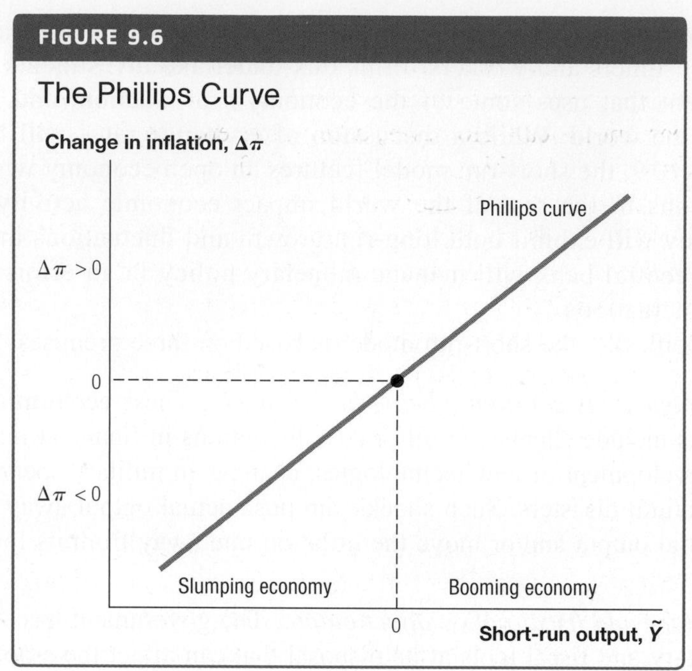

FIGURE 9.6
The Phillips Curve

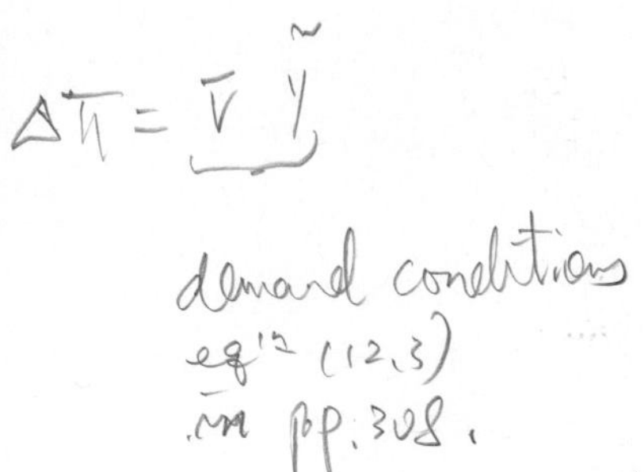

positive—that is, inflation will increase. In contrast, if output is below potential so that $\tilde{Y}$ is negative, the change in inflation will be negative, so inflation will be falling over time.

What is the intuition behind this dynamic trade-off? First, consider a booming economy and the rise in inflation that it generates. In this case, actual output is greater than potential output: firms are producing more than they can sustain in the long run. But how can firms produce *more* than potential output? The fact is, our terminology is unfortunate and somewhat confusing: you might think that "potential" output should always be just beyond reach, but this is not what economists mean by potential output.

Let's take an example. Each December, a hot new toy—a furry robot pet or the latest computer game—becomes the "must-have" gift of the holiday season. The firm making the gift revs up its production line and keeps its workers overtime in an effort to meet the spike in demand. Routine maintenance of the production equipment may be deferred until later, just as you may put off changing the oil in your car during final exams. Workers may be asked to put in extra hours at 50 percent higher wages. With these temporary measures, the firm can expand its output in the short run. However, the price of the must-have gift rises in December, for at least two reasons. First, production is more costly, for example because of the higher wages associated with overtime. Second, even with the expanded output, furry robots are likely to remain scarce as frantic parents scramble to put happy smiles on their kids' faces. Prices rise to reflect this scarcity.

In a booming economy with output above potential, it's as if all firms are the lucky producers of the must-have gift, and every month is December. In this situation, firms raise prices—perhaps to cover the higher costs of production as they attempt to meet the higher demand, or to take advantage of high demand to make more profits. If the prevailing inflation rate is 5 percent, firms may raise their prices by 7 percent instead. However, a key difference in the booming economy is that *all* firms are doing this, not just a single furry toy maker. When all firms raise their prices by 7 percent, the inflation rate goes up.

Alternatively, when output is below potential and the economy is in a recession, firms see little demand for their products and are faced with laying off workers. They will be restrained in raising their prices. If the prevailing inflation rate is 5 percent, they may raise their prices by only 3 percent in an effort to sell more output. When all firms behave this way, the inflation rate falls, just as the Phillips curve predicts.

How the Short-Run Model Works

In the following examples, we will assume that policymakers are free to set short-run output $\tilde{Y}$ to whatever level they like. How this works will be the topic of the next two chapters. But for the moment, take it as given: by choosing the appropriate monetary policy, the Federal Reserve can cause the economy to boom or undergo a recession.

Now suppose the year is 1979. In part because of the large increases in oil prices engineered by OPEC, the inflation rate is spiking, as we saw in Figure 9.5. Because of the costs of inflation discussed in Chapter 8, policymakers have a mandate to reduce inflation. So what do they do?

According to the Phillips curve in Figure 9.6, the only way to reduce the rate of inflation is to reduce output. This is exactly what happened in 1979. The Federal Reserve, chaired by Paul Volcker, decided to tighten monetary policy by raising interest rates sharply. This tight monetary policy plunged the economy into a deep recession, for reasons we will study closely in the coming chapters (in particular, the high interest rates depressed business investment and consumer spending on goods like cars and mortgages—goods that typically require large loans). Short-run output fell to -5 percent. Faced with such a sharp decline in the demand for their products, firms moderated their price increases, and workers moderated their wage increases. The inflation rate fell dramatically, to below 5 percent in just a few years.

Many other recessions can be interpreted in this same fashion. The rate of inflation creeps upward, either because of shocks to inflation or, as we will see in later chapters, because monetary policy is not appropriate. Eventually, inflation becomes high enough that the Federal Reserve tightens monetary policy to bring it under control, causing a recession.

Now look back at the Phillips curve in Figure 9.6 and answer the following question: What would happen if policymakers tried to stimulate the economy to keep actual output above potential year after year? One interpretation of the 1970s is that policymakers did exactly this, in part because they didn't believe the costs of inflation were high and in part because they thought the Phillips curve was very flat (so that a boom would not raise inflation by much).

Each data point shows the change in inflation and the level of short-run output in the given year. The slope of the line is about 1/2—output that is 2 percent above potential is associated with an increase in the inflation rate of about 1 percentage point.

FIGURE 9.7

Measuring the Phillips Curve, 1960–2009

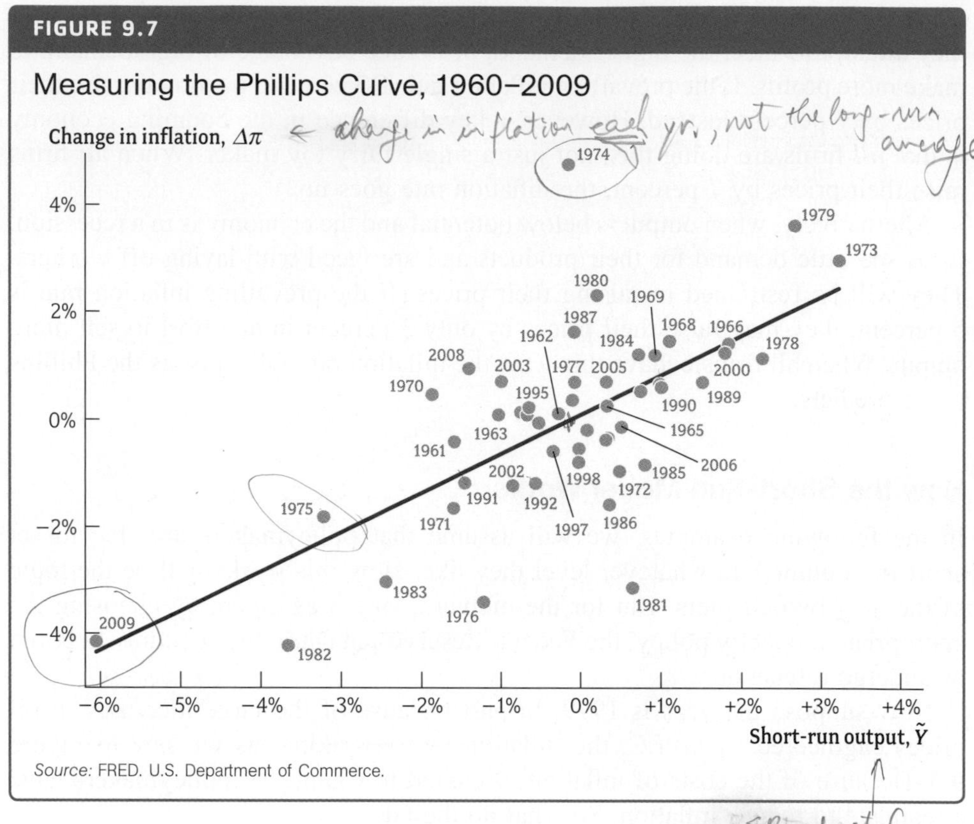

Source: FRED. U.S. Department of Commerce.

The Empirical Fit of the Phillips Curve

Figure 9.7 shows the empirical version of the Phillips curve for the U.S. economy since 1960; that is, it plots historical data on the change in inflation and short-run output for each year. As shown in the graph, in years when output is above potential, the inflation rate has typically risen. Conversely, when the economy is slumping, the inflation rate has typically declined. On average, the slope of this relationship is about 1/2, so that when output exceeds potential by 2 percent, the inflation rate rises by about 1 percentage point. The data point for 2009, in the lower left part of the figure, provides a nice illustration. Actual output was far below potential, and the inflation rate declined sharply. Compare to Figure 9.5 to see this more directly.)

The graph also shows that in many years, the change in the inflation rate has been higher or lower than what the Phillips curve predicts. In part, this is because of shocks. For example, in both 1974 and 1979, oil prices rose sharply on world markets, leading the U.S. inflation rate to rise by more than would be implied by its level of output.

Summary

Summarized in one sentence, *the short-run model says that a booming economy leads the inflation rate to increase, and a slumping economy leads the inflation rate to fall.* Through monetary and fiscal policy, the government has tools at its disposal to influence the state of the economy and thereby influence inflation.

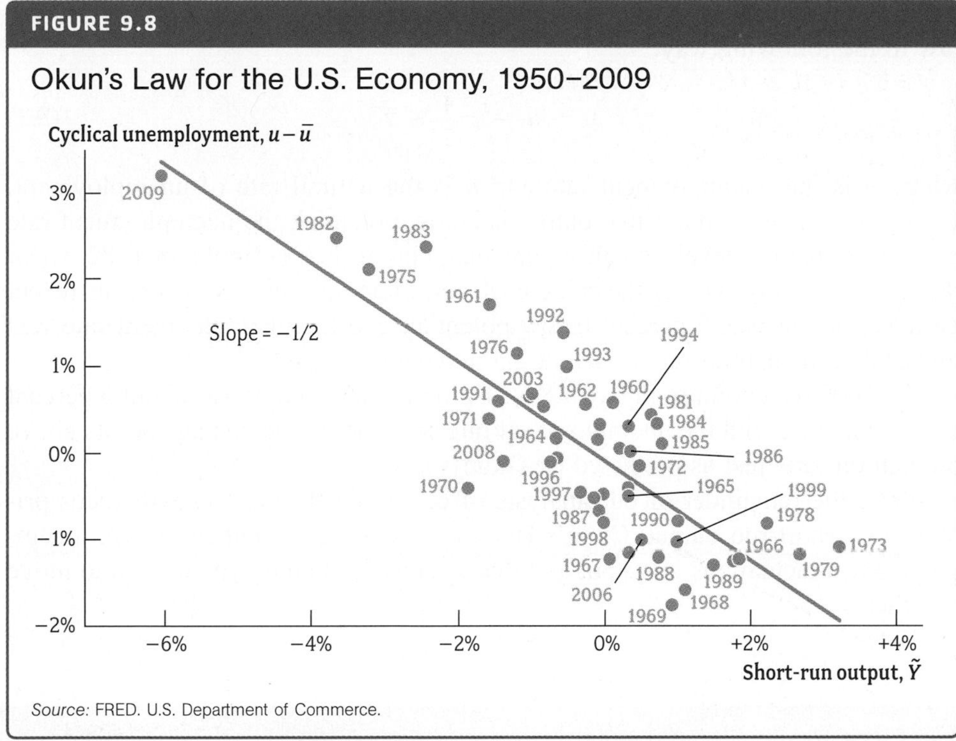

FIGURE 9.8

Okun's Law for the U.S. Economy, 1950–2009

Source: FRED. U.S. Department of Commerce.

Okun's law says that for each percentage point that output is below potential, the unemployment rate exceeds its long-run level by half a percentage point. The long-run (natural) unemployment rate $\bar{u}$ is measured as the average rate in the surrounding period (see Figure 7.2).

9.4 Okun's Law: Output and Unemployment

When analyzing economic fluctuations, we could focus on either output or unemployment. A recession, for example, is a time when output is below potential and unemployment is high; a boom is a time when output is above potential and unemployment is low. To keep the analysis simple, however, in these short-run chapters we will focus on output rather than unemployment.

Fortunately, there's a way to move back and forth between these approaches, known as "Okun's law."[4] This law in its modern form is shown in Figure 9.8, which presents data for the U.S. economy. The horizontal axis plots short-run output $\tilde{Y}$, while the vertical axis plots cyclical unemployment, defined as the difference between the current unemployment rate and the natural rate of unemployment. This natural rate is analogous to potential output: it's the rate of unemployment that prevails in the long run.

What we see in Figure 9.8 is a tight, negative relationship between output and unemployment. If output is above potential, the economy is booming and the unemployment rate is low. If output is below potential, the economy is in a

[4] This law is named after Arthur Okun, an economist on the Council of Economic Advisers under President John F. Kennedy. In part, Okun was trying to help the CEA convince Kennedy to cut taxes to stimulate the economy, and translating the change in the unemployment rate that might result into dollars was an important part of the argument.

recession and unemployment is high. We can summarize Figure 9.8 and **Okun's law** in the following way:

$$u - \bar{u} = -\frac{1}{2} \times \tilde{Y}, \tag{9.3}$$

where u is the unemployment rate and $\bar{u}$ is the natural rate of unemployment. For each percentage point that output is below potential, the unemployment rate exceeds its natural level by half a percentage point. For example, in 1982, when the U.S. economy was in the middle of one of its deepest recessions in recent decades, output was 5 percent below potential, and the unemployment rate was higher than its natural rate by about 2.5 percentage points.

The 2009 data point in Figure 9.8 is also remarkable. GDP was about 6 percent below potential, and the unemployment rate was about 3 percentage points above the natural rate, just as predicted by Okun's law.

While the remainder of our analysis of economic fluctuations will focus primarily on short-run output, Okun's law lets us connect this analysis with unemployment. Fluctuations in output and fluctuations in unemployment tend to move together.

CASE STUDY

Can the Macroeconomy Predict Presidential Elections?

Ray Fair, an economist at Yale University, has studied the extent to which macroeconomic statistics can be used to predict the outcomes of presidential elections in the United States. Perhaps surprisingly, a simple statistical formula predicts election outcomes with intriguing accuracy, correctly forecasting 10 of the last 13 presidential races. Moreover, in 2 of the 3 races where the model gave the wrong prediction, the race was extremely close (in 1960 and 1968); the only time it missed the mark widely was Clinton's defeat of Bush in 1992.

Fair's analysis predicts elections on the basis of several variables, including whether a sitting president is running for reelection, which party currently holds the White House, and such statistics as the growth rate of real GDP in the 9 months preceding the election and the rate of inflation that has prevailed over the current presidential term. For each percentage point of real GDP growth, the incumbent party's candidate is predicted to receive an extra 0.7 percentage points of the popular vote. And for each percentage point of inflation, the incumbent party's candidate is predicted to lose an extra 0.7 percentage points.

Table 9.1 shows the forecasts of the popular vote using Fair's statistical model as well as the actual popular vote for elections going back to 1960. For example, in 2008, macroeconomic statistics predicted that Obama would win 51.9 percent of the (two-party) popular vote. In fact, he won 53.4 percent. While the forecast did

TABLE 9.1

Macroeconomic Forecasts of Presidential Elections

Year	Incumbent party	Challenger	–Incumbent vote share– (percent) Actual	Predicted	Accuracy
1960	Nixon	**Kennedy**	49.9	50.9	**missed (close)**
1964	**Johnson**	Goldwater	61.3	61.3	**correct**
1968	Humphrey	**Nixon**	49.6	50.1	**missed (close)**
1972	**Nixon**	McGovern	61.8	58.4	**correct**
1976	Ford	**Carter**	48.9	49.5	**correct**
1980	Carter	**Reagan**	44.7	45.7	**correct**
1984	**Reagan**	Mondale	59.2	62.1	**correct**
1988	**Bush**	Dukakis	53.9	50.5	**correct**
1992	Bush	**Clinton**	46.5	50.9	**missed**
1996	Clinton	Dole	54.7	53.0	**correct**
2000	Gore	**Bush**	50.3	49.6	**correct (?)**
2004	**Bush**	Kerry	51.2	54.6	**correct**
2008	McCain	**Obama**	46.6	48.1	**correct**

Source: Ray Fair, "Presidential Vote Equation–2008 Post Mortem"; see http://fairmodel.econ.yale.edu.

For each presidential election since 1960, the table shows the actual vote share captured by the candidate running for the incumbent party as well as the share predicted by macroeconomic variables.

not precisely nail the vote share, it did correctly predict that Obama would win the election. As another example, in 2000, Professor Fair forecast that Gore would win 49.6 percent of the popular vote, narrowly losing the election. Instead, Gore won 50.3 percent, but still lost the election because of differences between the popular vote and the electoral college.

Fair provides a Web site where you can explore predictions for both presidential and congressional elections. See http://fairmodel.econ.yale.edu.

9.5 Filling in the Details

The next five chapters are devoted to the study of short-run economic fluctuations. Chapter 10 jumps right into the most significant macroeconomic event of recent years: the global financial crisis and the economic downturn that hit much of the world. We will discuss the basic facts of the crisis and use the intuitive understanding of the short-run model developed in this chapter to shed light on these facts.

Then, in the next several chapters, we develop the short-run model in more detail. For example, we will learn the answer to a crucial question that has been pushed aside in this overview: how do monetary policy and fiscal policy affect output? Here we have simply assumed that policymakers can choose whatever output they'd like. The next several chapters will explain how this works.

Chapter 11 adds a new component to the analysis, the *IS curve*. The IS curve says that an economy's output in the short run depends negatively on the real interest rate. A high real interest rate reduces the demand for investment by both firms and households—for example, loans to businesses and mortgages on new housing are more expensive when interest rates are high. The reduction in investment demand reduces overall demand in the economy, pushing actual output below potential. High real interest rates therefore reduce current output.

Chapter 12 then introduces the MP curve, which shows how monetary policy affects the real interest rate. In most advanced economies today, monetary policy is set in terms of a short-term nominal interest rate. In the United States, this interest rate is the federal funds rate. Under some circumstances, changes in this nominal interest rate lead to changes in the real interest rate. Since the real interest rate influences output in the short run (through the IS curve), monetary policy therefore affects output.

Chapters 12 and 13 will combine the Phillips curve with these two additional components—the IS curve and the ability of policymakers to set the real interest rate. The result will be a fully worked-out version of the short-run model. Culminating our study of the short run, Chapter 14 then examines the global financial crisis and the dramatic economic downturn of 2008 and beyond. We will see how the short-run model, augmented to include interactions with the financial system, can help us make some sense of these remarkable events.

CHAPTER REVIEW

SUMMARY

1. The long-run model determines potential output and the long-run rate of inflation. The short-run model determines current output and current inflation.
2. In any given year, output consists of two components: the long-run component associated with potential output $\bar{Y}_t$, and a short-run component associated with economic fluctuations $\tilde{Y}_t$. The latter component is called short-run output and is a key variable in our short-run model.
3. Another way of viewing $\tilde{Y}$ is that it is the percentage difference between actual and potential output. It's positive when the economy is booming, and negative when the economy is slumping. A recession is a period when actual output falls below potential, so that short-run output becomes negative.
4. In the slump associated with a recession, the cumulative loss in output is typically about 6 percent of GDP—about \$2,800 per person or \$11,000 per family of four. The gains from eliminating fluctuations in short-run output are smaller than this, however, because of the benefits associated with a booming economy.

5. An important stylized fact of economic fluctuations is that the inflation rate usually falls during a recession. This fact lies at the heart of our short-run model in the form of the Phillips curve. The Phillips curve captures the dynamic trade-off between output and inflation: a booming economy leads to a rising inflation rate, and a slumping economy to a declining inflation rate.
6. The essence of the short-run model is that the economy is hit with shocks, which policymakers may be able to mitigate, and inflation evolves according to the Phillips curve. Policymakers use monetary and fiscal policy in an effort to stabilize output and keep inflation low and steady. This task is made difficult by the fact that potential output is not readily observed, and the economy is always being hit by new shocks whose effects are not immediately obvious.
7. Okun's law, which allows us to go back and forth between short-run output and the unemployment rate, says that a one percentage point decline in output below potential corresponds to a half percentage point increase in the unemployment rate.

KEY CONCEPTS

annualized rate
economic shocks
the Great Depression
long-run trend
Okun's law
the Phillips curve
recession
the short run
short-run fluctuation
short-run output

REVIEW QUESTIONS

1. How do the long-run model and the short-run model fit together? What is the purpose of each model?
2. Why do we measure short-run output $\tilde{Y}$ in percentage terms rather than in dollar terms?
3. Before the latest financial crisis and recession, when was the largest recession of the last 50 years, and what was the cumulative loss in output over the course of the slowdown?
4. What are some recent shocks that have hit the macroeconomy?
5. How can you "see" the Phillips curve operating in the graph of inflation in Figure 9.5?
6. Why is Okun's law a useful rule of thumb to keep in mind when analyzing our short-run model?

EXERCISES

smartwork.wwnorton.com 

1. Using the "Country Snapshots" data file, plot per capita GDP over time for two countries. Drawing upon Wikipedia and/or other data sources, write a paragraph for each country, discussing the general causes of the major fluctuations in per

capita GDP. What shocks appear to be most important in explaining fluctuations in economic activity for the countries you chose? Be sure to document your sources carefully.

2. **Overstimulating the economy:** Suppose the economy today is producing output at its potential level and the inflation rate is equal to its long-run level, with $\bar{\pi} = 2\%$. What happens if policymakers try to stimulate the economy to keep output above potential by 3% every year? How does your answer depend on the slope of the Phillips curve?

3. **The slope of the Phillips curve:** Draw a graph with a steep Phillips curve and a graph with a gently sloped Phillips curve.
   - **(a)** Explain how the two economies respond differently to a boom and to a slump.
   - **(b)** What are some factors that might influence the slope of the Phillips curve?
   - **(c)** Do you think the slope of the Phillips curve has changed over time in the U.S. economy? Consider the United States in the 1970s versus today.

4. **An oil shock:** Consider an economy that begins with output at its potential level and a relatively high inflation rate of 6%, reflecting some recent oil price shocks. As the head of the Federal Reserve, your job is to pick a sequence of short-run output levels that will get the rate of inflation back down to 3% no later than three years from now. Your expert staff offers you the following menu of policy choices:

	–Short-run output–			–Inflation–		
Option	**Year 1**	**Year 2**	**Year 3**	**Year 1**	**Year 2**	**Year 3**
1	−6%	0	0	3%	3%	3%
2	−4%	−2%	0	4%	3%	3%
3	−2%	−2%	−2%	5%	4%	3%

   - **(a)** According to these numbers, what is the slope of the Phillips curve?
   - **(b)** If you as a policymaker cared primarily about output and not much about the inflation rate, which option would you recommend? Why?
   - **(c)** If you cared primarily about inflation and not much about output, which option would you recommend? Why?
   - **(d)** Explain the general trade-off that policymakers are faced with according to the Phillips curve.

5. **A productivity boom:** Suppose the economy exhibits a large, unexpected increase in productivity growth that lasts for a decade. Policymakers are (quite reasonably) slow to learn what has happened to potential output and incorrectly interpret the increase in output as a boom that leads actual output to exceed potential. Suppose they adjust macroeconomic policy so that the *mismeasured* level of short-run output is zero.
   - **(a)** What happens to the true amount of short-run output $\tilde{Y}$?
   - **(b)** What happens to inflation over time?

(c) This problem outlines a concern economists have had in recent years after the large increase in productivity growth that started around 1995. Now consider the opposite problem: Suppose productivity growth declines for a decade. What would be predicted to happen? Has this ever happened to the U.S. economy?

6. Measuring $\bar{Y}_t$ and $\tilde{Y}_t$: A real-world problem faced by policymakers, forecasters, and businesses every day is how to judge the state of the economy. Consider the table below, showing hypothetical measures of real GDP in the coming years, starting at a level of $17.0 trillion in 2015.

Year	Actual output Y_t	Potential output $\bar{Y}_t$	$Y_t - \bar{Y}_t$	Short-run output $\tilde{Y}_t$	Growth rate of actual output $\%\Delta Y$
2015	17.0				
2016	17.6				
2017	18.0				
2018	17.9				
2019	18.9				
2020	20.0				
2021	21.0				

Now fill in the remaining columns of the table by answering the following questions.

(a) What is potential output in 2015? You could call this a trick question, since there's no way for you to know the answer! In a way, that's the main point: fundamentally, we have to take some other measurements and make some assumptions. Suppose your research assistant tells you that in 2015, business surveys, unemployment reports, and recent years' experience suggest that the economy is operating at potential output. So go ahead and write 17.0 for potential in this year.

(b) Assume potential output grows at a constant annual rate of 3.5%, and complete the remainder of the table.

(c) Comment on the state of the economy in each year. When does the economy enter a recession? When does the recession end?

(d) How is your answer in part (c) related to the growth rate of actual output in the last column of the table?

7. Okun's law: Suppose the economy has a natural rate of unemployment of 5%.

(a) Suppose short-run output over the next four years is +1%, 0%, −1%, and −2%. According to Okun's law, what unemployment rates would we expect to see in this economy?

(b) Consider another economy in which the unemployment rate over the next three years is 6%, 7%, and then 4%. According to Okun's Law, what are the levels of short-run output $\tilde{Y}$ in this economy?

WORKED EXERCISE

2. **Overstimulating the economy:** Figure 9.9 shows the Phillips curve in this case. Since output exceeds potential, inflation is increasing according to the Phillips curve: $\Delta\pi > 0$.

   Suppose the slope of the Phillips curve is 1. In this case, the inflation rate rises by 3 percentage points each year. For example, if it starts at 2%, then it's 5% in year 1, 8% in year 2, and 11% in year 3. The cost of maintaining output above potential is that the inflation rate keeps increasing.

   If the slope is even higher, then the rate of increase is also higher—inflation rises faster when the Phillips curve is more steeply sloped.

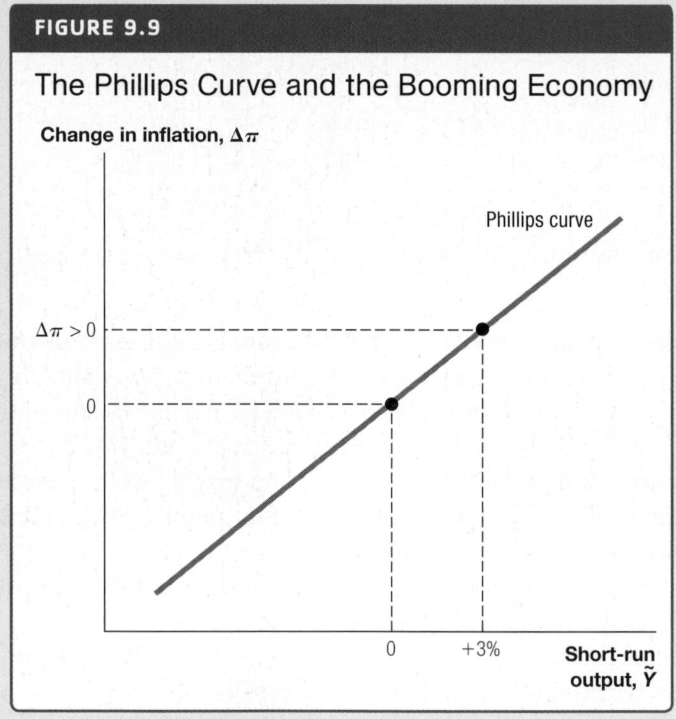

CHAPTER 10

THE GREAT RECESSION: A FIRST LOOK

OVERVIEW

In this chapter, we learn

- the causes of the financial crisis that began in the summer of 2007 and then pushed the U.S. and world economies into the deepest recession in many decades.
- how this recession compares to previous recessions and previous financial crises in the United States and around the world.
- several important concepts in finance, including *balance sheet* and *leverage*.

> Wednesday is the type of day people will remember in quant-land for a very long time. Events that models only predicted would happen once in 10,000 years happened every day for three days.
>
> —MATTHEW ROTHMAN

10.1 Introduction

By many measures, the financial crisis of 2007 to 2009 caused the deepest recession in the U.S. and world economies in more than 50 years. Commercial and investment banks, which earned enormous profits during the run-up of housing prices in the first half of the decade, had literally "bet the bank" on securities backed by mortgages. The virtually unprecedented decline in housing prices starting in 2006 roiled financial markets and reshaped Wall Street. Financial giants such as Bear Stearns, Lehman Brothers, Merrill Lynch, Wachovia, Washington Mutual, Fannie Mae, Freddie Mac, and AIG suffered colossal losses, resulting either in outright failure or in emergency rescue by the government. The last two remaining investment banks, Goldman Sachs and Morgan Stanley, converted to bank holding companies. They and other titans such as Citigroup, Bank of America, and Wells Fargo accepted $25-billion capital infusions from the government and were the beneficiaries, either directly or indirectly, of enormous financial interventions and loan guarantees by the Federal Reserve, the U.S. Treasury, and other governmental agencies in the United States and around the world.

The crisis that began on Wall Street migrated to Main Street, pushing the U.S. economy into a recession in December 2007. Rising from a low of 4.4 percent in March of that year, the unemployment rate rose steadily, peaking at 10.1 percent in October 2009. U.S. employment declined by more than 6 percent, the largest decline of the postwar era. World GDP declined in 2009 for the first time in more than half a century. Not since the Great Depression had such financial panic and macroeconomic turmoil so thoroughly infected the world. And while a repeat of the Depression was avoided, the "Great Recession," as it is coming to be called, shook the U.S. and world economies in ways that almost no one thought was possible.

The financial crisis and ensuing recession have forced economists to rethink our understanding of financial markets and macroeconomic fluctuations. Something that almost no mainstream economist thought could happen did. Understanding why and how will ultimately require a decade or more of research. But some of the basic lessons and forces at work are already becoming clear. And while changes to our understanding of macroeconomics will surely be required, much of the infrastructure that has been built by past research remains intact.

Epigraph: Quoted in Kaja Whitehouse, "One 'Quant' Sees Shakeout for the Ages—'10,000 Years,'" *Wall Street Journal*, August 11, 2007.

This chapter provides an overview of the financial crisis. We begin by discussing the events that led up to the crisis and documenting the macroeconomic shocks that struck the economy before and during the financial crisis. Next, we consider data on macroeconomic outcomes like inflation, unemployment, and GDP to highlight the basic effect of these shocks.

The chapter then studies how financial factors impact the economy. We introduce several important financial concepts, especially balance sheets and leverage. Clearly, there was a crisis among financial institutions tied to a decline in the value of their assets and the effect this had on their solvency in the presence of leverage. But the crisis also struck household balance sheets through a decline in their assets, notably housing and the stock market. As a result, households cut back their consumption, reducing the economy's demand for goods and services. Finally, the balance sheets of both the U.S. government and the Federal Reserve played starring roles in current events. The Congressional Budget Office projects that federal debt as a ratio to GDP will double over the next decade, from 41 percent to 82 percent, in part because of the financial crisis.[1] And the Federal Reserve more than doubled the size of its balance sheet, pursuing unconventional means to ensure liquidity in financial markets. In this sense, the Great Recession is tightly linked to balance sheets throughout the economy—for financial institutions, for households, for governments, and for the Federal Reserve.

10.2 Recent Shocks to the Macroeconomy

What shocks to the macroeconomy caused the global financial crisis? A natural place to start is with the housing market, where prices rose at nearly unprecedented rates until 2006 and then declined just as sharply. We also discuss the rise in interest rate spreads (one of the best ways to see the financial crisis in the data), the decline in the stock market, and the movement in oil prices.

Housing Prices

At the heart of the financial crisis was a large decline in housing prices. In the decade leading up to 2006, housing prices grew rapidly before collapsing by more than 30 percent over the next three years, as shown in Figure 10.1. Fueled by demand pressures during the "new economy" of the late 1990s, by low interest rates in the 2000s, and by ever-loosening lending standards, prices increased by a factor of nearly 3 between 1996 and 2006, an average rate of about 10 percent per year. Gains were significantly larger in some coastal markets, such as Boston, Los Angeles, New York, and San Francisco.

Alarmingly, the national index for housing prices in the United States declined by 33 percent between the middle of 2006 and April 2009. This is remarkable because it is by far the largest decline in the index since its inception in 1987.

[1] Congressional Budget Office, "A Preliminary Analysis of the President's Budget and an Update of CBO's Budget and Economic Outlook," March 2009.

After rising sharply in the years up to 2006, housing prices fell dramatically.

FIGURE 10.1

A Bursting Bubble in U.S. Housing Prices?

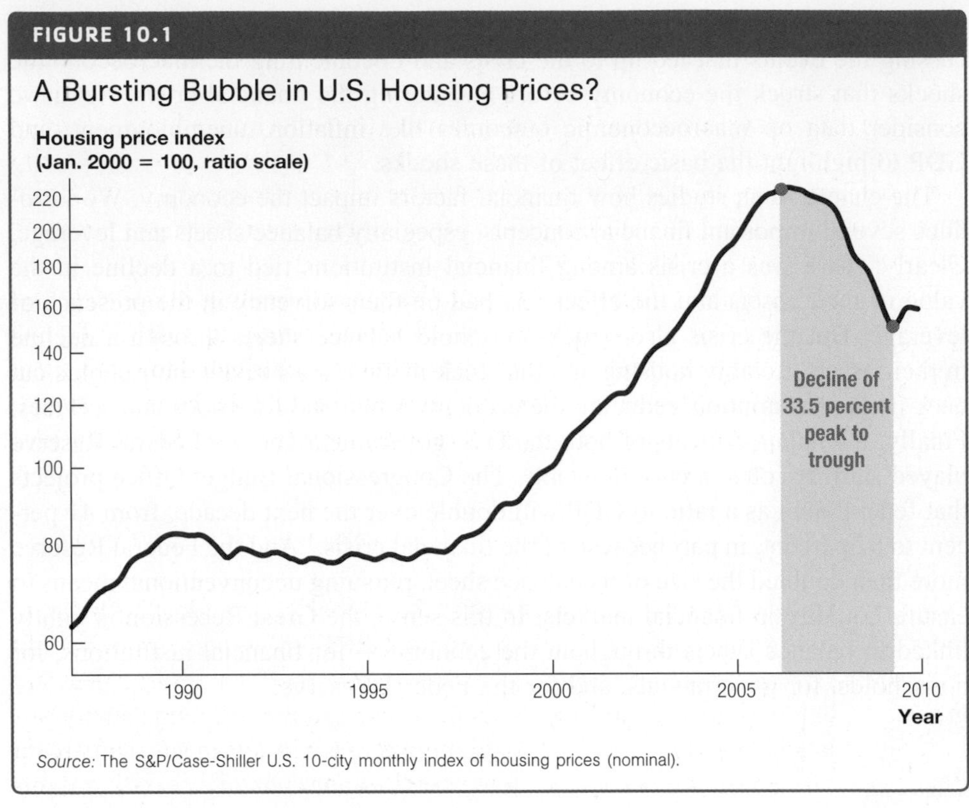

Source: The S&P/Case-Shiller U.S. 10-city monthly index of housing prices (nominal).

By comparison, the next largest decline was just 7 percent during the 1990–91 recession.

What caused the large rise and then sharp fall in housing prices? The answer brings us to the financial turmoil in recent years.

The Global Saving Glut

In March 2005, before he chaired the Federal Reserve, Ben Bernanke gave a speech entitled "The Global Saving Glut and the U.S. Current Account Deficit." With the benefit of hindsight, we can now look at this speech and see one of the main causes of the sharp rise in asset prices. The genesis of the current financial turmoil has its source, at least to some extent, in financial crises that occurred a decade ago.

In this speech, Governor Bernanke noted that financial crises in the 1990s prompted an important shift in the macroeconomics of a number of developing countries, especially in Asia. Prior to the crises many of these countries had modest trade and current account deficits. Essentially, they were investing more than they were saving, and this investment was financed by borrowing from the rest of the world. For rapidly growing countries, this approach has some merit: they will be richer in the future, so it makes sense to borrow now in order to maintain consumption while investing to build new highways and equip new factories.

For a variety of reasons (discussed in more detail in Chapter 19), these countries experienced a series of financial crises in the 1990s—Mexico in 1994, Asia in 1997–98, Russia in 1998, Brazil in 1999, and Argentina in 2002. The result was a sharp decline in lending from the rest of the world, steep falls in the value of their currencies and stock markets, and significant recessions. After the crises, these countries increased their saving substantially and curtailed their foreign borrowing, instead becoming large lenders to the rest of the world—especially to the United States. While developing countries on net borrowed $88 billion in 1996 from the rest of the world, by 2003 they were instead saving a net $205 billion into the world's capital markets.

Bernanke argued that this reversal produced a **global saving glut**: capital markets in advanced countries were awash in additional saving in search of good investment opportunities. This demand for investments contributed to rising asset markets in the United States, including the stock market and the housing market. One way this happened was through the creation of mortgage-backed securities, as we see in the next two sections.

Subprime Lending and the Rise in Interest Rates

Lured by low interest rates associated with the global saving glut, by increasingly lax lending standards, and perhaps by the belief that housing prices could only continue to rise, large numbers of borrowers took out mortgages and purchased homes between 2000 and 2006. These numbers include many so-called "subprime" borrowers whose loan applications did not meet mainstream standards—for example, because of poor credit records or high existing debt-to-income ratios. According to *The Economist*, by 2006 one fifth of all new mortgages were subprime.[2]

The extent to which lending standards apparently deteriorated is stunning. In his speech to the American Economic Association in January 2010, Bernanke highlighted the range of exotic mortgages that allowed people with very little income to borrow large sums to purchase houses. As long as housing prices increased, these mortgages were secure: the borrower rapidly accumulated equity in the house that could be taken out in a refinance, allowing the mortgage to be repaid. By 2006, these exotic mortgages, which had been negligible just six years earlier, accounted for a large fraction of new mortgages. Housing prices rose, lending standards deteriorated, more people borrowed to buy houses, and this drove prices even higher.[3]

Against this background and after more than two years of exceedingly low interest rates, the Federal Reserve began to raise its Fed funds target—the rate charged for overnight loans between banks—as shown in Figure 10.2. Between May 2004 and May 2006, the Fed raised its interest rate from 1.25 percent to 5.25 percent in part because of concerns over increases in inflation. (This was arguably a reasonable policy—according to the Taylor rule, interest rates were too low in

[2] An excellent early summary of the subprime crisis and the liquidity shock of 2007 can be found in "CSI: Credit Crunch," *The Economist*, October 18, 2007.

[3] See Ben S. Bernanke, "Monetary Policy and the Housing Bubble," speech given at the Annual Meeting of the American Economic Association, Atlanta, Georgia, January 3, 2010. A fascinating account of these events is also provided in Michael Lewis, "The End," *Portfolio.com*, November 11, 2008. For more details, see Lewis's *The Big Short: Inside the Doomsday Machine* (New York: Norton, 2010).

After keeping interest rates very low from 2002 to 2004, the Fed raised rates sharply over the next two years. Following the financial turmoil that began in August 2007, the Fed cut interest rates even more sharply, ultimately driving the Fed funds rate all the way to zero for well over a year.

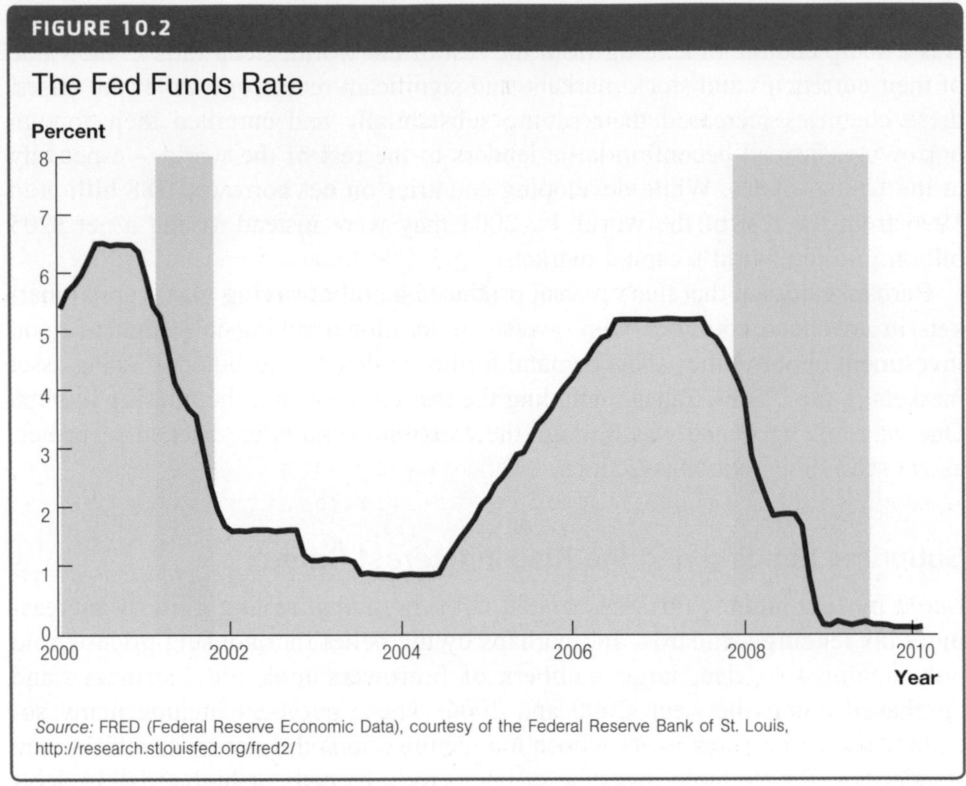

FIGURE 10.2

The Fed Funds Rate

Source: FRED (Federal Reserve Economic Data), courtesy of the Federal Reserve Bank of St. Louis, http://research.stlouisfed.org/fred2/

the preceding years, and the Fed raised them to a more reasonable level. This will be further discussed below.) Higher interest rates generally lead to a softening of the housing market, as borrowing becomes more costly. In an environment with subprime borrowers facing mortgages whose rates were moving from low teaser rates to much higher market rates, the effect on housing prices was even more severe. According to Chairman Bernanke, by August 2007, nearly 16 percent of subprime mortgages with adjustable rates were in default.[4] The problem then spiraled, as low housing prices led to defaults, which, in a vicious cycle, lowered housing prices even more.

The Financial Turmoil of 2007–2009

To understand the financial turmoil that followed, it helps to appreciate a (generally valuable) innovation in finance known as **securitization**. Like a decadent buffet at an expensive hotel, securitization involves lumping together large numbers of individual financial instruments such as mortgages and then slicing and dicing them into different pieces that appeal to different types of investors. A hedge fund may take the riskiest piece in the hope of realizing a high return. A pension fund may take a relatively safe portion, constrained by the rules under which it operates. The resulting pieces go by many names and acronyms, such

[4] Ben S. Bernanke, "The Recent Financial Turmoil and Its Economic and Policy Consequences," speech given at the Economic Club of New York, October 15, 2007.

as mortgage-backed securities, asset-backed commercial paper, and collateralized debt obligations (CDOs).[5]

In principle, combining large numbers of assets can diversify the risk associated with any individual asset. For instance, one subprime mortgage may be especially risky; but if you put thousands together and only a few default, the aggregate instrument will be mostly insulated. In the case of the subprime crisis, however, the underlying mortgages proved to be significantly riskier than most investors realized. Banks that generated the mortgages sold them off and did not have to bear the consequences if their particular mortgages went bad; as a result, lending standards deteriorated. Moreover, securitization is based to a great extent on the supposition that a large fraction of mortgages will not go bad at the same time. After all, the history of the U.S. housing market was that while some regions experienced large declines, the overall national market was relatively stable. When the Fed raised interest rates, more and more subprime mortgages went under, housing prices fell nationwide, and this led to even more defaults. Securitization did not (and cannot) insulate investors from aggregate risk.

Remarkably, the investors who were holding these mortgage-backed securities often turned out to be the large commercial and investment banks themselves. The collapse of the dot-com stock market bubble in 2000 did not cause a financial crisis because the stock market risk was diversified across a huge number of investors. In contrast, a relatively small number of financial institutions held a large amount of mortgage-backed securities, putting their solvency at risk. One would have thought that these sophisticated financial institutions would have had all the right incentives to recognize the problems with deteriorating lending standards and the nearly unprecedented rise in housing prices. The only way this house of cards could continue to hold together was if housing prices continued to rise. And yet for reasons that are somewhat difficult to understand, many of these financial institutions wound up on the wrong side of the housing bubble.

As sophisticated financial instruments were developed and traded, it became difficult to know how much exposure an individual bank had to this risk. In August 2007, these forces came to a head, and banks sharply increased the interest rates that they charged one another: if Bank A worries that Bank B is backed by a large number of bad mortgages, it will demand a premium to lend money or may not lend at all. There was a "flight to safety" as lenders decided to place their funds in U.S. Treasury bills—government bonds that mature in one year or less, sometimes called "T-bills"—instead of lending to other banks. As a result, the spread between T-bill yields and interbank lending rates rose dramatically, as shown in Figure 10.3. What had been a modest premium of 0.2 to 0.4 percentage points rose sharply to between 1.0 and 1.5 percentage points. If the yield on T-bills was 2.0 percent, banks might lend to one another at 2.3 percent before the crisis. Once the crisis started, these rates rose to as much as 3.5 percent, and the amount of lending dropped, producing a classic example of a **liquidity crisis**—a situation in which the volume of transactions in some financial markets falls sharply, making it difficult to value certain financial assets and thereby raising questions

[5] A quick visit to Wikipedia can provide more details on these and other financial instruments.

The rate at which banks borrow and lend to one another rose sharply in August 2007 during the subprime crisis and then spiked in September 2008 with the collapse of Lehman Brothers.

FIGURE 10.3

Liquidity and Risk Shocks since August 2007

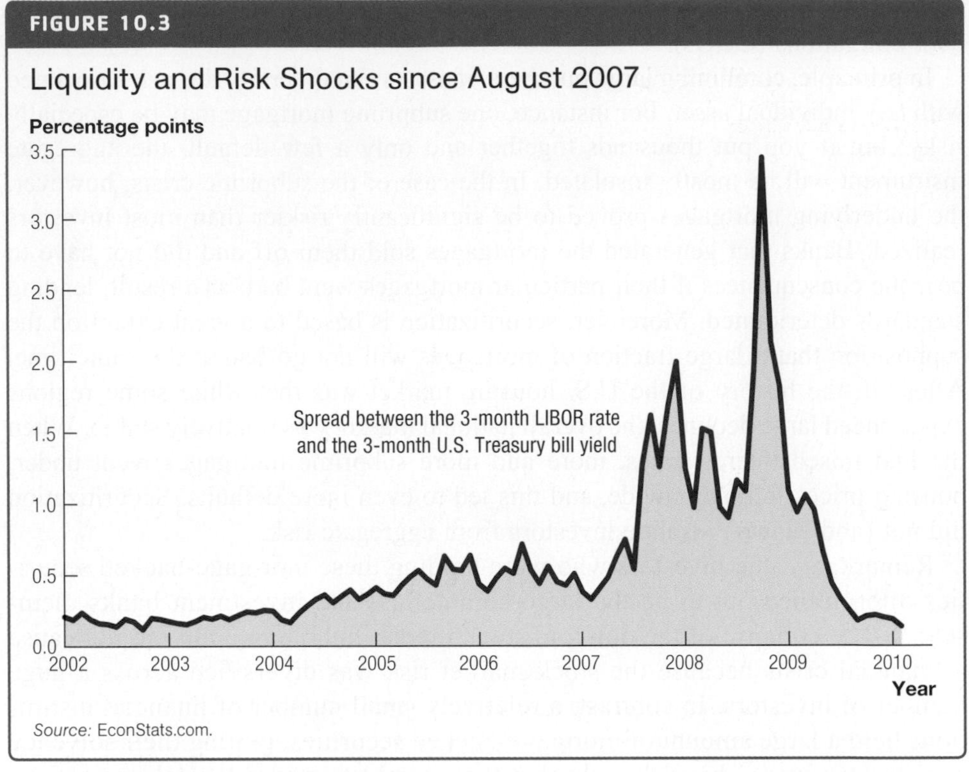

Source: EconStats.com.

about the overall value of the firms holding those assets. In September 2008, the crisis intensified, and the risk premium exploded from around 1.0 percentage point to more than 3.5 percentage points. Panic set in, and the end of Wall Street investment banking was nigh.

In the course of two weeks in September 2008, the government took over the mortgage companies Fannie Mae and Freddie Mac, Lehman Brothers collapsed into bankruptcy, Merrill Lynch was sold to Bank of America, and the Federal Reserve organized an $85 billion bailout of AIG. Treasury Secretary Henry Paulson and Fed Chair Ben Bernanke met with congressional leaders to outline the $700 billion Troubled Asset Relief Program (TARP), with Bernanke warning, "If we don't do this, we may not have an economy on Monday."[6]

Financial markets declined sharply during this time, as shown in Figure 10.4. The S&P 500 stock price index fell by more than 50 percent from its recent peak in 2007, placing it below levels from a decade earlier.

Oil Prices

If the decline in housing prices and the financial crisis were not enough, the economy also suffered from large movements in oil prices.

After nearly two decades of relative tranquility, oil prices rose in mid-2008 to levels never seen before. These prices are shown in Figure 10.5. From a low of about $20 per barrel in 2002, oil prices peaked at more than $140 per barrel

[6] This crisis period is laid out in vivid detail in Joe Nocera, "As Credit Crisis Spiraled, Alarm Led to Action," *New York Times*, October 1, 2008, p. A1.

FIGURE 10.4

The S&P 500 Stock Price Index (Real)

Source: Robert Shiller, www.econ.yale.edu/~shiller/data.htm

The real value of the S&P 500 stock price index declined by more than 50 percent between its peak in November 2007 and March 2009.

during the summer of 2008. This sevenfold increase is comparable in magnitude to the oil shocks of the 1970s. Other basic commodities such as natural gas, coal, steel, corn, wheat, and rice also featured large price increases. Then, spectacularly, oil prices declined even more sharply so that by the end of 2008 they hovered around $40 per barrel.

Why did these prices rise and then fall so sharply? It is instructive to consider the case of oil more carefully. First, world oil consumption increased significantly during this same period of sharply rising prices. For example, during the first half of 2008, a decline in oil consumption among OECD countries (including the United States) was more than offset by increases in China, India, and the Middle East. Rising prices coupled with rising quantities are a classic sign of an outward shift in demand, and it appears that rising demand—throughout the world but especially among some rapidly growing emerging economies—was a major driving force behind the increase in the prices of basic commodities. Shorter-term factors such as supply disruptions, macroeconomic volatility (in the United States, China, and elsewhere), and poor crop yields appear to have played a role in exacerbating the price movements. The economic slowdown associated with the global financial crisis then relieved this demand pressure—at least partially—which goes some way toward explaining the recent declines. Nevertheless, it is difficult to justify both $140 per barrel in the summer of 2008 and $40 per barrel just a few months later as both being consistent with fundamentals. Some speculative elements may have played a role as well.[7]

[7] On the recent sharp swings in oil prices, see James Hamilton's "Oil Prices and Economic Fundamentals," online at Econbrowser, July 28, 2008, and his more detailed study, "Understanding Crude Oil Prices," NBER Working Paper 14492, November 2008.

Oil prices rose by more than a factor of 6 between 2002 and July 2008, roughly comparable to the increase in the 1970s. Remarkably, prices then fell off a cliff, returning to the $40-per-barrel range.

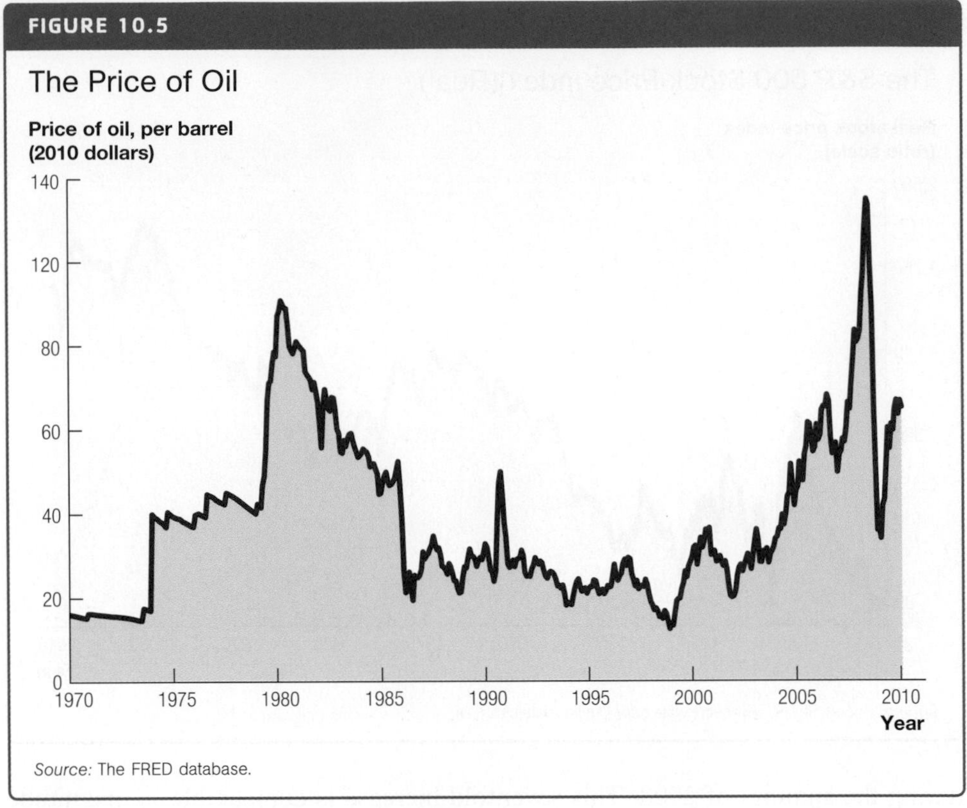

FIGURE 10.5

The Price of Oil

Source: The FRED database.

10.3 Macroeconomic Outcomes

Following the sharp increase in oil prices, the large decline in housing prices, and the ensuing financial turmoil, the macroeconomy entered a recession in December 2007. The recession first showed up in employment, as shown in Figure 10.6. Total nonfarm employment peaked at 138 million in 2007. By February 2010, nearly 8.5 million jobs had been lost.

The recession showed up a bit later in short-run output. As seen in Figure 10.7, short-run output turned sharply negative in the last quarter of 2008 and then bottomed out in the middle of 2009, falling more than 6 percent below potential. The recession can also be seen in the unemployment rate in Figure 10.8. From a low in 2007 of 4.4 percent, the unemployment rate rose sharply, peaking at more than 10 percent toward the end of 2009.

A Comparison to Previous Recessions

Table 10.1 provides an alternative perspective on the current recession. This table shows some key statistics in two ways: averaged over previous recessions going back to 1950, and for the current recession. For example, during a typical recession, GDP falls by about 1.7 percent. In the recent recession, however, real GDP declined by more than twice as much—3.7 percent.

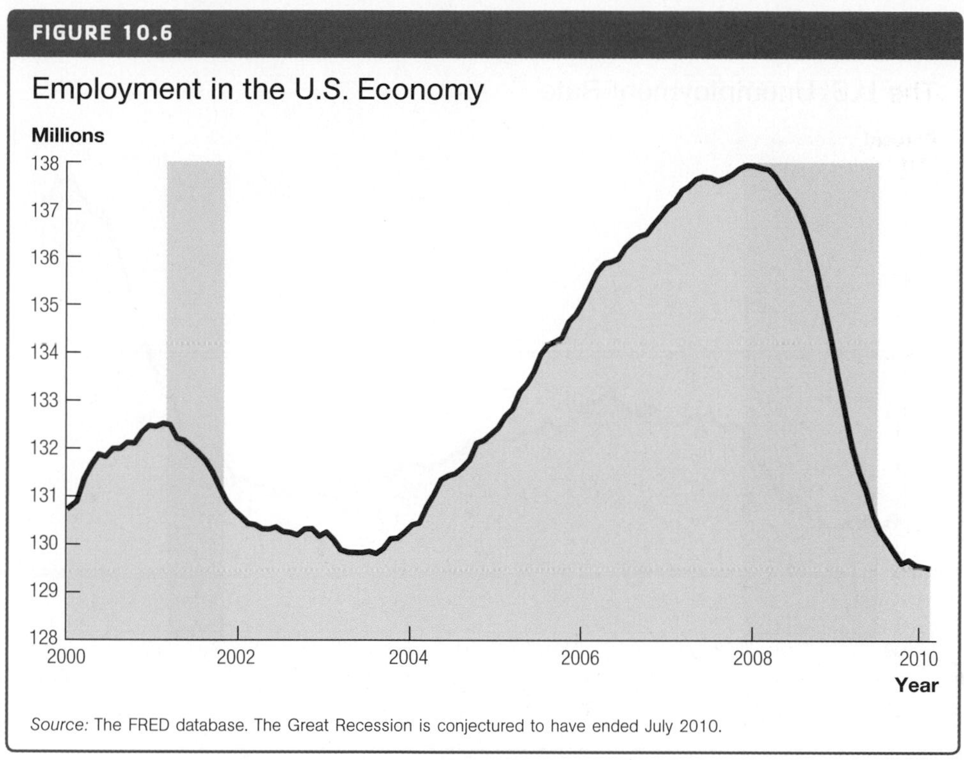

Source: The FRED database. The Great Recession is conjectured to have ended July 2010.

Total nonfarm employment peaked in December 2007, the date the recession is said to have started, at more than 138 million. More than 8.4 million jobs were lost during the recession.

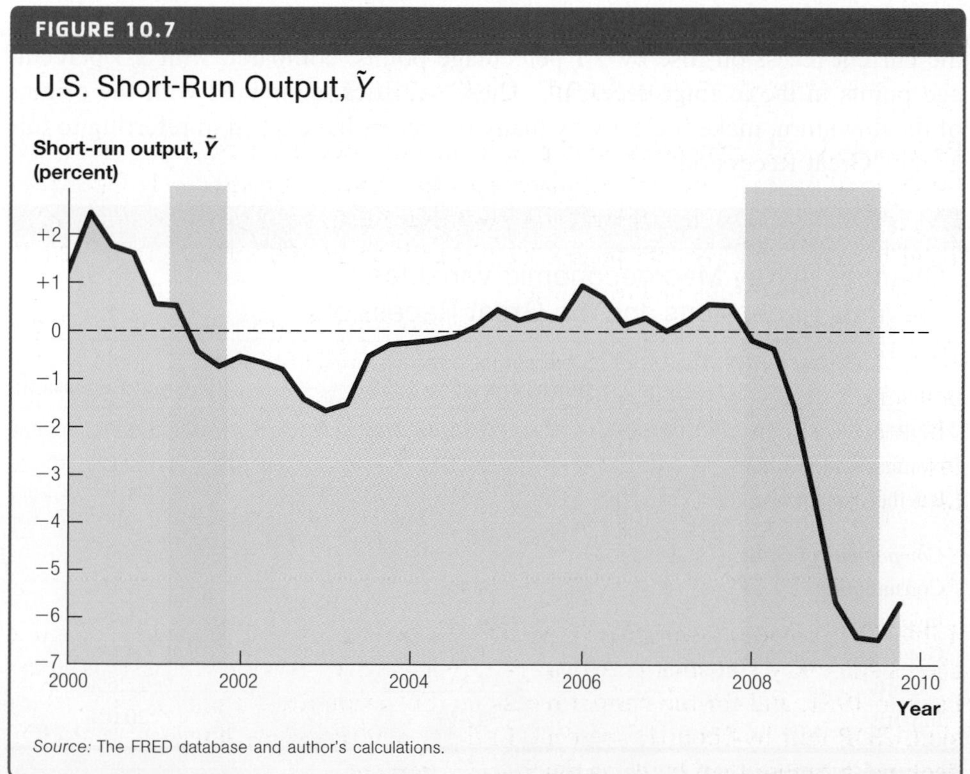

Source: The FRED database and author's calculations.

After its initial resilience to the financial crisis, the real economy declined sharply. At the bottom of the recession, real GDP was more than 6 percent below potential.

The unemployment rate rose sharply during the recent recession, peaking at 10.1 percent in October 2009.

FIGURE 10.8

The U.S. Unemployment Rate

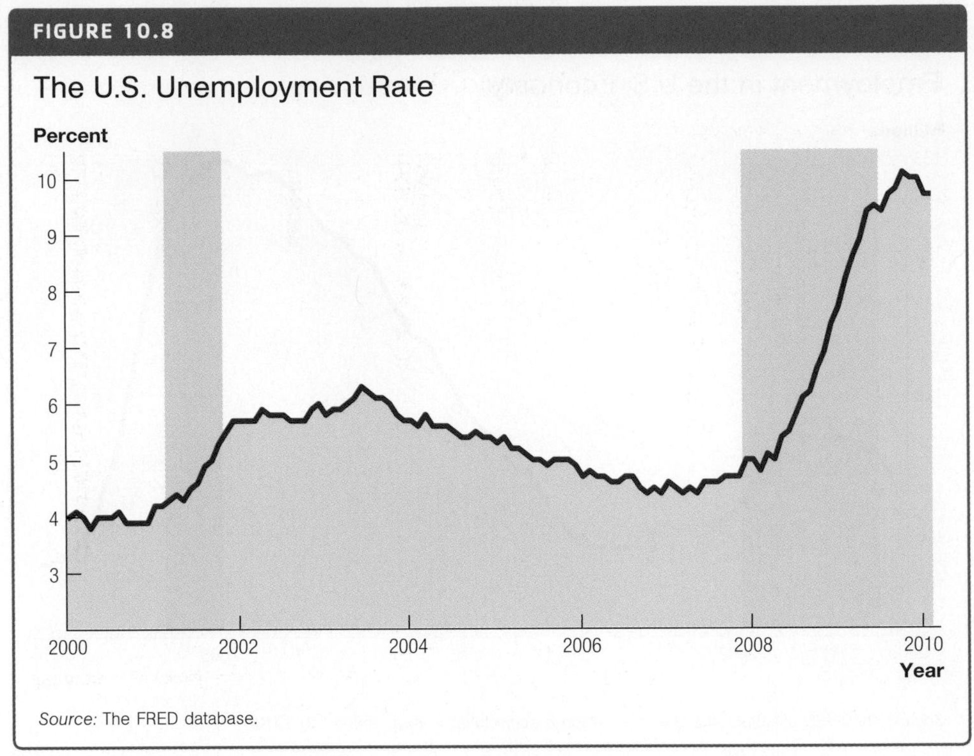

Source: The FRED database.

The employment measures clearly indicate the severity of this recession. Nonfarm employment fell about three times as much as normal—by 6.1 percent, compared with a typical fall of 2.1 percent. Similarly, the unemployment rate in the current recession rose by 5.1 percentage points, compared with 2.5 percentage points in the average recession. These statistics, combined with the origins of the downturn, make it clear why many observers have taken to referring to this as the "Great Recession."

The Great Recession is substantially larger than the average recession since 1950, on virtually every dimension.

TABLE 10.1

Changes in Key Macroeconomic Variables: Previous Recessions and the Great Recession

	Average of previous recessions since 1950	The Great Recession
GDP	−1.7%	−3.7%
Nonfarm employment	−2.1%	−6.1%
Unemployment rate	2.5	5.1
Components of GDP		
Consumption	0.4%	−1.9%
Investment	−14.7%	−31.4%
Government purchases	1.2%	4.0%
Exports	−1.5%	−12.6%
Imports	−4.4%	20.0%

Source: The FRED database.

FIGURE 10.9

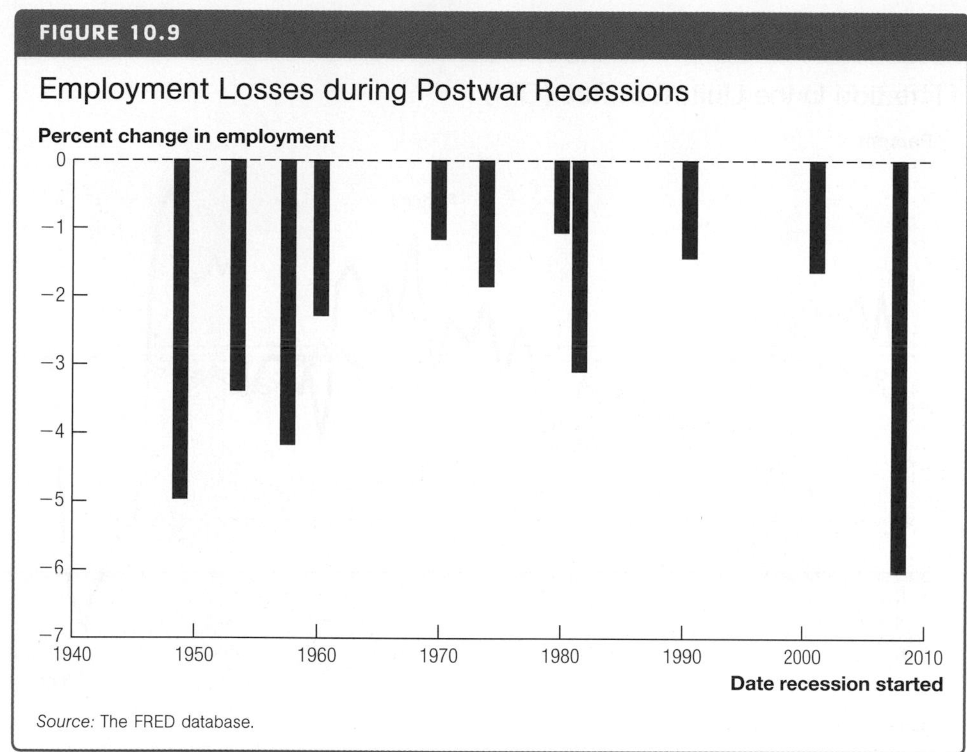

Source: The FRED database.

The decline in employment of more than 6 percentage points during the Great Recession is the largest employment loss in many decades.

The remainder of Table 10.1 explores the components of GDP and shows an important way in which the recent recession is atypical. On average during the last half century, recessions were characterized by a relatively stable level of consumption—it actually rose by the small amount of 0.4 percent. The severity of the current recession is already evident in consumption, which fell by 1.9 percent. In most recessions, households seek to smooth their consumption even though GDP is declining. This recession, however, has been led in part by declines in consumption itself. One explanation for this behavior is that the large declines in housing and the stock market have reduced household wealth substantially. This is a decline in permanent income, and consumption has fallen accordingly.

Investment and exports fell very sharply, much more than in the typical recession. Government purchases of goods and services are the one bright spot, having risen by 4.0 percent, in part due to efforts by the government to stimulate the economy.

As one final indication of the severity of the Great Recession, consider Figure 10.9, which shows the total percentage change in employment from the start of each recession since 1948 until employment hits its trough. The 6-percent loss in employment in the Great Recession is the largest in the postwar era.

Inflation

Figure 10.10 shows inflation since 2000, both for "all items" and for the so-called "core" items that exclude food and energy prices. The overall inflation rate shows a sharp swing in 2008, driven in large part by the movements in energy prices.

Twelve-month inflation rates rose sharply during the first half of 2008, driven largely by the price of energy and food, peaking in July 2008 at 5.5 percent. Declining oil prices then reversed this trend, and prices actually declined in the twelve months preceding June 2009. Excluding food and energy, inflation has been more stable, featuring a gradual decline.

FIGURE 10.10

Inflation in the United States (CPI)

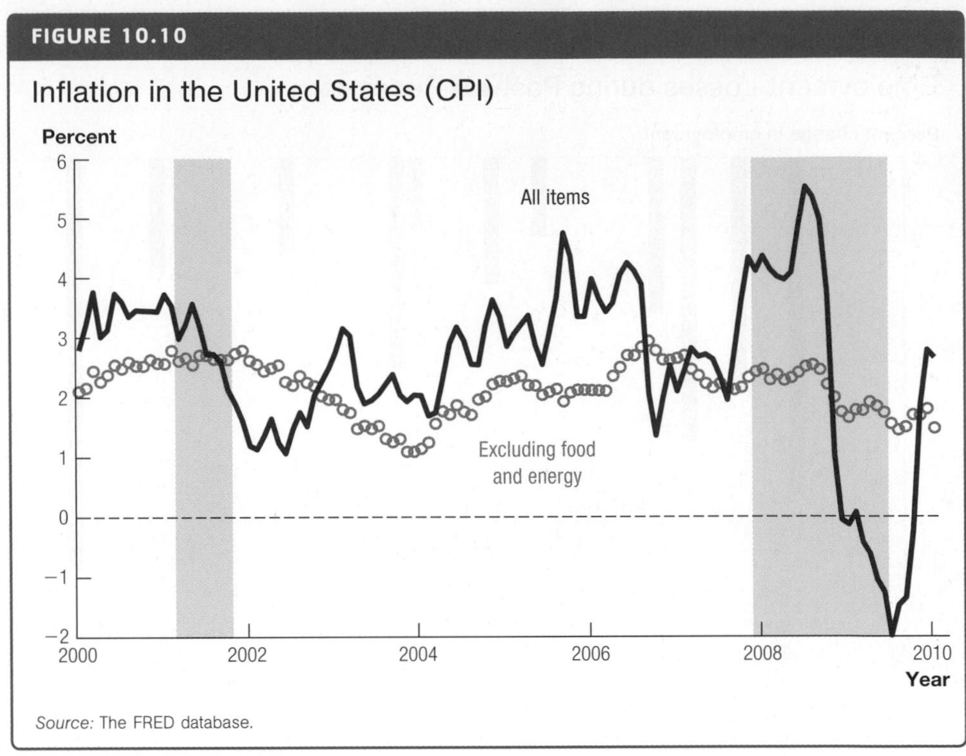

Source: The FRED database.

The rise in the price of oil in the first half of the year leads the inflation rate to peak at about 5.5 percent in the middle of the year. The sharp decline in the price of oil actually produced a negative inflation rate temporarily during the middle of 2009.

In contrast, the core inflation rate has been much smoother. Core inflation was just over 2.0 percent during the last several years. In the recent recession, inflation declined slightly, a pattern that continued into 2010.

CASE STUDY

A Comparison to Other Financial Crises

How does the U.S. experience compare to outcomes in other financial crises, and what might the future hold? Carmen Reinhart and Kenneth Rogoff have gathered data on many of the major financial crises that have hit the world in the last century, including the Great Depression, Japan in the 1990s, Sweden in 1991, and the Asian financial crisis of 1997. They've studied closely how a financial crisis affects the macroeconomy along a number of key dimensions. Their results are summarized in Table 10.2.

TABLE 10.2

Average Outcomes of Twentieth-Century Financial Crises

Economic statistic	Average outcome
Housing prices	−35%
Equity price	−56%
Unemployment	+7 percentage points
Duration of rising unemployment	4.8 years
Real GDP	−9.3%
Duration of falling GDP	1.9 years
Increase in real government debt	+86%

Source: Carmen Reinhart and Kenneth Rogoff, "The Aftermath of Financial Crises," Harvard University working paper, December 2008.

Financial crises are typically quite long and very costly.

The bottom line of their historical study is that financial crises are typically quite long and very costly to the economy. For example, the unemployment rate rises on average by 7 percentage points over the course of almost 5 years, government debt nearly doubles, and real GDP declines by close to 10 percent. While there is variation around these averages—some crises are shorter and shallower while others are longer and deeper—these data suggest that during the "typical" financial crisis, outcomes are comparable to or slightly worse than what we've seen to date in the United States.

The Rest of the World

Another important feature of the financial crisis is that it was global in scope. The advanced countries of the world—including Japan, Germany, the United Kingdom, and France—all suffered deep recessions.

Table 10.3 shows the sharp declines in real GDP experienced throughout the United States, industrialized Asia, and Western Europe during 2009. Even the rapid growth in China and India was slowed temporarily. In 2009, real GDP declined for the world as a whole, the first time this has happened in many decades.

The table also shows forecasts from the International Monetary Fund (IMF) for real GDP growth in 2010. Real GDP is expected to increase throughout the world. The IMF expects U.S. growth to reach 2.7 percent for the year, a rate still below its average growth rate in the last decade.

There are at least two important implications of the global nature of this financial crisis. First, it means that exports were not a major source of demand for the United States or for any other country. In the 1990s, Japan could hope that demand from the rest of the world would mitigate its slump. Such hope is not available for the world as a whole. In fact, declines in export demand from the rest of the world have been an important drag on GDP growth in many countries. Second,

The Great Recession was a worldwide event. Western Europe and Japan were hit even harder by the recession than was the United States, while China and India saw temporary slowdowns in their rapid growth.

TABLE 10.3

Percentage Change in Real GDP around the World

	2009	2010 (forecast)
Japan	−5.3	1.7
United Kingdom	−4.8	1.3
Euro area	−3.9	1.0
United States	−2.5	2.7
Asian NICs	−1.2	4.8
China	+8.7	10.0
India	+5.6	7.7
World	−0.8	3.9

Source: IMF World Economic Outlook Update, January 26, 2010.

the global nature of the crisis emphasizes that the Great Recession is markedly different from much of what has come before.

10.4 Some Fundamentals of Financial Economics

To understand the financial crisis, it is helpful to have some familiarity with several basic concepts in finance. As mentioned earlier, the recent crisis was in many ways a balance-sheet crisis. This section explains what a balance sheet is, how the equity or net worth of a company is determined, and the important concept of leverage and how it makes companies and individuals very sensitive to relatively small declines in asset prices.

Balance Sheets

Many of the basic issues involved in the financial crisis can be illuminated by focusing on the **balance sheet** of financial institutions, other companies, and households. As an example, consider the balance sheet of a hypothetical bank, displayed in Table 10.4. This hypothetical bank is modeled very loosely on the large commercial banks, like Citigroup or Bank of America.[8] A balance sheet consists of two columns. On the left are the **assets** of the institution—items of value that the institution owns. On the right are the **liabilities**—items of value that the institution owes to others.

In our example, the bank has three categories of assets. It has $1,000 billion of loans that it has made (such as mortgages or loans to businesses). It has $900 billion in investments—for example, the bank may own some Treasury bonds, some mortgage-backed securities, and some collateralized debt obligations. Finally, the

[8] To see their actual balance sheets, take a look at http://finance.yahoo.com/q/bs?s=BAC, for example.

TABLE 10.4

A Hypothetical Bank's Balance Sheet (billions of dollars)

Assets		Liabilities	
Loans	1,000	Deposits	1,000
Investments	900	Short-term debt	400
Cash and reserves	100	Long-term debt	400
Total assets	2,000	*Total liabilities*	1,800
		Equity (net worth)	200

The net worth of a company is the difference between its total assets and its total liabilities. Because net worth is usually small relative to assets, a modest decline in the value of assets can render a company bankrupt.

bank has $100 billion in cash and reserves—including reserves that it is required to hold on deposit with the Federal Reserve. The total assets of the bank are, therefore, $2,000 billion, or $2 trillion.

On the liability side, our hypothetical bank also has three categories. The main liability of most banks are the deposits that households and businesses have made. These deposits are a liability to the bank—they are funds owed to someone else. In our example, the bank has $1,000 billion of deposits. It also may have borrowed funds from other financial institutions, which are another kind of liability. Here, the bank has $400 billion in short-term debt (for example, 30-day commercial paper) and $400 billion in long-term debt (such as 10-year corporate bonds). These liabilities total $1,800 billion.

The reason this is called a balance sheet is that the two columns must balance. And the key category that makes them balance is called **equity**, or **net worth**, or simply **capital**. Equity is the difference between total assets and total liabilities and represents the value of the institution to its shareholders or owners (and hence is owed to someone else, which is why it is reported on the liability side of the balance sheet). In our example, the bank has a net worth of $200 billion.

Banks are subject to various financial regulations, for reasons that will become clear in a moment. For example, a **reserve requirement** mandates that banks keep a certain percentage, such as 3 percent, of their deposits in a special account ("on reserve") with the central bank. Similarly, a **capital requirement** mandates that the capital (net worth) of the bank be at least a certain fraction of the bank's total assets, such as 6 percent. For the hypothetical bank shown in Table 10.4, the bank appears to have about 10 percent of its deposits held in reserves (and cash), and capital is 10 percent (=200/2,000) of total assets. So this bank satisfies both the reserve requirement and the capital requirement in our example.

Leverage

In an unforgettable scene from the 1967 movie *The Graduate*, Dustin Hoffman plays a young man, Benjamin, who gets career advice from one of his father's business associates, Mr. McGuire:

MR. MCGUIRE: I want to say one word to you. Just one word.

BENJAMIN: Yes, sir.

MR. MCGUIRE: Are you listening?
BENJAMIN: Yes, I am.
MR. MCGUIRE: Plastics.

If this scene were playing out today as an explanation for the financial crisis, the one word would be "leverage." This word is largely responsible for the financial regulations outlined above and is at the heart of how a relatively small shock to the entire wealth of the United States can be turned into a global financial crisis.

Leverage is the ratio of total liabilities to net worth. For our hypothetical bank, this leverage ratio is 9 (=1800/200). For every $10 of assets the bank holds, $9 is essentially financed by borrowing and only $1 is financed by money put up by the shareholders. Leverage, then, magnifies any changes in the value of assets and liabilities in terms of the return to shareholders.

To see why, consider what happens to our bank if it has a good year and its investments go up in value by $100 billion, from $900 billion to $1,000 billion. These investments have earned a return of 11 percent (=100/900). After the good year, the bank's total assets are now $2,100 billion, and its equity rises from $200 billion to $300 billion. The gain of $100 billion in equity, however, represents a 50 percent increase! The 11 percent return on investments gets magnified into a 50 percent return to shareholders because of leverage.

A more familiar example of leverage is associated with a homeowner's mortgage. The new homeowner may put 20 percent down and borrow 80 percent of the value of the new home. If the house initially costs $500,000, the homeowner starts with $100,000 in equity in the house. Now think about what happens if the price of the house rises by 10 percent, to $550,000. Now the homeowner has $150,000 of equity and has made a 50 percent gain on his or her investment. The reason the 10 percent price increase turns into a 50 percent gain to the homeowner is because the original investment is leveraged through the mortgage.

That's the great appeal of leverage: when prices are going up, a modest gain on a house or other investment can be turned into a huge gain on the owner's initial equity. But there is a downside to leverage as well. In the mortgage example, the downside is easy to see: if house prices fall by 10 percent instead of rising by 10 percent, the homeowner loses 50 percent of his or her equity.[9] If prices fall by 20 percent, the entire equity is lost. Leverage magnifies both the gains and the losses on investments.

Returning to our bank example, suppose market prices were to fall sharply so that the bank's investments were worth $600 billion instead of $900 billion. Total assets would also fall by $300 billion, to a new level of $1,700 billion. Even though the total value of assets has only fallen by 15 percent, this change in market prices would entirely wipe out the bank's equity: net worth would go from +$200 billion to −$100 billion. The assets owned by the bank would no longer be large enough to cover the liabilities that the bank owes to others. In this situation, we say the bank is **insolvent** or **bankrupt**. When a bank or firm is highly leveraged, a given percentage change in the value of its assets has a much larger proportional effect on its net worth. This magnification is a result of leverage.

Before the financial crisis, major investment banks had leverage ratios that were even higher than in these examples. For example, when Bear Stearns collapsed,

[9]The price of the house falls from $500,000 to $450,000, resulting in a loss of $50,000. The homeowner's equity, therefore, declines from its original level of $100,000 to $50,000, a 50 percent loss.

its leverage was 35 to 1.[10] Roughly speaking, the major investment banks owned complex investment portfolios, including significant quantities of soon-to-be toxic assets, that were financed with $3 of their own equity and $97 of borrowing. Given this extraordinary leverage, major investment banks were in such a precarious position that a relatively small aggregate shock could send them over the insolvency edge.

Bank Runs and Liquidity Crises

Another classic version of a financial crisis that is easy to understand using balance sheets is a **bank run**. During the Great Depression of the 1930s, depositors worried about the possibility that banks might go under and not be able to return their deposits. This sometimes led all depositors to converge on the bank at once to demand their deposits back. Looking at the balance sheet in Table 10.4, one can see the problem. The bank has only $100 billion in cash and reserves on hand to repay the depositors. The majority of the bank's assets are held in loans and investments, relatively illiquid forms that are hard to turn into cash quickly at fair value. To repay all of its depositors, the bank may be forced to call in outstanding loans and to immediately sell some of its investments. To the extent that these actions cause the values of these assets to fall, the bank run itself may result in the bank having negative equity, a kind of self-fulfilling prophecy. In 1933, the Federal Deposit Insurance Corporation (FDIC) was set up to provide government insurance for deposits, a measure that has largely eliminated this kind of bank run.

A related problem on the liability side occurred in the recent financial crisis, however. In this case, the deposits were not the problem but, rather, the short-term debt. Financial institutions often have relatively large amounts of short-term debt, in part to provide liquidity as they manage their deposits, loans, and investments. An example is commercial paper, which is often traded with maturities of one week or less. Banks may borrow in the commercial-paper market to fund the "cash" entry on the asset side of their balance sheet, which is used to manage their day-to-day commitments. In the last months of 2008 following the collapse of Lehman Brothers, financial institutions became extraordinarily worried about lending money via commercial paper to other financial institutions that might become insolvent. Interest rates on commercial paper rose sharply by more than 5 percentage points, and access to this form of liquidity was sharply curtailed. To fund their daily operations, banks might then have been forced to sell some of their less liquid assets at "fire sale" prices, reducing their net worth—potentially all the way to insolvency.

Financial Wrap-Up

Leverage is like the genie that emerges from the magic lamp. When asset prices are rising, leverage can turn a 10 percent return into a 50 percent return. In the period leading up to the current financial crisis, the genie was granting wishes, and financial institutions earned huge profits by expanding their leverage. When firms take leveraged bets that pay off 9 times out of 10, they can have long runs of seemingly amazing returns.

[10] Roddy Boyd, "The Last Days of Bear Stearns," *Fortune*, March 31, 2008.

The problem occurs when the genie—inevitably—catches you in a mistake. The declines in housing prices and the stock market combined with leverage to threaten the solvency of many financial institutions. Because the financial system is so integrated—financial institutions borrow and lend large sums with each other every day in normal times—problems in a few banks can create a **systemic risk** for the financial system as a whole. Paul O'Neill, a former Treasury secretary under President George W. Bush, summarized this risk with an apt analogy: if you have ten bottles of water and one is poisoned but you don't know which, no one drinks water.[11]

The global financial crisis and the Great Recession have their roots in the bubble that developed in the housing market in the early 2000s. An increase in global savings, low interest rates, and a substantial deterioration of lending standards led to an enormous increase in housing prices. The collapse of this bubble nearly took down the entire financial structure, built as it was on a system of leverage and securitization. The Great Recession was the macroeconomic consequence. And, at some level, we are fortunate that it was not even worse.

10.5 Going Forward

In Chapter 14, we will revisit the global financial crisis and the recent recession. In the next few chapters, however, we develop the basic insights of the macroeconomics of the short run. The short-run model we study is the culmination of more than 80 years of research into the causes of economic fluctuations. The insights that this framework delivers are crucial to understanding booms and recessions as well as the rise and fall of moderate inflation. They will also provide an essential foundation for comprehending the basic facts we've laid out in this chapter, the facts of what will (we hope!) prove to be the most significant downturn in our lives—the Great Recession.

CHAPTER REVIEW

SUMMARY

1. The U.S. economy has suffered several major shocks in recent years. Initially these shocks included a large decline in house prices and a spike in the prices of oil and other commodities.
2. The decline in house prices reduced the value of mortgage-backed securities. Because of leverage, this threatened the solvency of a number of financial institutions, including major investment banks. Risk premiums rose sharply on many kinds of lending, and the stock market lost about half its value.

[11] Deborah Solomon, "Market Leader: Questions for Paul O'Neill," *New York Times*, March 30, 2008.

3. These shocks combined to put the U.S. economy and many economies throughout the world into a financial crisis and a deep recession, by some measures the most severe since the Great Depression.
4. Balance sheets are an accounting device for summarizing the assets, liabilities, and net worth (or equity) of an institution. This can be a bank, a household, or a government, for example.
5. Leverage is the ratio of liabilities to equity. Financial institutions are typically highly leveraged; for example, $10 of assets may be financed by $1 of equity and $9 of debt, a leverage ratio of 9 to 1. Major investment banks before the financial crisis were even more highly leveraged, on the order of 35 to 1.
6. Leverage magnifies both returns and losses, so that small percentage changes in the value of assets or liabilities can be enough to entirely wipe out equity, causing an institution to become insolvent, or bankrupt.
7. During the height of the financial crisis, the solvency of numerous financial institutions was called into question. Because financial firms are interlinked through a complex web of loans, insurance contracts, and securities, problems in a few financial institutions can create problems in many others, which is called systemic risk.

KEY CONCEPTS

assets
balance sheet
bank run
bankruptcy
capital
capital requirement
equity
global saving glut
insolvency
leverage
liabilities
liquidity crisis
net worth
reserve requirement
securitization
systemic risk

REVIEW QUESTIONS

1. By roughly how much did housing prices fall during the financial crisis? What about the stock market?
2. How severe was the Great Recession? What pieces of economic data would you cite to support your answer?
3. What is a balance sheet? What is net worth?
4. What is leverage, and why is it so important in understanding the financial crisis?

EXERCISES

smartwork.wwnorton.com 

1. **The latest data on the financial crisis:** Pick two figures from this chapter, and update them to include the latest available data. What does this tell you about how the economy has evolved in response to the financial crisis?

2. **The current state of the European economy:** By now, you are relatively familiar with recent economic events in the United States. But what about Europe? Write two paragraphs about the state of the economy in the Euro area over the last several years. What has happened to inflation, real GDP growth, and unemployment? What about a key policy interest rate set by the European Central Bank (ECB)? (*Hint*: The ECB sets several key interest rates, including a "deposit rate"—the interest rate the ECB pays on deposits from banks—and a "lending rate"—the interest rate it charges for overnight loans. All are useful and interesting. To keep us all on the same page, let's look at the lending rate.) An extremely helpful resource for this exercise is the ECB's Statistical Data Warehouse: http://sdw.ecb.europa.eu. (You may find it convenient to make a brief table of this data or even to copy some of the ECB's graphs.)

3. **Leverage in the financial system:** Choose two financial institutions, and look up their balance sheets online. (For example, Yahoo! Finance provides these data in an easily accessible form at http://finance.yahoo.com/q/bs?s=GS.) What is the leverage ratio of the two companies you've chosen? For each $100 of assets, how much is financed with equity and how much with debt? By what percentage would assets have to decline in value to bankrupt these financial institutions?

4. **Systemic risk:** Consider the following balance sheets for two hypothetical financial institutions, bank B and bank C:

Bank B's Balance Sheet

Assets		Liabilities	
Cash	1,000	Deposits	1,400
Loan to bank C	500		
Total assets	???	*Total liabilities*	???
		Equity (net worth)	???

Bank C's Balance Sheet

Assets		Liabilities	
Mortgage-backed securities	800	Deposits	200
		Loan from bank B	500
Total assets	???	*Total liabilities*	???
		Equity (net worth)	???

(a) Fill in the missing entries in the balance sheets (denoted ???).
(b) What is the leverage ratio in each bank?
(c) Suppose housing prices fall sharply and the mortgage-backed securities held by bank C fall in value to only $500. What happens to bank C's net worth?
(d) The shortfall in bank C's equity means that it cannot repay the loan it received from bank B. Assume bank C pays back as much as it can, while still making good on its deposits. What happens to the net worth of bank B?
(e) Discuss briefly how this is related to systemic risk.

CHAPTER 11

THE IS CURVE

OVERVIEW

In this chapter, we learn

- the first building block of our short-run model: the IS curve, which describes the effect of changes in the real interest rate on output in the short run.
- how shocks to consumption, investment, government purchases, or net exports – "aggregate demand shocks" – can shift the IS curve.
- a theory of consumption called the life-cycle/permanent-income hypothesis.
- that investment is the key channel through which changes in real interest rates affect GDP in the short run.

> A softening in housing markets would likely be one of many adjustments that would occur in the wake of an increase in interest rates.
>
> —ALAN GREENSPAN

11.1 Introduction

Every six to eight weeks, the Federal Reserve Board of Governors holds an important meeting that is followed carefully by businesspeople, political leaders, and even young couples thinking about buying a new house. Cable news channels report the outcome during live broadcasts. No other discussion of economics garners this much attention, so what makes these meetings so important? The answer is that the Federal Reserve sets a particular interest rate—called the federal funds rate—at these meetings. And by effectively setting the rate at which people borrow and lend in financial markets, the Fed exerts a substantial influence on the level of economic activity in the short run.[1]

This chapter explains how and why movements in interest rates affect the economy in the short run. The key relationship that captures this interaction is called **the IS curve**, one of the important building blocks of our short-run model.

The basic story we will tell is this:

$$\uparrow \text{interest rate} \Rightarrow \downarrow \text{investment} \Rightarrow \downarrow \text{output} \tag{11.1}$$

An increase in the real interest rate raises the cost of borrowing for businesses and households. Firms respond by reducing their purchases of machines and buildings. Consumers respond by reducing their borrowing to buy new houses. Both of these channels reduce investment. And this reduction in investment leads firms to produce less, lowering the level of output in the short run.

The IS curve, then, captures the fact that high interest rates reduce output in the short run, and the channel through which this reduction occurs is investment. The letter I in fact stands for investment; we'll get to the S in a case study later on. Graphically, this negative relationship between interest rates and short-run output is summarized in Figure 11.1.

In this chapter, we first learn the economics underlying the IS curve. Next, we look at several examples of how this curve can help us understand short-run

Epigraph: Speaking as chair of the Federal Reserve, May 6, 2004.

[1] While not exactly page-turners that you'll want to take to the beach with you, a number of interesting accounts of what happens "inside" the Fed have been published recently. Two of these are Laurence H. Meyer's *A Term at the Fed: An Insider's View* (New York: HarperCollins, 2004) and Bob Woodward's *Maestro: Greenspan's Fed and the American Boom* (New York: Simon and Schuster, 2000).

FIGURE 11.1

Introducing the IS Curve

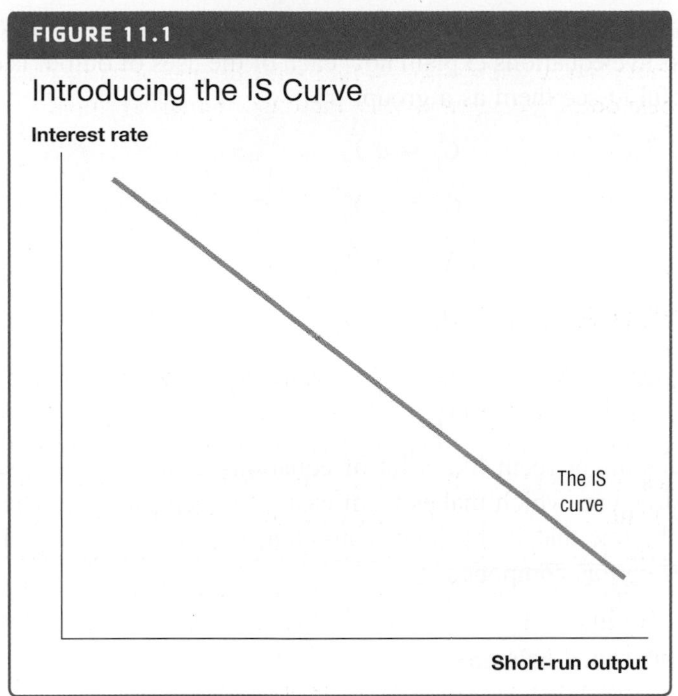

The IS curve captures the fact that high interest rates reduce output in the short run. This occurs because high interest rates make borrowing expensive for firms and households, reducing their demand for new investment. The reduction in demand leads to a decline in output in the economy as a whole.

fluctuations in output. Finally, we analyze in more detail the consumption, investment, fiscal policy, and trade components that make up the IS curve.

11.2 Setting Up the Economy

To develop a long-run model of economic growth, we constructed a simple economy and analyzed how that economy behaved. The result was a model that we could use to shed light on important economic questions. In the coming chapters, we will do the same thing for the short-run model.

The IS curve is a key building block of the short-run model. We will develop it as if it were its own "mini model." The equation that serves as the foundation for the IS curve is the national income identity that we first encountered in Chapter 2:

$$Y_t = C_t + I_t + G_t + EX_t - IM_t. \tag{11.2}$$

This equation shows that the economy's output Y_t can be used in one of four ways: as consumption C_t, for investment I_t, for government purchases G_t, or for net exports $EX_t - IM_t$. Although this is the traditional way of writing the equation, you might find it easier to understand in the form $Y_t + IM_t = C_t + I_t + G_t + EX_t$. In this version, the left side is total resources available to the economy (production plus imports), and the right side is total uses (consumption, investment, government purchases, selling the goods to foreigners in the form of exports).

At this point, we have one equation and six unknowns: Y_t, C_t, I_t, G_t, EX_t, and IM_t. The next five equations explain how each of the uses of output is determined, and it's helpful to see them as a group:

$$C_t = \bar{a}_c \bar{Y}_t \tag{11.3}$$

$$G_t = \bar{a}_g \bar{Y}_t \tag{11.4}$$

$$EX_t = \bar{a}_{ex} \bar{Y}_t \tag{11.5}$$

$$IM_t = \bar{a}_{im} \bar{Y}_t \tag{11.6}$$

$$\frac{I_t}{\bar{Y}_t} = \bar{a}_i - \bar{b}(R_t - \bar{r}). \tag{11.7}$$

Though this might seem like a lot of equations, note that the first four share a common structure, which makes them easier to keep track of. The investment equation is the one that is different, consistent with the emphasis the short-run model places on this component.

Consumption and Friends

Equations (11.3) to (11.6) say that consumption, government purchases, exports, and imports each depend on the economy's potential output $\bar{Y}_t$. An important assumption in the short-run model is that the level of potential output is given exogenously. That is, $\bar{Y}_t$ is not an endogenous variable in the short-run model; we think of it as already having been determined by our long-run model.

Equation (11.3) says that consumption is a constant fraction of potential output, given by the parameter $\bar{a}_c$. As an empirical benchmark, $\bar{a}_c$ is about 2/3, as roughly 2 out of every 3 dollars of GDP goes toward consumption. This equation also has an economic justification. Agents in our economy consume a constant fraction of potential output. You may remember that this simple behavioral rule was exactly what we assumed in our long-run model.

Now recall that potential output is much smoother than actual output (see Figure 9.2 on p. 230). Combined with our consumption equation, this fact has the interesting economic implication that consumption is smoother than GDP. What does this mean? Consider a shock that reduces current output and causes a recession. While actual GDP declines, potential output $\bar{Y}_t$ is unchanged, since it is determined by the long-run model. According to equation (11.3), then, consumption will not change either. During a recession, people may keep their consumption at a steady level by drawing on their savings, for example. Shocks to income are "smoothed" out to keep consumption steady. This result is related to a theory of consumer behavior known as the permanent-income hypothesis, which will be discussed later in the chapter.

Equations (11.4) through (11.6) look much like the consumption equation. Government purchases, exports, and imports are all assumed to be constant fractions of potential output, given by the parameters $\bar{a}_g$, $\bar{a}_{ex}$, and $\bar{a}_{im}$. These four equations are the simplest assumptions we can make that still deliver a realistic and economically informative model. But they all have an economic justification as well and will prove to be surprisingly rich in their implications.

The Investment Equation

The investment equation, (11.7), is different. It's made up of two parts. The first is the $\bar{a}_i$ parameter, reflecting the long-run fraction of potential output that goes to investment. If this were the only term, the investment equation would look like the others.

The last part is what's new, and it indicates how the interest rate enters the model. In particular, the amount of investment depends on the gap between the real interest rate R_t and the marginal product of capital $\bar{r}$. The real interest rate R_t is the rate at which firms can save or borrow. For example, R_t might equal 10 percent, implying that firms can borrow \$100 today if they are willing to pay back \$110 next year (assuming there is no inflation).

The marginal product of capital $\bar{r}$ is familiar from the long-run model: it reflects the amount of additional output the firm can produce by investing in one more unit of capital. Our short-run model takes $\bar{r}$ to be an exogenous parameter, like $\bar{Y}_t$, determined by the long-run model. Since the marginal product of capital is constant along a balanced growth path, we don't include a time subscript on $\bar{r}$. (In contrast, since potential output $\bar{Y}_t$ is growing over time, we do include a time subscript there.)

The key assumption embedded in equation (11.7) is that the amount of investment that firms in the economy undertake depends on the gap between the real interest rate R_t and the marginal product of capital $\bar{r}$. If the marginal product of capital is low relative to the real interest rate, then firms are better off saving their retained earnings in the financial market (for example, by buying U.S. government bonds). Alternatively, if the marginal product of capital is high relative to the real interest rate, then firms would find it profitable to borrow at the real interest rate and invest the proceeds in capital, leading to a rise in investment.

To be more concrete, suppose $R_t = 10\%$ and $\bar{r} = 15\%$. Now suppose a firm borrows 100 units of output at this 10 percent rate, invests it as capital, and produces. The extra 100 units of capital produce 15 units of output, since the marginal product of capital is 15 percent. The firm can pay back the 10 units it owes in interest and keep a profit of 5 units. In this scenario, one would expect firms to invest a relatively large amount.[2]

This discussion also helps us understand the $\bar{b}$ parameter, which tells us how sensitive investment is to changes in the interest rate. A high value for $\bar{b}$ means that small differences between the interest rate and the marginal product of capital lead to big changes in investment.

In the long run, the real interest rate must equal the marginal product of capital. This is what we saw in our long-run model: firms rent capital until the marginal product of capital is equal to the interest rate. In our short-run model, we allow the marginal product of capital to differ from the real interest rate. The reason for this is that installing new capital to equate the two takes time: new factories must be built and brought online, and new machines must be set up. When the Federal Reserve changes interest rates, the change is instantaneous but the marginal

[2] In this example, firms would always want to borrow more and more. But in practice, there are costs to changing the capital stock: for example, a new factory has to be built and new machines have to be installed, both of which take time. These adjustment costs help to limit the amount of investment firms decide to undertake in such a situation.

TABLE 11.1

The Setup of the Economy for the IS Curve

Endogenous variables: $Y_t, C_t, I_t, G_t, EX_t, IM_t$	
National income identity:	$Y_t = C_t + I_t + G_t + EX_t - IM_t$
Consumption:	$C_t = \bar{a}_c \bar{Y}_t$
Government purchases:	$G_t = \bar{a}_g \bar{Y}_t$
Exports:	$EX_t = \bar{a}_{ex} \bar{Y}_t$
Imports:	$IM_t = \bar{a}_{im} \bar{Y}_t$
Investment:	$\frac{I_t}{\bar{Y}_t} = \bar{a}_i - \bar{b}\,(R_t - \bar{r})$
Exogenous variables/parameters: $\bar{Y}_t, \bar{r}, \bar{a}_c, \bar{a}_i, \bar{a}_g, \bar{a}_{ex}, \bar{a}_{im}, \bar{b}$	
Exogenous for now (until next chapter): R_t	

product of capital doesn't change until new capital is installed and put to use. When $R_t = \bar{r}$ in the long run, the investment share of potential output is $\bar{a}_i$. So this $\bar{a}_i$ parameter plays the same role for investment that $\bar{a}_c$ did for consumption.

In contrast to the marginal product of capital $\bar{r}$, which we're assuming is exogenous in the short-run model, the real interest rate R_t is an endogenous variable. Notice that it has no bar on top. We will determine the real interest rate in Chapter 12, where it will constitute the second building block of the short-run model. In this chapter, however, we take R_t as given, or exogenous. In a sense, it would be appropriate to place a bar over R_t here and then remove it in Chapter 12, but this would be somewhat tedious and might create some confusion. The important thing to remember is that R_t will be endogenized in Chapter 12 but is exogenous for now.

Table 11.1 summarizes the setup of the economy for the short-run model at this point, with six endogenous variables—Y_t, C_t, I_t, G_t, EX_t, and IM_t—and six equations. In spite of the table's intimidating look, the model solves out quite easily, as we will see next.

11.3 Deriving the IS Curve

To derive the relationship between output and the interest rate shown in the IS curve (Figure 11.1), we first divide the national income identity in equation (11.2) by the level of potential output:

$$\frac{Y_t}{\bar{Y}_t} = \frac{C_t}{\bar{Y}_t} + \frac{I_t}{\bar{Y}_t} + \frac{G_t}{\bar{Y}_t} + \frac{EX_t}{\bar{Y}_t} - \frac{IM_t}{\bar{Y}_t} \tag{11.8}$$

Now we substitute our five equations for C_t, I_t, G_t, EX_t, and IM_t into the right side of this equation, which yields

$$\frac{Y_t}{\bar{Y}_t} = \bar{a}_c + \bar{a}_i - \bar{b}(R_t - \bar{r}) + \bar{a}_g + \bar{a}_{ex} - \bar{a}_{im}. \tag{11.9}$$

The final step in deriving the IS curve is to recall (from Chapter 9) the definition of short-run output $\tilde{Y}_t$: the percentage by which current output Y_t differs from potential output $\bar{Y}_t$:

$$\tilde{Y}_t \equiv \frac{Y_t - \bar{Y}_t}{\bar{Y}_t}. \tag{11.10}$$

To get short-run output on the left side of equation (11.9), we just need to subtract 1 from both sides of that equation:

$$\underbrace{\frac{Y_t}{\bar{Y}_t} - 1}_{\tilde{Y}_t} = \underbrace{\bar{a}_c + \bar{a}_i + \bar{a}_g + \bar{a}_{ex} - \bar{a}_{im} - 1}_{\bar{a}} - \bar{b}(R_t - \bar{r}). \tag{11.11}$$

And this gives the equation for the IS curve:

$$\tilde{Y}_t = \bar{a} - \bar{b}(R_t - \bar{r}) \tag{11.12}$$

where $\bar{a} \equiv \bar{a}_c + \bar{a}_i + \bar{a}_g + \bar{a}_{ex} - \bar{a}_{im} - 1$, a combination of the various demand parameters.

This is our IS curve. Relative to the six-equation model we just solved, it's fairly simple: just a straight, downward-sloping line that relates short-run output to the interest rate. And having derived the equation first, we understand it more fully. Now we'll see how it works.

As we assumed in Figure 11.1, an increase in the real interest rate R_t leads to a decline in short-run output (or output, for short). Firms find it more expensive to borrow in order to purchase capital equipment. Households see mortgage rates go up, which results in a reduction in demand for new housing, which is also part of investment. Through the national income identity, this decline in investment reduces output.

Equation (11.12) exhibits two innovations relative to the basic diagram from the start of this chapter. For one, it is really the gap between the real interest rate R_t and the marginal product of capital $\bar{r}$ that matters for output. The reason for this, as discussed above, is that firms can always earn the marginal product of capital on their new investments.

But now we also have the parameter $\bar{a}$ entering the IS equation. Recall that $\bar{a} \equiv \bar{a}_c + \bar{a}_i + \bar{a}_g + \bar{a}_{ex} - \bar{a}_{im} - 1$. That is, this parameter is really a combination of the parameters from the various demand equations. To understand this equation, consider the case where the economy has settled down at its long-run values; that is, $Y_t = \bar{Y}_t$, so output is at potential and $\tilde{Y}_t = 0$. In the long run, as we've seen, the real interest rate prevailing in financial markets is equal to the marginal product of capital, so that $R_t = \bar{r}$. In this case, the IS equation reduces to a simple statement that $0 = \bar{a}$. The reason is straightforward: when output is equal to potential, the sum $C + I + G + EX - IM$ is equal to $\bar{Y}$, and therefore the share parameters $\bar{a}_c + \bar{a}_i + \bar{a}_g + \bar{a}_{ex} - \bar{a}_{im}$ must add up to 1. In the long run, then, $\bar{a} = 0$.

In fact, our baseline IS curve will respect this long-run value. We will think of $\bar{a} = 0$ as the default case. However, shocks to the economy can push $\bar{a}$ away from 0 in the short run. Because $\bar{a}$ is derived from the demand equations for consumption, investment, and so on, we call it the **aggregate demand shock**. In the next section, we will see how aggregate demand shocks can shift the IS curve and cause fluctuations in economic activity.

CASE STUDY

Why Is It Called the "IS Curve"?

The IS curve was first introduced during the Great Depression by John R. Hicks, who won the Nobel Prize in economics in 1972.[3] With this curve, Hicks provided a mathematical version of Keynes's *General Theory of Employment, Interest, and Money* that has played an important role in macroeconomics ever since.

"IS" stands for "investment equals savings." To see how this statement is related to the IS curve, consider once again the national income identity, $Y = C + I + G + EX - IM$.

First, rearrange the equation as

$$Y - C - G + (IM - EX) = I.$$

Now, add and subtract tax revenues T from the left side of this equation to get

$$\underbrace{(Y - T - C)}_{\text{private saving}} + \underbrace{(T - G)}_{\text{government saving}} + \underbrace{(IM - EX)}_{\text{foreign saving}} = I. \tag{11.13}$$

The sum of saving in the U.S. economy—by the private sector, by the government, and by foreigners (by shipping us more goods than we ship them)—is equal to investment. The national income identity, which is at the heart of the IS curve, thus requires that total saving be equal to total investment. We will revisit this equation again in Chapter 17, when we look at budget deficits and government saving, and again in Chapter 18, when we study the trade balance and foreign saving.

11.4 Using the IS Curve

The Basic IS Curve

Now that we have derived the IS equation, we can illustrate it in a graph and gain additional insights that were glossed over in the introduction. The basic IS curve shown in Figure 11.2 captures the negative relationship between the real interest rate and output in the short run. The curve is drawn for the benchmark of no aggregate demand shock, so $\bar{a} = 0$. Therefore, short-run output $\tilde{Y}_t$ is 0 at

[3] John R. Hicks, "Mr. Keynes and the 'Classics': A Suggested Interpretation," *Econometrica*, vol. 5 (April 1937), pp. 147–59.

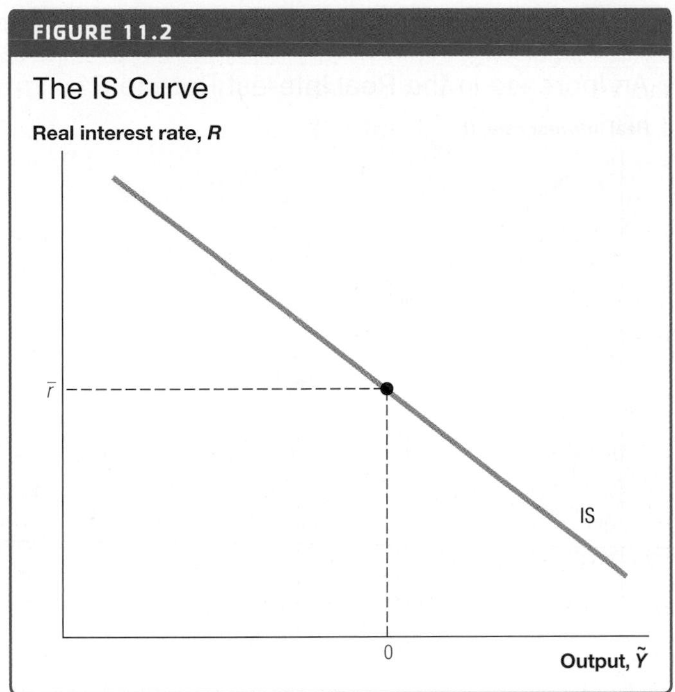

FIGURE 11.2

The IS Curve

This graph shows the IS curve

$$\tilde{Y}_t = \bar{a} - \bar{b}\,(R_t - \bar{r})$$

in the benchmark case of no aggregate demand shocks, so that $\bar{a} = 0$.

the point where the real interest rate equals its long-run value $\bar{r}$. That is, actual output is at potential.

Given that the equation is $\tilde{Y}_t = \bar{a} - \bar{b}(R_t - \bar{r})$, we are thinking of output as a function of the interest rate. But the graph puts output (the endogenous variable) on the horizontal axis. Wouldn't it be more natural to switch things around and put output on the vertical axis? Absolutely! If these are your instincts, they are right on target. However, we will resist these instincts for two reasons. First, we will make R_t an endogenous variable in the next chapter, and one of our endogenous variables must go on the horizontal axis. Second, the long-standing tradition in economics is to put the price on the vertical axis and the quantity on the horizontal axis—think about supply and demand.

The Effect of a Change in the Interest Rate

Now consider an economic experiment in our model. Suppose the real interest rate in financial markets increases. In Chapter 12, we will see how the Federal Reserve could make this happen; but for now, take it to be an exogenous change.

Central banks control the nominal interest rate, but the IS curve depends on the real interest rate. We address this distinction in Chapter 12.

Is this increase a movement along the IS curve or a shift of the curve? The answer is clear when we think about what we have graphed. The IS curve is a plot of how output changes as a function of the interest rate, so a change in the real interest rate is most certainly a movement along the curve.

Figure 11.3 illustrates this experiment. We assume the economy begins at its long-run values, so output is at potential and the real interest rate is initially equal to the marginal product of capital. An increase in the real interest rate then causes the economy to move up the IS curve, from point A to point B, so that short-run output declines.

An increase to R' in the real interest rate is a *movement along* the IS curve that moves the economy from *A* to *B*, resulting in a decline in output in the short run.

FIGURE 11.3

An Increase in the Real Interest Rate to R'

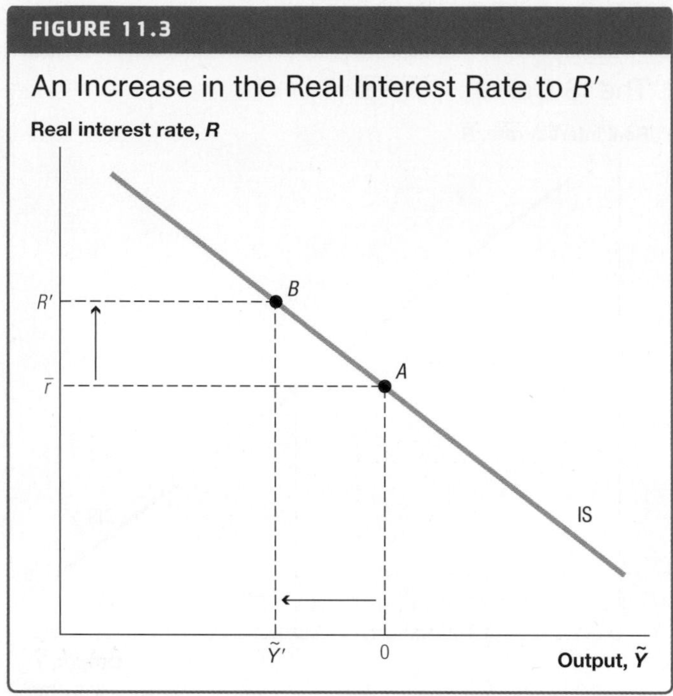

What is the intuition for the decline in output? By now the answer should start to sound familiar: the higher interest rate raises borrowing costs, reduces demand for investment, and therefore reduces output below potential.

Consider the same experiment from the point of view of the IS equation,

$$\tilde{Y}_t = \bar{a} - \bar{b}(R_t - \bar{r}). \tag{11.14}$$

Suppose we assume $\bar{a} = 0$, $\bar{b} = 2$, $R = \bar{r} = 5\%$, and $R' = 6\%$ (the increased interest rate). With these values, the economy begins with output at potential, so $\tilde{Y} = 0\%$. When the real interest rate rises by 1 percentage point, what happens to short-run output? Plugging these numbers into the IS curve yields the answer: output falls to -2 percent, so the economy is 2 percent below potential.

In fact, with these parameter values, each percentage point increase in the real interest rate reduces short-run output by 2 percentage points. This results directly from the fact that $\bar{b}$, the sensitivity of investment to the interest rate, equals 2. If $\bar{b}$ were higher, the IS curve would be flatter, and a given change in the interest rate would be associated with an even larger change in output. Why? Because investment is more sensitive to interest rates in this case.

An Aggregate Demand Shock

Now consider another experiment. Suppose improvements in information technology (IT) lead to an investment boom: businesses become optimistic about the future and increase their demand for machine tools, computer equipment, and factories at any given level of the interest rate. If you look back at Table 11.1, you'll see that this situation most naturally corresponds to an increase in $\bar{a}_i$: this parameter changes the amount of investment associated with any given level of the interest rate.

FIGURE 11.4

An Aggregate Demand Shock

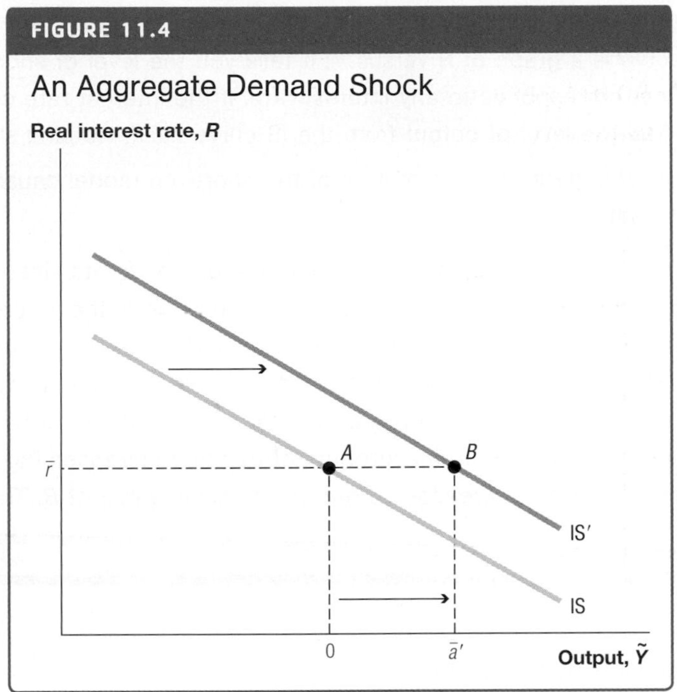

The figure shows the effect of a positive aggregate demand shock that raises $\bar{a}$ from 0 to $\bar{a}'$. The IS curve shifts out, moving the economy from point *A* to point *B* and increasing output above potential.

How does the IS curve respond when $\bar{a}_i$ increases? The aggregate demand shock parameter $\bar{a}$ rises to some value greater than zero. That is, the experiment we are considering is a *positive* aggregate demand shock. Is this a movement along the IS curve or a shift in the curve? Recall that the IS curve shows output as a function of the real interest rate. So if $\bar{a}$ increases to some positive value $\bar{a}'$, this means output is higher at every interest rate. If we look again at the IS curve equation, $\tilde{Y}_t = \bar{a} - \bar{b}(R_t - \bar{r})$, we see that for any given real interest rate R_t, output is higher when $\bar{a}$ increases. This means the IS curve shifts out.

The old and new IS curves are shown in Figure 11.4. Notice in the figure that the new IS curve passes through point B. At this point, $R_t = \bar{r}$ and output is $\bar{a}'$, as the equation implies. Aggregate demand shocks generally translate one-for-one into changes in short-run output. If $\bar{a}_i$ increases by 1 percent, for example, then $\bar{a}$ rises from 0 to 1 percent as well, and output rises above potential by 1 percentage point.

CASE STUDY

Move Along or Shift? A Guide to the IS Curve

The IS curve is a graph of the relationship between the real interest rate *R* and short-run output $\tilde{Y}$. The following guide should help you to understand when the curve shifts versus when the economy moves along the IS curve.

- A change in R shows up as a movement along the IS curve. Why? Because the IS curve is a graph of R versus $\tilde{Y}$; it tells you the level of short-run output that corresponds to any interest rate. If the interest rate changes, you simply read the level of output from the IS curve itself. Nothing shifts.
- Any other change in the parameters of the short-run model causes the IS curve to shift.

Changes in any of the aggregate demand parameters ($\bar{a}_c$, $\bar{a}_i$, etc.) lead to a change in $\bar{a}$. The amount of output associated with any given value of the interest rate then changes, so the IS curve must shift. Increases in $\bar{a}$ shift the IS curve out, increasing output in the short run. Decreases in $\bar{a}$ shift the IS curve in, reducing output.

What happens if $\bar{r}$ increases? Consider the equation for the IS curve: $\tilde{Y} = \bar{a} - \bar{b}$ $(R_t - \bar{r})$. An increase in the marginal product of capital $\bar{r}$ increases the demand for investment and therefore increases output at any given value of R. Therefore, the IS curve shifts out.

A Shock to Potential Output

As we saw in our study of long-run growth, shocks to the economy such as the discovery of a new technology or an earthquake that destroys a substantial amount of capital can change potential output $\bar{Y}_t$. And since $\bar{Y}_t$ is an exogenous variable in our setup of the IS curve, it is useful to think about how the IS curve is affected by such changes in potential output.

Since potential output $\bar{Y}_t$ doesn't enter our equation $\tilde{Y}_t = \bar{a} - \bar{b}(R_t - \bar{r})$, shocks to potential output therefore leave the IS curve unchanged. There is no movement along the curve and no shift of the curve. Short-run output $\tilde{Y}_t$ is unaffected by a change in potential output.

The reason for this result is that shocks to potential output in our setup change actual output by the same amount. For example, the discovery of a new technology raises potential output but it also raises actual output. The destruction of capital in an earthquake reduces potential output but also reduces actual output, since less capital is available for use in production. These changes exactly match so that short-run output—the gap between actual and potential output—is unchanged.[4]

It is important to notice, however, that a new technology or an earthquake may change more than just the $\bar{Y}_t$ parameter. For example, the discovery of a new technology may raise the marginal product of capital $\bar{r}$, leading to an increase in investment demand as firms attempt to build new plants to take advantage of the new technology.[5] This would shift the IS curve out and stimulate the economy.

---

[4] Mathematically, the reason is that an increase in potential output raises current consumption according to the consumption equation. It has the same effects on investment, government purchases, and net exports, leading to an increase in demand that matches the increase in potential output.

[5] Recall that the marginal product of capital is the extra amount of output produced if a firm increases its capital stock by one unit. This marginal product increases if total factor productivity (technology) is higher or if there are more workers in the firm. It decreases as more and more capital is used. (See section 4.2 in Chapter 4.)

Interestingly, an earthquake also raises the marginal product of capital and thus has the same effect: it reduces actual and potential output, but typically leads to an increase in short-run output as investment demand is stimulated by the increase in $\bar{r}$.

Other Experiments

Most other experiments we can consider using the IS curve fit nicely into one of two cases: either they involve a change in the interest rate, like our first experiment, or they involve a shift of the IS curve, like the second one.

For example, suppose a large recession hits Europe or Japan, and foreigners decide to reduce their demand for U.S. goods. Looking back at Table 11.1, we see that the natural way to think of this shock is as a temporary decline in $\bar{a}_{ex}$: potential output hasn't changed, so the only way exports of U.S. goods can fall is if $\bar{a}_{ex}$ declines.

Now what happens? The decline in $\bar{a}_{ex}$ leads to a decline in $\bar{a}$ in the IS curve, which causes the IS curve to shift in. The recession in Europe or Japan thus causes output to fall below potential in the United States, so there is an international transmission of the recession. This case is similar to the aggregate demand shock studied in Figure 11.4, only here the IS curve shifts in instead of out.

Other experiments can be analyzed in similar ways. What might lead to changes in $\bar{a}_c$ or $\bar{a}_g$, and how would these affect the IS curve and the economy? What happens if the real interest rate is lowered? Exercises at the end of the chapter will help you translate similar real events that transpire in the economy into the appropriate changes in the IS curve.

11.5 Microfoundations of the IS Curve

The IS curve is based on the demands for consumption, investment, government purchases, exports, and imports specified by the five equations in Table 11.1. Here we provide an overview of the underlying microeconomic behavior that gives rise to these relationships—the *microfoundations* for these equations. These microfoundations will be examined in further detail in Chapters 15 through 19.

An important principle to bear in mind in this discussion is that aggregation tends to average out departures from the model that occur at the individual level. For example, the consumption of a particular family or the investment of a particular firm may be subject to whims that are not part of our model. But these whims will average out as we consider the collection of consumers and firms in the economy as a whole.

Consumption

How do individuals decide how much of their income to consume today and how much to save? The starting point for the modern theory of consumer behavior is a pair of theories developed in the 1950s by two Nobel Prize–winning economists:

the permanent-income hypothesis, developed by Milton Friedman, and the closely related life-cycle model of consumption, formulated by Franco Modigliani (1985 winner).

Both theories begin with the observation that people seem to prefer a smooth path for consumption to a path that involves large movements. For example, most people prefer to eat one bowl of ice cream per day rather than seven bowls on Monday and none for the rest of the week. This is nothing more than an application of the standard theory of diminishing marginal utility. **The permanent-income hypothesis** applies this reasoning to conclude that people will base their consumption on an average of their income over time rather than on their current income. For example, if you take an unpaid vacation, your income falls sharply but your consumption generally remains steady. Similarly, construction workers or farmers who engage in seasonal work, workers who become unemployed, and even lucky people who win the lottery all tend to smooth their consumption.

The life-cycle model of consumption applies this same reasoning to a person's lifetime. It suggests that consumption is based on average lifetime income rather than on income at any given age. When people are young and in school, their consumption is typically higher than their income (they may receive money from their parents). As people age and their income rises, their consumption rises more slowly and they save more. Then when they retire, income falls, but consumption remains relatively stable: people live off of the savings they accumulated while middle-aged. This stylized pattern is shown in Figure 11.5.

The basic insight from the life-cycle/permanent-income (LC/PI) hypothesis is that people smooth their consumption relative to their income. The simple consumption equation from Table 11.1, $C_t = \bar{a}_c \bar{Y}_t$, incorporates this insight by setting consumption proportional to potential output rather than to actual output. If actual output moves around while potential output remains constant, the LC/PI hypothesis would lead us to expect consumption to remain relatively steady as

According to the life-cycle model, consumption is much smoother than income over one's lifetime.

FIGURE 11.5

The Life-Cycle Model of Consumption

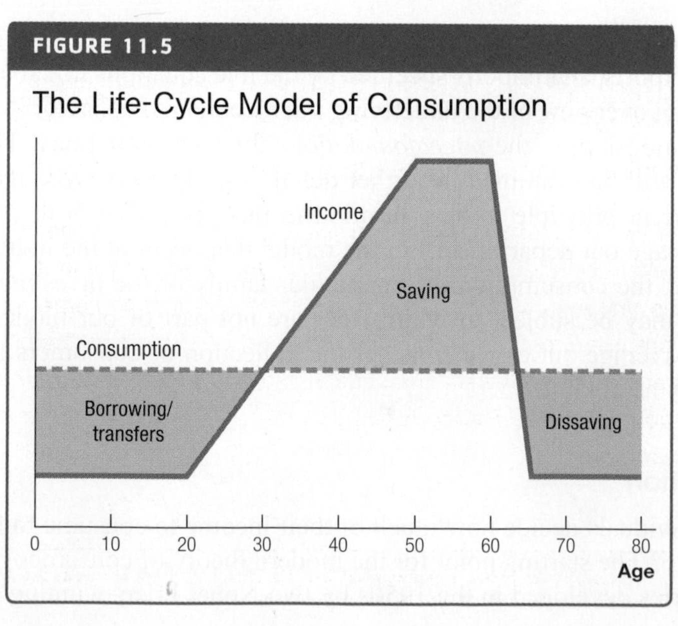

people use their savings to smooth consumption. Strict versions of the hypothesis imply that predictable movements in potential output should also be smoothed, so our simple consumption equation only partially incorporates the insights from the LC/PI hypothesis.

How successful is the LC/PI model at explaining individual consumer behavior? The answer appears to be mixed. Chang-Tai Hsieh of the University of Chicago has examined the behavior of consumers in Alaska in response to two shocks: the annual payment from the State of Alaska's Permanent Fund and the annual payment of federal tax refunds.[6] The Permanent Fund pays out a large sum of money each year to every resident of Alaska based on oil revenues; the general size of the payment is known through experience, and the exact size is announced 6 months before it's actually made. The LC/PI hypothesis predicts that consumption should not change when the Permanent Fund check is received, but that consumers should have already taken it into account when planning their consumption pattern a year in advance. And this is exactly what Hsieh finds. On the other hand, Hsieh finds that the very consumers who smooth their consumption in response to the Permanent Fund payment don't fully smooth their tax refund: during the quarter in which tax refunds arrive, consumption rises by about 30 cents for every dollar of tax refund. He interprets this evidence as suggesting that the LC/PI hypothesis works well for large and easy-to-predict changes in income but less well for small and harder-to-predict shocks.

In summary, consumption by individuals likely depends on their permanent income and their stage in the life cycle. However, it is also sensitive to transitory changes in income. At the aggregate level, our simple approach of assuming that consumption is proportional to potential output is a rough compromise that works fairly well, at least as a first pass. The fact that consumption may respond to temporary changes in income, however, leads to an interesting and important insight. This is what we turn to in the next section.

CASE STUDY

Permanent Income and Present Discounted Value

In considering the LC/PI model, we have used the phrase "average income" rather loosely. We said people base their consumption on their permanent income rather than on current income, where "permanent income" refers to some average value. To be more precise, what we really mean is this: people base their consumption on the constant income stream that has the same present discounted value as the actual income stream. The constant income stream is, not surprisingly, called **permanent income**.

[6]Chang-Tai Hsieh, "Do Consumers React to Anticipated Income Changes? Evidence from the Alaska Permanent Fund," *American Economic Review*, vol. 93, no. 1 (March 2003), pp. 397–405.

That's quite a mouthful, so let's take it more slowly. First, recall the concept of *present discounted value* from Chapter 7. The present discounted value is the single amount today that has the same value as the entire income stream. Suppose Janet has an income stream that generally rises over time but occasionally falls, during spells of unemployment, unpaid vacations, and so on. As we did with your human capital, we could compute the present discounted value of her income stream. And if Janet wants to smooth consumption, we could calculate the constant level of consumption that has the same present discounted value as her lifetime income stream. This constant level is her permanent income.

By borrowing and lending at the appropriate times, Janet could consume a constant amount equal to her permanent income. Because of diminishing marginal utility, this smooth path is preferred to the fluctuating path of actual income. The fact that permanent income and actual income have the same present discounted value ensures that whatever borrowing and lending occurs over time is acceptable and doesn't violate Janet's budget constraint.

Multiplier Effects

What if we consider more seriously the possibility that aggregate consumption responds to temporary changes in income? An important economic phenomenon called a "multiplier" emerges in this case. Suppose we modify our consumption equation slightly, so that

$$\frac{C_t}{\bar{Y}_t} = \bar{a}_c + \bar{x}\tilde{Y}_t. \tag{11.15}$$

The consumption equation now includes an additional term that is proportional to short-run output. Now when the economy booms temporarily, consumption rises; the amount by which it rises depends on the parameter $\bar{x}$. For reasons we will see in a moment, we assume $\bar{x}$ is between 0 and 1.

If you derive the IS curve with this new consumption equation, you will find:[7]

$$\tilde{Y} = \underbrace{\frac{1}{1-\bar{x}}}_{\text{multiplier}} \times \underbrace{(\bar{a} - \bar{b}(R_t - \bar{r}))}_{\text{original IS curve}}. \tag{11.16}$$

[7]The derivation follows exactly the same steps as with the original IS curve. After dividing the national income identity by $\bar{Y}$ and subtracting 1 from both sides, we get

$$\underbrace{\frac{Y_t}{\bar{Y}_t} - 1}_{\tilde{Y}_t} = \bar{a} + \bar{x}\tilde{Y}_t - \bar{b}(R_t - \bar{r}).$$

Subtracting $\bar{x}\tilde{Y}_t$ from both sides and then dividing by $1 - \bar{x}$ gives the new IS curve in equation (11.16).

This equation looks much like our standard IS curve, but with one key difference: there is now a **multiplier** on the aggregate demand shock and interest rate term, $1/(1 - \bar{x})$. Since $\bar{x}$ is between 0 and 1, the multiplier is larger than 1. For example, if $\bar{x} = 1/3$, then the multiplier is equal to $\frac{1}{2/3} = 1.5$.

This means that an aggregate demand shock that increases $\bar{a}$ to +2% will raise output in the short run by $1.5 \times 2\% = 3\%$. Similarly, an increase in the interest rate that reduces output by 1 percent in our original IS curve will now reduce output by 1.5 percent because of the multiplier.[8]

What is the economic intuition for this multiplier? The answer is important. Suppose an increase in the interest rate reduces investment by 1 percentage point. In our original formulation of the IS curve, short-run output falls by 1 percentage point (relative to potential), and that's the end of the story. Now, however, more interesting things happen. The reduction in investment may cost some construction workers their jobs. This unemployment leads the workers to reduce their consumption—they may hold off buying new cars and televisions, for example. Car dealers and television makers then feel squeezed and may themselves lay off some workers. These workers reduce consumption themselves, and this in turn may impact other firms. What we see is a long chain of effects resulting from the original reduction in investment. A shock to one part of the economy gets multiplied by affecting other parts of the economy.

The math behind this multiplier is actually quite interesting (see footnote 9, below). Overall, the main point to remember is that the IS curve can involve feedback that leads to "vicious" or "virtuous circles": a shock to one part of the economy can multiply to create larger effects.[9]

Another important thing to note about the multiplier is that it doesn't really change the overall form of the IS curve. The curve still has the form of an aggregate demand shock plus a term that depends on the gap between the interest rate and the marginal product of capital. The only difference is that the coefficients of the IS curve (the intercept and the slope) can be larger in magnitude because of multiplier effects. For this reason and to keep things simple, we will generally continue to write the IS curve as $\tilde{Y}_t = \bar{a} - \bar{b}(R_t - \bar{r})$, while recognizing that $\bar{a}$ and $\bar{b}$ may be larger than the underlying aggregate demand and investment parameters because of multiplier effects.

---

[8] That is, suppose $\bar{b} = 1/2$ and the real interest rate R rises by 2 percentage points. In the original formulation of the IS curve, output would fall by 1 percent. With the multiplier, it falls by 1.5 percent.

[9] Suppose a shock reduces $\bar{a}$ by 1 percentage point. The direct effect is to reduce output by 1 percentage point. But from our new consumption equation (11.15), when output is reduced by 1 percentage point, this leads consumption to fall by $\bar{x}$ percentage points. This in turn reduces output by another $\bar{x}$ percentage points. So the total effect on output at this point is $1 + \bar{x}$ percentage points, larger than the original 1 unit shock. But the extra $\bar{x}$ unit reduction in output reduces consumption further, so that output is reduced again, and so on. The general pattern is something like this:

$$\downarrow \tilde{Y} \Rightarrow \downarrow C \Rightarrow \downarrow \tilde{Y} \Rightarrow \downarrow C \Rightarrow \ldots$$

In other words, we get something like a "vicious circle." Mathematically, the sum of all these effects is $1 + \bar{x} + \bar{x}^2 + \bar{x}^3 + \ldots$ But this is just the geometric series, which adds up to $1/(1 - \bar{x})$. And this is our multiplier.

Investment

There are two main determinants of investment at the firm level, both of which appear in the simple investment equation (11.7). The first is the gap between the real interest rate and the marginal product of capital. If a semiconductor manufacturing company has a high return on capital relative to the real interest rate that prevails in financial markets, then building an additional fabrication plant will be profitable; the firm will increase its investment.

An important issue faced by the firm is how to calculate this return on capital. In a simple model, the return is just the marginal product of capital net of depreciation; just such an example was given in Chapter 5, in connection with the Solow model. A richer framework may also include corporate income taxes, investment tax credits, and depreciation allowances. Intuitively, such taxes and subsidies have to be taken into account when computing the rate of return.[10]

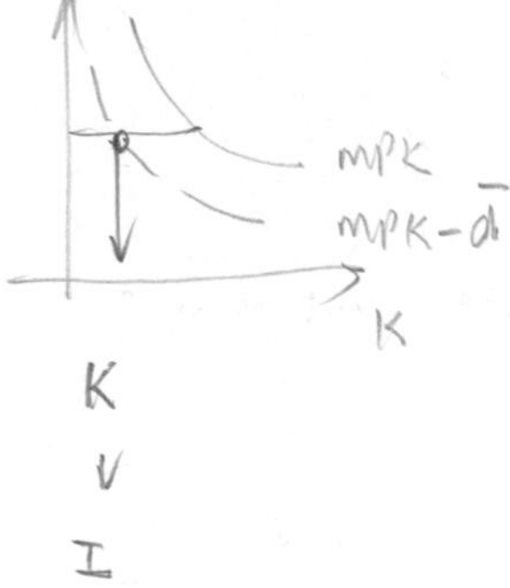

The second main determinant of investment is a firm's **cash flow**,[11] the amount of internal resources the company has on hand after paying its expenses. A firm with a high cash flow finds it easy to finance additional investment, while a firm with a low cash flow may be forced to borrow in financial markets. It's generally more expensive for firms to borrow to finance investment than it is to use their own internal funds, because of what are known as "agency problems."

Agency problems, studied extensively in microeconomics, occur when one party in a transaction holds information that the other party does not possess. For example, a firm may know that its niche in the industry is particularly vulnerable over the coming year, so it will want to borrow: if the firm does well that year, it can pay back the loan, but if it fails, it can declare bankruptcy. This is a problem of **adverse selection**. Alternatively, after a firm borrows a large sum of money, it may engage in particularly risky investments, again knowing that if the investments succeed, the firm will make lots of money, while if they fail, the firm can declare bankruptcy. This is a problem of **moral hazard**. Knowing these potential problems exist, banks and other lenders to a firm will be careful how they lend and at what rate.

Although it may not be apparent at first, our baseline equation for investment (11.7) does include a term that captures some of these cash flow considerations. If we rewrite the equation as

$$I_t = \bar{a}_i \bar{Y}_t - \bar{b}(R_t - \bar{r})\bar{Y}_t, \tag{11.17}$$

the cash flow effect can be seen in the presence of potential output $\bar{Y}_t$. The aggregate cash flow in the collection of firms in the economy is probably related to potential output, so this is a useful place to start. We might do better by adding another term that involves short-run output $\tilde{Y}_t$. If you think about it carefully, you may realize that this would be another way to incorporate a multiplier in our

[10]Exactly how government policies affect investment was studied by Robert E. Hall and Dale Jorgenson in "Tax Policy and Investment Behavior," *American Economic Review*, vol. 57 (June 1967), pp. 391–414.

[11]The importance of cash flow for investment spending was emphasized by Steven Fazzari, Glenn Hubbard, and Bruce Petersen in "Financing Constraints and Corporate Investment," *Brookings Papers on Economic Activity* (1988), pp. 141–95.

model, much like the $1/(1 - \bar{x})$ multiplier in equation (11.16). In the end, we are left with an IS curve that takes the same basic form as the original, but that provides another justification for multiplier effects.

Government Purchases

Government purchases of goods and services affect short-run economic activity in two ways: as a shock that can function as a source of fluctuations and as a policy instrument that can be used to reduce fluctuations.

As we saw in Chapter 2, the government is an important source of demand for goods and services in the economy. In the United States, for example, government purchases account for about 20 percent of GDP in recent years. Fluctuations in this share—because of changes in military expenditures during wartime, say, or because of an increase in spending engineered by Congress before an election—can produce significant effects on the economy. Such fluctuations are naturally captured as a temporary change in $\bar{a}_g$ in the baseline equation (11.4).

Some government purchases are discretionary. The government may use this discretion to expand fiscal policy when shocks have caused the IS curve to shift back, in an effort to restore the demand for goods and services back to potential output. For example, it can decide when to build more highways or schools and when to hire more firefighters and economists. The government may also choose to increase $\bar{a}_g$ in response to another shock that would otherwise push the economy into a recession.

A canonical example of discretionary fiscal policy is the American Recovery and Reinvestment Act of 2009. This \$797-billion fiscal stimulus bill, enacted shortly after President Obama took office, featured a wide range of spending measures, including spending on highways, education, and research and development, as well as grants to state governments.

Discretionary fiscal policy is not limited to purchases of goods and services, however. Another instrument available on the fiscal side is tax rates. For example, in 1961 President Kennedy established the investment tax credit, in which the government provides a temporary offset to taxes that corporations pay for every dollar they invest. This credit can lead firms to invest today instead of in the future, potentially raising $\bar{a}_i$, and it has been used by several administrations since then when faced with a slack economy. As another example, in June 2001 President Bush signed the Economic Growth and Tax Relief Reconciliation Act into law, cutting personal income tax rates by several percentage points. While the rationale for these tax cuts had more to do with long-term issues, the tax cuts themselves were enacted when the economy was in a recession and played a role in strengthening the economy over the next year.

An alternative and increasingly important fiscal instrument is transfer spending, in which the government transfers resources away from some individuals and toward others. Many of these transfers automatically increase when the economy goes into a recession. For instance, the unemployment insurance program naturally becomes more important when the economy weakens, helping to mitigate the decline in income faced by people when they lose their job. Spending on welfare programs and Medicaid also increases automatically. Because the additional spending provided by these programs occurs automatically and because they generally help stabilize the economy, these spending mechanisms are known as **automatic stabilizers**.

The impact of fiscal policy on the economy depends crucially on two additional considerations. First, there is the problem of timing. Discretionary changes such as programs to put people to work building highways or investment tax credits are often put in place only with considerable delay: legislation must be drafted, enacted by Congress, and approved by the executive branch. By the time the policy is in place, the shock it was designed to mitigate may have passed.

The second consideration is more subtle but important. As we have seen, the government faces a budget constraint, just like any household or firm. If it decides to increase spending today, then either it must reduce spending in the future or it must raise taxes at some point to pay for the higher spending. It's subject to what is often called **the no-free-lunch principle**: higher spending today must be paid for, if not today then at some point in the future. But clearly the additional taxes or the reduction in future spending serves as a drag that offsets at least some of the positive impact on the economy of a fiscal stimulus today.

This consideration can be illustrated in a simple example. Suppose the government decides to improve the highway system and increases government purchases by \$500 million. On the one hand, this shows up as an increase in $\bar{a}_g$ and therefore an increase in G_t. But the no-free-lunch discipline imposed by the government's budget constraint means that this increased spending must be paid for somehow: the government can increase taxes by \$500 million today or borrow the money today and repay it (plus interest) in the future. When it repays in the future, it must raise taxes to cover the initial \$500 million plus the interest.

According to the permanent-income hypothesis, what matters for your consumption today is the present discounted value of your lifetime income, after taxes. In this case, the present value of your lifetime income doesn't depend on whether the government collects the taxes this year or next year; it will be lower in either case. So consumption should also be lower, perhaps completely offsetting the increased government spending. The notion that what matters for consumption is the present value of what the government takes from consumers rather than the specific timing of the taxes is called **Ricardian equivalence**.[12]

On the other hand, it could be that the increased highway spending today is simply a change in the timing of spending—so that future highway spending will be reduced. In this case, the new spending doesn't involve an increased tax burden; it's much like the change in the timing of investment spending produced by the investment tax credit. Permanent (after-tax) income would not change, so neither would consumption. The increased demand for goods today by the government would therefore stimulate the economy.

As an empirical matter, if the government increases its purchases by \$100 billion today, what is the net effect on the position of the IS curve? The honest answer is that it depends—on exactly how the change in spending today is

[12] David Ricardo, writing in *On the Principles of Political Economy and Taxation* in 1817, was one of the first economists to recognize this possibility. Robert Barro of Harvard University formalized similar insights in "Are Government Bonds Net Wealth?" *Journal of Political Economy*, vol. 82, no. 6 (November–December 1974), pp. 1095–1117.

expected to be financed, on how well this financing is understood, and on the state of the economy. Most economists accept the following characterization of the effects of fiscal policy. First, an increase in government purchases financed by an increase in taxes of the same amount will have a modest positive impact on the IS curve, raising output by a small amount in the short run. Second, an increase in spending today financed by an unspecified change in taxes and/or spending at some future date will shift the IS curve out by a moderate amount, perhaps by as much as 50 cents for each dollar increase in spending. Third, these effects can be even larger during a recession, when a significant fraction of an economy's resources are underutilized. In that case, a reasonable estimate is that the IS curve shifts out by between 75 cents and a dollar for each dollar of spending. Unfortunately, substantial uncertainty surrounding the precise magnitude of the short-run effects of fiscal policy remains. One example of this uncertainty is given in the next case study.[13]

The difficulty of getting the timing right and the discipline imposed by the no-free-lunch principle of the government budget constraint serve to limit the use of discretionary fiscal policy in practice, except in severe situations.

CASE STUDY

The Macroeconomic Effects of the American Recovery and Reinvestment Act of 2009

When this $797-billion fiscal stimulus program was passed in 2009, economists offered a wide range of opinions about how successful the program would be. Some economists, like Christina Romer, the chair of President Obama's Council of Economic Advisers, suggested that the effects would be large, in part because the economy was in a deep recession, when one might suspect the effects of fiscal policy would be greatest. Others, such as Robert Barro of Harvard University and John Taylor of Stanford University, were more skeptical, emphasizing the offsetting negative effect of future tax increases.

Figure 11.6 shows the analysis of the American Recovery and Reinvestment Act of 2009 (ARRA) put forward by the Congressional Budget Office (CBO) in February 2009. The CBO is a highly regarded, nonpartisan part of the federal government that advises Congress on spending and tax issues. The CBO analysis shows forecasts for the unemployment rate under various scenarios. In the absence of a stimulus package, the CBO suggested that the unemployment rate would peak at 9.0 percent and then decline slowly over the next five years.

[13] The effects may be even larger when the nominal interest rate is "stuck" at zero—the so-called "zero lower bound"; see Chapter 14. For an excellent overview of the effects of fiscal policy in the short run, see Alan J. Auerbach and William G. Gale, "Discretionary Fiscal Policy," *Journal of Economic Perspectives*, forthcoming.

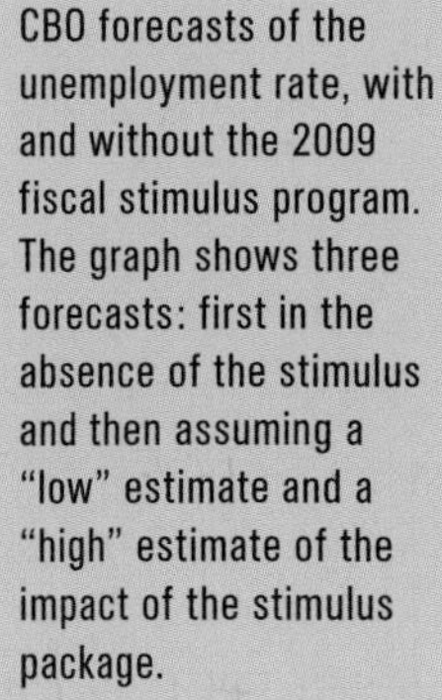
CBO forecasts of the unemployment rate, with and without the 2009 fiscal stimulus program. The graph shows three forecasts: first in the absence of the stimulus and then assuming a "low" estimate and a "high" estimate of the impact of the stimulus package.

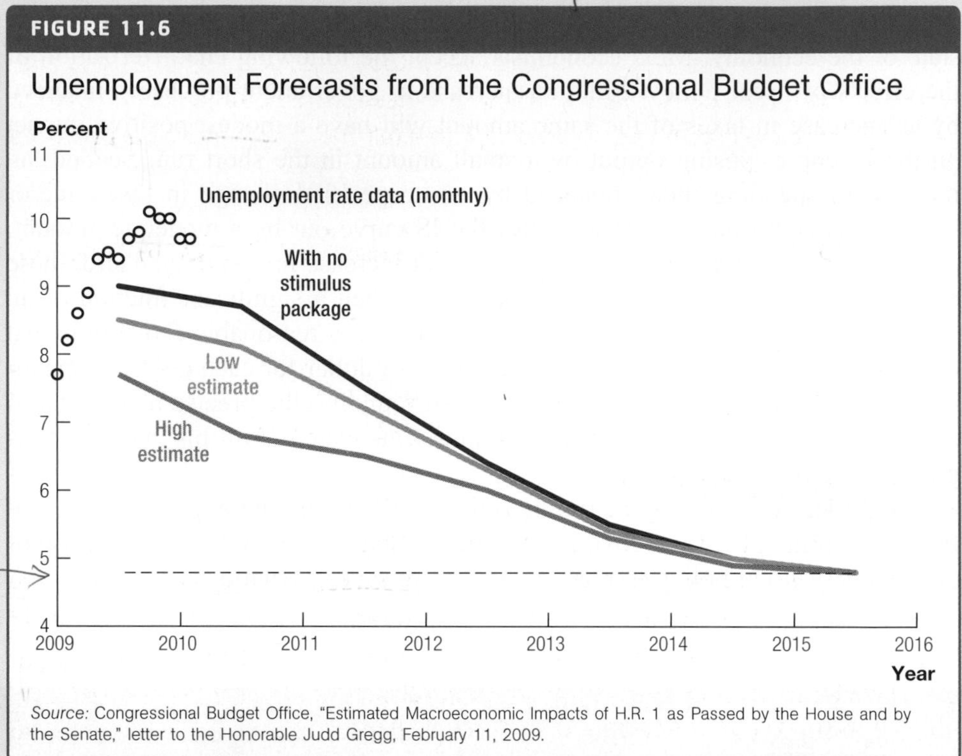

Source: Congressional Budget Office, "Estimated Macroeconomic Impacts of H.R. 1 as Passed by the House and by the Senate," letter to the Honorable Judd Gregg, February 11, 2009.

The CBO then also provided two forecasts including the impact of the stimulus—a "low estimate" based on pessimistic assumptions about the short-run effects of fiscal policy, and a "high estimate" based on optimistic assumptions. Notice that even in the best-case scenario, the recession was projected to be long and deep, with unemployment remaining high for several years. Nevertheless, the fiscal stimulus was estimated to improve the economy substantially relative to the case of no stimulus package.

There is one other piece of data shown in Figure 11.6—the actual unemployment rate—and its behavior is quite remarkable. The observed path of the unemployment rate generally lies *above* even the "no stimulus package" estimates of the CBO. For example, the average unemployment rate in 2009 was about 9.3 percent, whereas the CBO estimate in the case of no stimulus was only 9.0 percent.

What should we make of this discrepancy? Unfortunately, the answer is not clear. It could be that the fiscal stimulus was much less effective than expected, supporting the case made by opponents of the stimulus. Alternatively, it could be that the basic forecasts of the path of the unemployment rate in the absence of the stimulus were too optimistic. Maybe the fiscal stimulus had relatively large effects on unemployment, and the unemployment rate would have been even higher absent the legislation.

A final point on the American Recovery and Reinvestment Act worth mentioning is that when this package was proposed and enacted during the early months of 2009, there was enormous uncertainty about the macroeconomic consequences of the financial crisis. A severe economic depression, with unemployment rising well above 10 percent and GDP declining by 10 percent was a distinct possibility. One of the key purposes of the ARRA was to reassure households and businesses that policy makers were prepared to do whatever it took to avoid this worst-case scenario. While it is difficult to quantify exactly to what extent the ARRA contributed to reducing the sense that the economy was in free fall, this may in fact have been one of its most important accomplishments.

CASE STUDY

Fiscal Policy and Depressions

The most famous example of U.S. discretionary fiscal policy is the New Deal program put in place during the Great Depression. Between 1929 and 1934, the share of government purchases in the economy expanded sharply from 9 percent to 16 percent. This discretionary policy was followed by an enormous expansion in military expenditures during World War II, which raised the share of government purchases to 48 percent—a dramatic increase in demand that led the economy to boom. In fact, as shown back in Figure 1.6 of Chapter 1, output rose substantially above potential, reaching a peak in 1945.

As a counterexample, consider the case of Japan during the last two decades. The Japanese economy experienced rapid growth for several decades following World War II. However, this exceptional performance screeched to a halt in 1990. In an unprecedented turnaround, the stock market in Japan declined by 60 percent between December 1989 and August 1992. And a real estate bubble that in 1991 valued the land under the emperor's palace—an area less than a square mile—at the same amount as all the land in California gradually burst during the following years.[14] Whereas between 1960 and 1990 per capita GDP grew at an average annual rate of 5.4 percent, between 1990 and 2000 this growth rate slowed to only slightly more than 1 percent.

One response by the Japanese government to this tremendous slowdown in growth was a large fiscal expansion: government spending as a share of GDP rose from 32 percent in 1990 to 38 percent in 2000. The expansion was financed primarily by increased borrowing, and Japan saw its small budget surplus in 1990 change to large budget deficits in the early 2000s that reached 8 percent of GDP. This policy does not appear to have been successful at pulling the Japanese economy out of its slump, perhaps in part because of the perceived future tax burden associated with the fiscal expansion.

[14] The facts about the stock market and real estate values are taken from Douglas Stone and William Ziemba, "Land and Stock Prices in Japan," *Journal of Economic Perspectives,* vol. 7, no. 3 (1993), pp. 149–65.

Net Exports

In deriving the IS curve, we specified simple demand functions, equations (11.5) and (11.6), for exports and imports: both are a constant fraction of potential output. This means that net exports, $EX - IM$, are also a constant fraction of potential output. Another name for net exports is the trade balance. If net exports are positive, the economy exports more than it imports and runs a trade surplus. Conversely, if imports are larger, the economy imports more than it exports and there is a trade deficit.

The trade balance is the main way that economies throughout the rest of the world influence U.S. economic activity in the short run. An increase in the demand for U.S. goods in the rest of the world—an increase in $\bar{a}_{ex}$—stimulates the U.S. economy by shifting the IS curve out. On the other hand, if Americans divert some of their demand away from U.S. goods and toward foreign goods by demanding more imports (an increase in $\bar{a}_{im}$), this shifts the IS curve back in, reducing output below potential. These basic mechanisms are at work in our short-run model.

Other issues related to exports and imports won't be touched on here. For example, as discussed in Chapter 2, the U.S. economy has been running a sizable trade deficit in recent years. What are the medium-run implications of this deficit for the economy? How do exchange rates fit into our short-run model? These more general issues will be discussed in detail in Chapters 18 and 19.

11.6 Conclusion

In this chapter, we've derived one of the key building blocks of our short-run model: the IS curve. This relationship tells us how and why changes in the real interest rate affect economic activity in the short run. As we saw, the key mechanism works through investment. Higher interest rates raise the cost of borrowing to firms and households and reduce the demand for investment spending; firms reduce their business investment, and consumers reduce their housing investment. Through multiplier effects, these changes can affect the economy more broadly, for example by leading to reductions in consumption.

In Chapter 12, we study how the central bank controls the real interest rate in the short run. Through the IS curve, we will then understand how the Federal Reserve can influence the level of GDP in the short run. Once we combine this insight with the Phillips curve, we will essentially have completed our development of the short-run model.

CHAPTER REVIEW

SUMMARY

1. The IS curve describes how output in the short run depends on the real interest rate and on shocks to aggregate demand.

2. When the real interest rate rises, the cost of borrowing faced by firms and households increases, leading them to delay their purchases of new equipment, factories, and housing. These delays reduce the level of investment, which in turn lowers output below potential. Therefore, the IS curve shows a negative relationship between output and the real interest rate.
3. Shocks to aggregate demand can shift the IS curve. These shocks include (a) changes in consumption relative to potential output, (b) technological improvements that stimulate investment demand given the current interest rate, (c) changes in government purchases relative to potential output, and (d) interactions between the domestic and foreign economies that affect exports and imports.
4. The life-cycle/permanent-income hypothesis says that individual consumption depends on average income over time rather than current income. This serves as the underlying justification for why we assume consumption depends on potential output.
5. The permanent-income theory does not seem to hold exactly, however, and consumption responds to temporary movements in income as well. When we include this effect in our IS curve, a multiplier term appears. That is, a shock that reduces the aggregate demand parameter by 1 percentage point may have an even larger effect on short-run output because the initial reduction in output causes consumption to fall, which further reduces output.
6. A consideration of the microfoundations of the equations that underlie the IS curve reveals important subtleties. The most important are associated with the no-free-lunch principle imposed by the government's budget constraint. The direct effect of changes in government purchases is to change $\bar{a}_g$. However, depending on how these purchases are financed, they can also affect consumption and investment, partially mitigating the effects of fiscal policy on short-run output.

KEY CONCEPTS

adverse selection
aggregate demand shock
automatic stabilizers
cash flow
the IS curve
the life-cycle/permanent-income hypothesis of consumption
moral hazard
multiplier effects
the no-free-lunch principle
permanent income
Ricardian equivalence

REVIEW QUESTIONS

1. What role does the IS curve play in our short-run model? What kind of economic questions does it allow us to analyze?
2. Why does the IS curve slope downward?
3. What are some examples of changes in the economy that would lead to movements along the IS curve? What are some changes that would shift the IS curve?

4. For the development of the rest of the short-run model in the next two chapters, we could just present the equation for the IS curve, $\tilde{Y}_t = \bar{a} - \bar{b}(R_t - \bar{r})$, and omit the six equations and six unknowns that allowed us to derive the curve. Why, however, do you think the underlying setup of the economy might prove useful?

5. What are three insights you gained from studying the microfoundations of the IS curve?

6. Why is the relationship between output and the real interest rate called the "IS curve"?

EXERCISES

smartwork.wwnorton.com 

1. **Calculations with the IS curve:** Suppose the parameters of the IS curve are $\bar{a} = 0$, $\bar{b} = 3/4$, $\bar{r} = 2\%$ and the real interest rate is initially $R = 2\%$. Explain what happens to short-run output in each of the following scenarios (consider each separately):
   - **(a)** The real interest rate rises from 2% to 4%.
   - **(b)** The real interest rate falls from 2% to 1%.
   - **(c)** $\bar{a}_c$ increases by 1 percentage point.
   - **(d)** $\bar{a}_g$ decreases by 2 percentage points.
   - **(e)** $\bar{a}_{im}$ decreases by 2 percentage points.

2. **Analyzing macroeconomic events with the IS curve (I):** Consider the following changes in the macroeconomy. Show how to think about them using the IS curve, and explain how and why GDP is affected in the short run.
   - **(a)** The Federal Reserve undertakes policy actions that have the effect of lowering the real interest rate below the marginal product of capital. (We will learn how this can occur in Chapter 12.)
   - **(b)** Consumers become pessimistic about the state of the economy and future productivity growth.
   - **(c)** Improvements in information technology increase productivity and therefore increase the marginal product of capital.

3. **Analyzing macroeconomic events with the IS curve (II):** Consider the following changes in the macroeconomy. Show how to think about them using the IS curve, and explain how and why GDP is affected in the short run.
   - **(a)** The government offers a temporary investment tax credit: for each dollar of investment that firms undertake, they receive a credit that reduces the taxes they pay on corporate income.
   - **(b)** A booming economy in Europe this year leads to an unexpected increase in the demand by European consumers for U.S. goods.
   - **(c)** U.S. consumers develop an infatuation with all things made in New Zealand and sharply increase their imports from that country.
   - **(d)** A housing bubble bursts, so that housing prices fall by 20% and new home sales drop sharply.

4. **Government purchases:** Suppose Congress and the president decide to increase government purchases today, say for national defense. Explain how this affects the IS curve. How does your answer depend on the way in which the spending is financed and on the extent to which Ricardian equivalence holds?

5. **Social Security transfers:** Suppose the government announces an increase in Social Security transfers. Which aggregate demand parameter is affected? How and why is it affected? How does this increase affect the graph of the IS curve? How does your answer depend on the way in which the spending is financed and on the extent to which Ricardian equivalence holds?

6. **Natural disasters:** Suppose a large earthquake destroys many houses and buildings on the West Coast, but fortunately results in little loss of life. Show how to think about this event using the IS curve. Explain how actual output, potential output, and short-run output are affected in the short run, and why.

7. **Consumption and the multiplier:** Show how to derive an IS curve that includes the consumption multiplier. That is, show how to derive equation (11.16). Draw a graph of the original IS curve and the IS curve that includes the multiplier. Which one is flatter, and why?

8. **Imports and the multiplier:** The amount of goods that the U.S. economy imports might depend on the current state of the economy as well as on potential GDP: for example, when the economy is booming, imports usually rise. To incorporate this channel into the model, suppose the import equation is given by

$$\frac{IM_t}{\bar{Y}_t} = \bar{a}_{im} + \bar{n}\tilde{Y}_t.$$

Assume the remainder of the model is unchanged from the original setup, as in Table 11.1.

(a) Derive the IS curve for this new specification.

(b) What is the economic explanation for why the $\bar{n}$ parameter shows up in the denominator of the new IS curve? Notice that an aggregate demand shock that increases $\bar{a}$ by 1 percentage point now has a *smaller* effect on output than it did in the original IS curve. Why?

9. **Consumption and the real interest rate:** According to the life-cycle/permanent-income hypothesis, consumption depends on the present discounted value of income. An increase in the real interest rate will make future income worth less, thereby reducing the present discounted value and reducing consumption. To incorporate this channel into the model, suppose the consumption equation is given by

$$C_t = \bar{a}_c\bar{Y}_t - \bar{b}_c(R_t - \bar{r})\bar{Y}_t.$$

Assume the remainder of the model is unchanged from the original setup, as in Table 11.1.

(a) Derive the IS curve for this new specification.

(b) How and why does it differ from the original IS curve? (*Hint*: Think about the slope of the IS curve.)

10. The permanent-income theory of consumption: According to the permanent-income hypothesis, how does your consumption change in each of the following scenarios? (The first question is answered for you.) To keep things simple, suppose the interest rate is 10% and you will live forever. Feel free to give answers that involve approximations.

(a) A distant aunt that you never knew dies and leaves you \$100,000 in her will. *Answer: Consumption rises today and in the future by a constant amount, equal to the "permanent-income equivalent" of the \$100,000. Since you live forever, you can raise your consumption by the amount of interest earned on the bequest. So consumption rises in every period by 0.10 × \$100,000 = \$10,000.*[15]

(b) You receive an unexpected promotion today that raises your income permanently by \$5,000 per year.

(c) To balance its budget, the government levies a one-time tax this year that costs you \$10,000.

(d) You win a lottery, which pays you a one-time amount of \$10 million today.

(e) You win a different lottery, which pays you a one-time amount of \$10 million, but the payment is made 5 years from now.

WORKED EXERCISES

2. Analyzing macroeconomic events with the IS curve (I): To get started, recall the equation for the IS curve:

$$\tilde{Y}_t = \bar{a} - \bar{b}(R_t - \bar{r}).$$

(a) When the Federal Reserve reduces the real interest rate so that it falls below the marginal product of capital, this is a movement along the IS curve. The result is shown in Figure 11.7. Because firms can borrow at a rate below the marginal product of capital, investment is stimulated, causing short-run output to increase as the economy moves from point *A* to point *B*.

(b) In our model, consumers' becoming pessimistic about the future of the economy can be represented as a decline in $\bar{a}_c$, which reduces the aggregate demand parameter $\bar{a}$. The reduction causes the IS curve to shift back, as shown in Figure 11.8. If we hold the real interest rate constant, this reduction in aggregate demand leads output to fall in the short run, from point *A* to point *B*. In fact, output falls one-for-one with the aggregate demand shock, so if $\bar{a}_c$ falls by 2 percentage points, then so does short-run output.

---

[15] Notice that this is only an approximation: the present discounted value of an annual flow of \$10,000 starting from today is actually \$100,000 × (1 + *R*) if *R* is the interest rate, so \$10,000 per year is a little high. If interest were compounded continuously instead of annually, the \$10,000 answer would be exactly correct.

FIGURE 11.7

A Reduction in the Real Interest Rate

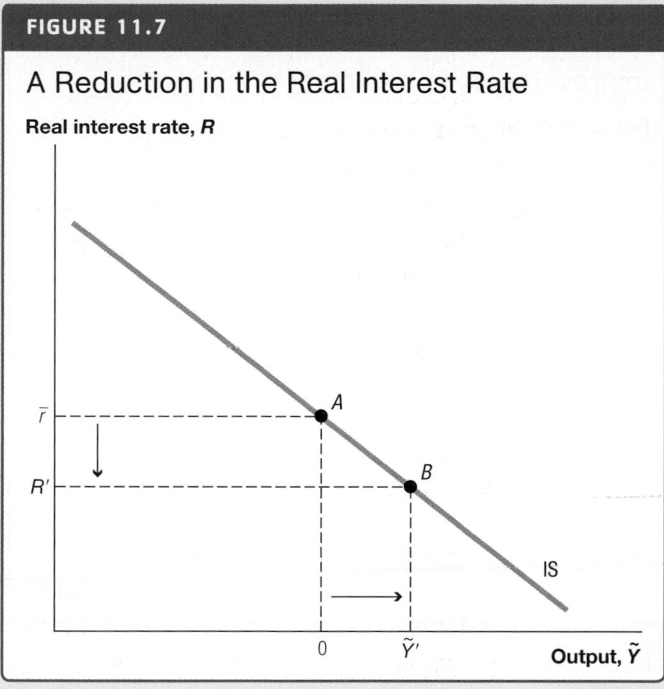

(c) Improvements in information technology cause the marginal product of capital $\bar{r}$ to increase. After this occurs, the real interest rate is lower than the marginal product of capital. This means firms wish to borrow at the low interest rate to take advantage of the high marginal product of capital, so investment demand goes up, stimulating the economy.

(b)

FIGURE 11.8

Pessimistic Consumers

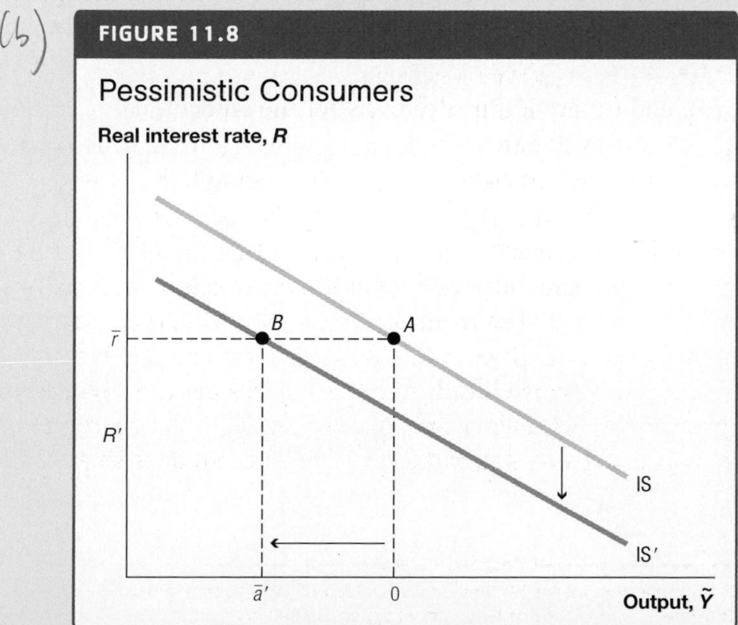

(c)

FIGURE 11.9

Improvements in Information Technology

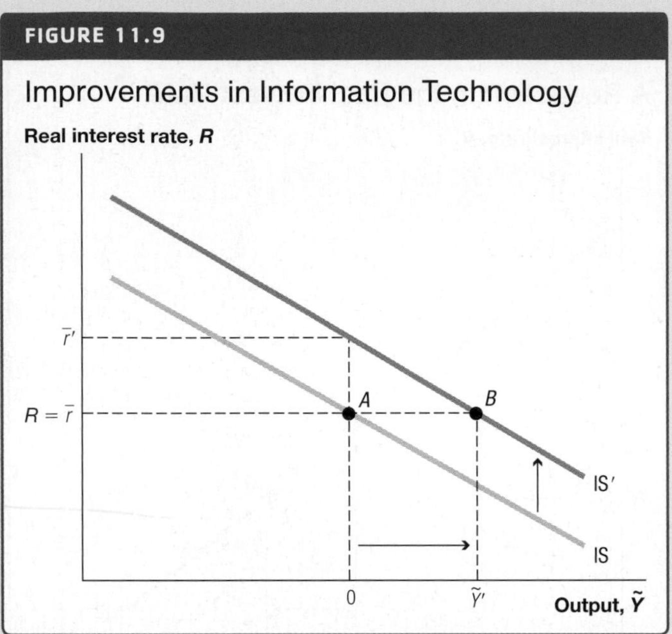

As shown in Figure 11.9, short-run output $\tilde{Y}$ is zero at the point where the real interest rate is $\bar{r}$. Since $\bar{r}$ increases, this means the IS curve shifts up, and the economy moves from point *A* to point *B*.

10. The permanent-income theory of consumption:

(a) Answer given in exercise.

(b) This one should be relatively easy. Consumption rises today and in the future by a constant amount. How much? Your income has gone up by $5,000 per year, so your consumption rises by this same amount each year.

Parts (c), (d), and (e) are left as exercises for the student.

CHAPTER 12

MONETARY POLICY AND THE PHILLIPS CURVE

OVERVIEW

In this chapter, we learn

- how the central bank effectively sets the real interest rate in the short run, and how this rate shows up as the MP curve in our short-run model.
- that the Phillips curve describes how firms set their prices over time, pinning down the inflation rate.
- how the IS curve, the MP curve, and the Phillips curve make up our short-run model.
- how to analyze the evolution of the macroeconomy—output, inflation, and interest rates—in response to changes in policy or economic shocks.

Our mission, as set forth by the Congress, is a critical one: to preserve price stability, to foster maximum sustainable growth in output and employment, and to promote a stable and efficient financial system that serves all Americans well and fairly.

—BEN S. BERNANKE

12.1 Introduction

How does a central bank go about achieving the lofty goals summarized by Chairman Bernanke in the quotation above? This question becomes even more puzzling when we realize that the main policy tool used by the Federal Reserve is a humble interest rate called **the federal funds rate**. The fed funds rate, as it is often known, is the interest rate paid from one bank to another for overnight loans. How does this very short-term nominal interest rate, used only between banks, have the power to shake financial markets, alter medium-term investment plans, and change GDP in the largest economy in the world?

Recall that the IS curve describes how the real interest rate determines output. So far, we have acted as if policymakers can pick the level of the real interest rate. This chapter introduces the "MP curve," where MP stands for "monetary policy." This curve describes how the central bank sets the nominal interest rate and then exploits the fact that real and nominal interest rates move closely together in the short run. We then revisit the Phillips curve (first introduced in Chapter 9), which describes how short-run output influences inflation over time.

The short-run model consists of these three building blocks, as summarized in Figure 12.1. Through the MP curve, the nominal interest rate set by the central bank determines the real interest rate in the economy. Through the IS curve, the real interest rate then influences GDP in the short run. Finally, the Phillips curve describes how economic fluctuations like booms and recessions affect the evolution of inflation. By the end of the chapter, we will therefore have a complete theory of how shocks to the economy can cause booms and recessions, how these booms and recessions alter the rate of inflation, and how policymakers can hope to influence economic activity and inflation.

The outline for this chapter closely follows the approach taken in Chapter 11. After adding the MP curve and the Phillips curve to our short-run model, we combine these elements to study one of the key episodes in U.S. macroeconomics during the last 30 years, the Volcker disinflation of the 1980s. In the last part of the chapter, we step back to consider the microfoundations for the MP curve and the Phillips curve, helping us to better understand these building blocks of the short-run model.[1]

Epigraph: Upon being sworn in as chair of the Federal Reserve, February 6, 2006.

[1] The MP curve building block is a recent addition to the study of economic fluctuations and is advocated by David Romer, "Keynesian Macroeconomics without the LM Curve," *Journal of Economic Perspectives*, vol. 14 (Spring 2000), pp. 149–69. Formal microfoundations for the short-run model have been developed in detail in recent years. See Michael Woodford, *Interest and Prices* (Princeton, N.J.: Princeton University Press, 2003), for a detailed and somewhat advanced discussion.

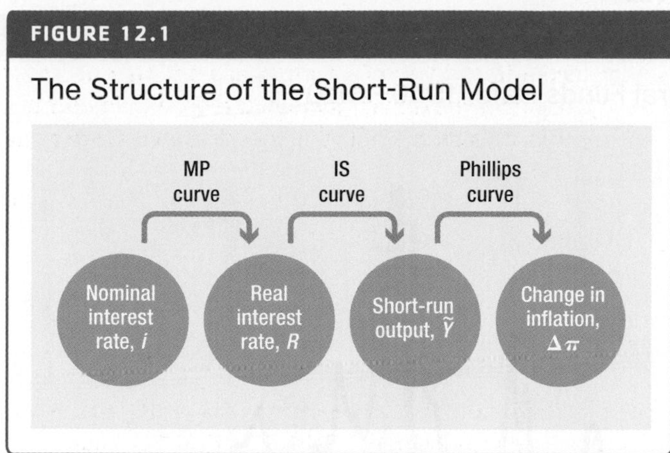

FIGURE 12.1
The Structure of the Short-Run Model

For the most part, this chapter studies conventional monetary policy. That is, the chapter considers how the central bank influences the economy during the usual course of booms and recessions by adjusting its target interest rate. In Chapter 14, we will see that such conventional policy was a crucial part of the Fed's response to the financial crisis of 2007–2009. The severity of that crisis, however, prompted the Fed to pursue unconventional policies as well. We tackle these different approaches in turn. This chapter (and the next) analyzes the state-of-the-art view of conventional monetary policy as it has been applied in the past and as it will surely be applied in the future. Chapter 14 then considers the unconventional policy actions the Fed undertook during the financial crisis and the Great Recession.

12.2 The MP Curve: Monetary Policy and Interest Rates

In many of the advanced economies of the world today, the key instrument of monetary policy is a short-run nominal interest rate, known in the United States as the fed funds rate. Since 1999, the European Central Bank has been in charge of monetary policy for the countries in the European Monetary Union, which include most countries in Western Europe (the exceptions being Great Britain and some of the Scandinavian countries). Monetary policy with respect to the euro, the currency of the Monetary Union, is set in terms of a couple of key short-term interest rates.

Figure 12.2 plots monthly data on the fed funds rate since 1960. The fed funds rate shows tremendous variation, ranging from a low of essentially zero during the recent financial crisis to a high of nearly 20 percent in 1981.

How does the Federal Reserve control the level of the fed funds rate? One way to think about the answer is given below; a more precise explanation is provided in Section 12.6. For a number of reasons, large banks and financial institutions routinely lend to and borrow from one another from one business day to the next

The fed funds rate has fluctuated enormously over the last 50 years, ranging from its recent lows of nearly zero to a high of nearly 20 percent during 1981.

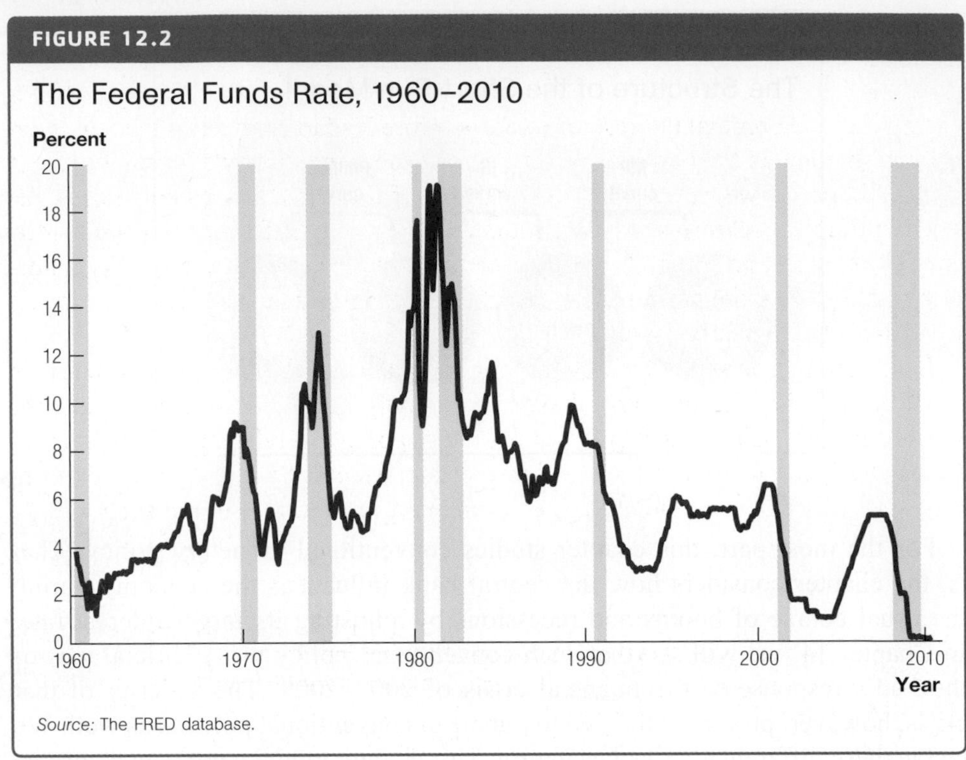

FIGURE 12.2

The Federal Funds Rate, 1960–2010

Source: The FRED database.

through the Fed. In order to set the nominal interest rate on these overnight loans, the central bank states that it is willing to borrow or lend any amount at a specified rate. Clearly, no bank can charge more than this rate on its overnight loans—other banks would just borrow at the lower rate from the central bank.

But what if the Bank of Cheap Loans tries to charge an even lower rate? Well, other banks would immediately borrow at this lower rate and lend back to the central bank at the higher rate: this is a pure profit opportunity (sometimes called an *arbitrage opportunity*). Whatever limited resources the Bank of Cheap Loans has would immediately be exhausted, so this lower rate could not persist. The central bank's willingness to borrow and lend at a specified rate pins down the overnight rate.

In Chapter 11, however, we saw that it's the real interest rate that affects the level of economic activity. For example, it is the real interest rate that enters the IS curve and determines the level of output in the short run. How, then, does the central bank use the nominal interest rate to influence the real rate?

From Nominal to Real Interest Rates

The link between real and nominal interest rates is summarized in the Fisher equation, which we encountered in Chapter 8. The equation states that the nominal interest rate is equal to the sum of the real interest rate R_t and the rate of inflation π_t:

$$i_t = R_t + \pi_t. \tag{12.1}$$

Rearranging this equation to solve for the real interest rate, we have

$$R_t = i_t - \pi_t. \tag{12.2}$$

Changes in the nominal interest rate will therefore lead to changes in the real interest rate as long as they are not offset by corresponding changes in inflation.

At this point, we make a key assumption of the short-run model, called **the sticky inflation assumption**: we assume that the rate of inflation displays inertia, or stickiness, so that it adjusts slowly over time. In the very short run—say within 6 months or so—we assume that the rate of inflation does not respond directly to changes in monetary policy.

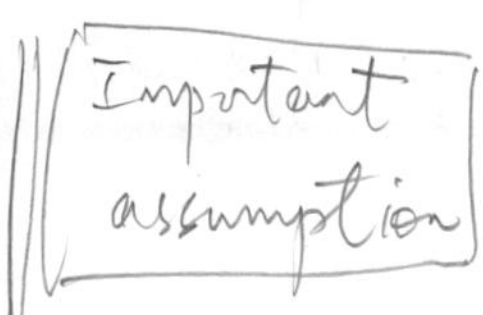

This assumption of sticky inflation is a crucial one, to be discussed below in Section 12.5. For the moment, though, we simply consider its implications, the most important being that changes in monetary policy that alter the nominal interest rate lead to changes in the real interest rate. Practically speaking, this means that central banks have the ability to set the real interest rate in the short run.

CASE STUDY

Ex Ante and Ex Post Real Interest Rates

A more sophisticated version of the Fisher equation replaces the actual rate of inflation with expected inflation:

$$i_t = R_t + \pi_t^e$$

where π_t^e denotes the rate of inflation people expect to prevail over the course of year *t*.

Suppose you are an entrepreneur with a new investment opportunity: you have a plan for starting a new Web site that you believe will provide a real return over the coming year of 10 percent. At the start of the year, you can borrow funds to finance your Internet venture at a nominal interest rate of i_t. Should you undertake the investment? Well, the answer depends on what you *expect* the rate of inflation to be over the coming year, just as the Fisher equation suggests. The point is that you have to do the borrowing and investing before you know what rate of inflation prevails in the coming year, so it is the expected rate of inflation that affects your decision.

In principle, then, we could use the Fisher equation to calculate two different versions of the real interest rate. By subtracting expected inflation from the nominal interest rate, we get a measure of the *ex ante* real interest rate investors expect to prevail: $R_t^{ex\ ante} = i - \pi_t^e$. Alternatively, by subtracting the realized inflation rate from the nominal interest rate, we recover the *ex post* real interest rate that was actually realized: $R_t^{ex\ post} = i - \pi_t$. (*Ex ante* is Latin for "from before" and *ex post* for "from after.")

This distinction can be important in some circumstances. For example, as discussed above, investors use expected inflation when deciding which investments to undertake: as an Internet entrepreneur, you would compare $R_t^{ex\ ante}$ with the project's real return of 10 percent in deciding whether or not to make the investment. It is the *ex ante* real interest rate that is relevant for investment decisions. However, for our short-run model of the economy, this distinction is not crucial and will be ignored in what follows.

The IS-MP Diagram

We illustrate the central bank's ability to set the real interest rate with **the MP curve**, shown in Figure 12.3, which simply plots the real interest rate that the central bank chooses for the economy. In the graph, the central bank sets the real interest rate at the value R_t, and the MP curve is represented by a horizontal line.

The figure also plots the IS curve that we developed in Chapter 11. Together, these curves make up what we call **the IS-MP diagram**. As shown in the graph, when the real interest rate is set equal to the marginal product of capital $\bar{r}$, and when there are no aggregate demand shocks so $\bar{a} = 0$, short-run output is equal to zero. That is, the economy is at potential.

What happens if the central bank decides to raise the interest rate? Figure 12.4 illustrates the results of such a change. Because inflation is slow to adjust, an increase in the nominal interest rate raises the real interest rate. Since the real interest rate is now above the marginal product of capital, firms and households cut back on their investment, and output declines. This simple example shows the way in which the central bank can cause a recession.

The MP curve represents the choice of the real interest rate made by the central bank. In this graph, we've assumed the central bank sets the real interest rate equal to the marginal product of capital $\bar{r}$.

FIGURE 12.3

The MP Curve in the IS-MP Diagram

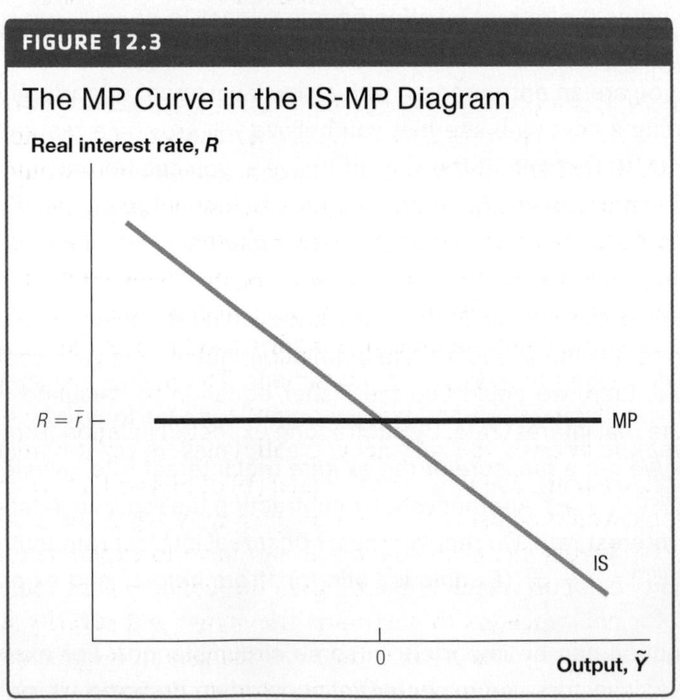

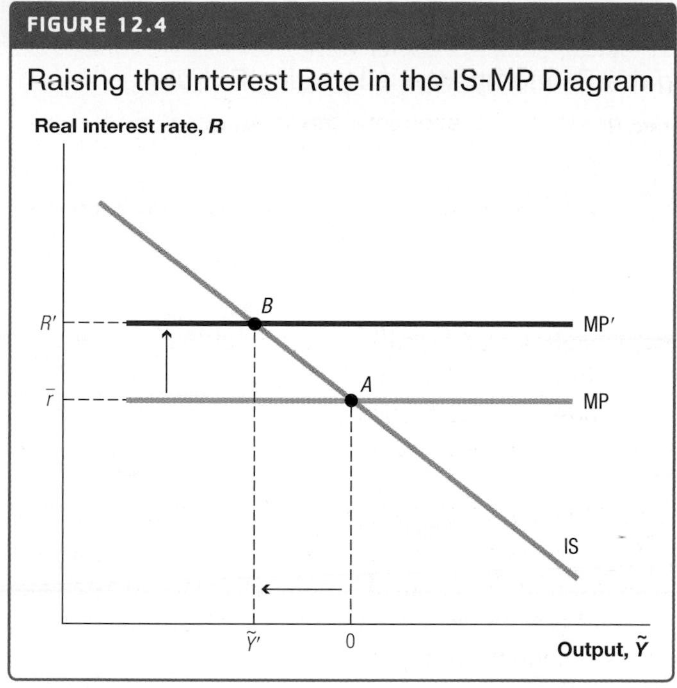

FIGURE 12.4

Raising the Interest Rate in the IS-MP Diagram

When the central bank raises the real interest rate, the economy enters a recession, moving from point *A* to point *B*.

Example: The End of a Housing Bubble

To see another example of how the IS-MP diagram works, let's consider the bursting of a housing bubble. Suppose that housing prices had been rising steadily for a number of years, but have suddenly declined sharply during the last year. Policymakers suspect that a housing bubble has now burst and fear that the decline in household wealth and consumer confidence will push the economy into a recession.

We might model this episode as a decline in the aggregate demand parameter $\bar{a}$ in the IS curve. As shown in Figure 12.5, this decline causes the IS curve to shift backward, so that at a given real interest rate the economy would move from its initial point *A* to a point *B*, where output is below potential and $\tilde{Y}$ is negative. (The -2% number shown in the graph is just chosen as an example.)

Now suppose that in response, the central bank lowers the nominal interest rate. The stickiness of inflation ensures that the real interest rate falls as well. As it falls below the marginal product of capital $\bar{r}$, firms and households take advantage of low interest rates to increase their investment. The higher investment demand makes up for the decline in $\bar{a}$ and pushes output back up to potential.

By lowering the interest rate sufficiently, policymakers can stimulate the economy, moving it to a point like *C*, shown in panel (b) of Figure 12.5. In the best case, the central bank would adjust monetary policy exactly when the housing bubble collapses, and in theory the economy would not have to experience a decline in output. In practice, though, such fine-tuning of the economy is extremely difficult: it takes time for policymakers to determine the nature and severity of the shock that has hit the economy, and it takes time for changes in interest rates to affect investment demand and output. Economists who study monetary policy believe

The negative shock leads to a recession, as the economy moves from point *A* to point *B*.

The Fed responds by stimulating the economy with lower interest rates, moving output back to potential as the economy moves to point *C*.

FIGURE 12.5

Stabilizing the Economy after a Housing Bubble

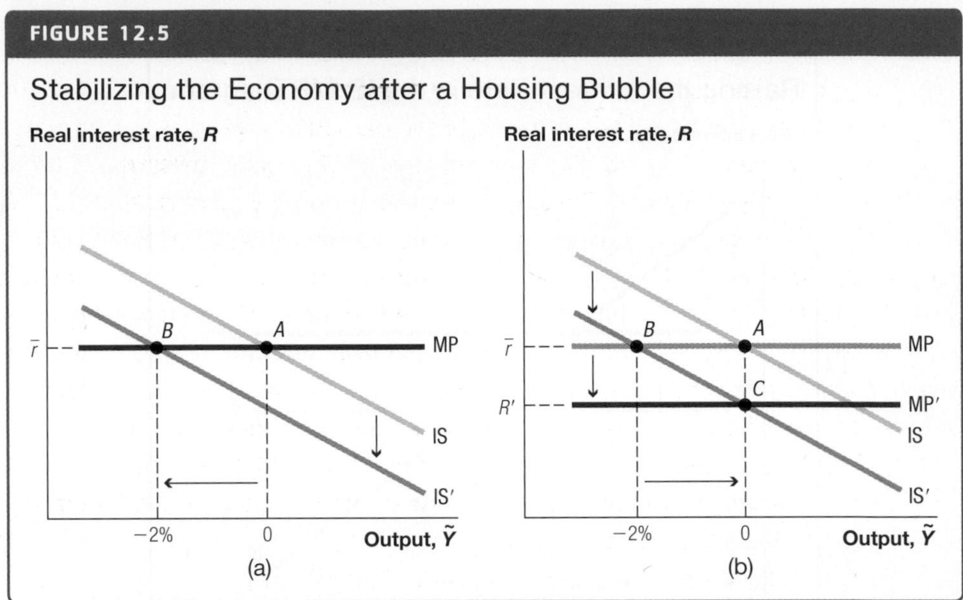

it takes 6 to 18 months for changes in interest rates to have substantial effects on economic activity. Nobel laureate Milton Friedman famously remarked that monetary policy affects the economy with "long and variable lags."

Despite this important caveat, it remains the case that in our simple model, monetary policy could in principle completely insulate the economy from aggregate demand shocks. In fact, one could argue that the Fed had just such an example in mind in the mid 2000s, when considering the possibility that a housing bubble might burst. At some level, it seemed plausible that the Fed's standard toolkit would be able to mitigate much of the fallout from such a shock. In Chapter 14, we'll see what went wrong.

CASE STUDY

The Term Structure of Interest Rates

So far, this book has discussed the nominal interest rate as if it were a single rate, but this is not the case. A quick look at the financial pages of any newspaper reveals a menu of rates: the fed funds overnight rate, a 3-month rate on government Treasury bills, a 6-month rate, a 1-year rate, a 5-year rate, a 10-year rate, and the nominal rate on 30-year mortgages. How do these interest rates fit together?

The different period lengths for interest rates make up what is called **the term structure of interest rates**. The rates are related in a straightforward way. To see how, suppose you have $1,000 that you'd like to save for the next 5 years. There are different ways you can do this. You could buy a government bond with a 5-year maturity, which would guarantee you a certain nominal interest rate for 5 years. Alternatively, you could buy a 1-year government bond today, get a 1-year return, and then roll the resulting money into another 1-year bond next year. If you repeat this every year for the next 5 years, you will have earned a series of 1-year returns.

Which investment pays the higher return, the single 5-year government bond or the series of 1-year bonds? The answer had better be that they yield the same return, given our best expectations, or everyone would switch to the higher-return investment. This means that the 5-year government bond pays a return that's in some sense an average of the returns on the series of 1-year bonds. If financial markets expect short-term interest rates to rise over the next 5 years, then the 5-year rate must be higher than today's 1-year rate. Otherwise the two approaches to investing over the next 5 years could not yield the same annualized return.

This example illustrates the key to the term structure of interest rates: interest rates at long maturities are equal to an average of the short-term rates that investors expect to see in the future.

When the Federal Reserve changes the overnight rate in the fed funds market, interest rates at longer maturities may also change. Why? There are two main reasons. First, financial markets generally expect that the change in the overnight rate will persist for some time. When central banks raise interest rates, they generally don't turn around and lower them immediately. Second, a change in rates today often signals information about the likely change in rates in the future. For example, look back at the target-level curve of the fed funds rate from 2004 to 2006 shown in Figure 12.2. In these years, there was a prolonged sequence of small increases, which may have suggested that the rate was likely to rise for a sustained period. This would have caused long-term interest rates to rise as well.

12.3 The Phillips Curve

We are now ready to turn to the final building block of the short-run model, **the Phillips curve**. The overview of the model in Chapter 9 provided an introduction to this curve, but here we look at it in more depth.

Suppose you are the CEO of a large corporation that manufactures plastic goods, such as the molds surrounding LCD computer screens or the nylon threads that get turned into clothing. For each of the last three years, the inflation rate has remained steady at 5 percent per year, and GDP has equaled potential output. This year, however, the buyers of your products are claiming that the economy is weakening. The last few months' worth of orders for your plastic goods are several percent below normal.

In normal times, you'd expect prices in the economy to continue to rise at a rate of 5 percent, and you'd raise your prices by this same amount. However, given the weakness in your industry, you'll probably raise prices by less than 5 percent, in an effort to increase the demand for your goods.

This reasoning motivates the price-setting behavior that underlies the Phillips curve. Recall that $\pi_t \equiv (P_{t+1} - P_t)/P_t$: that is, the inflation rate is the percentage change in the overall price level over the coming year. Firms set the amount by which they raise their prices on the basis of their expectations of the economywide inflation rate and the state of demand for their product:

$$\pi_t = \underbrace{\pi_t^e}_{\text{expected inflation}} + \underbrace{\bar{v}\tilde{Y}_t}_{\text{demand conditions}}. \tag{12.3}$$

Here, π_t^e denotes **expected inflation**—the inflation rate that firms think will prevail in the rest of the economy over the coming year.

To understand this equation, suppose all firms in the economy are like the plastics manufacturer. They expect the inflation rate to continue at 5 percent, but slackness in the economy persuades them to raise their prices by a little less, say by 3 percent, in an effort to recapture some demand. If all firms behave this way, actual inflation in the coming year will be 3 percent—equal to the 5 percent expected inflation less an adjustment to allow for slackness in the economy. Short-run output $\tilde{Y}_t$ enters our specification of the Phillips curve in equation (12.3) to capture this slackness effect.

What determines how much inflation firms expect to see in the economy over the coming year? To start, we assume that these expectations take a relatively simple form:

$$\pi_t^e = \pi_{t-1}. \tag{12.4}$$

That is, firms expect the rate of inflation in the coming year to equal the rate of inflation that prevailed during the last year. Under this assumption, called **adaptive expectations**, firms adjust (or adapt) their forecasts of inflation slowly.

Another way of saying this is that expected inflation embodies our sticky inflation assumption. Firms expect inflation over the next year to be sticky, or equal to the most recent inflation rate. In many situations, this is a reasonable assumption, and it is a convenient one to make at this point. However, thinking carefully about how individuals form their expectations and about the consequences of this for macroeconomics has led to some Nobel Prize–winning ideas in the last few decades. We will return to these intriguing possibilities at the end of this chapter and in the next. For now, though, we stick with our assumption of adaptive expectations because it is simple and useful.

Combining these last two equations—equations (12.3) and (12.4)—we get the Phillips curve:

$$\pi_t = \pi_{t-1} + \bar{v}\tilde{Y}_t. \tag{12.5}$$

The Phillips curve describes how inflation evolves over time as a function of short-run output. When output is at potential so that $\tilde{Y}_t = 0$, the economy is neither booming nor slumping and the inflation rate remains steady: inflation over the next year equals expected inflation, which is equal to last year's inflation. However, if output is below potential, the slumping economy leads prices to rise more slowly than in the past. Alternatively, when the economy is booming, firms are producing more than potential. They raise prices by more than the usual amount, and inflation increases: π_t is more than π_{t-1}.

FIGURE 12.6

The Phillips Curve

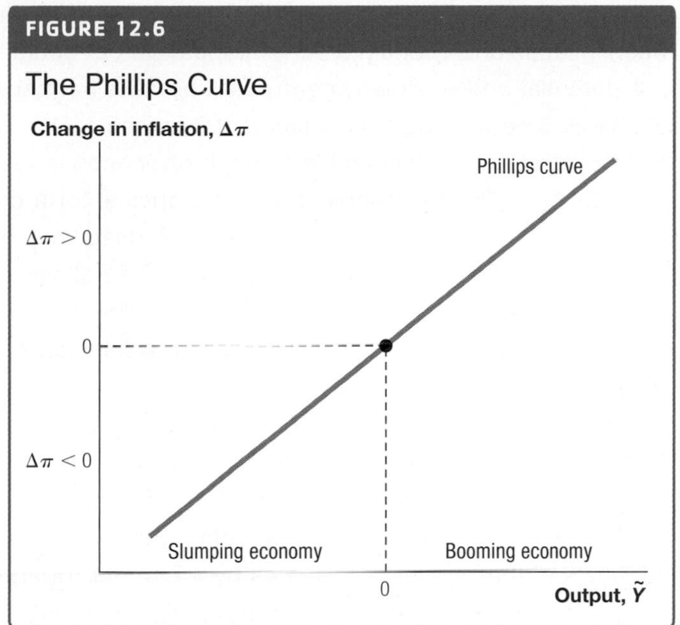

According to the Phillips curve, when the economy booms, inflation rises; when the economy slumps, inflation falls.

Following our standard notation, let $\Delta\pi$ denote the change in the rate of inflation: $\Delta\pi_t = \pi_t - \pi_{t-1}$. Then the Phillips curve can be expressed succinctly as

$$\Delta\pi_t = \bar{v}\tilde{Y}_t. \tag{12.6}$$

When the economy booms, inflation rises. When the economy slumps, inflation falls. Graphically, the Phillips curve is shown in Figure 12.6.

The Phillips curve describes how the state of the economy—short-run output—drives changes in inflation. The parameter $\bar{v}$ measures how sensitive inflation is to demand conditions; it governs the slope of the curve. If $\bar{v}$ is high, then price-setting behavior is very sensitive to the state of the economy. Alternatively, if $\bar{v}$ is low, then it takes a large recession to reduce the rate of inflation by a percentage point.

CASE STUDY

A Brief History of the Phillips Curve

The Phillips curve is named after A. W. Phillips, an economist at the London School of Economics who studied the relationship between wage inflation and economic activity in the late 1950s.[2] Phillips originally postulated that the *level* of inflation—rather than the change in inflation—was related to the level of economic activity.

[2] See A. W. Phillips, "The Relationship between Unemployment and the Rate of Change of Money Wages in the UK, 1861–1957," *Economica*, vol. 25 (1958), pp. 283–99.

On this basis, conventional wisdom in the 1960s held that there was a permanent trade-off between inflation and economic performance. Output could be kept permanently above potential and unemployment could be kept permanently low by allowing inflation to be 5 percent per year instead of 2 percent.

At the end of the 1960s, in a remarkable triumph of economic reasoning, Milton Friedman and Edmund Phelps proposed that this original form of the Phillips curve was mistaken. Friedman and Phelps argued that efforts to keep output above potential were doomed to fail. Stimulating the economy and allowing inflation to reach 5 percent would raise output temporarily, but eventually firms would build this higher inflation rate into their price changes, and output would return to potential. The result would be higher inflation with no long-run gain in output.

Moreover, efforts to keep output above potential would lead to rising inflation. Firms would raise their prices by ever-increasing amounts in an attempt to ease the pressure associated with producing more than potential output. If current inflation were 2 percent, they would raise prices by 3 percent. In the next year, seeing a 3 percent rate of inflation, they would raise prices by 4 percent if output remained high. Firms would constantly try to outpace the prevailing rate of inflation if output exceeded potential. Rather than being stable, the inflation rate itself would rise over time.

This economic reasoning was vindicated by the rising inflation of the 1970s that came about, at least in part, as policymakers tried to exploit the logic of the original Phillips curve. The modern version of the Phillips curve advocated by Friedman and Phelps—the version in our short-run model—has played a key role in macroeconomic models ever since. Partly for this contribution, Edmund Phelps was awarded the Nobel Prize in economics in 2006; Friedman had already won the prize 30 years earlier.[3]

Price Shocks and the Phillips Curve

Most of the time in our short-run model, the inflation rate follows the dynamics laid out above. Occasionally, however, it can be subject to shocks. For example, the oil **price shocks** of the 1970s and the late 2000s can be viewed as leading to a temporary increase in the rate of inflation.

We introduce such shocks into the model by adding them to the price-setting equation, (12.5), which leads to our final specification of the Phillips curve:

$$\pi_t = \pi_{t-1} + \bar{v}\tilde{Y}_t + \bar{o} \qquad (12.7)$$

[3] See Milton Friedman, "The Role of Monetary Policy," *American Economic Review*, vol. 58 (March 1968), pp. 1–17; and Edmund S. Phelps, "Money-Wage Dynamics and Labor Market Equilibrium," *Journal of Political Economy*, vol. 76 (1968), pp. 678–712.

This equation says that the actual rate of inflation over the next year is determined by three things. The first is the rate of inflation that firms expect to prevail in the rest of the economy; with our assumption of adaptive expectations, this is equal to last year's inflation rate. The second is the usual adjustment for the state of the economy $\bar{v}\tilde{Y}_t$. The third is a new term: a shock to inflation, denoted by $\bar{o}$ (to suggest oil price shocks, which might occur, for example, if oil prices in the world market increase sharply).

Rewriting in terms of the change in the inflation rate, we have

$$\Delta\pi_t = \bar{v}\tilde{Y}_t + \bar{o}. \qquad (12.8)$$

Just as with the aggregate demand shock $\bar{a}$ in the IS curve, we will think of the price shock $\bar{o}$ as being zero most of the time. When a shock hits the economy that raises inflation temporarily, this will be represented by a positive value of $\bar{o}$.

A rise in oil prices has an immediate and highly visible impact on many prices in the economy: the price of gasoline, the cost of an airline ticket, the cost of heating a home during the winter. Some of these effects are direct, while others show up indirectly. For example, consider how an oil price shock affects you as the plastics manufacturer. Petroleum is a key input into the production of plastics. So if oil prices rise, so does the cost of one of your key inputs. Rather than raise prices by the usual 5 percent rate of inflation, you will raise them by this amount *plus* an additional amount to reflect the increase in cost. The rise in oil prices can get passed through to a broader range of goods in this fashion.

Graphically, an oil price shock produces a temporary upward shift in the Phillips curve, as shown in Figure 12.7. Notice that even when output is at potential, the inflation rate will increase because of this shock.

FIGURE 12.7

An Oil Price Increase

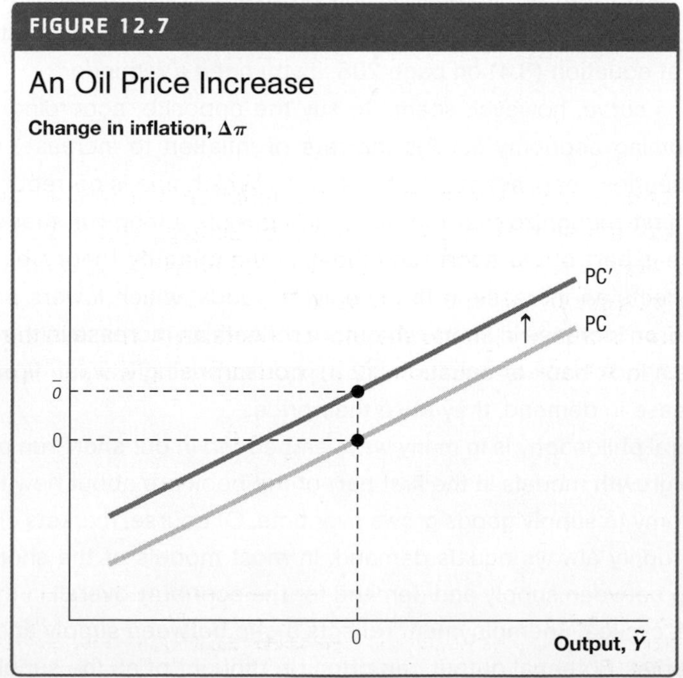

An increase in oil prices causes a temporary upward shift in the Phillips curve (PC).

Cost-Push and Demand-Pull Inflation

In addition to the canonical example of oil shocks, the price shock term in the Phillips curve can reflect changes in the price of any input to production; an increase in the world price of steel, for example, would have similar effects in Japan. More generally, these price shocks are called **cost-push inflation**, because the cost increase tends to push the inflation rate up. To parallel this terminology, the basic effect of short-run output on inflation in the Phillips curve—the $\bar{v}\tilde{Y}_t$ term—is called **demand-pull inflation**: increases in aggregate demand in the economy raise (pull up) the inflation rate.

Another important source of price shocks to the Phillips curve comes from the labor market. In many countries, unions bargain to set wages for certain time periods. If a union contract specifies a particularly large increase in wages during the coming year, this increase can feed into the prices set by firms, and $\bar{o}$ would temporarily be positive in our model. On the other hand, the arrival of a large pool of new immigrants may reduce the bargaining power of workers and lead to smaller-than-expected increases in wages. Inflation would be reduced, and $\bar{o}$ would temporarily be negative.

CASE STUDY

The Phillips Curve and the Quantity Theory

Here's a puzzle. In Chapter 8, we studied the quantity theory of money. According to Milton Friedman, inflation is caused by "too much money chasing too few goods." We found that an increase in the growth rate of real GFP would reduce inflation—goods are growing faster relative to money, so the inflation rate falls. Take a look back at equation (8.4) on page 206, if you need a reminder.

The Phillips curve, however, seems to say the opposite: according to equation (12.7), a booming economy causes the rate of inflation to *increase*, not decline. These two theories, then, seem directly at odds. Which one is correct?

We must first recognize that the quantity theory is a long-run model, while the Phillips curve is part of our short-run model. In the quantity theory, an increase in real GDP reflects an increase in the *supply* of goods, which lowers prices. In the Phillips curve, an increase in short-run output reflects an increase in the *demand* for goods—take a look back at equation (12.3); not surprisingly, when firms are faced with an increase in demand, they raise their prices.

This general philosophy is in many ways embedded in our short-run and long-run models. The growth models in the first part of the book are about how the capacity for the economy to supply goods grows over time. Of course, markets clear in those models, so supply always equals demand. In most models of the short run, there can be a gap between supply and demand for the economy overall in the short run. For example, cyclical unemployment reflects a gap between supply and demand in the labor market. Potential output can often be thought of as the supply of output, and short-run output can be thought of as the gap between supply and demand, with the view that output is determined by demand in the short run. Notice that this is consistent with the view that prices do not always adjust immediately to clear markets, a view implied by our assumption of sticky inflation.

The answer to our question, then, is that the quantity theory supply-driven view holds in the long run. In the short run, however, an increase in short-run output reflects an increase in demand that raises inflation.

12.4 Using the Short-Run Model

We are now ready to put the pieces of our short-run model together and see how they combine to determine the time path of output and inflation in the economy. To do this, we will consider two examples that are of particular interest. The first concerns **disinflation**, a sustained reduction in inflation to a stable, lower rate. This example studies how the economy moved from a period of high and uncertain inflation in the 1970s to an extended period of more than two decades of low and stable inflation. The second example analyzes the causes of **the Great Inflation** of the 1970s and considers how misinterpreting that decade's productivity slowdown contributed to the rising inflation. As background to both examples, look again at the graph of U.S. inflation over time, shown in Figure 12.8.

FIGURE 12.8

Inflation in the United States, 1960–2009

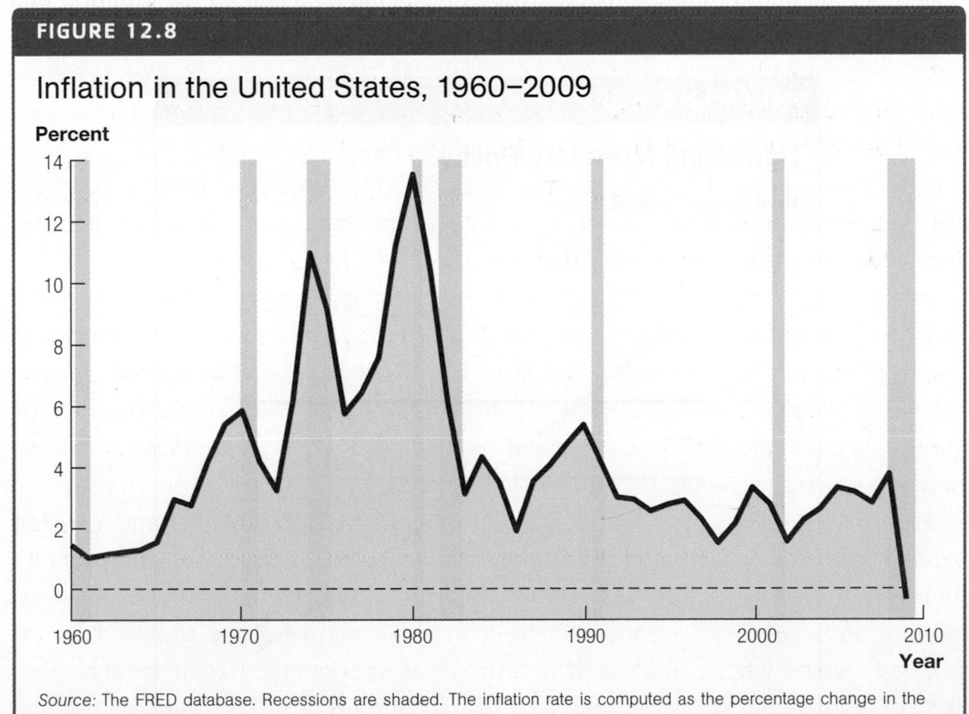

Source: The FRED database. Recessions are shaded. The inflation rate is computed as the percentage change in the consumer price index.

Recessions typically lead the inflation rate to decline, a fact embodied in the Phillips curve.

The Volcker Disinflation

Paul Volcker was appointed to chair the Federal Reserve Board of Governors in 1979. In part because of the oil shocks of 1974 and 1979 and in part because of an excessively loose monetary policy in previous years, inflation in 1979 exceeded 10 percent and appeared to be headed even higher. Volcker's job was to bring it back under control. Over the next several years, inflation did decline; armed with our short-run model, how do we understand this decline?

From our long-run theory of inflation, we know that at some level reducing the rate of inflation requires a sharp reduction in the rate of money growth. This "tight monetary policy" is equivalent to an increase in the nominal interest rate. (You may already understand how this works, or this statement may be unclear at this point; the last section of this chapter will develop the link between money and interest rates.) If the classical dichotomy holds in the short run as well as the long run, that may be all that's required: slowing the rate of money growth might slow inflation immediately. However, because of the stickiness of inflation, the dichotomy is unlikely to hold exactly in the short run, so the increase in the nominal interest rate, as we have seen, will result in an increase in the real interest rate.

The effect on the economy of a rise in the real interest rate is shown in Figure 12.9. Faced with a real interest rate that's higher than the marginal product of capital, firms and households put their investment plans on hold. The decline in investment demand leads output to fall, from point *A* to point *B*, and the economy goes into a recession. To be concrete, let's assume that short-run output falls to −2 percent.

Now turn to the Phillips curve, shown in Figure 12.10. The recession causes the change in the inflation rate to become negative. That is, it causes the inflation rate

The Federal Reserve raises the nominal interest rate. Because the classical dichotomy doesn't hold in the short run, this action raises the real interest rate and causes a decline in output.

FIGURE 12.9

Tightening Monetary Policy

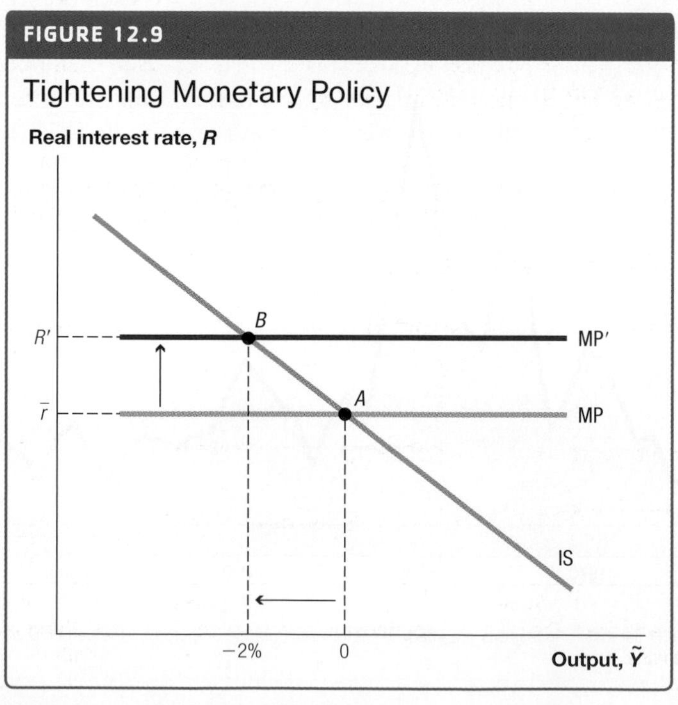

FIGURE 12.10

A Recession and Falling Inflation

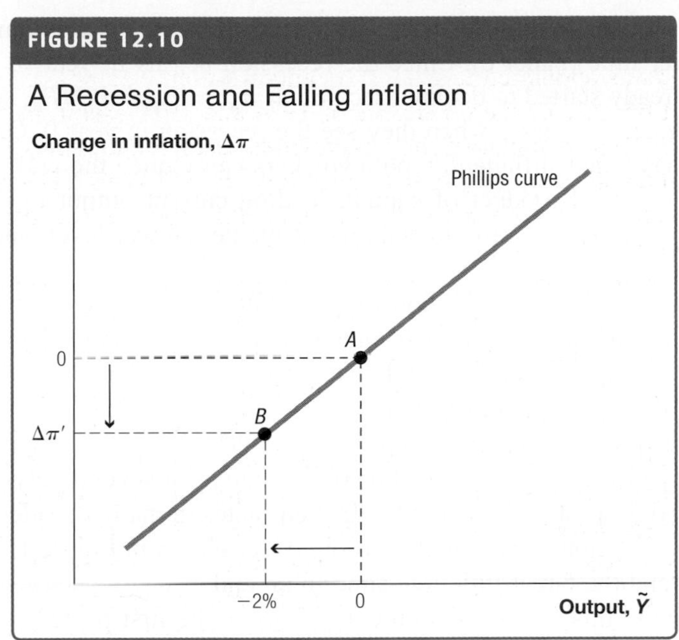

The Fed causes a recession, leading the economy to jump from point *A* to point *B*, where the change in the inflation rate is negative.

to decline. Why? Firms see the demand for their products fall, so they raise prices less aggressively in an effort to sell more. Instead of raising prices by 10 percent, they may raise them by only 8 percent, so the inflation rate begins to fall.

In principle, a Volcker-style policy can keep the real interest rate high, with output remaining below potential, until inflation falls to a more appropriate level, say 5 percent. The cost is a slumping economy and the high unemployment and lost output this entails; the benefit is a lowering of the inflation rate. The dynamics of the economy will then look something like what's shown in Figure 12.11.

In this graph, we assume the Volcker policy starts at date 0 and continues until time t^* (panel a). While the real interest rate is high, output stays below potential

FIGURE 12.11

The Disinflation over Time

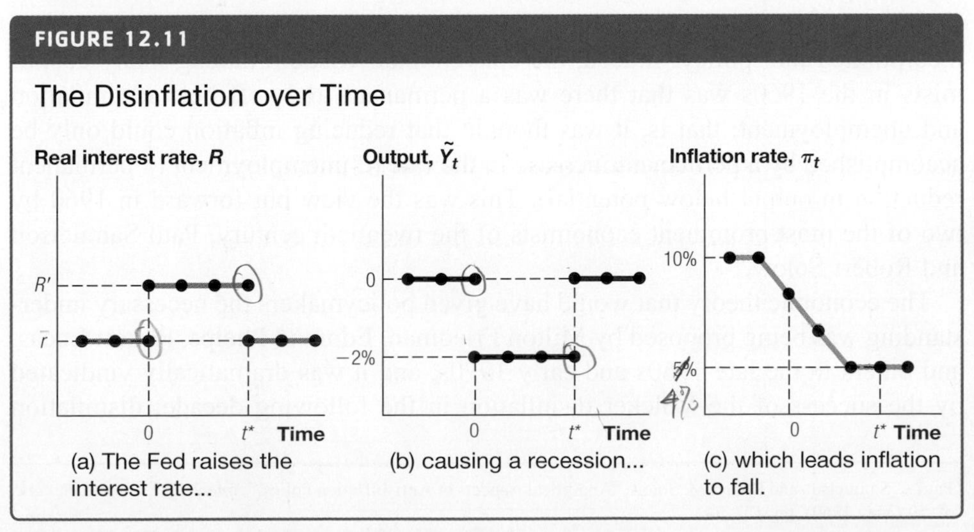

(a) The Fed raises the interest rate... (b) causing a recession... (c) which leads inflation to fall.

(panel b). Through the Phillips curve, this leads the rate of inflation to decline gradually over time (panel c). Since the recession begins in year 0, inflation in year 0 has already started to decline: recall that $\pi_0 = (P_1 - P_0)/P_0$, so that firms are setting prices for year 1 when they see the recession in year 0. Once the rate of inflation has fallen sufficiently, policymakers can reduce the real interest rate back to the marginal product of capital, leading current output to rise back to potential. This causes inflation to stabilize at the new lower level, and the disinflation is complete.

In the actual Volcker disinflation of the 1980s, the changes to the economy were large and dramatic. Mortgage interest rates rose to more than 20 percent for a time, causing demand for new housing to plummet. The prime lending rate charged by banks to their most creditworthy clients—which has been below 5 percent in recent years—reached 19 percent in 1981 and led to sharp drops in new investment by firms. Output fell well below potential for several years, producing the largest and deepest recession in the United States in many decades. However, the effects on inflation were equally profound. As shown in Figure 12.8, inflation fell quickly, and the Great Inflation came to an end.

But where did this Great Inflation come from in the first place?

The Great Inflation of the 1970s

Inflation in the United States and in many other industrialized countries was relatively low and stable in the 1950s and 1960s. At the end of the 1960s, however, it began to cycle up dramatically in the United States. From a low of about 2 percent per year in the early 1960s, inflation rose to peak at more than 13 percent in 1980.

A combination of at least three factors contributed to this rise. First are the oil shocks of 1974 and 1979, which occurred as OPEC coordinated to raise oil prices. We incorporated price shocks like this ($\bar{o}$) into our Phillips curve earlier in the chapter.

Second, in hindsight it seems clear that the Federal Reserve made mistakes in running a monetary policy that was too loose. As we have seen, the modern version of the Phillips curve that appears in our short-run model hadn't yet been incorporated into policy. Indeed, the conventional wisdom among many economists in the 1960s was that there was a permanent trade-off between inflation and unemployment: that is, it was thought that reducing inflation could only be accomplished by a permanent increase in the rate of unemployment (a permanent reduction in output below potential). This was the view put forward in 1960 by two of the most prominent economists of the twentieth century, Paul Samuelson and Robert Solow.[4]

The economic theory that would have given policymakers the necessary understanding was being proposed by Milton Friedman, Edmund Phelps, Robert Lucas, and others in the late 1960s and early 1970s, and it was dramatically vindicated by the success of the Volcker disinflation in the following decade: disinflation

[4] Paul A. Samuelson and Robert M. Solow, "Analytical Aspects of Anti-Inflation Policy," *American Economic Review*, vol. 50 (May 1960), pp. 177–94.

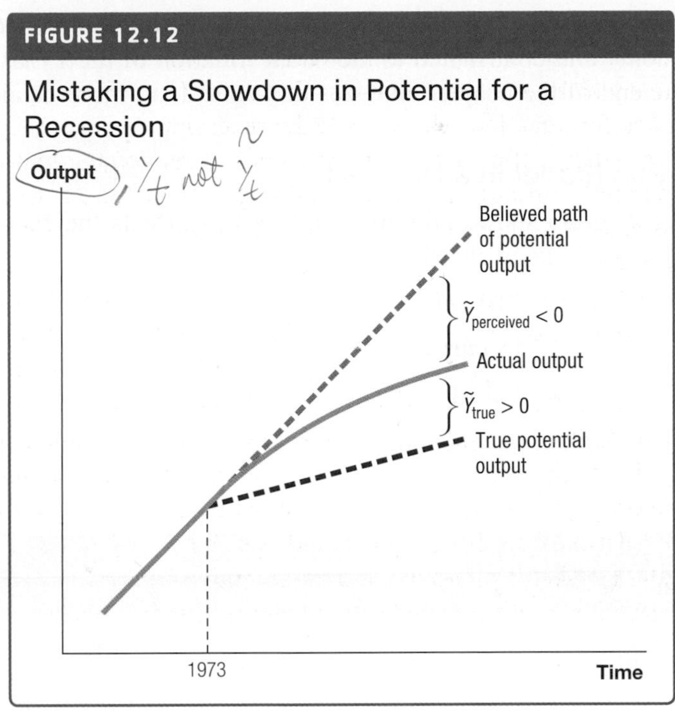

FIGURE 12.12

Mistaking a Slowdown in Potential for a Recession

The graph shows a stylized version of what happened in the 1970s. Because of the productivity slowdown, potential output grows more slowly. Policymakers assume potential output is growing at the same rate as before. They interpret the slowdown in GDP as a recession and stimulate the economy with lower interest rates. This mistake raises GDP above true potential and causes inflation to rise.

required a temporary recession, not a permanent reduction in output. Three years after the recession, the economy was booming again and unemployment was back to normal.

A third contributing factor to the Great Inflation of the 1970s was that the Federal Reserve did not have perfect information about the state of the economy. With hindsight, it's clear that a substantial and prolonged productivity slowdown occurred starting in the early 1970s. At the time, policymakers naturally considered this a temporary shock; they believed the economy was going into a recession, in the sense that output was falling below potential. Instead, the productivity slowdown was a change in potential output, and not something that monetary policy could overcome.[5]

It is instructive to study this third factor more closely through the lens of the short-run model. Figure 12.12 shows a stylized version of the situation in the 1970s. Potential output was growing sluggishly because of a productivity slowdown, and this slowed growth in actual output. However, policymakers didn't understand this and assumed potential output was growing at the same rate as before. They thought that $\tilde{Y}_t$ was becoming negative, when in fact it was remaining at zero.

In response to the perceived negative demand shock, policymakers lowered interest rates to stimulate the economy. Output rose, and policymakers believed they had done a good job. In truth, though, the lower interest rates pushed output above potential. Through the Phillips curve, this led to higher inflation. Thus,

[5] For a careful exposition and analysis of this view, see Athanasios Orphanides, "Monetary-Policy Rules and the Great Inflation," *American Economic Review*, vol. 92 (May 2002), pp. 115–20.

mistaking the slowdown in potential output for a recession, policymakers stimulated the economy and contributed to the Great Inflation of the 1970s. A worked exercise at the end of the chapter analyzes this episode in more detail.

The Short-Run Model in a Nutshell

The following diagram shows how monetary policy affects the economy, using the three building blocks of the short-run model:

$$\begin{array}{ll} \text{MP curve} & \uparrow i_t \Rightarrow \uparrow R_t \\ \text{IS curve} & \uparrow R_t \Rightarrow \downarrow \tilde{Y}_t \\ \text{Phillips curve} & \downarrow \tilde{Y}_t \Rightarrow \downarrow \Delta\pi_t \end{array}$$

Be sure you can explain the economic reasoning underlying each step.

CASE STUDY

The 2001 Recession

The late 1990s were characterized by what's called the "new economy." The Nasdaq stock index began at a level of 750 at the start of 1995 and peaked at more than 5,000 in March 2000. But then the economy hit a large bump: over the next two and a half years, the market lost more than 78 percent of its value.

As shown in Figure 12.13, the end of this remarkable run in the stock market coincided with the beginning of a sharp slowdown in economic activity. Although

The semiofficial dates of the recession are shaded (March 2001 through November 2001); but clearly the economy was already weak in early 2000 following the collapse of the dot-com stocks. Notice how quickly GDP recovers, while employment doesn't return to its peak level until early 2005. This experience has been called the "jobless recovery."

FIGURE 12.13

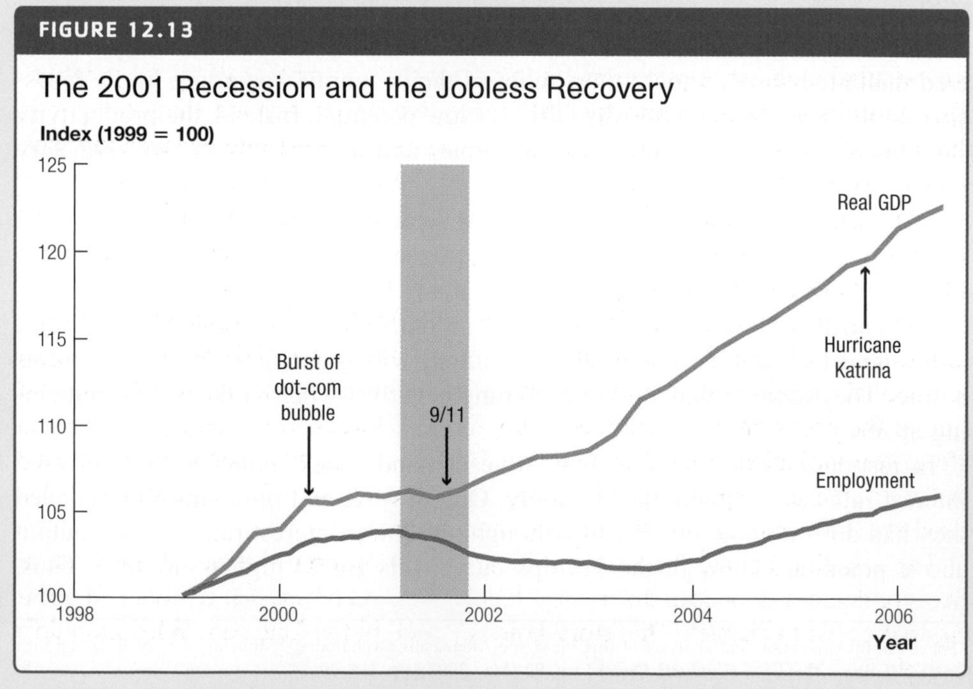

the economy did not peak until March 2001 according to the National Bureau of Economic Research, real GDP growth was slowing significantly at this time, and the economy presumably fell below potential output. Interestingly, by the time of the terrorist attack on New York and Washington, D.C., on September 11, 2001, the recession was nearly over, and real GDP growth was already returning.

The 2001 recession is also remarkable because of its "jobless recovery." In contrast to the strong return of GDP after the recession, employment continued to fall through late 2003. Indeed, employment did not return to its pre-recession peak until early 2005. Our model—through Okun's law—assumes that employment and GDP move together, and typically this is a reasonable assumption. The recession of 2001 and the jobless recovery provide an important exception to this rule.

Also worth noting in this graph are the effects of Hurricane Katrina at the end of August 2005, which devastated New Orleans and much of the Gulf Coast. GDP growth slowed slightly during the quarter of the hurricane but picked up sharply in the next quarter, roughly returning the economy to trend. The data on aggregate employment show little effect from the hurricane. Such small effects may be partly explained by the large size of the U.S. economy and the stimulus associated with donations and the rebuilding efforts.

12.5 Microfoundations: Understanding Sticky Inflation

An essential element of our short-run model is the assumption of sticky inflation. This assumption is built into the MP curve, where we assume that changes in the nominal interest rate lead to changes in the real interest rate because inflation doesn't adjust immediately. Sticky inflation is also central to the formulation of the Phillips curve. Expected inflation adjusts slowly over time in part because actual inflation adjusts slowly. Thus, sticky inflation is behind our assumption of adaptive expectations as well.

The assumption of sticky inflation brings us back to the classical dichotomy (discussed in Chapter 8). Recall that according to the classical dichotomy, changes in nominal variables have only nominal effects on the economy, so that the real side of the economy is determined solely by real forces. If monetary policy is to affect real variables, it must be that the classical dichotomy fails to hold, at least in the short run. Explaining this failure is one of the crucial requirements of a good short-run model, and the task of this section.

The intuition behind the classical dichotomy is quite powerful: if the Federal Reserve decides to double the money supply, then all prices can double and nothing real needs to change. This story holds up well in the long run. Why shouldn't it apply in the short run as well?

The Classical Dichotomy in the Short Run

As we learned in Chapter 8, for the classical dichotomy to hold at all points in time, all prices in the economy, including all nominal wages and rental prices, must adjust in the same proportion immediately. The best way to explain how this may not happen is to consider a specific example. Suppose you are the owner and manager of the local pizza parlor. On a daily basis, your job involves a number of important concerns:

- Are there adequate supplies of ingredients?
- Are you getting the best deal possible on those ingredients?
- Have any new restaurants opened down the street?
- Are the workers doing their jobs in a professional, friendly manner?
- Is the oven working correctly?
- Where is the most recent order of pizza boxes, and are you going to run out this weekend?
- Is the money you make on a given day kept in a safe place?

Given these concerns and the changing economic conditions constantly faced by the pizza parlor, we might think pizza prices should change every day. But of course they don't, and one reason is that it would simply be too costly and time-consuming to gather information on every detail affecting the restaurant and to figure out the correct price every single day. That is, there are costs of setting prices associated with *imperfect information* and *costly computation*. In the ideal competitive world often envisioned in introductory economics, prices adjust immediately to all kinds of shocks. In practice, however, prices are set by firms. These firms are hit by a range of shocks of their own, and monetary policy is perhaps one of the least important. In general and on a day-to-day basis, it's better for you as manager to spend your time trying to make sure the pizza parlor is doing a good job of making and selling pizzas than to worry about the exact state of monetary policy. Every couple of months (or more or less frequently, depending on the rate of inflation and the shocks hitting the pizza business), you may sit down and figure out the best way to adjust prices.[6]

Another example of imperfect information concerns monetary policy itself. If the Fed announces that it's doubling the money supply and explains this process clearly, then perhaps we could imagine the massive coordination of prices being successful. In practice, however, monetary policy changes are much more subtle.

For one thing, they are announced as changes in a short-term nominal interest rate. The amount by which the money supply has to change to implement this interest rate change depends in part on a relatively unstable money demand curve, as we will see at the end of this chapter.

In addition to imperfect information and costly computation, a third reason for the failure of the classical dichotomy in the short run is that many *contracts* set prices and wages in nominal rather than real terms. For the classical dichotomy to

[6] For some implications of this reasoning, see N. Gregory Mankiw and Ricardo Reis, "Sticky Information versus Sticky Prices: A Proposal to Replace the New Keynesian Phillips Curve," *Quarterly Journal of Economics*, vol. 117, no. 4 (November 2002), pp. 1295–1328.

hold in the pizza example, the wages of all the workers, the rent on the restaurant space, the prices of all the ingredients, and finally the prices of the pizzas must all increase in the same proportion. The rental price of the restaurant space is most likely set by a contract. There may also be wage contracts; such contracts were more important in the United States 30 years ago when unions were more prominent, but they remain important in a number of other countries today.

A fourth reason is *bargaining costs* associated with negotiating over prices and wages. Are the workers going to risk their jobs to argue for a slight increase in wages driven by some change in monetary policy they've read about in the newspaper? And even if they do, what prevents the pizza owner from responding, "Yes, but let me tell you about the other changes that are also occurring: a new restaurant is opening down the street, the rent I am paying is going up by even more than 2 percent, and demand for pizza is down, so while we are negotiating your wages, let's raise them by 2 percent because of the change in monetary policy, but let's cut them by 6 percent because of these other changes." This kind of bargaining is costly and difficult, and certainly not beneficial to engage in on a daily basis.

Finally, social norms and money illusion may prevent the classical dichotomy from prevailing in the short run. *Social norms* include conventions about fairness and the way in which wages are allowed to adjust. *Money illusion* refers to the fact that people sometimes focus on nominal rather than real magnitudes. Because of social norms and money illusion, people may have strong feelings about whether or not the nominal wage can or should decline, regardless of what's happening to the overall price level in the economy.

Adam Smith's invisible hand of the market works well on average, but at any given place and time, there's no reason to think that prices and wages are set perfectly. Moreover, given the information and computation costs of setting prices perfectly, it's probably best in some sense for prices not to move precisely in response to every shock that hits a firm or a region. For all the reasons given above, the classical dichotomy fails to hold in the short run.

CASE STUDY

The Lender of Last Resort

One of the many famous scenes in the 1946 movie *It's a Wonderful Life* features the citizens of Bedford Falls crowding into the Building and Loan, the bank owned by Jimmy Stewart's character, George Bailey. Worried that the bank has insufficient funds to back its deposits, people race to withdraw their funds so as not to be left with a worthless claim. Similar scenes are not uncommon in American history; during the Great Depression, nearly 40 percent of banks failed between 1929 and 1933.[7]

---

[7] George G. Kaufman, "Bank Runs," *The Concise Encyclopedia of Economics*, www.econlib.org/library/Enc/BankRuns.html.

One of the roles of the central bank is to ensure a sound, stable financial system in the economy. It does this in several ways. First, the central bank ensures that banks abide by a variety of rules, including maintaining a certain level of funds in reserve in case depositors ask for their money back. Second, it acts as the "lender of last resort": when banks experience financial distress, they may borrow additional funds from the central bank. In the United States, this borrowing occurs at the discount window, and the interest rate paid on such loans is called the *discount rate*.

Following the bank failures of the Great Depression, the United States adopted a system of *deposit insurance*. Small- and medium-sized deposits—typically up to $100,000—were now insured by the federal government, and this insurance nearly eliminated bank failures between 1935 and 1979.

In the 1980s, a new round of failures emerged, this time spurred in part by the presence of deposit insurance and by regulatory mistakes. Financial institutions called savings and loans (S&Ls) that were in financial trouble as a result of the high inflation of the 1970s found it profitable to gamble on high-risk/high-return investments. If those gambles paid off, the S&Ls would emerge from difficulty. If they did not pay off, deposit insurance would limit the losses to depositors. While these high-risk gambles paid off for some, the overall result was the failure of hundreds of S&Ls. Overall, the S&L crisis cost the government (and taxpayers) more than $150 billion.[8]

12.6 Microfoundations: How Central Banks Control Nominal Interest Rates

In order to apply our short-run model, it is enough to simply assume the central bank can set the nominal interest rate at whatever level it chooses. Still, the details of how the bank goes about this are interesting as well, and they resolve an important question: when we speak of "monetary policy" and "tight money," where exactly is the money?

The answer is that the way a central bank controls the level of the nominal interest rate is by supplying whatever money is demanded at that rate. The remainder of this section explains this statement.

Consider the market for money. In Chapter 8, we saw that the quantity theory of money determines the price level—the rate at which goods trade for colored pieces of paper—in the long run, assuming velocity is constant. For our short-run model, we are going to flip this around. Because of the assumption of sticky

[8] George A. Akerlof and Paul M. Romer, "Looting: The Economic Underworld of Bankruptcy for Profit," Brookings Papers on Economic Activity (1993), pp. 1–73. See also Howard Bodenhorn and Eugene N. White, "Financial Institutions and Their Regulation," in *Historical Statistics of the United States: Millennial Edition* (Cambridge: Cambridge University Press, 2006).

inflation, the rate of inflation—and therefore tomorrow's price level—doesn't respond immediately to changes in the money supply. But how, then, can the money market clear? Through a change in the velocity of money driven by a change in the nominal interest rate.

In particular, *the nominal interest rate is the* **opportunity cost** *of holding money*—the amount you give up by holding the money instead of keeping it in a savings account. Suppose you are deciding how much currency to carry around in your wallet on a daily basis, or how much money to keep in a checking account that pays no interest as opposed to a money market account that does pay interest. If the nominal interest rate is 1 percent, you may as well carry around currency or keep your money in a checking account. But if it's 20 percent, we would all try to keep our funds in the money market account as much as possible. This means that the demand for money is a decreasing function of the nominal interest rate.

As we saw in Chapter 8, the central bank can supply whatever level of currency it chooses. Call this level M^s, where s stands for the supply of money. Now consider the supply-and-demand diagram for the money market, as shown in Figure 12.14. A higher interest rate raises the opportunity cost of holding currency and reduces the demand for currency (M^d). The money supply schedule is simply a vertical line at whatever level of money the central bank chooses to provide.

The nominal interest rate is pinned down by the equilibrium in the money market, where households are willing to hold just the amount of currency that the central bank supplies. If the nominal interest rate is higher than i^*, then households would want to hold their wealth in savings accounts rather than currency, so money supply would exceed money demand. This puts pressure on the nominal interest

FIGURE 12.14

How the Central Bank Sets the Nominal Interest Rate

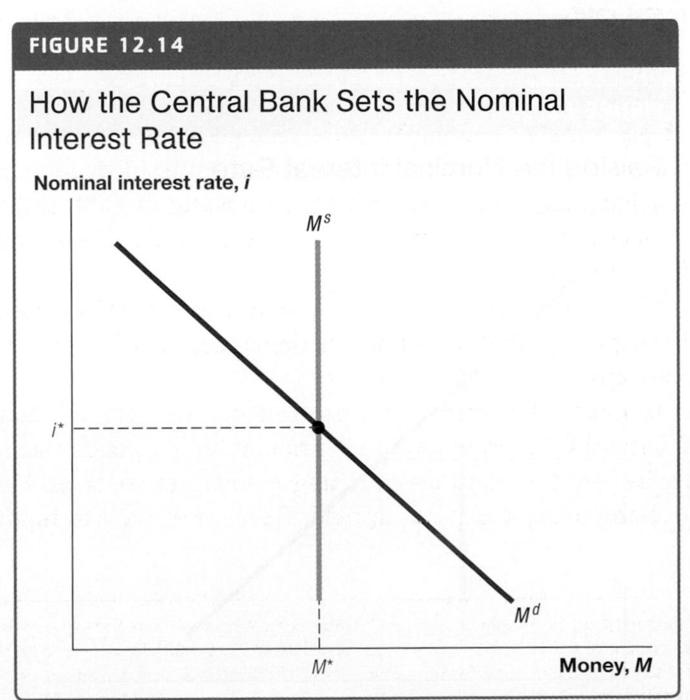

The central bank controls the supply of money (M^s). The demand for money (M^d) is a decreasing function of the nominal interest rate: when interest rates are high, we would rather keep our funds in high-interest-earning accounts than carry them around. The *nominal interest rate* is the rate that equates money demand to money supply.

rate to fall. Alternatively, if the interest rate is lower than i^*, money demand would exceed money supply, leading the nominal interest rate to rise.

Changing the Interest Rate

Now suppose the Fed or the European Central Bank wants to raise the nominal interest rate. Look again at Figure 12.14 and think about how the central bank would implement this change.

The answer, shown in Figure 12.15, is that the central bank reduces the money supply. As a result, there is now an excess of demand over supply: households are going to their banks to ask for currency, but the banks don't have enough for everyone. Therefore, they are forced to pay a higher interest rate (i^{**}) on the savings accounts they offer consumers, to bring the demand for money back in line with supply. A reduction in the money supply—"tight" money—thus increases the nominal interest rate.

Why i_t Instead of M_t?

As mentioned in Section 12.2, in advanced economies like the United States and the European Monetary Union, the stance of monetary policy is expressed in terms of a short-term nominal interest rate. Why do central banks set their monetary policy in this fashion rather than by focusing on the level of the money supply directly?

Historically, central banks did in fact focus directly on the money supply; this was true in the United States and much of Europe in the 1970s and early 1980s, for example. Beginning in the 1980s, however, many central banks shifted to a focus on interest rates.

The central bank can raise the nominal interest rate by reducing the money supply (a tightening of monetary policy).

FIGURE 12.15

Raising the Nominal Interest Rate

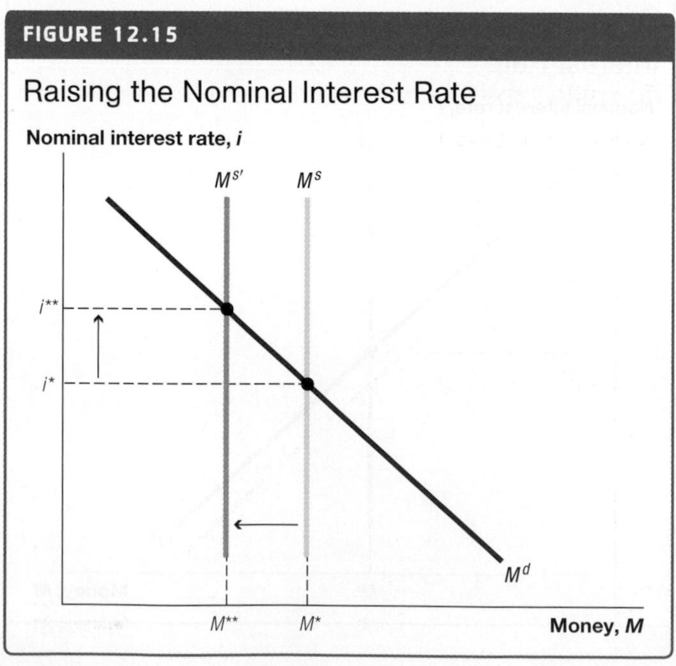

To see why, first recall that a change in the money supply affects the real economy through its effects on the real interest rate. The interest rate is thus crucial even when the central bank focuses on the money supply.

Second, the money demand curve is subject to many shocks. In addition to depending on the nominal interest rate, the money demand curve also depends on the price level in the economy and on the level of real GDP—the price of goods being purchased and the quantity of goods being purchased. Changes in the price level or output will shift the money demand curve. Other shocks that shift the curve include the advent of automated teller machines (ATMs), the increasing use of credit and debit cards, and the increased availability of financial products like mutual funds and money market accounts. With a constant money supply, the nominal interest rate would fluctuate, leading to changes in the real interest rate and changes in output if the central bank did not act.

By targeting the interest rate directly, the central bank automatically adopts a policy that will adjust the money supply to accommodate shocks to money demand. Such a policy prevents the shocks from having a significant effect on output and inflation and helps the central bank stabilize the economy.

In terms of a supply-and-demand diagram, the money supply schedule is effectively horizontal at the targeted interest rate. The central bank pegs the interest rate by its willingness to supply whatever amount of money is demanded at that interest rate. This is shown graphically in Figure 12.16. Here, shifts in the money demand curve will not change the interest rate.

In summary, central banks often express the stance of monetary policy in terms of a short-term nominal interest rate. They set this nominal interest rate by being willing to supply whatever amount of money is demanded. A monetary expansion (a "loosening" of monetary policy) increases the money supply and lowers the

FIGURE 12.16

Targeting the Nominal Interest Rate

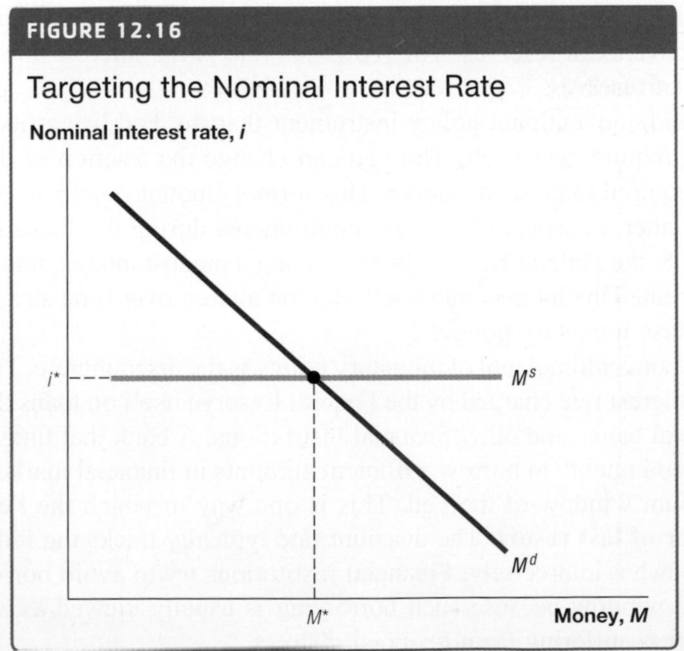

The central bank can peg the nominal interest rate at a particular level by being willing to supply whatever amount of money is demanded at that level. That is, it makes the money supply schedule horizontal.

nominal interest rate. A monetary contraction (a "tightening" of monetary policy) reduces the money supply and leads to an increase in the nominal interest rate.

Changes in short-term rates can affect interest rates that apply over longer periods. This is true either if financial markets expect the changes to hold for a long period of time or if the changes signal information about future changes in monetary policy.

12.7 Inside the Federal Reserve

The details of how the Federal Reserve interacts with the banking and financial systems are intricate. Indeed, many colleges have a separate course on money and banking that goes into these intricacies in great detail. However, the main points turn out to be relatively straightforward, as we shall see in this section.

Conventional Monetary Policy

The Federal Reserve has three conventional tools for exercising monetary policy: the fed funds rate, reserve requirements, and the discount rate. The main tool is the one we have focused on in this chapter—the fed funds rate. The other two tools are seldom used but shed important light on the workings of the central bank.

Traditional banks accept deposits from some customers and make loans to others. Central banks typically have **reserve requirements** that apply to these banks. That is, banks are required to hold a certain fraction of their deposits in special accounts ("in reserve") with the central bank itself. These special accounts are known as **reserves**. Historically, these reserve accounts paid no interest, so banks tried to hold as little as possible in reserves, preferring to lend out funds or hold them in interest-bearing instruments. The fed funds market, in fact, is the market through which banks that are short of reserves on any given day can borrow from banks that have extra reserves. The fed funds rate is the interest rate charged on these loans of reserves.

The second conventional policy instrument that the Fed has at its disposal is this reserve requirement itself. The Fed can change the fraction of deposits that banks are required to hold on reserve. This formal amount is seldom changed, but the Fed did alter an aspect of reserve requirements during the financial crisis. In October 2008, the Federal Reserve began paying a modest interest rate on reserves of 0.25 percent. This interest rate itself may be altered over time as a way for the Fed to exercise monetary policy.

The final conventional tool of monetary policy is the discount rate. The **discount rate** is the interest rate charged by the Federal Reserve itself on loans that it makes to commercial banks and other financial institutions. A bank that finds itself short of reserves and unable to borrow sufficient amounts in financial markets may turn to the discount window of the Fed. This is one way in which the Fed functions as the **lender of last resort**. The discount rate typically tracks the fed funds rate, though somewhat imprecisely. Financial institutions try to avoid borrowing from the discount window because such borrowing is usually viewed as a signal that the borrower is suffering from financial distress.

During the financial crisis of 2007 to 2009, the Federal Reserve and other central banks around the world used these conventional policies extensively. The policies were no doubt useful but proved insufficient for dealing with the severity and scope of the financial crisis, prompting central banks around the world to pursue unconventional monetary policies. The Federal Reserve, for example, purchased more than \$1 trillion of assets from financial institutions. These unconventional actions will be discussed further in Chapter 14.

Open-Market Operations: How the Fed Controls the Money Supply

The main way in which central banks affect the money supply is through **open-market operations**, in which the central bank trades interest-bearing government bonds in exchange for currency reserves. Suppose the Fed decides to reduce the money supply by \$10 million. The open-market operations desk at the Federal Reserve Bank of New York will announce that it is selling \$10 million of government bonds, such as 3-month Treasury bills. A financial institution will buy these bonds in exchange for currency or reserves. This transaction reduces the monetary base of the economy. In order to find a buyer for the bonds, the interest rate they pay may have to adjust upward so that financial institutions are willing to hold the extra bonds instead of the currency.

Alternatively, if the Fed wishes to expand the money supply and lower the nominal interest rate, it will offer to buy back government bonds in exchange for a credit in the buyer's reserve account.

How does the interest rate adjust? It turns out that the interest rate is implicit in the price of the bonds. Each bond comes with a face value of \$100, which means the bondholder will be paid \$100 on the date that the bond comes due. The bonds sell at a discount. For example, a bond that is due in one year's time may sell at a price of \$97. At this price, the investor earns a return of \$3 in one year's time in exchange for an investment of \$97. The implied yield on the bond over the next year is then $3/97 = 3.1\%$. This is the nominal interest rate implied by the bond price. So when the Fed buys or sells government bonds, the price at which the bonds sell determines the nominal interest rate.

12.8 Conclusion

This chapter has derived the short-run model, consisting of the IS-MP diagram and the Phillips curve. Policymakers exploit the stickiness of inflation so that changes in the nominal interest rate lead to changes in the real interest rate; the latter changes influence economic activity in the short run. Through the Phillips curve, the booms and recessions that are induced alter the evolution of inflation over time. Such a model can be used to understand the Great Inflation of the 1970s and the Volcker disinflation that followed during the early 1980s. More generally, it provides us with a theory of how economic activity and inflation are determined in the short run and how they evolve dynamically over time.

The assumptions of sticky inflation and adaptive expectations have important implications for our model. In particular, they firmly tie the hands of policymakers. If the central bank wants to reduce inflation, the only way it can is by pushing output below potential. In contrast, if there were no sticky inflation and adaptive expectations, the central bank could, conceivably, simply announce that it would be pursuing a policy to lower inflation, and all firms could reduce the rate at which they raise their prices. The inflation rate could be lowered with no change in output or any other real quantity.

But this latter scenario is not the case in our short-run model. We've assumed that inflation (and firms' expectations of inflation) evolves gradually and only as a function of short-run output. The only way to reduce inflation systematically is by slowing the economy. This raises an interesting and important possibility that the central bank may want to take actions to change the expectations firms have about inflation. If expectations *can* be changed by policymakers, it may be possible to reduce inflation without large recessions—and not just in a model but in the real economy. This is one of several Nobel Prize–winning ideas that were developed during the last several decades, and we will consider them more extensively in Chapter 13.

CHAPTER REVIEW

SUMMARY

1. The short-run model consists of the IS curve, the MP curve, and the Phillips curve.
2. Central banks set the nominal interest rate. Through the MP curve—and because of sticky inflation—they thus control the real interest rate. The real interest rate then influences short-run output through the IS curve. The IS-MP diagram allows us to study the consequences of monetary policy and shocks to the economy for short-run output.
3. The Phillips curve reflects the price-setting behavior of individual firms. The equation for the curve is $\pi_t = \pi_{t-1} + \bar{v}\tilde{Y}_t + \bar{o}$. Current inflation depends on expected inflation (π_{t-1}), current demand conditions ($\tilde{Y}_t$), and price shocks ($\bar{o}$).
4. The Phillips curve can also be written as $\Delta\pi_t = \bar{v}\tilde{Y}_t + \bar{o}$. This equation shows clearly that the change in inflation depends on short-run output: in order to reduce inflation, actual output must be reduced below potential temporarily. The Volcker disinflation of the 1980s is the classic example illustrating this mechanism.
5. Three important causes contributed to the Great Inflation of the 1970s: the oil shocks of 1974 and 1979; a loose monetary policy resulting in part from the mistaken view that reducing inflation required a permanent reduction in output; and a loose monetary policy resulting from the fact that the productivity slowdown was initially misinterpreted as a recession.

6. Central banks control short-term interest rates by their willingness to supply whatever money is demanded at a particular rate. Through the term structure of interest rates, long-term rates are an average of current and expected future short-term rates. This structure allows changes in short-term rates to affect long-term rates.

KEY CONCEPTS

adaptive expectations
cost-push inflation
demand-pull inflation
discount rate
disinflation
expected inflation
the federal funds rate
the Great Inflation
the IS-MP diagram
lender of last resort
the MP curve
open-market operations
opportunity cost
the Phillips curve
price shocks
reserves
reserve requirements
the sticky inflation assumption
the term structure of interest rates

REVIEW QUESTIONS

1. Figure 12.1 presents a summary of the short-run model. Explain each step in this diagram.
2. What is the economic justification for the sticky inflation assumption? What role does this assumption play in the short-run model?
3. How does a central bank influence economic activity in the short run?
4. What is the relevance of Milton Friedman's phrase "long and variable lags" to this chapter?
5. What is the Phillips curve? What role does it play in the short-run model? Explain the role played by each term in the equation for the Phillips curve.
6. What policy change did Paul Volcker implement, and how did it affect interest rates, output, and inflation over time?
7. Why do central banks often exercise monetary policy by targeting an interest rate rather than by setting particular levels of the money supply?

EXERCISES

smartwork.wwnorton.com 

1. **How the Fed affects investment:** The Federal Reserve exercises monetary policy by means of a very short-term, overnight nominal interest rate. Explain how changes in this overnight nominal rate influence longer-term real interest rates, and thus investment.
2. **Lowering the nominal interest rate:** Suppose the Fed announces today that it is lowering the fed funds rate by 50 "basis points" (that is, by half a percentage point). Using the IS-MP diagram, explain what happens to economic activity in the short run. What is the economics underlying the response in the economy?

3. **A consumption boom:** Using the IS-MP diagram, explain what happens to the economy if there is a temporary consumption boom that lasts for one period.
   - (a) Initially, suppose the central bank keeps the nominal interest rate unchanged.
   - (b) Suppose you are appointed to chair the Federal Reserve. What monetary policy action would you take in this case and why? Refer to the IS-MP diagram.

4. **No inflation stickiness:** Suppose the classical dichotomy holds in the short run as well as in the long run. That is, suppose inflation is not sticky but rather adjusts immediately to changes in the money supply.
   - (a) What effect would changes in the nominal interest rate (or the money supply) have on the economy?
   - (b) What effect would an aggregate demand shock have on the economy?
   - (c) What about an inflation shock?

5. **Your day as chair of the Fed (I):** Suppose you are appointed to chair the Federal Reserve. Your twin goals are to maintain low inflation and to stabilize economic activity—that is, to keep output at potential. Why are these appropriate goals for monetary policy? (*Hint*: What happens if the economy booms?)

6. **Your day as chair of the Fed (II):** With the goal of stabilizing output, explain how and why you would change the interest rate in response to the following shocks. Show the effects on the economy in the short run using the IS-MP diagram.
   - (a) Consumers become pessimistic about the state of the economy and future productivity growth.
   - (b) Improvements in information technology increase productivity and therefore increase the marginal product of capital.
   - (c) A booming economy in Europe this year leads to an unexpected increase in the demand by European consumers for U.S. goods.
   - (d) Americans develop an infatuation with all things made in New Zealand and sharply increase their imports from that country.
   - (e) A large earthquake destroys many houses and buildings on the West Coast, but fortunately results in little loss of life.
   - (f) A housing bubble bursts, so that housing prices fall by 20% and new home sales drop sharply.

7. **The summary diagram:** The end of Section 12.4 contains a summary of the short-run model. Explain the economic reasoning that underlies each step in this summary.

8. **An oil price shock (hard):** Suppose the economy is hit by an unexpected oil price shock that permanently raises oil prices by $50 per barrel. This is a temporary increase in $\bar{o}$ in the model: the shock $\bar{o}$ becomes positive for one period and then goes back to zero.
   - (a) Using the full short-run model, explain what happens to the economy in the absence of any monetary policy action. Be sure to include graphs showing how output and inflation respond over time.

(b) Suppose you are in charge of the central bank. What monetary policy action would you take and why? Using the short-run model, explain what would happen to the economy in this case. Compare your graphs of output and inflation with those from part (a).

9. **Immigration and inflation:** Suppose a large number of new immigrants enter the labor market. Assume this increase in the supply of labor provides a drag on wage increases: wages rise by less than the prevailing rate of inflation over the next year. Use the short-run model to explain how the economy responds to this change.

10. **The consumption boom revisited:** Go back to exercise 3 and explain what happens in the full short-run model (including the Phillips curve and allowing the economy to evolve over time). Do this for both parts (a) and (b), and be sure to provide graphs of output and inflation over time.

11. **Changing the slope of the Phillips curve:** Suppose the slope of the Phillips curve—the parameter $\bar{v}$—increases. How would the results differ from the Volcker disinflation example considered in the chapter? What kind of changes in the economy might influence the slope of the Phillips curve?

12. **The productivity slowdown and the Great Inflation:** Using the IS-MP diagram and the Phillips curve, explain how the productivity slowdown of the 1970s may have contributed to the Great Inflation. In particular, answer the following:
    - **(a)** Suppose growth in actual output is slowing down, as shown in Figure 12.12. Policymakers believe this is occurring because of a negative shock to aggregate demand. Explain how such a shock would account for the slowdown using an IS-MP diagram.
    - **(b)** With this belief, what monetary policy action would policymakers take to stabilize the economy? Show this in the IS-MP diagram, as perceived by policymakers.
    - **(c)** In truth, there was a slowdown in potential output, as also shown in Figure 12.12. Show the effect of monetary policy on short-run output in the "true" IS-MP diagram.
    - **(d)** Show the effect of this monetary policy in a graph of the Phillips curve. Explain what happens.
    - **(e)** How will policymakers from parts (a) and (b) know they have made a mistake?

13. **The new economy of the late 1990s:** Between 1995 and 2000, the U.S. economy experienced surprisingly rapid growth, termed the "new economy" by some observers. Was this a change in potential output or short-run output? Alan Greenspan, Fed chairman, argued it was a change in potential and did not raise interest rates to slow the economy. At the time, many economists thought this was a mistake. Look back at the data on inflation in Figure 12.8 to form your own opinion. Write a brief memo (one page or less) either defending or criticizing Greenspan's position. Be sure to use the graphs of the short-run model to make your case.

14. **E-commerce and monetary policy:** In the context of the money supply-and-demand diagram, explain the effects of financial innovations like e-commerce

and the increased prevalence of credit card readers in stores. Are the effects possibly related to the fact that central banks in most countries express monetary policy in terms of a target for the nominal interest rate?

WORKED EXERCISES

4. No inflation stickiness:

(a) Recall that the classical dichotomy says that real variables in the economy are determined entirely by real forces and are not influenced by nominal changes. In this case, a change in monetary policy that changes the nominal interest rate will affect inflation immediately and leave the real interest rate—and therefore the rest of the real economy—unchanged. In the absence of sticky inflation, changes in monetary policy have only nominal effects, not real effects.

(b) Recall that the IS curve is entirely a relationship between real variables in the economy and has nothing to do with the classical dichotomy. So in the IS-MP diagram, the IS curve would still shift in the presence of an aggregate demand shock.

What would differ is the ability of monetary policy to insulate the economy from such shocks. Since monetary policy could no longer affect the real interest rate, the MP curve would be stuck at the marginal product of capital $\bar{r}$. Aggregate demand shocks would then push the economy around, causing booms and recessions. For example, in response to the bursting of a housing bubble, the economy would respond as in panel (a) of Figure 12.5. Monetary policy could not implement the changes associated with panel (b).

(c) Similarly, inflation shocks like a change in oil prices could affect the inflation rate. If inflation were not sticky, the inflation rate would potentially move around even more. What would be different in this case is that monetary policy could respond to the rate of inflation with no fear of causing a recession. If the central bank didn't like the current rate of inflation, it could simply adjust monetary policy to deliver the desired rate.

12. The productivity slowdown and the Great Inflation:

(a) Policymakers believe that the slowdown in growth is caused by a negative aggregate demand shock that reduces output below potential. This is straightforward to analyze in an IS-MP diagram, as shown in Figure 12.17(a).

(b) Perceiving a negative shock to aggregate demand, policymakers react by lowering the real interest rate, in the belief that they are restoring output to potential (panel b).

(c) In truth, of course, there has been no negative aggregate demand shock, so the IS curve has not shifted. The stimulation of the economy by the

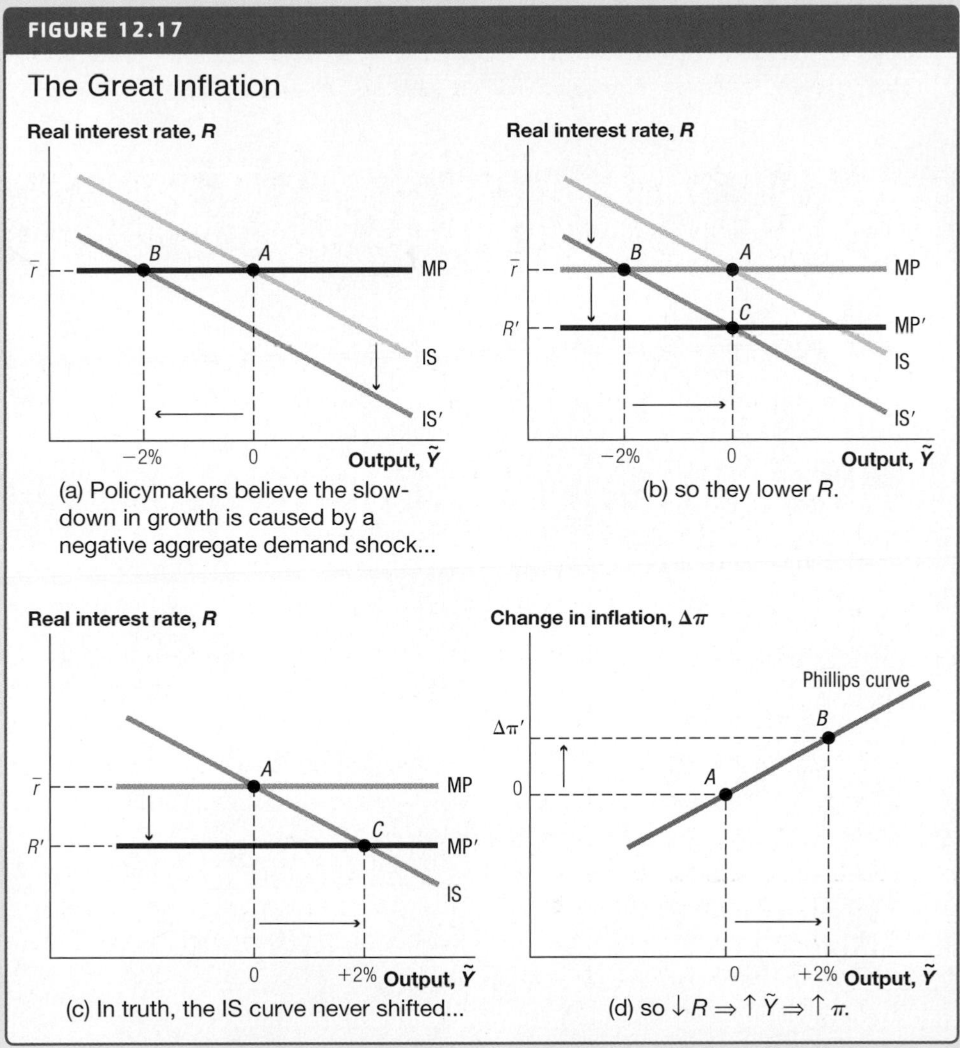

(a) Policymakers believe the slowdown in growth is caused by a negative aggregate demand shock...

(b) so they lower R.

(c) In truth, the IS curve never shifted...

(d) so $\downarrow R \Rightarrow \uparrow \tilde{Y} \Rightarrow \uparrow \pi$.

Fed moves the economy down the original IS curve, raising output above potential rather than restoring the economy to potential (panel c).

(d) Since output is above potential, firms raise their prices by more than the original rate of inflation, leading the rate of inflation itself to increase. This is dictated by the Phillips curve (panel d). At this point, we have explained how misconstruing the productivity slowdown as a negative aggregate demand shock could have led to the Great Inflation: the Fed stimulates the economy in an effort to move it back to potential. In fact, this leads output to rise above potential, which raises inflation.

(e) The key indicator that the central bank has made a mistake is that inflation rises. In the absence of any other shocks, this would be a strong indication that output is above potential. The experience of the 1970s, however, was not so clear because of the presence of oil shocks, which would also tend to increase inflation. Learning about the productivity slowdown and the mistakes in policy thus took longer than was ideal.

CHAPTER 13

STABILIZATION POLICY AND THE AS/AD FRAMEWORK

OVERVIEW

In this chapter, we learn

- that in the presence of a systematic monetary policy, we can combine the IS curve and the MP curve to get an aggregate demand (AD) curve.
- that the Phillips curve can be reinterpreted as an aggregate supply (AS) curve.
- how the AD and AS curves represent an intuitive version of the short-run model that describes the evolution of the economy in a single graph.
- the modern theories that underlie monetary policy, including the debate over rules versus discretion and the importance of expectations.

Experience shows that low and stable inflation and inflation expectations are also associated with greater short-term stability in output and employment, perhaps in part because they give the central bank greater latitude to counter transitory disturbances to the economy.

—BEN S. BERNANKE

13.1 Introduction

Could we replace Chairman Bernanke with a robot? This may sound more like the plot of a new Hollywood blockbuster than like a serious question. However, there is an important sense in which this question goes to the heart of modern monetary policy. By the end of the chapter, you will see that while no one would truly take such a proposal seriously—one need look no further than the extraordinary actions taken by the Fed in response to the recent financial crisis to see the importance of some discretion—it has more merits than you might have expected.

Chapters 11 and 12 contain the nuts and bolts of the short-run model: the MP curve (reflecting the central bank's choice of the real interest rate), the IS curve (showing how this real interest rate determines short-run output), and the Phillips curve (relating today's output to the evolution of inflation). We have used these ingredients to analyze how the economy behaves when it's bombarded by various shocks, including shocks to aggregate demand and to inflation. And we have seen that policymakers can change monetary policy to help buffer the economy against these shocks.

Up until now, though, we have considered these policy changes on a case-by-case basis: we analyzed how the economy responds when hit with a given shock, and developed the appropriate policy response. Imagine doing this for the various kinds of shocks that can possibly hit the economy and formulating a systematic policy in response. What would this policy look like?

That's the basic question we consider in this chapter, and the answer is called a monetary policy rule. We begin by considering a simple policy rule that makes the real interest rate a function of the inflation rate. We will examine the performance of the economy when such a rule is in place and see that it has some desirable properties—namely, that it stabilizes output and inflation in response to a broad range of shocks. The last part of the chapter steps back to consider some important issues that arise in the short-run model, such as *why* systematic monetary policy might be important to a successful stabilization policy.

Epigraph: Speaking as chair of the Federal Reserve Board of Governors, February 15, 2006.

13.2 Monetary Policy Rules and Aggregate Demand

The short-run model consists of three basic equations, summarized here:

IS curve:	$\tilde{Y}_t = \bar{a} - \bar{b}(R_t - \bar{r})$.
MP curve:	The central bank chooses R_t.
Phillips curve:	$\Delta\pi_t = \bar{v}\tilde{Y}_t + \bar{o}$.

There is an essential trade-off in the model: high short-run output leads to an increase in inflation. By choosing the level of the real interest rate R, the central bank effectively chooses how to make this trade-off.

A **monetary policy rule** is a set of instructions that determines the stance of monetary policy for a given situation that might occur in the economy. For example, a simple rule might make the real interest rate a function of the inflation rate: if inflation is high, the interest rate should be raised by a certain amount. More generally, monetary policy rules might depend on short-run output and even on aggregate demand and inflation shocks, in addition to the rate of inflation.

A simple monetary policy rule we will consider in this chapter is

$$R_t - \bar{r} = \bar{m}(\pi_t - \bar{\pi}) \tag{13.1}$$

In this rule, the stance of monetary policy depends on current inflation π_t, as well as on an inflation target $\bar{\pi}$. We will see eventually that this inflation target corresponds to the "steady-state" rate of inflation in our short-run model.

The policy rule sets the real interest rate according to whether inflation is currently above or below the target. If inflation is above its target level, the rule says the real interest rate should be high, so policymakers should tighten monetary policy. Conversely, if inflation is below its target level, the rule says the real interest rate should be low, so as to stimulate the economy.

The parameter $\bar{m}$ governs how aggressively monetary policy responds to inflation. If inflation is one percentage point higher than the target, the rule says the real interest rate should be raised above the marginal product of capital by $\bar{m}$ percentage points. For example, with $\bar{m} = 1/2$, an inflation rate that is two percentage points above the target would lead policymakers to raise the real interest rate by one percentage point. While we will also consider more sophisticated monetary policy rules, it turns out that many central banks, including the Federal Reserve, conduct policy in a way that's closely approximated by this simple one.

The AD Curve

Consider how the short-run model behaves if we replace the MP curve with the monetary policy rule in equation (13.1). In particular, suppose we combine this monetary policy rule with the IS curve. We substitute for the $R_t - \bar{r}$ term in the IS curve with the rule itself, which says this interest rate gap depends on inflation.

This leads to an equation that makes short-run output a function of the rate of inflation, which we'll call the **aggregate demand (AD) curve**:

$$\left.\begin{array}{l}\text{IS curve: } \tilde{Y}_t = \bar{a} - \bar{b}(R_t - \bar{r}) \\ \text{policy rule: } R_t - \bar{r} = \bar{m}(\pi_t - \bar{\pi})\end{array}\right\} \Rightarrow \text{AD curve: } \tilde{Y}_t = \bar{a} - \bar{b}\bar{m}(\pi_t - \bar{\pi}).$$

The aggregate demand curve is shown in Figure 13.1. A slightly odd feature of this graph is that short-run output is on the horizontal axis instead of the vertical. The reason for this is reminiscent of our choice with the IS curve and is the same as in a standard supply-and-demand diagram: we have two endogenous variables, so one must be on the horizontal axis.

The AD curve describes how the central bank chooses short-run output based on the rate of inflation. If inflation is above its target level, then the central bank raises the interest rate to push output below potential. The reasoning is that as the economy softens, inflation will be restrained in the future.

Why is this relation called the aggregate demand curve? Think about a standard demand curve in a particular market, say the market for hamburgers. This is a downward-sloping curve with the price of hamburgers on the vertical axis and the quantity of hamburgers on the horizontal. The aggregate demand curve is superficially similar, in that it's a downward-sloping curve in a graph between quantities and prices. However, the economics behind the AD curve is fundamentally different. While the market demand curve for hamburgers describes the quantity of hamburgers demanded by consumers at each different price, the AD curve describes how the central bank sets short-run output for each different rate of inflation.

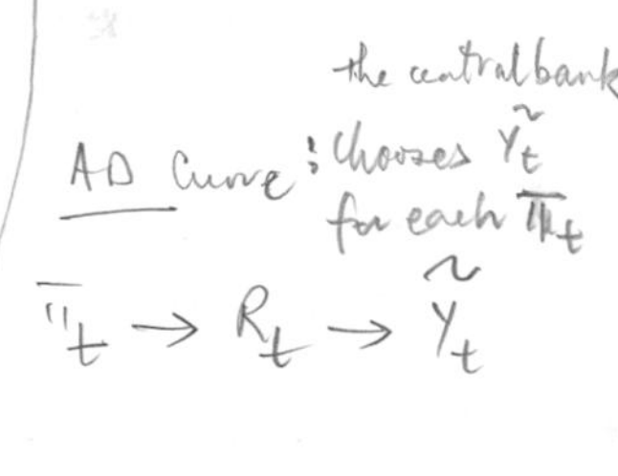

Another reason for calling this the aggregate demand curve is that it's built up from the demand side of the economy. Through the IS curve, consumption,

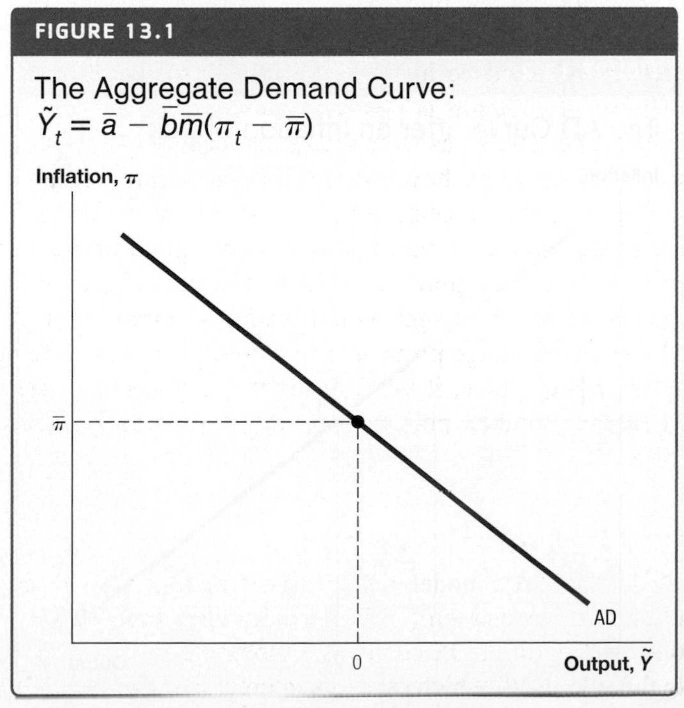

The aggregate demand curve describes how the central bank chooses short-run output based on the current inflation rate. If inflation is above its target, the bank raises interest rates and pushes output below potential. If inflation is below its target, the bank stimulates the economy. The curve is drawn for the standard case of no aggregate demand shock; that is, $\bar{a} = 0$.

investment, government purchases, and foreign demand for goods and services are central components of the curve. Moreover, we will see later how shocks to the aggregate demand parameter $\bar{a}$ can shift the curve.

Moving along the AD Curve

Suppose the economy begins in steady state and then is hit by a shock that raises the inflation rate from $\bar{\pi}$ to a higher value π'. What happens? The answer is shown graphically in Figure 13.2. If the central bank sees an inflation rate higher than its target $\bar{\pi}$, the monetary policy rule dictates an increase in interest rates. The higher interest rates cause a reduction in investment and a slowdown in economic activity—a movement along the AD curve.

As mentioned earlier, the parameter $\bar{m}$ measures how aggressive monetary policy is in fighting inflation. For example, a high value of $\bar{m}$ prescribes a sharp increase in interest rates if inflation rises, leading to a deep recession. In this case, the AD curve is relatively flat, as shown in Figure 13.3; a 1 percentage point increase in the inflation rate dictates a large decline in short-run output.

What would happen if the value of $\bar{m}$ were small instead of large? Try drawing the AD curve for yourself in this case.

Shifts of the AD Curve

We have seen that changes in π_t represent movements along the AD curve, and changes in $\bar{m}$ alter its slope. What about changes in the other parameters? The most important are changes in the aggregate demand parameter $\bar{a}$ and changes in the target rate of inflation $\bar{\pi}$. As we will see in later examples, changes in these

A change in inflation is a movement along the AD curve, since the curve is a plot of output versus the inflation rate. Seeing an increase in inflation, the monetary policy rule dictates that the central bank increase the interest rate, thereby reducing short-run output.

FIGURE 13.2

The AD Curve after an Inflation Shock

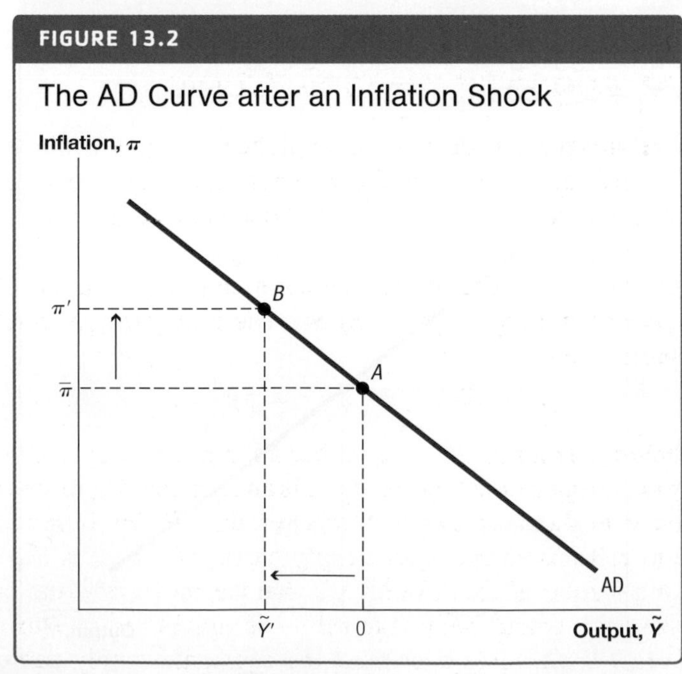

FIGURE 13.3

An Aggressive Monetary Policy Rule

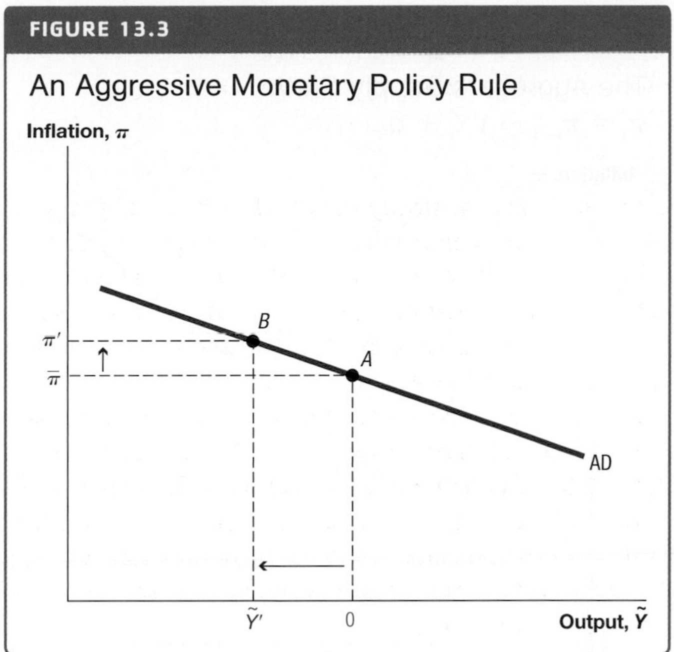

A high value of $\bar{m}$ means the monetary policy rule produces a large recession in order to fight a given increase in the inflation rate, leading to a flat AD curve.

parameter values shift the AD curve. That is, they change the level of short-run output that the central bank desires at any given inflation rate.

To summarize, changes in inflation move the economy along the AD curve. Aggregate demand shocks and changes in the central bank's target for inflation shift the AD curve.

13.3 The Aggregate Supply Curve

Because we have an aggregate demand curve plotted on a graph of inflation versus output, we naturally need an upward-sloping aggregate supply curve on the same graph—the economic intuition that has been honed into you in previous courses nearly requires it!

This requirement will be met by relabeling an existing equation: the Phillips curve. That is, our **aggregate supply (AS) curve** is simply the price-setting equation used by firms in the economy:

$$\text{AS curve:}\quad \pi_t = \pi_{t-1} + \bar{v}\tilde{Y}_t + \bar{o}. \qquad (13.2)$$

Notice the following: holding π_{t-1} fixed (after all, it has already been determined by the time period t begins), the Phillips curve is an equation that relates the current rate of inflation π_t to short-run output. Moreover, this relation is upward-sloping, so it's natural to call this an aggregate supply curve, as shown in Figure 13.4.

An interesting feature of the AS curve is that the intercept—the point in the graph where short-run output is equal to zero—is equal to π_{t-1}. This means that if the inflation rate is changing over time, the aggregate supply curve will shift

The aggregate supply curve is simply another name for the Phillips curve. Plotted in ($\tilde{Y}$, π) space, the curve is upward-sloping: higher output today leads firms to raise their prices by more, leading to a higher rate of inflation today. The plot assumes no inflation shocks; that is, $\bar{o} = 0$.

FIGURE 13.4

The Aggregate Supply Curve: $\pi_t = \pi_{t-1} + \bar{v}\tilde{Y}_t + \bar{o}$

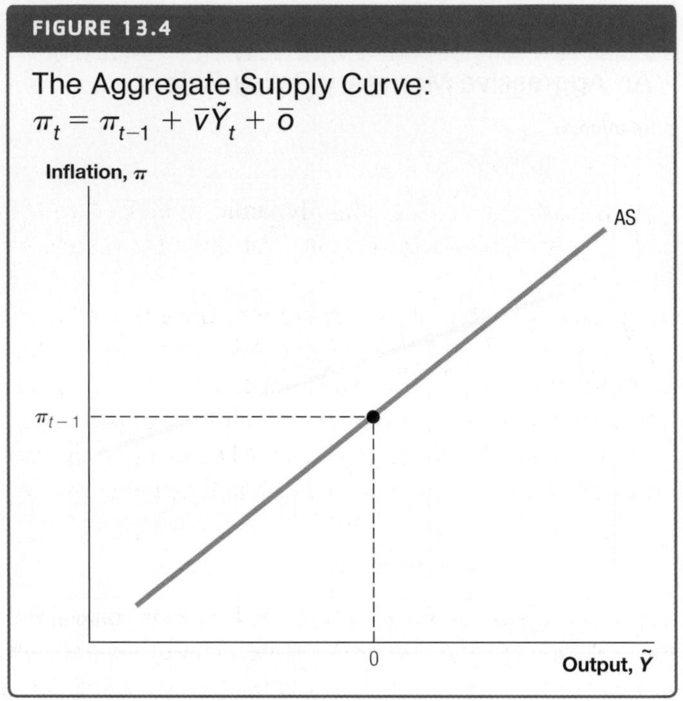

over time, an important feature of our model. The curve may also shift because of inflation shocks—for example, if $\bar{o}$ becomes positive for a period.

Finally, recall *why* there is a π_{t-1} term in the Phillips curve. From Chapter 12, you may remember that this term reflects expected inflation. We've assumed that the expected inflation rate in the coming period is equal to last period's inflation rate. When there are no inflation shocks and when output is at potential, firms simply expect the current rate of inflation to continue. This interpretation of π_{t-1} as expected inflation plays a crucial role in what follows.

13.4 The AS/AD Framework

We can now combine the aggregate demand and aggregate supply curves to create a more elegant version of our short-run model. Mathematically, the two curves are

$$\text{AD curve: } \tilde{Y}_t = \bar{a} - \bar{b}\bar{m}(\pi_t - \bar{\pi}) \tag{13.3}$$

$$\text{AS curve: } \pi_t = \pi_{t-1} + \bar{v}\tilde{Y}_t + \bar{o} \tag{13.4}$$

We have two equations and two unknowns, π_t and $\tilde{Y}_t$. Because this is a dynamic model, solving it is more complicated than just solving two equations—there's also the π_{t-1} term to worry about. But everything works out nicely, as we see next.

The Steady State

We first consider the steady state of this dynamic model. Recall that in steady state, the endogenous variables are constant over time and there are no shocks to the economy ($\bar{a} = 0$ and $\bar{o} = 0$).

In this case, the steady state is easy to solve for. Since the inflation rate must be constant, we have $\pi_t = \pi_{t-1} = \pi^*$. From the AS curve, we see that this implies that short-run output must be zero in steady state: $\tilde{Y}^* = 0$. Then, substituting this solution into the AD curve, we see that when output is at potential, $\pi^* = \bar{\pi}$.

Intuitively, then, the steady state of our AS/AD model is the point where the inflation rate is equal to the central bank's target and actual output is at potential.

The AS/AD Graph

The AS/AD framework is shown in Figure 13.5. Following our standard practice, we assume the economy begins in steady state. Therefore, the inflation rate is $\bar{\pi}$, and it has been at this level for several years. The π_{t-1} term in our AS curve is therefore also equal to $\bar{\pi}$. The graph is quite similar, at least superficially, to a standard supply-and-demand diagram. The aggregate supply curve slopes upward, the aggregate demand curve slopes downward. The vertical axis represents the inflation rate (the percentage change in the price level), and the horizontal axis measures short-run output.

FIGURE 13.5

The AS/AD Framework

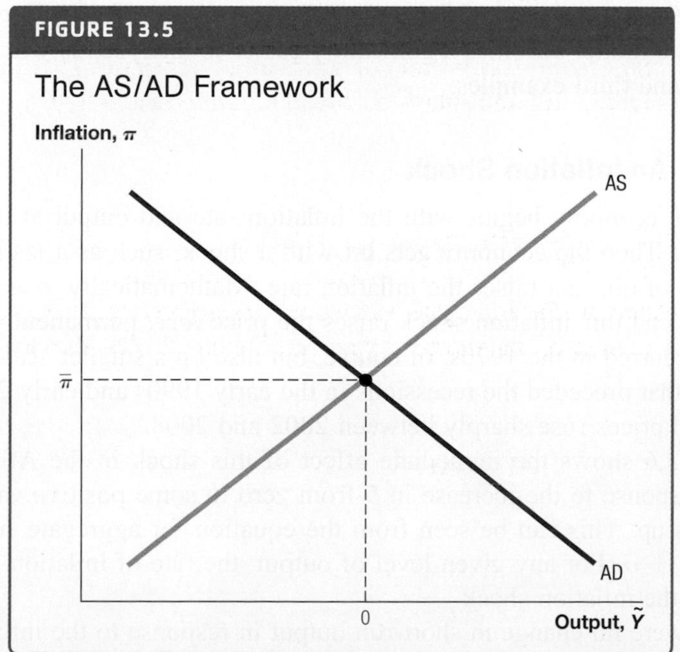

The aggregate supply curve is plotted under the assumption that the economy begins in its steady state, so that $\pi_{t-1} = \bar{\pi}$.

Be sure you understand *why* the AD curve slopes downward and the AS curve slopes upward. The economic explanations of the slopes are quite different from their microeconomic counterparts in a standard supply-and-demand diagram. The AD curve slopes downward because of the response of policymakers to inflation. If the central bank observes a high rate of inflation, the monetary policy rule dictates an increase in the real interest rate. The high interest rate reduces output by reducing investment demand in the economy. Essentially, policymakers slow the economy when they see a high rate of inflation because they know that this will eventually bring inflation back down.

The AS curve slopes upward as an implication of the price-setting behavior of firms embodied in the Phillips curve. When actual output exceeds potential, firms struggle to keep production in line with the high demand—like the firm that manufactures the best-selling toy during the holiday season. Firms therefore raise their prices by more than the usual amount in an attempt to cover increased production costs, like overtime pay. When all firms raise their prices this way, inflation increases. There is thus a positive relation between output and inflation embodied in the AS curve.

13.5 Macroeconomic Events in the AS/AD Framework

The AS/AD version of the short-run model conveniently allows us to analyze the dynamics of inflation and output in a single familiar diagram. We will see how by studying three macroeconomic events: a shock to prices, a disinflation, and an aggregate demand shock. As we go through the first event in detail, the dynamics in the model may seem somewhat tedious. However, after you appreciate what is going on, the model becomes significantly easier to analyze, as will be clear by the second and third examples.

Event #1: An Inflation Shock

Suppose the economy begins with the inflation rate and output at their steady-state values. Then the economy gets hit with a shock, such as a lasting increase in the price of oil, that raises the inflation rate. Mathematically, $\bar{o}$ is positive for one period, and this inflation shock raises the price *level* permanently. This kind of shock occurred in the 1970s, of course, but also on a smaller scale during the Gulf Wars that preceded the recessions in the early 1990s and early 2000s. More recently, oil prices rose sharply between 2002 and 2008.

Figure 13.6 shows the immediate effect of this shock in the AS/AD framework. In response to the increase in $\bar{o}$ from zero to some positive value, the AS curve shifts up. This can be seen from the equation for aggregate supply: $\pi_t = \pi_{t-1} + \bar{v}\tilde{Y}_t + \bar{o}$. For any given level of output, the rate of inflation is increased because of the inflation shock.

If there were no change in short-run output in response to the inflation shock, the inflation rate would increase one-for-one. However, the monetary policy rule

FIGURE 13.6

The Initial Response to an Inflation Shock

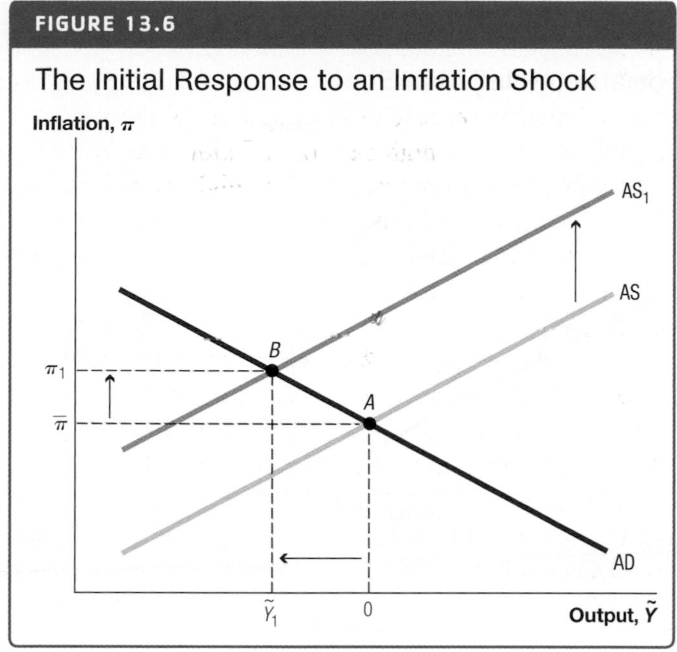

This graph shows the initial response of the economy to an inflation shock: $\bar{o}$ becomes positive for one period, causing the AS curve to shift up. This raises the inflation rate, and the monetary policy rule engineers a slowdown in economic activity.

dictates that the increase in inflation be fought by an increase in the real interest rate, leading short-run output to decline. Therefore, the economy jumps from point *A* in the graph to point *B*, leading to both high inflation and a softening of the economy. This **stagflation**—stagnation of economic activity accompanied by inflation—is exactly what happened in the U.S. economy in response to the oil shocks of the 1970s.

Now think about what happens in the period following the inflation shock. Because we assumed the shock happened for only a single period, $\bar{o}$ is equal to zero from now on. You might think, then, that the AS curve should shift back to its original position. But it doesn't. Why not? Recall that the AS curve is given by the equation

$$\pi_t = \pi_{t-1} + \bar{v}\tilde{Y}_t + \bar{o},$$

where initially $\pi_{t-1} = \bar{\pi}$, since we assumed the economy started in steady state. Now, however, $\pi_1 > \bar{\pi}$, so the AS curve in period 2 is

$$\pi_2 = \pi_1 + \bar{v}\tilde{Y}_2 + \bar{o}.$$

Since $\bar{o} = 0$, if $\tilde{Y}_2$ were equal to zero, inflation would continue at the higher rate π_1: that is, the AS curve for period 2 crosses the $\tilde{Y} = 0$ point at an inflation rate of π_1, which is larger than $\bar{\pi}$. This is shown graphically in panel (a) of Figure 13.7. What is the economics of the situation? First, recall that expected inflation in this setup is given by last period's inflation: $\pi_t^e = \pi_{t-1}$. The high inflation created by the oil shock raises expected inflation. These high expectations adjust only slowly because of our assumption of sticky inflation, which slows down the return of the AS curve to its original position.

FIGURE 13.7

Two Periods after an Inflation Shock

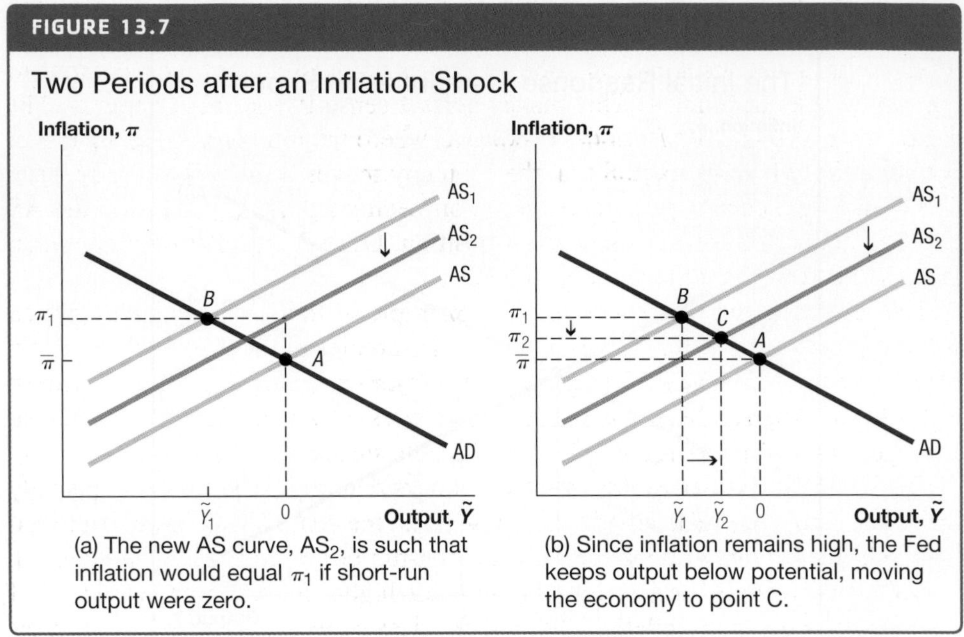

(a) The new AS curve, AS$_2$, is such that inflation would equal π_1 if short-run output were zero.

(b) Since inflation remains high, the Fed keeps output below potential, moving the economy to point C.

In period 2, the economy moves from point *B* to point *C*, shown in panel (b). The slumping economy leads inflation to fall, but only gradually. As a result of the decline in inflation, the monetary policy rule increases output somewhat (leaving it below potential), so the economy is improving.

Figure 13.8 shows the situation in period 3. Once again, the AS curve shifts back toward its original position. However, the presence of an inflation rate greater than $\bar{\pi}$ leads expected inflation to exceed the target rate. The economy gradually adjusts toward steady state, moving to point *D*.

In period 3, expected inflation falls further, shifting the AS curve closer to its original position, and the economy moves to point *D*.

FIGURE 13.8

Three Periods after an Inflation Shock

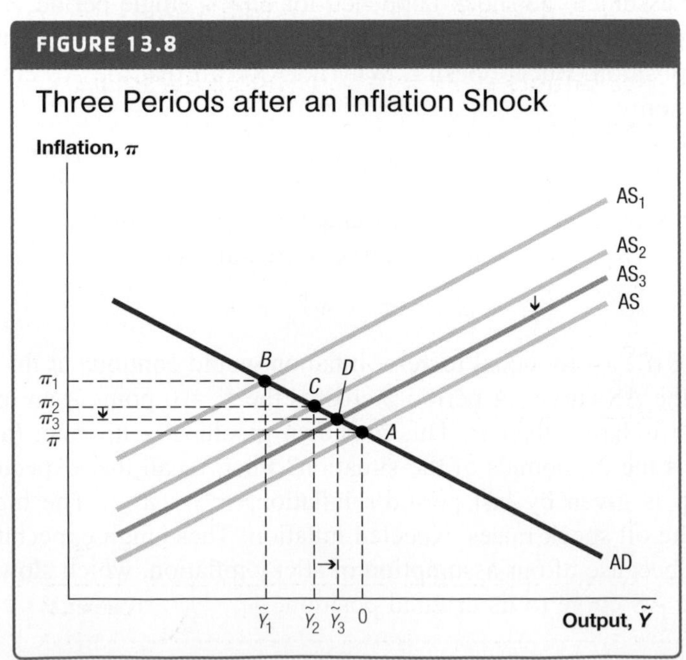

Figure 13.9 provides a way of summarizing the dynamics of inflation and output in the AS/AD framework. The economy initially jumps from point A to point B when the inflation shock hits, and then it moves gradually over time back toward the steady state at point A. This makes perfect sense if you think about it. The steady state of this AS/AD model is point A, where inflation is $\bar{\pi}$ and output is at potential. So it is quite natural that the economy moves back to this steady state. The adjustment occurs as expected inflation declines gradually, causing the AS curve to shift back toward its original position. Our sticky inflation assumption is at the heart of this gradual adjustment.

The careful reader will notice that the principle of transition dynamics, which we first encountered in the long-run model, also applies in the AS/AD framework: the movement back toward the steady state is fastest when the economy is furthest from its steady state. Then, as we saw in Figures 13.7 and 13.8, the movement back gets slower as the economy approaches its steady state.

The lesson from this event is that price shocks that raise inflation are especially insidious. First, they raise inflation directly. Next, the central bank induces a recession to bring the inflation rate back to its long-run target. Even though the shock lasts for only a single period, inflation remains higher for an extended period of time, because of sticky inflation. The shock raises expected inflation, and it takes a prolonged slump in the economy to get these expectations back to normal. The economy suffers stagflation—stagnation and inflation simultaneously—just as it did in the 1970s.

Event #2: Disinflation

Now consider a change in the monetary policy rule itself, similar to the Volcker disinflation of the 1980s. Suppose the economy begins in a steady state that features a

FIGURE 13.9

The Effects of an Inflation Shock: Summary

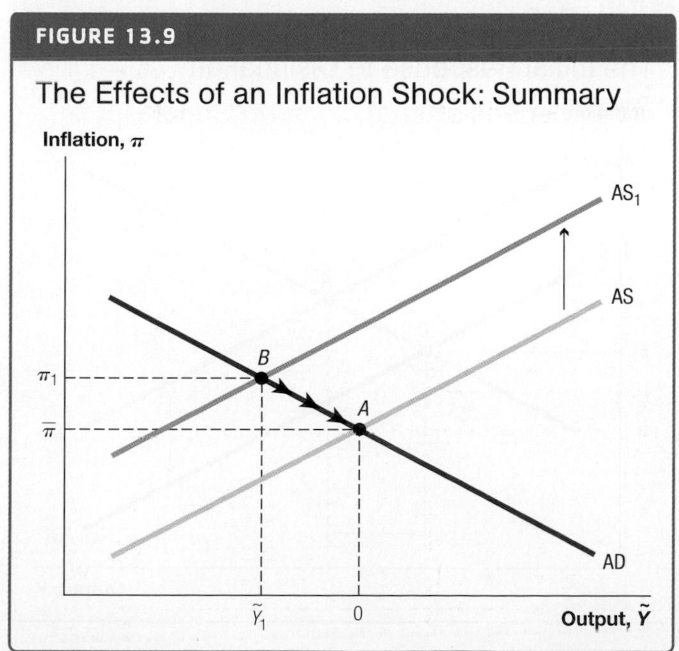

A positive inflation shock–a one-time increase in $\bar{o}$ that lasts for a single period–causes the AS curve to shift up and leads the economy to jump from point A to point B. The monetary policy rule dictates a decline in output in order to fight this inflation. Through the Phillips curve, the slumping economy causes inflation to come down gradually, shifting the AS curve back toward its original position bit by bit. The economy transits slowly back to its steady state at point A (the transitional shifts are indicated with arrows).

moderately high rate of inflation $\bar{\pi}$. Policymakers then decide to reduce the inflation target to a new, lower level $\bar{\pi}'$. How does the economy respond over time?

To analyze this event, first recall the AS and AD equations:

$$\text{AS curve:} \quad \pi_t = \pi_{t-1} + \bar{v}\tilde{Y}_t + \bar{o}.$$
$$\text{AD curve:} \quad \tilde{Y}_t = \bar{a} - \bar{b}\bar{m}(\pi_t - \bar{\pi}).$$

The only place that the inflation target $\bar{\pi}$ appears in the model is in the AD curve, so whatever change occurs will initially involve this curve.

Does the AD curve shift? By studying the equation itself, you should be able to conclude that the answer is yes. At any given inflation rate π_t, the output level associated with the policy rule is reduced. This means that the AD curve shifts down immediately following the policy change, as shown in Figure 13.10.

With the new monetary policy rule in place, the initial rate of inflation, the old target rate of $\bar{\pi}$, is viewed as being too high. The new rule then calls for an increase in interest rates, causing a slowdown and a reduction in inflation. The economy jumps from point *A* to point *B*, leading to an inflation rate of π_1. This rate is somewhere in between the old target and the new one.

To analyze what happens to the economy over time, we again apply the principle of transition dynamics: after a shock that moves the economy away from its steady state, it will transit back gradually to its steady state. The only subtlety here is that the change in the monetary policy rule means that the steady-state rate of inflation has now changed: the new steady-state rate is the lower target $\bar{\pi}'$.

Look at Figure 13.10: by how much did the AD curve shift when the new policy rule was adopted? From the equation, we see that the new AD curve is such that when actual output is at potential, inflation is $\bar{\pi}'$. This new steady state is labeled as point *C* in Figure 13.11, which also shows the transition to the new steady state.

The graph shows the initial response of the economy to a change in the monetary policy rule that targets a lower level of inflation $\bar{\pi}'$. The reduction in the inflation target shifts the AD curve down: at any given inflation rate, the output level associated with the policy rule is reduced.

FIGURE 13.10

The Initial Response to Disinflation

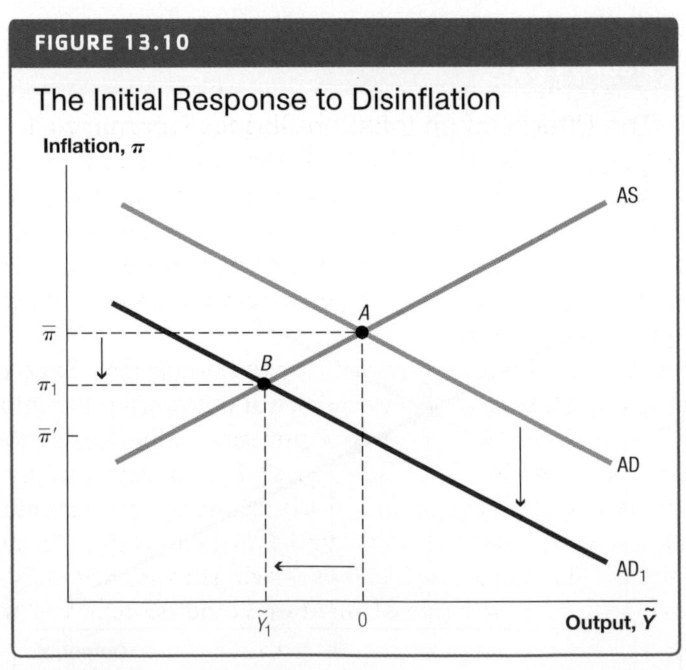

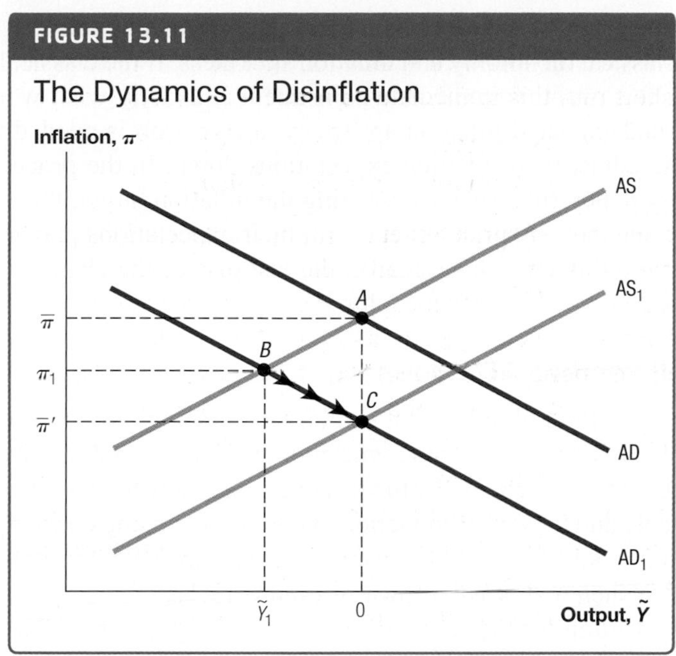

FIGURE 13.11

The Dynamics of Disinflation

Over time, transition dynamics take the economy from point *B* to the new steady state at point *C*. This occurs as the AS curve gradually shifts downward. More formally, the AS curve shifts down as it did in event #1 in Figures 13.7 and 13.8.

When you are solving economic problems in general, the intuition of transition dynamics is an extremely helpful guide to how the economy will evolve. This intuition suggests that the economy will move gradually over time, in Figure 13.11, from point *B* to point *C*. But how do we know that this is really what occurs?

The answer is seen by studying the AS curve. Just as in the first event, the change in the rate of inflation from $\bar{\pi}$ to π_1 causes the AS curve to shift in the following period. Firms adjust their expectations for inflation to take into account the new, lower rate; their expected rate of inflation now becomes π_1 rather than $\bar{\pi}$, so the AS curve shifts down. Since inflation is still above the target, the central bank keeps actual output below potential, leading the inflation rate to fall further. To keep things simple, Figure 13.11 (like Figure 13.9) doesn't show the actual shifts of the AS curve but instead represents them with the arrows of transition dynamics. Nevertheless, the shifts in the AS curve look just like they did in Figures 13.7 and 13.8. These dynamics occur over time until the economy moves to its new steady state at point *C*. Inflation is permanently reduced from $\bar{\pi}$ to $\bar{\pi}'$, and short-run output returns to zero.

In thinking through this event, something important may have occurred to you. If the central bank simply announces that it is lowering the inflation target from $\bar{\pi}$ to $\bar{\pi}'$—say from 10 percent to 5 percent—why doesn't the economy jump immediately to the lower inflation rate? If policymakers made such an announcement and if all price setters in the economy bought into it and set expected inflation to $\bar{\pi}'$, the economy would in fact jump immediately from point *A* to point *C*. The AD and AS curves would shift immediately and simultaneously, and the new, lower rate of inflation could be achieved with no loss in output.

If you think about this possibility, you will see that it reflects the tension between the classical dichotomy and inflation stickiness. If the classical dichotomy holds in the short run, this immediate adjustment is exactly what would happen. But if actual and expected inflation are sticky, a recession is needed to convince price setters to adjust their inflation expectations down. In the process of changing a monetary policy rule, such as lowering the inflation target, the credibility of policymakers and the way price setters form their expectations play critical roles. We will return to this important issue in the last part of the chapter.

Event #3: A Positive AD Shock

Another important kind of shock that can hit the economy is a positive aggregate demand shock. For example, an economic boom in Europe could create an increase in demand there for U.S. goods. Or the discovery of a new technology could make Americans richer and improve production in the future, raising consumption today. Either situation would lead to a temporary increase in $\bar{a}$. The initial response of the economy to such a shock is shown in Figure 13.12.

Recall the equation for the AD curve: $\tilde{Y}_t = \bar{a} - \bar{b}\bar{m}(\pi_t - \bar{\pi})$. The initial effect of an increase in $\bar{a}$ is to shift the AD curve out: at any given level of inflation, the output level associated with the higher value of $\bar{a}$ has increased. This means the economy jumps from point A to point B. Seeing the increase in demand for their goods, firms increase prices, so inflation picks up to some extent. Some of the aggregate demand shock appears in the form of higher output and some in the form of higher inflation.

How does the economy evolve over time after the initial impact of the shock? Your intuition about transition dynamics should suggest that the AS curve will

The AD curve shifts up following a positive AD shock (an increase in $\bar{a}$). The increase in demand leads to higher output and higher inflation, and the economy moves from point A to point B.

FIGURE 13.12

A Positive AD Shock

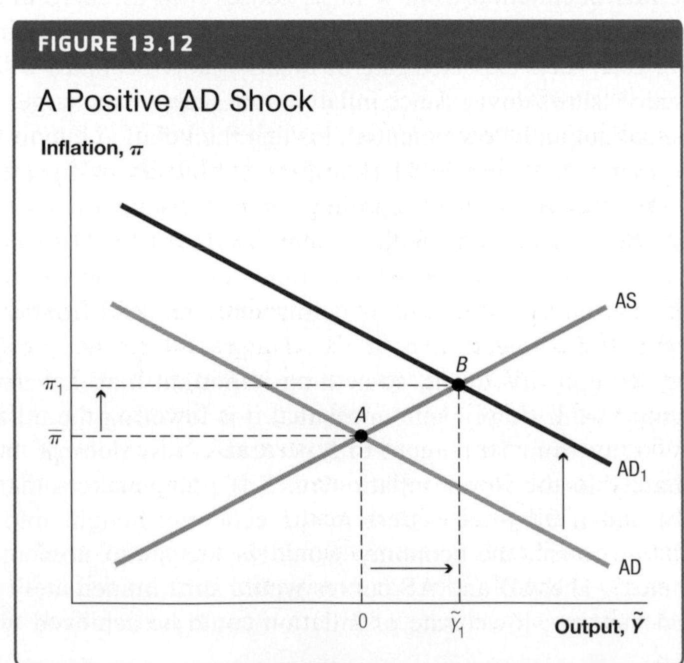

FIGURE 13.13

Dynamics as the AS Curve Shifts

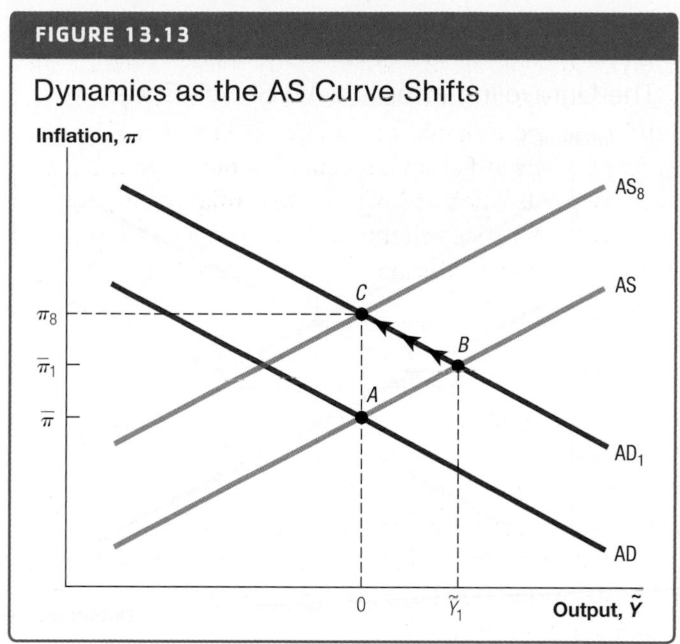

Transition dynamics occur as the AS curve shifts to restore output to potential—but this time at an inflation level that exceeds the steady-state level!

gradually shift until the economy moves back to its original steady state. But if you take a close look at Figure 13.12, you'll see that this isn't possible. If the AS curve shifts to the right, the inflation rate will decline but output will increase. If it shifts to the left, output will decline toward zero, but inflation will rise.

So what happens? First, consider the equation for the AS curve:

$$\pi_t = \pi_{t-1} + \bar{v}\tilde{Y}_t + \bar{o}.$$

The level of inflation associated with zero output (and no inflation shocks) is given by π_{t-1}. Since inflation is above $\bar{\pi}$ in period 1, firms expect higher inflation in the future, so the AS curve shifts upward over time. And since firms expect higher inflation, the inflation rate associated with zero output rises. Transition dynamics thus push the economy toward a higher level of inflation and reduce output toward zero. These dynamics are shown graphically in Figure 13.13. The economy moves gradually over time from point *B* to point *C*. (In the graph, this movement occurs after eight periods of time, but that time label is somewhat arbitrary.)

At point *C*, short-run output is zero; therefore the inflation rate is stable: $\pi_t = \pi_{t-1} + 0 + 0$. As long as nothing else changes, the economy will remain at point *C*. Next, from the AD equation, we see that $0 = \tilde{Y} = \bar{a} + \bar{b}\bar{m}(\pi - \bar{\pi})$. Solving this equation for the level of inflation, we find that $\pi^C = \bar{\pi} + \bar{a}/\bar{b}\bar{m}$. That is, the inflation rate exceeds its steady-state rate by an amount that depends on the aggregate demand shock. (The notation π^C denotes the inflation rate at point *C*; in the figure, this is also labeled π_8.)

Point *C* features an inflation rate that exceeds the central bank's target rate of $\bar{\pi}$. The economy is therefore not in steady state here, so this can't be the end of the story. But then what can change to move the economy back to the steady state at point *A*?

The return to steady state occurs once the AD shock is over. First, the AD curve shifts back to its original position, leading the economy to jump from point *C* to point *D*. Then transition dynamics gradually take the economy from point *D* back to the original steady state at point *A*.

FIGURE 13.14

The Unraveling after the AD Shock Ends

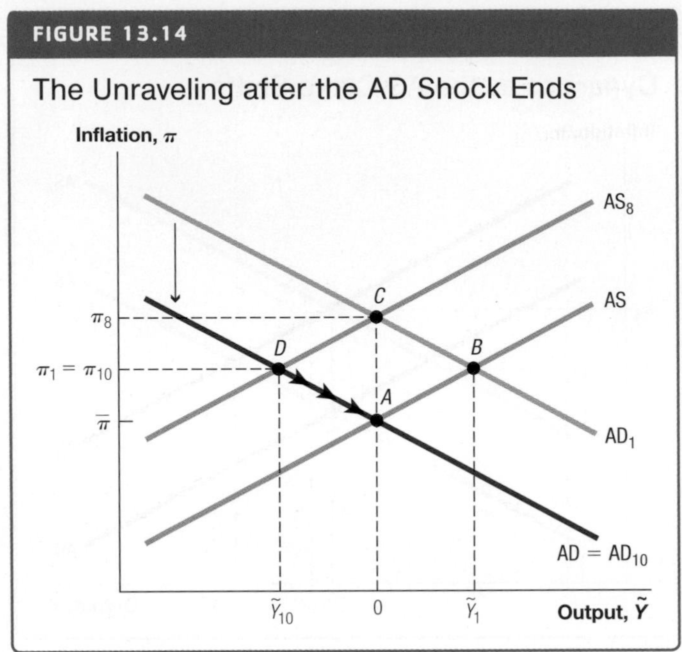

Aggregate demand shocks are by their very nature temporary; the long-run value of $\bar{a}$ is equal to zero. (Why? Remember that in the long run the consumption, investment, government purchases, and net exports shares of potential output must sum to 1.) If a European boom stimulates U.S. exports, for example, the shock will end when the European boom subsides. When this happens, the AD curve shifts back to its original position, and the economy jumps from point *C* to point *D*, as shown in Figure 13.14. Notice that since output was already zero, this is like a negative shock, and it causes output to fall below zero—there is a recession. This change in turn puts downward pressure on inflation. The standard transition dynamics then take the economy back to steady state as lower inflation reduces expected inflation and causes the AS curve to shift back gradually to its original position. Over time, the economy moves back to point *A*, slowly sliding down the original AD curve.

The complete behavior of the economy in response to the positive aggregate demand shock is summarized in Figure 13.15. An important assumption here is that the AD shock remains positive for several periods. As soon as the shock ends, the AD curve will shift back to its original position. In this example, we've allowed the economy to get all the way back to potential (at point *C*) before the shock ends, but the shift back could possibly occur sooner. For example, the European boom that increases demand for U.S. exports could end before the U.S. economy reaches point *C*.

The main lesson from this study of an aggregate demand shock is that booms are matched by recessions. The economy initially benefits from a boom. But it causes inflation to rise, and the only way inflation is brought back down is by a recession. In some "average" sense, the economy doesn't really gain in terms of output: the boom and recession offset each other. But the costs associated with

FIGURE 13.15

A Positive AD Shock: Summary

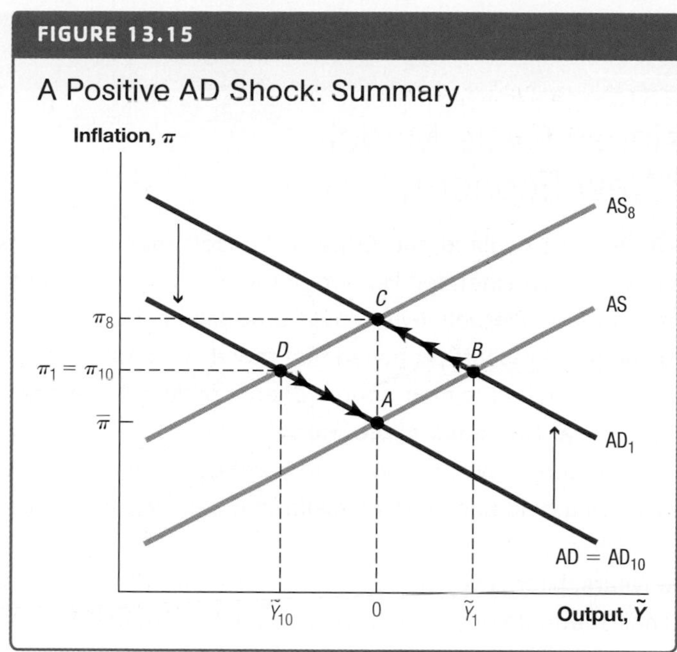

This graph summarizes the dynamics of the economy following a positive AD shock: a jump from *A* to *B*, transition dynamics to *C*, a jump from *C* to *D*, and finally transition dynamics back to the original steady state at *A*.

the higher inflation are real and represent a net loss to the economy. People would be better off staying at point *A* forever, rather than going through this cycle and suffering from temporarily high inflation. It is for this fundamental reason that central banks seek to stabilize short-run output.

Further Thoughts on Aggregate Demand Shocks

The careful reader may have been bothered by the previous section's discussion of the effect of an aggregate demand shock. After all, we know from Chapter 12 that in principle, monetary policy can be used to insulate the economy from aggregate demand shocks—we saw this in the housing bubble example (Section 12.2). By adjusting the real interest rate appropriately, short-run output can be kept at zero, so there is no reason for the economy to go through the kind of cycle just described.

This is a completely appropriate concern. The problem arises because the simple monetary policy rule specified here responds only to inflation and not to changes in output. (We'll consider this point further in Section 13.7.)

The main response to this concern, though, is that there is a difference between the economic model and reality. In practice, when a shock hits the economy, it may take a while for policymakers to understand exactly its magnitude and nature. For example, what are the aggregate demand consequences of Hurricane Katrina or the war in Iraq? When such an event occurs, the consequences aren't immediately obvious. It's also the case that monetary policy may not affect the economy immediately. Our analysis of the aggregate demand event, then, should help us understand how the economy behaves in response to realistic aggregate demand shocks that can be only imperfectly offset.

CASE STUDY

Real Business Cycle Models and the "New Economy"

In the early 1980s, Finn Kydland and Edward Prescott made a surprising discovery. They found that in an extended version of the Solow growth model, variations in the level of total factor productivity could produce realistic fluctuations in the economy. Kydland and Prescott proposed that these "technology shocks," as they came to be called, could be the main source of economic fluctuations. Their framework was called a **real business cycle model** because fluctuations were driven by real forces in the economy, as opposed to nominal changes in monetary policy. At the time, this was a bold and startling claim that set off a flurry of research and controversy.[1]

Twenty-five years later, Kydland and Prescott's contribution is more clearly understood. Their methodology for studying economic fluctuations has had a tremendous influence on modern research, and both were awarded the 2004 Nobel Prize in economics. Research in macroeconomics today often takes some version of the extended Solow model as the starting point for studying economic fluctuations. Various "frictions" to the economy such as sticky inflation or problems in the labor market, together with monetary policy rules, are added to this framework to produce a rich model of economic fluctuations with complete microfoundations. The model allows a range of shocks—including taxes, technological changes, government spending, international factors, price shocks, and changes in monetary policy—to influence economic activity over time. Modern descendants of the real business cycle model are now called "dynamic, stochastic [random] general equilibrium" (DSGE) models, in part because both real and nominal shocks can play important roles.

How do these DSGE models relate to our short-run model? Mathematically, the DSGE models are more complicated; you need graduate-level classes in economics to understand them. Some versions come up with predictions that are generally in line with the predictions of the short-run model, while others lead to some discrepancies, either between the models or between models and data. An important area of current research focuses on how to resolve these difficulties.

One of the significant unresolved issues is whether fluctuations in GDP are due mostly to fluctuations in potential output or to fluctuations in short-run output. As we learned in Chapter 9, separating out these differences can be quite hard in practice. Yet the task is crucial, not only for our academic understanding, but also for

[1] Their original paper, "Time to Build and Aggregate Fluctuations," appeared in *Econometrica* in 1982.

policymaking. For example, in the late 1990s, U.S. GDP grew so rapidly that people spoke of the "new economy." Policymakers had to decide whether this rapid growth was due to technological changes that moved potential output (and therefore didn't threaten to raise inflation) or was due to an aggregate demand shock that raised short-run output and would likely increase inflation.

Many macroeconomists were of the view that at least some of the changes represented an increase in short-run output that raised the specter of higher inflation. To his credit, Alan Greenspan, an early adherent of the "new economy" view, ascribed most of the gains in output to technological changes and thus opposed raising interest rates to slow the economy. Since inflation did not increase substantially at the end of the 1990s, most economists today believe he made the right call.

Such questions—and more generally providing detailed microfoundations for the theory of economic fluctuations—make for a very active branch of research in macroeconomics today.[2]

13.6 Empirical Evidence

This section evaluates the empirical predictions of our short-run model when monetary policy is dictated by the simple inflation-based policy rule. We consider two pieces of evidence: the implied path for the fed funds rate and the time paths for inflation and output.

Predicting the Fed Funds Rate

"So, where do you think interest rates are headed?" When you return home for vacation and tell your parents you're taking an economics class, questions like this are sure to follow. The truth of the matter is that if you knew for sure, you'd be a very rich person. Nevertheless, our simple monetary policy rule, $R_t - \bar{r} = \bar{m}(\pi_t - \bar{\pi})$, does provide some guidance.

The first thing to notice is that our policy rule applies to the real interest rate, not the nominal interest rate. Fortunately, the Fisher equation tells us how to go back and forth between these two; we just need to add the rate of inflation to the real interest rate to get the nominal rate. Then, the monetary policy rule implies that the nominal interest rate is

$$i_t = R_t + \pi_t = \bar{r} + \pi_t + \bar{m}(\pi_t - \bar{\pi}). \qquad (13.5)$$

[2] For more details, consult the following references: Robert E. Lucas Jr., *Models of Business Cycles* (New York: Basil Blackwell, 1987); Edward C. Prescott, "Nobel Lecture: The Transformation of Macroeconomic Policy and Research," *Journal of Political Economy*, vol. 114 (April 2006), pp. 203–35; David Romer, *Advanced Macroeconomics* (New York: McGraw-Hill, 2006), Chapter 4.

The graph shows the actual and predicted level for the fed funds rate. The predicted level is computed using the monetary policy rule with a coefficient of $\bar{m} = 1/2$. We also assume $\bar{r} = 2\%$ and $\bar{\pi} = 2\%$.

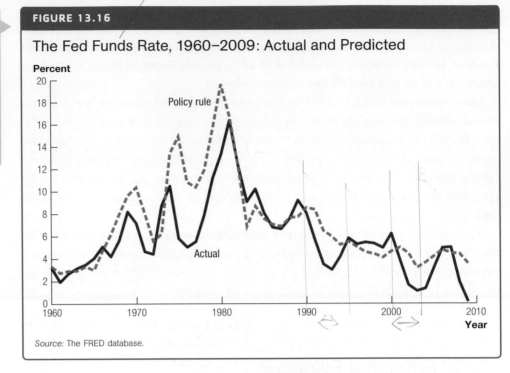

FIGURE 13.16

The Fed Funds Rate, 1960–2009: Actual and Predicted

Source: The FRED database.

Next, to implement this equation, we need to pick values for the parameters. In the early 1990s, John Taylor of Stanford University suggested picking parameter values that were all functions of the number 2: $\bar{r} = 2\%$, $\bar{m} = 1/2$, and $\bar{\pi} = 2\%$.[3] That is, we assume the real interest rate is constant at 2 percent, and that an increase in inflation of 1 percentage point causes the central bank to raise the real interest rate by 1/2 a percentage point. This means the nominal interest rate rises by 1½ percentage points—more than one-for-one with inflation—so that the real interest rate rises with inflation. And we assume the target rate of inflation $\bar{\pi}$ is also equal to 2 percent.

If we take these parameter values along with data on the inflation rate, we can compute the fed funds rate predicted by our monetary policy rule. As we can see from Figure 13.16, overall our simple policy rule produces a surprisingly accurate picture of the actual behavior of the fed funds rate.

A key place where the policy rule and the actual fed funds rate give different answers is the period from the late 1960s until 1980. During this period, the fed funds rate was substantially less than the rate implied by the policy rule. One interpretation of this gap is that monetary policy was excessively loose during this period, which contributed to rising inflation during the 1970s.

If you look closely, you will also see that the Fed also departs from this very simple policy rule during recessions: in the early 1990s, in the early 2000s, and in 2009, the Fed set interest rates much lower than our simple policy rule predicts.

[3] The Taylor rule, as it is called, included short-run output as well as the inflation rate in the monetary policy rule. You will analyze the Taylor rule in an exercise at the end of the chapter. See John Taylor, "Discretion versus Policy Rules in Practice," *Carnegie-Rochester Conference Series on Public Policy*, vol. 39 (1993), pp. 195–214.

There is a good explanation for this. The actual version of the Taylor rule includes a short-run output term as well as an inflation term. That is, when the economy is in a recession, the Taylor rule dictates that the fed funds rate be lowered even further. We will discuss this richer version of the Taylor rule in an exercise at the end of this chapter and then again in Chapter 14.

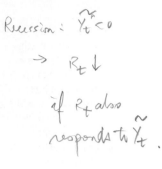

Inflation-Output Loops

A robust feature of the short-run model is that the economy follows counterclockwise loops in a plot with the inflation rate on the vertical axis and output on the horizontal axis. We can see this easily in Figure 13.15, where the economy was hit with an aggregate demand shock, but it was also true in the inflation shock example, Figure 13.9. If we had considered a negative aggregate demand shock or a negative shock to inflation, the same pattern would have been apparent. The intuition for these loops is straightforward. First, positive short-run output leads the inflation rate to rise. Second, a rise in inflation leads policymakers to reduce output. These basic forces produce the counterclockwise movements in the graph.

How well does this prediction hold up empirically? The answer is shown in Figure 13.18. If you follow the years, you'll observe the counterclockwise evolution of the economy. When the economy booms, inflation increases. When the inflation rate is high, the central bank slows the economy, short-run output declines, and inflation falls. This key prediction of the short-run model thus receives strong support from the data.

Also readily apparent in these figures is the fact that 2009 is such a large "outlier": short-run output is sharply negative, and inflation is already low. An implication of the counterclockwise loop pattern is that there will be downward pressure on inflation in coming years, which could even push the inflation rate negative. This is called **deflation** and, for reasons that will be discussed in Chapter 14, it can be particularly harmful to an economy. The Federal Reserve is well aware of this threat and is keeping a watchful eye on inflation.

CASE STUDY

Forecasting and the Business Cycle

Our analysis of the short-run model suggests that economists have a solid understanding of economic fluctuations. We might then expect that they would be able to forecast the time path of the economy with reasonably good precision, to the satisfaction of businesses, Wall Street investment banks, and policymakers, among others. Unfortunately, the truth of the matter is quite different!

Economic forecasts are made by professional economists each quarter (four times a year), and because GDP for a given quarter is not known until well after the quarter is over, the forecasts begin with the level of GDP in the current quarter. To

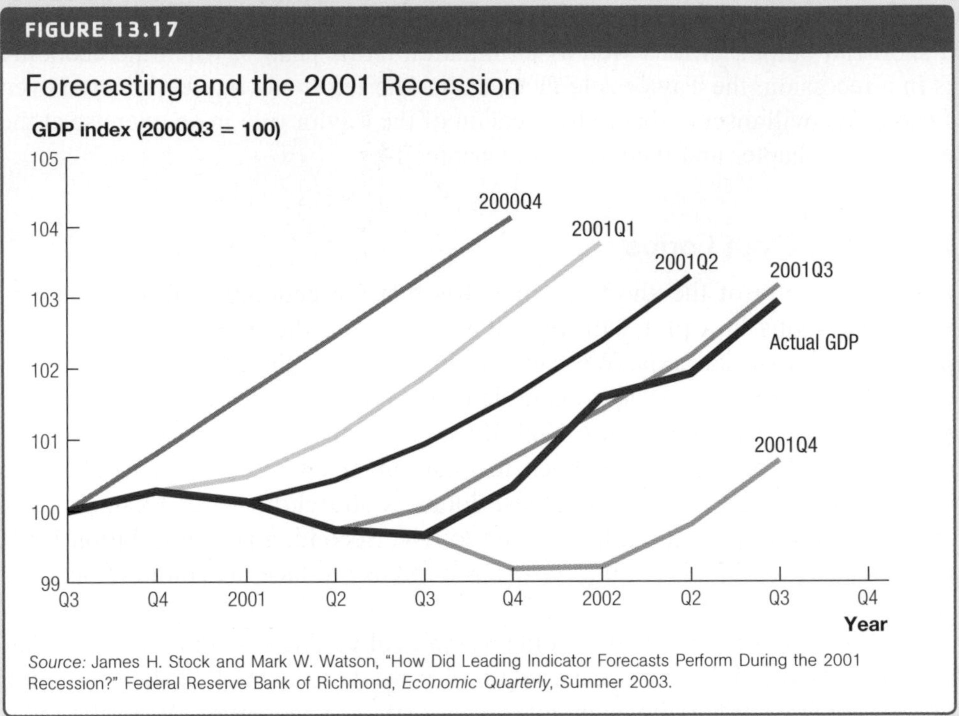

The heavy red line shows the actual path of GDP. The other lines show the average predicted path that professional forecasters expected the economy to follow. (Different paths are shown according to the quarter in which the forecast was made.) Forecasts by professional economists consistently missed the onset and continuation of the recession. Moreover, once they finally predicted that the recession would continue, following the 9/11 terrorist attack, the economy recovered rapidly. Forecasting is extremely difficult!

construct these forecasts, economists study a large number of economic variables that have proved useful in predicting the time path of the economy in the past, called **leading economic indicators**. Examples include the fed funds rate, the term structure of interest rates (such as the difference between the 10-year rate and the 30-day rate), new claims for unemployment insurance, and the number of new houses being built.

Consider the forecasts of the path of real GDP around the time of the 2001 recession, as shown in Figure 13.17. There are three remarkable characteristics of this figure. First, the forecasts fail to predict the onset of the recession, despite the fact that they were made after the sharp decline in the stock market associated with the bursting of the dot-com "bubble" in March 2000. Second, after the recession begins, the forecasts miss its continuation for the next three quarters: they keep predicting the recovery will begin in the current quarter, which it fails to do. Finally, when the forecasts predict the recession will continue in the fourth quarter of 2001, the recovery begins. Overall, professional forecasts have an extremely difficult time predicting the "turning points" of the economy.

The third feature of the forecasts is related to the terrorist attacks on September 11, 2001. Following these attacks, forecasters were pessimistic about the coming time path of the economy—this is the curve labeled "2001Q4" in the graph. But remarkably, the economy had already begun to recover, and the recovery looked much like the time path forecasters were expecting before the attacks occurred.

FIGURE 13.18

Inflation-Output Loops in the U.S. Economy

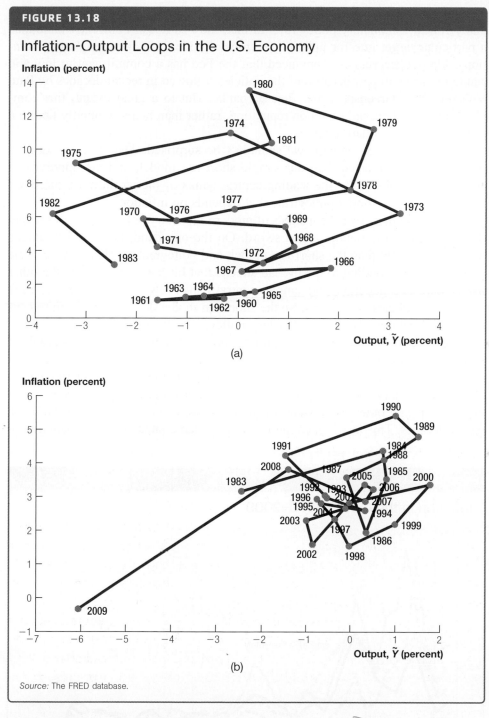

(a)

(b)

Source: The FRED database.

The U.S. economy, confirming a key prediction of the short-run model, follows counterclockwise inflation-output loops over time. A booming economy tends to raise inflation. High inflation is often followed by a recession to bring inflation down.

13.7 Modern Monetary Policy

We have seen that monetary policy in the United States can be described as following a systematic approach, at least in the last three decades. And we have noted that this approach can be characterized in terms of a simple monetary policy rule.

It may come as a surprise, then, to learn that the Federal Reserve does *not* officially follow a monetary policy rule. In fact, the Fed doesn't currently announce a particular target rate for inflation, even as a guide to its own long-term intentions. Many observers are convinced that the Fed has a commitment to low and stable inflation, in part because of the policies followed in recent decades by Paul Volcker, Alan Greenspan, and Ben Bernanke. But to a great extent, this commitment is implicit and based on reputation, rather than being explicitly tied to a particular rule or inflation target.

At a deeper level, perhaps we shouldn't be surprised. The U.S. economy is much more complicated than our simple short-run model, and the hundreds of economists employed by the leading central banks of the world must surely do more than obey a simple policy rule that depends on inflation.

This section discusses the insights of modern monetary policy. We will see that these insights are a double-edged sword. On the one hand, the world is indeed more complicated than the short-run model, and policymakers should have some discretion in responding to the myriad shocks that hit the economy. On the other hand, there is a general move among central banks toward being more explicit about their policies and targets. So the short-run model does indeed seem to capture many features of modern monetary policy.

Before we delve into monetary policy, look first at Figure 13.19, a graph of inflation in certain industrialized countries. A great deal of (well-deserved) credit is given in the United States to Paul Volcker and Alan Greenspan for running an effective monetary policy for the last 30 years. What's also true, however, is that inflation rates in other industrialized countries have been equally well-behaved in recent decades. This fact is even more striking when compared with inflation rates

Inflation was high in the 1970s in many advanced countries. Central banks there succeeded in lowering inflation substantially by the 1980s.

FIGURE 13.19

Inflation in the OECD, 1970–2009

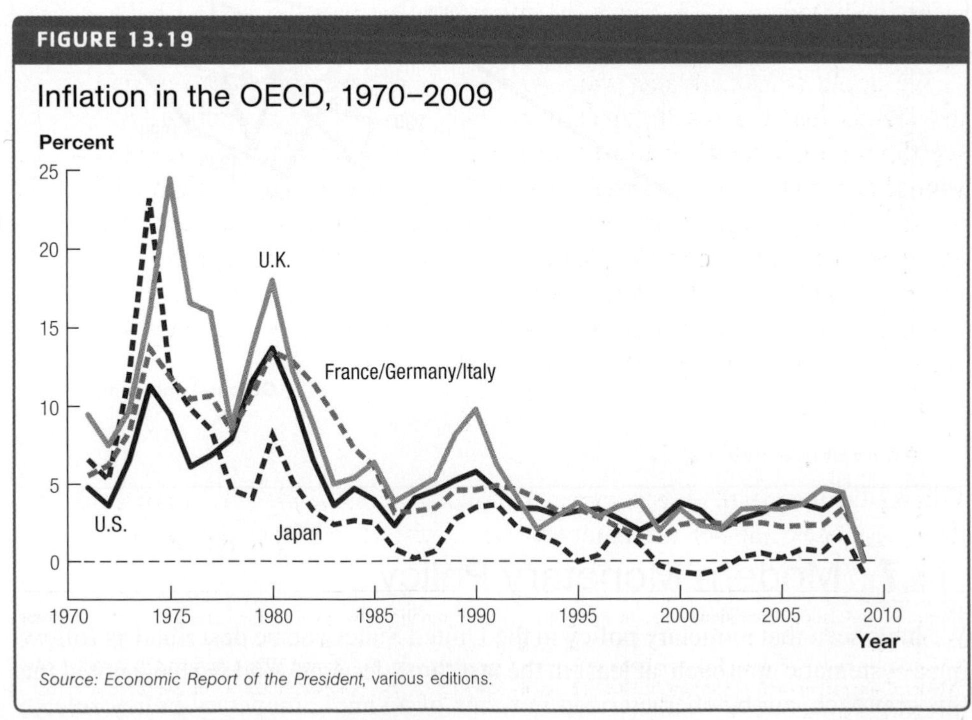

Source: Economic Report of the President, various editions.

in these countries in the 1970s: in both the United Kingdom and Japan, for example, inflation rates peaked at more than 20 percent per year during the early 1970s.

A precise accounting of the taming of inflation in these industrialized countries is not available. Some economists attribute part of the decline to good luck: the large oil shocks of the 1970s, for example, haven't been repeated. But it's also the case, as we have seen, that economists today have a better understanding of how to conduct effective monetary policy than they had in the 1960s and 1970s, thanks to academic research and practical experience. We turn now to some of the academic ideas that have contributed to this successful policy.[4]

More Sophisticated Monetary Policy Rules

No central bank in the world mechanically follows a simple monetary policy rule like the one considered in this chapter. Nevertheless, these rules are extremely useful. For one thing, policy rules, as we saw in the previous section, do provide a surprisingly accurate characterization of monetary policy in the United States; the same is true in other countries as well. And the rules may prove useful as guidelines, even if they're not followed mechanically, both to financial markets and to central bankers themselves. Central banks can depart from the guidelines when their superior information about the state of the economy renders such departures prudent. As we will see shortly, these rules-as-guidelines may play an important role in helping the central bank stabilize the economy and maintain low inflation.

The monetary policy rule we've been considering depends only on inflation and not at all on short-run output. At first glance, this may seem odd: shouldn't the central bank's focus be on stabilizing output when the economy goes into a recession? Does the sole focus on inflation mean that the central bank doesn't care about short-run output in some sense?

We could consider richer monetary policy rules in the short-run model, but the fact is that the result typically resembles our AS/AD framework. (You'll see this in a couple of exercises at the end of the chapter.) The reason for this similarity is that even our simple rule *implicitly* puts weight on short-run output. In our model, changes in short-run output lead to changes in inflation (recall the aggregate demand shock we studied in Section 13.5). Because the policy rule responds to changes in inflation, it implicitly responds to the changes in output that cause inflation to change. This is the basic reason why even our simple rule delivers such reasonable and realistic results.

Rules versus Discretion

Would we ever want to program our monetary policy rule into a computer and then step back and let the computer be in charge of monetary policy? Or, to

[4] For a more detailed discussion of recent thought in economic policy, two useful references are Christina Romer and David Romer, "The Evolution of Economic Understanding and Postwar Stabilization Policy," in *Rethinking Stabilization Policy* (Federal Reserve Bank of Kansas City, 2002), pp. 11–78; and V. V. Chari and Patrick J. Kehoe, "Modern Macroeconomics in Practice: How Theory Is Shaping Policy," *Journal of Economic Perspectives*, vol. 20 (Fall 2006), pp. 3–28.

return to the question posed at the beginning of the chapter, could we replace Ben Bernanke with a robot? The obvious answer is no. It's impossible to allow for every shock and combination of shocks that may hit the economy. Events in the real world are much more complicated than the simple shocks in our model, and some discretion by policymakers will always be valuable in these situations. The recent financial crisis provides a perfect example of this point. But a less stringent version of the question is worthy of consideration: is there any benefit to committing to a systematic policy?

Finn Kydland and Edward Prescott won their Nobel Prize in 2004 partly for answering this question.[5] Their answer is summarized nicely in an analogy to Homer's epic poem *The Odyssey*. In the poem, Ulysses has his sailors bind him to the mast of his ship and fill their own ears with wax before sailing past the island of the Sirens, so that the crew won't be tempted by the Sirens' enchanting music. This commitment to a policy prevents the crew from steering the ship to its destruction on the island's rocky coast.[6]

Kydland and Prescott suggest that a similar dilemma, known as a **time consistency problem**, is faced by central banks. After firms and workers have formed their expectations about inflation and built these expectations into their contracts and pricing strategies, central bankers have an incentive to pursue an expansionary monetary policy so that the economy will boom. Firms and workers, however, will anticipate the expansionary monetary policy and build *that* into their prices. The result will be a high rate of inflation with no benefit on the output side. If policymakers can commit to not exploiting the inflation expectations of firms and workers, the economy can benefit from a lower average level of inflation. This result is exactly what an explicit and credible monetary policy rule can accomplish.

Another example of the time consistency problem concerns investments. After firms undertake large investments, policymakers may be tempted to tax these investments. However, if they know that policymakers will respond in this fashion, firms will logically be reluctant to invest in the first place. Even if policymakers say they won't tax the investment tomorrow, once tomorrow comes, they have an incentive to renege on their promise. That is, their promise is not "time consistent."

Policymakers can overcome these time consistency problems by committing themselves to the right policy, as Ulysses did on his ship. In addition to explicit policy rules, credibility and a reputation for making the right long-run choices can also help policymakers overcome such problems.

The Paradox of Policy and Rational Expectations

The ultimate goal that we'd like macroeconomic policy to attain is relatively straightforward: full employment, output at potential, and low, stable inflation. The great paradox of monetary policy is that the best way a central bank can achieve

[5] Finn E. Kydland and Edward C. Prescott, "Rules Rather Than Discretion: The Inconsistency of Optimal Plans," *Journal of Political Economy*, vol. 85 (June 1977), pp. 473–91.

[6] Ben Bernanke gave this analogy in a speech in 2003, when he was a governor of the Federal Reserve, but not the chair; see footnote 11 for the reference.

this goal may be to focus on maintaining low inflation and to show a willingness to engineer large recessions in order to achieve that end. The mere presence of a policymaker who is willing to generate recessions to fight inflation may make the need to use that policy less likely, thereby leading to the joint goals of economic stability and low inflation.

How might such a policy show up in our short-run model? A tough stance on inflation shows up in the monetary policy rule as a high value of $\bar{m}$: the policymaker raises interest rates sharply in response to a modest increase in inflation, producing a large recession. To see how such a policy keeps inflation low, we need to reconsider how workers and firms form their expectations about inflation.

Up until now, we've been working with adaptive expectations: we've assumed that expected inflation between period t and period $t + 1$ is simply given by last period's inflation:

$$\pi_t^e = \pi_{t-1}.$$

In some ways, this is a strange assumption to make. For example, the central bank's target rate of inflation $\bar{\pi}$ makes no appearance in this equation. We might have thought that the expected rate of inflation would depend directly on the target rate. More generally, if the central bank changes its monetary policy rule, this equation says that the expected rate of inflation will not change. Our motivation for this assumption was the stickiness of inflation, and for many purposes, this is a useful benchmark.

It is also important, however, to consider another benchmark: **rational expectations**, a concept emphasized in a series of papers by Robert E. Lucas, the 1995 winner of the Nobel Prize in economics.[7] Under rational expectations, people use all information at their disposal to make their best forecast of the coming rate of inflation. This information may include the costs that tend to make inflation sticky. But it may also include the central bank's target rate of inflation $\bar{\pi}$ and any announcements the bank may make about its future target. So if a credible central bank changes its policy rule, expected inflation may adjust directly.

In the presence of rational expectations, the central bank's willingness to fight inflation becomes a crucial determinant of expected inflation. If firms know that the central bank will fight aggressively to keep inflation at a low rate, no matter what the consequences, then they will be much less likely to raise prices sharply in response to an inflation shock. That is, the knowledge that policymakers will reduce the rate of inflation back to $\bar{\pi}$ quickly means that price setters will do some of this hard work for them.

Recall that apart from shocks and departures of output from potential, the inflation rate in the economy is pinned down by what firms *expect* the inflation rate to be: $\pi_t = \pi_t^e$. To the extent that policymakers can influence, or *manage*, these expectations, they can reduce the costs of maintaining a low target level of inflation. This is one of the most important lessons of modern monetary policy, and we now explore it in more detail.

---

[7] See, for example, Robert E. Lucas Jr., "Expectations and the Neutrality of Money," *Journal of Economic Theory*, vol. 4 (April 1972), pp. 103–24; and "Econometric Policy Evaluation: A Critique," *Carnegie-Rochester Conference Series on Public Policy*, vol. 1 (1976), pp. 19–46.

The central bank lowers its target rate of inflation from 4% to 2%, shifting the AD curve back. With adaptive expectations, this would cause a recession that would gradually shift the AS curve down, as we saw in event #2. However, by coordinating expected inflation so that it falls to 2% immediately, the central bank achieves a disinflation with no loss in output.

FIGURE 13.20

Costless Disinflation by Coordinating Expectations

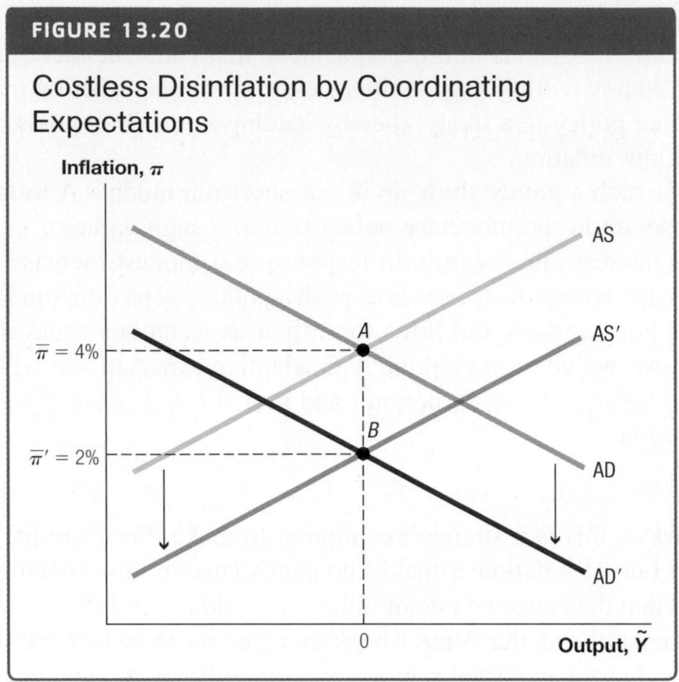

Managing Expectations in the AS/AD Model

To incorporate the insights of rational expectations into our AS/AD framework, we drop the assumption of adaptive expectations and rewrite the AS curve with π_t^e instead of π_{t-1}:[8]

$$\pi_t = \pi_t^e + \bar{v}\tilde{Y}_t + \bar{o}. \tag{13.6}$$

Now consider the following change in monetary policy. Suppose the Federal Reserve announces that it wishes to lower inflation from a current target of $\bar{\pi} =$ 4% to a new target of $\bar{\pi}' = 2\%$. If people believe the new target will prevail and set $\pi^e = 2\%$, what happens to inflation and output?

The answer is shown in Figure 13.20. The change in the target rate of inflation causes the AD curve to shift down. In the standard AS/AD model with adaptive expectations, this result would lead to a recession that would eventually cause inflation to fall to the new, lower target. However, if expectations adjust immediately so that $\pi^e = 2\%$, the AS curve shifts down immediately to the new target. The economy, by moving from point A to point B, achieves the lower rate of inflation without undergoing a costly recession.

This example illustrates the fundamental importance of expectations in the conduct of monetary policy. To the extent that the central bank can coordinate people's expectations of inflation, it can maintain low and stable inflation without the need for recessions. Such coordination requires credibility and transparency on the part of the central bank. Although extremely difficult to achieve, it represents an important and valuable goal.

[8] This was our original specification of the Phillips curve, which you can check by looking back at equation (11.3) on page 000.

CASE STUDY

Rational Expectations and the Lucas Critique

In the 1970s, macroeconomic models were based entirely on simple assumptions about expectations, such as adaptive expectations. Then, in 1976, Robert Lucas applied the theory of rational expectations in a powerful way to these models, in what has become known as **the Lucas critique**.[9] The Lucas critique says that it is inappropriate to build a macroeconomic model based on equations in which expectations are not consistent with the statistical properties of the underlying economy. For example, when a credible central bank announces a change in its monetary policy rule, expected inflation changes directly. Any model based on adaptive expectations could thus lead to incorrect predictions. The Lucas critique has had a profound impact on macroeconomic theory: modern models have internalized it so that they incorporate the theory of rational expectations explicitly.

In practice, we might wonder if workers and firms are in fact fully rational and able to figure out exactly the implications of policy changes for the expected rate of inflation. And even if they are, do the costs of making these computations still mean that inflation (and therefore expected inflation) will adjust slowly? Such questions remain the subject of economic research. Nevertheless, the principles of the Lucas critique are powerful, and the lessons it implies for coordinating expectations are central to modern monetary policy.

Inflation Targeting

How can central banks improve their management of inflation expectations? They could announce an explicit monetary policy rule, even though such rules are often too simple to capture the richness of the information possessed by central banks and the range of shocks that can hit the economy. Or they could take a step in that direction by adopting an explicit target rate of inflation.

A large and growing list of countries—the United Kingdom, Australia, Brazil, Canada, Mexico, New Zealand, and Sweden among them—follow the latter course. In the United Kingdom, the government instructs the Bank of England to aim for a target rate of inflation of 2.5 percent, and this target appeared to have played an important role in stabilizing inflation at a low level.[10] Central banks are not required to deliver the target rate of inflation in every period, but rather apply it over a medium- to long-term horizon.

---

[9] See the 1976 paper cited in footnote 7.

[10] See, for example, Mervyn King, "What Has Inflation Targeting Achieved?" in Ben Bernanke and Michael Woodford, *The Inflation Targeting Debate* (Chicago: University of Chicago Press, 2004).

An obvious advantage of an explicit inflation target is that it helps to anchor inflation expectations. When firms are deciding how to set their prices after a temporary inflation shock, the target rate may serve as a focal point and allow firms and workers to coordinate efforts in keeping inflation low, thereby reducing the need for large declines in output. In addition, an explicit inflation target may actually make it easier for the central bank to stabilize output. When the central bank eases monetary policy to stimulate the economy, if firms and workers understand the commitment to the long-run inflation rate, they won't be tempted to deviate from their standard price-setting behavior, and this will allow the monetary stimulus to exert its desired short-term effect on output.

As of this writing, the Federal Reserve does not make public an explicit target for the inflation rate. Nevertheless, a number of prominent monetary economists—including Ben Bernanke before he became chair of the Federal Reserve—have advocated a move to a more explicit target rate. To Bernanke, inflation targeting is a matter of what he calls **constrained discretion**. In the short run, the central bank has the flexibility to respond to shocks to the economy in order to ensure the stability of output and inflation. Over the long term, however, it maintains a commitment to a particular rate of inflation.[11] In any case, it's a reasonable bet that more information about the Federal Reserve's goals for inflation will be made public in the coming years.

CASE STUDY

Choosing a Good Federal Reserve Chair

The person who chairs the Federal Reserve Board of Governors is one of the two most important economic policymakers in the United States (the other being the president). Some chairs—such as William McChesney Martin Jr. in the 1950s and early 1960s, Paul Volcker in the 1980s, and Alan Greenspan in the 1990s—have proved highly successful. Others have not. Mariner Eccles, the chair in the late 1930s, pursued a monetary policy that prolonged the Great Depression and resulted in a large deflation. Arthur Burns (1970–78) and G. William Miller (1978–79) presided over the Great Inflation of the 1970s.

What makes some chairs more successful than others? Christina Romer and David Romer of the University of California at Berkeley argue that policymakers' views about how the economy works play a crucial role.[12] In the successful cases, policymakers held a conviction that inflation brought high costs and offered

[11] Ben Bernanke, "A Perspective on Inflation Targeting," March 25, 2003 (www.federalreserve.gov/boarddocs/speeches/2003/20030325/default.htm).

[12] Christina D. Romer and David H. Romer, "Choosing the Federal Reserve Chair: Lessons from History," *Journal of Economic Perspectives* (Winter 2004), pp. 129–62.

realistic views about the impact of monetary policy on economic fluctuations. In contrast, Fed chairs in the 1930s and 1970s held views at odds with our modern understanding of macroeconomics. For example, Arthur Burns believed there was little that monetary policy could do in the 1970s to stem the tide of rising inflation.

Equally interesting, Romer and Romer found that these views were expressed in writings, speeches, and testimony given by the policymakers *before* they were appointed chair. The lesson is a simple one: knowledge of macroeconomics is essential to a successful reign by the chair of the Federal Reserve. Writing in 2004, the authors conclude, "The way to choose a good Federal Reserve chair is to read what candidates have said about how the economy operates and ask them about their economic beliefs. If what a candidate says is unrealistic or poorly reasoned, move on to another candidate or risk a replay of the 1930s or the 1970s" (p. 130). By this criterion, the selection in 2006 of Ben Bernanke—a Princeton University professor of macroeconomics with extensive experience as a policymaker—as the new chair appears to have been an extremely solid decision.

13.8 Conclusion

The taming of inflation in many advanced countries of the world during the last 30 years is one of the great accomplishments of monetary policy. A credible, transparent commitment by central banks to a low rate of inflation is one of the keys to this victory. Such a commitment helps to anchor the inflation expectations of firms and workers, so that temporary shocks to inflation are deflected quickly.

Moreover, the commitment to low inflation makes it easier for the central bank to achieve another goal of stabilization policy: keeping actual output at potential. The widespread knowledge that the central bank has a commitment to low and stable inflation allows it to stimulate the economy to fight adverse shocks and downturns, without provoking self-fulfilling fears of a general rise in inflation. Indeed, after the United States suffered its most severe recession since the Great Depression in 1980–82, an improved monetary policy focused on taming inflation helped bring about the two longest economic expansions in recorded history, back-to-back (see Figure 9.3 in Chapter 9). This successful period has been labeled **the Great Moderation** because of the relative tranquility of the macroeconomy during this time.[13]

Of course, the term *the Great Moderation* seems quaint from the perspective of today: it is not much of a "moderation" if it is followed by the Great Recession! While our understanding of the forces underlying booms, recessions, and

[13] For example, see the "Remarks by Governor Ben S. Bernanke at the Meetings of the Eastern Economic Association," Washington, D.C., February 20, 2004, archived at www.federalreserve.gov.

financial crises remains incomplete, it is also clear that macroeconomics has made substantial progress during the last several decades. In the next chapter, though, we will see how this understanding was put to the test by the Great Recession.

CHAPTER REVIEW

SUMMARY

1. Monetary policy often follows a systematic approach that can be characterized as a monetary policy rule. In the simple rule explored in this chapter, $R_t - \bar{r} = \bar{m}(\pi_t - \bar{\pi})$, the central bank increases the real interest rate whenever inflation exceeds a particular target. Although it's difficult to imagine such a simple rule reflecting the real world, it turns out to describe monetary policy in the U.S. economy over the last few decades reasonably well.

2. Combining a monetary policy rule with the IS curve leads to an aggregate demand (AD) curve, which describes how the central bank chooses the level of short-run output based on the current rate of inflation. When the central bank sees a high rate of inflation, it raises interest rates to slow down economic activity, reducing output below potential. The equation for the AD curve is $\tilde{Y}_t = \bar{a} - \bar{b}\bar{m}(\pi_t - \bar{\pi})$.

3. The aggregate supply (AS) curve, another name for the Phillips curve, tells us that the current rate of inflation depends positively on short-run output. A booming economy leads firms to raise their prices by more than last period's rate of inflation, leading to an even higher rate of inflation over the coming year. The equation for the AS curve is $\pi_t = \pi_t^e + \bar{v}\tilde{Y}_t + \bar{o}$.

4. In the basic AS/AD framework, we assume expected inflation adjusts slowly, or is sticky. In other words, we have adaptive expectations, so that $\pi_t^e = \pi_{t-1}$.

5. The AS/AD framework is quite intuitive. In a single graph, it allows us to study such shocks to the economy as inflation shocks, aggregate demand shocks, and changes in the inflation target. The graph shows how inflation and short-run output evolve over time. In general, the principle of transition dynamics applies, and the economy moves gradually back to its steady state after a shock. These dynamics are driven by the slow adjustment of expected inflation and show up as shifts in the AS curve.

6. Modern monetary policy recognizes that managing inflation expectations is an important key to stabilizing the economy. The theory of rational expectations says that in order to determine future inflation, people analyze all information that is available to them. Systematic monetary policy, reputation, and inflation targets are tools that central banks use to help them manage inflation expectations. By anchoring inflation expectations, central banks can achieve low inflation and stable output in the least costly fashion.

KEY CONCEPTS

aggregate demand (AD) curve
aggregate supply (AS) curve
constrained discretion
deflation
the Great Moderation
inflation expectations
inflation-output loops
inflation targets
leading economic indicators
the Lucas critique
monetary policy rules
rational expectations
real business cycle model
rules versus discretion
stagflation
time consistency problem

REVIEW QUESTIONS

1. How is a monetary policy rule helpful for understanding U.S. monetary policy?
2. Why does the AD curve slope downward? Why does the AS curve slope upward? How is the AS/AD graph like a standard supply-and-demand diagram? How is it different?
3. What are some examples of shocks that shift the AD curve? What about the AS curve?
4. What is the fundamental source of transition dynamics in our AS/AD framework? Why does the economy take several periods before returning to its steady state following a shock?
5. Why do inflation-output loops appear counterclockwise?
6. Why are inflation expectations so important to modern monetary policy? What are several ways that central banks try to manage inflation expectations?

EXERCISES

smartwork.wwnorton.com 

1. **A simple monetary policy rule:** Consider the policy rule employed in the chapter: $R_t - \bar{r} = \bar{m}(\pi_t - \bar{\pi})$, where we assume $\bar{r} = 2\%$, $\bar{m} = 1/2$, and $\bar{\pi} = 2\%$.
   - **(a)** Compute the level of the (nominal) interest rate implied by this rule when the inflation rate takes the following values: 10%, 5%, 2%, 1%.
   - **(b)** Repeat part (a) when $\bar{m} = 1$ instead. Explain why you get different answers.
2. **Predicting the fed funds rate:** Obtain data on the inflation rate for the most recent 12-month period possible (the FRED database at the Federal Reserve Bank of St. Louis is an excellent resource). Use this inflation rate and this chapter's monetary policy rule to determine what fed funds rate the policy rule indicates. How does this rate compare with the current fed funds rate? If they are different, why do you think that's the case? (*Hint*: Be sure that you are comparing two nominal rates; our simple rule corresponds to a real rate.)

3. **A negative oil price shock:** It is common to blame some of the poor macroeconomic performance of the 1970s on the rise in oil prices. In the middle of the 1980s, however, oil prices declined sharply. Using the AS/AD framework, explain the macroeconomic consequences of a one-time negative shock to the inflation rate, as might occur because of a sharp decline in oil prices.

4. **The oil price shocks of 2006–2009:** Between 2006 and the middle of 2008, oil prices rose sharply—from around \$60 to more than \$140 per barrel. By the end of 2008, however, oil prices had fallen even more sharply, to just over \$40 per barrel. Think of these events as two separate shocks.
   - **(a)** What, precisely, are the two shocks? (For the purpose of this question, let's ignore the significant role played by the financial crisis itself.)
   - **(b)** Using the AS/AD framework, explain how the macroeconomy would evolve in response to these shocks.

5. **A decline in foreign demand for U.S. goods:** Suppose the European and Japanese economies succumb to a recession and reduce their demand for U.S. goods for several years. Using the AS/AD framework, explain the macroeconomic consequences of this shock, both immediately and over time.

6. **Reinflation in Japan:** In the late 1990s and early 2000s, inflation was actually negative in Japan (look back at Figure 13.19). This question asks you to explore a change in policy to achieve a *higher* inflation rate.

   Consider an economy that begins with output at potential and an inflation rate of $\bar{\pi}$, so the economy begins in steady state. A new chair of the central bank decides to raise the long-run inflation target to $\bar{\pi}'$ (greater than the original $\bar{\pi}$). Show how the economy responds over time, using the AS/AD framework. Comment on your results.

7. **The slope of the AS curve:**
   - **(a)** Why does the AS curve slope upward?
   - **(b)** If the AS curve were more steeply sloped, how would the economy respond differently to aggregate demand shocks (shocks to $\bar{a}$)?
   - **(c)** If the curve were more steeply sloped, how would the economy respond differently to aggregate supply shocks (shocks to $\bar{o}$)?
   - **(d)** What kind of economic changes in the economy would lead the curve to be more steeply sloped?

8. **The slope of the AD curve:**
   - **(a)** Why does the AD curve slope downward?
   - **(b)** If the AD curve were more steeply sloped, how would the economy respond differently to aggregate demand shocks (shocks to $\bar{a}$)?
   - **(c)** If the curve were more steeply sloped, how would the economy respond differently to aggregate supply shocks (shocks to $\bar{o}$)?
   - **(d)** What kind of economic changes in the economy would lead the curve to be more steeply sloped?

9. The Taylor rule: John Taylor of Stanford University proposed the following monetary policy rule:

$$R_t - \bar{r} = \bar{m}(\pi_t - \bar{\pi}) + \bar{n}\tilde{Y}_t.$$

That is, Taylor suggests that monetary policy should increase the real interest rate whenever output exceeds potential.

(a) What is the economic justification for such a rule?

(b) Combine this policy rule with the IS curve to get a new aggregate demand curve. How does it differ from the AD curve we considered in the chapter? Consider the response of short-run output to aggregate demand shocks and inflation shocks.

10. A monetary policy rule that completely offsets aggregate demand shocks: Our monetary policy rule responds only to shocks to the inflation rate. We saw in Section 13.5 that this means that aggregate demand shocks can cause the economy to undergo a "boom-recession" cycle. Create your own monetary policy rule that would insulate the aggregate economy complctely from aggregate demand shocks—so that neither inflation nor output would change if an aggregate demand shock hit the economy. Explain why your policy works. (*Hint*: Assume that policymakers can observe the aggregate demand shocks directly.)

11. Crowding out: Consider a simplified version of the Taylor rule, where monetary policy depends only on short-run output:

$$R_t - \bar{r} = \bar{n}\tilde{Y}_t.$$

(a) Draw an IS-MP diagram, but instead of the usual MP curve, plot the simplified version of the Taylor rule. You might label this curve MPR for "monetary policy rule."

(b) Now consider the effect of a positive aggregate demand shock in the IS-MPR diagram. (An example might be a fiscal stimulus.) Compare and contrast the effect of this shock on the economy in the standard IS-MP diagram versus the IS-MPR diagram. Why is the result different?

(c) Economists refer to the result in the IS-MPR diagram as "crowding out." What gets crowded out and why?

12. The coefficient on inflation in the nominal version of the policy rule: Consider the policy rule for the nominal interest rate in equation (13.5). Draw a graph with the inflation rate on the horizontal axis and the nominal interest rate on the vertical.

(a) What is the slope of this line? Is it larger than 1 or less than 1?

(b) Suppose the slope were the reverse of what you answered in part (a): larger or less than 1. Explain what this implies about the response of nominal interest rates to inflation in a good monetary policy rule.

13. Deflation: The Japanese economy at the end of the 1990s and into the 2000s experienced several years of deflation (see Figure 13.19). Again, recall the monetary policy rule employed in the chapter: $R_t - \bar{r} = \bar{m}(\pi_t - \bar{\pi})$, where $\bar{r} = 2\%$, $\bar{m} = 1/2$, and $\bar{\pi} = 2\%$.

(a) Compute the level of the (nominal) interest rate implied by this policy rule when the inflation rate takes the following values: 1%, 0%, −1%.
(b) Is it possible for the nominal interest rate to be negative? Why or why not?
(c) What does your answer to part (b) mean about monetary policy during a deflation?
(d) If a central bank wants to end the deflation and stimulate the economy, as in the case of Japan in the late 1990s, what can it do?

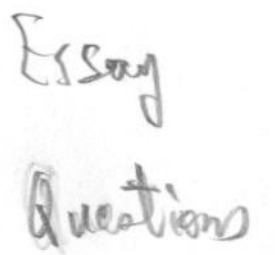

14. Analyzing remarks by the Federal Reserve chair: Suppose your job is to explain Federal Reserve policy to the CEO of a corporation. Look at a speech by the Fed chair on www.federalreserve.gov/newsevents/. Write a brief memo to your CEO explaining one of the key points of the speech. Use the diagrams of the AS/AD framework if you like; your CEO is a former economics major. (Be sure to indicate which speech you're analyzing.)

15. Can the Fed permanently increase employment? "The Federal Reserve is obsessed with inflation, so much so that it ignores the fact that millions of American workers are unemployed. We need a Fed that fights for American jobs. We need a Fed that views any unemployment as too much unemployment, rather than worrying about whether inflation is 2% or 3%." In a one-page essay, discuss the merits and demerits of this viewpoint, using graphs and equations when helpful.

16. Revisiting the inflation shock (hard): Reread the inflation shock example (event #1) in Section 13.5. Suppose the size of the shock is $\bar{o}_0$.

(a) In the AS/AD graphs describing the response of the economy to the inflation shock, we labeled the initial response of inflation as π_1 and initial output as $\tilde{Y}_1$. What are the values of these key points in terms of the parameters of the model? That is, by how much does output fall, and what is the initial inflation rate?
(b) Now suppose the parameters of the AS and AD curves take the following values: $\bar{o}_0 = 2\%$, $\bar{a} = 0$, $\bar{b} = 1/2$, $\bar{m} = 1/2$, $\bar{v} = 1/2$, and $\bar{\pi} = 2\%$. Solve for the value of short-run output and the inflation rate for the first three years following the shock.
(c) Comment briefly on your results.

17. Revisiting the effect of the booming European economy (hard): Reread the aggregate demand shock example (event #3) in Section 13.5. Suppose the parameters of the AS and AD curves take the following values: $\bar{a} = 2\%$, $\bar{b} = 1/2$, $\bar{m} = 1$, $\bar{v} = 1/2$, and $\bar{\pi} = 3\%$. Solve for the value of short-run output and the inflation rate for the first three years following the shock. For this problem, assume the aggregate demand shock lasts for more than three years. Comment on your results.

WORKED EXERCISES

9. The Taylor rule:

(a) Taylor's rule features a key property that—at least on the surface—makes it appear preferable to the simple policy rule considered in this chapter. In particular, it says that the central bank should respond directly to short-run output. If the economy goes into a recession, this rule dictates a lowering of interest rates to stimulate the economy. In contrast, our policy rule changes interest rates only *after* the softening of the economy has affected inflation. This exercise asks you to consider how this direct response to output changes the model relative to the indirect response we've been considering.

(b) To derive the new AD curve, we substitute the Taylor rule into the basic IS curve. Recall that the equation for the IS curve is $\tilde{Y}_t = \bar{a} - \bar{b}(R_t - \bar{r})$. Making the substitution for the interest rate term gives

$$\tilde{Y}_t = \bar{a} - \bar{b}\bar{m}(\pi_t - \bar{\pi}) - \bar{b}\bar{n}\tilde{Y}_t.$$

We can then collect the $\tilde{Y}_t$ terms on the left side to get

$$(1 + \bar{b}\bar{n})\tilde{Y}_t = \bar{a} - \bar{b}\bar{m}(\pi_t - \bar{\pi}).$$

Finally, dividing by $1 + \bar{b}\bar{n}$ leads to our new AD curve:

$$\tilde{Y}_t = \frac{\bar{a}}{1 + \bar{b}\bar{n}} - \frac{\bar{b}\bar{m}}{1 + \bar{b}\bar{n}}(\pi_t - \bar{\pi}).$$

Two things to notice about this equation: First, if $\bar{n} = 0$, we are back to our original AD curve, just as you'd expect. Second, because $1 + \bar{b}\bar{n}$ is greater than 1, the new AD curve shows *more muted responses* to aggregate demand shocks and to changes in the inflation rate—the new AD curve is steeper.

Why is this? The policy rule now says to stimulate the economy whenever there is a recession. This softens the impact of aggregate demand shocks and makes the central bank less harsh in fighting inflation. Notice also, however, that the overall form of the AD curve is just the same as the one we studied in the chapter. The difference is really just a matter of degree (muting the effects). This is why we are somewhat justified in sticking with the simpler formulation in the main text.

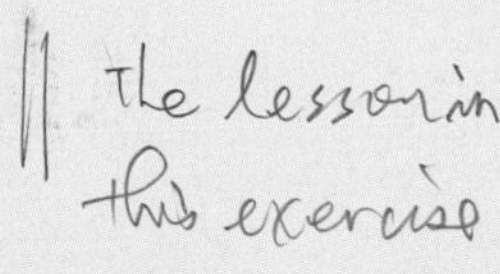

13. Deflation:

(a) From equation (12.5), the nominal interest rate is given by

$$\begin{aligned} i_t = R_t + \pi_t &= \bar{r} + \pi_t + \bar{m}(\pi_t - \bar{\pi}) \\ &= 2\% + \pi_t + 1/2 \times (\pi_t - 2\%) \\ &= 1\% + 3/2 \times \pi_t. \end{aligned}$$

Using this formula, we get the following results:

Inflation	Nominal interest rate
1%	2.5%
0%	1.0%
−1%	−0.5%

(b) It's *not* possible for the nominal interest rate to be negative. Think about it. The nominal interest rate is the rate that the bank pays you for the privilege of having access to your money. Suppose the bank tried to charge you 0.5% per year on your savings account instead of paying interest, so the effective nominal interest rate was −0.5%. You could always keep your money under your mattress or in a lock box in the bank and earn a zero nominal interest rate. (Well, in highly dangerous circumstances, we could imagine banks charging you a fee for protecting the property right you have to your money, but those circumstances don't apply here.)

(c) The fact that nominal interest rates can't be negative poses a dilemma for a country like Japan during a deflation. The policy rule says to stimulate the economy with negative interest rates, but the most Japan can do is lower the interest rate to zero. In fact, this is basically what the Bank of Japan did—short-term nominal interest rates were reduced to extremely low levels.

Notice that with a deflation, the economy would like to create some inflation. The problem is that it appears difficult to make monetary policy sufficiently "loose" to achieve this goal.

(d) At some level, governments are good at generating inflation, so deflation should not be a serious problem. Japan tried to use fiscal policy to stimulate the economy and created large budget deficits and a large national debt. One thing the government could do is print money to pay for its government spending. We know from the quantity theory of money that if the central bank prints enough money, it should be able to generate inflation. Another way the central bank can stimulate the economy is to reduce long-term interest rates by buying 10-year bonds instead of short-maturity bonds.

Many observers worried in the early 2000s that a problem similar to Japan's could someday affect the United States, particularly when the inflation rate was low. Overall, however, most economists believe there are enough tools at the disposal of the U.S. government and the central bank for creating inflation that deflation should not be a serious problem. This reasoning is being tested once again in recent years as the Great Recession puts downward pressure on inflation at a time when inflation is already quite low.

CHAPTER 14

THE GREAT RECESSION AND THE SHORT-RUN MODEL

OVERVIEW

In this chapter, we

- introduce financial considerations—a risk premium—into our short-run model and use this framework to understand the Great Recession.
- study deflation, bubbles, and the Federal Reserve's balance sheet as we deepen our understanding of the financial crisis.
- consider various actions that policymakers took in response to these events.

> When banking stops, credit stops, and when credit stops, trade stops, and when trade stops—well, the city of Chicago had only eight days of chlorine on hand for its water supply. . . . The entire modern world is premised on the ability to buy now and pay later.
>
> —MICHAEL LEWIS, *THE BIG SHORT*

14.1 Introduction

In the fall of 2008, a financial tsunami crashed through the world's financial sector, taking down century-old financial institutions and creating mass panic in financial markets. In under a month, the stock market declined by a third, wiping out trillions of dollars of wealth. Near the height of the panic on a weekend in late September, Chairman Bernanke met with congressional leaders and warned, "If we don't do this [the Troubled Asset Relief Program], we may not have an economy on Monday."[1]

What began as a modest problem in a small corner of the mortgage market spread far beyond Wall Street. World GDP declined in 2009 for the first time in decades, and the U.S. and world economies succumbed to the Great Recession. The unemployment rate peaked at more than 10 percent in the United States and seems likely to remain high for years to come. Why? How do we make sense of these events?

The answers to these questions are not entirely clear, and macroeconomic research has its plate full in the coming years. Nevertheless, using our short-run model, the broad outlines of the crisis can be understood.

We begin this chapter by adding a key financial component to the IS/MP and AS/AD frameworks. In particular, we show how the financial crisis generated a huge wedge between the fed funds rate—the rate set by policymakers—and the rate at which businesses and households borrow. Interest rates spiked, and a number of credit markets ceased to function. As a result, investment declined sharply, ultimately dropping by more than 30 percent. This large shock to aggregate demand was compounded by declines in the stock market and the housing market, which in turn reduced household wealth and consumption, providing a second channel through which aggregate demand plummeted.

The second part of the chapter considers the actions that policymakers took in response to the crisis. The Federal Reserve lowered interest rates all the way to zero. However, this conventional policy proved to be insufficiently effective because of the increased interest-rate wedges in financial markets. The Fed then pursued a range of unconventional policies as well, ultimately adding more than

---

Epigraph: Michael Lewis, *The Big Short: Inside the Doomsday Machine* (New York: Norton, 2010), p. 222.

[1] Joe Nocera, "As Credit Crisis Spiraled, Alarm Led to Action" *New York Times*, October 1, 2008, p. Al.

$1 trillion in loans to financial institutions and purchases of assets like mortgage-backed securities to its balance sheet. The government was involved in other ways as well, ranging from the $700 billion Troubled Asset Relief Program (TARP) to the $787 billion fiscal stimulus package passed as the American Recovery and Reinvestment Act of 2009.

This chapter considers the economics underlying the policy responses to the global financial crisis. Along the way, we make contact with several pathologies that can infect the macroeconomy, including deflation, bubbles in financial markets, and that most famous of all financial crises, the Great Depression.

14.2 Financial Considerations in the Short-Run Model

A Risk Premium

In Chapters 9 through 13, we assumed that the Fed could effectively set the real interest rate at which firms borrow and lend. As a starting point—and in normal times—this is a good assumption. But, as we suggested in Figure 10.3, one of the key channels through which the financial crisis affected the economy was by creating a substantial spread between the interest rate on government securities and the interest rate at which firms and households borrow.

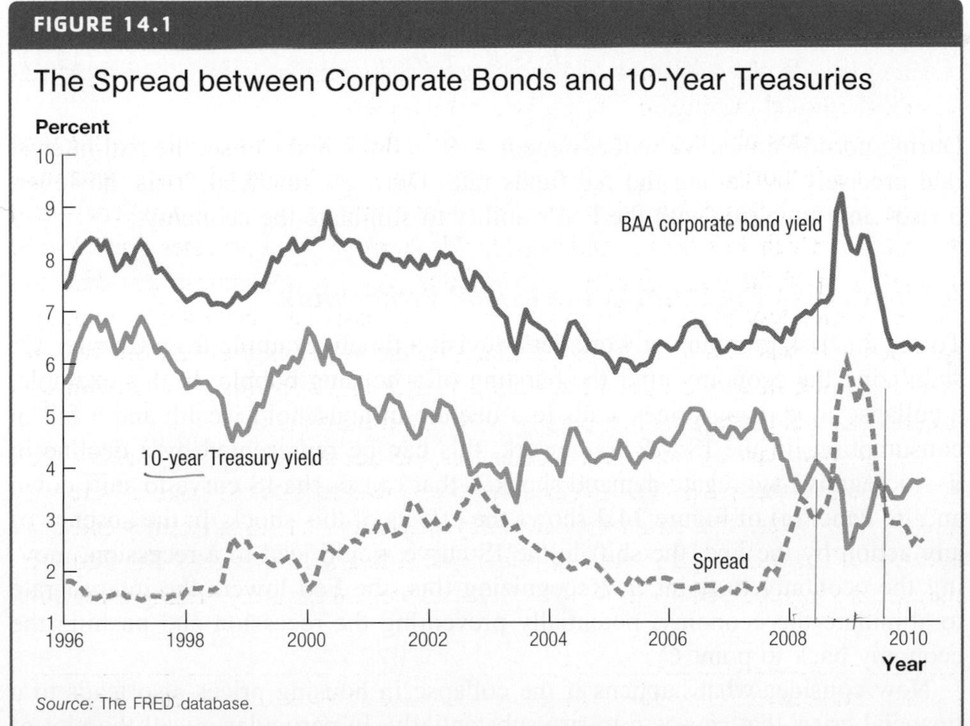

FIGURE 14.1

The Spread between Corporate Bonds and 10-Year Treasuries

Source: The FRED database.

Despite the large decline in the interest rate on government securities, the interest rate for corporate borrowing rose rather than declined during the financial crisis.

While Figure 10.3 showed this spread for loans with a 3-month maturity, Figure 14.1 illustrates it for corporate bonds of a much longer maturity. BAA-rated corporate bonds (investment-grade bonds with a "medium" grade for risk) typically have a yield that is about 2 percentage points higher than 10-year Treasury bonds. Between 2007 and 2008, however, this spread rose sharply, reaching more than 6 percentage points in December 2008. Ten-year Treasury yields fell substantially between 2006 and 2008 as the Fed cut interest rates. But contrary to their usual historical pattern, the yield on corporate bonds rose instead of fell.

This pattern can be found throughout financial markets in late 2008 and early 2009: afraid that borrowers might have trouble repaying their loans, lenders demanded a **risk premium**. For example, if one believes there is a 2 percent chance that Citigroup will default on its loans during the next year and pay back only 50 cents on the dollar, one may ask for an extra 1 percent in interest to compensate for this risk.

The interest-rate spread in Figure 14.1 also illustrates something else that is very important: even though the Fed cut the fed funds rate all the way to zero in an effort to stimulate the economy, the rate at which firms and households borrow to finance investment was rising instead of falling. Despite the extensive efforts of the Federal Reserve, interest rates moved in the wrong direction, deepening instead of mitigating the downturn.

To incorporate this discussion into our short-run model, let $\bar{p}$ represent the exogenous risk premium that sits between the fed funds rate R^{ff} and the real interest rate at which firms borrow in financial markets:

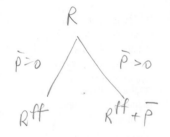

$$R = R^{ff} + \bar{p} \tag{14.1}$$

During normal times, we will assume $\bar{p} = 0$, and the Fed can set the real interest rate precisely by setting the fed funds rate. During a financial crisis, however, $\bar{p}$ rises and interferes with the Fed's ability to stimulate the economy.

A Rising Risk Premium in the IS/MP Framework

To see this risk premium at work, let's revisit a timely example from Chapter 12: stabilizing the economy after the bursting of a housing bubble. In this example, a collapse in housing prices leads to a decline in household wealth and a fall in consumption. In the IS/MP framework, this can be represented by a decline in $\bar{a}$—a negative aggregate demand shock—that causes the IS curve to shift down and in. Panel (a) of Figure 14.2 shows the effects of this shock. In the absence of any action by the Fed, the shift in the IS curve would lead to a recession, moving the economy to point B. Recognizing this, the Fed lowers the interest rate to stimulate the economy, potentially preventing the recession and pushing the economy back to point C.

Now consider what happens if the collapse in housing prices also leads to a financial crisis that causes $\bar{p}$ to rise substantially. In particular, recall the plot of

FIGURE 14.2

A Housing Bubble and a Financial Crisis

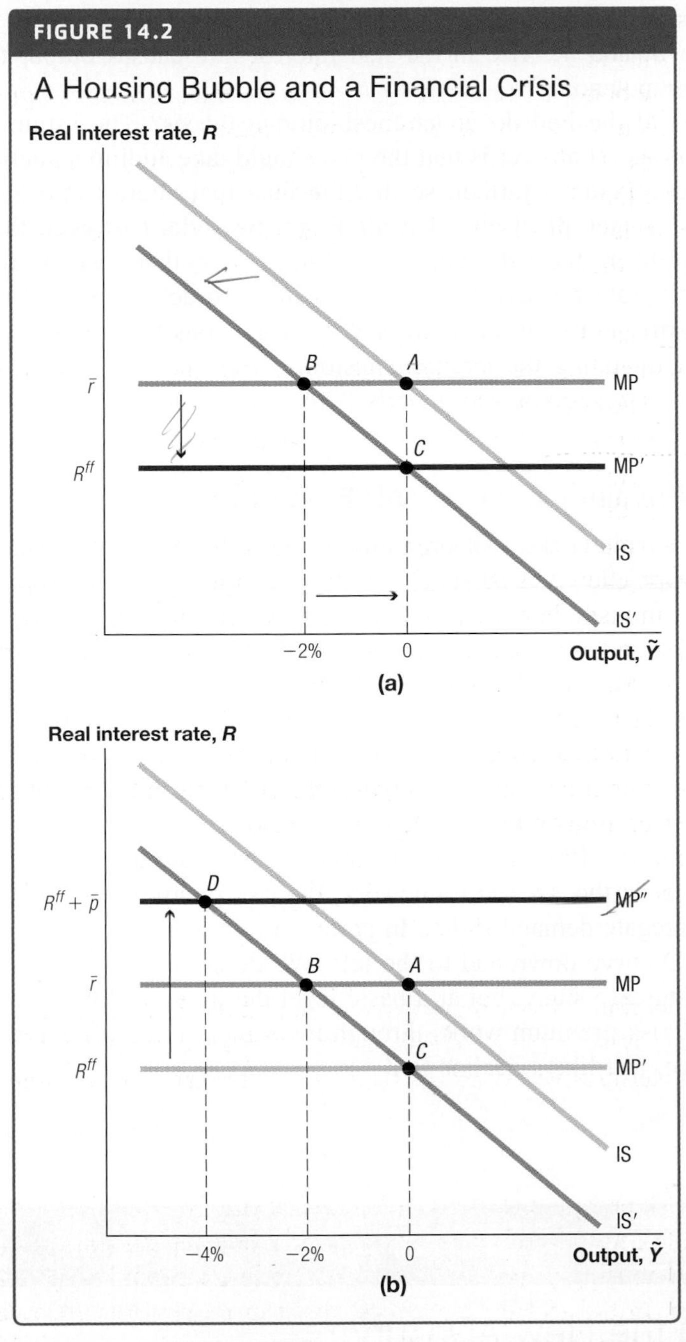

(a) The collapse of a housing bubble causes the IS curve to shift back, producing a recession at point *B*. In response, the Fed lowers the fed funds rate, pushing the economy back to its potential at point *C*.

(b) The financial crisis raises interest rates despite the Fed's efforts, producing a deep recession at point *D*.

corporate bond rates in Figure 14.1, where we saw that the borrowing cost to firms rose sharply during the financial crisis despite the huge reductions in the fed funds rate.

Panel (b) of Figure 14.2 shows what happens if the rise in the risk premium is enough to cause the real interest rate to increase, despite the Fed's actions. In this case, the economy moves to a point like *D*, where the recession is deepened by the conspiring of the two shocks. The decline in consumption pushes the economy to B, and the rise in the real interest rate causes output to fall even further below potential.

What should the Fed do under these circumstances? The astute reader will notice that a natural answer is that the Fed should take additional actions and cut the fed funds rate even further, so that the final real interest rate is sufficiently low. This is, in fact, precisely what the Fed tried to do. However, this approach ran into a problem: the fed funds rate fell to zero, so there was no room for the Fed to cut the rate further. As we discuss in more detail below, this is one of the main justifications for the additional policy actions taken by the Fed and the government, including the large expansion of the Fed's balance sheet and the fiscal stimulus package passed in early 2009.

The Risk Premium in the AS/AD Framework

We can also include the risk premium in our AS/AD framework. Recall that this framework allows us to study the dynamics of short-run output and inflation together in a single graph. The aggregate demand (AD) curve combines the IS/MP analysis with a standard monetary policy rule, and the aggregate supply (AS) curve is a standard Phillips curve.

How does the risk premium fit into this analysis? From the previous section, we know that the risk premium shows up in our short-run model via the IS curve: while the Fed sets the fed funds rate, the rate at which firms and households can borrow is equal to this rate *plus* the risk premium.

Because the IS/MP structure feeds into the aggregate demand curve, it is not surprising that in the AS/AD framework, the risk premium functions just like a negative aggregate demand shock. In particular, an increase in the risk premium shifts the AD curve down and to the left. We derive this result carefully in the accompanying case study, but at a basic level the intuition for this result should be clear: the risk premium works through investment in the IS curve, so it shifts the AD curve, just like a decline in $\bar{a}$.

CASE STUDY

Deriving the New AD Curve

Recall from Chapter 13 that the AD curve is derived by combining the IS/MP analysis with a standard monetary policy rule. In the presence of a risk premium, the key equations for this derivation are

The IS curve:	$\tilde{Y}_t = \bar{a} - \bar{b}(R_t - \bar{r})$
The monetary policy rule:	$R_t^{ff} - \bar{r} = \bar{m}(\pi_t - \bar{\pi})$
The risk premium equation:	$R_t = R_t^{ff} + \bar{p}$

Combining the risk premium equation and the monetary policy rule gives

$$R_t - \bar{r} = \bar{p} + \bar{m}(\pi_t - \bar{\pi}).$$

Substituting this into the IS curve yields the new AD curve:

$$\text{The new AD curve:} \quad \tilde{Y}_t = \underbrace{\bar{a} - \bar{b}\bar{p}}_{\text{AD shock}} - \bar{b}\bar{m}(\pi_t - \bar{\pi}). \qquad (14.2)$$

Notice that this equation looks exactly like our familiar AD curve except that now the risk premium acts like another shock. A higher risk premium works like a negative shock to aggregate demand (a decline in $\bar{a}$).

Figure 14.3 shows how the economy responds in the AS/AD framework to the shocks associated with the financial crisis. In particular, one can focus on two related shocks: (1) a decline in housing prices and equity prices that reduces household wealth, and (2) a rise in the risk premium at which firms and households borrow. Both shocks cause the AD curve to shift down and to the left. The result is a deep recession that leads the inflation rate to fall below its target. Over time, the AS curve gradually shifts down as the recession leads firms to moderate their price increases.

This analysis also makes clear an important further risk associated with the Great Recession. Inflation was already low—somewhere around 2 percent—when the recession began. In the AS/AD framework, the recession leads inflation to fall further, raising the possibility that inflation might become negative—a situation, known as **deflation**, that turns out to be fraught with danger.

FIGURE 14.3

The Financial Crisis in the AS/AD Framework

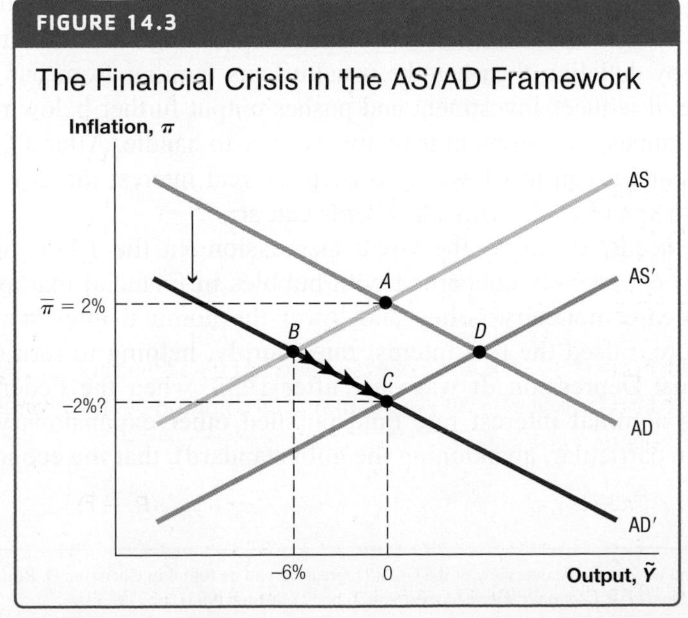

The large negative AD shocks associated with the financial crisis cause a deep recession, and the economy moves from *A* to *B*. The recession causes inflation to fall over time, shifting the AS curve down and moving the economy gradually to point *C*. Because inflation was already relatively low at 2% before the financial crisis, this decline could potentially lead to deflation.

When should the AS/AD framework be used, and when is the IS/MP–Phillips curve approach more appropriate?

When should the AS/AD framework be used, and when is the IS/MP–Phillips curve approach more appropriate? The key point is that the AS/AD framework assumes that a well-designed monetary policy rule is being implemented. When this is the case, the AS/AD framework is preferable, especially because the dynamics of the economy can be tracked in a single graph. In situations where such a policy rule is not operating, however, the IS/MP–Phillips curve approach is superior. This can occur if there is deflation, as we will see next, or if the central bank is not following the basic tenets of good monetary policy, as was the case in the 1970s and during the Great Depression.

The Dangers of Deflation

To motivate our concern about deflation, we need look no further than the worst macroeconomic disaster in U.S. history, the Great Depression. The shocks that caused the Great Depression were magnified by deflation; had there been no deflation, there probably would not have been a Great Depression.

To understand why, recall the Fisher equation that relates real and nominal interest rates:

$$i_t = R_t + \pi_t,$$

where i_t is the nominal interest rate, R_t is the real interest rate, and π_t is the rate of inflation. We can rearrange this equation to solve for the real interest rate, since this is the key rate that feeds into the IS curve and influences the real economy:

$$R_t = i_t - \pi_t. \qquad (14.3)$$

When inflation is positive, it lowers the real interest rate. However, notice what happens when inflation is negative: it raises the real interest rate. Why is this? When there is deflation, the price level is falling. So when it comes time for you to repay a \$100 loan in a year, you will be paying it back with dollars that are worth more than when you borrowed them. The ensuing rise in the real interest rate caused by deflation then has the usual effects familiar from our analysis of the IS curve: it reduces investment and pushes output further below potential.

In normal times, this problem is relatively easy to handle. After all, the central bank sets i_t, and it can just lower i_t to keep the real interest rate low. However, there are two situations in which problems can arise.

The first occurred during the Great Depression. In the 1930s, the Federal Reserve was excessively concerned with bubbles in financial markets and was reluctant to ease monetary policy and lower the nominal interest rate. Deflation, therefore, raised the real interest rate sharply, helping to turn a recession into the Great Depression. It was only after 1933, when the Federal Reserve lowered the nominal interest rate (and pursued other expansionary monetary policies—in particular, abandoning the gold standard), that the economy turned around.[2]

[2] A fascinating and very readable overview of the Great Depression can be found in Christina D. Romer, "The Nation in Depression," *Journal of Economic Perspectives*, vol. 7, no. 2 (Spring 1993), pp. 19–39.

The second and more pernicious situation in which deflation can lead to problems occurs when the nominal interest rate is already low. To see why, we first note something remarkable: nominal interest rates cannot be negative. Why not? Suppose your bank tried to pay you an interest rate of −3 percent on your deposits. That is, if you leave $100 in the bank for the year, they return $97 to you rather than paying you a positive rate of interest. What would you do? Well, you can always keep your money at home and earn a nominal interest rate of zero. This possibility makes it difficult for the Fed to lower interest rates once the **zero lower bound** is approached. But this means deflation will raise the real interest rate, because the central bank cannot lower nominal rates further.

To drive this point home, suppose the nominal interest rate has been reduced to zero. In this case, the Fisher equation from (14.3) becomes

$$R_t = -\pi_t.$$

When the inflation rate is +3 percent, the real interest rate is −3 percent, providing a substantial stimulus to the economy to help it emerge from a recession. If the marginal product of capital is 1 percent, a real interest rate of −3 percent will sharply raise the demand for new investment. Now consider what happens if there is a deflation so that, say, π_t is −2 percent. In this case, the real interest rate is +2 percent, and the central bank cannot push it any lower. Since this real interest rate is above the marginal product of capital, firms and households do not wish to invest. Deflation curtails the ability of conventional monetary policy to stimulate the economy.

Such a situation is an example of a **liquidity trap**, a term that refers to the inability of monetary policy to lower the nominal interest rate below zero. When there is deflation as well, the liquidity trap is easy to see: because the real interest rate is high, firms and households do not wish to borrow. The liquidity provided by monetary policy gets "trapped" inside banks and cannot stimulate the economy.

Progress in understanding monetary policy means we have successfully avoided the first situation. But during the financial crisis, the Fed cut the fed funds rate all the way to zero. So one danger of deflation is that it could raise the real interest rate faced by firms and households, because the Fed might have trouble reducing nominal rates further.

Let's first discuss why this would be a problem and then consider the tools that the Fed has at its disposal to make sure something like this does not happen.

The problem is easiest to see in the IS/MP framework. In fact, the effects of deflation very much mimic the analysis of the risk premium that we have already conducted: deflation causes the real interest rate to rise, which reduces investment and pushes the economy deeper into a recession. Look at Figure 14.2 for an example.

What is pernicious about deflation, however, is that these dynamics can *destabilize* the economy. Deflation may result from a recession that makes inflation negative through the standard short-run dynamics. But the deflation then raises the real interest rate, which deepens the recession. This, in turn, causes inflation to become even more negative, which raises the real interest rate further and makes the recession even worse. This situation is ominously known as a **deflationary spiral** because the usual stabilizing forces of the macroeconomy no longer come into play. The Worked Exercise at the end of this chapter (exercise 2) illustrates these forces in the context of the Great Depression.

What can be done to avoid such a situation? The first remedy is to stimulate the economy with monetary policy to the extent that this is possible. When the zero lower bound becomes a problem, though, other policies may be needed. This is one of the key justifications for a fiscal stimulus. Central banks may also attempt to use monetary policy in unconventional ways. For example, they can print money and buy financial securities like asset-backed commercial paper, mortgage-backed securities, or long-term nominal bonds, seeking to lower interest rates in these other markets. In fact, these are exactly the policies the Federal Reserve pursued during the crisis, as we will see in the next section.

Another important tool in fighting inflation is the management of inflation expectations. Notice that one of the key forces that causes inflation to decline between points *B* and *C* in Figure 14.3 is the fact that our simple analysis is based on adaptive expectations, where $\pi^e = \pi_{t-1}$. If, instead, the central bank has a strong reputation for keeping inflation stable and close to a target level, such as 2 percent, expectations may keep inflation from spiraling lower and lower.

14.3 Policy Responses to the Financial Crisis

The Taylor Rule and Monetary Policy

A natural place to start evaluating current policies is the Taylor rule. Recall that the Taylor rule is a more sophisticated version of the monetary policy rule we used extensively in Chapter 13. Our simple policy rule specifies the fed funds rate as a function of the gap between the current inflation rate and some target rate. The Taylor rule goes further by letting the current level of short-run output also influence the setting of the fed funds rate. Figure 14.4 shows both the actual fed funds rate and the rate predicted by a Taylor rule. In addition, the figure shows the data on inflation and short-run output that are used in the Taylor rule.

There are three important things to take away from this graph. First, at least on the surface, monetary policy during the financial crisis appears to be quite expansionary, with the fed funds rate lying consistently below what the Taylor rule would suggest. However, this view is misleading. Because of the large increase in the risk premium, what appears to be a low fed funds rate has not translated into lower interest rates for firms and households (see Figure 14.1).

Second, if there is a problem with Fed policy in the years leading up to the financial crisis, it may be that the fed funds rate was kept too low for too long. Between 2003 and 2006, for example, the fed funds rate was substantially lower than the prescription of the Taylor rule. Together with the global saving glut, these low rates may have contributed to the run-up in housing prices.[3]

[3] This point is developed more fully in John Taylor, "The Financial Crisis and the Policy Responses: An Empirical Analysis of What Went Wrong," Stanford University working paper, November 2008.

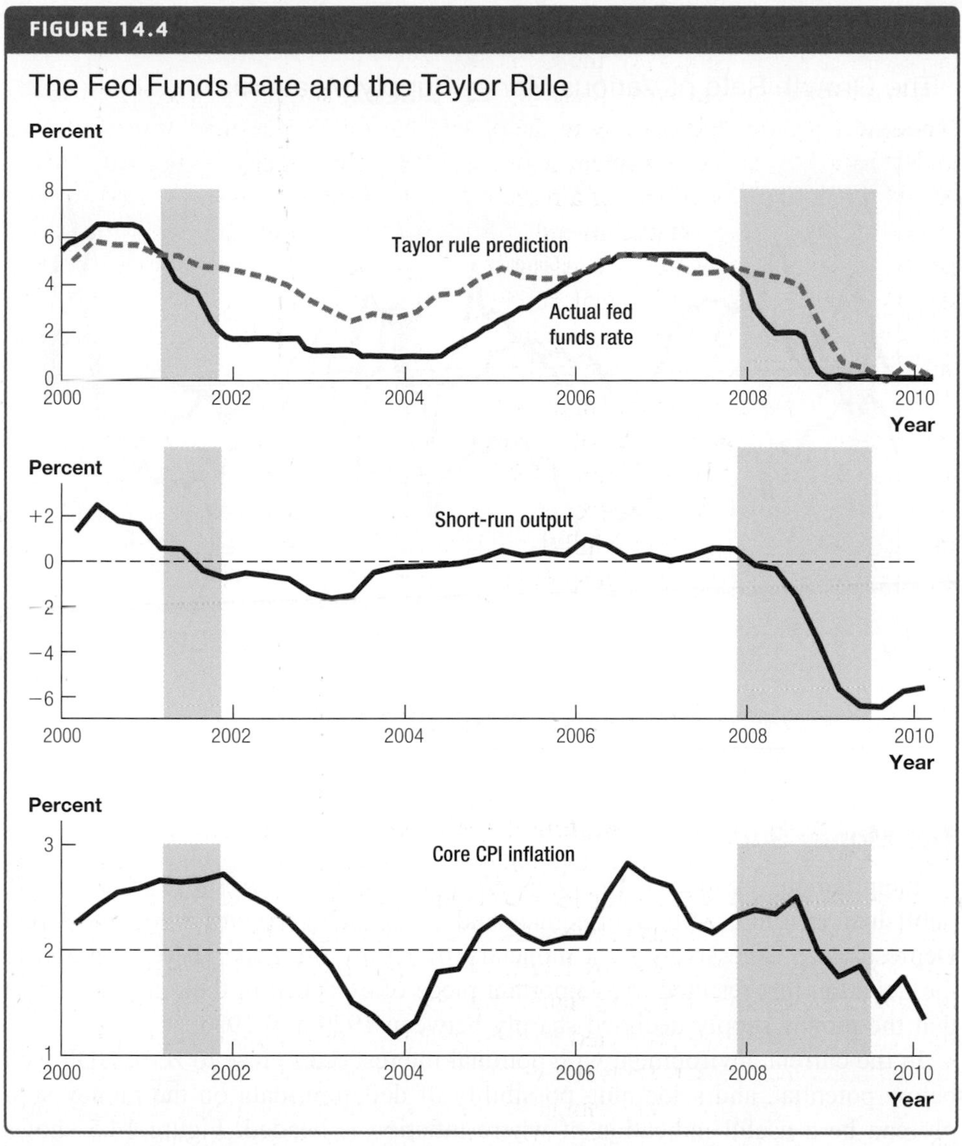

The first panel shows the actual fed funds rate and the target suggested by a mainstream Taylor rule that includes both inflation and short-run output. In particular, the Taylor rule puts equal weights of 1/2 on inflation and short-run output in determining the real interest rate and is based on a target rate for inflation of 2 percent; in nominal terms, the rule can be expressed as $i_t = 1\% + 1.5\pi_t + 0.5\tilde{Y}_t$. Inflation is measured for the last 12 months using the CPI excluding food and energy.

Finally, one of the reasons given for the low fed funds rate in 2003 was that the Fed was very concerned about the possibility of deflation at that time. The reasons for such a concern are apparent in Figure 14.4. The macroeconomy remained weak throughout 2002 and into 2003, and this had a large effect on inflation. The inflation rate fell from more than 2.5 percent at the start of 2002 to just over 1 percent at the end of 2003.

This serves to emphasize the current worry about the possibility of deflation. In 2009–2010, GDP is substantially below potential and seems likely to stay that way in the coming year, possibly putting strong downward pressure on inflation.

Various measures of the money supply all exhibit rapid growth by the end of 2008, suggesting that the mistakes made by the Federal Reserve during the Great Depression are not being repeated today.

FIGURE 14.5

The Growth Rate of Various Money Supply Measures

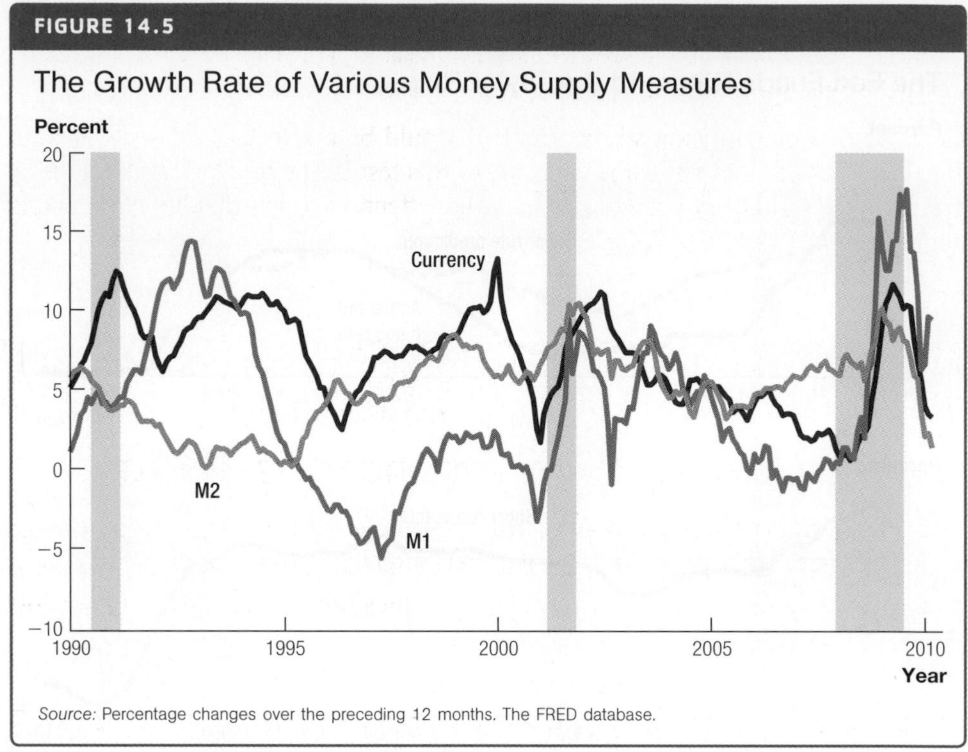

Source: Percentage changes over the preceding 12 months. The FRED database.

The Money Supply

In their famous treatise *A Monetary History of the United States, 1867–1960*, published in 1963, Milton Friedman and Anna Schwartz attributed the Great Depression to excessively tight monetary policy by the Federal Reserve and to the deflation that resulted. An important piece of evidence in their argument was that the money supply declined sharply between 1929 and 1933.

In the current environment with nominal interest rates close to zero, GDP well below potential, and a looming possibility of deflation, data on the money supply can be a useful indication of where inflation is headed. Figure 14.5 shows the growth rate of various measures of the money supply, ranging from a narrow measure that just counts currency to the broader measures of M1 and M2 that include checking accounts, savings accounts, and certificates of deposit (CDs). Reassuringly, each of these measures exhibited rapid growth by the end of 2008 and into 2009, suggesting that the Federal Reserve is focused on preventing a deflation and stimulating the economy. Other actions by the Fed also indicate an attempt to coordinate inflation expectations on a positive rate of inflation around 2 percent, thus helping to avoid a deflation.[4]

Speaking in 2002 at a celebration of Milton Friedman's 90th birthday, then-Governor Bernanke had this to say:

[4] For example, the Federal Open Market Committee (FOMC) recently began reporting their expectations of inflation between 4 and 6 years from the date of their policy meetings. This was interpreted as an effort to coordinate expectations on positive rates of inflation. See www.federalreserve.gov.

> Let me end my talk by abusing slightly my status as an official representative of the Federal Reserve. I would like to say to Milton and Anna: Regarding the Great Depression. You're right, we did it. We're very sorry. But thanks to you, we won't do it again.[5]

Certainly, no one anticipated that the Fed would be put to the test so soon after Bernanke spoke. And while the outcome of this test is not entirely certain, at least the measures of money growth that drew the attention of Friedman and Schwartz suggest that Bernanke is being true to his word.

CASE STUDY

Should Monetary Policy Respond to Asset Prices?

With the benefit of hindsight, it appears to most observers that there was a bubble in the housing market in the mid-2000s. What should monetary policy do if policymakers suspect there may be a bubble? Should they raise interest rates in an effort to bring asset prices down?

FIGURE 14.6

The Price-Earnings Ratio in the Stock Market

Source: Robert Shiller, www.econ.yale.edu/~shiller/data.htm

Whenever the ratio of stock prices to company earnings gets too far away from its mean, it tends to revert back. Notice that this measure reached its two highest peaks in 1929 and 2000.

[5] Ben Bernanke, "On Milton Friedman's Ninetieth Birthday," November 8, 2002.

Following the dot-com crash in stock prices in 2000, then-Governor Bernanke gave a speech entitled "Asset-Price 'Bubbles' and Monetary Policy" (speech to the New York Chapter of the National Association for Business Economics, October 15, 2002). There, Bernanke reviewed this question in light of the stock market crash of 1929 and the Great Depression. In particular, he argued that (1) it is often difficult to tell if there is a bubble in real time, and (2) even if it is known that there is a bubble, standard monetary policy is too coarse an instrument to be used to manage bubbles. For example, excessive concern by policymakers about bubbles was an important cause of the Great Depression, in Bernanke's view.

Figure 14.6 shows the ratio of stock prices to "earnings" (an average of an accounting measure of corporate profits over the preceding decade). This kind of statistic has been used by Robert Shiller of Yale University to argue that there was a bubble in the stock market in the late 1990s. In standard models in financial economics, stock prices should be equal to the present discounted value of future profits. Shiller points out that whenever the price-earnings ratio gets exceptionally high, prices usually come down again to restore the ratio to something like its average value. Notice that the price-earnings ratio was even higher in 2000 than in 1929.

A similar picture can be drawn for the housing market, which certainly makes it appear that there was a bubble by 2006. For example, Figure 14.7 shows real home prices—home prices deflated by the consumer price index—back to 1950.

By nearly any measure, the appreciation of home prices between 2000 and 2006 was unusual.

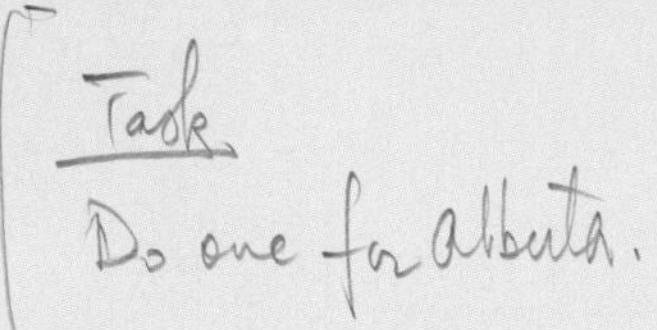

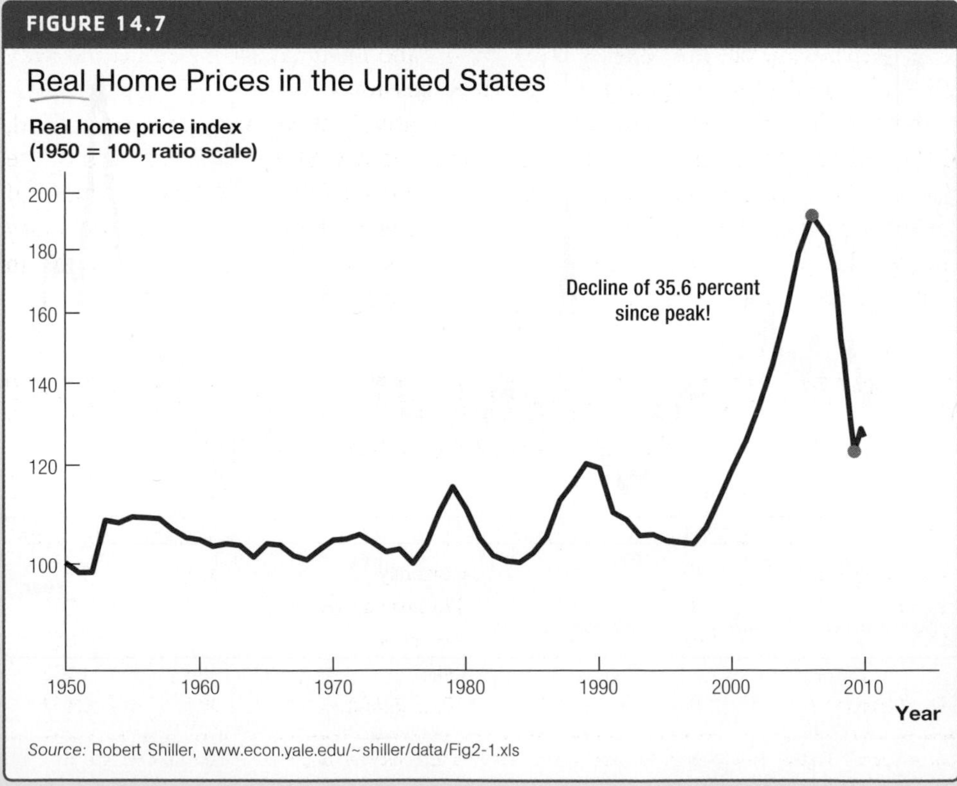

FIGURE 14.7

Real Home Prices in the United States

Source: Robert Shiller, www.econ.yale.edu/~shiller/data/Fig2-1.xls

The period since 2000 is clearly exceptional. Moreover, previous episodes of rapidly rising real home prices were often followed by real declines.

In 2002, Bernanke suggested that instead of using monetary policy to manage bubbles, policymakers should use more precise instruments, such as capital requirements and the regulation of lending standards. The relatively mild recession in 2001 that followed the crash in stock prices in 2000 provided some reassurance that monetary policy could adequately respond to bubbles after the fact. It will be interesting to see how this position gets reconsidered by policymakers in light of the Great Recession.

The Fed's Balance Sheet

Given the failure of conventional monetary policy to stimulate the economy, the Federal Reserve and the Treasury have created myriad new policies to provide liquidity and capital to financial institutions. Examples include allowing these institutions to swap less liquid financial instruments for Treasury securities, the provision of liquidity to the large government-sponsored mortgage companies Fannie Mae (the Federal National Mortgage Association) and Freddie Mac (the Federal Home Loan Mortgage Corporation), and direct capital injections through the Troubled Asset Relief Program (TARP).

Because so many different programs are involved, it can be difficult to get a sense of their overall magnitude. One illuminating exercise is to consider the balance sheet of the Federal Reserve. This balance sheet, summarized in Table 14.1, reflects two different times: May 2007, before the financial crisis began, and May 2009, essentially the bottom of the Great Recession.

In May 2007, the Fed's balance sheet was relatively straightforward and, indeed, almost trivial. Total assets and total liabilities were $906 billion. The bulk of the assets were U.S. Treasury securities, and the bulk of the liabilities consisted of currency held by the public. This situation reflects the mechanics of monetary policy whereby the Fed essentially buys and sells U.S. government bonds in exchange for currency in order to set the fed funds rate.

TABLE 14.1

The Federal Reserve's Balance Sheet (billions of dollars)

Assets			Liabilities		
	May 2007	*May 2009*		*May 2007*	*May 2009*
U.S. Treasuries	790	569	Currency	814	905
Loans	0	553	Treasury accounts	5	276
Other	116	1,050	Reserves	7	858
			Other	80	133
Total assets	906	2,172	*Total liabilities*	906	2,172

Source: Federal Reserve Release H.4.1. See also James Hamilton's "Econbrowser" blog entry "Federal Reserve Balance Sheet," December 21, 2008.

The Federal Reserve has expanded its balance sheet by more than $1 trillion to fight the financial crisis.

In responding to the financial crisis, however, the Fed dramatically reshaped its balance sheet. First, the size of the balance sheet—total assets and liabilities—more than doubled, growing by more than $1 trillion. Second, the composition of assets and liabilities changed significantly. On the asset side, the Fed expanded its lending to the rest of the economy, not only to financial institutions but also to nonfinancial corporations. This lending came either in the form of loans or through the purchase of securities like commercial paper. The numerous programs undertaken by the Fed are consolidated in the balance sheet that we present in Table 14.1 into just two categories: "Loans" and "Other." A more nuanced version of these assets is displayed in the rainbow of colors in Figure 14.8. This figure emphasizes the spectacular change in both the size and composition of the Fed's balance sheet that occurred during the financial crisis.

On the liability side, it is important to note that, by and large, the Fed did not finance this additional lending by printing money. The amount of currency outstanding, for example, was higher by only about 10 percent, or $90 billion, as can be seen in Table 14.1—this despite the fact that assets grew by more than $1 trillion. Instead, these funds came from two sources: borrowing from the U.S. Treasury and excess reserves from the banks themselves. In essence, the Fed bought commercial paper or securitized loans from financial institutions and paid for these purchases by crediting their reserve accounts. What is unusual is that these banks then kept the funds as reserves with the Fed rather than lending them out to the private sector. There are two related reasons for this. First, the

In response to the financial crisis, the Fed radically expanded its balance sheet. Assets grew from about $900 billion in May 2007 to more than $2.3 trillion in April 2010, with the Fed purchasing a range of securities and making a large volume of loans to the private sector.

FIGURE 14.8

Financial Assets of the Federal Reserve

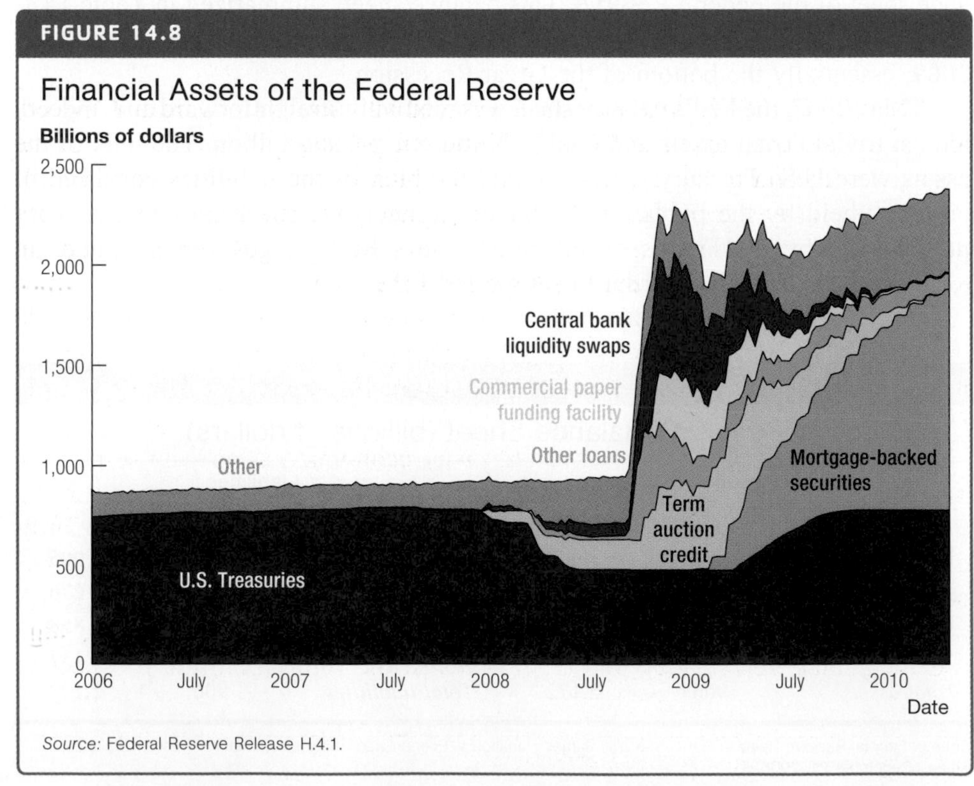

Source: Federal Reserve Release H.4.1.

banks were worried about their own balance sheets and reluctant to make risky loans that might not be repaid in full. Second, the Fed began paying interest on excess reserves, making this a safe and profitable place for banks to keep their funds. By adjusting the interest rate paid on these excess reserves, the Fed can control the extent to which its balance-sheet actions translate into additional currency (and the inflation with which this would presumably be associated, at least in the long run). Interestingly, these balance-sheet actions by the Fed have been much larger in magnitude than the funds made available by Congress and the Treasury through the TARP, which was funded at $700 billion and which is discussed next.

The Troubled Asset Relief Program

At the urging of then Treasury Secretary Henry Paulson and Fed Chair Ben Bernanke, Congress passed the Troubled Asset Relief Program (TARP) in the fall of 2008. This program established a $700 billion fund to be used by the Treasury to purchase and insure assets held by financial institutions in an effort to strengthen the financial system and encourage lending. Funds were ultimately used to purchase equity in banks and other financial institutions, to guarantee loans to those institutions, and even to bail out some U.S. automakers.

While many observers at the time expected this program to incur heavy losses, this apparently will not be the case. Estimates as of April 2010 suggest that the losses will likely be around $89 billion.[6]

Fiscal Stimulus

On February 17, 2009, President Obama signed into law the American Recovery and Reinvestment Act of 2009, a $787 billion package designed to stimulate aggregate demand in the economy. The final plan includes more than $250 billion in tax cuts and more than $500 billion in new government spending on such things as unemployment benefits, infrastructure, education, health care, and aid to state and local governments. According to the Congressional Budget Office (CBO), about $185 billion of the stimulus will occur in 2009, with another $400 billion in 2010. Because of these and other changes in government spending and revenues, the federal deficit rose in 2009 to about 10 percent of GDP, up sharply from only 3 percent in 2008.

Given the macroeconomic situation, many economists supported some kind of fiscal stimulus. With the fed funds rate at zero, short-run output turning sharply negative, and deflation a possibility, a large fiscal stimulus seemed prudent. The main areas of disagreement among economists concerned the types of spending and the relative weight on tax cuts versus new spending. The Ricardian equivalence argument, discussed in Chapter 10, was also a factor: high spending must be financed by higher taxes in the future, and the prospect of

[6] http://www.reuters.com/article/idUSTRE63B05N20100412.

these taxes may reduce the current impact of the stimulus package. Temporary measures that seek to change the timing of production—such as a temporary investment tax credit or a temporary cut in payroll taxes—might overcome some of these concerns.[7]

Financial Reform

With the worst of the Great Recession apparently behind us, a last important policy topic is financial reform. What changes to the financial system will minimize the likelihood of another financial crisis and ensure the least amount of damage, should another crisis occur?

This is a complex question that requires careful thought and a sophisticated answer. Some of the deepest causes of the financial crisis are not entirely understood. For example, economists do not understand why the prices of stocks and houses are so volatile, and how and why bubbles in these asset markets occur. It is likely that the nature of the best financial reform depends on the answers to these and related questions.

Nevertheless, some of the general principles of financial reform are relatively clear. First and foremost, a key downside to the way in which the financial crisis was handled by policymakers is that it has made problems of **moral hazard** more severe.

What do we mean by this statement? As discussed in Chapter 10, one of the key ways that the financial system made record profits in the years leading up to the financial crisis was through leverage. Financial institutions took \$3 of their own funds and \$97 of borrowed funds to make \$100 worth of risky investments. As long as the investments paid off, companies earned huge returns on their \$3 investment. However, when these risky investments turned sour, the financial institutions did not suffer the full financial consequences of their bets. Many of these institutions were deemed too systemically important to fail or **too big to fail**, and they were bailed out by various government policies. Financial institutions are all too happy to undertake these "heads, I win; tails, the economy loses" types of bets, but this is clearly not in the interests of the economy as a whole. Economists refer to this as a moral hazard problem. Unfortunately, absent financial reform, the bailouts of the financial sector have served to make these bets look even more attractive to financial institutions. Absent reform, the risks of a serious financial crisis in the future have probably gone up rather than down.

This is not to say that the various policies that stabilized the financial sector at the peak of the crisis were not beneficial. It seems that they were. However, something that is beneficial overall may still involve costs, and this is surely the case with the bailouts of the financial sector.

To understand some of the basic issues involved, it is helpful to see how firms fail under normal circumstances. A standard remedy when liabilities exceed assets

[7] For example, see Mark Bils and Pete Klenow, "Further Discussion of a Temporary Payroll Tax Cut during Recession(s)," Stanford University, December 12, 2008.

in a firm is for the firm to file for bankruptcy. A judge or some other government entity steps in and reorganizes the firm if possible so that it can resume its business. The essential way the reorganization works is as follows. Equity (net worth) is already zero or even negative, so the stockholders have lost their entire investment. Debt is then "reorganized" into new equity claims. That is, debt is written down to zero, and the former debtholders are given equity claims in the newly reorganized firm. Essentially, the value of the debt at the time of the reorganization becomes the new equity in the new firm.

In the context of a financial crisis, this approach has a number of appealing features. First, the stockholders and bondholders in the financial firms that have magnified the crisis bear the brunt of the cost of putting the financial institutions back on their feet; the cost to taxpayers is minimized. Second, the banks are recapitalized and should emerge with a willingness and an ability to lend. A potential problem with this approach, however, is that if not handled carefully, it could severely interfere with the functioning of financial markets. The panic following the collapse of Lehman Brothers in September 2008 is an all-too-vivid reminder of what can go wrong.

What, then, should financial reform look like? A group of expert financial economists who call themselves the Squam Lake Group have recently suggested the following guidelines:

- **Create a systemic regulator.** Each country should have one primary regulator, such as the central bank, charged with monitoring systemic risk in financial markets. Importantly, this systemic regulator would be responsible for enforcing the other elements of financial reform.
- **Enhance capital requirements.** Financial institutions are already subject to capital requirements: they are required to maintain capital (equity) that is above a certain percentage of assets. (This can be viewed as a restriction on leverage.) This minimum percentage should be raised so that financial institutions have a larger "cushion" in case the value of their assets declines suddenly. Also, larger or more complex financial institutions should face higher capital requirements.
- **Link executive compensation to long-term performance.** The compensation of senior management in systemically important financial institutions should be tied, at least in part, to the long-term performance of the firms. Because of systemic risk, this link must be tighter than shareholders themselves would privately enforce.
- **Require convertible debt.** Systemically important financial institutions might also be required to issue a significant amount of a new, hybrid debt instrument that converts to equity when certain prespecified crisis conditions arise. This hybrid is called convertible debt. When the value of equity in such a firm falls significantly, this debt would convert to equity, recapitalizing banks at no cost to taxpayers. Bondholders and shareholders would themselves bear the costs of financial problems, minimizing the likelihood of taxpayer bailouts. This convertible debt functions like an automated, limited version of the reorganization that occurs in bankruptcy, but it should not have the

negative effect of interfering with the functioning of financial markets that a more formal reorganization would entail.

- **Require "living wills."** Finally, some important financial institutions will inevitably fail. A living will—a set of instructions for how this failure should be carried out to keep to a low level the disruption to financial markets—would minimize the effects of such a failure.[8]

The direct cost of bailing out financial institutions was only a small portion of the overall cost of the global financial crisis. And the bulk of these costs were borne by people outside the finance industry. The main cost is measured in lost jobs and forgone GDP—that is, in the macroeconomic losses inflicted around the world by the Great Recession. Financial reform is needed to ensure that this does not happen again or, at the very least, to mitigate the severity and frequency of future problems.

CASE STUDY

Macroeconomic Research after the Financial Crisis

A strong case can be made that macroeconomists failed the country and the world in September 2008. Indeed, the president of the Federal Reserve Bank of Minneapolis, macroeconomist Narayana Kocherlakota, makes precisely this case in a recent article.[9] Kocherlakota points out that policymakers needed a "playbook" to guide them during the peak of the financial crisis, and modern macroeconomic research did not furnish them with one. Worse, macroeconomic research failed to provide the kind of analysis and rules that could have prevented the financial meltdown in the first place.

Kocherlakota's diagnosis of why macroeconomists failed is especially illuminating. He observes that media reports of this failure tend to focus on a caricature, dividing economists into those that favor active government intervention in the macroeconomy and those that do not. Instead, claims Kocherlakota, the truth about macroeconomic research is both more nuanced and more optimistic. Both these caricatures and the failures of macroeconomics during the financial crisis largely have the same root cause: macroeconomic research has historically been limited by technology.

To understand this statement, note that "modern" macroeconomic models—models with solid microfoundations, based on explicit decisions made by firms

[8] See Kenneth R. French et al., *The Squam Lake Report: Fixing the Financial System* (Princeton, N.J.: Princeton University Press, 2010). Some of their recommendations are discussed at www.squamlakegroup.org.

[9] See Narayana R. Kocherlakota, "Modern Macroeconomic Models as Tools for Economic Policy," *The Region: Federal Reserve Bank of Minneapolis*, (May 2010).

and households—largely first appeared during the 1980s. These models were so complicated that they had to be solved on computers, and computers were so limited in power that only relatively simple macroeconomic models could be solved. Primarily because of this constraint, these early models featured settings where Adam Smith's invisible-hand theorem held: any fluctuations in macroeconomic activity were efficient, and government efforts to stabilize the economy would reduce welfare.

As research progressed and computing power exploded, increasingly sophisticated models have been analyzed. The latest versions of these models include many frictions, such as sticky inflation and limited financial markets. Consumers are heterogeneous—some are rich, some are poor—and financial markets are imperfect. This means that a rise in unemployment can be especially harmful to certain segments of the economy in large part because they cannot insure themselves fully against that possibility. Such models, to varying extents, allow the government to play an important role in limiting inefficient fluctuations in macroeconomic activity.

While there are clearly a number of shortcomings in modern macroeconomic research, this view of the limitations is fundamentally optimistic. There has been a sharp increase in macroeconomic research focused on economic fluctuations and financial imperfections. With a combination of better computers and better theories, this research should pay off with a better understanding of the causes of financial crises and the rules and policies that could prevent them.[10]

14.4 Conclusion

The global financial crisis will likely go down in history as the largest recession in the United States and the rest of the world since the Great Depression. Rudi Dornbusch, professor of economics at MIT at the end of the twentieth century, once remarked of U.S. recessions, "None of the postwar expansions died of old age, they were all murdered by the Fed."[11] What Dornbusch meant is that the Federal Reserve engineered most of the postwar recessions in order to bring down inflation.

The Great Recession was different. It was not intentionally engineered by the Fed to lower inflation. Instead, it was a balance-sheet crisis, reflected in the balance sheets of financial institutions, households, the Federal Reserve, and even the government itself. It is much more reminiscent of the Great Depression than any other recession in postwar history.

---

[10] The Fall 2010 issue of the *Journal of Economic Perspectives* contains an enlightening and readable symposium of five papers on "Macroeconomics after the Financial Crisis."

[11] Quoted in "Of Shocks and Horrors," *The Economist*, September 26, 2002.

Macroeconomic performance over the next five years remains very uncertain. Whatever happens in the coming years, it is worth remembering a key fact about the Great Depression, in evidence on the cover of the *Macroeconomics* textbook and displayed more clearly in Figure 1.6. Even something as earthshaking as the Great Depression essentially left the long-run GDP of the United States largely unaffected. Something so seemingly world-changing was, in the end, only temporary.

CHAPTER REVIEW

SUMMARY

1. Despite reducing the fed funds rate from over 5 percent before the crisis to between 0 percent and 0.25 percent in 2009, many of the interest rates at which firms and households can borrow were *higher* in 2009 than they were before the crisis. This reflects a rise in the risk premium that sits between the fed funds rate and other lending rates.
2. Small increases in the risk premium can theoretically be offset by the central bank lowering its target rate. When the target rate reaches zero, however, this option is no longer available. This characterizes the situation in 2008–09 and is one justification for the additional "unconventional" measures undertaken by the Federal Reserve.
3. A rising risk premium can be analyzed in the IS/MP–Phillips curve and AS/AD frameworks. The AS/AD framework is best suited to "normal" times when a well-designed monetary policy rule is functioning. In abnormal situations—deflation, for instance, or when the zero lower bound on nominal interest rates is binding, or when the basic tenets of good monetary policy are not being pursued—the IS/MP approach is superior.
4. Holding the nominal interest rate constant, deflation raises the real interest rate. This is particularly a problem if the nominal interest rate is already at zero; in that case, it cannot be pushed lower, and the real interest rate rises with the amount of deflation. A recession causes inflation to fall, and deflation raises the real interest rate, which deepens the recession. This can produce a vicious cycle from which it can be hard to escape.
5. Faced with the threat of deflation and a fed funds rate that is essentially zero, policymakers pursued a range of unconventional policies, including the Troubled Asset Relief Program (TARP), the Fed's direct purchases of mortgage-backed securities and commercial paper, and the fiscal stimulus program.
6. Going forward, thoughtful and prudent financial reform is needed.

KEY CONCEPTS

bubbles
deflation
deflationary spiral
the Federal Reserve's balance sheet
financial reform
fiscal stimulus
liquidity trap
moral hazard
risk premium
too big to fail
toxic assets
zero lower bound

REVIEW QUESTIONS

1. What is a risk premium, and what role do such premiums play in the financial crisis? How does the risk premium enter the IS/MP diagram and the AS/AD framework?
2. Why is the Great Recession best understood in the IS/MP–Phillips curve framework instead of the AS/AD framework?
3. What is deflation, and what problems does deflation pose for the macroeconomy? How does deflation interact with the zero lower bound for nominal interest rates?
4. Throughout much of the financial crisis, the fed funds rate was substantially lower than what a Taylor rule for monetary policy would seem to indicate. Why?
5. Describe the Fed's balance sheet in "normal" times. How did it change during the financial crisis? Why?
6. What are three financial reforms that policymakers are considering to improve the functioning of the financial system?
7. What justification can one give for a fiscal stimulus in the current financial crisis?

EXERCISES

smartwork.wwnorton.com 

1. **A financial crisis:** Suppose the economy starts with GDP at potential, the real interest rate and the marginal product of capital both equal to 3 percent, and a stable inflation rate of 2 percent. A mild financial crisis hits that raises the risk premium from zero to 2 percent.
   (a) Analyze the effect of this shock in an IS/MP diagram.
   (b) What policy response would you recommend to the Federal Reserve? What would be the effect of this policy response on the economy?
   (c) How would your answer to part (b) change if the financial crisis were very severe, raising the risk premium to 6 percent?
   (d) What other policy responses might be considered in this case?

2. **The Great Depression:** The "Roaring Twenties" led to an enormous run-up in stock prices. By 1928–29, policymakers at the Federal Reserve had become

concerned that there was a bubble in the stock market. In response, they tightened monetary policy by raising interest rates sharply. Answer the following questions:

(a) In an IS/MP diagram, show the effect on the economy of the increase in interest rates by the Fed.
(b) This policy had the desired effect of "popping" the stock market bubble, and stock prices fell sharply at the end of 1929 and into 1930. This created uncertainty in markets about the future, which, together with the loss in stock-market wealth, reduced consumption and investment. Show this second shock in your original IS/MP diagram.
(c) What is the effect of these two shocks on inflation? Show this in a graph of the Phillips curve. In the late 1920s, the average inflation rate was approximately zero. What will happen to the inflation rate over time in response to the shocks in parts (a) and (b)?
(d) Suppose the Federal Reserve left the nominal interest rate unchanged in response to the changes in inflation from part (c). What further change would have occurred in the IS/MP diagram?
(e) Summarize what you learn from this exercise about the Great Depression.

3. **Predicting the fed funds rate:** Consider the following simple monetary policy rule:

$$R_t - \bar{r} = \bar{m}(\pi_t - \bar{\pi}) + \bar{n}\tilde{Y}_t.$$

In the following questions, you are asked to gather data on inflation and short-run output to feed into this policy rule. A good resource for the data you will need is the FRED database of the St. Louis Fed, available at http://research.stlouisfed.org/fred2/

(a) Pick some reasonable values for the parameters of this policy rule, and explain why you chose these values.
(b) Obtain data on the CPI inflation rate for the most recent 12-month period possible (you may include food and energy in your CPI calculation or not—your choice). Discuss briefly this value of the inflation rate.
(c) Create an estimate of $\tilde{Y}_t$ for the U.S. economy. Explain how to construct this estimate, and discuss its value. You may find it helpful to use the series GDPPOT from the FRED database.
(d) Use these data and the monetary policy rule you specified above to see what fed funds rate the policy rule indicates. How does this compare to the current fed funds rate? *Hint*: Be sure that you are comparing two nominal rates; the simple rule above only gives you the real portion.
(e) If the rates are different, why do you think that is the case? What would you recommend to the Fed, based on your calculation?

4. **Government policy and the financial crisis:** Based on what you've learned, pick one policy action undertaken by the U.S. government in response to the financial crisis. In a half-page essay, explain the policy action and the rationale behind the policy. Also, discuss briefly a possible criticism of the policy action.

5. **Reading the minutes of the FOMC:** The Federal Open Market Committee (FOMC) is the formal name of the group chaired by Bernanke that meets every six weeks or so to set monetary policy in the United States. Immediately after the meeting, the FOMC issues a statement, consisting of a few paragraphs, that summarizes its position. Then, three weeks later, the FOMC releases the minutes of its meeting. These minutes contain extensive details about the issues that were discussed in the meeting.

   Suppose your job is to explain Federal Reserve policy to the CEO of a corporation. Do a Web search for the latest FOMC minutes. Then answer the questions below:

   (a) What action did the FOMC take, if any, regarding the level of the fed funds rate? Why did it make this choice?
   (b) Pick a paragraph or two from the FOMC minutes, and quote it in your answer. Using the short-run model, explain, using graphs and words, the economic consequences of the events in the paragraph(s) you've quoted. You do not need to analyze anything else in the economy; just focus on what you've chosen.
   (c) Pick one other thing that is mentioned in the minutes that you do not understand (for example, a term with which you are unfamiliar). Do some research to discover its economic significance, and explain it in two or three sentences.

6. **The current state of the European economy:** Write a couple of paragraphs about the state of the economy in the euro area over the last several years. What has happened to inflation, real GDP growth, and unemployment? What about a key policy interest rate set by the European Central Bank (ECB)? (*Hint*: The ECB sets several key interest rates, including a "deposit rate"—the interest rate that the ECB pays on deposits from banks—and a "lending rate"—the interest rate it charges for overnight loans. All are useful and interesting. To keep everybody on the same page, consider the lending rate.) An extremely helpful resource for this exercise is the ECB's Statistical Data Warehouse, which you can find using a search engine. In answering this question, it may be helpful to copy some of the ECB's graphs.

WORKED EXERCISE

2. **The Great Depression:**

   (a) When the Fed tightened monetary policy in 1928–29, it raised interest rates. In Figure 14.9, this is shown in the movement of the economy from point *A* to point *B*, which caused a small slowdown in economic activity by reducing investment.
   (b) The stock market bubble then popped, which created tremendous uncertainty in the economy, further reducing consumption and investment. This is modeled as a negative aggregate demand shock (a lower $\bar{a}_c$ and $\bar{a}_i$),

FIGURE 14.9

The Great Depression in the IS/MP Framework

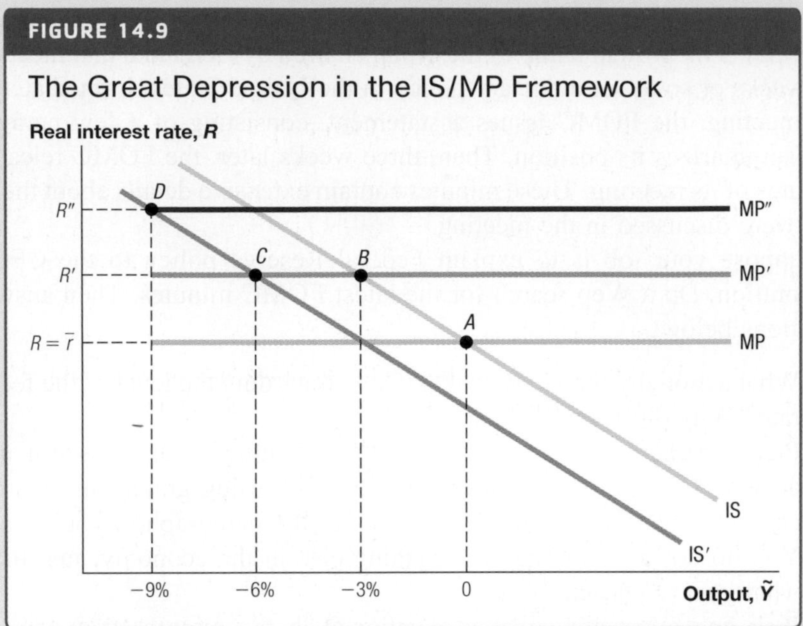

which shifts the IS curve down and to the left, depressing economic activity further as the economy moves from *B* to *C*.

(c) The Phillips curve is shown in Figure 14.10. The recession in the economy caused the inflation rate to decline. Because the inflation rate was already approximately zero, the decline through the Phillips curve led to *deflation*—a negative inflation rate.

FIGURE 14.10

The Phillips Curve and the Great Depression

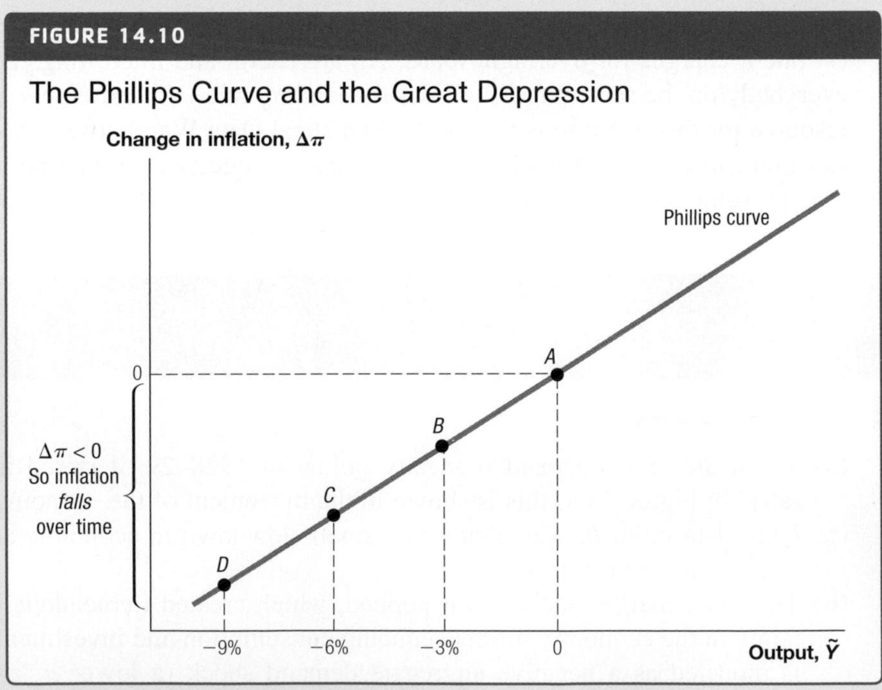

(d) If the Fed had left the nominal interest rate unchanged, then the deflation would have caused the real interest rate to rise even further. To see this, recall the Fisher equation, $i_t = R_t + \pi_t$, which can be rearranged to yield $R_t = i_t - \pi_t$. If i_t does not change, then a decline in π_t will cause the real interest rate to increase. This is shown in the original IS/MP diagram in Figure 14.9 by another shift up in the MP schedule. The economy moves from *C* to *D*, causing yet another decline in short-run output. The combination of these three factors caused a large shortfall in output—that is, the Great Depression.

(e) This exercise reveals how a sequence of events can conspire to reduce GDP below potential by a significant amount (the exact numbers in this exercise—thc −3 percent, −6 percent, and −9 percent—are just examples). Moreover, we see the vicious circle between deflation and depression that can continue to push the economy further below potential unless some other change breaks this dynamic. In the actual Great Depression, the Fed devalued the dollar by breaking from the gold standard, which is essentially an "unconventional policy" that allowed the Fed to increase the money supply substantially and create some inflation, ending the deflationary spiral.

PART 4

APPLICATIONS AND MICROFOUNDATIONS

CHAPTER 15

CONSUMPTION

OVERVIEW

In this chapter, we study

- the neoclassical consumption model, in which individuals choose the time path of their consumption to maximize utility.
- how this standard model leads to a benchmark solution in which consumption is proportional to an individual's total wealth, including current financial wealth and the present value of current and future labor income.
- the heterogeneity in consumer behavior at the microeconomic level; some individuals, often the rich, tend to follow the permanent-income hypothesis, while others, often the poor, have consumption that is quite sensitive to current income.
- additional facts about aggregate consumption, including the decline in the personal saving rate and the rise in the debt-income ratio in recent decades.

> Consumption is the sole end and purpose of all production.
>
> —ADAM SMITH

15.1 Introduction

Consumption accounts for more than two-thirds of GDP, more than \$10 trillion in the U.S. economy. This spending results from the economic decisions of over 100-million households as they purchase food, clothing, houses, vacations, refrigerators, cars, and health care. What key economic forces shape their decisions?

The models considered in this book until now treat consumption in a very simple way. In the Solow model, individuals save a constant fraction of their income. According to the main short-run model, people consume a constant fraction of potential output. In reality, however, things are more complex.

In this chapter, we develop what is sometimes called the **neoclassical consumption model.** Individuals choose consumption at each moment in time to maximize a lifetime utility function that depends on current and future consumption. People recognize that income in the future may differ from income today, and such differences influence consumption today.

The neoclassical model that we explore in this chapter is a fundamental building block of modern macroeconomics. The neoclassical model is to consumption as the Solow model is to the study of economic growth. This workhorse model allows us to develop a better, more intuitive understanding of the microfoundations of consumption that were summarized in Chapter 10. There, we outlined the insights from the permanent-income hypothesis of Milton Friedman and the life-cycle model of consumption of Franco Modigliani. Here, we provide careful microfoundations for these frameworks and assess their empirical relevance.

15.2 The Neoclassical Consumption Model

The first insight of the neoclassical consumption model is that one can make a great deal of progress by thinking of time as involving only two periods: today and the future. People may earn income today and in the future, they consume today and in the future, and a key decision they have to make is how much to consume today versus how much to consume in the future. This is the essence of the neoclassical model.

The consumption model is based on two main elements: an intertemporal budget constraint and a utility function. We discuss each of these in turn.

The Intertemporal Budget Constraint

Consider a consumer named Irving (after Irving Fisher, one of the great economists of the first half of the twentieth century and one of the originators of the neoclassical consumption model). Suppose that as of this moment Irving has **financial wealth** equal to f_{today}. For example, this financial wealth would include Irving's savings account balance and his holdings of stocks and bonds. Irving earns labor income y_{today} today and y_{future} in the future. Letting c denote consumption, Irving faces the following two budget constraints:

$$c_{today} = y_{today} - (f_{future} - f_{today}) \tag{15.1}$$

$$c_{future} = y_{future} + (1 + R) f_{future}. \tag{15.2}$$

Both equations have the form "consumption equals income less saving." The first equation applies to "today," and $f_{future} - f_{today}$ represents Irving's saving for the future—the amount he sets aside to increase the balance in his financial accounts. The second equation applies to the future, the second (and last) period of the model. In this case, Irving earns labor income y_{future} but also earns interest on his financial wealth. Because this is the last period of life, there is nothing to save for, and Irving consumes all of his income and wealth at that point.

Combining these two equations yields Irving's **intertemporal budget constraint**:[1]

$$\underbrace{c_{today} + \frac{c_{future}}{1 + R}}_{\text{present value of consumption}} = \underbrace{\underbrace{f_{today}}_{\text{financial wealth}} + \underbrace{y_{today} + \frac{y_{future}}{1 + R}}_{\text{human wealth}}}_{\text{total wealth}}. \tag{15.3}$$

This equation says that the present discounted value of consumption must equal total wealth. That is, Irving's consumption is constrained by the total resources that will be available to him in the present and in the future. These resources include his existing financial wealth f_{today}. But they also include his **human wealth**—the present discounted value of labor income $y_{today} + \frac{y_{future}}{1 + R}$.

These equations suggest that Irving's consumption in any given year can be very different from his income. (Indeed, if you are a student, your consumption this year probably exceeds your income.) Irving is allowed to save for the future, if he desires; but he can also borrow against his future labor income. What must be true is that the present value of consumption equals the present value of lifetime resources.

Utility

We assume that Irving chooses his consumption today and in the future in order to maximize utility. For this to make sense, we have to explain how consumption

[1] Rewrite the second equation as $f_{future} = (c_{future} - y_{future})/(1 + R)$, and substitute this result into the first equation.

affects utility. The standard assumption in macroeconomics is that consumption delivers utility through a **utility function**. For example, if Irving consumes some amount c in a given period, we assume that he receives $u(c)$ units of utility, sometimes called "utils." We also assume that Irving gets more utility whenever his consumption is higher, but that consumption runs into diminishing returns. That is, consumption exhibits **diminishing marginal utility**: each additional unit of consumption raises utility by a smaller and smaller amount. Diminishing marginal utility is intuitive and applies to all kinds of consumption. Eating dinner at a fancy restaurant one night during the week is a special treat; after seven nights in a row, however, another night out seems much less desirable. An example of such a utility function is shown in Figure 15.1. Diminishing marginal utility is reflected in the curvature of the utility function, which gets flatter and flatter as consumption increases.

Because Irving consumes in two periods, utility depends on consumption today and consumption in the future. A natural way to express this is with the following lifetime utility function:

$$U = u(c_{\text{today}}) + \beta u(c_{\text{future}}). \tag{15.4}$$

Irving's lifetime utility depends on how much he consumes today and how much in the future. The parameter β is some number—such as 1.0 or 0.9—that captures the weight that Irving places on the future, relative to today. For example, if $\beta = 1$, then Irving treats utils received today and in the future equally. Alternatively, if $\beta < 1$, a given flow of utility is worth more when it occurs today. Economists often think of β as capturing the extent to which consumers are patient.

FIGURE 15.1

Flow Utility $u(c)$

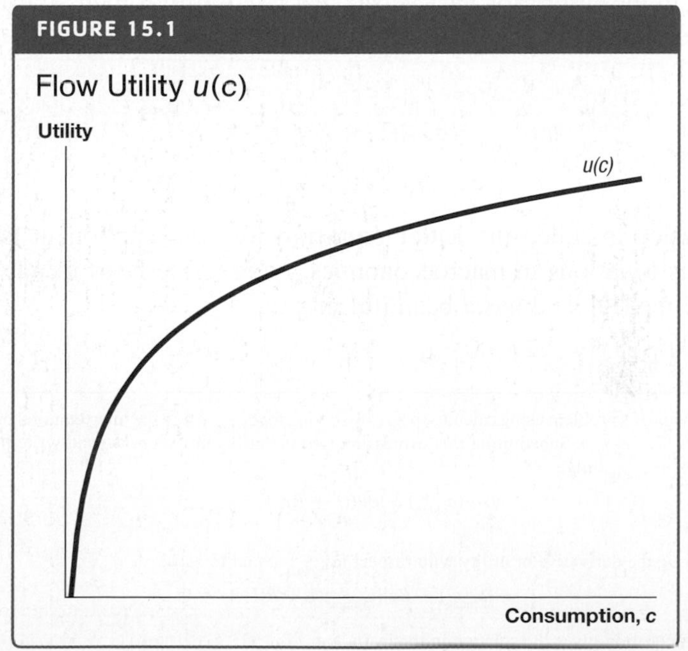

A consumption level of c delivers a flow of utility to the consumer of $u(c)$. Utility rises when c increases, but the amount of the increase gets smaller and smaller, reflecting diminishing marginal utility.

Choosing Consumption to Maximize Utility

We've now completed the setup of the neoclassical consumption model. Irving gets utility from consuming in each period, as in equation (15.4), and he must choose his consumption to satisfy the intertemporal budget constraint in equation (15.3). The model is closed by assuming that Irving chooses his consumption so as to maximize utility, subject to his budget constraint:

$$\max_{c_{\text{today}},\, c_{\text{future}}} \quad U = u(c_{\text{today}}) + \beta u(c_{\text{future}}), \text{ subject to}$$
$$c_{\text{today}} + \left(\frac{c_{\text{future}}}{1 + R}\right) = \overline{W}, \tag{15.5}$$

where we've defined $\overline{W} \equiv f_{\text{today}} + y_{\text{today}} + \left(\frac{y_{\text{future}}}{1 + R}\right)$. That is, $\overline{W}$ denotes total wealth, the sum of financial wealth and human wealth.

Solving this problem requires calculus, and the solution is derived step-by-step in the footnote below. However, the solution turns out to be intuitive. In fact, walking through the intuition will allow you to get the solution yourself without going through the details.[2]

First, look at the utility function. If Irving consumes a little more today, the extra utility he gets is the marginal utility of consumption today, which we can write as $u'(c_{\text{today}})$. Alternatively, Irving can consume a little more tomorrow, in which case he gets the marginal utility of consumption tomorrow (adjusted by the discount parameter): $\beta u'(c_{\text{future}})$.

Now recall the logic of the intertemporal budget constraint. The essence of this constraint is that Irving can consume 1 unit today or can save that unit and consume $1 + R$ units in the future. If he's maximized utility, Irving must be indifferent between consuming today or in the future. Why? Because if moving consumption from today to the future (or vice versa) increased utility, then Irving would not be at a maximum. This key indifference condition can be stated as

$$u'(c_{\text{today}}) = \beta(1 + R)u'(c_{\text{future}}). \tag{15.6}$$

This expression is called the **Euler equation** for consumption. It is one of the most famous equations in macroeconomics, lying at the heart of advanced macroeconomic models, and has a beautiful intuition.

---

[2] To solve the consumer's problem using calculus, begin by solving for c_{future} using the intertemporal budget constraint: $c_{\text{future}} = (1 + R)(\overline{W} - c_{\text{today}})$. Substituting this expression into the utility function, we can write the maximization problem in terms of c_{today} only:

$$\max_{c_{\text{today}}} u(c_{\text{today}}) + \beta u((1 + R)(\overline{W} - c_{\text{today}})).$$

We solve by setting the derivative of utility with respect to c_{today} equal to zero:

$$u'(c_{\text{today}}) + \beta u'(c_{\text{future}})(1 + R)(-1) = 0.$$

Rearranging this equation gives the solution in the main text.

The Euler equation essentially says that Irving must be indifferent between consuming one more unit today on the one hand and saving that unit and consuming it in the future on the other. If Irving consumes today, he gets the marginal utility of consumption today—the left-hand side of the equation, $u'(c_{\text{today}})$. If Irving saves that unit instead, he gets to consume $1 + R$ units in the future, each giving him $u'(c_{\text{future}})$ extra units of utility. Because this utility comes in the future, it must be discounted by the weight β. That's the right side of the Euler equation. The fact that these two sides must be equal is what guarantees that Irving is indifferent to consuming today versus consuming in the future.

Another way to see that this equation must hold is to think about what would happen if it did not. For example, let's first suppose that $u'(c_{\text{today}})$ were larger than $\beta(1 + R)u'(c_{\text{future}})$. This means that the marginal utility of consumption today is higher than the value Irving gets from consuming the extra unit (plus interest) in the future. In this case, Irving should reduce consumption in the future and raise it today. That will increase overall lifetime utility. This reallocation should occur until Irving is just indifferent between consuming an extra unit today and consuming that unit plus interest in the future. That's what the Euler equation says.

Alternatively, if we supposed that $u'(c_{\text{today}})$ were smaller than $\beta(1 + R)u'(c_{\text{future}})$, the story would go in the other direction. If the marginal utility of consumption today is lower than it would be in the future, Irving should reduce consumption today and raise it in the future. That would increase overall lifetime utility.

Solving the Euler Equation: Log Utility

In order to get an explicit solution for consumption, we need to specify a functional form for the utility function $u(c)$. A common choice is the logarithmic function:[3] $u(c) = \log c$. In fact, the specific curve drawn in Figure 15.1 is exactly this case. The reason this case is so common is that it has a very nice property:

If $u(c) = \log c$, then the marginal utility of consumption is $u'(c) = \frac{1}{c}$.

If you are familiar with calculus, then you will understand why this statement is true. If you are not familiar with calculus, do not be concerned—just take the statement as a fact that you can use.

Using the fact that $u'(c) = 1/c$, the Euler equation in (15.6) can be written as

$$\frac{1}{c_{\text{today}}} = \beta(1 + R)\frac{1}{c_{\text{future}}}. \tag{15.7}$$

Rearranging this equation slightly leads to another very intuitive result:

$$\frac{c_{\text{future}}}{c_{\text{today}}} = \beta(1 + R). \tag{15.8}$$

[3] By this, we mean the natural logarithm. We follow the convention in economics in denoting the natural logarithm as "log."

Notice that the left-hand side of this equation is just the growth rate of consumption (plus 1). Equation (15.8), therefore, says that Irving chooses his consumption so that the growth rate of consumption is the product of the discount parameter and the interest rate that he can earn on his saving. If Irving is very impatient, he places less weight on future utility (a lower β), and consumption growth is lower. On the other hand, a higher interest rate raises the return to saving, and consumption growth is faster.

In fact, writing the Euler equation in terms of consumption growth reveals another deep insight into macroeconomics: it explains why interest rates and growth rates are often similar numbers, like 2 percent. In the partial equilibrium consumption problem that Irving is solving, Irving takes the value of the real interest rate R as given and chooses any consumption growth rate he wishes. The economy as a whole consists of a bunch of people like Irving, we might suppose, and in general equilibrium, the real interest rate and the growth rate of the economy are both endogenous variables, as we saw in the growth models in Chapters 4 through 6. The Euler equation then explains how these two variables are related. In fact, the general equilibrium interpretation of the Euler equation switches the logic around in a way. In general equilibrium, a Solow/Romer-type model pins down the growth rate of the economy. The Euler equation then determines the interest rate that Irving faces.

An example may help illustrate how this works. Suppose the growth rate of the economy—and, therefore, of consumption—is 2 percent per year, which we think of as coming from some long-run growth model. Suppose to start that $\beta = 1$. In this case, the Euler equation implies that the real interest rate will also be 2 percent, exactly equal to the growth rate. To the extent that consumers prefer to get their utility today instead of in the future, β may be less than 1 and, therefore, the real interest rate will be a little higher than 2 percent. What's key here is that *the Euler equation explains how interest rates and growth rates are linked.*

Solving for c_{today} and c_{future}: Log Utility and $\beta = 1$

The Euler equation in equation (15.8) is one equation but features two unknowns, c_{today} and c_{future}. Therefore, to solve for consumption today and in the future, we need one more equation. What is it? The answer is the original intertemporal budget constraint in equation (15.5).

Because it is helpful to see these two equations together, we repeat them here:

$$\frac{c_{future}}{c_{today}} = \beta(1 + R) \qquad \text{(Euler equation)}$$

$$c_{today} + \frac{c_{future}}{1 + R} = \overline{W}. \qquad \text{(IBC)}$$

Now consider the case where $\beta = 1$. In this case, these two equations can be solved easily just by looking at them closely. In particular, the Euler equation implies that $\frac{c_{future}}{1 + R} = c_{today}$, so consumptions are equal (in present value). Plugging this result into the intertemporal budget constraint immediately implies

$$c_{\text{today}} = \frac{1}{2} \cdot \overline{W} \tag{15.9}$$

and

$$c_{\text{future}} = \frac{1}{2} \cdot (1 + R)\overline{W}. \tag{15.10}$$

For log utility and $\beta = 1$, then, Irving consumes one-half of his wealth today and saves the other half. In the future, he can consume the remainder of his wealth together with the interest it has earned. Solving the model when $\beta \neq 1$ is not much more difficult; this problem is considered in an exercise at the end of the chapter.

The Effect of a Rise in *R* on Consumption

How does consumption respond to a rise in the interest rate? As a starting point for answering this question, consider the solution in equation (15.9) that we just derived in the special case of log utility. At first glance, it may appear that a change in the interest rate will leave consumption unaffected. But that is not quite right. In particular, recall that total wealth $\overline{W}$ depends on the interest rate because it includes the present discounted value of labor income (look back at the text following equation 15.5). A higher interest rate will reduce this present value, therefore reducing consumption in the case of log utility. This force is called the *wealth effect* of a higher interest rate, because it works through the total wealth term.

You may also recall from your study of microeconomics that changes in interest rates often involve both a *substitution effect* and an *income effect*. In the case of log utility, these effects offset each other, which is why the interest rate does not appear explicitly in equation (15.9). When utility takes a different form, however—one example is the square root of consumption—these effects enter. The substitution effect of a higher interest rate is that current consumption is now more expensive (because saving will lead to even more consumption in the future), so consumers will tend to reduce their consumption today. The income effect says that consumers are now richer—because their current saving leads to more income in the future—which makes them want to consume more today. In general, a higher interest rate can either raise or lower current consumption, because these effects work in opposite directions.

15.3 Lessons from the Neoclassical Model

The neoclassical consumption model allows us to understand better several issues related to consumption that were originally raised in Chapter 11. It also offers some new lessons, which are discussed below.

The Permanent-Income Hypothesis

In discussing the microfoundations for consumption in Chapter 11, we introduced Milton Friedman's **permanent-income hypothesis**. According to this view, consumption depends on some average value of income, rather than on current income. In strong versions of the hypothesis, we said, consumption might depend on the present discounted value of income.

The neoclassical consumption model provides a way of making this statement precise. In particular, we see from equation (15.9) that consumption is proportional to a consumer's overall wealth, $\overline{W} = f_{\text{today}} + y_{\text{today}} + \frac{y_{\text{future}}}{1+R}$. However, this total wealth depends on the present discounted value of income (the last two terms). The permanent-income hypothesis, then, is one implication of the neoclassical consumption model.

The intuition behind the permanent-income result is that consumers wish to smooth their consumption over time. This desire is embedded in the utility function $u(c)$. To begin, suppose $\beta = 1$ and $R = 0$, and consider Figure 15.2. Suppose Irving could consume c_1 today and c_2 in the future or could consume the average of these two values in both periods. Because of diminishing marginal utility, Irving prefers to smooth consumption and take the average in both periods. Now consider what happens if $R > 0$. From the Euler equation, we know that this change leads consumption to grow over time. Because of Irving's basic desire to smooth consumption, he must be paid a positive interest rate not to keep consumption constant.

How does Irving respond to a temporary increase in income? Suppose y_{today} rises by \$100. Equation (15.9) implies that Irving's consumption will rise by only 1/2 as much as the increase in income, or \$50. Irving saves the remainder and consumes it in the future, smoothing out the burst of income.

In this simple example, the value of 1/2 is called the **marginal propensity to consume**: if income temporarily goes up by \$1, consumption rises by 1/2 that

Suppose Irving could either consume c_1 today and c_2 in the future or could consume the average of these two values in both periods. Because of diminishing marginal utility, Irving prefers to smooth consumption and take the average in both periods. That is, lifetime utility is higher when Irving gets $u(\bar{c})$ in both periods, rather than $u(c_1) + u(c_2)$. (This assumes $\beta = 1$ and $R = 0$, so these results can be shown easily in a simple graph.)

FIGURE 15.2

The Desire to Smooth Consumption

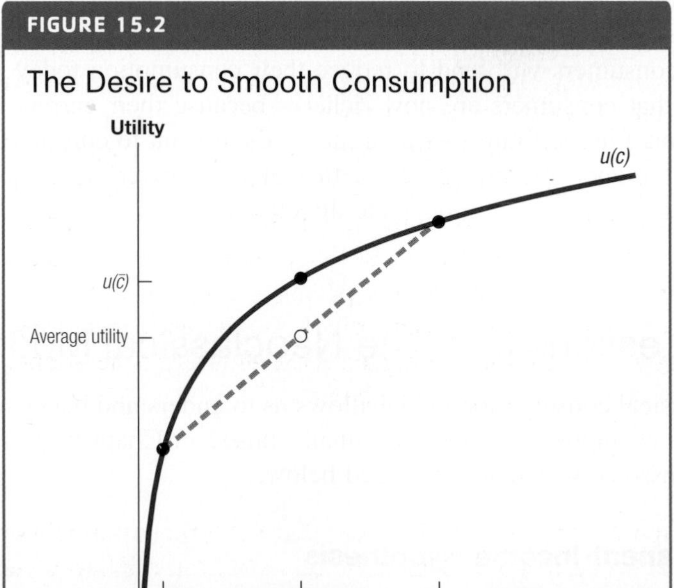

amount. Similarly, the marginal propensity to consume out of financial wealth is also 1/2.

In richer models, the marginal propensity to consume out of income differs from 1/2. For example, if we increase the number of periods in Irving's life—say to 3 periods or perhaps to 80 periods, where each period represents a year of life—then the marginal propensity to consume is approximately equal to 1 divided by the number of periods; this approximation is exact when $R = 0$ and $\beta = 1$. In other words, if Irving expects to live for another 50 years, the marginal propensity to consume out of another dollar of income will be something like 1/50. The general lesson from models in which the permanent-income hypothesis holds is that the marginal propensity to consume out of income or wealth is relatively small.

Ricardian Equivalence

The concept of **Ricardian equivalence**, first discussed in Chapter 11, can also be better understood in the neoclassical consumption model. The essence of the Ricardian approach to the government is that consumption depends on the present discounted value of taxes and is invariant to the timing of taxes.

To see this point, consider again the derivation of the intertemporal budget constraint from equation (15.5). While we did not emphasize it, the proper interpretation of y is as income *after taxes*. That is, taxes—both today and in the future—must be subtracted from the right-hand side of the intertemporal budget constraint. Lifetime wealth $\overline{W}$ is the present discounted value of resources net of taxes.

The Ricardian equivalence claim is that a change in the timing of taxes does not affect consumption. A tax cut today, financed by an increase in taxes in the future, will not affect consumption, if the Ricardian claim is true. This claim is almost trivial to see in our neoclassical model. Clearly, a change in the timing of taxes will leave $\overline{W}$ unchanged. Therefore, the consumer's maximization problem as specified in equation (15.5) will be unchanged, and there is no reason for consumption to change.

How well does Ricardian equivalence describe what happens empirically when the government changes the timing of taxes? It depends. For example, we will see that to the extent that consumers are limited by borrowing constraints, Ricardian equivalence need not hold. It can also break down when the tax cuts are given to people who differ from the people paying the higher taxes. This might occur because of a progressive tax system or because current generations are receiving a tax cut that will be paid for by higher taxes on future generations. These issues will be discussed in more detail in Chapter 17.

Borrowing Constraints

A key assumption of the neoclassical model is that Irving can freely save or borrow at the market interest rate R. This may be a good description of the opportunities available to many consumers, but there may also be some consumers who, for whatever reason, have no financial wealth and are unable to borrow in credit markets. Financial conditions could be bad in the economy as a whole; or perhaps the individual's credit history is not good, and no one will provide a loan.

In this case, the intertemporal budget constraint is no longer the correct constraint. Instead, the constraint on consumption for individuals with no financial wealth and no access to credit is much simpler:

$$c_{today} \leq y_{today}. \tag{15.11}$$

That is, Irving's consumption is constrained by the lack of borrowing opportunities to be no greater than his income.

If Irving is already consuming less than his income, then this constraint will not be binding: Irving is already saving, so not allowing him to borrow does not change anything. Alternatively, if Irving's current income is sufficiently low, he may wish to borrow. In this case, the borrowing constraint binds, and his consumption is constrained to equal his income: $c_{today} = y_{today}$.

Interestingly, the marginal propensity to consume from an extra dollar of income changes significantly when borrowing constraints are present. We saw earlier that the marginal propensity to consume when the permanent-income hypothesis holds is typically a small number, such as 1 divided by the number of periods of life remaining. In contrast, when borrowing constraints bind, consumption is exactly equal to income. If current income rises by $1, consumption rises by $1 as well, and the marginal propensity to consume is unity, much larger than before.

Consumption as a Random Walk

What happens if Irving's income is uncertain? No one knows what the future holds, and tomorrow Irving may receive a long-sought promotion that raises his income. Alternatively, his job may be outsourced, and he may become unemployed. There are two important insights that emerge from thinking carefully about consumption when income is uncertain. We discuss one now and one in the next subsection.

In the presence of uncertainty, the neoclassical model implies that consumption today depends on all information the consumer has about the present value of lifetime resources. Clearly, there is no way for the consumer to know if she will win the lottery 25 years from now. However, she may know that she is currently under consideration for a big promotion and will likely be earning substantially more income in the future than she is today. This information—and all other available information—should be reflected in her current consumption.

In 1978, Robert Hall of Stanford University developed this implication, commonly known as the **random walk view of consumption**.[4] Because all known information should be incorporated into current consumption, changes in consumption should be unpredictable. Apart from the general trend in consumption associated with the interest rate in the Euler equation, consumption should be equally likely to move up or down over time, at least if the permanent-income

[4]Robert E. Hall, "Stochastic Implications of the Life Cycle–Permanent Income Hypothesis: Theory and Evidence," *Journal of Political Economy*, vol. 86, no. 6 (December 1978), pp. 971–987.

hypothesis is correct. When an expected promotion arrives, the effect on consumption should be relatively small—after all, the promotion was expected, and so the extra future income should already be reflected in current consumption. On the other hand, an unexpected job loss may have a much larger effect on current consumption, particularly if the unemployment spell is expected to be long.

CASE STUDY

Consumption versus Expenditure

A key prediction of the basic neoclassical consumption model is that consumption should not change when a long-anticipated event comes to pass. For example, retirement typically does not come as a surprise and is in fact one of the most anticipated events in an individual's lifetime. According to the neoclassical consumption model, then, one would expect consumption to remain relatively unchanged when people retire. In fact, expenditures on consumption change quite markedly around this event–falling by around 17 percent (according to a study we will discuss momentarily). Such a large decline in consumption expenditures was for many years a long-standing puzzle from the standpoint of the neoclassical model.

This puzzle was recently solved by Mark Aguiar of the University of Rochester and Erik Hurst of the University of Chicago.[5] Aguiar and Hurst studied a novel data set of food diaries for a large number of households–these diaries record all the food each person in the household consumes over a certain period of time. Aguiar and Hurst showed that while expenditures on consumption do indeed decline sharply upon retirement, the food and calories that people actually consume show no such decline. Instead, households spend much more time shopping for food and preparing it themselves. The quantity and the quality of food actually consumed is maintained when individuals retire, even though the amount of money spent on food declines. So what initially appeared to be a puzzle for the neoclassical consumption model turns out to be quite supportive once consumption itself is studied, as opposed to money spent on consumption.

Precautionary Saving

The second key implication that arises when income is uncertain is that consumers may save to hedge against the possibility of a large drop in income, perhaps associated with unemployment or disability. This type of saving is called **precautionary saving**. Interestingly, such a consumer might save even when income

[5]Mark Aguiar and Erik Hurst, "Consumption versus Expenditure," *Journal of Political Economy*, vol. 113, no. 5 (October 2005), pp. 919–948.

and wealth are temporarily low, when the basic permanent-income hypothesis would suggest borrowing. Why? As long as the possibility remains that income could fall even further, consumers may engage in precautionary saving to insure themselves against that outcome. In fact, the recent financial crisis provides an excellent example of precautionary saving. As we will document carefully at the end of this chapter, saving rates rose sharply during the financial crisis, and precautionary motives are a logical part of the explanation.[6]

The precautionary-saving motive can, therefore, lead consumers to behave as if they face borrowing constraints even when they do not. That is, consumers with low income who look like they ought to be borrowing may save instead. Moreover, their consumption may be especially sensitive to their current income, just as in the case of a borrowing constraint. Precautionary saving and borrowing constraints, then, are two explanations for why the marginal propensity to consume out of income can be higher than the permanent-income hypothesis would dictate.

15.4 Empirical Evidence on Consumption

As we have seen, the neoclassical consumption model is rich and can lead to a range of outcomes. For individuals with sufficient wealth, consumption may obey the permanent-income hypothesis and follow a random walk with only news of changes in income leading to changes in consumption. On the other hand, individuals with low wealth or those who cannot borrow in credit markets may display much greater sensitivity to current income.

What does the evidence say? This section reviews a range of evidence on consumer behavior, including both microeconomic evidence from individual households and aggregate evidence about the macroeconomic properties of consumption.

Evidence from Individual Households

One of the most studied areas of macroeconomics in recent decades has been the determinants of consumption at the household level. This literature is too large to review in detail, but we summarize its three central findings here.[7]

First, the Euler equation and the permanent-income hypothesis provide a useful description of the consumption behavior of many households, particularly those with above-average wealth. The marginal propensity to consume out of a temporary income shock is low, and consumption smoothing is effective for these households.

[6] A nice introduction to precautionary saving can be found in Christopher D. Carroll, "A Theory of the Consumption Function, with and without Liquidity Constraints," *Journal of Economic Perspectives*, vol. 15, no. 3 (Summer 2001), pp. 23–46.

[7] In addition to the economists mentioned elsewhere in this chapter, others who have made important contributions include Mark Aguiar, Orazio Attanasio, Chris Carroll, Karen Dynan, Pierre-Olivier Gourinchas, Chang-Tai Hsieh, Erik Hurst, Miles Kimball, Dirk Krueger, David Laibson, Sydney Ludvigson, Annamaria Lusardi, Jonathan Parker, Fabrizio Perri, Luigi Pistaferri, Andrew Samwick, Nick Souleles, and Stephen Zeldes.

Second, there are also many households, especially those with low income and wealth, that behave as if they are borrowing-constrained or engaging in precautionary saving. For these households, consumption tracks income well, and the marginal propensity to consume from a temporary boost in income is high.

At this point, it is worth pausing to note something that plays a central role in modern economics: households are heterogeneous. By this, we mean that there is not a single type of household with a single marginal propensity to consume. Instead, the microeconomic side of consumption is much messier. Consumption is very sensitive to income for some households, while others are much more successful at smoothing consumption. This gives rise to aggregation issues: for example, the effect on aggregate consumption of a 1-percent increase in GDP depends on the distribution of heterogeneous households exhibiting a range of microeconomic responses. Neither the permanent-income hypothesis nor a simple equation in which consumption responds one-for-one to changes in income provides a good description of aggregate consumption for modern economies. The real world is somewhere in between. For example, it has been suggested that the average marginal propensity to consume in rich countries may be about 25 to 30 percent.[8]

The third and final lesson from the extensive research on household consumption is that there are many anomalies and departures from the neoclassical consumption model—and even from the basic view of households as rational economic agents, for that matter. One of the most active areas of economic research in the last decade is **behavioral economics**. This research blends insights from psychology, neuroscience, and economics in an effort to create a better understanding of how individuals make economic decisions. We discuss it in more detail in the accompanying case study.

CASE STUDY

Behavioral Economics and Consumption

A common assumption in economics is that the agents in our models are rational, forward-looking individuals who are extremely good at solving complicated economic problems. They are the kind of people who would get an A+ in all of their economics classes. It will not surprise you that most people in the world fall short of this high standard. So the question at the heart of behavioral economics is this: What happens if we build our models around more realistic behavioral assumptions? For example, what if people are not that good at solving math problems, are susceptible to emotional advertising, or are willing to spend a lot to avoid losses?

Behavioral approaches have been applied throughout economics. But one of the applications that has met with the greatest success is the theory of consumption

[8] This estimate comes from the paper by Chris Carroll cited in note 6, above.

and saving. David Laibson of Harvard University has proposed a simple modification of the behavior of our standard rational economic agents. In particular, based on a number of psychological experiments, Laibson considers the possibility that people are particularly concerned about the present. That is, they may be especially impatient when faced with decisions involving today versus the future (as opposed to comparing two different moments in the future). Laibson shows that under this assumption, consumption will be more sensitive to movements in income than the permanent-income hypothesis predicts. Such departures have been observed empirically. For example, some people seem to borrow excessively, using credit cards that have very high interest rates. Others may have trouble exerting the self-control required to save in response to large, temporary boosts in income.

Some of the most compelling evidence on the importance of behavioral considerations comes from 401(k) retirement plans. These employer-sponsored plans encourage employees to save a portion of their salaries for retirement by providing favorable tax treatment. Individuals can choose what fraction of their salary to save, up to a maximum, and can pick from a number of investment opportunities, including money market accounts and mutual funds. The default design of these plans turns out to have a tremendous impact on how individuals participate: default options are "sticky." For example, research shows that when employees are enrolled by default in a 401(k) plan, almost no one opts out, and participation is, therefore, almost 100 percent. In contrast, when new employees are not enrolled automatically, fewer than half participate during their first year employed. Another (in)famous example comes from the energy-trading company Enron. In 2000, current and past employees of the Enron Corporation held $2.1 billion in the firm's 401(k) retirement plan. An astounding 62 percent of these funds were invested in Enron's own stock, despite the fact that employees were allowed (and generally encouraged by financial advisers) to diversify their holdings. In just a few weeks at the end of 2001, Enron collapsed in bankruptcy due to accounting fraud. Shares that had traded at $83 each earlier in the year became worthless, and thousands of employees and retirees saw much of their retirement saving wiped out.[9]

Economists are working hard to create better models of economic behavior, and the insights from behavioral economics are playing an important role in this endeavor.[10]

[9]The examples in this paragraph are from two papers: James J. Choi, David Laibson, Brigitte C. Madrian, and Andrew Metrick, "Optimal Defaults," *American Economic Review,* vol. 93, no. 2 (May 2003), pp. 180–185. James Choi, David Laibson, and Brigitte C. Madrian, "Are Empowerment and Education Enough?: Underdiversification in 401(k) Plans," *Brookings Papers on Economic Activity,* vol. 2005, no. 2 (2005), pp. 151–198.

[10]For more on the application of behavioral economics to consumption, see George-Marios Angeletos, et al., "The Hyberbolic Consumption Model: Calibration, Simulation, and Empirical Evaluation," *Journal of Economic Perspectives*, vol. 15, no. 3 (Summer 2001), pp. 47–68. Broader overviews of behavioral economics can be found in two papers: Matthew Rabin, "Psychology and Economics," *Journal of Economic Literature,* vol. 36, no. 1 (March 1998), pp. 11–46; and Colin Camerer, George Loewenstein, and Drazen Prelec, "Neuroeconomics: How Neuroscience Can Inform Economics," *Journal of Economic Literature,* vol. 43, no. 1 (March 2005), pp. 9–64.

Aggregate Evidence

We noted in Chapter 2 that aggregate consumption as a share of GDP rose from about 63 percent in 1970 to 70 percent in 2008. This section provides more insight into how the consumption share of GDP increased so substantially.

According to Figure 15.3, households have increased their borrowing substantially in recent decades. In the 1970s and early 1980s, household debt was typically less than 50 percent of GDP. Beginning in the mid-1980s, however, this ratio began to rise, reaching about 67 percent of GDP in 2000 and then rising sharply to nearly 100 percent of GDP by 2009. In Chapter 10, we noted that the recent financial crisis was a balance-sheet crisis. Here, we see the large increase in household debt that is one element of that story.

The remarkable rise in household debt is paralleled by a large, steady decline in the personal saving rate, as shown in Figure 15.4. The **personal saving rate** is the ratio of personal saving to disposable income (i.e., income after paying taxes). This saving rate declined from more than 10 percent in much of the 1970s and early 1980s to less than 2 percent by 2007. One effect of the financial turmoil in recent years has been to increase the personal saving rate; during 2009, the rate averaged more than 4 percent.

These two figures illustrate that U.S. households have increased their borrowing and reduced their saving for much of the last two decades, choosing instead to consume more. Why have these changes occurred? Economists have proposed a number of explanations. One of the most widely held of these is that large gains in the stock market and housing market during the last several decades have reduced

FIGURE 15.3

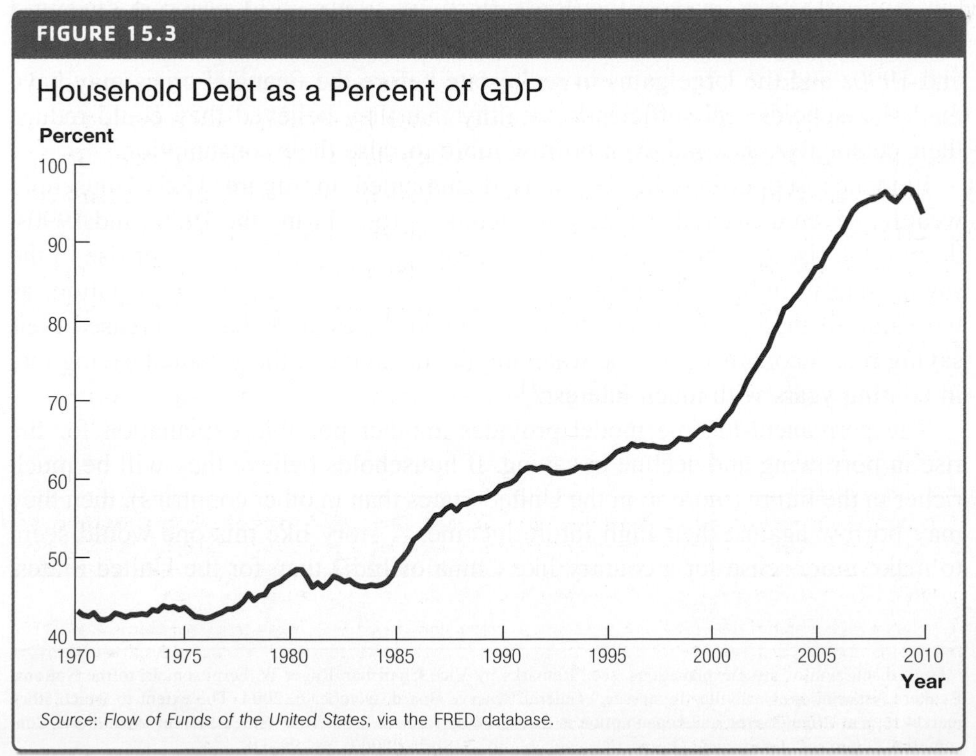

The ratio of debt accumulated by the household sector to GDP has doubled since 1970, rising very sharply between 2000 and 2008.

Between 1980 and 2008, the personal saving rate fell from about 10 percent to below 2 percent before rising in 2009.

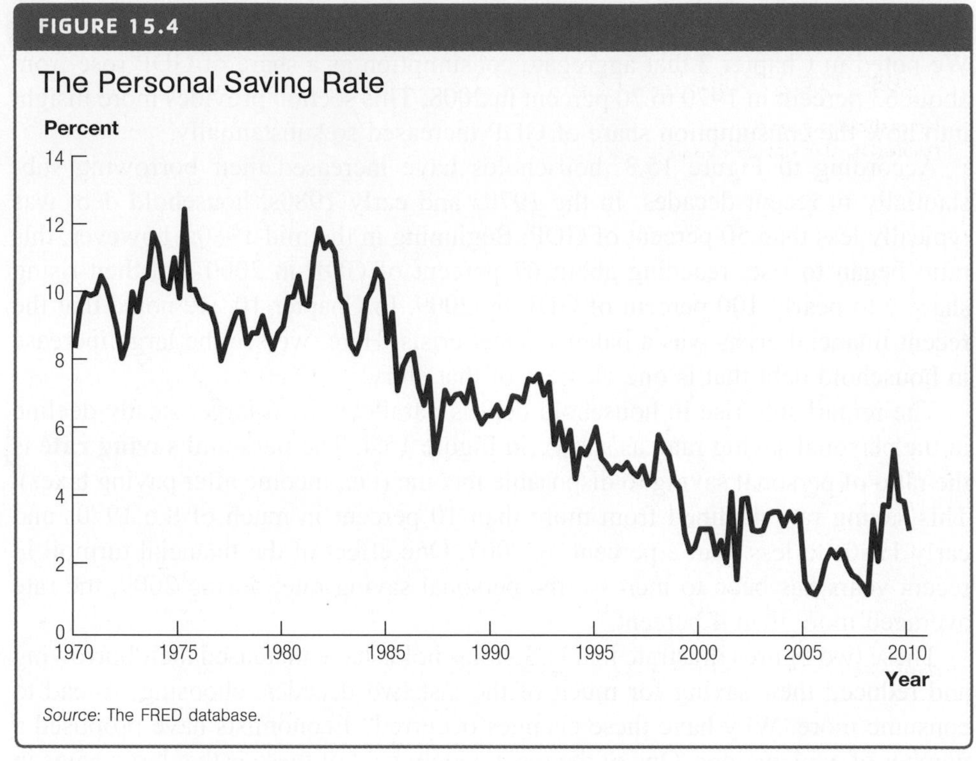

FIGURE 15.4

The Personal Saving Rate

Source: The FRED database.

the need for additional saving. The balance in your 401(k) plan can increase because you add more saving each month, or it can increase because the value of the assets being held has risen. The large gains in the stock market in the 1980s and 1990s and the large gains in real estate before the financial crisis may have made households feel sufficiently wealthy that they believed they could reduce their personal saving and even borrow more to raise their consumption.

Evidence supporting this claim is documented in Figure 15.5. Household wealth—even measured as a ratio to income—rose during the 1980s and 1990s, despite the rise in debt and the decline in saving. Similarly, the recent rise in the saving rate in light of the financial crisis is consistent with this explanation: as the value of their financial assets has declined, households have increased their saving rate. Economists will be watching the behavior of the personal saving rate in coming years with much interest.[11]

The permanent-income model provides another possible explanation for the rise in borrowing and decline in saving. If households believe they will be much richer in the future (more so in the United States than in other countries), then they may borrow against their high future income. A story like this one would seem to make more sense for a country like China or India than for the United States.

[11] For a discussion of these explanations, see "Remarks by Vice Chairman Roger W. Ferguson, Jr. to the National Bankers Association, Nashville, Tennessee," Federal Reserve Board, October 6, 2004. The extent to which stock market returns affect saving and consumption is discussed by James M. Poterba, "Stock Market Wealth and Consumption," *Journal of Economic Perspectives*, vol. 14, no. 2 (Spring 2000), pp. 99–118.

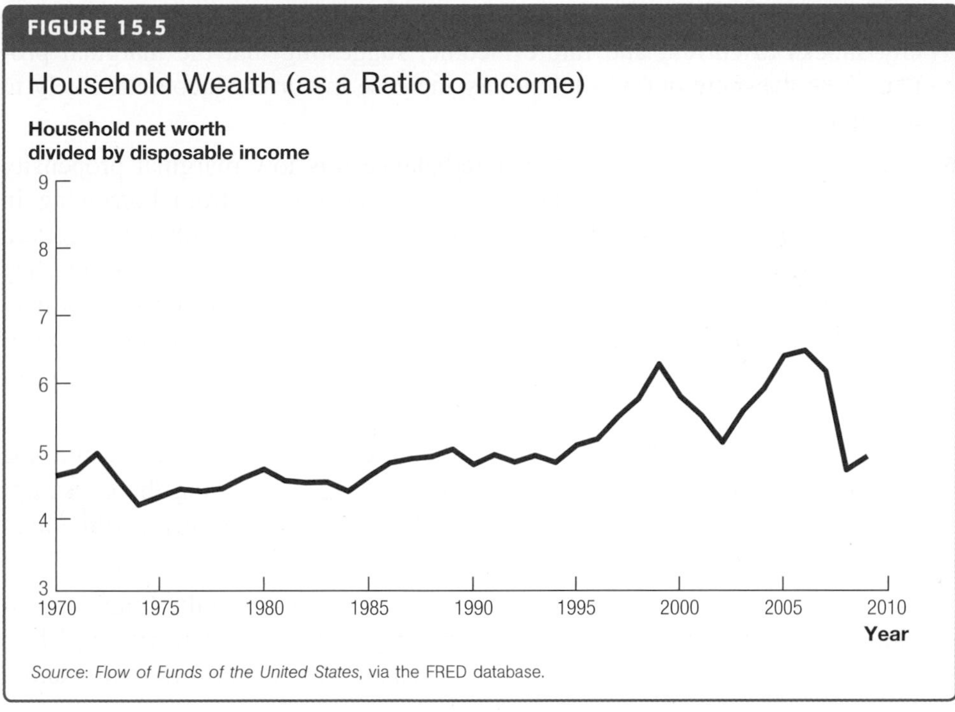

FIGURE 15.5

Household Wealth (as a Ratio to Income)

Source: *Flow of Funds of the United States*, via the FRED database.

Despite the rise in debt and the decline in saving, household wealth rose during the 1980s and 1990s. During the last decade, wealth declined following the dot-com stock market crash, recovered with the housing market boom, and then declined again back to its 1990 level following the collapse in financial markets, starting in 2008.

However, China's saving rate has been rising rather than falling. This story by itself, then, seems to get the facts backward. We will come back to this puzzle in Chapter 18, when we discuss international trade.

CHAPTER REVIEW

SUMMARY

1. The neoclassical consumption model is based on rational individuals who choose the time path of their consumption to maximize a utility function subject to their intertemporal budget constraint.
2. This problem is relatively easy to study when we consider only two periods, such as today and the future.
3. The solution to this basic problem is a version of the permanent-income hypothesis: consumption in each period is a fraction of total wealth, where total wealth includes financial resources, current income, and the present discounted value of future income.
4. This solution can also be expressed in terms of the Euler equation for consumption. This equation says that individuals are indifferent between consuming a little more today, on the one hand, or saving a little more and consuming the proceeds in the future.

5. A key implication of this result is that individuals will seek to smooth out any shocks to current and future income, suggesting that the marginal propensity to consume out of a temporary increase in current income is likely to be small.
6. There are two forces that may counterbalance this low marginal propensity to consume, however. Individuals who are constrained from borrowing in credit markets—perhaps because they have zero or low wealth and uncertain income—may set their consumption proportional to their income. Even if they are unencumbered by borrowing constraints, however, such individuals may engage in precautionary saving to insure themselves against the possibility of unemployment or disability and may, therefore, have a high marginal propensity to consume.
7. Empirical evidence, consistent with this theory, suggests that while the permanent-income model is a good benchmark for describing the consumption of well-off individuals, there are also many poorer consumers with a high marginal propensity to consume.
8. Behavioral economics provides a more nuanced approach to the study of individual behavior, incorporating insights from psychology and neuroscience. This literature highlights ways in which individuals depart, sometimes significantly, from neoclassical behavior.
9. Aggregate evidence on consumption during the 1980s and 1990s shows a rise in debt as a ratio to income and a decline in the personal saving rate. Despite these changes, household wealth as a ratio to income also rose during this period before falling back to its 1990 level in response to the recent financial turmoil.

KEY CONCEPTS

behavioral economics
borrowing constraints
diminishing marginal utility
Euler equation
financial wealth
flow utility
human wealth
intertemporal budget constraint
marginal propensity to consume
neoclassical consumption model
permanent-income hypothesis
personal saving rate
precautionary saving
random walk view of consumption
Ricardian equivalence
utility function

REVIEW QUESTIONS

1. What are the key building blocks of the neoclassical consumption model?
2. What is an intertemporal budget constraint, and where does it come from? What is the economic interpretation of the intertemporal budget constraint?
3. What is a lifetime utility function, and in what sense does it exhibit diminishing returns?

4. Summarize the main implications of the neoclassical consumption model for consumption and saving.

5. What is the Euler equation for consumption, and what is its economic interpretation?

6. How are interest rates and growth rates related according to the neoclassical consumption model, and why?

7. What is the marginal propensity to consume? How is it affected by borrowing constraints or precautionary saving issues?

8. Summarize the key facts about the behavior of the personal saving rate during recent decades, and place these facts in their macroeconomic context.

EXERCISES

smartwork.wwnorton.com 

1. **The neoclassical consumption model, a student's perspective:** Consider the special case solved in the text where $\beta = 1$ and utility takes the log form. Suppose the real interest rate is 5 percent. Let's give this consumer a financial profile that might look like that of a typical economics student: suppose initial assets are $f_{today} = \$5{,}000$, and the path for labor income is $y_{today} = \$10{,}000$ and $y_{future} = \$100{,}000$.

   (a) What is the individual's human wealth? Total wealth?
   (b) How much does a neoclassical consumer consume today and in the future?
   (c) By how much does consumption today rise if current labor income increases by \$10,000?
   (d) By how much does consumption today rise if future labor income rises by \$10,000? Why does your answer here differ from that in part (c)?
   (e) If the interest rate rises to 10 percent, what happens to total wealth and consumption today?
   (f) What happens to consumption if the student is constrained for some reason and cannot borrow today?

2. **The neoclassical consumption model, a retirement perspective:** Consider the special case solved in the text where $\beta = 1$ and utility takes the log form. Suppose the real interest rate is 5 percent. Let's give this consumer a financial profile that might look like that of a middle-aged college professor contemplating retirement: suppose initial assets are $f_{today} = \$50{,}000$, and the path for labor income is $y_{today} = \$100{,}000$ and $y_{future} = \$10{,}000$.

   (a) What is the individual's human wealth? Total wealth?
   (b) According to the neoclassical model, how much does the college professor consume today and in the future? How much does the college professor save today?
   (c) If current labor income rises by \$20,000, by how much will saving change?

(d) By how much does consumption today rise if future labor income rises by \$10,000?

(e) If the interest rate rises to 10 percent, by how much do total wealth and today's consumption change? By how much does saving change? Why are these effects so much smaller than in exercise 1?

(f) Would it matter if the professor could not borrow?

3. **Financial wealth and consumption:** Consider the neoclassical consumption model with log utility and $\beta = 1$. Suppose an individual begins with \$10,000 in stocks and \$30,000 of equity in her house, so that financial assets are $f_{today} = \$40{,}000$. Suppose her labor income stream is \$50,000, both today and in the future, and suppose the real interest rate is zero.

(a) What is c_{today} and c_{future}? How much does the consumer save today?

(b) Suppose the stock market booms, doubling in value. By how much do consumption and saving change today?

(c) Alternatively, suppose housing prices rise so that the individual's equity in her house rises to \$50,000. Now what happens to consumption and saving today?

(d) Discuss briefly how this exercise is related to the state of the U.S. economy around 2007.

4. **Interest rates and growth rates:** Consider the Euler equation for consumption for log utility, equation (15.8), and answer the following questions:

(a) If the real interest rate is 5 percent and $\beta = 1$, what growth rate for consumption will households choose?

(b) What if $\beta = 0.95$?

(c) Alternatively, suppose the long-run growth model means GDP per person will grow at a constant rate of 2 percent per year. Suppose $\beta = 0.95$. In order for the Euler equation to hold in this case, what value must the real interest rate take?

5. **The neoclassical consumption model with log utility and $\beta \neq 1$:** With log utility, the solution to the neoclassical consumption model is given implicitly by the two equations on page 408, the Euler equation and the intertemporal budget constraint:

$$\frac{c_{future}}{c_{today}} = \beta(1 + R)$$

$$c_{today} + \frac{c_{future}}{1 + R} = \overline{W}.$$

There, we solved these two equations for c_{today} and c_{future} in the special case where $\beta = 1$. This exercise considers the case where β differs from 1.

(a) Solve these two equations for c_{today} and c_{future} when $\beta \neq 1$.

(b) Verify that the solution matches what we obtained in the text when $\beta = 1$.

(c) When $\beta < 1$, is c_{today} higher or lower than when $\beta = 1$? Why?

6. **Ricardian equivalence:** Suppose that the government fears the economy might be heading into a recession and decides to cut income taxes today in an effort to prevent the recession.
   (a) How does the Ricardian equivalence argument apply in this case? How will consumption respond according to this argument?
   (b) How will your answer change if some individuals are borrowing-constrained?

7. **Inequality and the neoclassical consumption model:** As discussed extensively in Chapter 7, income inequality has risen in recent decades in the United States. This question considers the implications for consumption inequality.
   (a) Suppose a substantial part of the rise in inequality is due to the rising returns to education, so that more highly educated workers are permanently richer than less educated workers. According to the neoclassical consumption model, what would happen to consumption inequality? Why?
   (b) Alternatively, suppose that most of the rise in inequality is due to an increase in the frequency and magnitude of temporary shocks (like unemployment or temporary booms and busts in particular industries). What would happen to consumption inequality in this case? Why?

8. **Household debt and saving in the U.S. economy:** Figures 15.3 and 15.4 show household debt as a percentage of GDP and the personal saving rate. According to these graphs, the ratio of household debt to GDP in 2007, before the financial crisis took hold, was just under 100 percent. In the same year, the personal saving rate was 1.7 percent.
   (a) Using the FRED database hosted by the Federal Reserve Bank of St. Louis, obtain the latest values for these two statistics. How has the ratio of household debt to GDP changed since 2007? What about the personal saving rate? (*Hint*: search for the codes CMDEBT, GDP, and PSAVERT.)
   (b) Discuss some possible explanations for these changes.

WORKED EXERCISE

1. **The neoclassical consumption model, a student's perspective:**
   (a) Human wealth is the presented discounted value of labor income:

$$y_{\text{today}} + \frac{y_{\text{future}}}{1+R} = \$10{,}000 + \frac{\$100{,}000}{1.05} = \$105{,}238.$$

   Total wealth is the sum of financial wealth and human wealth, so we just add \$5,000 to our previous answer to get \$110,238.

   (b) According to the solution to the neoclassical consumption model in this case,

$$c_{\text{today}} = \frac{1}{2} \cdot \overline{W} = 0.5 \times \$110{,}238 = \$55{,}119$$

and

$$c_{\text{future}} = \frac{1}{2} \cdot (1 + R)\overline{W} = 0.5 \times 1.05 \times \$110{,}238 = \$57{,}875.$$

Notice how remarkable this is. Even though the student's income is only $10,000 today, her consumption is more than $55,000! Something to think further about: How is the student able to consume more than her income? Do you think students behave like this in reality? Why or why not?

(c) An increase in current labor income by $10,000 raises total wealth by this same amount. The marginal propensity to consume out of total wealth is 1/2 (since the solution for consumption is $c_{\text{today}} = \frac{1}{2} \cdot \overline{W}$). So consumption today rises by $5,000.

(d) Alternatively, if the rise occurs in the future, then total wealth increases by only the present value of $10,000, which is $10,000/1.05 = $9,524. Consumption rises by half this amount, or $4,762. The amount is smaller because future income is worth less than current income (because of the positive interest that can be earned).

(e) An increase in the interest rate will reduce consumption today because of the wealth effect: it lowers the present discounted value of labor income. With an interest rate of 10 percent, a calculation like that in part (a) indicates that human wealth is only $100,909, so that total wealth is only $105,909. Consumption today is, therefore, only $52,955.

(f) In this problem, the student's income is very low initially. Therefore, according to the neoclassical consumption model, she should borrow a large amount so that her current consumption lines up better with her high future income. If she is borrowing-constrained, however, this will not be possible. Instead, she will wish to consume as much as she can today, which will mean she consumes all her current resources: current labor income plus current financial assets, or $15,000. Notice two things. First, borrowing constraints can markedly change consumption. Second, they make consumption depend much more on current labor income.

CHAPTER 16

INVESTMENT

OVERVIEW

In this chapter, we study

- how firms determine investment in physical capital.
- the arbitrage equation, an important tool for analyzing any kind of investment.
- financial investment and a basic theory of prices in the stock market.

An investment in knowledge always pays the best interest.

—BENJAMIN FRANKLIN

There is no finer investment for any community than putting milk into babies.

– WINSTON CHURCHILL

The four most dangerous words in investing are "This time it's different."

– SIR JOHN TEMPLETON

16.1 Introduction

"Invest" is a word that is used frequently in economics, as the quotations above imply. One can invest in developing new ideas, as suggested by Benjamin Franklin. One can invest in human capital, as suggested by Winston Churchill. Or one can invest in financial assets, perhaps the most common use of this word in the business world.

Interestingly, none of these uses convey the most common meaning of "investment" in macroeconomics: investment in the national income accounting sense. In this context, investment refers to the accumulation of physical capital—roads, houses, computers, and machine tools. Nevertheless, each of these uses of the word "invest" captures something essential: it is by investing that our actions today influence our opportunities in the future.

There are two main reasons to study physical investment more closely. The first is evident in the recent financial crisis: investment fluctuates much more than consumption and falls disproportionately during recessions. Starting from its peak in 2006 at more than 17.5 percent of GDP, investment fell to just over 11 percent of GDP in mid-2009. The second reason for studying investment was already highlighted earlier: it is the key economic link between the present and the future. Broadly construed, investment in physical capital, human capital, and ideas lies at the heart of economic growth.

In this chapter, we begin by studying the economic forces that determine investment in physical capital. Starting with a narrow microeconomic question—How do firms make investment decisions?—we show how these microeconomic decisions aggregate to determine the evolution of an economy's capital stock and even the value of its stock market.

To study the determination of investment, we introduce a very important tool in economic analysis: the *arbitrage equation*. This equation turns out to apply to investment in its many different contexts, not just for physical capital. An arbitrage equation can be used to study investment in human capital, in new ideas, or even in financial assets.

We illustrate this point in the second half of the chapter by studying financial investment and the stock market. This provides us with an opportunity to see in detail what determines the price of a financial asset like a share of stock and what is meant by the notion of "efficient markets" in finance.

Finally, we end the chapter with a closer look at two components of physical investment—residential investment and inventory investment—both of which have played important roles in the recent recession. Not surprisingly, the arbitrage equation proves useful in these applications as well.

16.2 How Do Firms Make Investment Decisions?

Should Amazon build a new distribution center? Should Walmart open another store in Boston? Should Gino's East install a new pizza oven at its restaurant in Chicago? Each of these questions is fundamentally about how much a business should invest.

We studied this question in its simplest form in Chapter 4. There, we wrote down a profit-maximization problem for a firm that was choosing how much capital to install and how many workers to hire. The answer turned out to be straightforward: *a business should keep investing in physical capital until the marginal product of capital* (MPK) *falls to equal the rental price of capital, which we in turn argued equals the real interest rate.* Recall that a crucial part of this argument was that capital runs into diminishing returns. When the firm has very little capital, the marginal product of capital is high. If Gino's has only a single pizza oven, adding one more oven has a high return and substantially expands its ability to make pizzas. However, as Gino's adds more and more pizza ovens, the gain in production gets smaller and smaller: there are not enough customers to keep the ovens busy, and the store itself may be too small to handle more ovens. Maximizing profits requires Gino's to continue adding pizza ovens until the last dollar spent on ovens raises revenues by an amount equal to the interest rate.

Letting R denote this interest rate, the reasoning here can be expressed as a simple equation: a firm should invest until

$$MPK = R. \tag{16.1}$$

Reasoning with an Arbitrage Equation

Profit-maximization problems can occasionally become complicated and typically require calculus to analyze and solve. Fortunately, there is an elegant shortcut, a beautiful approach that applies to many investment problems—for capital, for ideas, and for financial investments. This approach uses an **arbitrage equation**.

Arbitrage equations consider two possible ways of investing money. They then take advantage of a powerful insight: if an investor is maximizing profits, then the two investments must yield the same return. Why? If one alternative yielded a higher return, the investor could not be maximizing profits. Taking a little money from the lower-return activity and switching it to the higher-return activity would make even more profit. So at a profit-maximizing position, active investments must yield the same return.

To see this in the simplest setting, return to Gino's and the pizza ovens. Instead of solving the full profit-maximization problem involving the choice of capital, labor, and other inputs, let's consider a slightly different problem.

Suppose the price of pizza ovens is p_k (short for the "price of capital"). Gino's can do two things with its cash on hand: it can put the money in the bank and earn the interest rate R, or it can buy pizza ovens. If the business is maximizing profits, then at the margin both options should yield the same profit; if buying pizza ovens earned a higher profit, then Gino's should do more of that.

Expressed mathematically, this means

$$\underbrace{R \cdot p_k}_{\substack{\text{return from} \\ \text{bank account}}} = \underbrace{MPK + \Delta p_k,}_{\substack{\text{return from} \\ \text{pizza oven}}} \tag{16.2}$$

where Δp_k denotes change in the price of pizza ovens: $\Delta p_k = p_{k,t+1} - p_{k,t}$.

On the left side of equation (16.2) is the return from taking p_k dollars and putting it into the bank for a year. This return is simply the interest earned on that sum. On the right side is the return from taking p_k dollars and investing in the oven. Gino's buys the oven and earns the marginal product of capital, *MPK*. At the end of the year, Gino's sells the oven. In addition to the marginal product, Gino's also makes a capital gain or loss on the oven, depending on whether the price went up or down. The amount of this capital gain is Δp_k.

To connect this result to Chapter 4, suppose we are considering investing an extra dollar—that is, let's normalize the initial price $p_{k,t} = 1$. In this case, we can rearrange equation (16.2) as

$$MPK = R - \frac{\Delta p_k}{p_k}. \tag{16.3}$$

This expression says that Gino's should invest in pizza ovens until the marginal product of capital falls to equal the difference between the interest rate and the growth rate of the price of ovens. Notice that if the price of ovens is constant (so $\Delta p_k = 0$), then this is the same as the solution we obtained in Chapter 4, repeated above in equation (16.1).

The User Cost of Capital

The result in equation (16.2) is even richer, however, because it applies even if the price of ovens is changing over time. This is worth considering in more detail. To begin, let's note an important definition: the growth rate of a price, $\Delta p_k/p_k$, is often called the **capital gain** (in percentage terms). Or, if we know the growth rate is negative, this can be called the **capital loss**.

Why might the price of ovens—or the price of physical capital in general—change? There are at least two reasons. First, suppose the oven depreciates as it gets used; recall that depreciation is the general "wear and tear" that reduces the amount or value of capital. Maybe we start the year with an oven worth \$10,000, but by the end of the year it is only worth \$8,000. In this case, we would expect the price to decline by 20 percent, a capital loss, so $\Delta p_k/p_k = -.20$. In fact, it is common to put this depreciation term in explicitly (as we did in the Solow model in Chapter 5). In this case, we would *add* the depreciation rate, $\bar{d}$, to the right side of equation (16.3)—equivalent to subtracting a negative price change. Then we'd reinterpret the price as the price of a unit of capital in its original condition, not having been used.

This leads to a second reason why a price might change. Think about what happens over time to the price of electronics. Because of rapid progress in the electronics industry, the price of many of these goods declines over time—consider cell phones, computers, or television sets. Calculators that cost $100 50 years ago can be had for a few dollars today. Along with depreciation, technological change is another reason why the price of capital goods might change.

The price of structures like factories or retail stores, in contrast, usually goes up over time. An important reason for this is that the land they are built on is becoming increasingly scarce, driving up their price.

Taking these considerations into account, we might include depreciation explicitly in equation (16.3) and write it as

$$MPK = \underbrace{R + \bar{d} - \frac{\Delta p_k}{p_k}}_{\text{user cost of capital}} \qquad (16.4)$$

The result from the simple framework in Chapter 4 was that firms should invest until the marginal product of capital falls to equal the interest rate. The more sophisticated framework here shows how to generalize this result. The lesson is for firms to invest until the marginal product of capital falls to equal the user cost of capital. The **user cost of capital** is the total cost to the firm of using one more unit of capital. In the framework of Chapter 4, this was just the interest rate—the cost of financial funds to the firm. Now, though, we see that the user cost also includes the depreciation rate and any capital gain or loss associated with a change in the price of capital. *A firm should invest in capital until the value of the extra output that capital produces falls to equal the user cost.*[1]

This condition is shown graphically in Figure 16.1. The marginal product of capital is plotted against the amount of capital owned by the firm. This marginal product falls as the capital stock rises, reflecting the diminishing marginal product of capital. The desired amount of capital for the firm to own occurs at the intersection of the marginal product with the user cost of capital. At this point, the extra output produced by one additional unit of capital is precisely enough to cover the extra cost of owning a unit of capital, the user cost.

[1] This approach to investment was developed by Dale W. Jorgenson, "Capital Theory and Investment Behavior," *American Economic Review*, vol. 53, no. 2 (May 1963), pp. 247–259; See also Robert E. Hall and Dale W. Jorgenson, "Tax Policy and Investment Behavior," *American Economic Review*, vol. 57, no. 3 (June 1967), pp. 391–414.

A firm should invest until the marginal product of capital falls to equal the user cost of capital. This implies a desired level of the capital stock, $K^{desired}$.

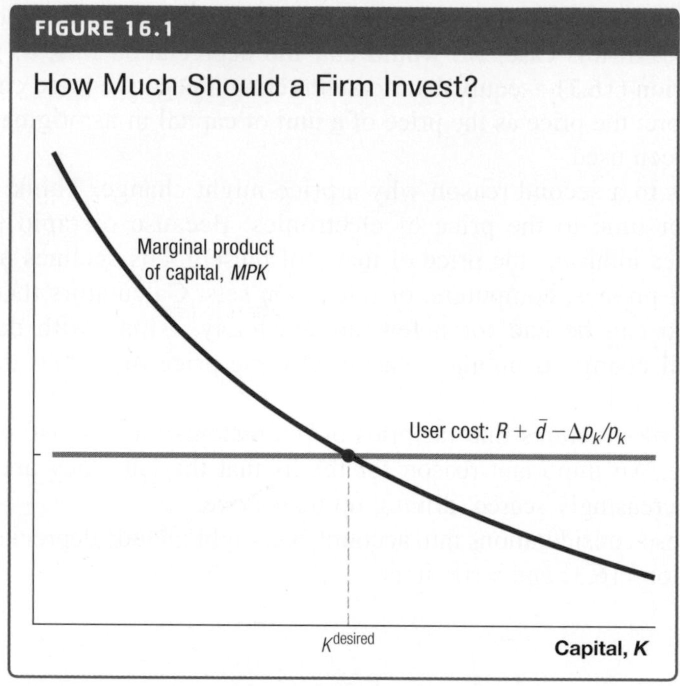

FIGURE 16.1

How Much Should a Firm Invest?

Example: Investment and the Corporate Income Tax

To see how this arbitrage approach and the user cost of capital are useful, let's work through an exercise. Suppose the economy starts with no taxes and then introduces a corporate income tax. As just one example, large corporations in the United States pay a federal tax rate of 35 percent on the income they earn. How does this tax affect a firm's desired capital stock and how much it invests?

To answer this question, we need to determine how a tax on corporate income affects the user cost of capital. For this, the arbitrage argument proves helpful. Letting τ denote the tax rate and keeping the initial price of capital normalized to 1, we now have

$$\underbrace{R}_{\text{cost of funds}} = \underbrace{(1 - \tau)MPK - \bar{d} - \frac{\Delta p_k}{p_k}}_{\text{return from investing in capital}}. \tag{16.5}$$

The cost of funds to the firm is the interest rate, R. What is the benefit to the firm of investing \$1 in capital? The firm earns the marginal product of capital but then has to pay taxes on these additional earnings. Net of taxes, this means the firm gets $(1 - \tau)$ MPK. The firm then loses some of the capital in depreciation and finally incurs a capital gain or loss.[2] Together, these terms make up the

[2]The careful reader will notice that the depreciation term should really be $\bar{d} \cdot p_{k,t+1}$—that is, it should be valued at the price at which the capital is sold rather than bought. The approach here is simpler and represents a traditional (and typically very accurate) approximation.

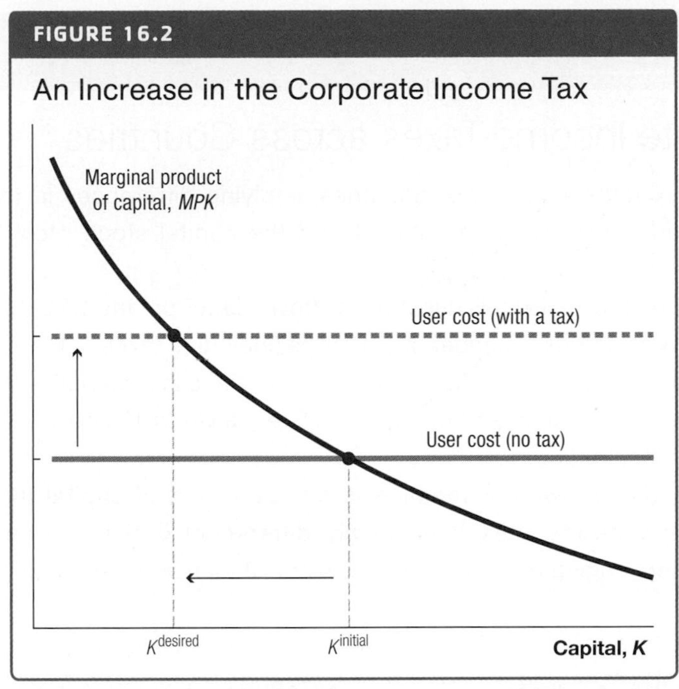

FIGURE 16.2

An Increase in the Corporate Income Tax

An increase in the corporate income tax from zero to some positive rate like 35 percent raises the user cost of capital; see equation (16.6). This requires the marginal product of capital to rise, which means the firm desires a smaller amount of capital.

return to investing in a unit of capital. If the firm is maximizing profits, the cost of investing equals the benefit, as shown in equation 16.5.[3]

We can now rewrite the arbitrage equation above as an expression that equates the marginal product of capital to the user cost of capital for this problem:

$$MPK = \underbrace{\frac{R + \bar{d} - \dfrac{\Delta p_k}{p_k}}{1 - \tau}}_{\text{user cost of capital}}. \tag{16.6}$$

Essentially, a corporate income tax *raises* the user cost of capital. For example, suppose that in the absence of taxes, the user cost of capital is 10 percent (e.g., a 2-percent real interest rate, an 8-percent depreciation rate, and no capital gain). Then a corporate tax rate of 35 percent ($\tau = .35$) would raise the user cost to more than 15 percent ($.10 \times 1/(1 - .35) \approx .153$). Because the extra output produced by a unit of capital is taxed, the marginal product of capital must be that much higher in order for the investment to be profitable. As shown in Figure 16.2, this higher user cost reduces the total amount of physical capital that the firm wishes to utilize.

[3] The argument here assumes that the firm does not pay any taxes on the capital gain associated with the changing value of the capital. This standard assumption is justified because most capital is held until it depreciates fully, and taxes are only paid on capital gains if and when they are realized.

CASE STUDY

Corporate Income Taxes across Countries

Corporate tax rates vary across countries, implying differences in the user cost of capital and, therefore, in investment and the capital stock. How large is this variation?

Table 16.1 helps answer this question. It shows data from the OECD on corporate income tax rates across a number of countries (including taxes at both the "federal" and "state" levels). The variation in corporate tax rates is remarkable, ranging from nearly 40 percent in Japan and the United States down to 12 and 15 percent in Ireland and Iceland, respectively.

The table also shows the variation in the user cost of capital that is implied by these corporate tax rates. Interestingly, differences in the user cost of capital appear smaller, ranging from about 10 percent in Japan and the United States down

Corporate tax rates (including state taxes) vary substantially across countries. Interestingly, the implied user cost of capital varies less.

TABLE 16.1

Corporate Income Tax Rates and the User Cost of Capital, 2009

Country	Corporate tax rate (percent)	User cost of capital (percent)
Japan	39.5	10.1
United States	39.1	10.0
France	34.4	9.3
Canada	31.3	8.9
Germany	30.2	8.7
Australia	30.0	8.7
Spain	30.0	8.7
Mexico	28.0	8.5
United Kingdom	28.0	8.5
Italy	27.5	8.4
Sweden	26.3	8.3
Finland	26.0	8.2
South Korea	24.2	8.0
Hungary	20.0	7.6
Turkey	20.0	7.6
Slovak Republic	19.0	7.5
Iceland	15.0	7.2
Ireland	12.5	7.0

Source: The OECD Tax Database, Table II.1. The user cost of capital for the United States is assumed to equal 10 percent, and the value in other countries is calculated by scaling this number by $1/(1-\tau)$. This user cost, therefore, omits other tax policies (like investment tax credits or depreciation credits) that may be important in practice.

to 7 percent in Ireland. These differences in user costs only take into account differences in corporate tax rates, so other differences among countries (say in other aspects of the tax system such as investment tax credits or credits for depreciation) could also be important.

From Desired Capital to Investment

The condition that firms invest until the marginal product of capital falls to equal the user cost pins down the desired capital stock—for example, as illustrated in Figure 16.1. The reason: the marginal product of capital is a decreasing function of the capital stock itself, holding other inputs constant. For instance, with the Cobb-Douglas production function considered in Chapter 4, $Y = \bar{A}K^{1/3}L^{2/3}$, the marginal product of capital is given by[4]

$$MPK = \frac{1}{3} \cdot \frac{Y}{K} = \frac{1}{3} \cdot \bar{A}\left(\frac{L}{K}\right)^{2/3}. \quad (16.7)$$

Clearly, the marginal product of capital declines as capital increases—this is the diminishing returns to capital.

To connect this expression to investment, recall the standard capital accumulation equation:

$$K_{t+1} = I_t + (1 - \bar{d})K_t. \quad (16.8)$$

This equation, which we studied extensively in Chapter 5, says that the change in the capital stock is equal to new investment less depreciation. If we replace K_t with a firm's initial capital stock and replace K_{t+1} with the firm's desired capital stock (obtained from, say, Figure 16.1 or 16.2, then this equation tells you how much investment the firm has to undertake over the next year in order to reach the desired level. If the desired capital stock exceeds the initial level, then the firm must undertake new investment. If the desired capital stock is less than the initial level—as would be the case after an increase in the corporate tax rate, for example—then the firm can invest a small amount and let depreciation bring the capital stock down or even sell off some of its capital.

In practice, the capital stock that a firm desires may far exceed its current capital—think about Amazon or Google when they were new firms and were expanding rapidly. It may take several years for a firm to reach its desired capital stock, and the path of investment will need to take into account installation costs and various costs associated with expanding the business.

That's the intuition for the connection. With a bit of math, we can make the connection more formally. Let *uc* denote the user cost of capital (say, the right

---

[4]You may recall that deriving this equation requires some calculus: the marginal product of capital is just the derivative of the production function with respect to K. If you are not comfortable with taking the derivative, just take the equation above as a statement of fact.

side of equation (16.4)). From equation (16.7), the marginal product of capital is $1/3 \cdot Y/K$, so the condition that the marginal product of capital equals the user cost means that

$$\frac{Y}{K} = 3 \cdot uc. \tag{16.9}$$

Next, let's rewrite the capital accumulation equation in (16.8) as follows:

$$\Delta K_{t+1} = I_t - \bar{d}K_t. \tag{16.10}$$

Dividing both sides of this equation by K_t gives

$$\frac{\Delta K_{t+1}}{K_t} = \frac{I_t}{K_t} - \bar{d}. \tag{16.11}$$

Then let's multiply and divide the first term on the right side by Y_t to get the investment rate:

$$\frac{\Delta K_{t+1}}{K_t} = \frac{I_t}{Y_t} \cdot \frac{Y_t}{K_t} - \bar{d}. \tag{16.12}$$

Finally, let's substitute $3 \cdot uc$ for Y/K and solve for the investment rate to find

$$\frac{I_t}{Y_t} = \frac{g_K + \bar{d}}{3 \cdot uc}. \tag{16.13}$$

This equation says that the investment rate depends on three main terms: the desired growth rate of the capital stock, $g_K \equiv \Delta K_{t+1}/K_t$; the depreciation rate; and the user cost of capital, uc. In particular, the investment rate depends inversely on the user cost: *a higher user cost of capital leads to a lower investment rate.*

This expression can also be usefully connected to our study of economic growth. In Chapters 5 and 6, we assumed that the investment rate was given by some constant, $\bar{s}$. Equation (16.13) provides the microfoundation for the investment rate. For example, it shows how higher taxes reduce the investment rate (via the user cost of capital). In fact, combining this result with the Euler equation from Chapter 15 and the growth models from Chapters 5 and 6, we have a full theory of the key macroeconomic variables in the long run. The growth models of Chapters 5 and 6 pin down the long-run growth rate, including the growth rate of capital. The Euler equation for consumption then pins down the long-run interest rate (and, therefore, the user cost of capital). The condition that the marginal product of capital equals the user cost pins down the capital-output ratio. Finally, equation (16.13) pins down the investment rate and, therefore, the consumption share of GDP as well. Those are the key endogenous variables in the macroeconomy, at least in a closed economy.

16.3 The Stock Market and Financial Investment

No doubt you have been confused at some point by the terms "capital" and "investment." In macroeconomics, these terms usually refer to the accumulation of physical capital. However, these words also are used frequently in finance: one might speak of financial capital, the capital (net worth) of a financial institution, or making a financial investment in a mutual fund.

While these are different uses of the terms "capital" and "investment," they share a deep connection, and one way to see that connection is by considering an arbitrage equation. We've already done this in the previous section for physical capital and physical investment. In this section, we turn to the financial concepts, which proves to be quite useful. For example, the arbitrage equation helps us to understand how financial markets price stocks (yet another word with separate but related meanings in macro- and financial economics).

The Arbitrage Equation and the Price of a Stock

The same arbitrage equation that governs how much a firm invests in physical capital can be used to study financial investments in financial assets like stocks. Suppose a (financial) investor has some extra money to invest. One option is to put the money into a saving account that pays an interest rate R. Alternatively, the investor can purchase a stock at price p_s, hold the stock for a year, and then sell it. This investment has two payoffs. First, the investor receives whatever dividend the stock pays: a **dividend** is a payment by a firm to its shareholders—think of it as a portion of the accounting profits earned by the firm. Second, when the investor sells the stock at the end of the year, the price may have changed: if the stock price goes up, the investor gets a capital gain; if the stock price goes down, the investor suffers a capital loss.

Importantly, let's suppose both investments are perfectly safe. That is, the investor knows what the dividend and capital gain will be; these are not uncertain. Obviously, this assumption does not generally hold in practice. In fact, much of the contribution of financial economics is in understanding risk and figuring out how that risk affects the prices of assets like stocks and bonds. For our brief excursion into finance, however, we will have to abstract from this important issue.[5] The simple model that results still conveys many useful insights about the pricing of stocks.

What is the arbitrage equation in this case? Someone investing p_s dollars in either the bank account or the stock must get the same financial return. This means

[5] It turns out that everything we will say is valid even in the presence of uncertainty, as long as one interprets the dividend and capital gain as expected values and as long as investors are risk-neutral. What this means, for example, is that investors place equal value on the following two options: \$100 for certain and a 50/50 chance at getting either \$200 or \$0. That is, investors do not care about risk. Of course, this is an unrealistic assumption in many cases.

$$\underbrace{R \cdot p_s}_{\substack{\text{return in} \\ \text{bank account}}} = \underbrace{\text{dividend} + \Delta p_s}_{\substack{\text{return from} \\ \text{the stock}}}. \tag{16.14}$$

The return from holding the stock is the sum of the dividend it pays plus the capital gain or loss. Notice that the dividend here plays the same role that the marginal product of capital played in the physical investment application: it is the key return if there is no change in the price of the asset.

In the application to physical capital, we assumed that the price of capital was known and used the arbitrage equation to determine the desired capital stock and the amount of investment. For the application to financial investment, we will use the equation differently—to tell us what determines prices in the stock market.

Dividing both sides of this arbitrage equation by the price of the stock leads to one of the most common ways to write the arbitrage equation:

$$R = \underbrace{\frac{\text{dividend}}{p_s}}_{\substack{\text{dividend return} \\ \text{(percent)}}} + \underbrace{\frac{\Delta p_s}{p_s}}_{\substack{\text{capital gain} \\ \text{(percent)}}}. \tag{16.15}$$

On the left is the *percentage* return in the bank account. On the right is the *percentage* return to buying the stock. The stock return is the sum of the dividend return (the dividend-price ratio) and the capital gain or loss in percentage terms.

Consider some simple numbers. Suppose the bank account pays an interest rate of 3 percent. Then the stock must also pay a total return of 3 percent. For example, it could be that the dividend yield is 2 percent and the capital gain is 1 percent.

Why does the stock have to yield a return of 3 percent? Think about what would happen if this were not true. If the stock paid more, everyone would invest in the stock and no one would invest in the bank account. The initial purchase price of the stock would rise, and this would reduce its return (via both the dividend yield and the capital-gain term). If the stock paid less, then everyone would put his or her money in the bank, no one would demand the stock, and its price would fall. This lower price would raise the return. The only way there is no arbitrage opportunity is if these two investments have the same return.

The key step at this point is to solve the arbitrage equation in (16.15) for the price of the stock. We do this by grouping the bank return and the capital-gain term together, and then inverting both sides of the equation.[6] This gives

---

[6]To derive the result, collect the interest rate and the capital gain on the same side of the equation to get

$$R - \frac{\Delta p_s}{p_s} = \frac{\text{dividend}}{p_s}.$$

Then bring p_s to the left side, and switch the difference between the interest rate and capital gain to the denominator on the right side.

$$p_s = \frac{\text{dividend}}{R - \dfrac{\Delta p_s}{p_s}} = \frac{\text{dividend}}{\text{interest rate} - \text{capital gain}}. \qquad (16.16)$$

This last equation is truly beautiful. It essentially says that the price of a stock will equal the present discounted value of the dividends that the stock will pay. To see this, suppose, first, that the capital-gain term is zero and the dividend is constant. For example, a stock may pay a dividend of \$10 per share each year. Then the price of the stock is just $10/R$, which turns out to be the present discounted value of \$10 paid forever (starting a year from now).[7] If the interest rate is 5 percent, the price of the stock is $10/.05 = \$200$ per share.

What happens if the dividend is not constant? Suppose the dividend starts out at \$10 per share but then grows over time at a constant rate g. (For example, $g = .02$ would be 2-percent growth.) Now look at equation (16.16) for the stock price, and notice something important: if the dividend is growing at a constant rate, then the growth rate of the stock price must equal the growth rate of the dividend. That is, the capital-gain term $\Delta p_s / p_s$ is also equal to the growth rate of the dividend, g.[8] This means that *when dividend growth is constant, the stock price equals the current dividend divided by* $R - g$. Observe what is going on here: when you discount a flow that is constant, you divided by R; when you discount a flow that is growing, you simply reduce the interest rate by the growth rate itself.

Going back to our numerical example, suppose the initial dividend is \$10, the interest rate is 5 percent, and the growth rate of the dividend (and, therefore, the stock price) is 2 percent. What is the price of the stock? The answer is $10/(.05 - .02) = 10/.03 \approx \$333$.

P/E Ratios and Bubbles?

Equation (16.16) tells us how stock prices should be determined according to a simple model. We can compare actual stock prices to the prices implied by our model. These could disagree either because the simple model is wrong—for example, it does not take sufficient account of risk—or because the stock prices themselves are somehow wrong—for example, there is a "bubble" in the stock market.

In fact, we've already seen a common way of making this comparison. Recall that in Chapter 14, we studied a diagram of the **price-earnings ratio** for the stock market as a whole in an effort to gauge if there might be bubbles in stock prices. With our simple model, we can now understand this graph, which we revisit here as Figure 16.3.

To understand this graph, return to equation (16.16), and divide both sides by the total earnings (earnings are essentially just accounting profits) of all companies in the S&P 500:

[7] If you need a reminder of why this is true, review worked exercise 4(c) in Chapter 7.

[8] To be more precise, the capital-gain term equals the dividend growth rate only if the capital-gain term is constant as well. One can think of this as holding in a steady state, or in the long run.

Whenever the ratio of stock prices to company earnings gets too far away from its mean, it tends to revert. Notice that this measure reached its two highest peaks in 1929 and 2000.

FIGURE 16.3

The Price-Earnings Ratio in the Stock Market

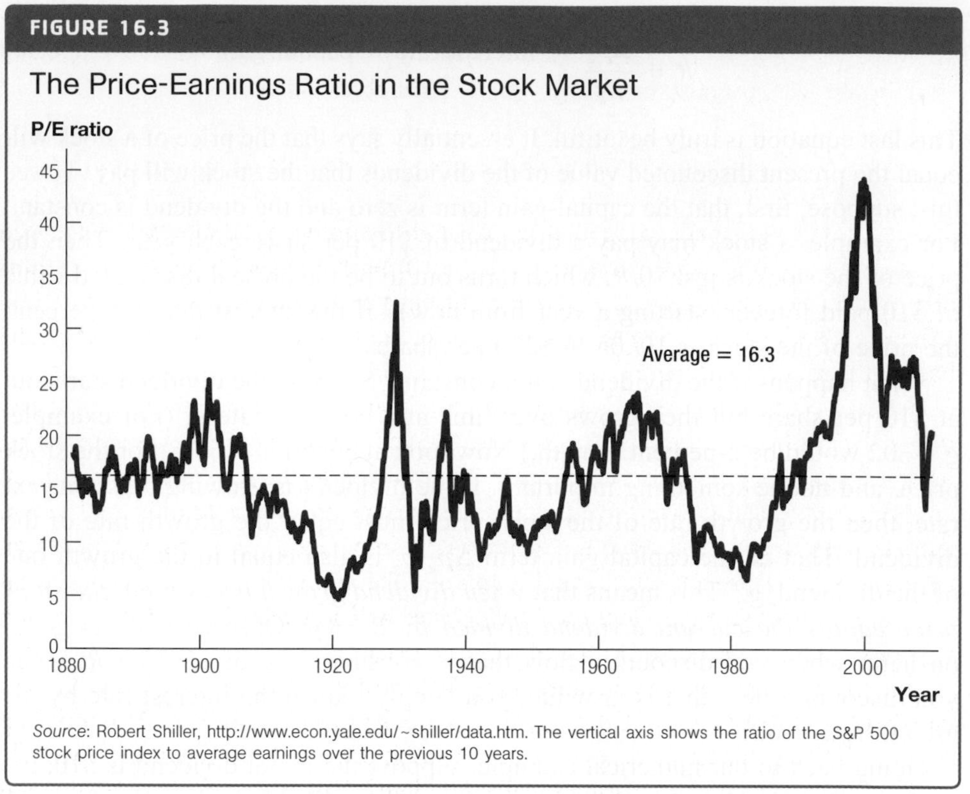

Source: Robert Shiller, http://www.econ.yale.edu/~shiller/data.htm. The vertical axis shows the ratio of the S&P 500 stock price index to average earnings over the previous 10 years.

$$\frac{p_s}{\text{earnings}} = \frac{\text{dividend/earnings}}{\text{interest rate} - \text{capital gain}}. \tag{16.17}$$

This equation says that the price-earnings ratio should equal the dividend-earnings ratio divided by $R - g$. Now take a look at Figure 16.3 to see what this ratio looks like in the data. This ratio is very volatile. In the early 1980s, this ratio was under 10; but then it rose sharply over the next 20 years, peaking in 2001 at more than 40; following the dot-com crash and the financial crisis, the ratio fell sharply to below 15.

How can we understand these movements? According to the simple model, the price-earnings ratio should be relatively stable to the extent that (1) the dividend-earnings ratio is stable and (2) the difference between the real interest rate and the growth rate of dividends is stable. One view is that the sharp increase in stock prices at the end of the 1990s reflects a bubble in stock prices. But an alternative view—and one that many observers were highlighting at the time when they were discussing the "new economy"—is that the difference between the interest rate and the growth rate of dividends declined because of faster growth, justifying an increase in the P/E ratio.

What this analysis emphasizes is that it's easy to draw a line at the average P/E ratio of 16.3 in Figure 16.3 and call any departures "bubbles." And there is certainly some merit to this approach. However, a more careful economic analysis of this ratio gives you solid economic reasons how and why the ratio might change. At any point, it may be difficult to know for sure if these fundamentals have changed or not, and this makes identifying potential "bubbles" a tricky enterprise.

Efficient Markets

This discussion of potential bubbles is related to another fundamental concept in finance, that of "efficient markets." A financial market is said to be **informationally efficient** if financial prices fully and correctly reflect all available information. When this is the case, it is impossible to make economic profits by trading on the basis of that information.

Let's stop and consider this more carefully. Suppose the price we are discussing is the price of a share of Google stock. And suppose Google is announcing its third-quarter profits next week, and experts expect this quarter to have been an extremely profitable one for Google. If markets are informationally efficient, then this expectation is already incorporated into Google's share price. When the announcement occurs in a week's time, if the announcement is exactly what everyone expected, then Google's stock price will not move—that information will have already been incorporated into the price.

According to this theory, the only thing that moves stock prices is news that was unexpected. But this means that at any time, a stock price is equally likely to move up or down. When this is the case, we say the stock price follows a **random walk**.[9]

Are financial markets informationally efficient? This is one of the fundamental questions in financial economics. The answer is "almost," and we learn a lot by studying this question closely.

The efficient-markets benchmark is an excellent starting point for understanding most financial markets. As one example, consider **mutual funds**. Such funds are collections of stocks and other financial assets that are held together in a large portfolio, small pieces of which are sold off to individual investors. Some of these mutual funds are "actively managed," meaning they are run by investment managers who are constantly buying and selling financial assets in an effort to deliver the highest possible return in the least risky way. Other mutual funds are "index funds." These funds are essentially managed by a simple computer program that imitates one of the major stock indexes, like Standard & Poor's 500 index or the Dow Jones Industrial Average. The actively managed funds usually charge higher fees—the investor must pay for the management skills of the team running the fund. An interesting question is whether or not this active management leads to higher returns. According to the efficient markets theory, one would not expect this to be the case—financial prices already reflect all available information, so the extra effort to "pick" winners and losers in the stock market will be wasted.

[9]If this discussion sounds familiar, it is because we said similar things about consumption under the permanent-income hypothesis in Chapter 15. In that case, consumption reflects all information about income and, therefore, only responds to news and follows a random walk. There is a nice mathematical similarity between consumption and stock prices.

In fact, this is what the evidence seems to suggest: by and large, actively managed mutual funds have lower returns than passive index funds. For example, according to Burton Malkiel, for the decade up to 2002, more than three-quarters of comparable, actively managed mutual funds failed to perform as well as the S&P 500 stock market index. Moreover, those that did beat the S&P cannot sustain their success: the best-performing funds of the 1980s underperformed the S&P index during the 1990s.[10]

While the efficient markets benchmark is a good starting point for understanding financial markets, it is not the final word. If the efficient markets hypothesis is viewed as a shiny new house, departures from this hypothesis can be thought of as dirt and mold that lies hidden in nooks and crannies and closets. Financial economists have explored the house in detail and documented with great care where the departures are hidden. For example, a tiny minority of mutual funds seem to beat the S&P 500 index with more persistence than the efficient markets hypothesis would predict. Financial markets also tend to display substantially more volatility—large swings in price—than can be justified based on fundamentals. The most extreme version of this are the "bubbles" that appear from time to time. Explanations of these departures are varied and include "behavioral" elements: economic players are not always perfectly rational calculating machines. In addition, there may be limits to the extent that skilled investors can bet against a bubble to take advantage of mispricing. This is illustrated by a famous quip that has gathered attention recently: "The market can stay irrational longer than you can stay solvent."[11]

CASE STUDY

Tobin's *q*, Physical Capital, and the Stock Market

James Tobin of Yale University, winner of the Nobel Prize in economics in 1981, developed the implications of a theory like the one we have explored for the relationship between investment and the stock market. In Tobin's approach, the only asset that a firm possesses is its capital; so, in the simplest case, the stock market value of the firm is the value of its capital stock. Now consider what happens when

[10]The sample considered here is of actively managed large-cap equity mutual funds, comparable in risk to the S&P 500. Malkiel is the author of one of the more famous popular books on financial markets, *A Random Walk down Wall Street: The Time-Tested Strategy for Successful Investing*, 9th ed. (New York: Norton, 2007). The findings reported in this paragraph are taken from an excellent overview of the efficiency of financial markets in Burton G. Malkiel, "The Efficient Market Hypothesis and Its Critics," *Journal of Economic Perspectives*, vol. 17, no. 1 (Winter 2003), pp. 59–82.

[11]Further discussion of some of the departures from efficient markets can be found in Robert J. Shiller, "From Efficient Markets Theory to Behavioral Finance," *Journal of Economic Perspectives*, vol. 17, no. 1 (Winter 2003), pp. 83–104. The quip is studied formally in a famous paper by Andrei Shleifer and Robert Vishny, "The Limits of Arbitrage," *Journal of Finance*, vol. 52, no. 1 (March 1997), pp. 35–55.

investing in physical capital involves adjustment costs. Replacing a broken-down machine may require stopping the assembly line for some time. Expanding the factory may require a significant amount of installation work. When such adjustment costs are important, the stock market value of the firm—the present discounted value of the profits it will earn today and in the future—can differ from the value of its capital. Why? Imagine that the firm develops a new product that raises its future profitability. With no adjustment costs, the firm should expand immediately. This expansion will reduce profitability because of diminishing returns. It should expand until the marginal product falls to equal the user cost and the value of the firm falls to equal the capital stock. In the presence of adjustment costs, this expansion will occur gradually instead of immediately, and the value of the firm may differ for a while from the value of its capital. This is the essence of Tobin's argument.

With this motivation, it is relatively easy to understand a key measure, known as **Tobin's *q***:

$$q = \frac{V}{p_k K} = \frac{\text{stock market value}}{\text{value of capital}}. \tag{16.18}$$

Tobin's q is the ratio of the stock market value of a firm to the value of its capital stock.

When q is larger than 1, the stock market signals that the value of the firm is greater than its capital, and the firm should invest in more capital. Alternatively, when q is less than one, the value of the firm is less than the value of its capital, and we would expect the firm to be "disinvesting." (That is, the owners could sell off the pieces of the firm, if its capital is worth more than its market value.)

This leads to two basic predictions. First, we should expect the value of a firm's q to be close to 1, at least apart from any short-run costs to adjusting capital. Second, the value of q should be a useful predictor of firm-level investment.

In practice, the first prediction has significant problems. If capital were the only asset owned by firms, we would expect values of q to be close to 1. However, firms also own their brand names (often called "goodwill" capital) and the ideas they have created, some patented, some not. Because these assets also have values that are capitalized into the stock market price, values for q often exceed 1.

Empirical evidence on the role of q in investment is mixed. The most careful studies looking at a large number of firms find that changes in tax policy, which are exogenous, change investment by affecting q and the user cost of capital. On the other hand, other factors that are not included in the theory so far—such as a firm's cash flow or access to financial markets and bank loans—also seem to play an important role.[12]

---

[12] A good overview of this evidence can be found in Kevin A. Hassett and R. Glenn Hubbard, "Tax Policy and Business Investment," in Alan J. Auerbach and Martin Feldstein, *Handbook of Public Economics*, 4 vols. (New York: Elsevier, 2002), III, ch. 20, pp. 1293–1343.

16.4 Components of Physical Investment

As discussed in Chapter 2, investment in the national accounts measures long-lasting goods that businesses and households purchase. In the United States, investment has averaged about 15 percent of GDP during the last decade or so. Investment is traditionally broken down into three basic categories, as shown in Figure 16.4.

- **Nonresidential fixed investment:** equipment and structures purchased by businesses. In recent years, this component accounted for about two-thirds of investment, about 11 percent of GDP.
- **Residential fixed investment:** new housing purchased by households.
- **Inventory investment:** goods that have been produced by firms but that have not been sold. An auto dealer has an inventory of cars on hand to sell to new customers. Inventory investment is the change in this stock of goods on hand. As shown in Figure 16.4, inventory investment is usually positive in normal times but turns negative during recessions.

Our discussion of physical investment at the start of this chapter did not distinguish among the components of investment. That discussion applies precisely to nonresidential fixed investment—the equipment and structures purchased by

Investment consists of three main components: nonresidential fixed investment (which includes equipment and structures purchased by businesses), residential investment (housing), and the change in inventories held by businesses.

FIGURE 16.4

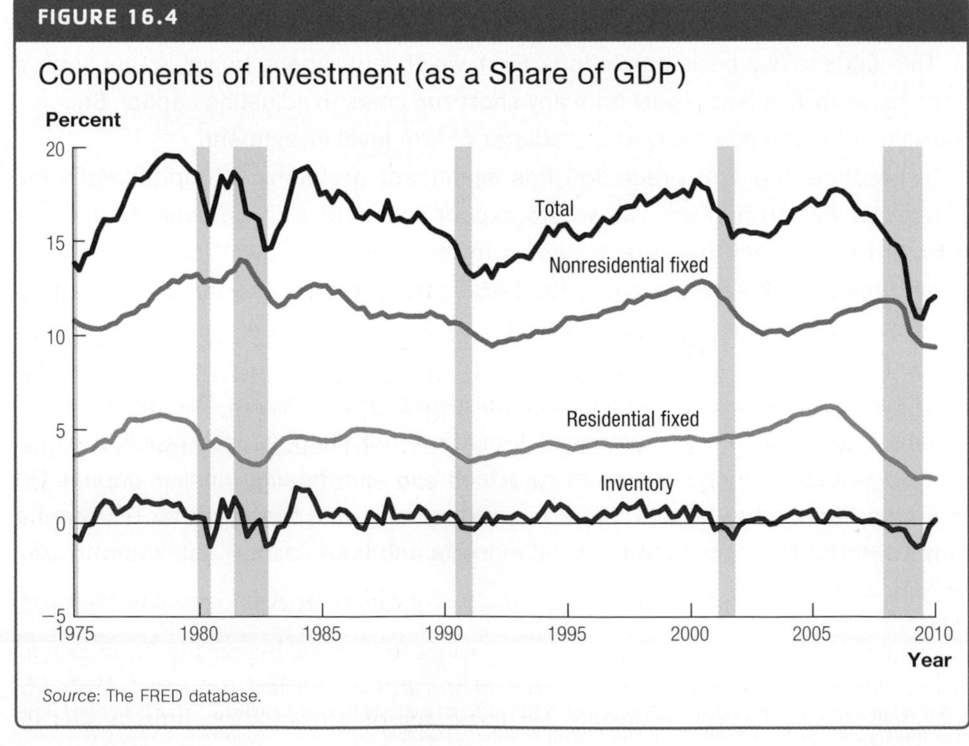

Source: The FRED database.

businesses. The two remaining categories of physical investment deserve additional consideration.

Residential Investment

Residential investment is the formal name for the construction of new housing, which is ultimately sold to households. As can be seen in Figure 16.4, housing investment played a large role in the financial crisis. Before the recent financial crisis, residential investment reached more than 6 percent of GDP. It then fell to less than half this amount during the depths of the recession.

Residential investment can be studied using the tools developed in this chapter. For example, consider the following arbitrage argument. Suppose some investor has \$20,000 to invest. She can put this in the bank and earn interest. Or she can use it as the downpayment on a \$100,000 condominium, rent out the condo for the year, and then sell it the following year and earn the capital gain (adjusted for depreciation). If this transaction involved no risk and if we ignore any transactions costs, these two options should yield the same return:

$$\underbrace{R \cdot \text{down payment}}_{\substack{\text{return from}\\ \text{saving the down payment}}} = \underbrace{\text{rent} - \bar{d}P^{\text{house}} + \Delta P^{\text{house}}}_{\substack{\text{return from}\\ \text{investing in condo}}} \tag{16.19}$$

Dividing both sides by the price of the condo, P^{house}, and solving yield

$$P^{\text{house}} = \frac{\text{rent}}{R \cdot \bar{x} + \bar{d} - \dfrac{\Delta P^{\text{house}}}{P^{\text{house}}}}, \tag{16.20}$$

where $\bar{x} \equiv \dfrac{\text{down payment}}{P^{\text{house}}}$ is the fraction of the purchase price that is given as a down payment, such as 20 percent. Notice that $\bar{x}$ is really just the inverse of leverage: if you put down \$20,000, you can buy a condo for \$100,000; thus, the leverage ratio is 5 and the down-payment ratio is 1/5 = 20 percent.

The equation we've just derived says that the price of a condominium is the present discounted value of the amount you can earn by renting out the condo. In this case, however, there are two reasons why the discounting is more complicated than just the interest rate. First, notice that the last term in the denominator, $\dfrac{\Delta P^{\text{house}}}{P^{\text{house}}}$, is the capital-gain term—the amount by which the condo price is expected to appreciate. The more you expect condo prices to rise, the higher the initial price. This is how, for example, a bubble in housing prices can feed on itself. Second, notice the role of $\bar{x}$. Suppose that for some reason (it could be innovations in financial markets, or it could just be the real estate industry doing something it shouldn't) the required down-payment rate on a condo falls from 20 percent to 10 percent: you can now lever your financial capital at a rate of 10 to 1 instead of 5 to 1. According to equation (16.20), condo prices will rise as a result of this change. A numerical exercise at the end of this chapter will show you that these effects can be large.

What we see here provides insight into housing prices in the last decade. Housing prices can rise because of financial innovations that allow that market to take advantage of higher leverage or if people believe that the rate of increase in housing prices has gone up.

Trying to figure out whether these changes are occurring for solid economic reasons or are possibly related to a bubble can be difficult. Notice that this discussion parallels our discussion about bubbles and the price-earnings ratio for the stock market in Section 3.2.

Inventory Investment

Inventories are goods that have been produced but have not yet been sold. Think about the goods on the shelf of a supermarket or the cars on a lot of an auto dealership. As can be seen in Figure 16.4, inventory investment is a small but very cyclical component of investment. In a booming economy, inventory investment is generally positive—firms are producing more goods than they are selling. In a recession, the opposite occurs: firms cut production sharply and run down their inventories.

There are several main motives that govern a firm's holding of inventories. First, firms may wish to engage in **production smoothing**. It is costly to ramp up production quickly when demand is high, so firms may wish to produce slightly more than they need during bad times and slightly less than they need during good times. Notice that if this force were dominant in the aggregate, it would imply that inventory investment is countercyclical. That is, firms would accumulate inventories during recessions. However, this is not what we see in Figure 16.4. Instead, inventory investment appears to be high when the economy is booming and low during recessions.

A second motive that helps to explain the procyclicality of inventories is the **pipeline theory**. That is, firms hold inventories as part of the production process itself. Consider the production of a laptop computer. The producer will have a collection of computer screens, flash drives, keyboards, and memory chips on hand—inventories of the laptop components. When demand goes up and the firm needs to ramp up production of laptops, its collection of components will naturally rise as part of the production process. This is one explanation for the procyclical behavior of inventory investment.

Another motive for holding inventories is **stockout avoidance**. Firms will hold inventories of final goods on hand to make sure they have these goods available when a customer wishes to make a purchase. Retail businesses such as supermarkets and bookstores certainly operate this way.

CASE STUDY

Inventories and Supply Chain Management

One of the places where information technology has had a substantial impact on business productivity is in the management of inventories, both of final goods and of materials and parts that make up the so-called "supply chain." A famous example is Walmart, the largest public company in the world in terms of revenues and the largest private employer in the United States. Walmart was an early adopter of information technology for managing inventories and networking suppliers. Computer networks link retail outlets with suppliers to ensure that new goods are ordered precisely when needed. Other techniques such as cross docking also keep inventories low: goods from various suppliers are unloaded at a distribution center and then directly loaded onto different trucks to get the goods to retail with little or no storage in between. Reduced inventories lead to lower costs and higher productivity.[13]

Steven Davis and James Kahn discuss the macroeconomic consequences of these improvements in inventory and supply chain management. For example, they document that the ratio of inventories to sales revenues for durable-goods manufacturing fell from more than 60 percent during much of the 1970s and early 1980s to less than 50 percent in the late 1990s and early 2000s. More controversially, Davis and Kahn argue that improvements in inventory management were an important factor in reducing the volatility of the U.S. macroeconomy in recent decades—the so-called "Great Moderation."[14]

CHAPTER REVIEW

SUMMARY

1. Investments of all kinds—in physical capital, in human capital, in new ideas, and in financial assets—are ways of transferring resources from the present to the future.

[13]For a general discussion of information technology and business productivity, see Erik Brynjolfsson and Lorin M. Hitt, "Beyond Computation: Information Technology, Organizational Transformation and Business Performance," *Journal of Economic Perspectives*, vol. 14, no. 4 (Autumn 2000), pp. 23–48.

[14]Steven J. Davis and James A. Kahn, "Interpreting the Great Moderation: Changes in the Volatility of Economic Activity at the Macro and Micro Levels," *Journal of Economic Perspectives*, vol. 22, no. 4 (Fall 2008), pp. 155–180.

2. The arbitrage equation is a fundamental tool in economics for studying investments of all kinds. It says that two investments of equal riskiness must have the same return (otherwise investors would flock to the activity with the higher return). Typically, this equation can be written in a form that says that the interest rate (a return in a bank account) is equal to the sum of a "dividend" return and a "capital gain" return, both in percentage terms.
3. Applying the arbitrage argument to physical capital leads to a key result: firms invest in physical capital until the marginal product of capital falls to equal the user cost of capital.
4. The user cost of capital is the total economic cost of using one unit of capital for one period. It typically involves the interest rate, the depreciation rate, and any capital gain or loss associated with a changing price of capital. It can be augmented to include effects from taxation.
5. Applying the arbitrage argument to financial investment leads to a simple theory of stock prices: the price of a stock is the present discounted value of dividends. This present value can typically be written as the ratio of the current dividend to the difference between the interest rate and the capital gain.
6. If financial markets are informationally efficient, then stock prices will reflect all publicly available information. Only unexpected "news" will change stock prices, making them equally likely to go up or down (apart from a "normal" return). This means that stock prices will follow a random walk.
7. Applied to residential investment (housing), the arbitrage argument says that the price of a house should equal the present discounted value of the amount that the house could be rented for, adjusting for leverage.
8. Inventory investment is highly procyclical, rising sharply in booms and falling precipitously in recessions. This likely reflects the pipeline story of inventories.

KEY CONCEPTS

arbitrage equation
capital gain
capital loss
dividend
informationally efficient
inventory investment
mutual funds
nonresidential fixed investment
pipeline theory
price-earnings ratio
production smoothing
random walk
residential fixed investment
stockout avoidance
Tobin's q
user cost of capital

REVIEW QUESTIONS

1. Why do economists use the terms "investment" and "capital" in very different contexts (physical investment and physical capital versus financial investment and financial capital)?

2. What is the arbitrage equation, and why is it useful in studying investment?
3. What is a capital gain, and what role does it play in the arbitrage equation?
4. What is the user cost of capital? How is this user cost related to investment in physical capital?
5. When is the value of the stock market equal to the value of the capital stock? How is this related to Tobin's q?
6. What is a "dividend return" and a "capital gain," and how do these terms enter the arbitrage equation when it is written in percentages?
7. In the simple theory developed in the chapter, why is the stock price equal to the dividend divided by interest rate (net of the capital gain)?
8. What determines the price-earnings ratio for a stock? What does this imply about detecting bubbles in the stock market?
9. What does it mean when economists say that the stock market is, at least to a great extent, "informationally efficient"?
10. How does the arbitrage equation help pin down the price of housing in our simple theory? What role does leverage play?

EXERCISES

smartwork.wwnorton.com 

1. **The user cost of capital:** Consider the basic formula for the user cost of capital in the presence of a corporate income tax. Suppose the baseline case features an interest rate of 2 percent, a rate of depreciation of 6 percent, a price of capital that rises at 1 percent per year, and a 0 percent corporate tax rate. Starting from this baseline case, what is the user cost of capital after the following changes?
   - **(a)** No changes—the baseline case.
   - **(b)** The corporate tax rate rises to 35 percent.
   - **(c)** The interest rate doubles to 4 percent.
   - **(d)** Both (b) and (c).

2. **Interest rates and the tax code:** An economy begins in steady state with an investment rate of 20 percent, a corporate tax rate of 25 percent, a real interest rate of 2 percent, a depreciation rate of 7 percent, and a price of capital that falls at an annual rate of 2 percent.
   - **(a)** What is the user cost of capital?
   - **(b)** Suppose the central bank tightens monetary policy, raising the real interest rate from 2 percent to 4 percent. By how much does the user cost of capital rise?
   - **(c)** How would your answer have differed if the corporate tax rate had been 0? Explain the effect that taxes have on the extent to which monetary policy affects the user cost of capital (and hence the investment rate).

3. **Investment and the corporate income tax:** Suppose the user cost of capital in an economy with no corporate income tax is 10 percent.
   - (a) What is the user cost if the corporate tax rate rises to 20 percent? 30 percent?
   - (b) Suppose an economy's steady state investment rate I/Y is 30 percent when the corporate tax rate is 0. What happens to this investment rate if the corporate tax rate rises to 20 percent? 30 percent?
   - (c) Are differences in corporate tax rates across countries a plausible explanation for the large variation in investment rates that we see in the data?

4. **Investment tax credits and the user cost of capital:** Consider the user cost of capital in the presence of taxes, starting with equation (16.5). Suppose the price of capital, p_k, is constant, so there is no capital-gain term. What is new, however, is an investment tax credit: rather than costing p_k, a unit of capital costs $(1 - ITC)p_k$. That is, the government subsidizes the purchase of new capital, and the amount of the subsidy is given by ITC. As just one example, in 1981, the U.S. government created a 10-percent investment tax credit to spur the economy out of its recession, so we might suppose $ITC = 0.10$.
   - (a) How does the arbitrage equation change in the presence of the investment tax credit?
   - (b) What is the user cost of capital in this case?
   - (c) What happens to the user cost of capital if the investment tax credit is exactly equal to the corporate income tax rate? Why?

5. **Total factor productivity and investment:** Suppose the TFP parameter, $\bar{A}$, increases permanently.
   - (a) What happens to the desired capital stock?
   - (b) What happens to investment?
   - (c) *Hard*: What happens to the investment rate in the long run? Why?

6. **Pricing stocks:** Suppose the initial dividend paid by a stock is \$10 per year. Let the interest rate and the growth rate of dividends be given by the table below:

Interest rate (percent)	Growth rate of dividends (percent)	Stock price
4	0.0	—
4	2.0	—
4	3.0	—
4	3.9	—
6	0.0	—
6	2.0	—
6	5.0	—

   - (a) For each case, compute the value of the stock according to the simple theory developed in the chapter.

(b) What happens as the growth rate of dividends gets closer and closer to the interest rate? Why?
(c) What does this imply about using a plot of the price-earnings ratio in the stock market to identify bubbles or the mispricing of individual stocks?

7. **Housing prices:** Suppose a condominium can be rented for \$1000 a month, it depreciates at 10 percent per year, and the annual interest rate is 5 percent. Let the down-payment rate and the annual growth rate of condominium prices be given by the table below:

Growth rate of condo prices (percent)	Down-payment rate, $\bar{x}$ (percent)	Price of the condo
0	20	—
2	20	—
5	20	—
10	20	—
5	100	—
5	10	—
5	5	—

(a) For each case, compute the value of the housing price according to the simple theory developed in the chapter.
(b) Based on your results, discuss the sensitivity of condo prices to the expected capital gain.
(c) Based on your results, discuss the sensitivity of condo prices to the down-payment rate.

8. **The price of a patent:** Let's use the arbitrage equation to determine the price of a patent in a simple setting. Let R denote the interest rate, let p_i denote the price of an "idea" that is under patent, and let *Prof* denote the extra profit that can be earned by a firm that owns this idea.
(a) Set up the basic arbitrage equation that will ultimately pin down the value of the patent. On the left side show the return from investing p_i dollars in a saving account. On the right, show the return from using these funds to purchase the patent.
(b) Solve this equation for the price of the idea.
(c) What is the economic interpretation of this result?

WORKED EXERCISES

1. **The user cost of capital:** Looking at equation (16.6), the user cost of capital when there is a corporate income tax is

$$uc = \frac{R + \bar{d} - \dfrac{\Delta p_k}{p_k}}{1 - \tau}.$$

(a) In the baseline case, this user cost is

$$uc = \frac{.02 + .06 - .01}{1 - 0} = .07,$$

or 7 percent.

(b) If the corporate tax rate is 35 percent instead of 0, the user cost rises to

$$uc = \frac{.02 + .06 - .01}{1 - .35} \approx .108,$$

or about 10.8 percent.

(c) On the other hand, if the tax rate remains 0 but the interest rate rises to 4 percent, the user cost rises to

$$uc = \frac{.04 + .06 - .01}{1 - 0} = .09,$$

or 9 percent.

(d) Finally, if we combine changes, (b) and (c), the user cost is

$$uc = \frac{.04 + .06 - .01}{1 - .35} \approx .138,$$

or 13.8 percent.

6. **Pricing stocks:** Looking back at equation (16.16), the formula for pricing stocks in our simple model is

$$p_s = \frac{\text{dividend}}{R - \frac{\Delta p_s}{p_s}}.$$

(a) Applying this formula to the numbers in the table leads to the following results for the first several rows (you can fill in the rest yourself):

Interest rate (percent)	Growth rate of dividends (percent)	Stock price
4	0.0	2.5
4	2.0	5.0
4	3.0	10.0
4	3.9	100.0
6	0.0	—
6	2.0	—
6	5.0	—

(b) As the growth rate of the dividend rises, the stock price rises. This makes sense: the stock is the present value of dividends; and if dividends are growing faster, then the stock will be worth more. Notice that as the growth rate of the dividend approaches the interest rate, the stock price rises very rapidly, reaching infinity in the limit! The reason is that the discounting and growth terms effectively cancel out, which is analogous to computing the present discounted value of $10 per year forever, when the interest rate and growth rate are 0. The present value is infinite.

(c) *Hint*: Take a look at Section 3.2 and Figure 16.3. Think about what would happen if the capital-gain term were to rise as a result of changes in the economy (say, the "new economy" of the late 1990s).

CHAPTER 17

THE GOVERNMENT AND THE MACROECONOMY

OVERVIEW

In this chapter, we consider

- government spending, taxation, budget deficits, and the debt-GDP ratio in the United States and around the world.
- the government's intertemporal budget constraint, which says that budget deficits today must be offset by budget surpluses in the future.
- the economic consequences of budget deficits.
- the fiscal problem of the twenty-first century: how to finance rising health expenditures.

There are 10^{11} stars in the galaxy. That used to be a huge number. But it's only a hundred billion. It's less than the national deficit! We used to call them astronomical numbers. Now we should call them economical numbers.

—ATTRIBUTED TO RICHARD P. FEYNMAN

17.1 Introduction

One of the key players in any macroeconomy is the government. In 2007—prior to the financial crisis—the ratio of government spending to GDP was more than 50 percent in Denmark, France, and Sweden. In the United States, the same ratio (including all levels of government) was 37 percent. What does the government spend this money on, how does it finance expenditures, and what are the consequences of the spending for the macroeconomy? These are the questions we take up in this chapter.

In our exploration of these questions, two main themes emerge. The first is the role of the government budget constraint. We first encountered this constraint in Chapter 8, where we saw that printing money is one way for the government to finance its expenditures. Here, we put the budget constraint to additional use. Governments are allowed to borrow or lend in any given year, and most have accumulated a sizable debt that must be repaid at some point. The government's budget must balance, not period by period but rather in present discounted value. Budget deficits today must be offset by budget surpluses in the future.

The second theme is what we call the "fiscal problem of the twenty-first century." The Congressional Budget Office in the United States prepares long-term forecasts of government spending, revenues, and debt under the assumption that current policies will remain unchanged. Recent forecasts suggest that current U.S. policies are unsustainable: they will result in an explosion of deficits and debt-GDP ratios over the next 75 years. Similar kinds of forecasts could be produced for most of the advanced countries of the world, indicating a huge, unsustainable increase in government borrowing.

What is the source of this worldwide problem, and what can be done about it? These are questions explored in the second half of the chapter.

17.2 U.S. Government Spending and Revenue

In 2008, total spending by all levels of government in the United States was equal to \$4.7 trillion, or more than \$15,000 per person. Spending by the federal government was \$3.0 trillion, or about \$9,800 per person. Table 17.1 details the composition of spending in the federal budget for that year.

TABLE 17.1

The U.S. Federal Government Budget, 2008

	Percentage of GDP	Dollars per person
Total expenditures	20.7	9,800
Health (including Medicare)	4.6	2,200
Social Security	4.3	2,030
National defense	4.3	2,020
Income security	3.0	1,420
Net interest	1.8	830
Other	2.7	1,290
Total revenues	17.5	8,290
Individual income taxes	7.9	3,760
Social insurance and retirement receipts	6.2	2,960
Corporate income taxes	2.1	1,000
Other	1.2	570
Budget deficit	3.2	1,510

Source: *Economic Report of the President*, 2010, Table B-34.

Federal spending in 2008 was just under 21 percent of GDP. Health, Social Security, and national defense were the three largest categories of spending, at over 4 percent each. Income security, which includes spending on welfare and unemployment insurance, totaled 3 percent, while interest payments on the outstanding debt amounted to 1.8 percent.

The table also shows how this spending was financed. More than 17 percent of GDP was collected in the form of tax revenues: 7.9 percent from personal income taxes, 6.2 percent from Social Security and Medicare taxes, and 2.1 percent from corporate income taxes.

The **budget balance** is the difference between tax revenues and spending. When taxes exceed spending, we say there is a **budget surplus**; when spending exceeds taxes, there is a **budget deficit**; and when the two are equal, the budget is **balanced**.

In 2008, there was a budget deficit equal to 3.2 percent of GDP. The only way a household could run up such a deficit would be if it "dissaved"—saved a negative amount—by selling some of its assets, or if it borrowed. The same is true of the government. The government owns many assets (like Yellowstone National Park, buildings and monuments, and large stockpiles of gold), but it usually does not sell these assets to finance the deficit. Instead, it borrows from lenders in the United States and abroad by selling government bonds. For example, a 10-year bond issued in 2008 may pay the holder $100 when it comes due in 2018. An investor may be willing to pay $55 for such a bond when it is issued; this amount is therefore loaned to the government. In 2008, the federal government issued $450 billion worth of new bonds to finance the budget deficit, more than $1,500 per person.

Spending and Revenue over Time

Figure 17.1 shows federal revenue and spending since 1930 for the U.S. economy. Notice that tax revenues were very small in the 1930s, on the order of 5 percent of GDP. Taxes rose sharply during World War II, reaching nearly 21 percent in 1944. The reason was the large increase in expenditures related to national defense. Total expenditures as a share of GDP peaked in 1943 and 1944 at just under 44 percent, with spending on national defense alone accounting for nearly 38 percent.

The decades following World War II featured spending and revenues of about 18 percent of GDP. Then, starting around 1970 or so, systematic budget deficits began to emerge. These deficits are shown more clearly in Figure 17.2 (bottom line). As a fraction of GDP, the deficits peaked at around 6 percent in 1983. Starting in 1998, surpluses made a brief reappearance before deficits again took over in 2002. In 2009 and 2010, the budget deficit reached 10 percent of GDP as government revenue fell sharply during the Great Recession and government expenditures rose considerably in an effort to resolve the crisis and stimulate the economy.

The Debt-GDP Ratio

When the government runs a deficit, it must borrow—by issuing government bonds—in order to finance its spending. For example, the government may sell $100 billion of 10-year government bonds to help cover the deficit in any given

FIGURE 17.1

U.S. Federal Government Revenue and Spending, 1934–2010

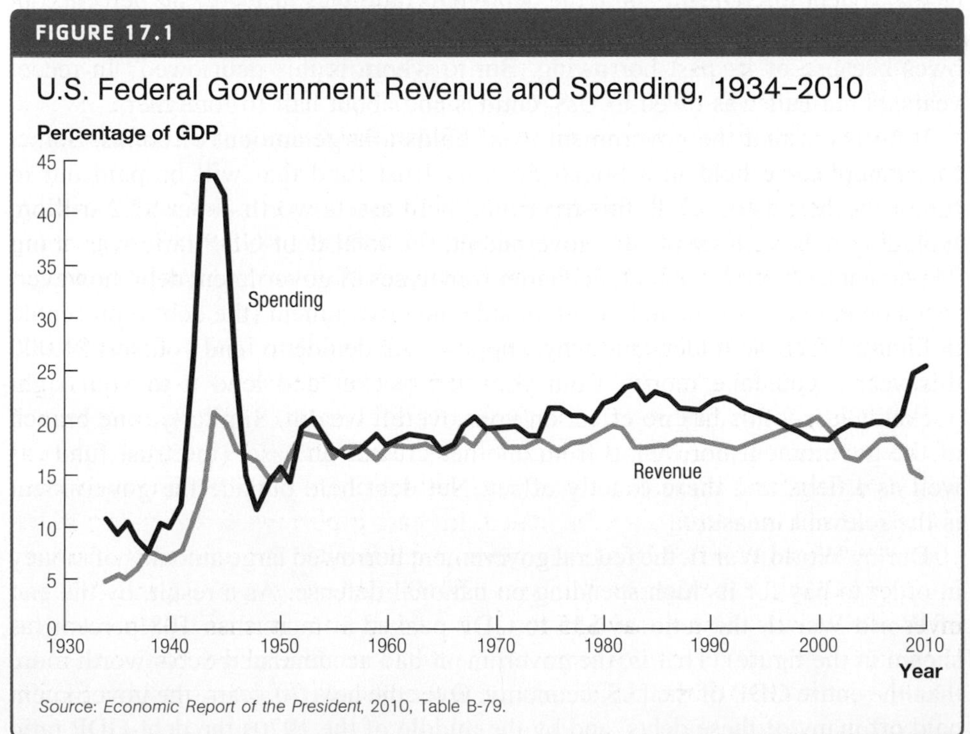

Source: Economic Report of the President, 2010, Table B-79.

In recent decades, federal government spending and revenue have averaged about 20 percent of GDP.

The top line is the ratio of federal debt held outside the government to GDP. The bottom line is the surplus or deficit for the federal budget, also as a percentage of GDP.

FIGURE 17.2

Federal Debt and Deficits in the United States, 1934–2010

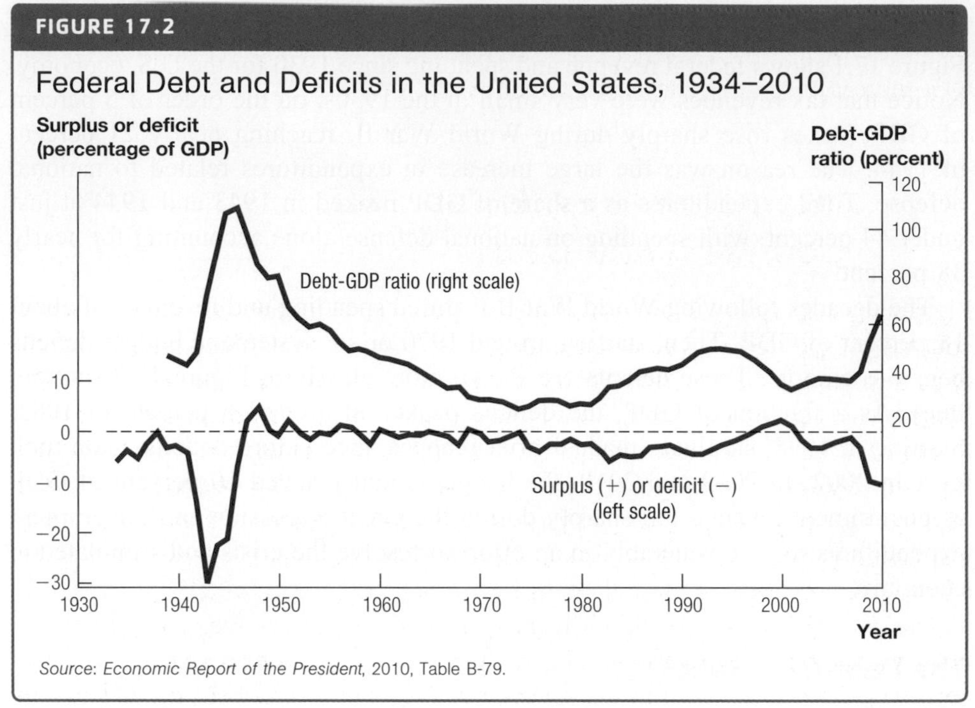

Source: *Economic Report of the President*, 2010, Table B-79.

year. The outstanding stock of bonds that have been issued in the past is called **government debt**. Figure 17.2 also shows the ratio of outstanding government (federal) debt to GDP. In 2005, the debt-GDP ratio was just over 37 percent, but this ratio rose to more than 60 percent in 2010. This is the amount the government owes because of its past borrowing. But to whom is this debt owed? In recent years, about half was owed to U.S. entities and about half to foreigners.

It turns out that the government itself holds a large amount of bonds. Some, for example, are held in a Social Security trust fund that will be paid out to future retirees; as of 2008, this trust fund held assets worth about $2.2 trillion. Including debt held inside the government, the total debt-GDP ratio was about 94 percent in 2010. Most macroeconomic analyses of government debt, however, focus on *net* debt, or the debt held outside the government (the debt represented in Figure 17.2). To understand why, suppose you decide to lend yourself $1,000 this year—you take money from your left pocket and lend it to your right pocket. Clearly this has no effect on your overall wealth. Similarly, one branch of the government borrowing from another creates an asset (the trust fund) as well as a debt, and these exactly offset. Net debt held outside the government is the relevant measure.

During World War II, the federal government borrowed large amounts of money in order to pay for its high spending on national defense. As a result, by the end of World War II, the ratio of debt to GDP peaked at more than 108 percent (as shown in the figure). That is, the government had accumulated debts worth more than the entire GDP of the U.S. economy. Over the next 30 years, the government paid off many of these debts, and by the middle of the 1970s the debt-GDP ratio had fallen to less than 25 percent. The emergence of large deficits starting at the end of the 1970s led the debt-GDP ratio to rise to just under 50 percent of GDP by 1994. It declined to around 33 percent by 2001, rose slightly until 2008, and then increased sharply during the Great Recession.

17.3 International Evidence on Spending and Debt

Figures 17.3 and 17.4 show government spending and debt-GDP ratios in some countries of the OECD. These data correspond to government spending at all levels (e.g., state and local spending as well as federal). Among the richer countries, the United States exhibits one of the lowest levels of overall government spending relative to GDP, about 41 percent. For the "Euro" countries (including France, Germany, Italy, and Spain), the average is 51 percent. The U.S. debt-GDP ratio today is typical of other rich countries, as seen in Figure 17.4. The ratio for the Euro countries is just under 60 percent, while in Japan, the ratio has risen sharply since 1991, from a low of about 13 percent to a high of more than 100 percent in 2010.

The debt-GDP ratio for South Korea, meanwhile, is negative. This means, in other words, that the government in South Korea is a net lender rather than a net borrower: it collects more in tax revenue than it spends and uses the balance to accumulate financial assets. Norway is another country in the OECD with a substantial negative debt-GDP ratio. Norway benefits from large government-owned petroleum and natural gas reserves, which boost its revenues and lead to budget

FIGURE 17.3

Government Spending around the World, 2009

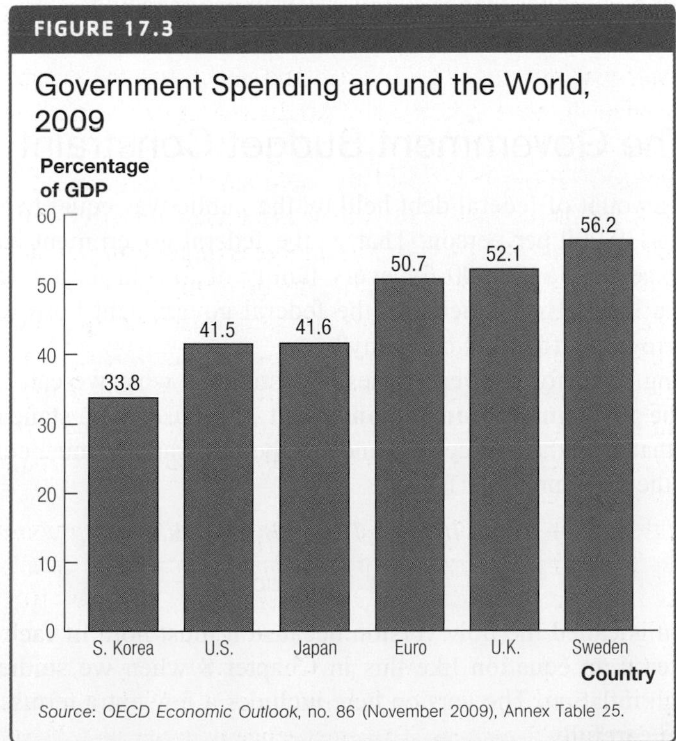

Source: OECD Economic Outlook, no. 86 (November 2009), Annex Table 25.

The graph shows general government spending (federal, state, and local) as a percentage of GDP. "Euro" denotes France, Germany, Italy, and Spain.

The figure plots general government debt held by the public, as a percentage of GDP.

FIGURE 17.4

Debt-GDP Ratios around the World, 1988–2010

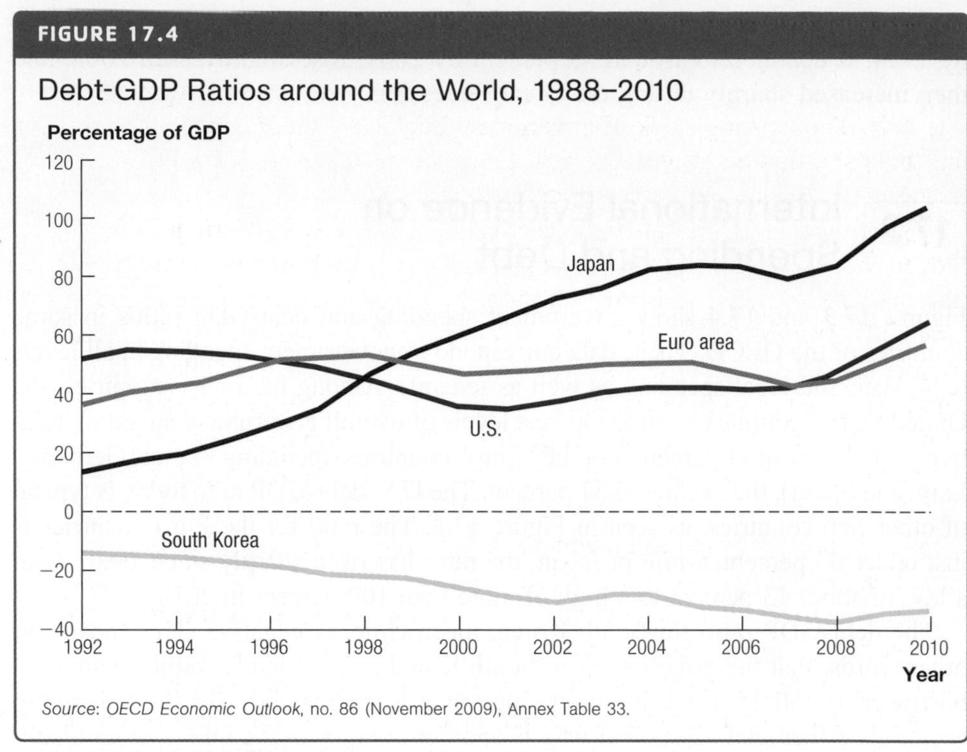

Source: *OECD Economic Outlook*, no. 86 (November 2009), Annex Table 33.

surpluses. Recognizing that these revenues will be depleted someday, the Norwegian government saves these surpluses as assets in a Government Petroleum Fund that can be used to finance future government spending.

17.4 The Government Budget Constraint

In 2010, the amount of federal debt held by the public was equal to \$9.3 trillion, or more than \$30,000 per person. That is, the federal government has borrowed an amount exceeding \$120,000 for every family of four in the United States. Is this a lot or a little? How much *can* the federal government borrow? And how does this borrowing affect the economy?

The starting point for answering these questions is what we can call the **flow version of the government budget constraint**. It is based on a standard accounting identity that says the sources of funds to the government must equal the uses of funds by the government. That is,

$$\underbrace{G_t + Tr_t + iB_t}_{\text{uses}} = \underbrace{T_t + \Delta B_{t+1} + \Delta M_{t+1}}_{\text{sources}}. \tag{17.1}$$

This equation is called the flow version because it must hold in each period. We first encountered an equation like this in Chapter 8 when we studied the fiscal causes of high inflation. The version here includes a few extra terms, so we'll go through them carefully.

The left side of the equation says that the government can use its funds to purchase goods and services, denoted G_t; for transfer payments, denoted Tr_t (unemployment insurance, Social Security, and welfare payments); and to pay interest on the debt. The existing stock of government debt is B_t (the B denotes "borrowing" or "bonds"); this is the stock of debt held at the start of period t. For simplicity, we assume the nominal interest rate is constant at i.

The right side of the equation describes the sources of government funds. The government can obtain funds through taxes T_t, which in the United States are the main source. It can also obtain them by borrowing. And since B_t is the total amount borrowed so far, ΔB_{t+1} is the amount of new borrowing; it can also be written as $\Delta B_{t+1} = B_{t+1} - B_t$. In other words, ΔB_{t+1} is the dollar value of the funds obtained by selling government bonds. Finally, the third source of funds is printing money: ΔM_{t+1} is the change in the stock of money—the amount of new money that is printed. To simplify our presentation, we will assume $\Delta M_{t+1} = 0$ for the rest of this chapter. That is, we assume none of the government finance comes about through printing money. As discussed in Chapter 8, this is a reasonable assumption for the United States.

We can simplify this budget constraint further by assuming transfer payments Tr_t are also zero. This is really just to make our notation easier; if you'd like, think of transfer payments as being included in G_t in what follows.

With these simplifications, the government budget constraint can be rearranged in a useful way. Since $\Delta B_{t+1} = B_{t+1} - B_t$, the budget constraint in equation (17.1) can be rewritten as

$$B_{t+1} = (1 + i)B_t + \underbrace{G_t - T_t}_{\text{deficit}}. \tag{17.2}$$

This equation says that the stock of debt at the start of next year is equal to the sum of three terms. The first is the stock of debt this year, including the required interest payments. The last two terms capture the extent to which current spending (G_t) exceeds tax revenues (T_t). That is, it is a measure of the budget deficit. Budget deficits cause the government debt to increase, other things being equal.

An important subtlety is involved here. Standard measures of budget deficits include interest payments on the government debt as a part of spending; this was true, for example, in Table 17.1. In studying the deficit, however, it proves convenient to separate out the interest payments, as we've done in equation (17.2). The measure $G_t - T_t$ is commonly referred to as the **primary deficit**, while $G_t + iB_t - T_t$ is called the **total deficit**. That is, the primary deficit excludes spending on interest, while the total deficit includes it. (A similar distinction—primary versus total—applies to the budget surplus and the budget balance.)

The Intertemporal Budget Constraint

Budget constraints play a central role in economics. Most of the insights to be gained from these constraints can be found by thinking about a simple example. Suppose an economy exists for two periods, period 1 and period 2. The world of this economy begins in period 1 and ends after period 2. What does the government budget constraint look like?

In this short-lived economy, there are actually two flow-version budget constraints, one for each period. If we apply the formula in equation (17.2), the budget constraint for period 1 is

$$B_2 = (1 + i)B_1 + G_1 - T_1. \tag{17.3}$$

All of the terms in this equation should make sense to you, except perhaps for B_1. This variable is the amount of debt that the government has outstanding when the economy starts. Even though our economy can't have accumulated any debt yet, this will prove a useful term. To see why, suppose we employed this model to study the United States. Period 1 could represent the country today, and period 2 could represent it in the future. A value of B_1 = \$5 trillion would capture the fact that the U.S. government begins today with a large outstanding debt.

There is a similar budget constraint for period 2:

$$B_3 = (1 + i)B_2 + G_2 - T_2 = 0. \tag{17.4}$$

But why do these terms now equal zero? The reason is that B_3 is the total amount the government owes at the beginning of period 3, but our economy ends after period 2. No one will be willing to make new loans to the government during period 2—they would never be repaid, since the world is coming to an end. Therefore, it must be the case that B_3 is equal to zero. This is simply another way of saying that all debts must be repaid before the world ends.

Now we are ready for an important result. We use the period 2 budget constraint to solve for B_2, and substitute the result back into the period 1 budget constraint. We are left with **the intertemporal budget constraint**:[1]

$$\underbrace{G_1 + \frac{G_2}{1 + i}}_{\text{pdv of spending}} + \underbrace{(1 + i)B_1}_{\text{initial debt}} = \underbrace{T_1 + \frac{T_2}{1 + i}}_{\text{pdv of taxes}} \tag{17.5}$$

To see how this equation gets its name, think about its interpretation. First, suppose $B_1 = 0$: when the economy begins, there is no outstanding government debt. In this case, the left-hand side of the equation is the present discounted value (pdv) of government spending: G_1 is spending today, and $G_2/(1 + i)$ is spending in the future. (We divide by $1 + i$ to compute the present value of the future spending.) So both terms on the left are valued as of period 1.

The right-hand side of the equation is the present discounted value of tax revenues. Therefore, the intertemporal budget constraint says that *the present discounted value of government spending must equal the present discounted value of tax revenues.*

[1] Here are the details of the derivation. If we use the period 2 budget constraint to solve for B_2, we find that $B_2 = (T_2 - G_2)/(1 + i)$. Now substitute this expression for B_2 back into equation (17.3). Collecting the spending terms on one side and the tax terms on the other gives the intertemporal budget constraint.

Now let's consider an economy where B_1 is allowed to differ from zero. Suppose $B_1 = \$5$ trillion, as is roughly the case in the U.S. economy today. What is the logic of the government budget constraint in this case? Here, the present value of tax revenues must be enough to cover current and future spending and to pay off the debt the economy starts with.[2]

According to this version of the intertemporal budget constraint, the present discounted value of uses of funds (spending plus paying off the initial debt) must equal the present discounted value of the sources of funds (taxes). Like the flow version, the intertemporal budget constraint yields a "uses = sources" interpretation, but now the uses and sources are measured in present discounted value.

An alternate version of the intertemporal budget constraint is also useful. Suppose we collect the tax and spending terms on the same side of the equation. In our two-period example, the intertemporal budget constraint in equation (17.5) can be written as

$$\underbrace{(T_1 - G_1)}_{\text{period 1 balance}} + \underbrace{\frac{(T_2 - G_2)}{1 + i}}_{\text{period 2 balance}} = \underbrace{(1 + i)B_1}_{\text{initial debt}}. \tag{17.6}$$

If $B_1 = 0$, the intertemporal budget constraint says that the present discounted value of the government's budget balance (the left-hand side of the equation) must equal zero. The government is allowed to borrow or lend in any given period. But what must be true is that any borrowing in period 1 gets offset by a surplus in period 2. If $T_1 - G_1$ is $-\$1{,}000$, then $T_2 - G_2$ must equal $+\$1{,}000$ in present discounted value. *The government's budget must balance—not period by period, but rather in a present discounted value sense.*

If, again, $B_1 = \$5$ trillion, the present discounted value of the budget balance going forward from today must be enough to pay off the initial stock of outstanding debt. Not only must future surpluses and deficits offset, but we must run more surpluses in the future in order to pay off the existing debt today. Higher taxes in the future are one implication of borrowing today.

Although our example entailed two periods, the logic of the intertemporal budget constraint applies no matter how many time periods there are. At the end of the chapter, you will get a chance to derive the constraint for a three-period economy.

17.5 How Much Can the Government Borrow?

When we think about the economic consequences of large deficits and high debt-GDP ratios, four issues arise: the importance of economic growth, the possibility of high inflation or default, intergenerational equity, and the extent to which deficits crowd out investment. Each is explored in turn below.

[2] You might ask yourself why B_1 is multiplied by $1 + i$ in the budget constraint. The answer is that we are valuing everything in period 1. Not only do we have to pay the debt balance B_1, we also have to pay the interest on the debt accumulated in the past.

Economic Growth and the Debt-GDP Ratio

The government budget constraint says that the amount the government can borrow is limited by the amount it can credibly be expected to pay back. But how much is this?

The answer depends in part on the size of an economy's GDP. After all, GDP is in some sense a measure of the total tax base that is potentially available. This explains why we often divide by GDP in presenting the facts about government debt. Can an economy borrow $1 trillion? If the economy is Kenya, maybe not, but if the economy is the United States, then the answer is certainly yes.

Is it possible for the stock of debt to be growing over long periods of time? This would seem to be a problem, but suppose GDP is growing even faster. In that case, the ratio of debt to GDP would be declining. If this trend continues, it will eventually be easy for the economy to satisfy its budget constraint: once the debt-GDP ratio falls to 1 percent, for example, the government could simply raise taxes for one period by 1 percent of GDP and pay off the entire debt.

As a simple analogy, consider how much money other people might be willing to lend to you. The amount surely depends on your income today and your income prospects in the future. If your future prospects look good, lenders may be willing to lend you a lot today even though your current income may be low. A high and growing stock of debt, on the other hand, would set off alarms. Lenders would worry about your ability to pay in the future, unless they had some independent evidence that your future prospects looked much better than your current ones. Countries operate in much the same way.

High Inflation and Default

If a country's debt-GDP ratio gets to be too high, lenders may become worried about the government's ability to repay its debt, and may stop lending. This will itself prevent government borrowing from growing too large, but it may also force the government to turn to the printing press in order to satisfy its budget constraint. At high and growing debt-GDP ratios, the possibility of high or even hyper inflation becomes a concern.

As soon as investors doubt the ability of the government to finance its spending, they may demand higher interest rates on new borrowing. These higher interest rates will compensate them for the possibility that the debt will be repaid with dollars that are worth less because of future inflation. The higher interest payments in turn make it more difficult for the government to satisfy its budget constraint and may precipitate a crisis. (Such a scenario was discussed in more detail in Chapter 8.)

In addition to causing inflation, problems with the budget constraint can also lead governments to **default** on their debt: that is, they declare that they will not repay certain debts, or will repay them at less than face value. This happened in a number of countries in Latin America during the early 1980s, as well as in Russia in 1998 and Argentina in 2002.

There is no magic level of the debt-GDP ratio that triggers such a calamity. In practice, the level varies with each economy based on historical experience, growth prospects, and the credibility of the government and central bank, among other factors. In 2001, the debt-GDP ratio in Argentina peaked at 65 percent just before its crisis, but other countries have exceeded this ratio without negative consequences. For example, the debt-GDP ratio in Japan has risen sharply since 1991, from a low of about 13 percent to a high of more than 100 percent in 2010 (see Figure 17.4). And the United States had an even higher debt-GDP ratio after World War II (see Figure 17.2), so there is nothing necessarily problematic with a ratio of 100 percent. Still, the time path of the debt-GDP ratio in Japan is not especially encouraging, and it seems unlikely that the debt-GDP ratio can continue to rise at this same rate for another decade.

Generational Accounting

By its very nature, a debt involves borrowing for the present and repaying in the future. To the extent that long time periods elapse between the borrowing and the repayment, it is possible that the people benefiting from the borrowing are not the same as the people doing the repaying. In this case, you could say that existing generations are borrowing from future generations.

Is this borrowing good or bad? Consider a previous episode of extensive borrowing in U.S. history. As we saw in Figure 17.2, by the end of World War II, the United States had a debt-GDP ratio of 108 percent. From an intergenerational standpoint, however, perhaps such heavy borrowing made good sense. The generation that fought World War II made large sacrifices, both in terms of lives lost and in terms of consumption per person during the war. By borrowing resources, the federal government was able to pass on some of the burden associated with fighting World War II to future generations. One can make the case that since future generations would benefit from the Allied victory in World War II, it was reasonable that they would share in the cost.

An approach to accounting that seeks to calculate the extent to which current policies are passing on tax burdens to future generations, known as **generational accounting**, was put together by Alan Auerbach, Laurence Kotlikoff, and their coauthors. As one example of this approach, the authors once determined that generations born in the 1980s and early 1990s would pay a lifetime tax rate of about 34 percent of their income under current fiscal policies. However, in order to satisfy the government budget constraint, all future generations would have to pay a lifetime tax rate of 71 percent.[3] Achieving equalized lifetime tax rates across generations would require a significant change in current fiscal policy. For example, as of the mid-1990s, all taxes at all levels of government would have to increase by 11.7 percent. Alternatively, all government transfers would have to be reduced by 24.9 percent. The basic point of generational accounting is that high and rising debt-GDP ratios imply higher tax rates on future generations.

What other intergenerational transfers are being made? Current generations are depleting nonrenewable natural resources like fossil fuels and may be passing on a serious problem in the form of global warming to future generations. On the other hand, future generations are likely to be much richer than current generations, in

[3] See Alan J. Auerbach, Jagadeesh Gokhale, and Laurence J. Kotlikoff, "Generational Accounting: A Meaningful Way to Evaluate Fiscal Policy," *Journal of Economic Perspectives*, vol. 8 (Winter 1994), pp. 73–94.

part because of the investments in capital, education, and research made by current generations. It is far from clear how these concerns net out, although it is certainly an important policy issue.

Deficits and Investment

Recall that in deriving the IS curve in Chapter 11, we noted that the national income identity requires that investment in an economy be equal to total saving. To see how we got this relation, let's first rearrange the national income identity as

$$Y - C + G + (IM - EX) = I.$$

We assume for the moment that all government spending is government purchases, so there are no transfer payments. This simplifies what follows without affecting the substance of the argument.

Now, add and subtract tax revenues T from the left side of the equation to get

$$\underbrace{(Y - T - C)}_{\text{private saving}} + \underbrace{(T - G)}_{\text{government saving}} + \underbrace{(IM - EX)}_{\text{foreign saving}} = I. \tag{17.7}$$

This equation says that there are three ways an economy's investment can be financed: saving from the private sector, saving by the government, and saving by foreigners. Saving by the private sector, $Y - T - C$, is the difference between income net of taxes (often called **disposable income**) and consumption. Saving by the government $(T - G)$, tax revenue less government spending, is the budget balance. And if the economy imports more goods and services than it exports, then these extra goods and services are also available for investment.

One source of concern about budget deficits is that if the government's savings are negative, this may reduce investment. Some of the savings by the private sector or by foreigners must then go to fund the government's borrowing, and these funds cannot be used for investment. Economists call this phenomenon **crowding out**: budget deficits may soak up saving in the economy and crowd out investment.

The crowding-out interpretation does not take into account the possibility that private or foreign saving might increase in response to the additional demand for funds by the government. Both possibilities are relevant. As discussed in Chapter 11 (see Section 11.5), the theory of Ricardian equivalence says that, holding the present value of government spending constant, the timing of taxes does not affect consumption. An important implication of this theory is that budget deficits need not crowd out investment. Instead, they will be offset exactly by higher private saving as individuals save to pay the future taxes implied by current budget deficits.

What about foreign saving? If the marginal product of capital is high in the United States but domestic savers don't have enough funds to take advantage of these opportunities, there may be plenty of foreign savers who will. To some extent, foreign saving *has* kept the investment rate close to its postwar average. We will explore this channel of saving in more detail in Chapter 18.

Whether government borrowing crowds out investment has been the subject of much research in economics, and the issue is still debated. Figure 17.5 shows the

FIGURE 17.5

U.S. Investment and the Budget Deficit, 1960–2009

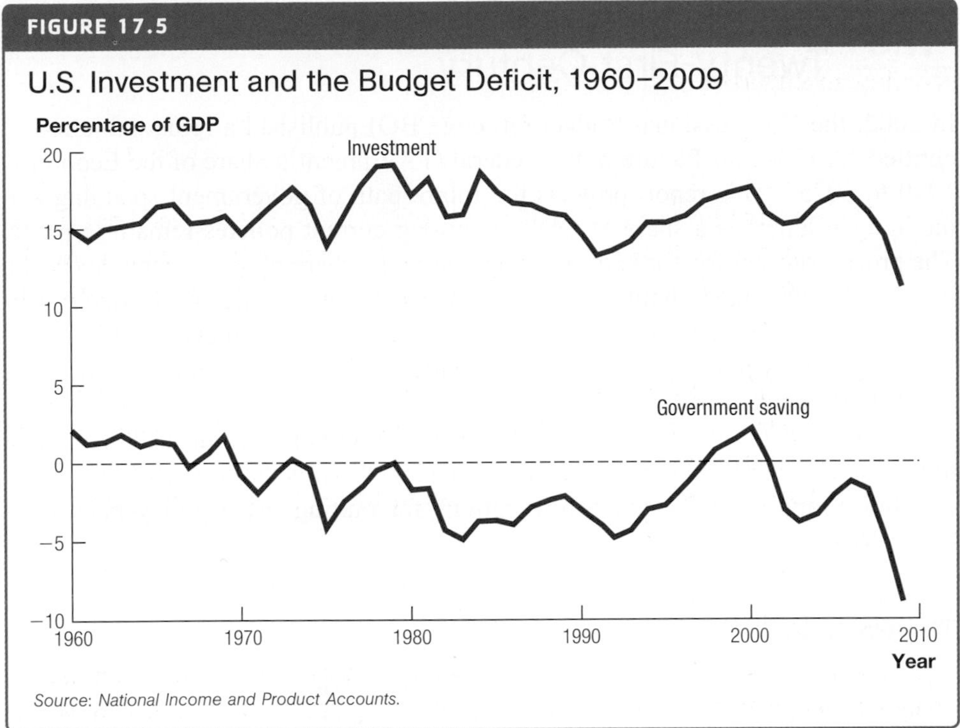

Source: National Income and Product Accounts.

Despite some correlation in the year-to-year movements in investment and government saving, the large budget deficits (negative government saving) since 1980 have not been associated with a lower average investment rate.

time series for investment and the budget deficit to help frame this debate. Notice that despite the emergence of relatively large budget deficits since the 1980s, the investment rate in this same period has not really declined. Still, there remains a high medium-term correlation between government saving and the investment share of GDP. For example, the decline in the budget deficit during the 1990s—a large rise in government saving—was accompanied by a rise in the investment share. Similarly, the reemergence of large deficits in recent years has been accompanied by a decline in the investment share.

The extent to which budget deficits crowd out investment is unclear, and there is no consensus on the answer in the economics literature. Private saving appears to increase by no more than 50 cents to offset each dollar of the budget deficit, and perhaps by even less.[4] We will return to this question again in Chapter 18, where we will see an important reason for the ambiguity.

To sum up: By most measures, the current U.S. debt-GDP ratio is not especially large. The ratio was much higher after World War II. It is also higher in many other advanced countries. There is some concern about current deficits possibly crowding out investment, although foreign saving has stepped in to some extent and has kept the investment rate close to its postwar average.

A source of great concern to many economists, however, is what current policies imply about future debts and deficits, as we see in the next section.

[4] See B. Douglas Bernheim, "Ricardian Equivalence: An Evaluation of Theory and Evidence," *NBER Macroeconomics Annual* (Cambridge, Mass.: MIT Press, 1987), pp. 263–304; and the *Economic Report of the President*, 1994.

17.6 The Fiscal Problem of the Twenty-First Century

In 2002, the Congressional Budget Office (CBO) published a remarkable report entitled "A 125-Year Picture of the Federal Government's Share of the Economy, 1950 to 2075." This report projects the future path of government spending and the budget deficit as a share of GDP, assuming current policies remain in place. The projections put forward are stunning: while the share of government spending in GDP has averaged about 19 percent since 1950, it is projected to rise drastically in coming decades, more than doubling to nearly 40 percent by 2075. With no change in tax policies, this rise in spending implies exploding budget deficits, reaching 20 percent of GDP by 2075.

The inescapable implication is that our current policies are unsustainable and must change substantially in the coming decades. What is the source of the unsustainability, and what are the policy options for putting fiscal policy back on a sound footing?

The Problem

Figure 17.6 summarizes the forecasts in the CBO's report. For the period 1950 to 2000, the figure plots actual numbers for the U.S. economy. For 2010 to 2075, the figure plots CBO projections under the assumption that current policies continue.

Rising entitlement spending – Social Security, Medicare, and Medicaid – is projected to raise federal spending well above revenues in coming decades. Actual data are plotted until 2000, CBO forecasts thereafter.

FIGURE 17.6

U.S. Federal Spending and Revenues, 1950–2075

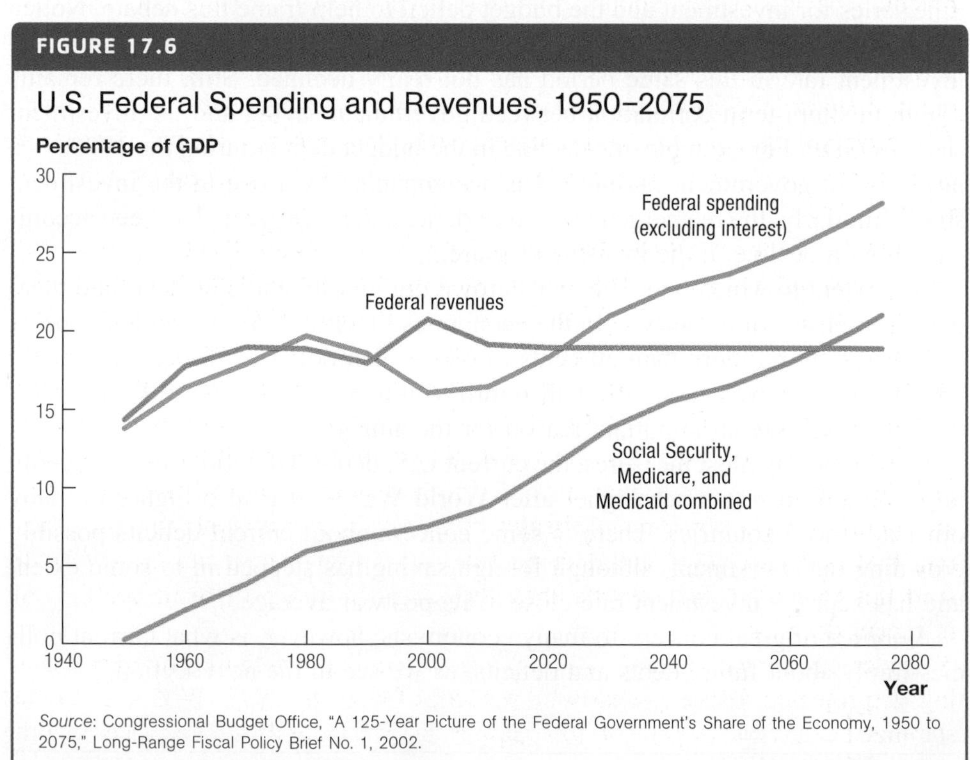

Source: Congressional Budget Office, "A 125-Year Picture of the Federal Government's Share of the Economy, 1950 to 2075," Long-Range Fiscal Policy Brief No. 1, 2002.

In general, the projections are based on reasonable assumptions for the future path of wages, the number of recipients of various entitlement programs, and spending per recipient. Importantly, notice that these projections were made long before the Great Recession and the associated financial crisis. So the problems outlined here were already an issue before the recent rise in the debt-GDP ratio. Recent events only exacerbate the problems.

As can be seen in the figure, the reason for the unsustainability of current policies is the projected rise in spending on three entitlement programs: Social Security, Medicare, and Medicaid. This entitlement spending rose from 0.3 percent of GDP in 1950 to 7.6 percent in 2000. Total federal spending (excluding interest) averaged about 19 percent of GDP over this period, so spending on health and retirement has thus risen from a negligible fraction to more than a third of the total.

What are the reasons for this rise? One is the increased generosity of the entitlement programs, and another is the larger fraction of the population that will be eligible for these benefits. In 1940, there were 8.6 people of working age for every person aged 65 and above; by 2000, the number had fallen by nearly half to 4.7. What is even more remarkable about federal spending on health and retirement, however, is the continuation of the trend in the CBO's projections. As shown in the figure, the fraction of GDP devoted to these programs will rise from 7.6 percent in 2000 to 13.9 percent in 2030 and 21.1 percent by 2075.

To put the rise of this entitlement spending in perspective, Figure 17.6 also plots federal revenues as a percentage of GDP. Like total federal spending, federal revenues have averaged about 18 or 19 percent of GDP since 1950. The CBO projections assume that if current policies continue, revenues will stabilize at 19 percent of GDP in the future. When entitlement spending was low, this left ample room for additional spending on defense, unemployment insurance, environmental protection, and federally funded research, among other things. However, the CBO projects that health and retirement spending by itself will exceed 19 percent of GDP by 2070.

Figure 17.7 breaks down the projections for the entitlement programs into health care and Social Security. The CBO projects Social Security expenditures to rise from 4.2 percent of GDP in 2000 to 6.2 percent in 2030, and then to level off. Social Security, then, accounts for some of the rise in spending—especially in the next 20 years—but it is not the primary source of the unsustainability of current policies. The main culprit is health. Expenditures on Medicare and Medicaid are projected to rise from 3.4 percent of GDP in 2000 to 7.7 percent in 2030 and then to 14.9 percent by 2075. A primary cause of this increase is an underlying assumption that health care costs per recipient will grow at a rate that is 1 percentage point faster than the rate of per capita GDP growth. And this rate is, in fact, slower than the actual rate of growth in health costs in recent decades.

Under current policies, total government spending (including interest spending) is projected to rise to nearly 40 percent of GDP by 2075. With tax revenue stabilized at around 19 percent, this implies an exploding deficit and an exploding ratio of debt to GDP.

The main culprit behind the rise in federal spending is health care. Actual data are plotted until 2000, CBO forecasts thereafter.

FIGURE 17.7

Components of Federal Spending, 1950–2075

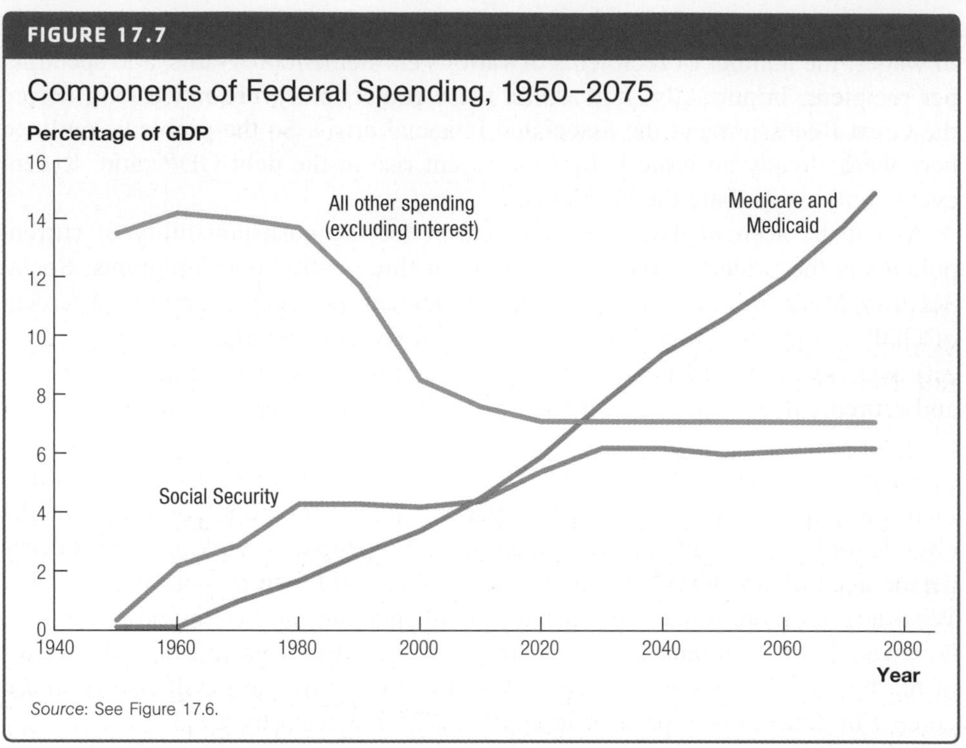

Source: See Figure 17.6.

CASE STUDY

Financing the Social Security Program

The Social Security program—along with personal savings and employer-provided pensions—plays a key role in allowing people to retire from the labor force and maintain their standard of living. The program was begun in the 1930s as part of Franklin D. Roosevelt's New Deal to combat the Great Depression; Social Security expenditures by the federal government now amount to more than 4 percent of GDP. This spending is financed by an employment tax on wage income, whose rate is currently 12.4 percent (half paid by workers and half by employers). To a great extent, current workers pay the Social Security benefits of the current elderly—a system known as **pay-as-you-go**.

As baby boomers age and retire, though, this pay-as-you-go system will come under increased pressure. The ratio of workers to retirees is projected to fall from the current level of 3.3 to 1 down to a ratio of 2 to 1 in coming decades. There will be more retirees to whom benefits are owed and fewer workers to pay for these benefits.

The economic size of this problem can be inferred from the CBO projections shown in Figure 17.7. Spending on Social Security will increase from about 4.2 percent of GDP to about 6 percent. Some combination of increased taxes and/or reductions in benefits will be needed to cover the gap.

The problem of financing Social Security receives a great deal of political and media attention, and deservedly so. Some difficult choices will have to be made. Nevertheless, the magnitude of the problem pales in comparison with the magnitude of the problem associated with financing health expenditures.

Possible Solutions

From an accounting standpoint, the possible ways to bring spending back in line with tax revenues are straightforward: either taxes have to rise or spending has to fall. Neither is an especially desirable option. Taxes have remained at or below 20 percent of GDP during virtually the entire history of the United States. In order to balance the budget, tax revenues would have to rise by about 9 percent of GDP by 2075.

In deciding among the options, it is important to step back and consider why Medicare and Medicaid spending are growing so rapidly. The aging of the population is only part of the reason. To understand this story, we start by documenting the rapid growth in health spending as a share of GDP throughout the world. Figure 17.8 shows this health share—not just by the government but for the economy as a whole—for five relatively rich OECD countries. As we can see, **health spending** is growing in virtually all advanced economies. It has grown quite rapidly within the United States, from about 5 percent of GDP in 1960 to more than 16 percent

FIGURE 17.8

Health Spending as a Share of GDP in Five Countries, 1960–2007

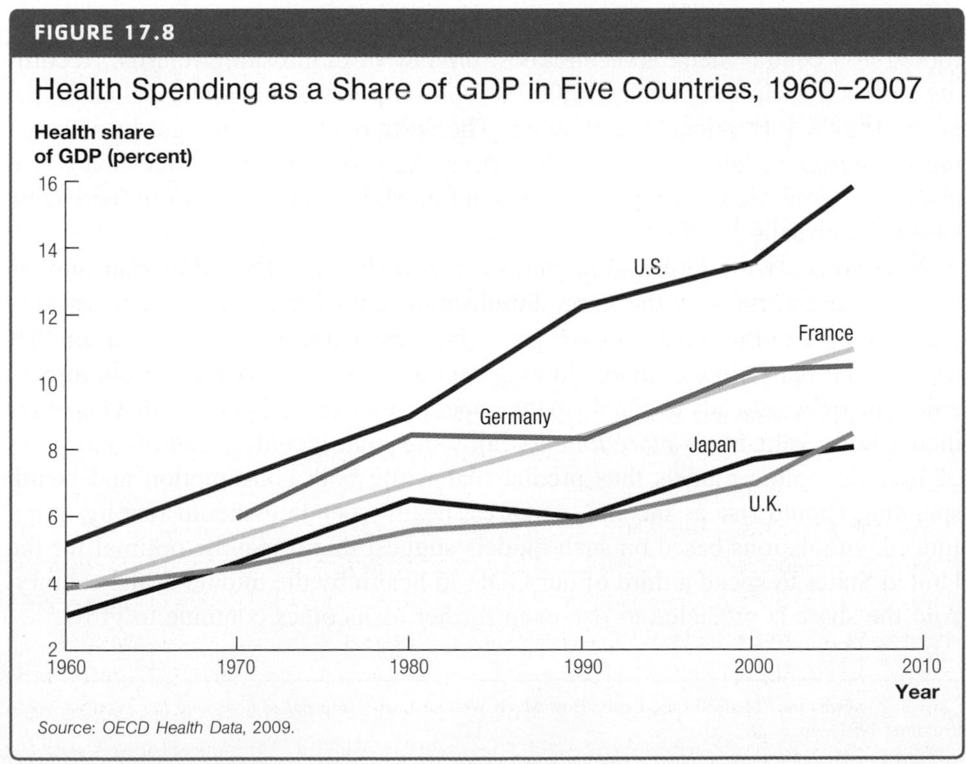

Source: OECD Health Data, 2009.

Health spending as a share of GDP has risen throughout the world.

today. The typical growth throughout the OECD is from about 4 percent in 1960 to about 8 percent by 2007.

Why is the fraction of GDP spent on health growing over time? In public policy discussions, much attention has focused on waste and fraud in the health care system, which clearly are harmful to the economy. But while this may account for some of the higher spending in the United States, the consensus among health economists is that it probably does not explain the fact that health spending is growing as a share of GDP in virtually all rich countries.

An important paper by Joseph Newhouse in 1992 surveyed a number of possible causes.[5] These included, besides the aging of the population, the rising cost of health insurance and anecdotes associated with doctors who induced patients to spend more on medical care than they really needed. But Newhouse found that the key factor was the advent of new, expensive medical technologies: MRIs, CT scans, new drugs, and other new medical procedures.

By itself, however, Newhouse's explanation raises other questions. People don't have to buy the new technologies if they don't want to, and, in fact, people don't have to invent them in the first place if they are not valuable. It thus seems likely that, at some level, the increasing share of GDP expended on health care reflects people's preferences.

Why might this be the case? Consider what happens when income grows over time, as it has in the United States and other industrialized countries. Consumption surely increases as income grows, and health spending probably rises as well. Because we are richer, we purchase more of all goods, including health care. But the key question is, Does health spending rise faster than consumption?

Perhaps surprisingly, standard models predict that it should. The prediction is rooted in a central theme in economics: the law of diminishing returns. According to this principle, the first $10,000 of consumption is incredibly valuable, the next $10,000 less valuable, and so on. The additional utility we get by increasing consumption falls as consumption rises. As people in the United States and elsewhere grow richer over time, consumption rises, and the return to increasing consumption falls.

Now consider the return to adding months of life. Adding additional months of life does not run into the same diminishing returns that increasing consumption within a month does. As we get richer, the marginal utility from another car, another television, or more clothing declines—there's barely enough time to enjoy the riches already available to the upper/middle class. Instead, what becomes increasingly valuable is *more time* to enjoy our high incomes—additional years of life. Economic models thus predict that while both consumption and health spending should rise as income increases, health spending should rise by more. Indeed, simulations based on such models suggest that it may be optimal for the United States to spend a third of our GDP on health by the middle of the century. And the share is predicted to rise even further as incomes continue to grow.[6]

[5] Joseph P. Newhouse, "Medical Care Costs: How Much Welfare Loss?" *Journal of Economic Perspectives*, vol. 6 (Summer 1992), pp. 3–21.

[6] Robert E. Hall and Charles I. Jones, "The Value of Life and the Rise in Health Spending," *Quarterly Journal of Economics*, February 2007, pp. 39–72.

The fiscal problem associated with rising health spending is clearly a difficult one to solve. If it were just a matter of increasing waste, one could argue that caps on spending and the elimination of waste might solve the problem. Instead, it seems likely that it is optimal for the health share of GDP to rise over time. Should the government play a large role in the provision of health care? In other advanced economies, where the government plays an even larger role in financing health spending, tax revenues will almost surely have to increase substantially to cover the rising health costs.

Eventually, as the health share continues to rise, it may be that alternative ways will have to be found to finance health care without raising taxes. Such alternatives might include private health insurance or mandated savings in individual health-spending accounts, although these alternatives may bring problems of their own. Determining how a society should finance rising health spending is likely to be one of the most important public policy questions we face over the next 50 years.[7]

17.7 Conclusion

Governments around the world play an important role in macroeconomics, as is evident from the relatively high shares of government purchases and spending relative to GDP. Many macroeconomic crises—including the Great Depression, the Great Inflation of the 1970s, and hyperinflations throughout the world—can be blamed at least in part on government mismanagement. In some cases, the fault may lie with monetary policy, antitrust policy, or bank regulation. However, in many cases, macroeconomic crises arise from problems with the government budget constraint. Economic growth is one of the magic elixirs that help to solve budget problems: a good example was the gradual but pronounced decline in the U.S. debt-GDP ratio following World War II.

One of the most important fiscal issues facing virtually all advanced economies of the world over the next 50 years is how to finance rapidly growing expenditures on health care. Here, the magic elixir of economic growth does not help but rather may be thought of as one of the causes of the problem. That is, as economic growth raises incomes, it may be desirable to spend an increasing fraction of our resources on health care. As people grow richer over time, one of the most valuable options for their spending is to purchase longer and better lives.

In the United States, government involvement in the financing of health care is substantial, and it is even larger in most other rich countries. Our current institutions—including the government and employer-provided health insurance—are likely to come under increasing strain in the next two decades, when new solutions for financing health care will be sorely needed.

---

[7] David Cutler, a professor at Harvard University, provides a nice general overview of these issues in his popular book *Your Money or Your Life: Strong Medicine for America's Health Care System* (New York: Oxford University Press, 2005).

CHAPTER REVIEW

SUMMARY

1. Prior to the Great Recession, the U.S. fiscal situation was relatively typical of recent decades: spending and taxes were low relative to most other rich countries, there was a modest budget deficit, and the debt-GDP ratio was not especially high.
2. The budget deficit rose sharply during the Great Recession, reaching more than 10 percent of GDP. The debt-GDP ratio rose to more than 60 percent. Neither number is dire in and of itself, but together they are more threatening given the next point.
3. This situation is likely to change significantly and for the worse in coming decades. The main reason is growth in transfer payments, especially for health care but also for Social Security.
4. The government's intertemporal budget constraint says that the budget must balance in a present discounted value sense. That is, the present discounted value of spending must equal the present discounted value of taxes, if the economy begins with no debt. To the extent that debt is initially present, tax revenues must exceed spending.
5. Very large debts are potentially problematic, leading to dangers of default and high inflation. However, there is no magic level of debt at which this occurs. An economy's size and growth prospects are important considerations, as is the ability of the government to collect taxes and restrain spending.
6. The extent to which government deficits crowd out investment is unclear. The Ricardian equivalence argument says that private saving should rise to offset temporary deficits, holding spending constant. This offset seems to be incomplete in the short run, however, as government saving and the investment rate move together.

KEY CONCEPTS

balanced budget
the budget balance
budget deficit
budget surplus
crowding out
the debt-GDP ratio
default
disposable income
the flow version of the government budget constraint
generational accounting
government debt
health spending
the intertemporal budget constraint
pay-as-you-go
primary deficit
total deficit

REVIEW QUESTIONS

1. How large is the current budget balance? What about the current debt-GDP ratio? Is the current fiscal situation especially troublesome? Why or why not?

2. Explain the flow version of the government budget constraint. Explain the government's intertemporal budget constraint.
3. How much can the government borrow?
4. What are three sources of saving that can be used to finance investment? What is "crowding out"?
5. What is the fiscal problem of the twenty-first century, and what are some possible solutions?

EXERCISES

smartwork.wwnorton.com 

1. **The U.S. federal budget:** Table 17.1 reports the composition of the federal budget as a percentage of GDP in 2008. Create a similar table using the latest available data from the *Economic Report of the President*. Has the composition of spending and taxes changed? What about the budget balance?

2. **The government's budget constraint:** What is the economic interpretation of the intertemporal budget constraint in equation (17.6)? Does this interpretation apply to the primary budget deficit or the total deficit? Why?

3. **The budget deficits of the 1980s and 2000s:** To what extent were the U.S. budget deficits of the 1980s and 2000s caused by higher spending versus lower tax revenues? Using the *Economic Report of the President*, explain which categories of spending or taxes were most responsible. As a share of GDP, what was the balance for the primary budget in 1985, 1999, 2006, and 2010? How does this compare with the total budget balance?

4. **The intertemporal budget constraint with three periods:** Consider an economy that exists for three periods: period 1, period 2, and period 3. In each period, the government must satisfy the budget constraint $B_{t+1} = (1 + i)B_t + G_t - T_t$.

   (a) Write this budget constraint for each period.
   (b) What must be true about B_4?
   (c) Using the result from part (b), solve the period 3 budget constraint for B_3, and substitute this back into the period 2 budget constraint.
   (d) Solve this new version of the period 2 budget constraint for B_2, and substitute the result back into the period 1 budget constraint.
   (e) At this point, you should have the intertemporal budget constraint for the three-period economy. Interpret this equation.

5. **The debt-GDP ratio:** This exercise allows you to use the government budget constraint to study how the debt-GDP ratio changes over time. Suppose a government has an initial debt of \$5 trillion, and the nominal interest rate is 5%.

   (a) If the government keeps its primary budget in balance, what is the growth rate of its debt? Why? [*Hint*: Look back at equation (17.2).]
   (b) If the government keeps its total budget in balance, what is the growth rate of its debt? Why?

(c) Suppose the country's GDP grows at 4% per year. What happens to the debt-GDP ratio over time in the two cases of parts (a) and (b)?

(d) Are the situations in part (c) sustainable? Why or why not?

6. **Ricardian equivalence and the government budget constraint:** Consider the intertemporal budget constraint in equation (17.5). Assume the interest rate is $i = 5\%$.

   (a) Suppose the government cuts taxes today by \$100 billion. Describe three possible ways the government can change spending and taxes to satisfy its budget constraint.

   (b) Suppose consumers obey the permanent-income hypothesis (discussed in Chapter 10). Would their consumption rise, fall, or stay the same for each of the alternatives considered in part (a)?

   (c) What happens to private saving, total saving, and investment in the three scenarios? Why? (Assume foreign saving does not change.)

7. **Debt-GDP ratios and economic crises:** The debt-GDP ratio in Belgium exceeded 120% in the early 1990s and has fallen to just over 80% more recently. Italy has had a debt-GDP ratio of about 100% for the last decade. The rapid rise in Japan's debt-GDP ratio was shown in Figure 17.4. Yet none of these economies experienced defaults or high inflation. In contrast, the debt-GDP ratio in Argentina peaked at 65% (up from 35% in 1996) and then a crisis struck, leading to default and other macroeconomic problems. How, broadly speaking, do we understand these very different outcomes?

8. **Deficits and investment:** Suppose the government decides to reduce taxes today by 1% of GDP, financed by higher borrowing, with the borrowing to be repaid 10 years from now with higher taxes. Discuss the various arguments about what effect this will have on the investment rate today.

9. **The fiscal problem of the twenty-first century:**

   (a) What is this problem? Is it limited to the United States?

   (b) To what extent is this fiscal problem driven by the Social Security program? By how much would taxes have to rise as a share of GDP in order to "solve" the Social Security problem?

   (c) How do you think the fiscal problem will likely be solved?

   (d) How would you suggest the problem be solved?

WORKED EXERCISE

5. **The debt-GDP ratio:**

   (a) The primary deficit is $G_t - T_t$: that is, it excludes interest payments. The government debt evolves according to

$$B_{t+1} = (1 + i)B_t + G_t - T_t.$$

So if the primary deficit is zero, the growth rate of the debt is just the interest rate i. In this case, the debt grows at 5% per year.

(b) The total (as opposed to primary) budget includes interest spending. If this budget is balanced, then $iB_t + G_t - T_t = 0$, and the level of debt is constant: its growth rate is 0. The change in the debt *is* the total budget balance.

(c) The growth rate of the debt-GDP ratio is equal to the growth rate of the debt minus the growth rate of GDP (this is just the growth rule for a ratio). If GDP grows at 4% per year, with the primary budget balanced, this means the debt-GDP ratio grows at a rate of 5% − 4% = 1%. In contrast, if the total budget is balanced, the debt-GDP ratio will decline at an annual rate of 4% per year.

(d) With GDP growth of 4%, the situation in part (a) is not sustainable: the debt-GDP ratio is growing, and eventually lenders will get worried about the ability of the economy to repay its debt. Something has to change. The situation in part (b), in contrast, is sustainable. The debt-GDP ratio declines relatively rapidly over time. If we wait long enough, GDP will be sufficiently high that it is quite easy to repay the debt. (For example, think about the case where the debt-GDP ratio falls to 0.01% of GDP.)

CHAPTER 18

INTERNATIONAL TRADE

OVERVIEW

In this chapter, we learn

- why countries trade goods and services, and why such trade can increase welfare.
- the roles of comparative advantage and risk-sharing in explaining trade between countries.
- the relationship between trade and the free flow of labor and capital across countries.
- that the U.S. trade deficit represents borrowing by the U.S. economy from the rest of the world, which must be repaid in the future.

> It is the maxim of every prudent master of a family never to attempt to make at home what it will cost him more to make than to buy. . . . If a foreign country can supply us with a commodity cheaper than we ourselves can make it, better buy it of them with some part of the produce of our own industry, employed in a way in which we have some advantage.
>
> —ADAM SMITH

18.1 Introduction

In the 1970s, some farmers in middle America (some say in Iowa) announced an amazing discovery: they had invented a new technology that would allow them to produce high-quality automobiles using nothing but corn as an input. To illustrate their new technology, the farmers traveled to San Francisco with train cars full of corn, loaded these onto a container ship, and told the assembled crowd to come back in a month. One month later, the crowd returned. When the train cars were opened, as if by magic, the corn had been replaced by brand-new, shiny cars.

This flight of fancy illustrates an important point: international trade can be viewed as an alternative technology for producing goods. In the old days, we could only produce cars by combining steel and autoworkers in Detroit. Then a new technology was discovered that would also allow us to "produce" cars with corn: the corn could be shipped to Japan and traded for cars. Discovering a new technology expands the production possibilities of an economy and offers an opportunity for increasing welfare, or economic well-being.

In this chapter, we analyze the effects of international trade on an economy. We begin by documenting some basic facts about trade, one of which is that the United States is running a large trade deficit, exceeding 5 percent of GDP in recent years. We are importing more goods and services than we are exporting. How do we evaluate this situation and its implications for the future?

We then consider four examples of international trade. The first makes the point that trade across countries is quite similar to trade across people within a country. The second considers the issue of trade deficits and how they can improve welfare. The third illustrates *comparative advantage*, one of the most important concepts in trade theory, while the fourth considers the relationship between trade and the free migration of labor.

The final part of the chapter uses these trade examples to shed light on the U.S. trade deficit. In particular, it outlines the relationship between saving, investment, and trade. We also look at the problem of *twin deficits*: the trade deficit and the government budget deficit.

Epigraph: From *The Wealth of Nations*, 1776.

Over the last 50 years, trade has become increasingly important in the U.S. economy.

FIGURE 18.1

U.S. Import and Export Shares of GDP, 1950–2009

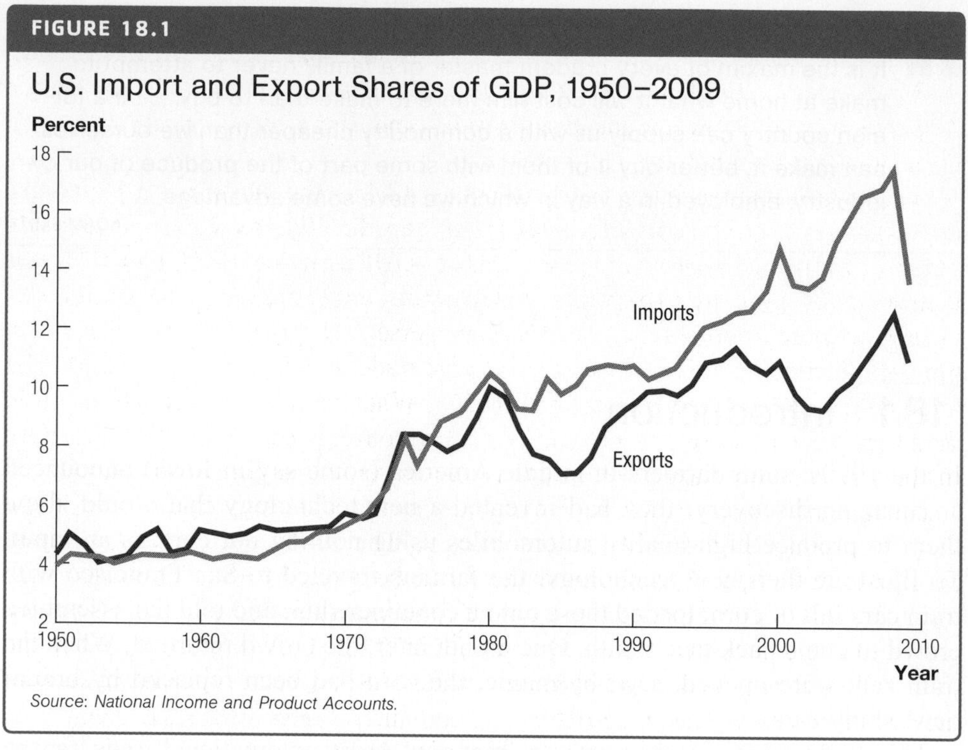

Source: National Income and Product Accounts.

18.2 Some Basic Facts about Trade

The first basic fact we consider is that international trade has increased dramatically over the last 50 years. Figure 18.1 shows this increase for the United States, but the same qualitative picture would emerge if we looked at a broad range of other countries.

In the United States, both imports and exports have risen from under 5 percent of GDP in the 1950s to as much as 12 or 17 percent of GDP before the financial crisis. Part of the explanation is a decline in the cost of transporting goods and services across countries. For example, average ocean freight charges per short ton declined from \$95 in 1920 to \$29 in 1990. An even sharper reduction is present in airline transportation: revenue per passenger-mile fell from 112 cents in 1930 to 11 cents in 2008. A three-minute phone call from New York to London cost more than \$250 in 1930, yet it can be made essentially for free today.[1]

Another part of the explanation for the rise in trade is a general decline in trade barriers such as tariffs and quotas throughout the world. As a result of international trade negotiations, the average worldwide tariff on manufacturing goods fell from about 14 percent in the early 1960s to 4 percent by 2000. Average tariff rates in many countries are now at relatively low levels.[2]

[1] These examples are taken from the *Economic Report of the President*, 1997, p. 243.

[2] The numbers for the worldwide tariff rate are taken from Kei-Mu Yi, "Can Vertical Specialization Explain the Growth of World Trade?" *Journal of Political Economy*, vol. 11, no. 1 (2003), pp. 52–102. Interestingly, though, Yi emphasizes that this decline in tariff rates is too small to explain much of the growth in world trade.

For most countries of the world, import and export shares of GDP are even larger than those in the United States. The shares in Canada, Chile, China, France, Germany, Russia, the United Kingdom, and Zimbabwe, for example, all exceed 20 percent of GDP. Argentina, Brazil, India, and Japan have import and export shares that are closer to the U.S. values.

Another interesting fact evident in Figure 18.1 is the widening gap between imports and exports. Figure 18.2 plots this gap directly by showing **the trade balance**, also called net exports, as a share of GDP. Between 1950 and 1975, the United States typically exhibited a trade surplus, exporting more goods and services than were imported. But the pattern reversed sharply after 1975. Since that time, the United States has experienced large trade deficits. Indeed, by 2006, the trade deficit had reached 5.7 percent of GDP. What explains the dramatic shift in the latter part of the twentieth century? What consequences does this shift have for the future? These are questions we will answer as the chapter develops.

An important observation in thinking about the U.S. trade deficit is that for the world as a whole, trade must be balanced. The world as a whole is a closed economy; the U.S. trade deficit must therefore be offset by trade surpluses in the rest of the world. Imagine the countries of the world grouped into two regions: the United States and the "Rest of the World." Then U.S. imports would equal, by definition, Rest of the World exports. And U.S. exports would equal Rest of the World imports. The trade deficit in the United States would be completely mirrored by a trade surplus in the Rest of the World.

To see where the Rest of the World's surplus comes from, consider Figure 18.3. The first bar for each country shows the country's trade balance as a share of GDP

FIGURE 18.2

The U.S. Trade Balance as a Share of GDP, 1950–2009

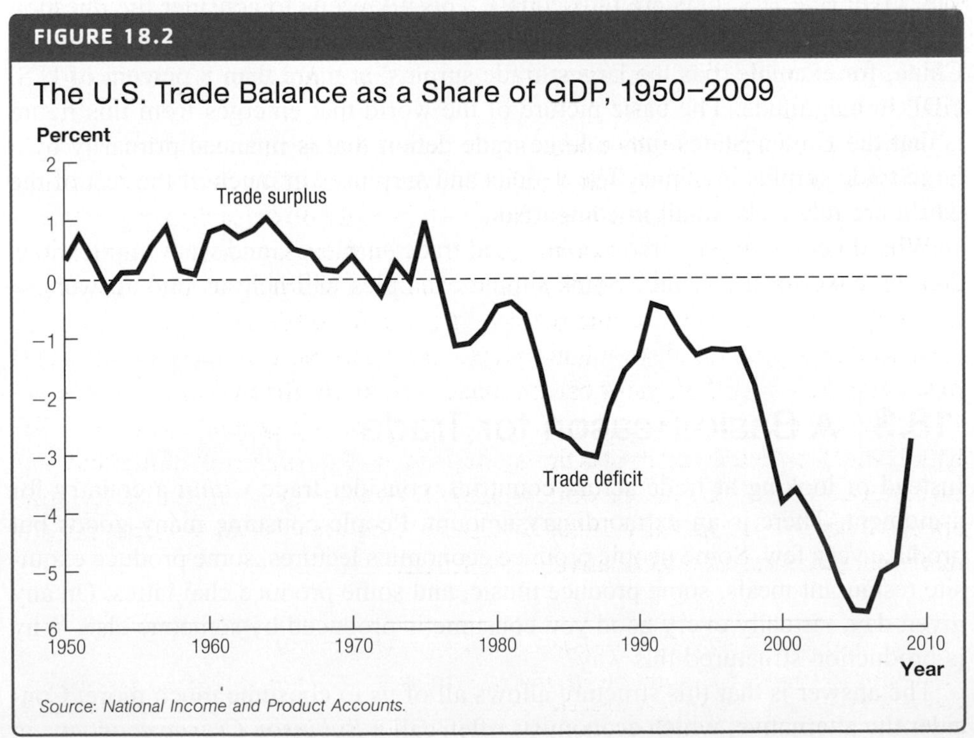

Source: National Income and Product Accounts.

The trade balance is another name for net exports: the difference between exports and imports. Large trade deficits reaching nearly 6 percent of GDP have emerged in the United States in recent years.

The first bar for each country shows the trade balance as a share of the country's GDP. The second bar represents the trade balance as a share of U.S. GDP. The U.S. trade deficit is financed by a trade surplus in the rest of the world.

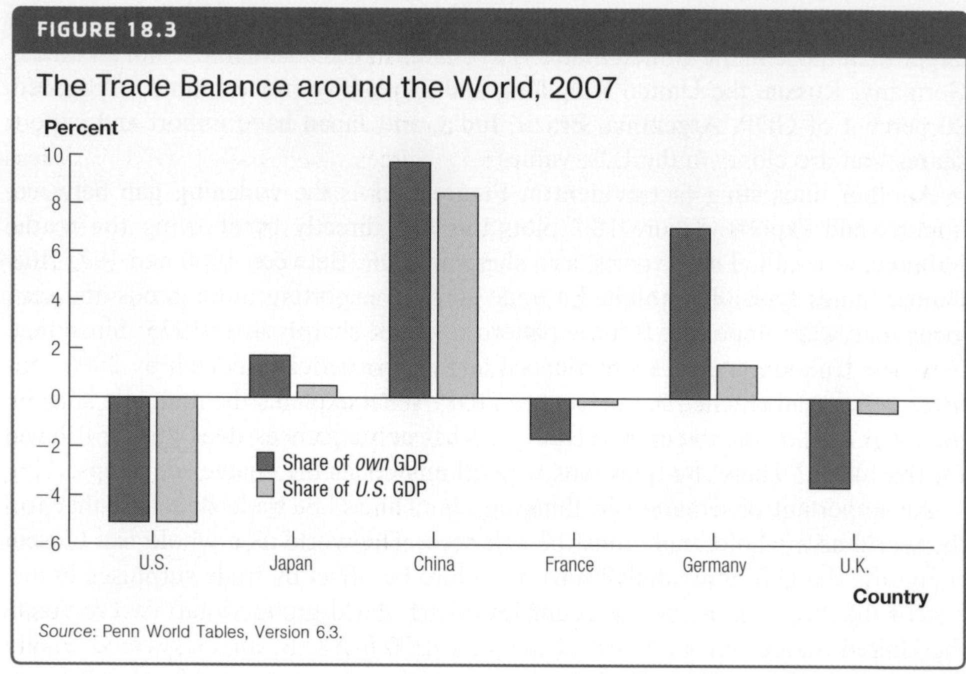

FIGURE 18.3

The Trade Balance around the World, 2007

Source: Penn World Tables, Version 6.3.

in the year 2007. The U.S. trade deficit that year was just over 5 percent of GDP. Japan, China, France, and Germany all ran trade surpluses, while the United Kingdom also experienced a trade deficit.

The second bar in the figure shows the country's trade balance as a share of *U.S.* GDP (the U.S. bars are thus equal). This allows us to consider the question of how the magnitude of the U.S. trade deficit is financed in the rest of the world. China, for example, has the largest trade surplus, at more than 8 percent of U.S. GDP in magnitude. The basic picture of the world that emerges from this figure is that the United States runs a large trade deficit that is financed primarily by a large trade surplus in China. The deficits and surpluses in much of the rest of the world are relatively small in comparison.

Why do countries run trade deficits and trade surpluses, and what implications do they have for the future? Some simple examples will help us find answers.

18.3 A Basic Reason for Trade

Instead of looking at trade across countries, consider trade *within* a country for a moment. There is an extraordinary amount. People consume many goods but produce very few. Some people produce economics lectures, some produce exquisite restaurant meals, some produce music, and some produce chai lattes. On any given day, virtually every good you consume is produced by someone else. Why is production structured this way?

The answer is that this structure allows all of us to consume much more. Consider the alternative, which economists often call a *Robinson Crusoe economy*, in which each person produces all the goods he or she consumes. If we were forced to eat crops that we farmed ourselves, make our own clothes, and provide our own medical services, most of us would be substantially worse off.

LeBron James, for example, specializes in playing basketball phenomenally well. He "trades" his performances on the court for the other goods and services he consumes. An alternative allocation of resources would have LeBron play less basketball, cook his own meals, build his own cars, and more generally live like Robinson Crusoe. But this would be a distinctly inferior way of organizing the economy. The basic motivation for international trade is the same as the motivation for trade within a country: people trade because they value goods that other people produce more at the margin than they value what they themselves own.

Consider a simple example of two island economies. Both countries are populated by people who like fish and bananas, and let's assume they prefer to consume equal quantities of both goods. But unfortunately, the islands are not endowed equally with fish and bananas. One island experiences poor weather for growing bananas but happens to be located in good fishing waters. The other enjoys an abundant supply of banana trees and good weather, but its geography makes it not a particularly good place to fish.

Suppose the first economy is endowed with 250 bananas and 750 fish, while the second is endowed with 750 bananas and 250 fish (these are annual, per capita quantities, and we assume the two islands have the same number of people). In the absence of trade across the islands, people of both islands would consume a bundle of goods that is less than ideal. Trade between the two yields an improvement in welfare: if the islands trade 250 fish for 250 bananas, consumers on both islands will be at their optimal consumption mix of 500 bananas and 500 fish.

So this is the first point about international trade: it is really no different from trade within a country, and gains from trade lie at the heart of economics. Just as welfare is increased when we allow people within an economy to trade the different goods they produce, qualitatively similar welfare gains are possible when there is trade between economies.

18.4 Trade across Time

In the banana-fish example, the pattern of trade is constant over time. Trade is *balanced*: that is, neither island is running a trade surplus or a trade deficit.[3] As we saw earlier, however, many countries exhibit trade deficits or surpluses. In the last 25 years, the United States has consistently run a trade deficit, while Japan has run a trade surplus. How do we understand these facts?

Consider two islands once again, but now suppose there is only a single good, wheat. Because of the vagaries of the weather, in some years one island enjoys an excellent harvest, while in other years the other island does. In odd years, Oddtopia reaps the good wheat harvest, which corresponds to 100 bushels of wheat, while in even years a hurricane hits Oddtopia, completely wiping out its wheat crop. Eventopia follows exactly the same pattern, but with the good harvest coming in even years. The harvests are shown in Table 18.1.

[3] To make this point more precise, we would have to calculate prices and value the trade of bananas for fish. We do something like this in Section 18.5 below.

TABLE 18.1

Wheat Harvests in Oddtopia and Eventopia

Year	1	2	3	4	5	6
			Wheat harvest			
Oddtopia	100	0	100	0	100	0
Eventopia	0	100	0	100	0	100
			Trade balance			
Oddtopia	+50	−50	+50	−50	+50	−50
Eventopia	−50	+50	−50	+50	−50	+50
			Consumption			
Oddtopia	50	50	50	50	50	50
Eventopia	50	50	50	50	50	50

The table shows the amount of wheat harvested every year in Oddtopia and Eventopia.

As is standard, we assume that the diminishing marginal utility of consumption means people in both countries would prefer to smooth their consumption over time. We also assume that wheat is perishable, so that it can't be stored over the years. In the absence of trade, then, the islanders would suffer from a terrible boom-bust cycle. What could be done to alleviate this problem?

Suppose each island takes half of its harvest during a good year and ships it to the other island as a loan. Oddtopia begins in year 1 by shipping 50 bushels of wheat to Eventopia. In return, the Oddtopians receive a promissory note from the Eventopians saying that they will repay the loan the next year. Sure enough, in year 2, the Eventopians ship half their harvest to Oddtopia to repay the debt. Oddtopia is happy with this arrangement because the repayment comes at exactly the time when its harvest is low.

In this example, international trade functions as intertemporal trade—that is, trade over time. This intertemporal trade allows the countries to smooth out the risk associated with a bad harvest. In good years, one country runs a trade surplus, as it exports wheat. In Table 18.1, this trade surplus is shown as a positive trade balance of 50 bushels. In bad years, the country runs a trade deficit, as it imports wheat (for a negative trade balance of 50 bushels). These flows of goods occur in parallel with financial transactions that document the lending and repayment of the loan, and both islands are better off because of this intertemporal trade. In particular, both enjoy a constant stream of consumption of 50 bushels of wheat even though their production fluctuates dramatically. International trade here allows for perfect **risk-sharing**.

The example also illustrates an important principle: *in the long run, trade must be balanced*. In our example, the average value of the trade balance is equal to zero for both countries. The presence of a trade surplus or deficit reflects international lending or borrowing. And, of course, no one is willing to lend unless they will be repaid. This means that trade must be balanced in the long run.

We could make this argument more precise by constructing an intertemporal budget constraint, as we did for government borrowing in Chapter 17 (the math is similar). In this case, though, the constraint would apply to the country as a whole rather than to the government. And the intertemporal budget constraint for a country says that the present discounted value of the trade balance must be equal to zero. Deficits today represent borrowing from the rest of the world that must be repaid by surpluses in the future.

Applied to the real world, this principle has a startling implication. Since the United States has been running a trade deficit for the last 25 years, the rest of the world has been lending goods and services to the United States for the last 25 years. The only way the rest of the world is willing to make these loans is if it knows the loans will be repaid. And the repayment should show up in a precise way; the United States must be expected to run large trade surpluses at some point in the future.

The implication of this reasoning can be seen by considering the national income identity. Recall that this identity says that $Y = C + I + G + NX$. Total production Y gets used as consumption, investment, government purchases, or net exports. Rewriting this identity, we see that

$$NX < 0 \Rightarrow C + I + G > Y. \tag{18.1}$$

That is, when a country is running a trade deficit so that it is importing more than it is exporting, $NX \equiv EX - IM$ is negative. From the national income identity, this means that the sum of the domestic uses of goods and services can exceed production.

But when the borrowing must be repaid, the inequalities switch the other way. At some point, net exports must be positive; the only way we repay the goods and services that other countries have sent us is by sending those goods and services back. And then we have

$$NX > 0 \Rightarrow C + I + G < Y. \tag{18.2}$$

That is, some of what is produced must be shipped abroad, leaving less available for domestic uses.

Running a trade deficit is not necessarily a bad thing. In our example, Eventopia and Oddtopia both benefit by being able to run trade deficits. The borrowing allows the people in both countries to smooth their consumption over time. More generally, a country can run a trade deficit (that is, it can borrow) when it expects rapid growth in the future, or when it has productive investments to make—knowing that at some point, the borrowing must be repaid.

18.5 Trade with Production

Our third example is the most involved, but the payoff is that it will allow us to look into a wide range of issues, including specialization and outsourcing. Here, our two countries are called the North and the South. We assume that people in these countries consume two goods, apples and computers, and they prefer to spend half of their budget on apples and half on computers.[4]

[4] If a denotes apples and c denotes computers, then an example of preferences that will deliver this result is $U = a^{1/2}c^{1/2}$, where U denotes utility.

TABLE 18.2

The Setup of the North-South Example

	North	South
Labor force	100	400
Number of apples one worker can produce	160	100
Number of computers one worker can produce	16	2

For the rest of the setup, look at Table 18.2. We assume the North is the smaller country, with a labor force of 100 workers, while the South contains 400 workers. The workers in the North, however, are more productive in both sectors than the workers in the South. A single worker in the North can produce either 160 apples or 16 computers, while a single worker in the South can only produce 100 apples or 2 computers.

The fact that the Northern workers are more productive at both activities is called an **absolute advantage**. One of the deep insights of economics is that even when one economy has an absolute advantage in producing all goods—as the North does in this example—there may still be gains from trade. Nobel Prize winner Paul Samuelson refers to this fact as a classic example of a fundamental result in economics that is far from obvious.

What makes gains from trade possible? Notice that the productivity advantage for the North is much larger in producing computers than in producing apples: a worker in the North can produce 8 times as many computers as a worker in the South, but only 1.6 times as many apples. In this case, we say the North has a **comparative advantage** in producing computers, and it's this advantage that allows room for trade, as we will see.

We now analyze these two economies under two different regimes. In the first regime, we assume both economies are closed to trade, a situation called **autarky**. In the second, we will open the economies up to trade and see what happens.

Autarky

Again, we are assuming that people in both countries spend half their income on apples and half on computers. Let w denote the wage of a worker, and assume each worker supplies one unit of labor, so that w is also the worker's income. Then,

$$\frac{\text{price of apples} \times \text{consumption of apples}}{\text{wage, } w} = \frac{1}{2} \tag{18.3}$$

and

$$\frac{\text{price of computers} \times \text{consumption of computers}}{\text{wage, } w} = \frac{1}{2}. \tag{18.4}$$

Next, we need to decide the units in which we will quote our prices: let's quote all of our prices in apples (the numéraire). So the price of an apple is 1 (apple), by assumption. If p denotes the price of a computer, then one computer costs p apples.

Now we use these assumptions to characterize the North and the South when there is no trade—under autarky. To use equations (18.3) and (18.4) to solve for the consumption of the two goods, we need to know the wage w and the price of computers p. We assume workers are free to work in either sector, producing either apples or computers. What must the wage be equal to? Well, since we are quoting our prices (including the wage) in units of apples, it must be the case that the wage is equal to the number of apples a worker can produce. From Table 18.2, this is just 160 apples in the North and 100 apples in the South; these are the wages in the two countries.

What about the price of a computer? One worker can produce either 160 apples or 16 computers in the North. It must be the case, then, that in the North the price of a computer is 10 apples (that is, 160/16). Why? If computers were more expensive, if they sold for, say, 100 apples, then everyone would want to produce computers, because one worker could produce 16 computers and sell them for 100 apples each, for a total income of 1,600 apples (as opposed to producing only 160 apples by working in the apple sector). Similarly, in the South, since one worker can produce either 100 apples or 2 computers, the price of a computer in the South must be 50 apples.

The wages and prices of computers in the North and South are summarized in Table 18.3. Notice that the wage is higher and computers are cheaper in the North than in the South. Both of these facts are consistent with the absolute advantage that the North has in producing both goods.

Now we can use these facts about wages and prices to find the consumption of apples and computers in the two countries. Looking back at equations (18.3) and (18.4), we see that since the price of an apple is 1 (apple) by assumption, the consumption of apples is just half the wage: 80 apples in the North, and 50 apples in the South. Similarly, the consumption of computers amounts to 8 computers in the North and 1 computer in the South. Half the workers in each country work to produce apples, and half work to produce computers.

The results are summarized in the bottom half of Table 18.3. Obviously, workers in the North are better off than workers in the South because they are better

TABLE 18.3

The North and the South under Autarky

	North	South
Wage, w	160 apples	100 apples
Price of a computer, p	10 apples	50 apples
Consumption of apples (per person)	80 apples	50 apples
Consumption of computers (per person)	8 computers	1 computer
Fraction of labor working to produce apples	50%	50%
Fraction of labor working to produce computers	50%	50%
Total production in the apple sector	8,000 apples	20,000 apples
Total production in the computer sector	800 computers	400 computers

at producing both computers and apples. Not much surprising has happened so far. This will change once trade is allowed.

Free Trade

Is there any clue in the autarky example that when trade *is* allowed, something interesting might occur? The key clue is that computers sell for different prices in the two regions: they are expensive in the South (50 apples) relative to the North (10 apples). Suppose you were allowed to trade in this world. You would want to buy computers in the North, where they are cheap, and sell them in the South, where they are expensive—an opportunity known as **arbitrage**. Unless the price of a computer adjusts, this would allow you the opportunity to make lots of money. It is exactly this opportunity that gives rise to the gains from trade.

In fact, this price difference is one of the defining features of comparative advantage: it implies that the North has a comparative advantage in producing computers. But it also implies that the South has a comparative advantage in producing apples. Why? Essentially, apples are cheap relative to computers in the South; in particular, apples are cheaper in the South than in the North.

A country has an *absolute* advantage over another in producing a particular good if it does so more cheaply. A country has a *comparative* advantage over another in producing a particular good if the relative price of that good–the price of the good relative to other goods produced in the economy–is lower.

The North is *relatively* good at producing computers and the South is relatively good at producing apples. If trade is allowed, the North might benefit from producing more computers and the South might benefit from producing more apples. Just like LeBron James, countries specialize in the goods they are best at producing.

So let's assume now that the North and the South completely specialize: the North puts all its workers into producing computers, and the South puts all its workers into producing apples. Since 100 workers each produce 16 computers, the North now produces 1,600 computers. And since 400 workers each produce 100 apples, the South now produces 40,000 apples. These facts are summarized in Table 18.4.

Solving for the world price of a computer is a little more complicated in the case of free trade. For now, we'll make an educated guess at the solution and then confirm that it is correct. The world now produces 40,000 apples and 1,600

TABLE 18.4

The North and South with Free Trade

	North	South
Fraction of labor working to produce apples	100%	100%
Fraction of labor working to produce computers	100%	100%
Total production in the apple sector	0 apples	40,000 apples
Total production in the computer sector	1,600 computers	0 computers
Wage, w	400 apples	100 apples
World price of a computer, p	25 apples per computer	
Consumption of apples (per person)	**200 apples**	50 apples
Consumption of computers (per person)	8 computers	**2 computers**

computers. In the autarky case, the price of a computer was given by the ratio of the production of apples to the production of computers (160/16 in the North, 100/2 in the South). Let's guess that this is also true for the world as a whole. Therefore, the price of a computer is 40,000/1,600 = 25 apples.

Now it is easy to derive the wages in the North and the South. In the South, the wage is simply 100 apples, as before, since this is the number of apples a worker can produce. In the North, a worker can produce 16 computers, and each computer is worth $p = 25$ apples, so the wage is $16 \times 25 = 400$ apples, much higher than the autarky wage of 160 apples.

Finally, to figure out welfare, we need to know how consumption changes. Our basic assumption that consumers in each country spend half their income on apples and half on computers still holds, so we can compute consumption using equations (18.3) and (18.4). Consumption of apples is just half the wage, since the price of an apple is 1. Northern workers thus eat 200 apples, and Southern workers eat 50 apples. Consumption of computers is half the wage divided by the price of a computer. So Northern workers consume 8 computers (200/25) and Southern workers consume 2 computers (50/25).

Notice that workers in both countries are better off. The world price of computers is higher than the autarky price in the North, and the Northern workers can use this higher price to buy more apples, 200 instead of 80. Similarly, the world price of computers is lower than the autarky price in the South, and Southern workers can therefore purchase more computers, 2 instead of 1.

Finally, we can check that our "guess" of the world price of computers was correct by confirming that the world markets for computers and apples clear. The world supply of computers is 1,600. The world demand is the sum of $8 \times 100 = 800$ in the North and $2 \times 400 = 800$ in the South, for a total of 1,600. The world supply of apples is 40,000. The world demand is the sum of $200 \times 100 = 20{,}000$ in the North and $50 \times 400 = 20{,}000$ in the South, for a total of 40,000. Since both markets clear at this world price, our guess was correct and we have successfully solved the model.[5]

Lessons from the Apple-Computer Example

The main lesson from this third example is the same one we learned in the original banana and fish example: allowing two countries to trade makes people in both countries better off. Before trade, computers were more expensive in the South than in the North, and apples were more expensive in the North than in the South. Trade allows people in the North to buy their apples in the South, where they are cheap. And trade allows people in the South to buy their computers in the North, where they are cheap. In this example, people in both countries are made better off by allowing free trade. This aspect of our example generalizes considerably. Indeed, one of the main lessons from international economics is that in the absence of frictions—more on this in a moment—trade improves efficiency and welfare.

[5] If the markets did not clear, then we could try a new guess. Or even better, we could write the supply and demand for computers as a function of the world price and solve for the price that clears the market.

Notice in particular that this is true of the South as well as the North. We might be tempted to think that the South is actually somewhat worse off: after all, trade "forces" Southern workers out of the high-tech computer sector and into the low-tech agricultural sector. Wouldn't the South be better off if it produced some computers? Our example shows why this is not the case: because the North is so much better at producing computers, it is cheaper for the South to buy computers from the North than to produce computers itself.

18.6 Trade in Inputs

There is another kind of institutional innovation that has the potential to improve welfare by even more than free trade. This innovation is to open economies up to the free migration of labor.

What happens in the North-South example if workers are allowed to work wherever they please? The answer is straightforward: wages are higher in the North than in the South, and so all the workers in the South would head north. Since the North has an absolute advantage at producing all goods, it is more efficient to have all production occur in the North. Whereas free trade is about comparative advantage, free migration is about absolute advantage.

The world economy with free migration of labor thus looks like the Northern economy under autarky: everyone is working in the North. So we can simply look back at the "North" column in Table 18.3 to see the outcome. The results are reproduced with more detail in Table 18.5. Since Northerners and Southerners are identical, their wages and consumption bundles are all the same.

Workers originally from the North see no change in their welfare relative to autarky. The economy exhibits constant returns to scale, so that adding new workers to the mix doesn't at all affect the welfare of the Northerners. However, access to the superior Northern productivity does improve the welfare of the workers from the South: they now consume 80 apples and 8 computers each instead of the 50 apples and 1 computer they had under autarky.

TABLE 18.5

Northern and Southern Workers with Free Migration

	Workers born in the North	Migrants from the South
Wage, w	160 apples	160 apples
Price of a computer, p	10 apples	
Consumption of apples (per person)	80 apples	80 apples
Consumption of computers (per person)	8 computers	8 computers
Fraction of labor working to produce apples	50%	
Fraction of labor working to produce computers	50%	
Total production in the apple sector	40,000 apples	
Total production in the computer sector	4,000 computers	

If we compare the two institutions from our North-South example, free trade and free migration, we find that Southern workers receive all the welfare gain under the free migration regime, while the welfare gain is shared under the free trade regime. Northern workers would therefore strictly prefer free trade to free migration: under free trade, the Northerners eat 200 apples each rather than just 80.

It is important to notice, however, that the world as a whole is more efficient under the free migration institution. Comparing Table 18.4 with Table 18.5 shows us that the world produces more output with free migration.[6] The reason is again the absolute advantage. Because the North exhibits higher productivity in both sectors, the efficient allocation of labor sends all workers to the North.

This means that with free migration, there is room for welfare to improve in both the North and the South. In moving from free trade to free migration, the gains to the South are larger than the losses to the North. In principle, then, the South could more than compensate the North for these losses and still achieve gains itself. Suppose the North charged an entry fee to Southern workers and transferred the revenue from these fees to the Northern workers. Since the gains to the South are larger than the losses to the North, there exists a range of fees that the North could charge that would make all workers in the world better off. An exercise at the end of the chapter will allow you to calculate such a fee.

Moving Capital versus Moving Labor

In our study of the Solow growth model in Chapters 4 and 5, we found that the gains from free capital mobility were relatively small, although the result wasn't expressed in quite that way. What we found was that poor countries are not really poor because they own too little capital (though this is true). Instead, the main reason they are poor is that they have very low total factor productivity. Allowing capital to flow to these low-productivity areas would not do much to solve the problem. As we saw, even if these regions possessed the same amount of capital (or the same investment rate) as the rich countries, they would still be poor.

Free migration—sometimes called "free labor mobility"—is more effective because it moves labor to the place where productivity is high. It therefore addresses the main problem directly and offers the possibility of much larger improvements in welfare. It may be quite hard to figure out how to increase productivity in Kenya, but if Kenyans were allowed to move freely to the United States and Western Europe, the evidence suggests that their wages would rise considerably.

There are certainly other considerations related to the free migration of labor. However, the potentially enormous gains to workers in very poor countries—and the fact that some of these gains can be shared with potential losers in the rich countries—must be taken into account in any discussion of the issue.[7]

[6] To be precise, the world produces more computers and the same number of apples. In other examples, the output of both goods can rise.

[7] On the potential wage gains, see Lutz Hendricks, "How Important Is Human Capital for Development? Evidence from Immigrant Earnings," *American Economic Review*, vol. 92 (March 2002), pp. 198–219. For more general discussions, see George J. Borjas, *Heaven's Door: Immigration Policy and the American Economy* (Princeton, N.J.: Princeton University Press, 2001), and the Summer 1995 issue of the *Journal of Economic Perspectives*.

18.7 The Costs of Trade

In the apple and computer example, the reallocation of workers in the North and the South occurs seamlessly. Apple farmers in the North become computer producers overnight, and computer makers in the South become farmers. In our model, both groups are made better off by this change, but the scenario has a somewhat unrealistic feel to it. Farmers in the North lose their jobs, and computer producers in the South lose theirs. Doesn't trade make these workers worse off? And couldn't these losses be large enough for trade to reduce welfare overall? In the model, the answer is no, because the workers immediately find better jobs in the other sector. In practice, however, it may be very difficult for farmers to become computer makers, and vice versa.

In reality, of course, there are often significant costs associated with switching jobs. Finding a new job may take time, and workers may go through spells of unemployment. Moreover, the skills of the farmers are not necessarily the same as the skills required to make computers. Many farmers may never be able to make the switch into the computer sector, at least not without significant new training.

How large are the job losses and reallocation costs associated with international trade? This is a difficult question to answer. Lori Kletzer of the University of California at Santa Cruz estimates that as many as 7.5 million workers in the manufacturing sector of the U.S. economy—including autoworkers in Michigan, steelworkers in Pennsylvania, and textile workers in North Carolina—may have lost their jobs because of competition from imports between 1979 and 2001. Because overall employment in these industries has been declining, the workers may be displaced for a long period of time.[8]

In richer models of international trade that incorporate these reallocation costs, the general finding is that trade can yield "winners" and "losers" within each country. The gains to the winners are typically larger than the losses to the losers. While some steelworkers may lose their jobs when steel is imported, the benefit is that everyone in the economy is able to buy cars at slightly lower prices. The job losses are typically concentrated in specific industries, while the benefits may be spread thinly over the entire economy. Large costs to relatively few steelworkers must be weighed against small benefits to hundreds of millions of consumers.

The fact that losses are concentrated on particular groups and regions while benefits are spread thinly across the economy creates a problem for capturing the gains from trade. On the one hand, free trade can, in principle, improve welfare for everyone. The winners could compensate the losers and there would still be additional gains to go around. On the other hand, when the benefits aren't shared, the costs associated with trade can be visible and substantial. Communities that have been founded on a particular industry can see sustained job losses, high unemployment rates, and significant changes in their way of life.

---

[8] See Lori G. Kletzer, "Globalization and Job Loss, from Manufacturing to Services," *Economic Perspectives*, Federal Reserve Bank of Chicago, Second Quarter 2005, pp. 38–46.

A first-order issue in capturing the gains from trade is therefore figuring out how best to share the benefits with the people who are most directly harmed. A strong social safety net and job-retraining programs are surely part of the solution. But how these should be designed and implemented is not well understood. Economists must do a better job on this front, as the case study below attests.

CASE STUDY

Outsourcing: Separating the Fiction and Fact

In recent years, concern over the outsourcing of U.S. jobs to foreign countries has received a great deal of political and popular attention. In previous decades, international trade led to the loss of blue-collar jobs in the United States, but now, so the argument goes, trade is climbing the ladder, and white-collar jobs are being exported as well. Why pay a computer programmer $75,000 per year in Silicon Valley when the same work can be done for a tenth the cost in Bangalore, India? Concerns over such outsourcing have been fueled by ominous forecasts of millions of high-tech jobs being moved overseas in the coming decade.

Gregory Mankiw, an economics professor at Harvard University, served as chair of the President's Council of Economic Advisers from 2003 to 2005. During his tenure, the council addressed the outsourcing debate in the 2004 *Economic Report of the President*:

> Outsourcing of professional services is a prominent example of a new type of trade. The gains from trade that takes place over the Internet or telephone lines are no different than the gains from trade in physical goods transported by ship or plane. When a good or service is produced at lower cost in another country, it makes sense to import it rather than to produce it domestically. This allows the United States to devote its resources to more productive purposes. (p. 25)

Mankiw and his colleagues were simply pointing out that the arguments of comparative advantage and free trade have not been repealed by the discovery of the Internet. Nevertheless, this conventional wisdom among economists set off a political backlash from both parties, as members of Congress and the president sought to distance themselves from the report. Sadly, economists have not done a sufficiently good job of educating the public on the benefits of free trade, and perhaps have not done enough to ensure that the benefits are shared in a way that the losses are not inappropriately concentrated.

As for the current debate over outsourcing, the evidence supports the conventional economic wisdom. Jagdish Bhagwati and Arvind Panagariya of Columbia University and T. N. Srinivasan of Yale University debunk the alarmists' claims in a *Journal of*

Economic Perspectives article entitled "The Muddles over Outsourcing."[9] The authors make two key points. First, the volume of jobs being outsourced is quite small when compared with the overall size of the U.S. economy. Even the most extreme estimates imply that only half of 1 percent of the relevant job pool is being outsourced.

Second, outsourcing has been going on for decades, and the gains outweigh the losses. As just one example, Matthew Slaughter of Dartmouth College studied the outsourcing of jobs by U.S. multinational corporations between 1991 and 2001.[10] During this period, he found, employment in the foreign affiliates of U.S. multinationals increased by 2.8 million jobs. However, employment in the United States by these same companies rose by even more, by 5.5 million jobs. For every job that was outsourced, the same companies created two domestic jobs. This is by no means proof that the outsourcing of jobs helped the U.S. economy; after all, it could be that these jobs were gained at the expense of other companies. But in weighing the costs of outsourcing, we should also consider the substantial gains associated with the "insourcing" of high-quality jobs to U.S. firms. Overall, the bulk of the empirical evidence suggests that trade and outsourcing are good for the economy as a whole.[11]

Trade allows economies to focus on activities in which they are more productive and hence provides long-term benefits. Again, this does not mean that there are no costs, only that the benefits to society as a whole outweigh the costs to those who lose.

More than 150 years ago, the French economist Frederic Bastiat wrote of a similar debate concerning the "ruinous competition" of a foreign rival in his satirical "Petition from the Manufacturers of Candles":

> We are suffering from the ruinous competition of a rival who apparently works under conditions so far superior to our own for the production of light that he is flooding the domestic market with it at an incredibly low price; for the moment he appears, our sales cease, all the consumers turn to him, and a branch of French industry whose ramifications are innumerable is all at once reduced to complete stagnation. This rival . . . is none other than the sun.

18.8 The Trade Deficit and Foreign Debt

Up to this point, we have analyzed various aspects of trade theory: why countries trade, why countries might run trade deficits, how trade promotes specialization, and how migration and trade are different approaches to productivity differences

---

[9] The article appears in the Fall 2004 issue on pp. 93–114.

[10] Matthew Slaughter, "Globalization and Employment by U.S. Multinationals: A Framework and Facts," *Daily Tax Report*, March 26, 2004.

[11] Exercise 6 at the end of the chapter provides an interesting qualification of this point.

across countries. With this theoretical background, we are ready to return to one of the key facts that began this chapter: the large and rising U.S. trade deficit. What we know from our trade models is that trade deficits can be good things, because they allow countries to smooth their consumption over time. A country may want to run a large trade deficit if it expects to be appreciably richer in the future. Actually, we need something more than this: it must be that a country's growth is expected to be faster than the growth rate in the world as a whole.

The large U.S. trade deficits, then, would be understandable if we thought the U.S. economy were likely to grow faster than the world as a whole in coming years. Do we think that? Probably not. As we saw earlier, the U.S. economy has grown more slowly than the world as a whole in the last 50 years, as much of the rest of the world develops.

Trade and Growth around the World

Let's revisit this prediction of the trade model: do countries that grow rapidly experience large trade deficits as they borrow against their future income to finance high levels of consumption today? Figure 18.4 shows the average trade balance for five rapidly growing countries in the world from 1990 until 2007. What we see here is quite striking. With one exception, the countries all show trade surpluses rather than deficits. This suggests that the "permanent-income hypothesis" version of trade theory—the idea that countries will borrow and run trade deficits when they are expecting rapid growth in order to smooth their consumption—may not hold up especially well.

What else could be going on? Maybe it is not rapid growth causing a large trade deficit, but instead a trade surplus that promotes rapid growth. That is, perhaps these countries are opening themselves up to international competition and forcing their

FIGURE 18.4

The Trade Balance in Rapidly Growing Countries, 1990–2007

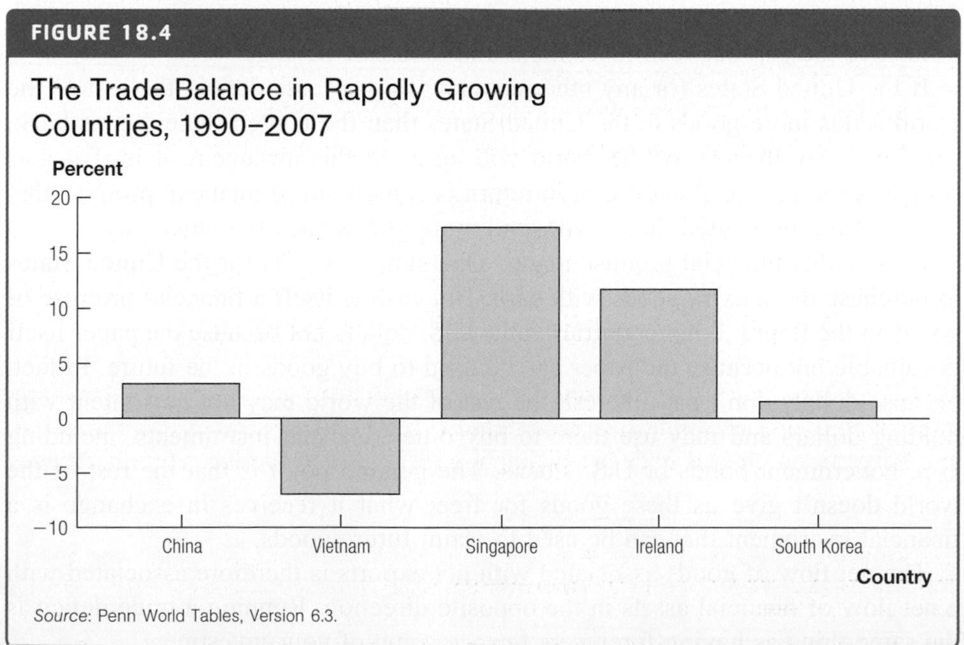

Source: Penn World Tables, Version 6.3.

The figure shows the average trade balance as a percentage of a country's own GDP for five rapidly growing countries in the world. These countries tend to have trade surpluses, not deficits.

firms to compete with the best producers in the world. They could be simultaneously rewarding firms that export a great deal with subsidies, and the subsidies may promote exports at the expense of imports, leading to a trade surplus.

The Twin Deficits

An alternative and useful perspective on trade deficits comes from looking at the national income identity, $Y = C + I + G + NX$. In Chapter 17, we saw that the national income identity implies that investment in an economy is equal to total saving:

$$\underbrace{(Y - T - C)}_{\text{private saving}} + \underbrace{(T - G)}_{\text{government saving}} + \underbrace{(IM - EX)}_{\text{foreign saving}} = I. \quad (18.5)$$

We can manipulate this relationship further by defining $S \equiv (Y - T - C) + (T - G)$ as domestic saving, equal to the sum of private saving and government saving. With this definition, we can rearrange the IS (investment = savings) version of the national income identity as

$$\underbrace{NX}_{\text{trade balance}} = \underbrace{S - I}_{\text{net capital outflow}} \quad (18.6)$$

This is an important version of the national income identity. It relates the international flow of goods, the trade balance, to the international flow of capital—the difference between domestic saving and investment. The United States runs a trade deficit; it also invests more than it saves. This version of the national income identity shows that these characteristics are really just two sides of the same coin: the trade deficit *is* the additional borrowing that the United States does to finance the gap between investment and domestic saving.

If the United States (or any other country) runs a trade deficit, the rest of the world sends more goods to the United States than the United States sends back. The only way the rest of the world will agree to this arrangement is if it gets something in return. What it gets in return is some kind of financial promise that in the future the United States will send more goods back the other way.

How is this financial promise made? One simple way is for the United States to purchase these extra goods with cash. But cash is itself a financial promise of goods in the future: other countries value U.S. dollars not because the paper itself is valuable but because the paper can be used to buy goods in the future. In fact, because dollars don't pay interest, the rest of the world may not be content with holding dollars and may use them to buy other financial instruments, including U.S. government bonds or U.S. stocks. The general point is that the rest of the world doesn't give us these goods for free; what it receives in exchange is a financial instrument that can be used to claim future goods.

The net flow of goods associated with net exports is therefore associated with a net flow of financial assets in the opposite direction. Running a trade deficit is the same thing as having foreigners finance some of your investment.

This last point helps us to see again why it is so puzzling that an economy like China's would run a trade surplus. China's economy is growing rapidly, and one would think that it would benefit tremendously from foreign investment. This is in fact the case: there is a lot of foreign investment in China. What is also true, however, is that China has so much domestic saving—the sum of private and government saving—that its domestic saving exceeds its investment. The result is that China ships some of its goods and services abroad and invests more abroad than foreigners invest in China.

The United States today is in the opposite situation. Our private saving is roughly equal to private investment, but a large budget deficit is paired with a large trade deficit, as shown in Figure 18.5. At the same time, however, the overall private investment rate has not really declined. Instead, foreigners have stepped in to provide the additional savings needed to cover the budget deficits. This was true in the 1980s, and the same thing appears to be occurring, at least partially, in recent years, as the large rise in the budget deficit is accompanied by a smaller decline in investment and an increase in the trade deficit. This phenomenon is called the emergence of the **twin deficits**.

Net Foreign Assets and Foreign Debt

The trade deficit represents borrowing by U.S. residents from the rest of the world. Regardless of how the borrowing affects investment, it will have to be repaid at some point in the future. One way of viewing this borrowing is that the trade deficits of the last 30 years or so will have to be offset by future trade surpluses.

FIGURE 18.5

U.S. Investment, Budget Deficit, and Trade Deficit, 1960–2009

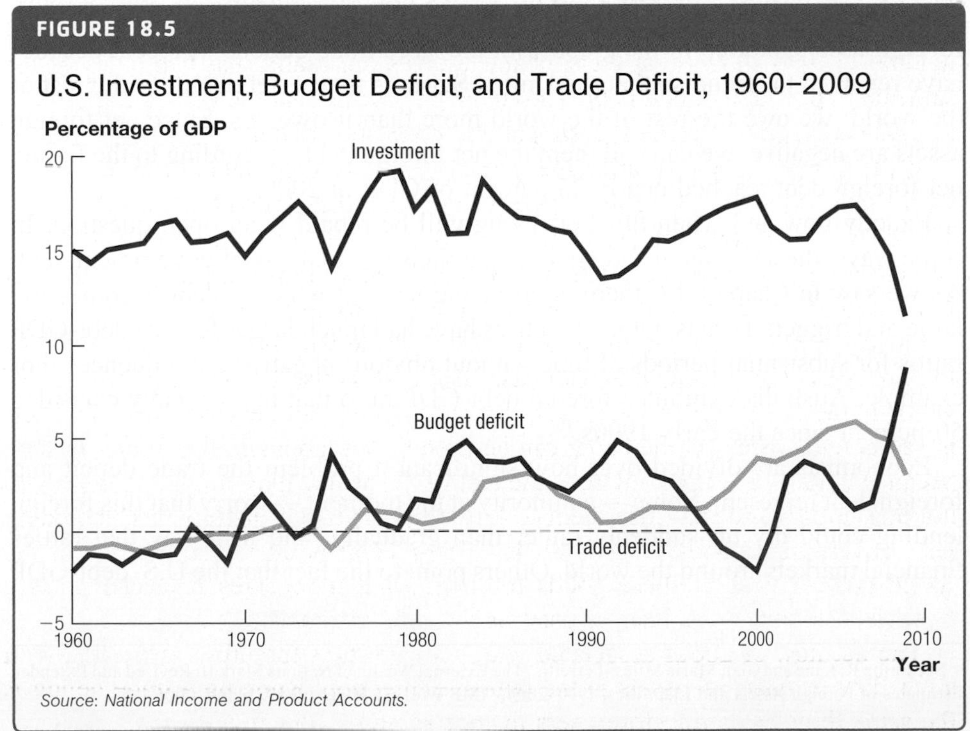

Source: National Income and Product Accounts.

Large budget deficits in the 1980s and more recently have not reduced investment substantially. Instead, investment has been financed increasingly by foreign saving–the trade deficit.

Up until 1986, the United States was a net creditor to the rest of the world: foreign assets held by U.S. entities exceeded U.S. assets held abroad. But with the large trade deficits of recent decades, the United States is now a net debtor to the rest of the world. The foreign debt reached nearly 25 percent of GDP in 2009.

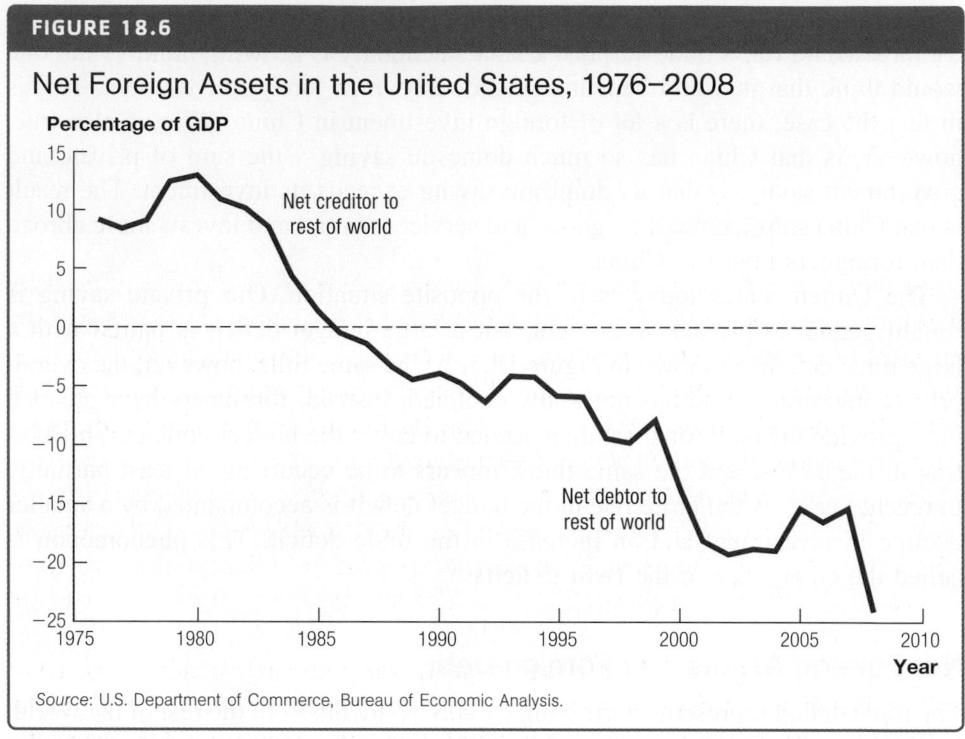

Source: U.S. Department of Commerce, Bureau of Economic Analysis.

Another way to look at it is shown in Figure 18.6. Up until 1986, the United States was a net creditor to the rest of the world: foreign assets held by U.S. entities exceeded U.S. assets held abroad. The difference between these two is **net foreign assets**, plotted in the graph. But the large trade deficits of recent decades have reversed the trend so that the United States is now a net debtor to the rest of the world: we owe the rest of the world more than it owes us. Since net foreign assets are negative, we can call them the net foreign debt. According to the figure, net foreign debt reached nearly 25 percent of GDP in 2009.

Exactly how and when this borrowing will be repaid is an open question. In some ways, the analysis of foreign debt parallels the analysis of government debt. As we saw in Chapter 17, there is no magic level at which a debt becomes too large and triggers a crisis. Other countries have had much larger foreign debt-GDP ratios for substantial periods of time without obvious negative consequences. For example, Australia exhibits a foreign debt-GDP ratio that has typically exceeded 50 percent since the early 1990s.[12]

Economists are divided over how significant a problem the trade deficit and foreign debt represent. Some—a minority at the moment—worry that this foreign lending could dry up suddenly rather than gradually, and in a way that rattles financial markets around the world. Others point to the fact that the U.S. debt-GDP

[12] See Philip R. Lane and Gian Maria Milesi-Ferretti, "The External Wealth of Nations Mark II: Revised and Extended Estimates of Foreign Assets and Liabilities, 1970–2004," IMF Working Paper 06/69, March 2006.

ratio is not especially large and suggest that a gradual adjustment is more likely. In Chapter 19, we will think more carefully about trade in the short-run model in order to study this adjustment.

18.9 Conclusion

Trade allows people in an economy to buy goods where they are cheapest and therefore improves economic efficiency. Just as the invention of the automobile put most horse-and-buggy operations out of business, however, trade can cause some types of jobs to disappear from an economy. In general, though, better jobs emerge to take their place, and the argument for free trade is similar to the argument for supporting the invention of the automobile.

The fact that trade often creates both winners and losers means that an important goal of public policy—a goal needed in order to maintain political support for free trade—is to find ways to redistribute some of the gains from the winners to the losers. Job-training programs and a solid social safety net are examples of such policies.

While trade in goods and services depends on comparative advantage (differences in prices across countries), the migration of labor depends on absolute advantage. With free migration, labor would flow from areas with low wages to areas with high wages. In principle, this migration could result in even larger welfare gains than free trade.

Finally, the emergence of the twin deficits—the government budget deficit and the trade deficit—in the U.S. economy over the last 25 years is somewhat disturbing. In theory, trade deficits can improve welfare by allowing countries to borrow when they expect the future to be better than average. In practice, however, the large deficits are starting to raise concerns among some economists.

CHAPTER REVIEW

SUMMARY

1. Since World War II, as tariffs and transportation costs have fallen, trade has become increasingly important to the world economy.
2. Imports have generally exceeded exports in the U.S. economy since the late 1970s, and the trade deficit reached 5.7 percent of GDP in 2006; it's the counterpart to a trade surplus in the rest of the world. The deficit allows domestic consumption, investment, and government purchases to exceed domestic production, with the excess financed by the rest of the world lending goods and services to the United States.

3. Trade between countries can be viewed as an extension of trade within a country. People specialize in production and trade in order to consume a broad range of goods. By specializing, both people and countries can focus on what they are best at, resulting in better efficiency. Trade can also be viewed as an alternative "technology" of production.
4. An important goal of public policy is to find ways (such as job-training programs) to redistribute some of the gains from the winners in an economy to the losers.
5. Trade deficits allow countries to smooth their consumption over time, much as the permanent-income hypothesis proposes. The intertemporal budget constraint applied to trade says that trade deficits today must be financed by surpluses in the future. Trade need not balance year by year, but it must balance in the long run.
6. Trade is based on comparative advantage: countries produce the goods they are best at producing, not in an absolute sense, but relative to other countries. If countries set different prices in autarky (when there is no trade), then free trade will allow them to buy goods where they are cheapest.
7. An alternative to trading goods is to allow the free flow of inputs, like labor and capital. While trade depends on comparative advantage, input flows depend on absolute advantage: inputs flow to where they earn the highest return. The efficiency gains from allowing the free migration of labor appear to be extremely large, based on the large total factor productivity differences across countries.
8. Trade deficits in the United States are a relatively recent phenomenon, emerging in the 1970s. The U.S. economy has gone from being a net lender to the rest of the world to being a net borrower. The amount of foreign debt (net of assets) owed by the United States reached nearly 25 percent of GDP in 2009. This number is large relative to recent U.S. history, but not relative to the debt ratios in other countries.

KEY CONCEPTS

absolute advantage
arbitrage
autarky
comparative advantage
net foreign assets
outsourcing
risk-sharing
trade balance
twin deficits

REVIEW QUESTIONS

1. Look around your dorm room and consider your daily life. About what fraction of goods and services that you come into contact with is produced domestically as opposed to abroad? How does this fraction compare with the fraction for the economy overall? If there is a difference, what do you think explains the difference?

2. In what sense does a trade deficit represent borrowing from the rest of the world?
3. Why do countries trade? What are the benefits and costs of trade?
4. Suppose there are two countries in the world, and one is better than the other at producing every good. Will the countries trade? Why or why not?
5. Discuss the extent to which the U.S. trade deficit and net foreign debt are serious economic problems.

EXERCISES

smartwork.wwnorton.com 

1. **Saving, investment, and trade:** China currently shows a high investment rate as well as a trade surplus. In what sense is there a tension between these two facts? What is odd about China's situation relative to conventional macroeconomic wisdom?

2. **The large trade surplus after World War II:** In the years following World War II, the United States briefly ran a trade surplus that peaked at about 5% of GDP in 1947. Use the national income identity (the investment = savings version) to provide a hypothesis that could explain what was going on.

3. **Comparative advantage and trade:** Suppose there are two goods in the world, beer and chips. The world consists of four economies: Elbonia, Genovia, Kinakuta, and Sodor. Labor is the only input into production, and one unit of labor can produce beer and chips in each of these economies according to the following table:

Country	Bottles of beer	Bags of chips
Elbonia	5	5
Genovia	5	10
Kinakuta	10	5
Sodor	10	10

   (a) Prices are expressed in units of bags of chips, so the price of a bag of chips is 1. What is the price of a bottle of beer in each economy when there is no trade?

   (b) Now suppose we let two countries trade with each other (keeping the others closed). There are six possible trading pairs: EG (Elbonia-Genovia), GK (Genovia-Kinakuta), KS, EK, GS, ES. For each case, explain who exports beer and who exports chips, and why.

4. **Trade in the apple and computer economy:** Consider the apple-computer trade example given in Section 18.5. Now suppose that because of a new technology, the North becomes even more productive at producing computers: one unit of labor can now produce 20 computers instead of 16.

   (a) Autarky: Redo Table 18.3 to reflect this change. Assume the other parameter values are unchanged.

(b) Free trade: Do the same thing for Table 18.4.
(c) Discuss the differences. How do the gains from trade change? Who benefits from the improvement in technology in the North?

5. **An improvement in Southern apples:** In the same apple-computer trade example given in Section 18.5, suppose that because of technology transfer, the South becomes just as productive as the North at producing apples: one unit of Southern labor can now produce 160 apples instead of 100.

   (a) Autarky: Redo Table 18.3 to reflect this change. Assume the other parameter values are unchanged.
   (b) Free trade: Do the same thing for Table 18.4.
   (c) Discuss the differences. How do the gains from trade change? Who benefits from the improvement in technology in the South?

6. **An improvement in Southern computers:**[13] Now suppose that the technological innovation occurs in the computer sector in the South: one unit of Southern labor can now produce 10 computers instead of 2. (Other parameters take their original values.)

   (a) Does the North still have a comparative advantage in producing computers? If we allow these two economies to trade, will there be any reason for them to trade? Explain.
   (b) How does this change affect the North? In particular, compare Northern economic performance before the Southern innovation with Northern economic performance after the innovation.
   (c) Discuss your findings. What do they mean for the case for free trade? (Be sure to note how the North would fare under autarky.)

7. **Trade in the apple and computer economy (hard):** Let's redo the trade problem with algebra instead of numbers. Suppose that one unit of labor produces x_n apples in the North and x_s apples in the South; one unit of labor can also produce z_n computers in the North and z_s computers in the South. The population of the North is given by L_n and the population of the South by L_s. We assume that x_n, x_s, z_n, z_s, L_n, and L_s are parameter values that are fixed numbers.

   (a) Autarky: Fill in Table 18.3 using these parameters.
   (b) Free trade: Fill in Table 18.4 as well.
   (c) In order to have the North specialize completely in producing computers and the South specialize completely in producing apples, the following condition on the parameters must hold:

$$\frac{x_s}{z_s} < \frac{L_s x_s}{L_n z_n} < \frac{x_n}{z_n}.$$

   Explain the intuition for this condition. (*Hint*: Look at the price of a computer; this is a very important point.)

[13] Paul Samuelson discusses an example like this one at length in "Where Ricardo and Mill Rebut and Confirm Arguments of Mainstream Economists Supporting Globalization," *Journal of Economic Perspectives*, vol. 18 (Summer 2004), pp. 135–46.

8. **Migration in the apple and computer economy:** In the apple-computer example, suppose people in the North have the right to charge an "entrance fee" to immigrants. Assume the world starts from the position of free trade and considers moving from free trade to free migration. Find an entrance fee (a certain number of apples and a certain number of computers paid each period) that the North can charge so that workers in both the North and the South will be better off.

9. **Politics and trade:** Suppose you are the economic adviser to a candidate running for the U.S. Congress. The candidate's district is historically a major producer of steel, and several steel mills have been shut down in recent years because of foreign competition. Hundreds of workers have lost their jobs. Draft a one-page speech on trade for the candidate to give in these areas.

WORKED EXERCISE

3. **Comparative advantage and trade:**

   (a) In Elbonia, one unit of labor can produce either 5 bottles of beer or 5 bags of chips. It must be the case that 1 bottle of beer trades for 1 bag of chips, so the price of beer is 1. Why? If the price were different, the economy would want to produce only beer or only chips. (For example, suppose 1 bottle of beer sold for 2 bags of chips. Then one unit of labor could produce 5 bottles of beer, which could be traded for 10 bags of chips. This would be better than producing chips directly, except for the fact that it means that no one would be producing chips! So this can't be an equilibrium.) But since consumers insist on enjoying both goods, both must be produced, so the price must be 1 in Elbonia.

   This same logic lets you calculate the price in the other economies. The price of beer in Genovia must be 2 bags of chips.

   (b) When the economies are closed, beer sells for 1 bag of chips in Elbonia but 2 bags in Genovia. Beer is expensive in Genovia, and chips are expensive in Elbonia. This means that Genovia has a comparative advantage in chips and will export chips. Elbonia has a comparative advantage in beer and will export beer.

   Using the prices in the closed economy, you should be able to determine the pattern of trade in a similar fashion for the other country pairs.

CHAPTER

19

EXCHANGE RATES AND INTERNATIONAL FINANCE

OVERVIEW

In this chapter, we learn

- how nominal and real exchange rates are determined, in both the short run and the long run.
- the key role played by the law of one price in determining exchange rates.
- how to incorporate exchange rates and a richer theory of the open economy into our short-run model.
- about international financial systems, including the gold standard, the Bretton Woods system, and the current system of floating exchange rates.
- the lessons from recent financial crises in Mexico, Asia, and Argentina.

19.1 Introduction

The world today, more than at any other time in history, is one of open economies. On any given day, financial flows around the world are an order of magnitude larger than total production on that day. International trade of goods and services exceeds 20 percent of GDP in nearly every country in the world.

This chapter continues Chapter 18's theme of international economics by studying exchange rates and international finance, both in the long run and in the context of a richer short-run model.

Relative to the simpler model of the open economy we have studied up until now, the description in this chapter includes two nice features. First, we are now able to devote more time to important topics such as the exchange rate and currency crises. Second, although the basic version of the short-run model covered in Chapters 9–14 continues to apply almost exactly when exchange rates are introduced, the model is now enriched in terms of the macroeconomic events we can study and the stories we can tell.

We begin by studying exchange rates and how they are determined, in both the long run and the short run. Next, we see how to incorporate exchange rates into the short-run model by learning how they influence the trade balance. Finally, the last part of the chapter explores the international financial system and different regimes countries may adopt for pinning down the exchange rate.

19.2 Exchange Rates in the Long Run

The Nominal Exchange Rate

In the United States, the currency is the dollar, in Japan the yen, in the United Kingdom the pound, in Mexico the peso, and in China the yuan. Until recently, most Continental countries in Western Europe had their own currency as well—the franc (France), the deutsche mark (Germany), the lira (Italy), and so on. Since 1999, however, a number of these countries have adopted a common currency, called the euro.

The **nominal exchange rate** is the rate at which one currency trades for another. For example, in mid-2010, $1 could be traded for 93 yen or 0.78 euros or 0.66 pounds. Viewed this way, the exchange rate is simply the price of a dollar. We will denote the nominal exchange rate by the letter E.

Figure 19.1 shows the yen-dollar and euro-dollar exchange rates since 1970. Between 1970 and 1995, the number of yen required to buy one dollar declined dramatically. In 1971, for example, 357 yen were required, but by 1995 the price had fallen to only 87 yen. This decline in the exchange rate—the decline in the price of a dollar—is called a **depreciation** of the dollar. Since 1995, the yen-dollar exchange rate has fluctuated, reaching as high as 133 yen per dollar in 1998 before dropping to 93 yen toward the middle of 2010.

In 1999, 0.92 euros were required to purchase a dollar. By the start of 2002, the dollar had risen in value to 1.15 euros. This rise is called an **appreciation** of

This graph of exchange rates shows the number of yen or euros that could be purchased with one dollar.

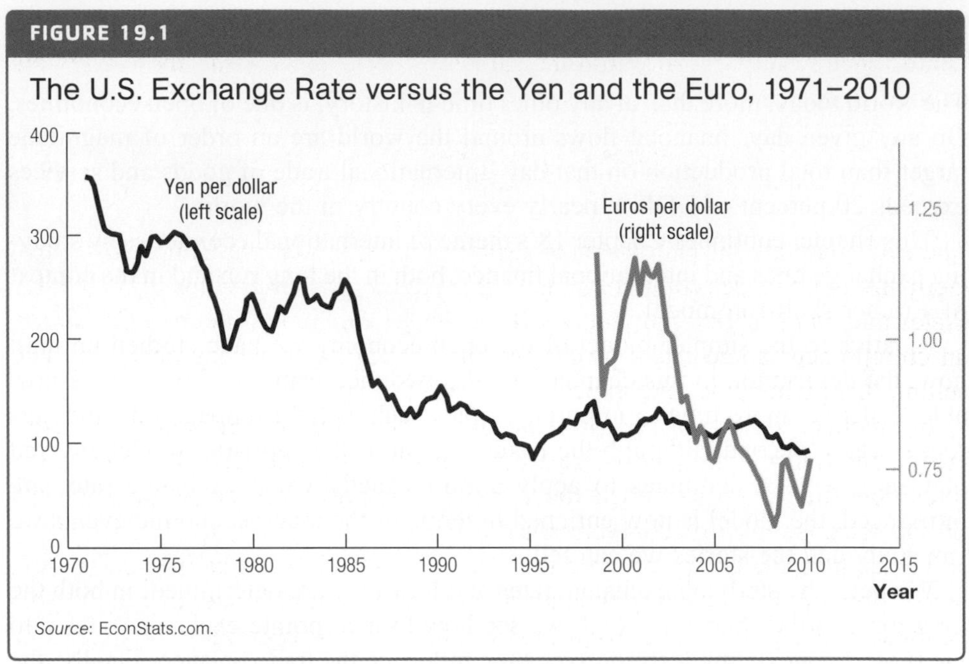

FIGURE 19.1

The U.S. Exchange Rate versus the Yen and the Euro, 1971–2010

Source: EconStats.com.

the dollar. Between 2002 and 2008, the dollar fell sharply againt the euro, reaching a low of 0.64 before strengthening during the financial crisis. By the middle of 2010, the dollar was at 0.78 euros.

What explains these movements in exchange rates over time, and what consequences do they have for the macroeconomy? These are among the questions we will explore.

The Law of One Price

In the long run, the nominal exchange rate is pinned down by the fact that goods must sell for the same price in every country. Suppose, for example, identical Toyota minivans sold for more in the United States than in Japan. Then Toyota could increase its profits by shipping minivans from Japanese car lots and selling them in the United States. Similarly, if computer chips sold for more in Germany than in Silicon Valley, Intel could increase its profits by selling more chips in Germany and fewer in the United States. We would not expect such opportunities for arbitrage to exist for long. Instead, **the law of one price** says that in the long run, goods must sell for the same price in all countries.

But what exactly does this mean? After all, computer chips in Germany are priced in euros, while in the United States they are priced in dollars. Here is where the exchange rate comes in. Let P denote the price of goods in the United States and P^w their price in a foreign country, Germany in this case. (The superscript w stands for "world.") And let E denote the exchange rate, measured as the number of units of foreign currency that can be purchased with one dollar.

With this notation, the law of one price can be written as

$$EP = P^w. \tag{19.1}$$

We are using the exchange rate to convert the price of computer chips in the United States and Germany into the same currency. If we write these units out explicitly, we have

$$E\,\frac{\text{euros}}{\text{dollar}} \times P\,\frac{\text{dollars}}{\text{chip}} = P^w\,\frac{\text{euros}}{\text{chip}}. \tag{19.2}$$

The exchange rate thus allows us to express prices in both the United States and Germany in euros per computer chip. This equation says that chips in the United States and chips in Germany must sell for the same number of euros. Otherwise, an entrepreneur could make profits by buying chips where they are cheap and selling them where they are expensive.

In practice, the law of one price need not hold exactly. Differences in taxes, tariffs, and transportation costs are all frictions that can interfere. Still, the departures from the law should reflect these frictions, and as a theoretical ideal, the law of one price is a useful economic construct.

To see how the law determines the level of the exchange rate in the long run, think about applying it more broadly to a country's entire basket of goods. That is, think of P and P^w as the overall price levels in two economies: P is the price of goods in the United States, and P^w is the price of goods in a foreign country (which we might call the "Rest of the World").

We know that the overall price level in an economy is determined in the long run by the quantity theory of money. This theory pins down P in the United States and P^w in the rest of the world, so the law of one price is left to pin down the level of the nominal exchange rate. If we use overbars to denote values in the long run, then the law of one price implies that the long-run level of the exchange rate is given by

$$\bar{E} = \frac{\bar{P}^w}{\bar{P}}. \tag{19.3}$$

That is, the nominal exchange rate is simply equal to the ratio of the price levels in the two economies in the long run. (If you're keeping track of units, they match up: E is euros per dollar, P^w is euros per good, and P is dollars per good, so the "per good" terms cancel on the right side.)

The quantity theory of money lends this model of the nominal exchange rate a nice, intuitive appeal. Recall that the quantity theory tells us that one of the key determinants of the price level in a country is the money supply in that country. Then the law of one price tells us that, at least in the long run, the level of the exchange rate is essentially determined by the number of pieces of paper with the word "euro" stamped on them versus the number of pieces of paper with the word "dollar" stamped on them.

The model also helps us understand the long-run depreciation of the dollar relative to the yen that we saw in Figure 19.1. Look back at this figure: what must be true about the price levels in Japan versus the United States according to the law of one price in equation (19.3)? If the nominal exchange rate E was falling over 25 years, it must be the case that P^w, the price level in Japan, was rising more slowly than P, the price level in the United States. Another way of saying this

Higher inflation in the United States than in Japan is one reason for the depreciation of the dollar relative to the yen since the 1970s.

FIGURE 19.2

Inflation in the United States and Japan, 1975–2009

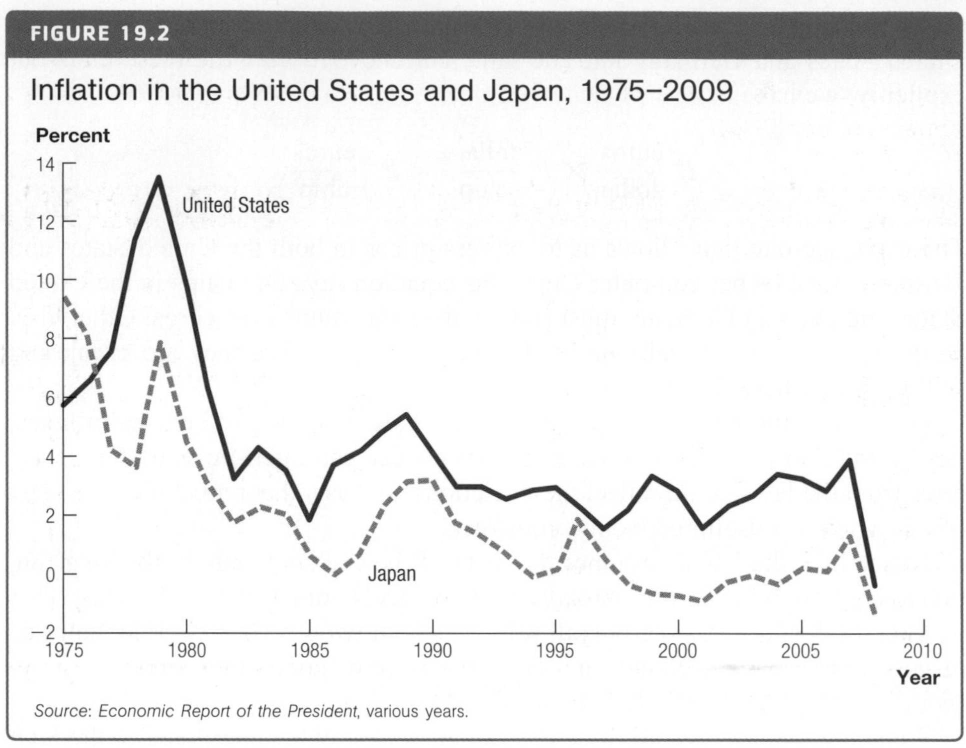

Source: Economic Report of the President, various years.

is that the inflation rate in the United States must have been significantly higher than it was in Japan.

Is this true? Yes—take a look at the inflation rates for these two economies, shown in Figure 19.2. One explanation for the depreciation of the dollar relative to the yen over the last 25 years is thus the different rates of inflation in the two economies.

CASE STUDY

The Big Mac Index

An excellent example of applying the law of one price is given by *The Economist* magazine's Big Mac Index. Using data provided by McDonald's, *The Economist* computes the dollar price of a Big Mac hamburger in various countries around the world. A summary of recent findings is reported in Table 19.1. In the United States, a Big Mac costs on average \$3.58. In the euro countries of Western Europe, in contrast, the cost is \$4.62, when the euro price is converted to dollars according to the current exchange rate. On the other hand, the price of a Big Mac in China is only \$1.83.

One lesson from this table is that the simple version of the law of one price fails to hold for Big Macs. Why might this be the case? First, it is conceivable that the exchange rate is over- or undervalued in different countries. For example, the fact that Big Macs are expensive in Europe could suggest that the euro is overvalued, so that one euro buys more dollars than it "should," pushing the price of burgers up. By this reasoning, the Chinese yuan is undervalued, so that the price of a Big Mac appears to be too low.

TABLE 19.1

The Big Mac Index

	Big Mac price in local currency	Exchange rate per dollar ($)	Big Mac price in dollars
United States	3.58 dollars	1.00 dollars/$	3.58
Euro area	3.35 euros	0.72 euros/$	4.62
Japan	321 yen	90.66 yen/$	3.54
Mexico	32.7 pesos	12.76 pesos/$	2.56
South Africa	18.3 rand	7.50 rand/$	2.44
Russia	71.5 rubles	29.90 rubles/$	2.39
Indonesia	21,060 rupiah	9,238 rupiah/$	2.28
China	12.49 yuan	6.83 yuan/$	1.83

Source: "Exchanging Blows," *The Economist*, March 17, 2010, and EconStats.com.

However, there are other important reasons for these price differences as well. Selling a Big Mac involves not only the price of hamburgers, pickles, and buns (tradable goods), but also the price of the real estate where the restaurant sits and the wage of the workers who sell the burgers (inputs that are not easily traded). In poor countries like China, real estate and labor are cheap, and this reality is reflected in the final sale of the hamburger. The law of one price applies only to goods that can be easily traded. Why? For goods that cannot be traded, it is not possible to buy low and sell high.

The Real Exchange Rate

If there is a "nominal" exchange rate, then there must be a "real" exchange rate. The **real exchange rate** is closely related to the law of one price. It is computed by adjusting the nominal exchange rate for the relative price level at home and abroad:

$$\text{real exchange rate} \equiv \frac{EP}{P^w}.$$

The units of the real exchange rate are given by

$$\frac{EP}{P^w} = E\,\frac{\text{euros}}{\text{dollar}} \times \frac{P\text{ dollars}}{\text{U.S. good}} \times \frac{1}{P^w\,\dfrac{\text{euros}}{\text{foreign good}}} = \frac{\text{foreign good}}{\text{U.S. good}}.$$

That is, the real exchange rate is simply the "real price" of U.S. goods: it is equal to the number of foreign goods required to purchase a single unit of the same U.S. good. If you recall that the nominal exchange rate is the price of the U.S.

currency, you can see the parallel. The nominal exchange rate gives the price at which currencies are exchanged, while the real exchange rate gives the price at which goods are exchanged.

The link to the law of one price is straightforward. If the law of one price holds, then foreign goods and U.S. goods should sell for the same price, so that the real exchange rate should equal 1. Since we believe, at least as a theoretical ideal, that the law of one price holds in the long run, then the real exchange rate should be equal to 1 in the long run as well:

$$R\bar{E}R = \frac{\bar{E}\bar{P}}{\bar{P}^{w}} = 1, \tag{19.4}$$

where *RER* denotes the real exchange rate and the overbars denote long-run values.

Summary

In the long run, the real exchange rate is pinned down by the law of one price: goods must sell at the same price in all locations. This means that the long-run value of the real exchange rate is equal to unity.

The long-run value of the nominal exchange rate then follows from this relationship and the quantity theory of money. In particular, the nominal exchange rate is determined by the relative nominal price of goods in two countries. Since the classical dichotomy holds in the long run, these price levels are themselves determined by money supplies. This result leads to the nice intuition that a key determinant of the level of the nominal exchange rate between two economies is the relative supplies of the different currencies.

CASE STUDY

Long-Run Trends in the Real Exchange Rate

Look closely at Figures 19.1 and 19.2, and you will see something that seems to contradict the law of one price. In particular, the nominal exchange rate for the dollar in terms of yen depreciates by *more* than the differences in inflation would seem to explain, at least up until around 1995. In fact, the inflation rate differs on average by only about a percentage point over this period. Notice that the dollar falls from about 350 yen to around 100 yen in only 25 years. This means that the real exchange rate for the dollar depreciates over this period. Or, alternatively, the real exchange rate for the yen appreciates. This fact is shown explicitly in Figure 19.3, which plots the real exchange rate between the United States and Japan: the price of U.S. goods, measured in terms of the number of Japanese goods that one U.S. good can buy, generally declined until 1995. But how can this happen over 25 years? Isn't this a sustained violation of the law of one price?

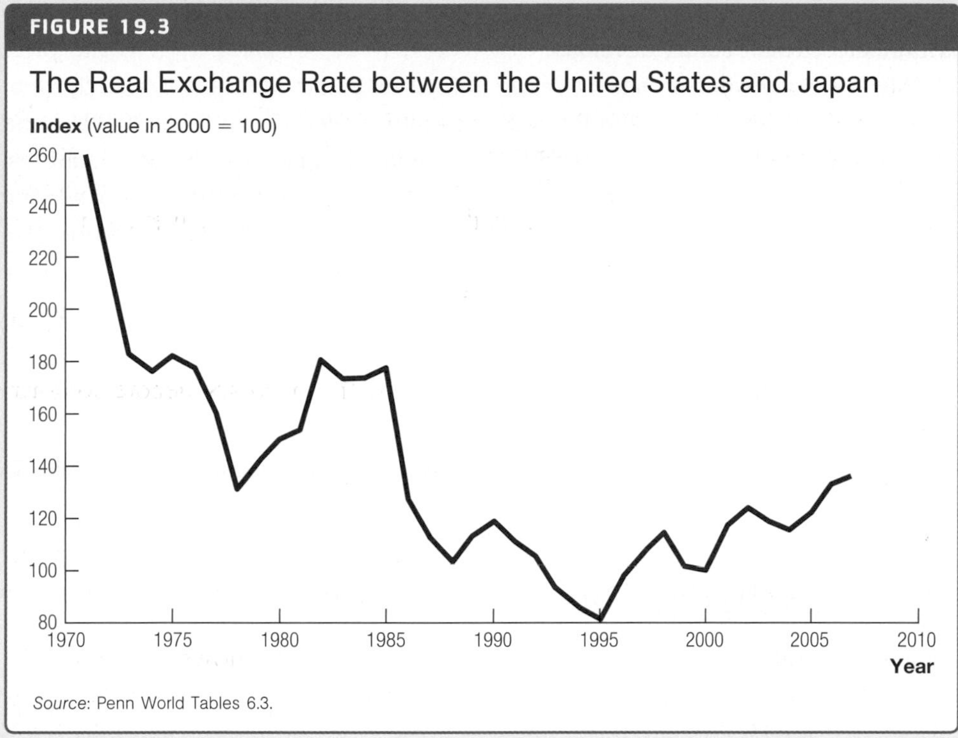

FIGURE 19.3

The Real Exchange Rate between the United States and Japan

Source: Penn World Tables 6.3.

The price of goods in the United States, measured in terms of Japanese goods, declined between 1971 and 1995, when Japan was growing rapidly. That is, the U.S. real exchange rate depreciated (or, equivalently, Japan's real exchange rate appreciated). Since 1995, U.S. goods have gotten more expensive as Japanese growth moderated.

The answer takes us to a more sophisticated understanding of real exchange rates. In particular, some goods in an economy are relatively easy to trade internationally: think about cars or cell phones or computers. Other goods are difficult to trade: think about haircuts or live musical performances or restaurant meals. Economists typically call these latter goods "nontraded," reflecting the fact that they are difficult to trade. One would expect the law of one price to apply to traded goods but not necessarily to nontraded goods. Why? Well, differences in the prices of nontraded goods cannot be arbitraged away since the goods cannot be bought where they are cheap and sold where they are expensive—by definition, they cannot be traded internationally.

Now consider what happens to prices in a rapidly growing economy such as Japan in the 1970s and 1980s. The law of one price dictates that the prices of traded goods should be the same in Japan and the United States. But nontraded goods can have different prices. In fact, as an economy grows rapidly, nontraded goods like haircuts, musical performances, and restaurant meals will naturally get more expensive over time: the wage is a key determinant of the prices of these goods, and as the economy develops, wages will rise. Rising wages then cause the price of nontraded goods to increase, at least as long as productivity growth is slow in these sectors, as is often the case. Since the real exchange rate reflects both traded goods and nontraded goods, one would expect the real exchange rate to rise as an economy develops: the price of traded goods may not change (because of the law of one price), but the price of nontraded goods will rise as the wage rises. This means that one would generally expect a country's real exchange rate to *appreciate* as the country develops.

This is exactly what we saw in Japan in Figure 19.3. In fact, this is exactly what we see across countries in the Big Mac index discussed above. Look closely, and you will see that poor countries tend to have cheaper Big Macs than rich countries, partly reflecting the prices of labor and land that are included in the price of serving a Big Mac in a restaurant. This phenomenon is known as the **Balassa-Samuelson effect**, named after two famous economists, Bela Balassa and Paul Samuelson. Notice that one implication of this force is that we should generally expect the real exchange rate in rapidly growing economies like China and India to appreciate over time as these economies develop. This prediction will prove important when, later in the chapter, we discuss China's exchange rate.

19.3 Exchange Rates in the Short Run

The Nominal Exchange Rate

What, then, determines exchange rates in the short run? To answer this question, we need to think about the main reasons people trade currencies. There are two. The first is to facilitate international trade. An American company that imports Italian olive oil, for example, makes its purchases in euros but earns its income in dollars; it therefore needs to convert one currency into another. The second reason is that traders in financial markets demand currency in order to make financial transactions. For example, a Japanese financial company may want to buy German government bonds, or a French holding company may purchase U.S. stocks.

It turns out that the volume of foreign exchange traded in financial markets is enormous. In April 2007, for example, the average amount of foreign exchange traded around the world was $4.0 trillion *per day*. To put this number into perspective, U.S. GDP for an entire year is $14.5 trillion, so that the amount of GDP produced on a given day is about $40 billion ($14.5 trillion divided by 365 days). More than 100 times the daily U.S. GDP thus trades hands in the foreign exchange market every day! And since the United States is about a quarter of world GDP, the average amount of foreign exchange traded on a given day exceeds 25 times the average amount of world production on that day.

The level of the nominal exchange rate between two currencies is pinned down by the trading of foreign exchange in the global market. We can view this market using standard supply-and-demand analysis: the supply of currencies is given by central banks, and international and financial market transactions create a demand for currencies. The exchange rate is the price of a currency that clears this market.

Given our emphasis on the central banks' practice of setting nominal interest rates rather than explicitly specifying a money supply, it is helpful to analyze the foreign exchange market in a slightly different way.

Suppose the Federal Reserve decides to increase the fed funds rate. When the nominal interest rate is raised in the United States, what happens to the value of the dollar and the exchange rate? Think about this from the perspective of global bond traders in London. Bonds in the United States now pay a higher interest rate than before, which attracts investors to purchase U.S. bonds. In order to make these purchases, our London traders need dollars, so the demand for U.S. dollars increases. The value of the dollar then rises; in other words, the dollar exchange rate appreciates. When the Fed increases interest rates in the United States, then, the dollar exchange rate appreciates, so that E increases. Another way of looking at this situation is that the United States has tightened monetary policy, so that the dollar is now scarcer than it was, leading its value to rise.

Now consider what happens if the Fed decides to reduce the fed funds rate instead. You should be able to figure out that the dollar exchange rate depreciates as a result, so that E declines.

This reasoning leads to an important relationship between monetary policy and the exchange rate:

Movements in the domestic nominal interest rate (holding the world interest rate constant) cause the nominal exchange rate to move in the same direction: $\uparrow i^{US} \Rightarrow \uparrow E$, *and* $\downarrow i^{US} \Rightarrow \downarrow E$.

The Real Exchange Rate

Although in the long run the real exchange rate is pinned down by the law of one price, in the short run the law may fail to hold. Why? The nominal exchange rate E is a financial market price, like a company's price in the stock market. In many economies—at least in those that do not maintain a fixed exchange rate—E changes by the minute and can exhibit large fluctuations; it therefore adjusts very quickly to financial news.

In contrast, our assumption of sticky inflation suggests that P and P^w adjust slowly over time. When a shock hits the economy, E moves immediately, while P and P^w adjust gradually, so that the real exchange rate EP/P^w can deviate from 1. Of course, this is equivalent to saying that the law of one price need not hold in the short run.

But what about the arbitrage argument? If goods sell for different prices, shouldn't goods be bought in one place and sold in another, so that an opportunity for pure profits exists? Transferring goods across countries is costly and requires time. In the long run, we might expect this arbitrage to occur, but should it occur in response to daily fluctuations in the nominal exchange rate? Probably not.

The assumption of sticky inflation means that unanticipated movements in the nominal exchange rate translate into movements in the real exchange rate in the short run. For example,

$$\uparrow E \Rightarrow \uparrow \frac{EP}{P^w}.$$

Table 19.2 provides a summary of how nominal and real exchange rates are determined in the long run and the short run.

TABLE 19.2

How the Exchange Rate Is Determined

		Long run	Short run
Nominal exchange rate	E	Pinned down by relative prices in the two economies; quantity theory of money.	Supply and demand in currency markets; moves in the same direction as i.
Real exchange rate	$\frac{EP}{P^w}$	Law of one price: $EP = P^w \Rightarrow \frac{EP}{P^w} = 1$	Sticky inflation means it moves with unanticipated changes in E.

19.4 Fixed Exchange Rates

Before 1973, many countries maintained a system of **fixed exchange rates**, in which the exchange rate of one currency for another was pegged to a particular level for some period. Even today, some developing countries and transition economies have chosen to peg their exchange rate to another currency. One of the most prominent examples is China, where the exchange rate was 8.28 yuan per dollar between 1998 and 2005. Another example is Argentina, which kept the peso pegged at 1 peso per dollar between April 1991 and December 2001.

How does a country maintain a fixed exchange rate, and what consequences does such a policy have for its economy? The discussion in Section 19.3 should give you a clue. Recall that in the long run, an economy's exchange rate is determined by the quantity theory of money. We saw, for example, that the long-run value of Argentina's exchange rate is given by

$$E \frac{\text{pesos}}{\text{dollar}} = \frac{P^{\text{Argentina}}\ \text{pesos/good}}{P^{\text{U.S.}}\ \text{dollars/good}}. \tag{19.5}$$

To maintain a fixed exchange rate, the price level in Argentina would have to move exactly with the price level in the United States. According to the quantity theory of money, the money supplies would have to change by the same amount.

Similarly, if the Fed decides to raise the fed funds rate, the only way the dollar-peso exchange rate will not move is if the nominal interest rate in Argentina changes by the same amount. *The central bank in Argentina must follow the monetary policy dictated by the Federal Reserve in the United States if it seeks to maintain a fixed exchange rate.*

Why would a country wish to cede control of its monetary policy to the Federal Reserve? One reason may be that the country has had trouble maintaining low and stable inflation in the past. A fixed exchange rate can be viewed as an attempt to "import" Alan Greenspan or Ben Bernanke as head of the country's central bank.

An understanding of the causes of high inflation, however, suggests that such an attempt may not always be successful. As we saw in Chapter 8, the main culprit behind a hyperinflation is typically not monetary policy but rather fiscal policy. Fixing the exchange rate may be a way to import another country's central banker, but it does not address the underlying fiscal causes of inflation. If these causes go unaddressed, a long-run commitment to a fixed exchange rate would seem questionable. In order to satisfy the government's budget constraint, a country may be tempted to print money and depart from the level of the pegged exchange rate. Historically, many pegs are undone for this and other reasons, and Argentina's latest peg, given up in January 2002, was no exception. The Argentinian peso depreciated sharply once the peg was relaxed; by mid-2007, Argentina's currency was trading at 3.1 pesos per dollar.

19.5 The Open Economy in the Short-Run Model

With our knowledge of exchange rates and (from Chapter 18) international trade, we are ready to incorporate exchange rates into a richer version of our short-run model.

The first step in extending the model is to include a more sophisticated theory of the trade balance. In our original version of the IS curve, we assumed the trade balance was a constant fraction of potential output. We now recognize that movements in the real exchange rate can influence trade in the short run.

Recall that the real exchange rate is the relative price of goods at home in terms of goods abroad. That is, it is measured in units of foreign goods per domestic good. If goods at home are expensive relative to goods abroad, so that the real exchange rate EP/P^w is high, then we would expect exports to be low and imports to be high: consumers and firms will seek to buy goods where they are cheapest. This suggests that an increase in the real exchange rate will reduce exports and increase imports, and therefore reduce net exports, $NX \equiv EX - IM$.

The connection between interest rates and exchange rates provides us with a link between interest rates and net exports. This is the key link we need in order to enrich our short-run model. In particular, we augment the net exports equation as follows:

$$\frac{NX_t}{\bar{Y}_t} = \bar{a}_{nx} - \bar{b}_{nx}(R_t - \bar{R}^w). \tag{19.6}$$

The baseline level of net exports in an economy is given by $\bar{a}_{nx}$, a parameter familiar from our original derivation of the IS curve in Chapter 11. This parameter can be thought of as the medium-run trade balance, dictated by, for example, international borrowing and lending concerns like those discussed in Chapter 18. The second term captures business-cycle considerations, and as anticipated above, it depends on the real interest rate. More specifically, it depends on the gap between the domestic real interest rate R_t and the foreign (rest of the world) real interest rate $\bar{R}^w$, which we take to be an exogenous parameter.

Consider first the role played by the domestic real interest rate. According to equation (19.6), an increase in the domestic real interest rate reduces net exports. The chain of reasoning that leads to this effect goes as follows:

$$\uparrow i \Rightarrow \uparrow R \text{ and } \uparrow E \Rightarrow \uparrow \frac{EP}{P^w} \Rightarrow \downarrow \frac{EX}{\bar{Y}} \text{ and } \uparrow \frac{IM}{\bar{Y}} \Rightarrow \downarrow \frac{NX}{\bar{Y}}.$$

Suppose the Fed raises the fed funds rate. As usual, this causes the real interest rate to rise. The high return attracts financial flows to the United States, increasing worldwide demand for dollars and causing the dollar to appreciate. Because of sticky inflation, the real exchange rate appreciates as well. This means that goods in the United States are relatively expensive, so that U.S. exports decline and imports increase, leading net exports to fall.

The role of the foreign real interest rate is now more easily understood. If the real interest rate in the rest of the world increases, U.S. assets look less desirable—just the opposite of the case we just considered. The dollar depreciates, causing the real exchange rate to depreciate. And U.S. goods are now cheap, so net exports increase.

The New IS Curve

The IS curve in our short-run model relates short-run output to the gap between the real interest rate and the marginal product of capital. For this reason, it is convenient to add and subtract the marginal product of capital $\bar{r}$ from the net exports equation (17.6), yielding

$$\frac{NX_t}{\bar{Y}_t} = \bar{a}_{nx} - \bar{b}_{nx}(R_t - \bar{r}) + \bar{b}_{nx}(\bar{R}^w - \bar{r}). \tag{19.7}$$

If you look closely at this equation, you will see that it really is just the same as (19.6)—the $\bar{r}$ terms cancel out.

The advantage of writing the net exports equation this way, though, is that it now depends on $R_t - \bar{r}$, just as investment does. And this is no accident. You may recall from equation (18.6) in Chapter 18 that the national income identity can be written as $NX = S - I$, or

$$S = I + NX.$$

Domestic saving S can be used for domestic investment or be invested abroad through net exports. Both are ways of deferring consumption to the future. An increase in U.S. interest rates makes borrowing in the United States expensive. This reduces investment in the United States and also reduces American willingness to invest in the rest of the world, where the world rate of return is unchanged. Therefore, net exports decline as well.

The fact that net exports enters the short-run model in exactly the same way as investment is very convenient. The IS curve for the open-economy model thus takes the same form as the IS curve for the original short-run model:

$$\text{IS curve: } \tilde{Y}_t = \bar{a} - \bar{b}(R_t - \bar{r}), \tag{19.8}$$

where now $\bar{a} \equiv \bar{a}_c + \bar{a}_i + \bar{a}_g + \bar{a}_{nx} - 1 + \bar{b}_{nx}(\bar{R}^w - \bar{r})$, and $\bar{b} \equiv \bar{b}_i + \bar{b}_{nx}$.

The interpretation of this equation is richer, however. The aggregate demand parameter $\bar{a}$ now involves an additional term that depends on the gap between the foreign real interest rate and the (world) marginal product of capital $\bar{r}$. In the long run, this gap must be zero, just as in the domestic economy. So the feature of the short-run model that $\bar{a} = 0$ in the long run is preserved. Now, though, a change in the real interest rate in the rest of the world creates an aggregate demand shock in the domestic economy. We will explore this event in more detail later in the chapter.

The most important thing to notice about this new IS curve is that it looks exactly like our old IS curve; the math is unchanged. The model we developed in the short-run section of this book—not only the IS curve but also the AS/AD framework—thus works exactly as before. The only difference is that now there are some additional parameters that can be shocked, and there are additional stories we can tell because of the effect that interest rates have on net exports. This additional richness will be apparent in the following examples.

Event #1: Tightening Domestic Monetary Policy and the IS Curve

In our first example, we ask, What happens to the IS curve when the central bank decides to raise interest rates to tighten monetary policy? The example is shown graphically in Figure 19.4.

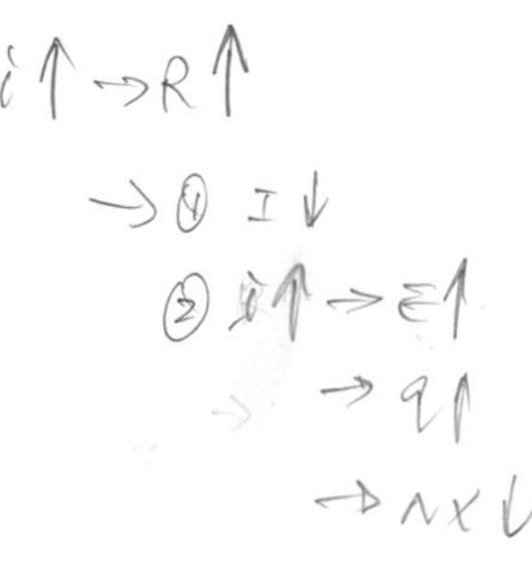

Because of sticky inflation, an increase in the nominal interest rate causes the real interest rate to rise. As can be seen from equation (19.8), the increase in the real interest rate then leads short-run output to decline.

What is the economic explanation for this decline in short-run output? There are two main forces at work in our enriched model. The first is the original one: since the real interest rate now exceeds the marginal product of capital, firms reduce their demand for investment, causing output to fall below potential.

The second force is a new one. The increase in the nominal interest rate leads to an increase in the demand for dollar-denominated financial assets, causing the dollar to appreciate. Because of sticky inflation, the real exchange rate appreciates as well, making U.S. goods expensive relative to foreign goods. Exports decline and imports rise. This fall in net exports is another reason why output falls below potential.

FIGURE 19.4

Increasing Interest Rates and the IS Curve

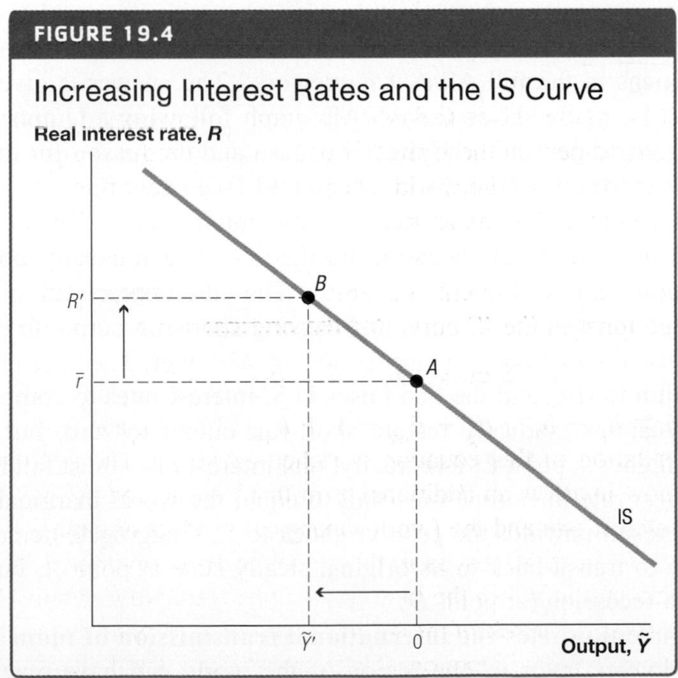

An increase in the domestic interest rate pushes output below potential, as the economy moves from point A to point B. In addition to the usual investment effects, there is an additional force working through trade. The high interest rate causes the dollar to appreciate, making U.S. goods expensive and reducing net exports.

Notice that qualitatively nothing has changed from our original analysis of the IS curve in Chapter 11. We still have a downward-sloping IS curve, and short-run output declines when interest rates go up. What *has* changed, however, is that there is an additional mechanism at work in the economy that causes short-run output to decline by even more for a given change in the interest rate. As a result, the IS curve is flatter when the short-run model is enriched to include the effect of exchange rates on the trade balance.

Event #2: A Change in Foreign Interest Rates

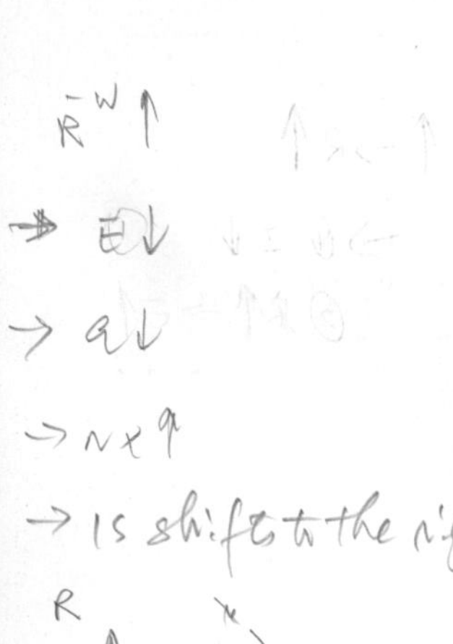

What is the effect on the United States if the European Central Bank raises interest rates in the euro area? To answer this question, we return to the net exports equation of our short-run model:

$$\frac{NX_t}{\bar{Y}_t} = \bar{a}_{nx} - \bar{b}_{nx}(R_t - \bar{r}) + \bar{b}_{nx}(\bar{R}^w - \bar{r}).$$

Mathematically, this equation implies that an increase in the foreign interest rate $\bar{R}^w$ will cause an increase in net exports in the United States.

Why would this occur? When the European Central Bank raises interest rates on euro-denominated assets, international investors will demand more euros and fewer dollars. This causes the euro to appreciate and the dollar to depreciate. Because of sticky inflation, the real exchange rate in the United States depreciates as well, leading the real price of U.S. goods to decline. As a result, net exports in the United States are stimulated.

In terms of our short-run model, this result causes the IS curve to shift out: for example, look back at the new IS curve in equation (19.8), where the $\bar{a}$ intercept parameter changes with the foreign interest rate. Holding the real interest rate in the United States constant, short-run output is now positive because of the stimulus from international monetary policy.

What happens in the full AS/AD framework? The answer is given in Figure 19.5, which essentially shows the AS/AD graph following a temporary positive shock to aggregate demand. The overall pattern and the reason for the dynamics should be clear from the analysis in Chapter 13 (see event #3).

What is different in this case is the economic interpretation. The positive shock to aggregate demand occurs because the tightening of monetary policy abroad leads to a stimulation of the U.S. economy. The euro appreciates, but the dollar depreciates, stimulating net exports and causing short-run output to rise.

Then the usual dynamics from an AD shock take over. The booming economy causes inflation to rise, and the Fed raises U.S. interest rates to combat the inflation. The dynamics gradually restore short-run output to zero, but inflation is temporarily higher at point *C*. Eventually, real interest rates must fall back in line: the real interest rate in Europe must fall to equal the world marginal product of capital. This result unwinds the positive shock to U.S. aggregate demand, leading the economy to transit back to its original steady state at point *A*, but only after undergoing a recession (at point *D*).

This example illustrates **the international transmission of monetary policy**. Changes in interest rates in one region of the world can have macroeconomic effects in other regions.

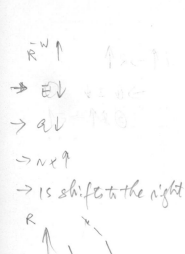

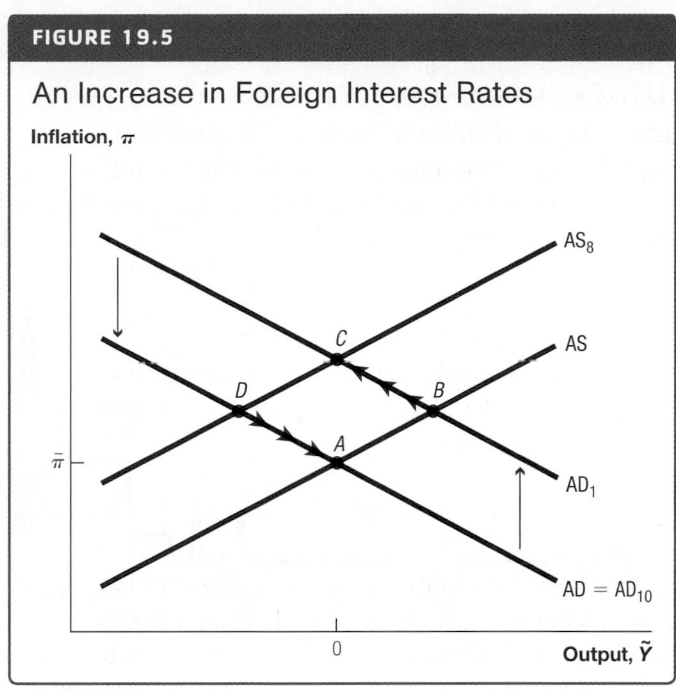

FIGURE 19.5

An Increase in Foreign Interest Rates

An increase in the foreign interest rate causes a temporary increase in $\bar{a}$. This is a positive aggregate demand shock that stimulates the economy in the short run (point *B*). The dynamics then follow the standard pattern: inflation rises and output returns to potential (*C*). Eventually, the foreign interest rate returns to the marginal product of capital, and the demand shock is unwound.

In applying this example to the real world, an important subtlety comes into play. Here, the increase in the European interest rate works through the exchange rate to stimulate the U.S. economy. In addition to this direct effect, however, there may also be another effect. The tight monetary policy in Europe may cause a recession there, which would reduce the demand for U.S. goods, perhaps causing a reduction in $\bar{a}_{nx}$ and shifting the AD curve back in. The net impact of these two effects is unclear, since they work in opposite directions. Your job as a student is to understand the various possibilities and be able to explain them clearly.

19.6 Exchange Rate Regimes

Broadly speaking, the history of the last two centuries of exchange rate "regimes"—the institutions that set exchange rates around the world—can be divided into three phases: the era of the gold standard, the era of the Bretton Woods system, and the modern era of **floating exchange rates**. Figure 19.6, a graph of the exchange rate between the British pound and the U.S. dollar since 1791, plots these three phases.

Before World War I (1914–18)—and especially in the half century leading up to the war—the international financial system was to a great extent based on what is called the gold standard, under which countries specified a fixed price at which they were willing to trade their currency for an ounce of gold. For example, starting in 1834, the United States pegged the price of gold at just under \$20.70 an ounce, while the United Kingdom pegged its price at 4.25 pounds. This meant that effectively you could trade \$1 for 1/20.7 ounces of gold, which could in turn

The graph shows the dollar exchange rate against the pound, together with the three main exchange rate regimes of the last 200 years.

FIGURE 19.6

The U.K.-U.S. Exchange Rate, 1791–2009

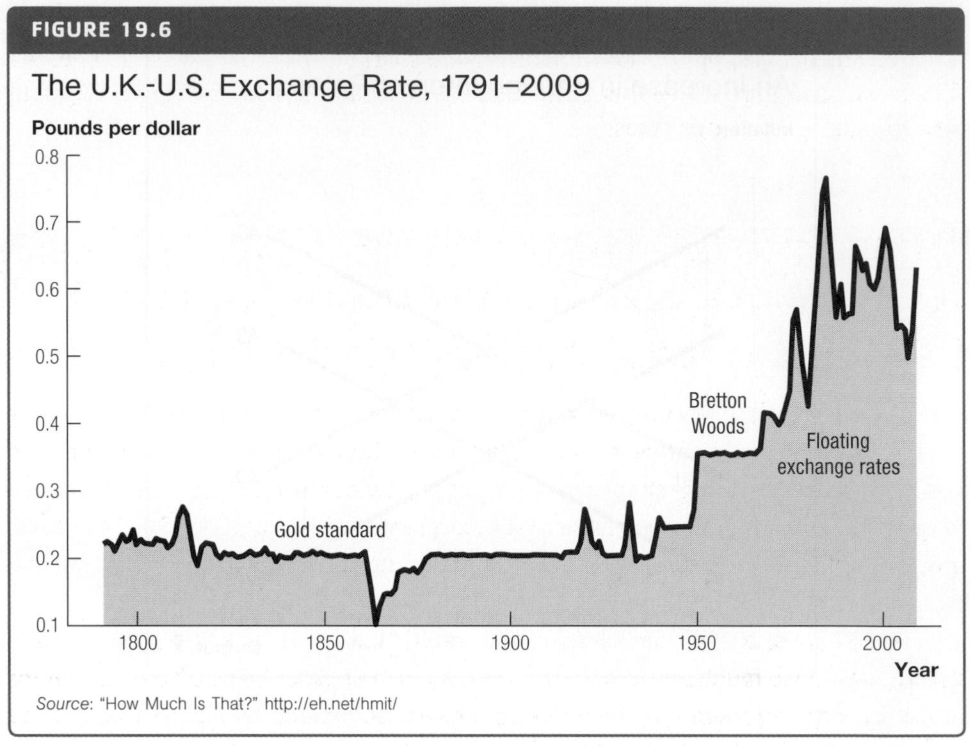

Source: "How Much Is That?" http://eh.net/hmit/

be traded for pounds at a price of 4.25 pounds per ounce. The implied exchange rate was

$$\frac{\$1}{\$20.70 \text{ per ounce}} \times £4.25 \text{ per ounce} = £0.205.$$

A quick glance at Figure 19.6 confirms that this was indeed the exchange rate between the pound and the dollar for more than an entire century.

The political, economic, and military havoc associated with World War I led to the breakdown of the gold standard and a period of financial instability. Indeed, this breakdown was partly responsible for the Great Depression of the 1930s. Then, in 1944, a blue-ribbon panel of financial economists met in Bretton Woods, New Hampshire, to fashion a new regime for the international monetary system. Under this regime—known as the Bretton Woods system—the United States pegged the price of gold at $35 per ounce, and most other economies specified a fixed exchange rate to the U.S. dollar. The gold standard was in essence replaced by a dollar standard.

Exchange rates were relatively stable following World War II until the early 1970s. The increase in inflation in the United States that had begun in the late 1960s put increasing pressure on the international financial system. The United States wanted to devalue its currency by pegging to a higher price of gold; other countries wanted the United States to raise interest rates and tighten monetary policy. In the early 1970s, this tension led the Bretton Woods system to collapse, as the United States revalued its currency. Since then, floating exchange rates have prevailed among the major currencies in the industrialized world. Monetary policies are not formally coordinated, and the value of the nominal exchange rate is determined by supply and demand in the markets for foreign exchange. As illustrated in Figure 19.6, this period has been characterized by large, frequent movements in exchange rates.

CASE STUDY

Does the Exchange Rate Matter in the Long Run?

Does the level of the nominal exchange rate matter in the long run? The answer is surely no. It would be rather easy for the United States to increase its exchange rate by a factor of 1,000 simply by adopting a new currency (blue dollars instead of green) and setting the quantities of the different-colored paper properly. Indeed, many countries that experience hyperinflations do exactly this once the original currency becomes worthless.

But if the level of the nominal exchange rate is unimportant in the long run, why does it receive so much attention? Partly because the exchange rate does matter for the short run. And there may be a deeper answer suggested by Figure 19.6. Notice that during the Civil War in the 1860s, the value of the dollar declined sharply. On the other hand, over the general course of the graph, the dollar appreciated relative to the pound. Both phenomena are consistent with the positive correlation between the value of the exchange rate and the overall performance of the economy. During the Civil War, economic performance suffered and the exchange rate declined in value. During the subsequent rapid growth that saw the United States overtake the United Kingdom as the richest country in the world, the currency appreciated.

However, as you learn throughout economics, correlation is not causality. In fact, the causality most likely goes the other way. Periods of solid macroeconomic performance are typically periods of low inflation. And periods of low inflation are generally associated with an appreciation in the value of the exchange rate (because other countries will typically not exhibit as sound a macroeconomic performance). While good macroeconomic performance and a strong currency go together, the most probable reason for this is that good macroeconomic performance leads to a strong currency rather than vice versa.

19.7 The Policy Trilemma

There are three natural goals related to the international monetary system that an open economy might like to achieve: (1) a stable exchange rate, (2) monetary policy autonomy, and (3) free flows of international finance. These goals are summarized graphically in Figure 19.7.

Open economies can choose at most two of the three characteristics at the vertices of the triangle. The policy choice is then dictated by the edge of the triangle defined by those two characteristics.

FIGURE 19.7

The Policy Trilemma in Open Economies

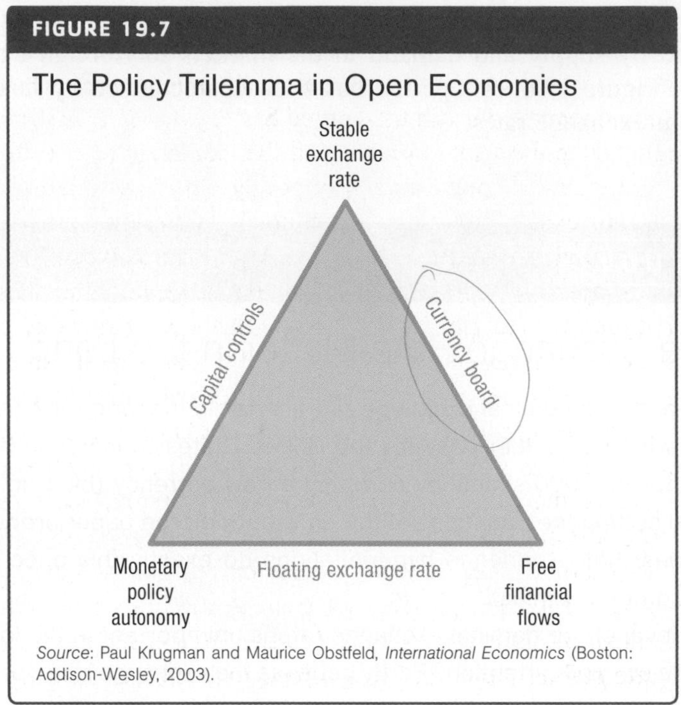

Source: Paul Krugman and Maurice Obstfeld, *International Economics* (Boston: Addison-Wesley, 2003).

A stable exchange rate is desirable in much the same way that a stable price level is desirable: it makes it easier for individuals and businesses to plan over time. Large movements in exchange rates can lead to large transfers of resources. This is especially true during periods of "currency crises," when exchange rates can depreciate by large amounts in a short period of time. College students from Mexico in the mid-1990s or from Asia in the late 1990s found that the dollar cost of their tuition rose dramatically as the Mexican peso, the Korean won, the Thai baht, and the Indonesian rupiah rapidly lost value. Firms in these countries that borrowed money that had to be repaid in dollars suddenly found that their debts had risen sharply.

Monetary policy autonomy (the ability of a country to set its own monetary policy) is desirable for the reasons outlined in our short-run model. Monetary policy is a tool that can be used in some circumstances to smooth out shocks to the economy.

Finally, free flows of international finance are desirable because they allow resources to be allocated most efficiently. If China or Mauritius sees an opportunity for high returns on its investments, it will benefit from the ability to borrow resources from the rest of the world in order to make the investments. International financial flows allow countries to borrow when times are bad in order to smooth consumption.

The remarkable feature of this **policy trilemma** is that at most only two of the three goals can be achieved in an economy. Countries must choose a single edge (two vertices) of the triangle shown in Figure 19.7, giving up on the goal that is opposite this edge, at the third vertex. For example, the United States sets its own monetary policy and features open capital markets with relatively free flows of international finance. It therefore has a floating exchange rate and must give up on the goal of a stable exchange rate. But why are the three goals mutually inconsistent? In the case of the United States, with a floating exchange rate, there is nothing that necessarily guarantees a stable exchange rate. Since the exchange rate depends on monetary policy in the United States *as well as in other countries*, changes in monetary policy abroad may lead the exchange rate to fluctuate even if the United States runs a sound monetary policy with low inflation.

The most famous example of a country choosing a currency board—along the right side of the triangle in Figure 19.7—was Argentina between 1991 and 2001. Under a currency board, an economy fixes its exchange rate and stands ready to trade its currency at the prescribed rate. If Argentina's exchange rate is 1 peso per dollar, then its central bank must hold a supply of dollars that it can exchange for pesos should any foreign exchange traders wish to make that trade. The central bank holds **foreign exchange reserves** (in Argentina's case, dollars and gold) so that the domestic currency is fully backed by the foreign exchange. For every peso in circulation, Argentina held a dollar's worth of foreign exchange reserves.

Between 1991 and 2001, Argentina's currency board pegged its exchange rate at 1 peso per U.S. dollar. Argentina also allowed reasonably open international financial flows. However, by pegging the peso to the dollar, the country effectively ceded control of its monetary policy to the United States. In order to keep the exchange rate stable, Argentina was forced to keep its monetary policy and interest rates in line with those in the United States. The cost of this policy choice was that Argentina could not use monetary policy to respond to shocks to its economy. The benefit was that Alan Greenspan was an excellent central banker who ensured low inflation in Argentina's economy, which had been wrecked by hyperinflations in the previous two decades.

If foreign exchange traders don't believe the fixed exchange rate will hold, they may start trading against the currency. They may, for example, sell their pesos in exchange for dollars, in the hope that at some point in the future the peso will be devalued and they can use their dollars to buy back the peso at a more favorable rate. However, as we will see below, some exchange rate crises occur when the central bank's stock of foreign reserves is not sufficient to exchange all the currency for dollars. In this case, the central bank, trying to defend a value of the exchange rate that is out of line with market fundamentals, can find its foreign reserves being drained quickly. If it runs low on reserves, it has no choice but to give in to the market and devalue the currency.

An example of an economy that operates at the left edge of the triangle in Figure 19.7 (capital controls) is China. Between 1996 and 2005, the Chinese yuan traded at a stable rate of 8.3 yuan per dollar. At the same time, China retained control of its monetary policy, by instituting tight controls on financial flows with the rest of the world. The government regulated the exchange rate and did not allow financial traders to trade large volumes of the currency in an open market. When the supply of a good is tightly regulated in this way, the regulator can set whatever price it wishes on the good.

To see how this works, consider a different good. Suppose you are the world's monopoly supplier of Mickey Mouse T-shirts. You can set whatever price you would like for the T-shirts and maintain that price forever. If you set the price very low, there will be excess demand for the shirts, and you will ration sales.

You can change the quantity of shirts that you sell (within bounds) to different levels and still maintain the fixed low price as long as there is excess demand. If you control the supply of the T-shirts, there is no market force that can require you to alter the price.

This is exactly what occurs when an economy operates with **capital controls**. Provided it holds the price of its currency—the exchange rate—artificially low, it is free to set its own monetary policy. It can supply whatever quantity of currency it chooses and maintain a fixed price. The cost of such a policy is that there are restrictions on financial flows. It is not the case that anyone who would like to trade dollars for yuan or vice versa can do so at a market rate of 8 yuan per dollar. Instead, the trading of the currency—just like the sale of Mickey Mouse T-shirts—is rationed.

Which Side of the Triangle to Choose?

Which side of the triangle should an economy choose? This is a difficult question, much debated by economists who study international finance. All three options have their merits and countries that follow them. Each policy choice also involves giving up on a desirable goal, and the costs and benefits associated with each choice may differ across countries and over time.

To help us understand the consequences of each choice, we will focus on three recent episodes: the 1994 currency crisis in Mexico, the Asian currency crisis in the late 1990s, and Argentina's decision to end its currency board and move to a floating exchange rate in 2002. The exchange rates for these episodes are plotted in Figure 19.8.

The exchange rate is normalized to 100 in the year 1991. The plot therefore shows the overall extent to which a currency has depreciated by a given year.

FIGURE 19.8

Depreciations during Several Currency Crises, 1991–2004

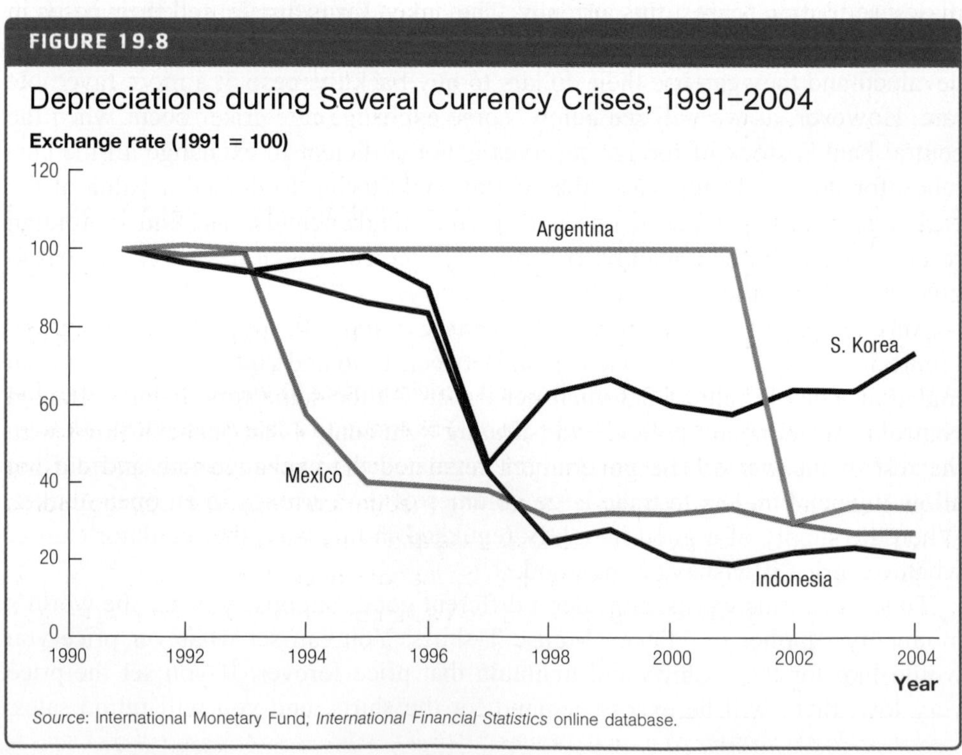

Source: International Monetary Fund, *International Financial Statistics* online database.

The Mexican Peso Crisis of 1994 In the 5 years leading up to 1994, Mexico exhibited steady economic growth, booming investment, and a relatively stable exchange rate of about 3 pesos per dollar. Some of the investment boom was financed by foreigners, however, and the trade deficit in Mexico was 4 to 5 percent of GDP in the early 1990s. Large capital flows and a stable exchange rate imply something like a currency board, according to the policy triangle in Figure 19.7.

By late 1994, political turmoil (including the assassination of political candidates) and the large foreign borrowing implied by the trade deficit led to fears of a devaluation of the peso. The Mexican central bank attempted to maintain the exchange rate for a while, leading to a loss in foreign reserves. Eventually foreign reserves fell to a very low level, and Mexico was forced to devalue the peso and let it float against the dollar. As shown in Figure 19.8, the peso fell sharply to only about 40 percent of its value before the crisis.

The Asian Currency Crisis of 1997 During the decades leading up to 1997, Asia was home to most of the fastest-growing countries in the world. A substantial part of this growth came about through high and rising investment rates. Before the 1990s, much of this investment was financed with domestic saving, but during the 1990s, Asian economies increasingly turned to foreign saving to finance part of their growth. By 1996, a number of these economies, including Thailand and Korea, were running large trade deficits.

Beginning in July 1997, currency speculation (see the case study below) led to sharp declines in Asian exchange rates as shown in Figure 19.8. They began first in Thailand, and then spread to South Korea, Indonesia, and Malaysia. With the benefit of hindsight, some economists point to weaknesses in the banking sectors of these economies and to government subsidies that supported banks that had made ill-advised loans. Many firms and banks had taken loans that were denominated in dollars, so that the decline in the value of the domestic currency made the loans much more costly to repay. The result was steep declines in economic activity and large recessions in a region that had previously been growing rapidly.

CASE STUDY

Hedge Funds, Financial Flows, and Financial Crises

In the months following the 1997 financial crisis in Asia, it was popular to pin the blame on global investors and hedge funds. For example, Malaysia's prime minister, Mahathir bin Mohamed, claimed that "all these countries have spent 40 years trying to build up their economies and a moron like [hedge-fund manager George] Soros comes along with a lot of money to speculate and ruins things."[1]

Hedge funds are private investment funds that can accept money only from relatively wealthy, accredited investors and, in exchange, are free to undertake risky

[1] Quoted in Sebastian Mallaby, "Hands off Hedge Funds," *Foreign Affairs*, January–February 2007.

investments with few regulations. These funds invest in stocks and bonds, but also in a range of more exotic financial instruments, including options, futures, derivatives, and swaps. By borrowing and then investing the proceeds, the funds can leverage up their base capital and take large bets about the direction and volatility of markets. There are a number of interesting economic examples involving hedge funds; two in particular deserve mention.

First is the spectacular collapse of a hedge fund called Long-Term Capital Management, or LTCM. This fund was started in 1994 and featured an impressive roster of founders, including Myron Scholes and Robert Merton, two financial economists who shared the Nobel Prize in economics in 1997. Using sophisticated financial analysis, the fund earned spectacular returns for several years. But then in 1998, it lost $4.8 billion, nearly setting off a financial crisis. In the words of Alan Greenspan, "Had the failure of LTCM triggered the seizing up of markets, substantial damage could have been inflicted on many market participants, including some not directly involved with the firm, and could have potentially impaired the economies of many nations, including our own."[2] But the Federal Reserve Bank of New York organized a meeting of LTCM's creditors to facilitate an orderly end to the hedge fund, and no financial crisis ensued.

The second example is related to exchange rates. In 1992, Britain attempted to maintain a fixed exchange rate vis-à-vis the major European currencies. However, inflation was substantially higher in Britain than in Germany, and the German Bundesbank was setting high interest rates to avoid inflation. Many financial market participants became convinced that Britain would have to devalue its currency, and took bets to that effect, selling the British currency "short" and offering to buy it back in the future. On September 16—Black Wednesday—the British central bank gave in, reducing the value of its currency. In the process, the British government suffered a loss of about 3.4 billion pounds, which was in turn a transfer to the hedge funds and investors speculating on the currency. Financier and philanthropist George Soros was one of the main speculators involved, and he is said to have netted a profit of more than $1 billion during the episode.

Like aspiring actors drawn to Hollywood, each year a new crop of MBAs and college graduates flock to Wall Street and London hoping to strike it rich with hedge funds. Also as in Hollywood, a few individuals become extraordinarily wealthy, while the rest—well, at least they don't usually end up waiting tables![3]

---

[2] Testimony before the Committee on Banking and Financial Services, U.S. House of Representatives, October 1, 1998.

[3] The sources for this summary, including the Wikipedia entries on "Hedge Funds" and "George Soros," make for interesting reading. Also see "Trillion Dollar Bet," a PBS documentary about the Black-Scholes option pricing formula that discusses the collapse of LTCM, available at www.pbs.org/wgbh/nova/ transcripts/2704stockmarket.html; and Malcolm Gladwell, "Blowing Up," *The New Yorker*, April 22 and 29, 2002, www.gladwell.com/archive.html.

The End of Argentina's Currency Board in 2001 Following decades of recurring hyperinflation, Argentina adopted a formal currency board in April 1991. As discussed above, the country pegged the peso to the dollar at an exchange rate of one for one. This policy, backed explicitly by gold and foreign reserves, was remarkably successful at ending the cycle of high inflation in Argentina. During the second half of the 1990s, inflation was on par with levels in the United States. Argentina also adopted free-market policies, including open capital markets, that led to substantial international financial flows. During the remainder of the 1990s, the country exhibited a modest trade deficit of just under 2 percent of GDP.

The currency crisis in Mexico in 1994 and the Asian financial crisis at the end of the 1990s led speculators to wonder if Argentina could maintain its exchange rate. Then in 1999, the value of the currency in Brazil—Argentina's main trading partner—declined, causing the Argentine peso to appreciate relative to the Brazilian currency, and producing a negative shock to aggregate demand through net exports. Unemployment crept up, as did government budget deficits. International lenders to Argentina began to worry about the country's ability to repay its debts, and interest rates on new borrowing rose sharply to incorporate this risk premium. As we have seen, the government budget constraint is often at the heart of inflation and financial crises, and this was the case in Argentina. Faced with high interest rates, Argentina defaulted on its government debt in late 2001. No longer able to access capital markets to finance its government spending, Argentina devalued the currency and ended its currency board, allowing the peso to float. As shown in Figure 19.8, the exchange rate fell precipitously to one-third its original value. The price level also increased, and inflation rose above 10 percent, but to its credit Argentina has managed to avoid high inflation.

The Future of Exchange Rate Regimes

A common theme from each of these examples is that stable exchange rates and free international capital markets can be difficult to maintain together for long periods of time, at least in developing economies. Part of the problem is that maintaining them requires tying the hands of monetary policy, which may be difficult if there are underlying problems with the government budget constraint. Another part of the problem may come from diverse trading partners. As we saw with Argentina, monetary policy dictated by Alan Greenspan preserved the value of the currency relative to the dollar. But a sudden depreciation of the currency in Brazil led to a sharp appreciation of the Argentinian currency, which hurt the economy.

Economists tend to be in favor of free flows of capital, but the Asian currency crisis has led some to question this policy. If currency speculators can bring enormous sums of money to bet on the depreciation of a currency in a short time, it is possible for a crisis to be created, or at least enhanced. Large bets can threaten to exhaust the foreign reserves of an economy and precipitate a crisis that might have been averted. China's current policy of keeping limits on capital flows in place can be viewed in this light.[4]

Countries continue to experiment with financial arrangements in order to find one that adequately balances the associated costs and benefits. It will be interesting to see how these experiments play out in coming decades.

CASE STUDY

The Euro

On January 1, 1999, a new currency—the euro—was introduced as the single currency of the 11 (now 16) countries of the European Monetary Union, which included France, Germany, Ireland, Italy, and Spain. The franc, the mark, the lira, and the other currencies of this group of countries have since disappeared, and the euro has taken their place as the common currency throughout much of Europe.

A single currency provides a number of benefits. Even more than with a currency board, the risks associated with fluctuations in the exchange rate are eliminated. In addition, the transaction costs of trade in the member countries are reduced—there is no longer a need to keep track of different currencies when trading between France, Germany, and Belgium, for example. Finally, a single central bank becomes responsible for the conduct of monetary policy, perhaps providing an assurance about the monetary policy that will apply across a range of countries. With nearly a decade of history in the books, the European Central Bank has quickly achieved a high degree of credibility and transparency in conducting monetary policy and coordinating inflation expectations.

There are also costs associated with a single currency. For one thing, as with a fixed exchange rate, individual countries lose control of their own monetary policies. With a single monetary policy for the countries of the European Union, policy cannot be targeted to particular regions that might be slumping when the rest of Europe is booming. This problem became acute in the years following the recent financial crisis, as illustrated by the problems in Greece in 2010: with a debt-GDP ratio exceeding 100 percent and a budget deficit in excess of 13 percent of GDP, bondholders became worried about the possibility that Greece might default on its debt. With its own currency, Greece could use monetary policy to help alleviate some of these problems. As part of the euro area, however, Greece does not possess this option. At the time of this writing, it is unclear how this thorny situation will be resolved. One clear consequence, however, is that the euro system itself is no longer perceived as an unqualified success.

---

[4] A helpful overview of these issues is provided by Kenneth Rogoff, "International Institutions for Reducing Global Financial Instability," *Journal of Economic Perspectives*, vol. 13 (Autumn 1999), pp. 21–42.

19.8 The Adjustment of the U.S. Trade Balance

As we have seen, the U.S. trade deficit in recent years exceeded 5 percent of GDP, and over the course of the last 30 years, the United States has gone from being a net lender to the rest of the world to being a net borrower. Net foreign debt owed by the United States to the rest of the world now exceeds 20 percent of GDP.

From the logic of intertemporal budget constraints, we know these deficits must be offset by trade surpluses in the future. How the adjustment back to trade surpluses is likely to occur, and what consequences this will have for the U.S. economy, is a matter of debate among macroeconomists.

Interestingly, some of the elements shared by the Mexican peso crisis of 1994, the Asian financial crisis of 1997, and the Argentinian financial crisis of 2001–02 also characterize the United States today. In particular, before its crisis, each country allowed relatively open capital markets and used these capital markets to finance a trade deficit. Some countries also ran high budget deficits. (The crises were marked by other problems as well, however, including political turmoil and structural banking problems.)

On the other hand, some countries with large trade deficits have experienced substantial depreciations without macroeconomic instability. A primary example of such a successful adjustment is the United States during the mid-1980s. Looking back at Figure 19.1, we can see the large depreciation of the dollar against the yen that occurred between 1985 and 1987, a period of strong macroeconomic performance.

Adjustment in the Short-Run Model

An interesting puzzle arises when we think about trade balance issues in the context of our short-run model. For example, if the U.S. trade deficit is to move to a surplus, there must be an increase in demand for U.S. exports, which stimulates net exports. By itself, this stimulation is a positive shock to aggregate demand, which might boost the economy. Indeed, this is what happened in the United States in the 1980s.

However, the currency crises analyzed in the previous section should give us pause. In particular, if the adjustment to a trade surplus occurs in the context of a crisis, we would expect to see negative effects on the economy in the short run.

Suppose, for whatever reason, the rest of the world became worried about the ability of the United States to pay back its foreign debt. Foreign countries might require higher interest rates on additional lending, and the U.S. trade deficit—which represents this lending—could disappear. While the Federal Reserve controls short-term interest rates between banks, a "risk premium"—a higher rate to compensate for the possibility that the loan may not be repaid—could emerge for government borrowing and raise interest rates in capital markets. This could have negative effects through the usual IS channels, reducing investment and consumption of durable goods. Overall, the result might be a negative shock to aggregate demand that outweighs the positive effects working through net exports.

Such a shock would also have reallocation effects: the United States would need to reduce C, I, and G back in line with domestic production if the rest of the world stopped lending goods to it. This reallocation would take the form of a reduction in demand for domestic consumption goods like construction and an increased demand for export goods like chemicals, aircraft, and computer technologies. Such a reallocation may involve unemployment and retraining.

Another interesting question is how large the effects of reallocation would be *quantitatively*. If the U.S. adjustment to a trade surplus were to occur gradually over time, it would likely be relatively smooth and may not have any significant consequences for short-run output or inflation. The reallocation of resources necessitated by moving from negative net exports to positive net exports would certainly be noticed, as some combination of consumption, investment, and government purchases would necessarily have to decline by more than 5 percent of GDP. On the other hand, if the adjustment had to occur quickly for some reason—as it did in Mexico, Asia, and Argentina—the macroeconomic consequences could be severe. Prominent international economists disagree on which form of adjustment, gradual or quick, is more likely. Increasingly, however, some economists appear to be worried about the likelihood of negative consequences.[5]

CHAPTER REVIEW

SUMMARY

1. The nominal exchange rate is the price of the domestic currency in units of foreign currency; for example, 115 yen can purchase \$1. The real exchange rate is the price of domestic goods in units of foreign goods; for example, it may take 1.3 foreign goods to purchase 1 domestic good.

2. In the long run, the value of the real exchange rate is pinned down by the law of one price: $EP = P^w$. Since the real exchange rate is just the ratio of prices at home and abroad, EP/P^w, the value of the real exchange rate is equal to 1 in the long run: goods have to sell for the same price. Frictions in the real world, however, prevent this law from holding exactly.

[5] For some of the concerns, see Maurice Obstfeld and Kenneth Rogoff, in Richard H. Clarida, *G7 Current Account Imbalances: Sustainability and Adjustment* (Chicago: National Bureau of Economic Research, 2007). More concerns are discussed by Brad Setser and Nouriel Roubini, "How Scary Is the Deficit?" *Foreign Affairs*, July–August 2005. A theoretical analysis suggesting a more sanguine view is Ricardo Caballero, Emmanuel Farhi, and Pierre-Olivier Gourinchas, "An Equilibrium Model of 'Global Imbalances' and Low Interest Rates," *American Economic Review*, vol. 98 (March 2008), pp. 358–93.

3. The fact that the real exchange rate equals 1 in the long run implies that the nominal exchange rate is pinned down by the domestic and foreign price levels. These in turn come from the quantity theory of money, which leads us to a quantity theory of the nominal exchange rate: in the long run, the nominal exchange rate is pinned down by the relative supplies of different currencies. If there are more green pieces of paper than blue pieces of paper, then green pieces will sell for a lower price.

4. Sticky inflation means that the law of one price can fail to hold in the short run. It also means that movements in the nominal exchange rate E translate to movements in the real exchange rate EP/P^w in the short run.

5. Interest rates and exchange rates move together. A tightening of monetary policy raises the short-term nominal interest rate. The high interest rates attract financial investors, increasing the demand for dollars and causing the exchange rate to appreciate.

6. A key determinant of imports and exports, and therefore of net exports, is the real exchange rate—the price of domestic goods (in units of foreign goods). If domestic goods become more expensive—if the real exchange rate goes up—then exports will fall and imports will rise. Net exports are therefore a decreasing function of the real exchange rate. Because exchange rates and interest rates move together, net exports are a decreasing function of the real interest rate.

7. The short-run model incorporating exchange rates works just like the short-run model analyzed in Chapters 9–14. Net exports behave much like investment: lending abroad is another way to defer consumption to the future. The experiments we can consider in the model that incorporates net exports, however, are richer. Quantitatively, the inclusion of exchange rates makes the economy more sensitive to interest rate changes.

8. The international financial system has been based on three different regimes in the last 150 years: the gold standard, the Bretton Woods system, and the current system of floating exchange rates.

9. The policy trilemma says that open economies can achieve at most two of the following three goals: stable exchange rates, monetary policy autonomy, and free flows of international finance.

KEY CONCEPTS

appreciation
Balassa-Samuelson effect
depreciation
capital controls
fixed exchange rate
floating exchange rate
foreign exchange reserves
the international transmission of monetary policy
the law of one price
nominal exchange rate
the policy trilemma
real exchange rate

REVIEW QUESTIONS

1. What is the difference between a nominal exchange rate and a real exchange rate?
2. Between 1970 and 1995, the dollar depreciated sharply versus the Japanese yen, while the average value of this exchange rate did not change much between 1995 and 2010. What might explain these facts?
3. Why would we expect the law of one price to hold in principle? Why might it fail to hold in practice?
4. Why do interest rates and exchange rates move in the same direction in the short run?
5. How and why are net exports and investment similar in the short-run model? Does this similarity make the IS curve steeper or flatter?
6. Why does a change in the foreign real interest rate lead to a shift of the AD curve?
7. Does the level of the exchange rate matter in the long run? Why or why not?
8. What is the policy trilemma, and why are countries restricted to one side of the triangle?

EXERCISES

smartwork.wwnorton.com 

1. **The Big Mac:** Look back at the Big Mac Index in Table 19.1. Compute the level of the exchange rate that would be needed to equalize the dollar price of the Big Mac across all countries. State whether each currency appears to be currently overvalued or undervalued relative to the dollar, and calculate the amount (as a percentage) by which the currency would need to appreciate or depreciate in order to equalize the price of a Big Mac.
2. **Net exports and the IS curve:** Consider the way in which net exports depend on the real exchange rate. Does the dependence of net exports on the real exchange rate make the IS curve steeper or flatter? What is the economic interpretation of this result?
3. **The depreciation of the dollar versus the yen:** Look back at equation (19.3) in Section 19.2.
   (a) Apply our growth rates rules (from Chapter 3) to this equation to express the growth rate of the exchange rate as a function of the inflation rate at home and abroad.
   (b) Between 1971 and 1995, U.S. inflation averaged 5.5% per year, while inflation in Japan averaged 4.5% per year. At what rate should we expect the dollar to depreciate against the yen between 1971 and 1995?

(c) Using Figure 19.1, make a rough calculation of the annual rate of depreciation of the dollar versus the yen. Do the numbers match up reasonably well?

(d) What must have been happening to the real exchange rate between 1971 and 1995? Can you think of any reason why this might have occurred?

4. **Fixed versus floating exchange rates:** Suppose Mexico wishes to fix its exchange rate relative to the U.S. dollar.

(a) If the Federal Reserve raises interest rates, what would happen to the peso-dollar exchange rate in the absence of any change in Mexican interest rates?

(b) Suppose Mexico wants to keep its interest rate fixed no matter what, maintain a fixed exchange rate, and allow open capital markets. What will happen when the United States raises interest rates? (*Hint*: What if the Mexican central bank holds a large number of dollars as foreign reserves in order to back its exchange rate?)

(c) Summarize what you learn from this exercise.

5. **Expansionary monetary policy in Europe:** Suppose the European Central Bank decides to stimulate the European economy by reducing interest rates there. Use the AS/AD model to explain how and why this affects the U.S. economy in the short run. How does the economy return to steady state?

6. **Imports and short-run output:** In addition to depending on the exchange rate (and therefore on the interest rate), imports may depend on short-run output: when the economy is booming, consumers tend to demand more foreign goods. To incorporate this result into our short-run model, suppose the new net exports equation is

$$\frac{NX_t}{\bar{Y}_t} = \bar{a}_{nx} - \bar{b}_{nx}(R_t - \bar{R}^w) - \bar{n}\tilde{Y}_t.$$

Derive the IS curve with this new equation, and explain how it differs from the standard IS curve in the short-run model.

7. **Currency crises and the demand for dollars:** Suppose there is a currency crisis in the rest of the world, leading to an increase in demand for U.S. dollars (a "flight to safety"). Use the AS/AD framework to explain the effects of this shock on the U.S. economy. Be sure to explain carefully how and why the shock enters the AS/AD model. (*Hint*: If the rest of the world would like more dollars, what does it have to give in exchange for those dollars?)

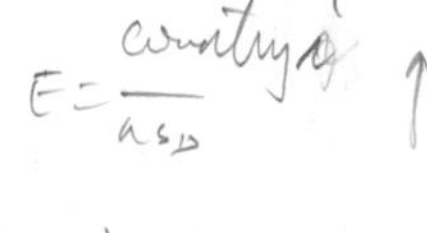

8. **The unwinding of the U.S. trade deficit:** Suppose some shock occurs to the U.S. economy that makes foreign investors more reluctant to hold U.S. assets. Use the AS/AD framework to explain the effects of this shock on the U.S. economy. Note: There are several possible answers to this question, depending on which effect dominates. Just be clear about the case you choose to analyze.

9. **The policy trilemma:** One could make a reasonable case that the United States in the last decade has been able to achieve all three goals of the policy trilemma: it sets its own monetary policy, it has open capital markets, and it has experienced a relatively stable exchange rate. Yet the chapter claimed that an open economy can only achieve two of these policy goals. How do we understand this apparent contradiction?

10. **Currency crises and macroeconomic performance:** Using the Country Snapshots data file (snapshots.pdf), study the macroeconomic performance of Mexico, Indonesia, and Korea following the financial crises in each region. How large were the declines in GDP per worker in each country, and how quickly did the regions recover?

11. **Advising a developing country:** Suppose you are appointed the international economic adviser to a small developing country. The country is deciding what kind of exchange rate and monetary policy regime to adopt. Provide your advice in a one-page policy memo, outlining the pros and cons of your position.

WORKED EXERCISES

4. **Fixed versus floating exchange rates:**

   (a) When the Federal Reserve raises interest rates, U.S. assets become more attractive than Mexican assets. This increases the demand for dollars and reduces the demand for pesos, putting pressure on the peso to depreciate.

   (b) In this hypothetical example, Mexico is attempting to violate the policy trilemma—trying to achieve all three goals simultaneously. At the old exchange rate, investors will want to trade their pesos for dollars to take advantage of the high U.S. interest rate. The Mexican central bank can finance these exchanges using its foreign reserves, but eventually Mexico will run out of dollars. As it runs out of dollars, it will be forced to reduce the value of the peso so as to stem the demand for these exchanges.

   (c) This example helps us to think about why all three goals of the policy trilemma cannot be achieved simultaneously, at least in the long run. It also shows how in the short run, a country may appear to be meeting all three goals if it is running down its supply of foreign reserves. This actually happened in Mexico in 1994.

8. **The unwinding of the U.S. trade deficit:**

   Many questions in international economics are tricky because there are often several "channels" at work; this exercise is an example.

   The direct answer is that the U.S. economy would *boom* following this flight away from the dollar. If foreigners want to hold fewer dollars, the dollar exchange rate will depreciate, stimulating net exports (and therefore the rest of the economy) and thereby causing the trade deficit to unwind. It seems odd that this is the basic effect at work, but we know that a reduction in the trade deficit *is the same thing* as an increase in net exports, and this is a positive stimulus to aggregate demand. You should be able to work out these effects in the AS/AD graph. (It will look much like Figure 19.5.)

In practice, we might suspect that such a lack of confidence in the dollar would not have purely stimulating effects on the economy. This is where our model is less successful than we might like, and a richer model is needed. The text discusses some channels through which other effects might work. For example, an increase in the "risk premium" on government debt could raise long-term interest rates, reducing investment and aggregate demand; see the discussion in section 19.8.

CHAPTER 20

PARTING THOUGHTS

OVERVIEW

In this chapter,

- we review the main insights of macroeconomics.
- we consider some of the unresolved questions that lie at the frontier of current macroeconomic research.

Physicists spend a large part of their lives in a state of confusion. It's an occupational hazard. To excel in physics is to embrace doubt while walking the winding road to clarity. The tantalizing discomfort of perplexity is what inspires otherwise ordinary men and women to extraordinary feats of ingenuity and creativity; nothing quite focuses the mind like dissonant details awaiting harmonious resolution. But en route to explanation–during their search for new frameworks to address outstanding questions–theorists must tread with considered step through the jungle of bewilderment, guided mostly by hunches, inklings, clues, and calculations. And as the majority of researchers have a tendency to cover their tracks, discoveries often bear little evidence of the arduous terrain that's been covered. But don't lose sight of the fact that nothing comes easily. Nature does not give up her secrets lightly.

–BRIAN GREENE

In any textbook or any course, there is an important but often hidden tension. On one side is the goal of explaining what the academic community has discovered about a particular subject. On the other side is our collective ignorance—the areas in any subject where significant topics are not well understood. By their nature, textbooks are good at conveying the former but often fail at conveying the latter.

This chapter attempts to lay out more clearly both sides of this tension. It summarizes some central lessons of macroeconomics, but also outlines the important areas in which our knowledge is lacking.

20.1 What We've Learned

1. *Standards of living in the long run are determined by rates of investment in physical and human capital, average hours worked per person, the economy's stock of technology and knowledge, and how productively the economy uses these inputs*. These determinants form the main lesson from our combined Solow-Romer model about levels of income and how they vary across countries.

The growth rate of standards of living in the long run hinges on the growth rate of knowledge. Because knowledge is nonrivalrous, the value of a new idea is not diminished by sharing it with a large number of people. Instead, per capita income is proportional in the long run to the total stock of knowledge. The continued discovery of new ideas, then, is fundamentally responsible for the continued increase in per capita income.

Epigraph: From *The Fabric of the Cosmos* (New York: Knopf, 2004), Chapter 16.

As poorer countries in the world grow richer, they will increasingly contribute new ideas to the world's stock of knowledge. Because of their size, China and India may play particularly important roles in this regard. For example, China and India each have as many people as the United States, Western Europe, and Japan combined. And as of 2008, China surpassed the United States to become the world's largest producer of Ph.D. degrees. Educational quality may suffer in the short run because of the rapid expansion of education in China and India, but we might expect these quality problems to disappear over time.[1] From a long-run perspective, the contributions to knowledge from the increase in worldwide research will benefit per capita incomes around the world. The prospects for economic growth over the next century look very solid, in part for this reason.

2. *Differences in growth rates across countries reflect the principle of transition dynamics.* Over long periods of time, countries may grow at different rates. For example, during the twentieth century, per capita GDP rose at 2.0 percent per year in the United States versus 1.5 percent in the United Kingdom. During the second half of the century, per capita GDP growth was 4.8 percent per year in Japan versus 2.2 percent per year in the United States.

Modern growth theory explains these differences in growth rates using the principle of transition dynamics. An economy that has reached its steady state will exhibit growth at a rate determined by the growth rate of world knowledge. However, economies that are below their steady-state position will grow rapidly, and those that are above their steady state will grow slowly. The last decade suggests that current policies in Japan are consistent with a steady ratio of Japanese-to-U.S. per capita GDP of something like 0.75. After World War II, however, Japan's income was only about 25 percent of the U.S. level. Its rapid growth between 1950 and 1990 reflects the closing of this gap. Growth models predict that as the gap closes, growth rates will slow down; this has in fact happened in Japan. Similarly, we would expect a gradual slowdown in the rapid growth rate of the Chinese economy as it approaches a new, higher steady-state position in the world income distribution.

3. *In the long run, the classical dichotomy holds: there is no long-run trade-off between inflation and real GDP.* In the long run, real GDP is determined by real forces in the economy, including those listed in #1 above (and in the Solow and Romer models). Inflation and the price level, on the other hand, are determined by the quantity theory of money. If there are more green pieces of paper floating around, the rate at which goods trade for pieces of paper will be higher. Similarly, if an economy prints money rapidly and exhibits a high rate of money growth, inflation will be high. This separation between the real and nominal sides of the economy, which holds in the long run, is called the classical dichotomy.

Another way of expressing the classical dichotomy is to say that in the long run, persistent inflation and persistent unemployment are separate problems with distinct causes. High inflation is, at least proximately, a monetary phenomenon. More

[1] See Richard Freeman, "Does Globalization of the Scientific/Engineering Workforce Threaten U.S. Economic Leadership?" NBER Working Paper No. 11457, June 2005.

fundamentally, inflation has real causes that are rooted in the government budget constraint. When a government cannot borrow (perhaps because it has recently defaulted on some of its debt) and when there is a large gap between taxes and spending, the government may be forced to print money to finance this gap.

The unemployment rate, on the other hand, is determined primarily by structural features of the labor market, at least in the long run. These features include hiring and firing costs and the structure of social insurance programs such as unemployment insurance, disability insurance, and welfare programs.

4. *In the short run, there is a trade-off between inflation and output.* At the root of this trade-off is the Phillips curve. Because of the difficulty of coordinating and managing expectations, inflation tends to adjust gradually over time, apart from shocks. One of the key forces governing the evolution of inflation is the state of economic activity. When the economy is in a recession, firms increase prices by less than the prevailing rate of inflation, so inflation declines. When the economy is booming, firms increase prices by more than the rate of inflation and inflation increases.

This inertia in inflation—which we call "sticky inflation"—has another important consequence for the macroeconomy: it means that the classical dichotomy does not hold in the short run. Changes in monetary policy, such as an increase in the nominal interest rate, can have real effects. For example, if the central bank decides to tighten monetary policy with a large increase in the nominal interest rate, sticky inflation means that this action results in an increase in the real interest rate as well. The higher real interest rate can affect investment demand and, through the exchange rate, net exports. These effects on domestic demand lead to changes in output.

5. *The credibility of the central bank in being willing and able to fight inflation is, somewhat paradoxically, of fundamental importance in stabilizing output.* Through the Phillips curve, one of the key ways that a central bank can reduce inflation is by causing a recession. This action will coordinate the economy's expectations toward a lower rate of inflation. A central bank that has established its credibility in being willing to take a strong stand against inflation can coordinate expectations more easily, reducing the need for recessions. Modern innovations in monetary policy such as increased transparency and explicit inflation targets are motivated by this same concern.

20.2 Significant Remaining Questions

While there is much about the economy that macroeconomists understand, a number of important questions remain unresolved. These questions lie at the frontier of economic research and are the subject of active study. We can hope that in the coming decades, macroeconomists will develop better, fuller answers.

1. *Why do countries have different investment rates, technologies, and total factor productivity levels?* Our study of economic growth documents that differences in investment rates and total factor productivity levels are key determinants of the large income differences across countries. But why do some countries have such low investment rates and TFP levels? Part of the explanation of low TFP is surely that the stock of ideas in poor countries is lower than the stock of ideas in rich countries, but why is this so?

Recent research has emphasized the importance of institutions like property rights and the rule of law. If the returns to investing in capital or technologies are especially low in a country because the true value cannot be captured by the investor, then investments in capital and technologies will be low. But then we must push the question one step deeper: why are property rights so poorly enforced in poor countries?

2. *What are the best institutions for achieving economic goals?* This question applies to a number of different areas. For example, what are the best institutions for encouraging the discovery and diffusion of new ideas? The discovery of new knowledge lies at the heart of economic growth. It is why people in the richest countries live twice as long as they did two or three hundred years ago, and why their standards of living are 50 times higher. Patent systems, prizes, organizations like the National Science Foundation, and subsidies to graduate training in the sciences and engineering are all ways of encouraging research. What combination of approaches is best? The mechanisms for encouraging the discovery and sharing of knowledge are themselves ideas that have been developed over time. Perhaps there are better mechanisms out there waiting to be discovered.

Similarly, how are ideas shared across countries, and what institutions would make such idea flows more efficient? As researchers in China, India, and elsewhere increasingly contribute to world knowledge, it will become more important to facilitate flows of knowledge around the world.

What are the best ways of capturing the welfare improvements made possible by free trade, free capital flows, and free immigration? These policies often produce winners and losers, even when the overall benefits exceed the costs. What institutions allow the gains from trade to be shared more broadly so that political support for it can be maintained?

Finally, what monetary institutions should an economy adopt? The last decade has seen substantial changes around the world in international financial systems, including the establishment of a currency board in Argentina and its subsequent abandonment, the Asian financial crises at the end of the 1990s, the adoption of a single currency in much of Europe, and the tight capital controls in China, one of the world's fastest-growing countries. What approach to international finance will allow economies to grow steadily and avoid future crises?

3. *How do we measure potential output—and therefore short-run output—in practice?* Potential output is a very useful theoretical construct. Unlike GDP or unemployment, however, we can't objectively measure it. When there is a shock to the economy and GDP declines, how much of the decline is due to a change in potential output and how much to a change in short-run output?

This question has serious implications. For example, the productivity slowdown of the 1970s reduced potential as well as actual output. The extent to which short-run output declined was presumably smaller than the decline in overall GDP.

Policymakers who did not appreciate that potential output had declined were tempted to stimulate the economy by more than was called for, thus contributing to a rise in inflation.

Similarly, during the end of the 1990s, economic growth associated with the "new economy" was particularly strong. The question arose as to how much of the gain was an increase in short-run output and how much was an increase in potential output. If it was mainly a short-run boom, then the policy response would call for an increase in interest rates to slow the economy back down and prevent a large rise in inflation. On the other hand, if potential output had changed, inflationary pressures would be minimized. Greenspan faced exactly this dilemma in the late 1990s, and one of the major accomplishments during his tenure at the Fed was the recognition early on that the new economy involved a change in potential rather than short-run output. Similar difficult but crucial decisions are faced by policymakers regularly.

4. *Why are financial markets susceptible to bubbles, and how should policymakers respond when bubbles appear to be present?* Given the rise in interest rate spreads in financial markets in 2008 and the collapse of the housing bubble, standard macroeconomic models do a reasonable job of explaining the large decline in economic activity that followed. Macroeconomics is much less successful at explaining why the housing bubble arose in the first place and why financial institutions became so leveraged and, therefore, so sensitive to the market downturn. Financial bubbles have been a recurrent feature of markets for centuries, so understanding their genesis and dynamics is important.

Even more important, however, is understanding how bubbles interact with the macroeconomy and how policymakers should reform financial regulation and respond to signs of excessive "froth" in financial markets in the future. Are current financial reforms sufficient, or has the experience of recent years merely reinforced the sense that leveraged investors can reap the benefits as markets rise but will be rescued when markets plunge? Such questions are at the top of the agenda for macroeconomic research in the coming decade.

5. *How should society best deal with the large looming fiscal problems associated with the aging of the baby boom generation and rising health expenditures?* If current policies remain in place, the U.S. government budget deficit will explode, reaching 20 percent of GDP by the year 2075. Part of the reason is spending on Social Security, but an even more important part is the government provision of health insurance through Medicare and Medicaid. Similar problems confront most other advanced countries.

Fiscal policy will have to change in major ways over the next half century. Either taxes will have to rise substantially or government spending on retirement programs and especially health care will have to be cut sharply, relative to current trends. Neither option is easy politically.

There are reasons to believe that health spending as a share of GDP will continue to rise over time. As people become richer, among the most valuable goods they can purchase are additional life and health. In the United States as well as other advanced countries, finding the best way to finance a rising health share is likely to be one of the central public policy problems over the next two decades.

20.3 Conclusion

In the quotation that opens this chapter, Brian Greene describes the deep-seated perplexity that exists for researchers at the frontier of physics. Much the same could be said about research in economics. Research—like education—is often fraught with confusion, and nothing comes easily.

The most rewarding experience we can have in academia occurs when seemingly mysterious concepts coalesce into understanding. Research offers the additional appeal that a researcher can be the first person in the world to comprehend some phenomenon. But a similar experience is at the heart of education. What everyone enjoys most about learning is that same feeling of discovery that occurs at the moment knowledge is first grasped. Even when much of economics is well-known by the experts, there is an exhilaration that comes from understanding something, if not new to the world, at least new to you.

I hope this book leads you to some of your own "aha" moments. And perhaps also to a bit of your own unease with the important problems that remain unsolved. Maybe this tantalizing discomfort will inspire you to seek out the answers.

Glossary

Page numbers are provided for terms in the Key Concepts lists at the end of each chapter.

absolute advantage One country has an absolute advantage over another in producing a particular good if it does so more cheaply. (p. 484)

accounting profit See *profit*. (p. 76)

AD (aggregate demand) curve The equation $\tilde{Y}_t = \bar{a} - \bar{b}\bar{m}(\pi_t - \bar{\pi})$. The AD curve shows the level of short-run output chosen by the central bank for a given rate of inflation. The AD curve is derived from the IS curve and a monetary policy rule that depends on the inflation rate. (p. 337)

adaptive expectations Expectations that are purely backward-looking and do not respond to news about the future. Under adaptive expectations, the expected rate of inflation over the coming year is given by the inflation rate that prevailed over the previous year. (p. 308)

aggregate Total, or pertaining to the entire economy.

aggregate demand curve See *AD curve*.

aggregate demand shocks Shocks to the economy that directly influence the short-run amount of consumption, investment, government purchases, or net exports. That is, they affect the amount of "demand" in the economy. Examples include news about the future that influences consumption or affects desired investment by firms, a recession in the rest of the world that reduces the demand for U.S. exports, and a change in government purchases. Aggregate demand shocks are captured by the $\bar{a}$ parameter in our short-run model. (p. 276)

aggregate supply curve See *AS curve*.

annualized rate The rate that would apply over an entire year. For example, if GDP increases by 1 percent during a single quarter, we would say it grew at an annualized rate of 4 percent. (p. 233)

appreciation A currency appreciates when it gains value relative to other currencies. That is, an appreciation is a rise in the exchange rate. (p. 503)

arbitrage Taking advantage of existing price differences to make a profit by buying at a low price and selling at a higher price. (p. 486)

arbitrage equation A mathematical expression that equates the returns from two different types of investment. For example, an investor may use \$100 to purchase shares of a company's stock or to purchase a government bond. If these two investments have the same underlying risk, then the arbitrage equation says that they should deliver the same return. (p. 427)

AS (aggregate supply) curve Another name for the Phillips curve equation $\pi_t = \pi_t^e + \bar{v}\tilde{Y}_t + \bar{o}$. We often assume adaptive expectations, so that $\pi_t^e = \pi_{t-1}$. The AS curve shows the rate of inflation that results from firms' pricing decisions. It depends on expected inflation, the level of short-run output, and price shocks. (p. 339)

asset Something of value that is owned. Financial assets include stocks, bonds, and savings accounts; a house is also an asset. (p. 262)

automatic stabilizer A policy stimulus that engages automatically when the economy goes into a recession, helping to mitigate the downturn. Unemployment insurance and welfare programs are examples. (p. 288)

autarky A situation in which a group of countries are not allowed to trade. (p. 484)

balanced growth path A situation in a growth model in which all economic variables grow at constant rates forever. (p. 146)

balance sheet An accounting tool with assets on the left side and liabilities and net worth on the right side; the two sides sum to the same value when net worth is included. (p. 262)

Balassa-Samuelson effect Productivity growth tends to be more rapid among traded goods than among non-traded goods, leading the relative price of non-traded goods to rise. In a developing country that is growing rapidly, this effect often manifests as an appreciation of the real exchange rate. (p. 510)

bank run A situation in which depositors or creditors worry about a bank's solvency and its ability to repay its deposits or short-term debt. Depositors and lenders may then withdraw their funds simultaneously. To the extent that the bank has illiquid assets, a worry about a bank run could be self-fulfilling. This concern is one motivation for deposit insurance by the government. (p. 265)

bankruptcy A legal event in which a bank or other company declares that it cannot pay its creditors, typically because the company is insolvent (its liabilities exceed its assets). (p. 264)

basis point A unit equal to 1/100 of 1 percent. For example, when the fed funds rate increases from 5 to 5.25 percent, we say it rose by 25 basis points.

bathtub model A model of the natural rate of unemployment in which the number of workers becoming unemployed is exactly offset by the number of unemployed persons who find new jobs. (p. 180)

behavioral economics A relatively recent field of economic research that blends insights from psychology, neuroscience, and economics in an effort to create a better understanding of how individuals make economic decisions. Behavioral economics emphasizes departures from perfectly rational, forward-looking behavior.

borrowing constraints Features of an economy that limit the ability of certain individuals to borrow, usually because they are viewed as being unlikely to repay a loan in a timely fashion.

bubble A situation in a market when the price rises above its fundamental value. (p. 380)

budget balance The difference between the government's sources of funds and its uses of funds; the difference between tax revenues and government spending. When this difference is positive, we say there is a "budget surplus"; when negative, we say there is a "budget deficit." See also *primary deficit or surplus*. (p. 454)

budget deficit See *budget balance*.

budget surplus See *budget balance*.

business cycle Short-run fluctuations in GDP, including recessions and booms.

capital The stock of machines, buildings, equipment, and factories in an economy. Somewhat confusingly, the word is also used to represent financial assets. For example, we speak of "international capital flows" in describing the flow of financial assets across countries. (p. 24)

capital (financial concept) See *net worth*. (p. 263)

capital accumulation The process by which the economy obtains its stock of capital, usually represented by the equation $\Delta K_{t+1} = I_t = \bar{d}K_t$. The capital stock is the cumulation of investment, adjusted for the depreciation that occurs over time. (p. 100)

capital controls Restrictions on financial flows across countries. Capital controls often take the form of restricting the free exchange of one currency for another. (p. 522)

capital gain The change (or percentage change) in the price of some asset, such as a stock or a house (p. 428)

capital loss The change (or percentage change) in the price of some asset, when that change is negative. (p. 428)

capital requirement Legal requirement that a financial institution have a certain ratio of its assets supported by capital (net worth) on its balance sheet—for example, 6 percent. (p. 263)

central bank The organization responsible for monetary policy in a country. The central bank in the United States is called the Federal Reserve.

central bank independence A modern idea for good monetary policy asserting that the central bank should be politically separate from the branches of the government responsible for spending and taxation. (p. 215)

chain weighting A method of computing real GDP that is robust to changes in relative prices over time. (p. 30)

classical dichotomy The notion that changes in nominal variables (like the money supply or the nominal interest rate) have only nominal effects on the economy. In particular, they do not affect real variables, such as the amount of real GDP. The classical dichotomy supposes that the nominal and real sides of the economy are largely separate. This is not quite accurate, however, as real variables *can* affect nominal variables—think about the quantity theory of money. (p. 204)

closed economy An economy that is not open to international trade.

Cobb-Douglas production function The production function $Y = K^a L^{1-a}$. We typically consider the case of $a = 1/3$. (p. 69)

comparative advantage One country has a comparative advantage over another in producing a particular good if the *relative* price of that good is lower in the first country. By relative price, we mean the price of the good relative to other goods produced in the economy. Under free trade, a country will export a good that it produces with a comparative advantage. (p. 484)

constant growth rule If a variable starts at some initial value y_0 at time 0 and grows at a constant rate $\bar{g}$, then its value at some future time t is given by $y_t = y_0(1 + \bar{g})^t$. (p. 46)

constant returns to scale The property of a production function that occurs when doubling all the inputs leads to exactly twice as much output. (p. 69)

constrained discretion A compromise in the "rules versus discretion" debate where policymakers use rules as guidelines to policy, only departing from them in exceptional circumstances. (p. 364)

consumer price index (CPI) A measure of how the cost of purchasing a given basket of consumer goods changes over time; the CPI is a common price index used when calculating inflation.

consumption The quantity of goods and services purchased by consumers (that is, by individuals as opposed to by businesses or by the government). In the national income accounts, housing is counted as investment rather than consumption, but other durable purchases such as automobiles are counted as consumption.

convergence The process of per capita income levels moving closer together over time. (p. 50)

cost-push inflation Inflation created by exogenous increases in the cost of production in any economy, such as an oil price increase; inflation that comes from shifts in the AS curve. (p. 312)

countercyclical Moving in the opposite direction of the business cycle. For example, the government budget deficit is often countercyclical, rising when the economy is in a recession.

crowding out Actions by the government may "crowd out" actions by the private sector. The typical example in macroeconomics is when government borrowing to finance a budget deficit uses up some of the economy's saving and crowds out investment. (p. 464)

cyclical unemployment The part of unemployment that moves over the business cycle, as distinct from frictional and structural unemployment. (p. 180)

debt-GDP ratio The ratio of government debt to GDP; a useful measure of the extent to which the government is borrowing to pay for its expenditures.

decreasing returns to scale A property of a production function that occurs when doubling all of the inputs leads to less than twice as much output. (p. 69)

deflate To convert a nominal value into a real value. Recall from Chapter 2 that a nominal value is equal to a real value times a price level. When we divide the nominal value by the price level to get the real value, we say we are deflating the nominal value. Commonly used deflators include the Consumer Price Index and the GDP deflator. (p. 31)

deflation A negative rate of inflation. Under deflation, the aggregate price level is declining over time. (pp. 207, 335)

deflationary spiral A situation in which deflation raises the real interest rate, causing a recession to deepen. This in turn causes inflation to decline, making the deflation worse, which further raises the real interest rate and worsens the recession. (p. 381)

demand-pull inflation Inflation created by a stimulus to demand conditions in the economy that leads firms to increase their prices; inflation that comes from shifts in the AD curve. (p. 312)

depreciation *In production*: The wear and tear that reduces capital during the production process. Machines wear out and buildings decay. *In international finance*: A currency depreciates when it loses value relative to other currencies. That is, a depreciation is a decline in the exchange rate. (pp. 25, 100)

depression An extremely severe recession; marked by rising unemployment.

devaluation A reduction in the value of a currency in a fixed exchange rate system.

development accounting The practice of using an economic model to account for differences in per capita GDP across countries. (p. 78)

diminishing marginal utility The concept of diminishing returns, applied to the utility function: when each additional unit of consumption raises utility by less and less (p. 405)

diminishing returns A property of production functions and utility functions. In production, individual inputs are typically subject to diminishing returns. That is, increasing a single input initially has a fairly large effect on output. But the effect diminishes as the quantity of the input grows. For example, adding sales clerks to an electronics store initially has a large effect on total sales. But each additional clerk will increase sales by a smaller and smaller amount (as they start to compete for and eventually annoy customers). (p. 79)

discount rate The interest rate charged by the central bank when lending to commercial banks. This rate is occasionally used explicitly for monetary policy, but typically it just follows the federal funds rate in the United States. (p. 326)

disinflation A sustained reduction in the inflation rate. A classic example of disinflation is the decline in inflation that occurred throughout advanced countries in the 1980s. (p. 313)

disposable income The amount of income remaining after taxes are subtracted. (p. 464)

dividend A payment by a firm to its shareholders. (p. 435)

DSGE models Dynamic, stochastic, general equilibrium models, frequently used in modern macroeconomic research.

economic fluctuations Movements in the aggregate economy over the short run; the term typically refers to movements in GDP.

economic growth The growth in standards of living that occurs over substantial periods of time.

economic profit See *profit*.

economic shocks See *shocks*.

efficiency wage A higher wage than is necessary to employ workers, paid in order to motivate workers to provide extra effort.

employment-population ratio The ratio of the number of people employed to the overall population of an economy. (p. 172)

endogenous Determined within the model itself (as opposed to *exogenous*).

endogenous variable One of the "unknowns," or outcomes, of a model. Examples include the level of output in the Solow model and the level of inflation in the short-run model. To solve a model is to solve for the endogenous variables as a function of the parameters and exogenous variables. (p. 10)

equilibrium A situation in which the markets in a model clear; that is, supply equals demand. (p. 73)

equity See *net worth*.

Euler equation A famous mathematical equation that characterizes the path of consumption when individuals are maximizing their utility. It says that the consumer must be indifferent between consuming an extra bit more today, on the one hand, and saving that bit and consuming it in the next period, on the other hand. (p. 406)

exchange rate The price at which currencies are traded. For example, $1 may trade for 0.8 euros. (p. 32)

excludability The extent to which someone has property rights over a good, legally permitting the good's use to be restricted. (p. 135)

exogenous Determined outside the model (as opposed to *endogenous*).

exogenous variable A component of an economic model that changes over time in an exogenous fashion. (p. 10)

expected inflation The rate of inflation that firms, workers, and consumers expect to prevail over some future period, such as the coming year. (p. 308)

factor shares The fractions of income paid to factors of production, such as 1/3 to capital and 2/3 to labor. (p. 74)

factors of production The inputs used in production, typically capital and labor.

federal funds rate Sometimes abbreviated as *the fed funds rate*, this is the interest rate at which banks borrow from and lend to each other on a day-to-day basis in the United States. In recent decades, the Federal Reserve has explicitly set this rate and used it as its key monetary policy instrument. (p. 300)

financial wealth The net financial assets (such as stocks, bonds, saving accounts and checking accounts) that an individual possesses. (p. 404)

fiscal Pertaining to government expenditures, revenue, or debt.

fiscal stimulus The use of fiscal policy, such as increased government spending or a decrease in taxes, to stimulate the economy.

Fisher equation $i_t = R_t + \pi_t$. The Fisher equation says that nominal interest rates are equal to real interest rates plus inflation. (p. 209)

fixed costs Production costs that are paid once and are independent of the scale of production. A typical example is the fixed cost of research that must be undertaken to invent a new idea. (p. 512)

fixed exchange rate An exchange rate is said to be *fixed* when its value is constant. (p. 512)

fixed rate loans Loans that are made at an interest rate that is constant over time (versus *variable rate loans*).

floating exchange rate An exchange rate that is allowed to fluctuate with market conditions. (p. 517)

flow A quantity that disappears after a period, in contrast to a stock, which survives (at least to some extent) over time. Stocks are the cumulation of flows. (p. 103)

flow budget constraint See *intertemporal budget constraint*.

flow utility The amount of utility an individual gets in a single period, in contrast to "lifetime" utility.

foreign exchange reserves Assets denominated in a foreign currency and held by a central bank. (p. 521)

frictional unemployment The part of unemployment that is due to people changing jobs for reasons unrelated to the business cycle, such as personal reasons or geographic preferences. (p. 180)

GDP deflator See *deflate*.

general equilibrium The situation in a market economy in which all markets clear at current prices and all interactions across markets are taken into account. (p. 73)

generational accounting A system of accounting for government spending and taxes that focuses on the amount of taxes each generation is asked to pay versus the benefits that each generation obtains from the government. (p. 463)

globalization A broad term used to describe the rising extent to which economies interact, for example through international trade and international financial flows. (p. 190)

global saving glut A term used by Ben Bernanke to refer to the increase in saving by many developing countries following the various financial crises of the late 1990s. (p. 251)

government budget constraint The government budget constraint specifies the "sources of funds equal uses of funds" for the government. It describes the ways the government can finance its spending, including by taxes, by borrowing, and by printing currency. (p. 214)

government debt The accumulated amount that a government owes, both to domestic residents and to foreigners, because of its past borrowing. (p. 456)

Great Depression The largest recession in modern U.S. economic history, the Great Depression was a worldwide slowdown in economic activity that started in 1929 and lasted more or less throughout the 1930s. Unemployment rates peaked at around 25 percent, and industrial production declined by more than 60 percent. (p. 229)

Great Divergence The increase in dispersion of incomes throughout the world associated with the fact that modern economic growth has taken hold in some countries but not in others. (p. 43)

Great Inflation The large rise in inflation rates that occurred throughout the advanced countries of the world in the late 1960s and 1970s. (p. 313)

Great Moderation The era since the early 1980s of relatively small fluctuations in economic activity, accompanied by low inflation. (p. 365)

gross domestic product (GDP) The market value of final goods and services produced by an economy during a period (typically a year). (p. 19)

gross national product (GNP) Similar to GDP, except based on ownership rather than on the physical location of production. Production by a U.S.-owned factory in Mexico counts as part of U.S. GNP and Mexican GDP.

growth accounting The practice of using the production function to account for growth in GDP over time in an economy, attributing shares to growth in capital, in labor, and in total factor productivity. (p. 152)

growth effect A change in the parameter of a growth model leading to a permanent change in the long-run growth rate. (p. 149)

growth rate The percentage change in a variable. For example, the growth rate of per capita GDP in the United States for the last century has averaged about 2 percent per year. (p. 44)

hedge To undertake additional financial transactions that limit the risk associated with the original transaction. For example, a person who borrows at a variable interest rate may turn around and lend some money at a variable interest rate as a hedge against movements in interest rates. (p. 252)

human capital The skills that individuals accumulate through schooling, experience, on-the-job training, and so on. Human capital raises an individual's productivity in the labor market and increases his or her wage. (p. 86)

human wealth The present discounted value of labor income (p. 404)

hyperinflation Extraordinarily high rates of inflation, such as 500 percent per year. (p. 199)

idea diagram Ideas → nonrivalry → increasing returns → problems with perfect competition. (p. 134)

ideas Economic goods can be divided into "ideas" and "objects." Ideas are recipes or instructions for making use of objects. Examples include the chemical formula for a new cancer drug, the blueprint for a new computer chip, and the management techniques used by Wal-Mart. (p. 133)

increasing returns to scale The property of a production function that occurs when doubling all of the inputs leads to more than twice as much output. A common instance of increasing returns occurs when one takes into account the nonrivalry of ideas. (p. 69)

indexing Tying a financial payment to a price index. For example, some firms provide annual cost-of-living adjustments that increase wages according to the inflation rate.

inflation expectations The rate of inflation that firms, workers, and consumers expect to prevail over some future period, such as the coming year.

inflation-output loops In a graph with inflation on the vertical axis and short-run output on the horizontal axis, the economy tends to move in a counterclockwise loop over time. This is true empirically for the U.S. economy and is also a prediction of the basic short-run model.

inflation rate The percentage change in the aggregate price level of an economy.

inflation targeting A modern approach to monetary policy that specifies an explicit target for the inflation rate as well as a general time frame over which that target will be achieved.

inflation tax The amount of funds the government obtains by issuing new money; another name for *seignorage*. It can be viewed as a tax paid by holders of existing currency who find that their currency is worth less in real terms because of the higher prices associated with inflation. (p. 214)

informational efficiency A financial market is said to be informationally efficient if financial prices fully and correctly reflect all available information. (p. 439)

input A generic name for a factor of production, such as capital or labor.

insolvency A situation in which the liabilities of a bank or other company exceed its assets. (p. 264)

institutions Features of an economy that shape the allocation of resources, including property rights, the legal system, and the rules and regulations governing individual behavior. (p. 87)

intertemporal budget constraint Budget constraints come in two flavors. They can be expressed as a "flow" constraint that applies in each year or as a single intertemporal constraint. The intertemporal form says that the constraint holds in a present discounted value sense. For example, applied to the government, the intertemporal budget constraint says that the present discounted value of tax revenues must be enough to cover the present discounted value of government spending plus any initial outstanding debt. (p. 404)

inventory investment Goods that have been produced by firms but have not been sold. (p. 442)

investment New purchases of goods such as machines, equipment, buildings, and factories that typically last for several years and are used to produce other goods.

investment In macroeconomics, investment typically refers to purchases of new goods such as machines, equipment, buildings, or factories: these are purchases of goods that typically last for several years. The term investment can also be used in other ways. For example, a financial investment is the purchase of a financial asset that pays a return in the future. Chapter 16 explains how these different types of investment are related. (p. 426)

IS curve The equation $\tilde{Y}_t = \bar{a} - \bar{b}(R_t - \bar{r})$. The IS curve captures the influence of the real interest rate on economic activity in the short run. A high real interest rate reduces investment (firms and households face a higher cost of borrowing), which in turn reduces economic activity. (p. 270)

IS-MP diagram A key graph of the short-run model, showing how the level of the real interest rate influences economic activity. (p. 304)

job creation An economic measure of the labor market that counts the number of jobs created in a period. (p. 174)

job destruction An economic measure of the labor market that counts the number of separations between workers and their jobs during a period. (p. 174)

job finding rate The fraction of unemployed persons who find a new job during a certain period of time, such as a month. (p. 181)

job separation rate The fraction of workers who lose their jobs and become unemployed during a certain period of time, such as a month. (p. 181)

Laspeyres index A method of comparing real GDP at two points in time that uses prices from the earlier time period. (Compare *Paasche index*.) (p. 29)

law of one price The law stating that the same good must sell for the same price in a competitive market. (p. 504)

leading economic indicators Measures of economic activity used by economists in predicting the future path of the economy. Examples include the fed funds rate, the term structure of interest rates (such as the difference between the 10-year rate and the 30-day rate), new claims for unemployment insurance, and the number of new houses being built. (p. 356)

level effect A change in the parameter of a growth model that leads to a permanent change in the level of economic activity in the long run, but does not affect the long-run growth rate. An increase in the investment rate in the Solow model has a long-run level effect. (p. 150)

leverage The ratio of total liabilities to net worth. (p. 264)

liability An amount that is owed to someone else. A business may borrow money from a bank in order to expand, and this loan is a liability to the business (and an asset to the bank). (p. 262)

life-cycle model A theory of consumption proposed by Franco Modigliani that states that consumers base their consumption on their lifetime income instead of their current income. Hence, they typically borrow when young, save when middle-aged, and dis-save when retired. (p. 282)

liquidity crisis A situation in which the volume of transactions in some financial markets falls sharply, making it difficult to value certain financial assets and raising questions about the overall value of the firms holding those assets. (p. 253)

liquidity trap A situation in which the nominal interest rate is zero and there is deflation. In this case, the real interest rate is positive and the central bank cannot use conventional monetary policy (a lower interest rate) to stimulate the economy. Because the real interest rate is high, firms do not wish to borrow and "liquidity" (money) is "trapped" in financial institutions. (p. 381)

long run A long period of time, more than several years. In our models, the long run often refers to the steady state. (p. 12)

loose versus tight monetary policy Loose monetary policy refers to a situation where the central bank keeps interest rates low to stimulate the economy. The terminology is a legacy from a time when central banks focused more on the money supply. Low interest rates are obtained by expanding the money supply—by being "loose" with money instead of "tight." A tight monetary policy therefore corresponds to high interest rates that slow the economy.

Lucas critique In 1976, Robert Lucas argued that changes in policies will typically lead to changes in expectations and if models do not take these changes in expectations into account, they will make invalid predictions. (p. 363)

macroeconomics The study of collections of people and firms and how their interactions through markets determine the overall performance of the economy. (p. 5)

marginal cost The cost of making one additional unit of output.

marginal product The extra amount of output that is produced when one additional unit of the input is added, holding all the other inputs constant. (p. 70)

marginal propensity to consume The amount by which consumption goes up if an individual receives an extra dollar of income today. (p. 410)

market clearing A market is said to clear when the quantity that firms are willing to supply is equal to the quantity that consumers demand. The equilibrium price is the one that prevails when this clearing occurs.

menu cost A cost to firms of changing prices, associated with the way prices are displayed, such as reprinting a menu.

model A simple device used to help us understand a more complicated real-world phenomenon. In economics, models are often mathematical equations that may be represented in graphs. The supply-and-demand diagram is one of the most widely used models in economics. (p. 67)

monetary base A narrow definition of money in an economy, equal to the amount of currency in circulation plus the amount of reserves held by banks. (p. 203)

monetary policy rule A systematic, predetermined menu of monetary policy responses to economic conditions. For example, a simple rule sets the interest rate as a function of the observed rate of inflation. (p. 335)

money supply The amount of money supplied by the central bank. (p. 336)

mortgage A loan used to purchase property, such as a house. If the mortgage is not repaid, the property reverts to the lender.

MP curve In the IS-MP diagram, the MP curve is a horizontal line at the real interest rate chosen by the central bank. It is derived from the fact that the central bank sets a nominal interest rate, but because inflation adjusts slowly over time, the central bank effectively chooses the real interest rate. (p. 304)

multiplier effects The important concept in macroeconomics that the long-run effect of a change can be larger than the initial shock. For example, an increase in total factor productivity in the Solow model by 1 percent raises output by more than 1 percent in the long run. This is because higher productivity has a multiplier effect: it raises output directly, but this indirectly increases investment, which increases capital and therefore leads to even higher output. In extensions of our short-run model, a similar amplification of shocks can occur. For example, an aggregate demand shock may increase output directly, but then the higher income may stimulate consumption, which raises output indirectly. (p. 285)

mutual funds Collections of stocks and other financial assets that are held together in a large portfolio, small pieces of which are sold off to individual investors. (p. 439)

national income accounting The system through which economists measure GDP, consumption, investment, and so on, in an economy.

national income identity $Y = C + I + G + EX - IM$. The left side of this identity is GDP, and the right side describes the various ways this GDP can be used in the economy. (p. 21)

natural rate of unemployment A medium-to-long-run measure of the unemployment rate that would prevail if the economy were producing at its potential output level. There may be nothing "natural" about this rate. It may include unemployment that results from institutional and structural features of the labor market, such as hiring and firing costs. Includes both frictional and structural unemployment. (p. 180)

neoclassical consumption model A standard model of consumption in which individuals choose the time path of consumption to maximize their lifetime utility. The key constraint in this model is that the present discounted value of consumption must equal the present discounted value of resources available to the individual (financial wealth and human wealth). (p. 403)

net foreign assets The stock of financial claims on the rest of the world that a country accumulates (net of the financial claims on that country held by the rest of the world). In the mid-1980s, the United States went from having a positive stock of net foreign assets to having a negative stock. That is, it became a net debtor to the rest of the world. (p. 496)

net investment Some investment goes to replace the capital that is worn out through depreciation. Net investment is the amount of investment on top of this; it is equal to total (gross) investment, less depreciation. (p. 105)

net worth The difference between assets and liabilities. Also called "capital" or "equity." (p. 263)

neutrality of money The notion that changes in the money supply do not have real effects on the economy; they only affect nominal variables. (p. 209)

no-free-lunch principle A tenet which says that nothing of value comes for free and everything must be paid for. (p. 288)

nominal Valued in current prices (as opposed to *real*). (p. 27)

nominal exchange rate The price at which currencies are traded. For example, $1 may trade for 0.8 euros. (p. 503)

nominal GDP GDP valued using current prices (as opposed to *real GDP*). (p. 27)

nominal interest rate The rate at which a unit of currency, such as a dollar, can be traded for other units in the future. For example, a nominal interest rate of 5 percent says that a dollar today can be exchanged for $1.05 a year from now. (p. 209)

nonresidential fixed investment Equipment and structures used in production that are purchased by businesses. (p. 442)

nonrivalry Ideas are nonrivalrous in that one person's use of an idea does not, at a technological level, inhibit someone else's use of the idea. A pencil is rivalrous—if I am using it, you cannot use it simultaneously. But the chemical formula for a new malaria vaccine and the design for a new computer chip are nonrivalrous. One factory or a thousand factories can use the same design simultaneously. (p. 135)

numéraire The unit in which prices are quoted. For example, in an economy with apples and oranges, we may express all prices in units of apples. In the U.S. economy, little green pieces of paper are our *numéraire*. (p. 70)

objects Economic goods can be divided into "ideas" and "objects." Objects are the standard economic goods commonly studied in economics. They are rivalrous, meaning that one person's use of an object inhibits someone else's use. Examples include capital, labor, ice cream, and computers. (p. 133)

Okun's law The equation $u - \bar{u} = -{}^1\!/_2\, \tilde{Y}$. Okun's law allows us to think about economic fluctuations in terms of either output or unemployment. It says that a 2 percentage point decline in short-run output is associated with a 1 percentage point rise in the unemployment rate. (p. 240)

open economy An economy that can engage in international trade.

open-market operations The buying and selling of government bonds by the central bank. Open market operations are the chief day-to-day instrument that a central bank uses to manage the supply of money and short-term interest rates. (p. 327)

opportunity cost The amount of money one could earn by taking the best alternative action. The opportunity cost of going to college is the amount of income you could earn by working instead. (p. 323)

output A generic name for production or real GDP, often used when referring to production in a model economy.

outsourcing In international trade, *outsourcing* refers to closing down the domestic production of some good and importing the good instead. (p. 491)

Paasche index A method of comparing real GDP at two points in time that uses prices from the later time period. (Compare *Laspeyres index*.) (p. 29)

parameter A part of an economic model that stands for a particular number. Examples include the investment rate in the Solow model and the sensitivity of a central bank's monetary policy rule to inflation. We often study one-time changes in a parameter value to see how the economy responds. (p. 9)

Pareto optimal A situation in which no one can be made better off without someone being made worse off. (p. 138)

partial equilibrium The practice of studying one market at a time and ignoring effects that occur across markets.

per capita By or for each person. For example, per capita GDP refers to GDP divided by the population.

permanent income See *permanent income hypothesis*.

permanent income hypothesis A theory of consumption proposed by Milton Friedman which states that consumers base their consumption on some average measure of income rather than solely on current income. A strong version of the permanent income hypothesis says that consumers set consumption equal to the "flow value" of the present discounted value of their lifetime income (also called permanent income). (p. 282)

personal saving rate The ratio of personal saving to disposable income (i.e., income after paying taxes). (p. 417)

per worker Per member of the labor force. For example, GDP per worker refers to GDP divided by the labor force. In simple models, every person in the population works, so that "per worker" and "per capita" may be equivalent. Empirically, of course, this is not the case.

Phillips curve The equation $\Delta\pi_t = \bar{v}\tilde{Y}_t + \bar{o}$. Derived from the price-setting behavior of firms in the economy, the Phillips curve relates short-run output to the *change* in the inflation rate. In a booming economy, inflation increases; in a slumping economy, inflation declines. (p. 235)

pipeline theory A theory of inventory behavior where firms hold components and materials are part of the production process itself. This theory helps us understand why inventories are often procyclical. (p. 444)

policy rule A systematic, predetermined menu of policy responses to economic conditions. An example is a monetary policy rule that sets the interest rate as a function of the observed rate of inflation.

policy trilemma In international finance, a country can choose at most two of the following three goals: a stable currency, control of monetary policy, and free flows of international financial assets. (p. 520)

potential output The amount of output an economy would produce if all factors were fully employed and all prices were completely flexible. (p. 12)

precautionary saving The additional saving that arises to guard against the possibility of a large drop in income or wealth. (p. 413)

present discounted value (*or* present value) The value today of a financial amount that is paid in the future. For example, if i is the interest rate, the present discounted value of \$100 to be paid 5 years from today is $\$100/(1 + i)^5$. (p. 186)

price-earnings ratio The ratio of a stock price to an earnings measure (a rough measure of profits) for a company or set of companies. (p. 437)

primary deficit or surplus The primary budget balance does not include interest payments, while the total budget balance does. This distinction is useful when considering the government's intertemporal budget constraint. (p. 459)

principle of transition dynamics This key property of the long-run model says that an economy that starts below its steady state (or its balanced growth path) will grow rapidly until it reaches its steady state. Growth slows down as the gap between the economy's position and the steady state shrinks. (p. 119)

procyclical Moving in conjunction with the business cycle. For example, investment is procyclical—peaking when the economy booms.

production function The equation that describes how inputs such as capital and labor combine to produce an output good. The Cobb-Douglas production function $Y = K^{1/3}L^{2/3}$ is an example. (p. 68)

production smoothing A theory of inventory behavior where firms maintain a stable level of production, producing more than they sell when business is booming and less than they sell when business is slumping (p. 444)

productivity slowdown The decline in total factor productivity growth in the early 1970s that occurred throughout much of the world. (p. 153)

profit Economists distinguish between accounting profit and economic profit. Accounting profit refers to total revenues less payments to labor and is therefore equal to payments to capital. Accounting profit can be thought of as payments to the owners of the firm. Economic profit subtracts out payments to all factors, including capital. Under perfect competition, economic profits are zero: all revenue is paid out to some factor of production. (p. 20)

property rights The authority to control how a good is used.

quantity equation $M_tV_t = P_tY_t$. (p. 204)

quantity theory of money Based on the equation $M_tV_t = P_tY_t$. A central prediction of the theory is that the money supply is a key determinant of the price level. This means that the growth rate of the money supply is a key determinant of the inflation rate. (p. 204)

quota In international trade, a restriction on the quantity of imports.

random walk view of consumption An implication of the neoclassical consumption model: current consumption should reflect all available information, including expectations of future income. So the change in consumption should be unpredictable. (p. 412)

rational expectations In an economy subject to shocks, firms and consumers must form expectations about future values of inflation, wages, short-run output, and so on. Expectations are said to be rational when all available information for making these predictions is used in the most efficient way. (p. 361)

ratio scale A scale for the axis of a graph whose equally spaced labels rise by a constant ratio rather than by a constant number of units. For example, a ratio scale may have labels such as 1, 2, 4, 8, 16 (a ratio of 2) or 1, 10, 100, 1000 (a ratio of 10) instead of 1, 2, 3, 4. (p. 48)

real Relating to changes in actual quantities of goods and services, as opposed to "nominal."

real business cycle theory The theory of short-run economic fluctuations based on a Solow model that emphasizes real (as opposed to nominal) disturbance to the economy. This theory views shocks to total factor productivity as the key driving force behind economic fluctuations and de-emphasizes the role played by monetary policy.

real exchange rate The rate at which foreign and domestic goods are traded. The real exchange rate is the price of domestic goods (in units of foreign goods). If the real exchange rate is high, domestic goods are expensive. (p. 507)

real GDP GDP valued in a way to facilitate comparisons over time or across countries. As a simple example, real GDP may be computed by valuing production using 2006 prices in every year, so that nominal differences in prices are removed from the comparison. (p. 27)

real interest rate The rate at which current units of output can be traded for future units of output. For example, a real interest rate of 5 percent says that 1 unit of real consumption today can be exchanged for 1.05 units a year from now. Savers may earn this real interest rate by saving a unit of output, and borrowers must pay this real interest rate in order to borrow a unit of output. (pp. 104, 209)

recession The period of time when actual production in an economy falls below potential output and has not yet started to recover. (p. 230)

reserve requirement A mandate that financial institutions keep a certain fraction, such as 3 percent, of their deposits in a special account ("on reserve") with the central bank. (p. 263)

reserve requirement One of the tools of conventional monetary policy: banks are required to hold a certain percentage of deposits in a special account ("reserves") with the central bank. (p. 326)

reserves Funds that pay no interest that are held by banks in an account with the central bank. They are held "in reserve" in case many depositors seek to withdraw their deposits at the same time. (p. 203)

residential fixed investment New housing purchased by households. (p. 442)

resource constraint A fundamental relationship in an economy that constrains how resources can be allocated, such as $C_t + I_t = Y_t$ (p. 141) or $L_{yt} + L_{at} = \bar{N}$ (p. 99).

returns to education The increase in wages resulting from additional years of education. (p. 87)

Ricardian equivalence The hypothesis that the *timing* of taxes is not important for current economic activity—only the present discounted value of the taxes that need to be collected. In particular, a tax cut today that is financed by higher taxes in the future will have no effect on economic activity under Ricardian equivalence. The reason—related to the permanent income hypothesis—is that households care only about the present discounted value of their after-tax income, not about the particular timing of when the income or taxes happen to arrive. A tax cut today will be saved in order to pay the taxes in the future. Named after the early nineteenth-century classical economist David Ricardo. (p. 288)

risk premium An extra amount of money charged to compensate for the risk that a loan will not be repaid; for example, the interest rate on a loan may be higher by a percentage point or two because of risk. (pp. 376)

risk-sharing The spreading of rises and declines in the consumption of individuals across larger groups in order to smooth individual consumption. (p. 482)

rivalrous See *nonrivalry*.

Romer model A model of sustained economic growth that is driven by the discovery of new ideas. (p. 141)

Rule of 70 A simple rule for calculating how long it takes a variable growing at a constant rate of g% per year to double: the answer is approximately $70/g$. For example, if GDP grows at 7 percent per year, it will double about every 10 years. (p. 47)

rules versus discretion To what extent should monetary policy be governed by a predetermined rule versus chosen at the discretion of a policymaker? *Rules* may help to anchor inflation expectations, while *discretion* may be useful when there are unforeseen circumstances.

saving The difference between income and consumption. In a general sense, the national income identity tells us that saving equals investment. (p. 104)

securitization The process of pooling a group of financial instruments such as mortgages and then slicing them up in a different way and selling off the pieces. (p. 252)

seignorage The amount of funds the government obtains by issuing new money; another name for the *inflation tax*. (p. 214)

shocks Unexpected changes to the underlying parameters of a model. Also, unexpected changes in actual economies. Examples include the discovery of a new technology, a sudden rise in oil prices, a war, and an earthquake. (p. 235)

short run The "near term" in economics, typically a period of several months or perhaps up to two years (as opposed to the long run). (pp. 12, 228)

short-run output The portion of production not explained by the long-run trend. Short-run output is a key variable studied in the theory of economic fluctuations. It is commonly measured in percentage terms and denoted by the variable $\tilde{Y}$. For example, $\tilde{Y} = 1\%$ says that the economy is booming, with output 1 percent above potential. Similarly, $\tilde{Y} = -2\%$ says the economy is slumping, with output 2 percent below potential. (p. 229)

skill-biased technical change A change in the technology of production that favors skilled labor, in the sense that the wage of a skilled person rises by more than the wage of an unskilled person. (p. 190)

Solow diagram The key diagram used to study the Solow model. (p. 105)

Solow growth model A model key to understanding the macroeconomy in the long run. The Solow model emphasizes the roles played by capital and labor in production. (p. 98)

stagflation A combination of a weak economy (stagnation) and inflation. Typically used to describe the U.S. economy in the 1970s and early 1980s. (p. 343)

standard replication argument The standard way of justifying constant returns to scale in a production function. If we wish to double the production of cellphones, we can replicate the existing production setup exactly. That is, we build an identical factory, hire an identical number and type of workers, and use an identical collection of inputs. This should double output, providing a justification for constant returns. (p. 69)

steady state A situation in which all variables in a model are constant. In the Solow model, the steady state is the long-run outcome of the model. If the economy starts away from its steady state, it gradually moves toward it. (p. 106)

sticky inflation assumption The assumption that when firms set prices, for various reasons the prices respond slowly to changes in monetary policy. This leads the rate of inflation (the change in prices) to adjust gradually over time. (p. 303)

sticky prices The phenomenon that prices set by firms typically respond very gradually to changes in monetary policy.

stock A quantity that results from the cumulation of flows over time. A key example is the capital stock, which is the cumulation of investment (*a flow*) over time. (p. 103)

stock market A market in which ownership shares of firms are traded.

stockout avoidance A theory of inventory behavior where firms hold extra supplies of the goods they produce in order to avoid being sold out of the goods when customers wish to buy them. (p. 444)

structural unemployment The part of unemployment associated with the institutional features of an economy, including hiring and firing costs and the structure of the unemployment compensation system. (p. 180)

systemic risk Risk to the financial system or economy as a whole when financial institutions are integrated, leveraged, and subject to shocks that affect them as a group. (p. 266)

tariff A tax on imports.

technological change A change in the production function that lets a given quantity of inputs produce more output. An increase in TFP is a common example of technological change.

term structure of interest rates The collection of interest rates that apply to bonds of different maturities. There is an interest rate that prevails on loans over the next 1 month, 3 months, 6 months, 1 year, 10 years, and so on. (p. 306)

time consistency problem A situation in which decision-makers wish to reconsider decisions about the future that are made today once the future date arrives. For example, the government may say today that it will not tax capital in the future in order to encourage investment. But later, there will be an incentive to tax the capital that has already been put in place. (p. 360)

Tobin's *q* The ratio of the stock market value of a firm to the value of its capital stock.

"too big to fail" A phrase that refers to the possibility that regulators, worried about systemic risk, may be unwilling to let large financial institutions go into bankruptcy if they are highly integrated into the financial system. (p. 390)

total budget balance See *primary deficit or surplus*.

total factor productivity (TFP) The efficiency with which inputs are transformed into output. In the familiar production function used in this book, $Y = \bar{A}K^{1/3}L^{2/3}$, TFP is equal to the parameter $\bar{A}$. (p. 82)

toxic assets A phrase used in the latest financial crisis to refer to assets that have declined significantly in value, such as mortgage-backed securities, especially when this lower value may not yet be reflected in accounting statements and balance sheets.

trade balance Another name for net exports. A country that exports more than it imports runs a trade surplus. A country that imports more than it exports runs a trade deficit. (pp. 22, 479)

transaction costs Costs that must be paid in order for exchange to take place. A sales tax is an example.

transfer payments Payments that simply transfer resources from one person to another. Examples include unemployment insurance and social security expenditures.

transition dynamics See *principle of transition dynamics*.

twin deficits A trade deficit and a budget deficit, which sometimes occur together. (p. 495)

unemployment A spell in which someone who would like to be working is actively searching for a job but is not employed.

unemployment insurance Payments to individuals when they become unemployed, typically paid by the government.

unemployment rate The number of people who are unemployed as a fraction of the labor force. (p. 173)

user cost of capital The total cost to the firm of using one more unit of capital, which depends on the interest rate, the depreciation rate, the expected capital gain, and taxes. (p. 429)

utility function A mathematical function, usually written as $u(c)$, which shows how much utility a given amount of consumption delivers. (p. 405)

value-added The amount of new value a firm creates in production, equal to total revenues less the cost of intermediate goods that are used along the way. For example, the value-added by an automobile manufacturer is not the total value of the cars that are created, but rather this value less the amount paid for steel, tires, and other parts. (p. 26)

variable-rate loans loans that are made at an interest rate that can change over time with market conditions (versus "fixed-rate loans").

velocity of money The number of times a given piece of currency changes hands in a particular period (such as a year). Velocity plays a key role in the quantity theory of money. (p. 204)

wage rigidity A tendency for wages to move slowly or not at all; can apply to real or nominal wages. (p. 179)

welfare A general term used to refer to economic wellbeing. Also has a separate use to describe government programs to help economically disadvantaged people.

zero lower bound Refers to the fact that nominal interest rates cannot fall below zero (except in unusual circumstances). (p. 381)

Index

Note: Page numbers in italics refer to figures, tables, graphs, and other illustrative material

T

U

V

W

Y

Z